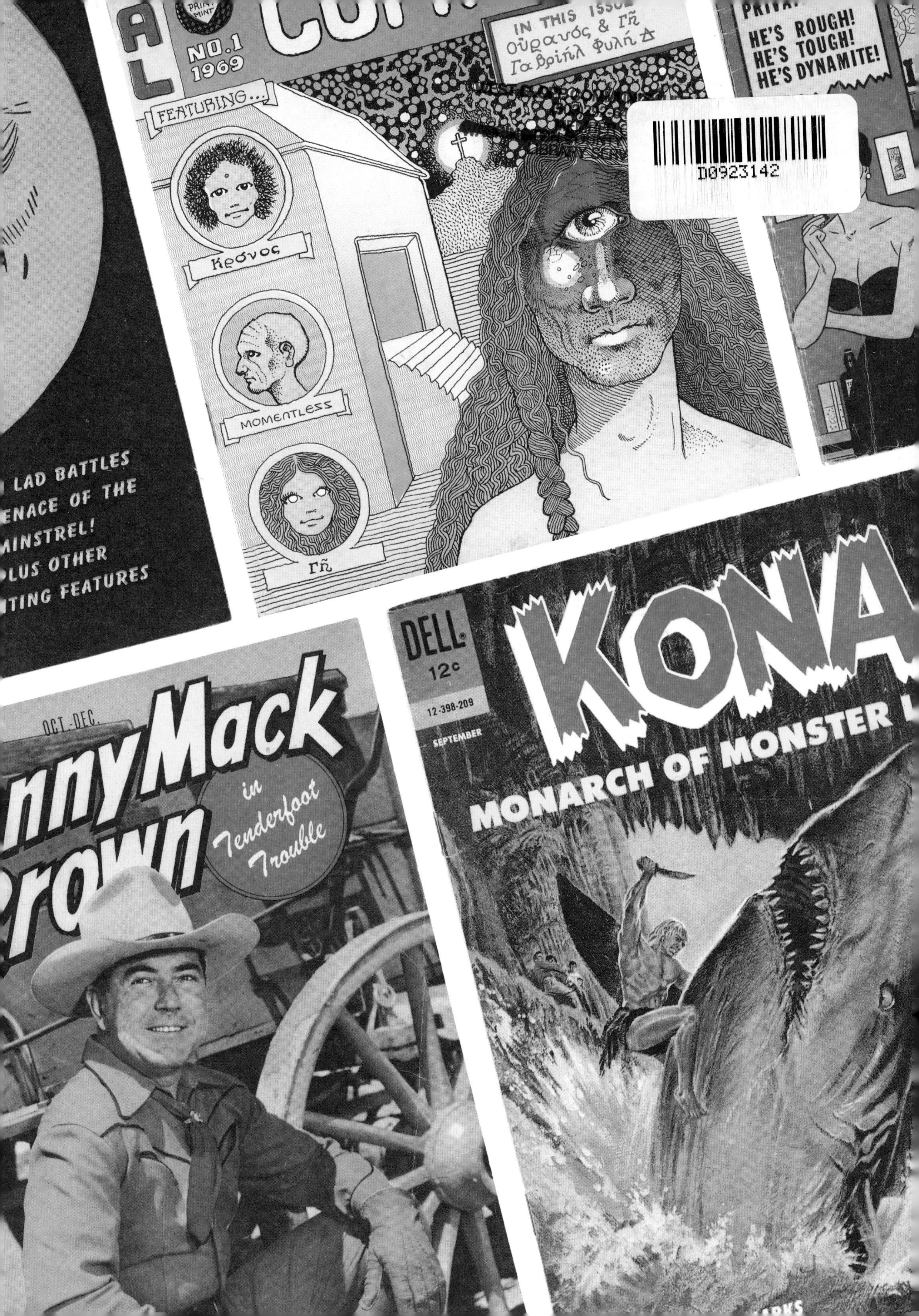
LAD BATTLES
ENACE OF THE
MINSTREL!
LUS OTHER
TING FEATURES
PRINT MINT
NO.1
1969
IN THIS ISSU
Οὐρανός & Γῆ
FEATURING...
Κρόνος
MOMENTLESS
Γῆ
HE'S ROUGH!
HE'S TOUGH!
HE'S DYNAMITE!
OCT.-DEC.
nnyMack
rown
in Tenderfoot Trouble
DELL
12¢
12-398-209
SEPTEMBER
KONA
MONARCH OF MONSTER

WEST SLOPE COMMUNITY LIBRARY
(503)292-6416
MEMBER OF
WASHINGTON COUNTY COOPERATIVE
LIBRARY SERVICES

Art in Time

ART in TIME

Unknown Comic Book Adventures, 1940–1980

Dan Nadel
PICTUREBOX, INC.

Abrams ComicArts, New York

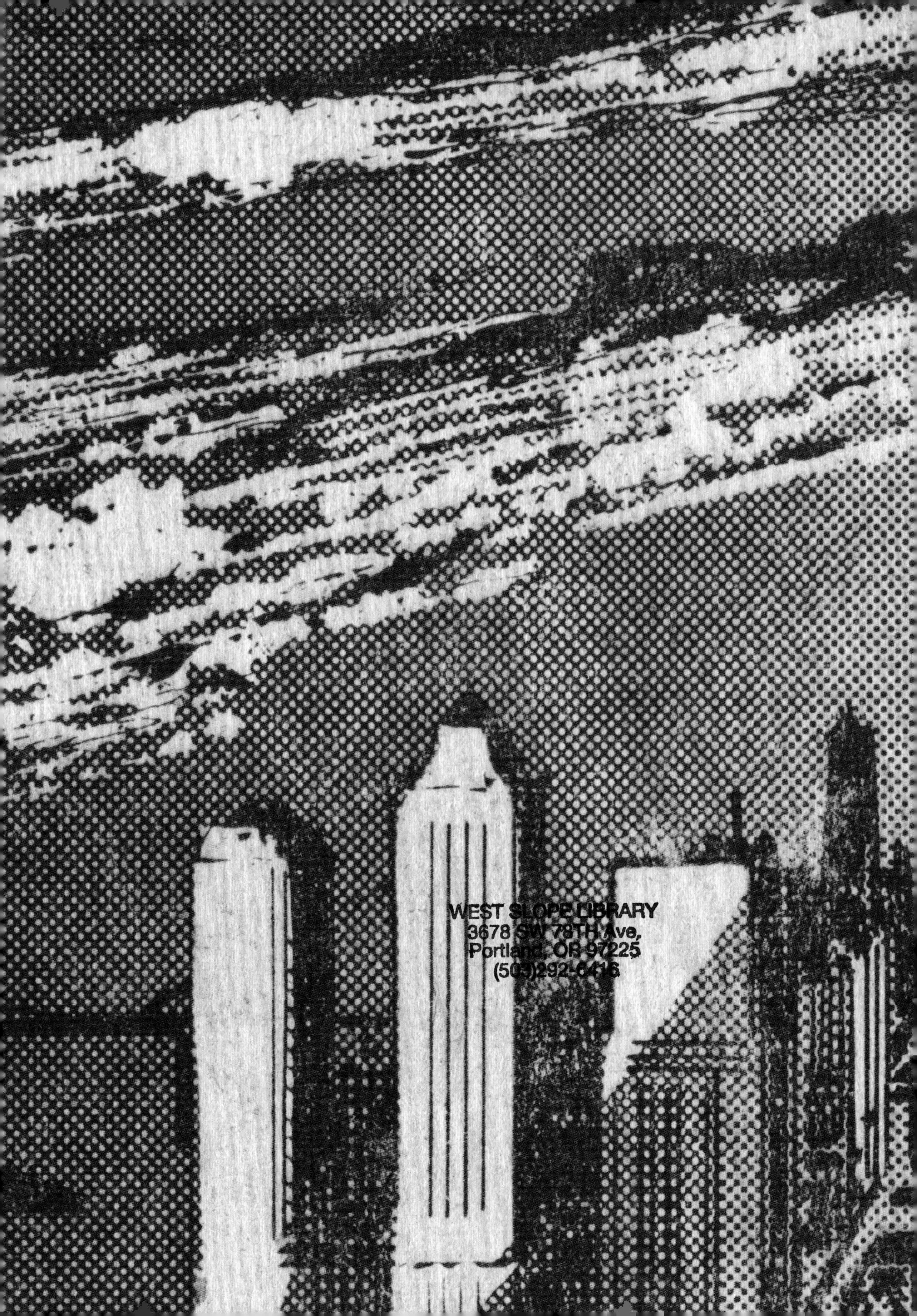

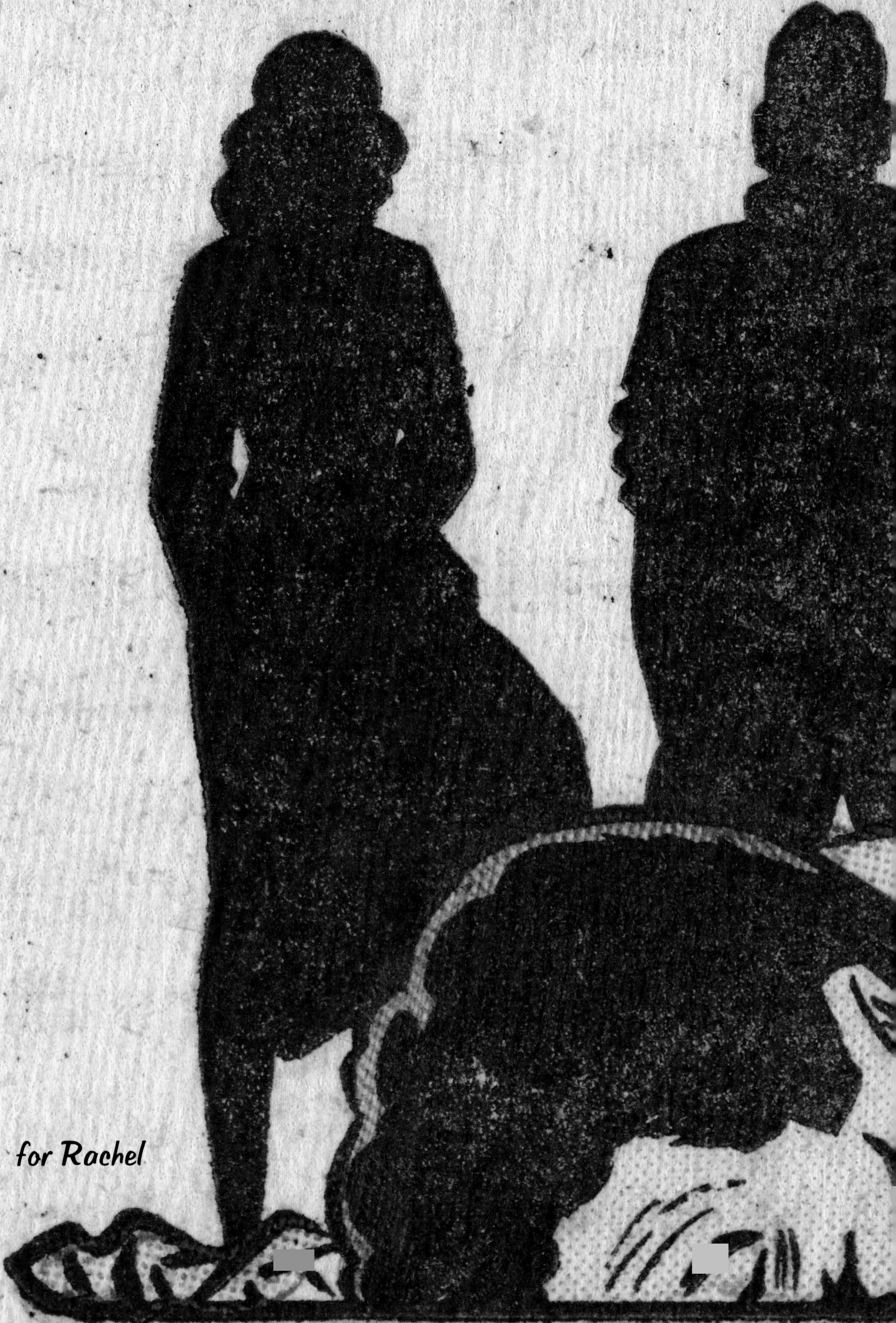

for Rachel

Contents

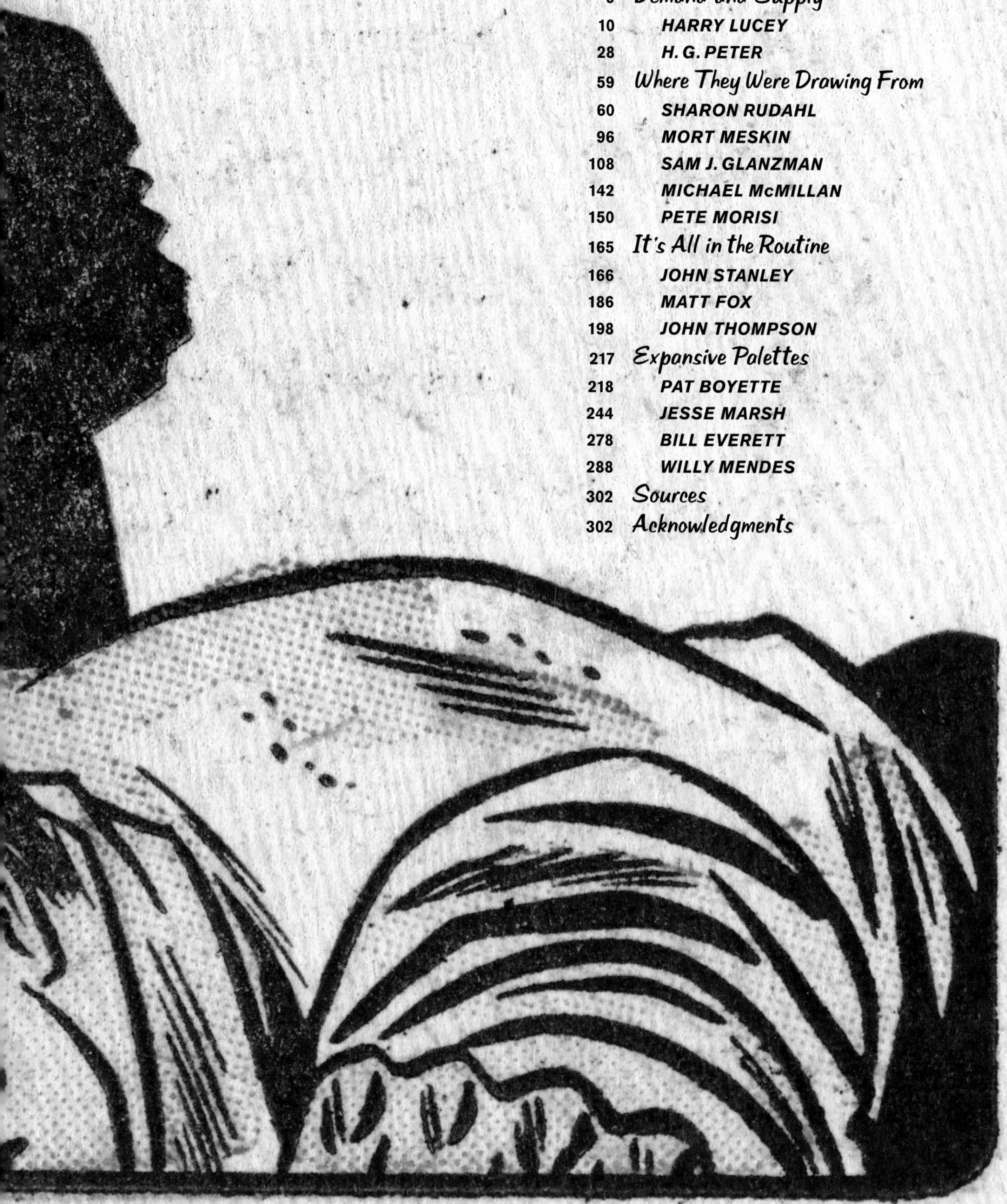

Introduction: Their Worlds

In 1953, comic book artist Wally Wood drew an E.C. Comics story called "My World," written by Al Feldstein. In it, an unseen narrator describes his daily experience of reality juxtaposed with panel after panel of spectacular fantasy scenes, consisting "of great space-ships that carry tourists on brief holidays to Venus or Mars or Saturn . . . My world can be ugly . . . Landing at night and entering my cities and killing and maiming and destroying . . . My world is what I choose to make it. My world is yesterday . . . Or today . . . Or tomorrow . . . For my world is the world of science-fiction . . . conceived in my mind and placed upon paper with pencil and ink and brush and sweat and a great deal of love for my world."

The final panel of the comic shows Wood smoking a cigarette at his drawing table, a bit wan. The image brings us back to the artist and the artist's world. The ownership of these worlds is powerful and terrifying. Envisioning and then exploring a world apart from the everyday, one with a different set of visual cues and designs, is a disorienting experience for the artist and reader. *Art in Time: Unknown Comic Book Adventures, 1940–1980* is, if nothing else, a testament to Wood's vision and his craft. The fourteen artists anthologized in these pages first built and then explored the lengths and depths of their worlds, using the genres of crime, Western, jungle, romance, psychedelic, science fiction, and super hero. They merit inclusion here primarily because their work transcends standard genre constraints through a combination of superior imagination and exquisite technique.

My previous book, *Art Out of Time: Unknown Comics Visionaries, 1900–1969*, was an attempt to broaden the conversation about the history and possibilities of comics. It focused on what, as of 2005, had been left out of the various "official" histories of comics. This new book is not a continuation of that project, but rather a companion. I am again focusing on cartoonists whose work has been marginalized or gone unrecognized, but this time I'm interested in exploring cartoonists like Harry Lucey (Archie) and John Stanley (Little Lulu), who became famous for only one aspect of their talents, as well as looking at the comic book itself as a medium (24 to 32 pages, stapled, printed on newsprint, and containing one or more stories of a fixed length determined by commercial constraints) and the popular genres it held.

The work in the pages that follow is resolutely a product of its time. Each story falls into a specific genre and historical context; each artist was

A Brief Comics Chronology

1924 Roy Crane introduces *Wash Tubbs*, which combines humor with adventure, as delineated by Crane's minimal, graceful line.

1934 *Terry and the Pirates*, by Milton Caniff, follows Crane's style combined with Caniff's filmic staging and chiaroscuro rendering, and becomes a hugely popular and influential comic strip.

Alex Raymond's *Flash Gordon* debuts on comics pages all over America.

1938 *Action Comics* no. 1 jump-starts the comic book boom with the first appearance of Superman.

1939 The character Sub-Mariner by Bill Everett first appears in *Marvel Comics* no. 1.

1940 *The Spirit* by Will Eisner debuts and swiftly becomes a jaunty and formally ambitious comic strip feature.

1941 *Reg'lar Fellers Heroic Comics* no. 7 includes the first appearance of H. G. Peter's Man O'Metal.

Wonder Woman, written by William Moulton Marston and drawn by H. G. Peter, makes her debut in *All Star Comics* no. 8.

Pep Comics no. 22 ushers Archie Andrews into the comics world.

very much influenced by, and was a part of, his or her comics and pop culture milieu, whether that was the popularity of film noir, dystopian science fiction, super heroes, or Westerns. Each of these artists also had a unique artistic vision of the world. There is a distinctly personal tone and even a joy to the work that makes these stories stand out from the stack of contemporaneous comic books. All the genres herein fall under the broad term "adventure," defined as a risky, uncertain activity undertaken to achieve a goal. Adventure, and the illustrative on-page physicality it engenders, is a wonderful use of the medium: time, bodies in motion, and negative space are all employed in a dynamic fashion to tell a story.

The comic book adventure story has its roots in the explosion of action comic strips in the 1930s, such as *Flash Gordon*, *Scorchy Smith*, *Terry and the Pirates*, and *Wash Tubbs*, the artists of which—Alex Raymond, Noel Sickles, Milton Caniff, and Roy Crane—were influenced by the work of illustrators like Howard Pyle, N. C. Wyeth, and Joseph Clement Coll. Crane pioneered a line-based style of elegant bodies in motion and precise timing; Raymond applied the swooning line work and theatrical staging of book illustration to narrative, while Sickles and Caniff took the chiaroscuro tones and dynamic camera angles of film and applied them, panel by panel, to comic strips. With the exception of underground artists John Thompson, Willy Mendes, and Sharon Rudahl, who inherited a separate set of countercultural influences, the artists within these pages, particularly Bill Everett, Harry Lucey, Mort Meskin, and Pete Morisi, emerged from the influence of those comic strips.

Many of these artists were well known for other work: As noted, Harry Lucey drew Archie and his pals for decades, while John Stanley chronicled Little Lulu's adventures. H. G. Peter was the founding artist for Wonder Woman, Bill Everett created the Sub-Mariner, and Jesse Marsh drew Tarzan. Others, like Pete Morisi, Matt Fox, Willy Mendes, and Michael McMillan, have been somewhat lost to history, while still others, including Mort Meskin and Pat Boyette, became "artist's artists," admired for their approaches but not identified with any one character or feature. The drawing in all of these examples is vital and helped to establish specific styles and illustrating methods. Coupled with heroic or horrific action, the representations here achieve a rare potency. They have physicality. They have flourish. They are not subtle. Sam J. Glanzman's on-paper heroics have the kind of slash-and-burn energy that H. C. Westermann wielded in

1945 — *Golden Lad* no. 1, by Mort Meskin, is published.

John Stanley begins writing the *Little Lulu* comic book.

1947 — Jesse Marsh begins drawing the *Tarzan* comic book.

1950 — E.C. Comics launches its adult-oriented comic book titles.

Harry Lucey's *Sam Hill* makes its debut.

***Johnny Mack Brown* no. 2 begins Jesse Marsh's seven-issue run on the comic book series.**

1952 — **Bill Everett's "Tidal Wave of Terror" is published in *Venus* no. 18.**

1953 — Wally Wood and Al Feldstein's "My World" appears in *Weird Science* no. 22.

***Dynamite* no. 3 features the debut of Johnny Dynamite with art by Pete Morisi.**

Matt Fox's "Meet the Bride" and "I Was a Vampire" are published.

1961 — *The Fantastic Four* no. 1, by Stan Lee and Jack Kirby, revitalizes the super-hero genre.

1962 — **Sam J.Glanzman's *Kona* is published.**

John Stanley's *Tales from the Tomb* has its one and only issue.

1967 **Pat Boyette's "Children of Doom" is published in *Charlton Premiere* no. 2.**

1968 *Zap* no. 1, by Robert Crumb, is published, sparking the underground comics revolution.

1969 ***Cyclops Comics*, by John Thompson, is released.**

1970 Barry Windsor-Smith helps set the standard for mainstream comics drawing with his work on *Conan the Barbarian*.

Jack Kirby begins his "Fourth World" saga at DC Comics.

1971 **Michael McMillan publishes his first comic, *Terminal Comics*.**

Willy Mendes releases *Illuminations*.

1975 Bill Griffith and Art Spiegelman's anthology, *Arcade: The Comics Revue*, begins its seven-issue run.

1976 Harvey Pekar publishes the first issue of *American Splendor*.

1980 **Sharon Rudahl's *The Adventures Of Crystal Night* is published.**

his drawings, while Bill Everett's brush line has a flourish unrivaled in comics except, perhaps, by Alex Raymond, though Everett's work seems more muscular and rooted in cartooning rather than illustration. And there is the undeniable urgency of John Thompson's attempts to communicate a budding cosmic consciousness and Willy Mendes's blue-eyed utopian adventures. There is something of the joyous searching of Beat artist and publisher Wallace Berman or the Grateful Dead band here: a groping forward for what's just beyond one's reach.

The final part of my criteria for including these specific comics in this volume is (even) more subjective. I am looking at this work in the context of its time and determining its merits by comparing it to like-minded work, but with an eye toward what has already been excavated and canonized. After all, there are plenty of comics that are just as good but have been healthily reprinted—artists like Jack Kirby, Alex Toth, and Jack Cole have plenty of pages in print. So, as ever, I was looking at who's been left out of recent publishing activity, or what was simply exceptional for its time and now passed over either because of what it is (a TV Western), or because it simply faded from time (like most underground comics by women). I'm also viewing the work as someone immersed in a certain kind of comic making that has emerged in the new millennium, primarily by artists from Providence, Rhode Island. These comics are genre-defying, drawing-based, and even ecstatic—they're looking for psychic and physical release on paper. Is my description perhaps a tad on the romantic side? Yes. But in these times, and in the times ahead, believing in art, whether the sheer wonder of Glanzman's Kona or the concrete justice of Morisi's Johnny Dynamite, is a worthwhile effort. I am not looking for the direct lineage of this recent work, because that would be reductive, but rather its equivalents—its antecedents. While this makes *Art in Time* a product of specific circumstances, comics history is such a fertile, under-explored ground that each book about the medium is essentially dated upon publication. But that only makes them all the more compelling. In my case, *Art Out of Time* and now *Art in Time* mark a certain time period—both in my own interest in the medium, and in the history of the history of the medium—which is really the story of the slow march toward a more open and inclusive understanding of what makes a compelling comic.

Art in Time is a stack of ideas about comics grouped by a series of criteria and bundled together by the theme of adventure. Taken together, the stories that follow illuminate and expand upon what Wally Wood and Al Feldstein so generously described in "My World": the immersive, intoxicating exploration of comic book worlds on paper.

—Dan Nadel, July 2009

Demand and Supply

One of the pleasures of making this kind of book is plucking characters like Harry Lucey's Sam Hill and H. G. Peter's Man O'Metal out of obscurity. Is there a secret society of fans for these characters? I doubt it. Both are fairly generic, even shallow versions of the suave detective and the brawny super hero, radically elevated by their respective creators' skill as cartoonists. These odd confluences of talent and material usually come about as happy meetings of *comics-the-business*— needing to churn out ever more product that in some way either apes popular culture (crime stories), or imitates itself (super heroes) in hopes of striking it rich—and *comics-the-medium* that chanced upon talented artists who could bring new life to the page. Sharon Rudahl is anomalous in this context. *The Adventures of Crystal Night*, a unique take on the science fiction genre, was published long after the underground comics revolution, but just before the alternative comics explosion of the early 1980s. This lack of commercial context is one reason her debut comic book never found an audience.

The supply of these artists is not infinite, but it's far wider than one would think. To properly view the pool, one just has to understand these cartoonists were not necessarily directors in the sense of controlling every aspect of a production, but rather capable craftsmen, and sometimes visionaries, who worked in, expanded, or even exploded formulaic genres as part of their daily chores. It was a job, after all.

HARRY LUCEY

(1913–79 / 80)

Like so many of the other men who entertained generations of children, Harry Lucey remains as anonymous in death as he was in life. Lucey attended the Pratt Institute in New York, and his career in comics began in the late 1930s. He bounced around various companies in the 1940s, drawing such characters and features as Madam Satan, Magno, *Crime Does Not Pay*, and even, for a handful of issues, *Captain America*. Beginning in 1950, Lucey drew *Sam Hill* for seven issues, creating some wonderful stories in the Roy Crane/Milton Caniff/Alex Toth tradition of lush brushwork and cinematic compositions.

Lucey spent most of his life drawing for MLJ, which published Archie, among other characters, and which later became Archie Publications. As one of the lead Archie artists, Lucey drew the freckle-faced teenager and his pals from the 1950s through the 1970s. Lucey took some breaks from the business to work for an advertising agency in St. Louis, but otherwise was dedicated to comics. In most years Lucey penciled and inked a page a day, often drawing the complete contents of the *Archie* comic book every month in the late 1950s and early 1960s.

Lucey's work is distinguished by his close attention to the body language, or acting, of every character he drew. Each aspect of a Lucey figure is drawn to express what that character is feeling at that moment. Posture, position, and facial expression are all geared toward maximizing that moment in the story, and Lucey was equally dedicated to refining the depiction of action with a minimum of lines. The character Sam Hill, an "Ex Ivy League halfback" private eye with a white streak in his hair, is rendered with loving precision and an acute attention to detail.

Lucey was certainly influenced by film noir's expressionist angles and perhaps by Will Eisner's *The Spirit*: The sixth page of "The Cutie Killer Caper" contains six panels, all drawn from a different angle—from below Sam Hill to over a cop's shoulder, to above

Hill and the cop, and finally to a level over-the-shoulder shot from behind Hill. Lucey, like Eisner and the filmmakers they both borrowed from, was seeking different ways to approach action sequences. The effect can be a bit jarring, but Lucey brings an economy of line and form to the proceedings that echoes the work of Roy Crane—allowing cartoon panels to show, rather than only tell the action. For example, Hill's wry expression on the seventh page is contrasted by the surprise of Mrs. Berkley and the fear of her lawyer. Each emotion is played out in their bodies, across their faces, and in an articulated space. Remove the words from a Lucey story and readers still know precisely how each character feels and what that means for the plot. This strong technique makes Lucey's cartoon characters seem alive on the page like few others, and gives Sam Hill an urgency that raises it above its obvious genre and cinematic influences.

Lucey never returned to Sam Hill after his final issue, and toward the 1960s he developed an allergy to graphite, reportedly wearing white gloves while drawing. In the 1970s he was diagnosed with Lou Gehrig's disease and, sometime later, cancer. He refused treatment for the latter and died in Arizona in the late 1970s or perhaps 1980.

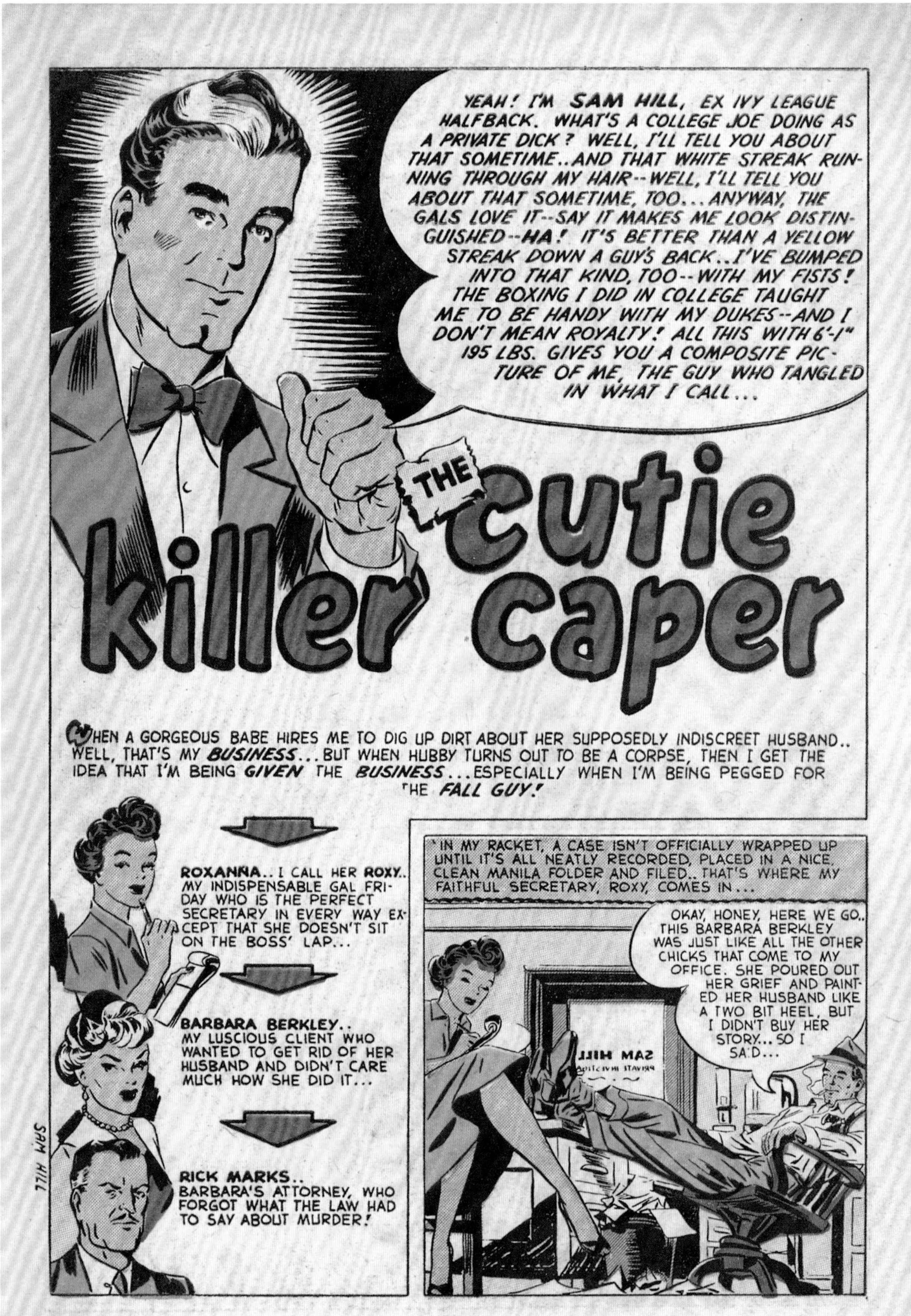
YEAH! I'M SAM HILL, EX IVY LEAGUE HALFBACK. WHAT'S A COLLEGE JOE DOING AS A PRIVATE DICK? WELL, I'LL TELL YOU ABOUT THAT SOMETIME..AND THAT WHITE STREAK RUNNING THROUGH MY HAIR--WELL, I'LL TELL YOU ABOUT THAT SOMETIME, TOO...ANYWAY, THE GALS LOVE IT--SAY IT MAKES ME LOOK DISTINGUISHED--HA! IT'S BETTER THAN A YELLOW STREAK DOWN A GUY'S BACK..I'VE BUMPED INTO THAT KIND, TOO--WITH MY FISTS! THE BOXING I DID IN COLLEGE TAUGHT ME TO BE HANDY WITH MY DUKES--AND I DON'T MEAN ROYALTY! ALL THIS WITH 6'-1" 195 LBS. GIVES YOU A COMPOSITE PICTURE OF ME, THE GUY WHO TANGLED IN WHAT I CALL...
THE cutie killer caper
WHEN A GORGEOUS BABE HIRES ME TO DIG UP DIRT ABOUT HER SUPPOSEDLY INDISCREET HUSBAND.. WELL, THAT'S MY BUSINESS...BUT WHEN HUBBY TURNS OUT TO BE A CORPSE, THEN I GET THE IDEA THAT I'M BEING GIVEN THE BUSINESS...ESPECIALLY WHEN I'M BEING PEGGED FOR THE FALL GUY!
ROXANNA..I CALL HER ROXY.. MY INDISPENSABLE GAL FRIDAY WHO IS THE PERFECT SECRETARY IN EVERY WAY EXCEPT THAT SHE DOESN'T SIT ON THE BOSS' LAP...
BARBARA BERKLEY.. MY LUSCIOUS CLIENT WHO WANTED TO GET RID OF HER HUSBAND AND DIDN'T CARE MUCH HOW SHE DID IT...
RICK MARKS.. BARBARA'S ATTORNEY, WHO FORGOT WHAT THE LAW HAD TO SAY ABOUT MURDER!
SAM HILL
IN MY RACKET, A CASE ISN'T OFFICIALLY WRAPPED UP UNTIL IT'S ALL NEATLY RECORDED, PLACED IN A NICE, CLEAN MANILA FOLDER AND FILED.. THAT'S WHERE MY FAITHFUL SECRETARY, ROXY, COMES IN...
OKAY, HONEY, HERE WE GO.. THIS BARBARA BERKLEY WAS JUST LIKE ALL THE OTHER CHICKS THAT COME TO MY OFFICE. SHE POURED OUT HER GRIEF AND PAINTED HER HUSBAND LIKE A TWO BIT HEEL, BUT I DIDN'T BUY HER STORY... SO I SAID...
SAM HILL
PRIVATE INVESTIGATOR

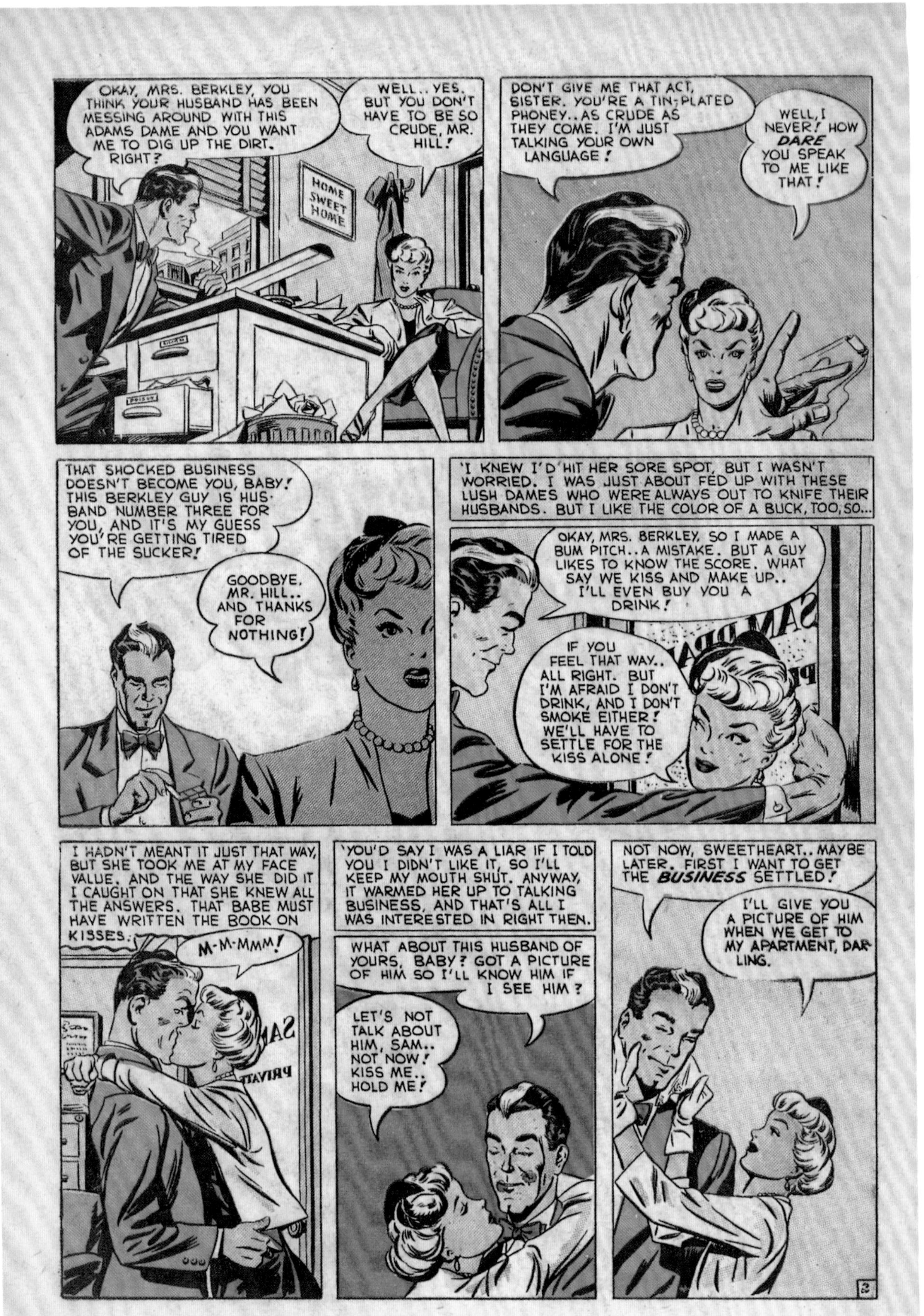
OKAY, MRS. BERKLEY, YOU THINK YOUR HUSBAND HAS BEEN MESSING AROUND WITH THIS ADAMS DAME AND YOU WANT ME TO DIG UP THE DIRT. RIGHT?
WELL.. YES. BUT YOU DON'T HAVE TO BE SO CRUDE, MR. HILL!
HOME SWEET HOME
DON'T GIVE ME THAT ACT, SISTER. YOU'RE A TIN-PLATED PHONEY.. AS CRUDE AS THEY COME. I'M JUST TALKING YOUR OWN LANGUAGE!
WELL, I NEVER! HOW DARE YOU SPEAK TO ME LIKE THAT!
THAT SHOCKED BUSINESS DOESN'T BECOME YOU, BABY! THIS BERKLEY GUY IS HUSBAND NUMBER THREE FOR YOU, AND IT'S MY GUESS YOU'RE GETTING TIRED OF THE SUCKER!
GOODBYE. MR. HILL.. AND THANKS FOR NOTHING!
'I KNEW I'D HIT HER SORE SPOT, BUT I WASN'T WORRIED. I WAS JUST ABOUT FED UP WITH THESE LUSH DAMES WHO WERE ALWAYS OUT TO KNIFE THEIR HUSBANDS. BUT I LIKE THE COLOR OF A BUCK, TOO, SO...
OKAY, MRS. BERKLEY, SO I MADE A BUM PITCH.. A MISTAKE. BUT A GUY LIKES TO KNOW THE SCORE. WHAT SAY WE KISS AND MAKE UP.. I'LL EVEN BUY YOU A DRINK!
IF YOU FEEL THAT WAY.. ALL RIGHT. BUT I'M AFRAID I DON'T DRINK, AND I DON'T SMOKE EITHER! WE'LL HAVE TO SETTLE FOR THE KISS ALONE!
I HADN'T MEANT IT JUST THAT WAY, BUT SHE TOOK ME AT MY FACE VALUE. AND THE WAY SHE DID IT I CAUGHT ON THAT SHE KNEW ALL THE ANSWERS. THAT BABE MUST HAVE WRITTEN THE BOOK ON KISSES.
M-M-MMM!
PRIVATE
'YOU'D SAY I WAS A LIAR IF I TOLD YOU I DIDN'T LIKE IT, SO I'LL KEEP MY MOUTH SHUT. ANYWAY, IT WARMED HER UP TO TALKING BUSINESS, AND THAT'S ALL I WAS INTERESTED IN RIGHT THEN.
WHAT ABOUT THIS HUSBAND OF YOURS, BABY? GOT A PICTURE OF HIM SO I'LL KNOW HIM IF I SEE HIM?
LET'S NOT TALK ABOUT HIM, SAM.. NOT NOW! KISS ME.. HOLD ME!
NOT NOW, SWEETHEART.. MAYBE LATER. FIRST I WANT TO GET THE BUSINESS SETTLED!
I'LL GIVE YOU A PICTURE OF HIM WHEN WE GET TO MY APARTMENT, DARLING.
3

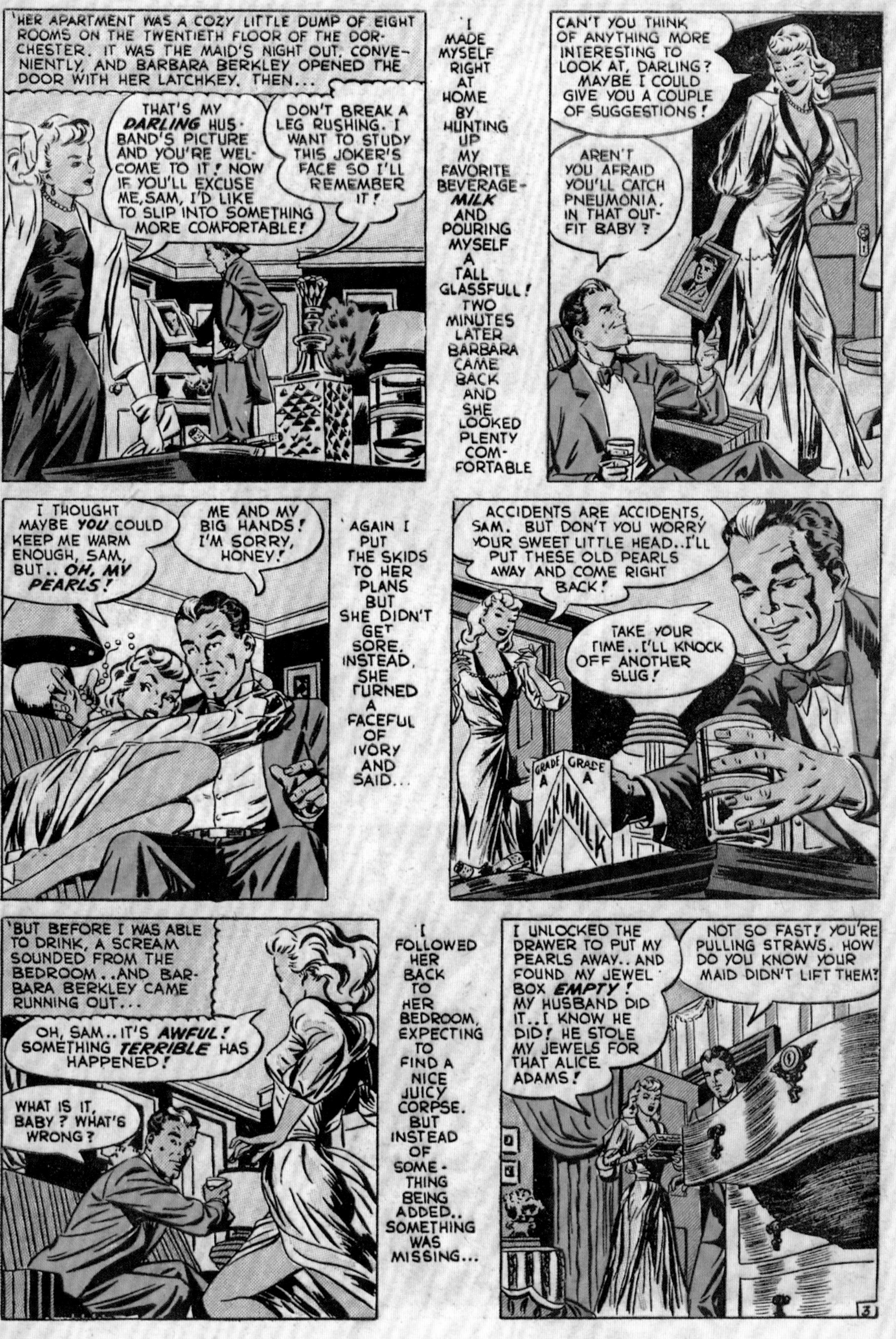
'HER APARTMENT WAS A COZY LITTLE DUMP OF EIGHT ROOMS ON THE TWENTIETH FLOOR OF THE DORCHESTER. IT WAS THE MAID'S NIGHT OUT, CONVENIENTLY, AND BARBARA BERKLEY OPENED THE DOOR WITH HER LATCHKEY. THEN...
THAT'S MY DARLING HUSBAND'S PICTURE AND YOU'RE WELCOME TO IT! NOW IF YOU'LL EXCUSE ME, SAM, I'D LIKE TO SLIP INTO SOMETHING MORE COMFORTABLE!
DON'T BREAK A LEG RUSHING. I WANT TO STUDY THIS JOKER'S FACE SO I'LL REMEMBER IT!
'I MADE MYSELF RIGHT AT HOME BY HUNTING UP MY FAVORITE BEVERAGE- MILK AND POURING MYSELF A TALL GLASSFULL! TWO MINUTES LATER BARBARA CAME BACK AND SHE LOOKED PLENTY COMFORTABLE
CAN'T YOU THINK OF ANYTHING MORE INTERESTING TO LOOK AT, DARLING? MAYBE I COULD GIVE YOU A COUPLE OF SUGGESTIONS!
AREN'T YOU AFRAID YOU'LL CATCH PNEUMONIA, IN THAT OUTFIT BABY?
I THOUGHT MAYBE YOU COULD KEEP ME WARM ENOUGH, SAM, BUT.. OH, MY PEARLS!
ME AND MY BIG HANDS! I'M SORRY, HONEY!
'AGAIN I PUT THE SKIDS TO HER PLANS BUT SHE DIDN'T GET SORE. INSTEAD, SHE TURNED A FACEFUL OF IVORY AND SAID...
ACCIDENTS ARE ACCIDENTS, SAM. BUT DON'T YOU WORRY YOUR SWEET LITTLE HEAD..I'LL PUT THESE OLD PEARLS AWAY AND COME RIGHT BACK!
TAKE YOUR TIME..I'LL KNOCK OFF ANOTHER SLUG!
GRADE A
GRADE A
MILK
MILK
'BUT BEFORE I WAS ABLE TO DRINK, A SCREAM SOUNDED FROM THE BEDROOM..AND BARBARA BERKLEY CAME RUNNING OUT...
OH, SAM.. IT'S AWFUL! SOMETHING TERRIBLE HAS HAPPENED!
WHAT IS IT, BABY? WHAT'S WRONG?
'I FOLLOWED HER BACK TO HER BEDROOM, EXPECTING TO FIND A NICE JUICY CORPSE. BUT INSTEAD OF SOMETHING BEING ADDED.. SOMETHING WAS MISSING...
I UNLOCKED THE DRAWER TO PUT MY PEARLS AWAY..AND FOUND MY JEWEL BOX EMPTY! MY HUSBAND DID IT..I KNOW HE DID! HE STOLE MY JEWELS FOR THAT ALICE ADAMS!
NOT SO FAST! YOU'RE PULLING STRAWS. HOW DO YOU KNOW YOUR MAID DIDN'T LIFT THEM?
3

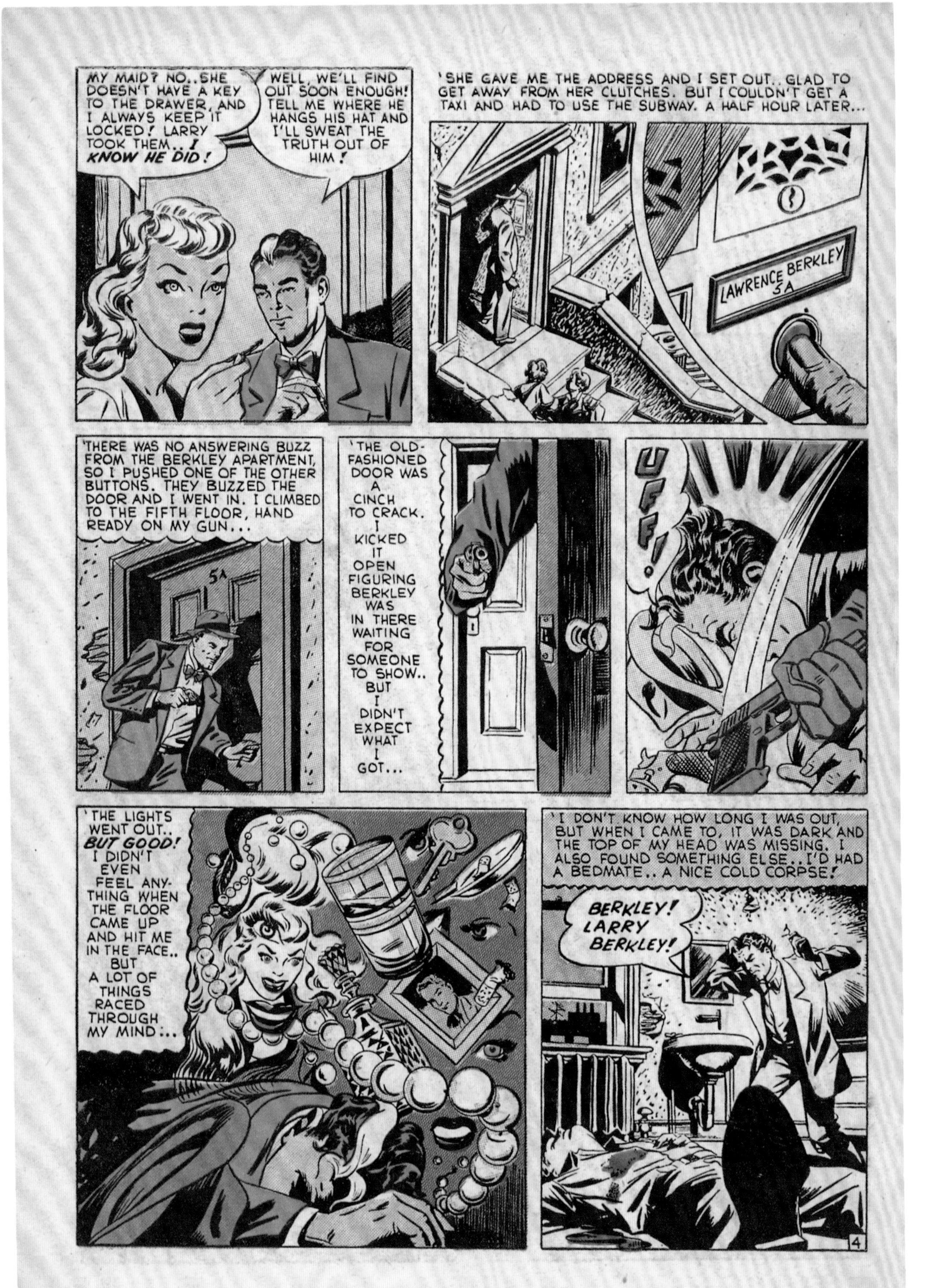
MY MAID? NO..SHE DOESN'T HAVE A KEY TO THE DRAWER, AND I ALWAYS KEEP IT LOCKED! LARRY TOOK THEM.. I KNOW HE DID!
WELL, WE'LL FIND OUT SOON ENOUGH! TELL ME WHERE HE HANGS HIS HAT AND I'LL SWEAT THE TRUTH OUT OF HIM!
'SHE GAVE ME THE ADDRESS AND I SET OUT.. GLAD TO GET AWAY FROM HER CLUTCHES. BUT I COULDN'T GET A TAXI AND HAD TO USE THE SUBWAY. A HALF HOUR LATER...
LAWRENCE BERKLEY 5A
'THERE WAS NO ANSWERING BUZZ FROM THE BERKLEY APARTMENT, SO I PUSHED ONE OF THE OTHER BUTTONS. THEY BUZZED THE DOOR AND I WENT IN. I CLIMBED TO THE FIFTH FLOOR, HAND READY ON MY GUN...
5A
'THE OLD-FASHIONED DOOR WAS A CINCH TO CRACK. I KICKED IT OPEN FIGURING BERKLEY WAS IN THERE WAITING FOR SOMEONE TO SHOW.. BUT I DIDN'T EXPECT WHAT I GOT...
UFF!
'THE LIGHTS WENT OUT.. BUT GOOD! I DIDN'T EVEN FEEL ANYTHING WHEN THE FLOOR CAME UP AND HIT ME IN THE FACE.. BUT A LOT OF THINGS RACED THROUGH MY MIND...
'I DON'T KNOW HOW LONG I WAS OUT, BUT WHEN I CAME TO, IT WAS DARK AND THE TOP OF MY HEAD WAS MISSING. I ALSO FOUND SOMETHING ELSE..I'D HAD A BEDMATE.. A NICE COLD CORPSE!
BERKLEY! LARRY BERKLEY!
4

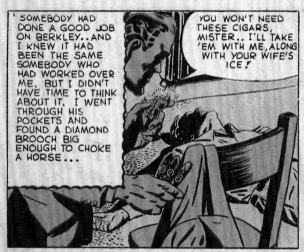

'SOMEBODY HAD DONE A GOOD JOB ON BERKLEY..AND I KNEW IT HAD BEEN THE SAME SOMEBODY WHO HAD WORKED OVER ME, BUT I DIDN'T HAVE TIME TO THINK ABOUT IT. I WENT THROUGH HIS POCKETS AND FOUND A DIAMOND BROOCH BIG ENOUGH TO CHOKE A HORSE...

YOU WON'T NEED THESE CIGARS, MISTER.. I'LL TAKE 'EM WITH ME, ALONG WITH YOUR WIFE'S ICE!

'THEN I DUG HIS WALLET OUT. IT HAD PLENTY OF DOUGH IN IT..ABOUT TEN GRAND..AND SOMETHING ELSE.. SOMETHING I DIDN'T EXPECT... A PICTURE OF HIS *WIFE*!

AND YOU WON'T NEED THE DOUGH EITHER. I'LL LEAVE THAT FOR THE COPS.. THE PICTURE I'LL TAKE, THOUGH!

'I STARTED TO GET OUT OF THERE..BUT THEN I NOTICED SOMETHING THAT MIGHT COME IN HANDY..A CIGARETTE BUTT...

HMM.. I WONDER!

'IT WAS HIGH TIME TO BEAT IT.. TO REPORT BACK TO BARBARA BERKLEY, BUT AS I OPENED THE DOOR...

COPS! THEY'VE GOT ME COLD!

'FOR A MINUTE I WAS LOST. IT WOULD BE THE HOT SQUAT IF THEY CAUGHT ME IN THE ROOM WITH A CORPSE! BUT THERE WAS NO OTHER DOOR! I DIVED FOR THE WINDOW...

I WAS FIVE FLIGHTS UP AND NO FIRE ESCAPE..JUST A LEDGE AROUND THE BUILDING. I SUCKED IN MY GUTS AND PRESSED BACK AGAINST THE BRICKS...

THERE'S THE STIFF.. JUST LIKE THE TIP SAID!

POOR PUNK! I WONDER WHO HE IS?

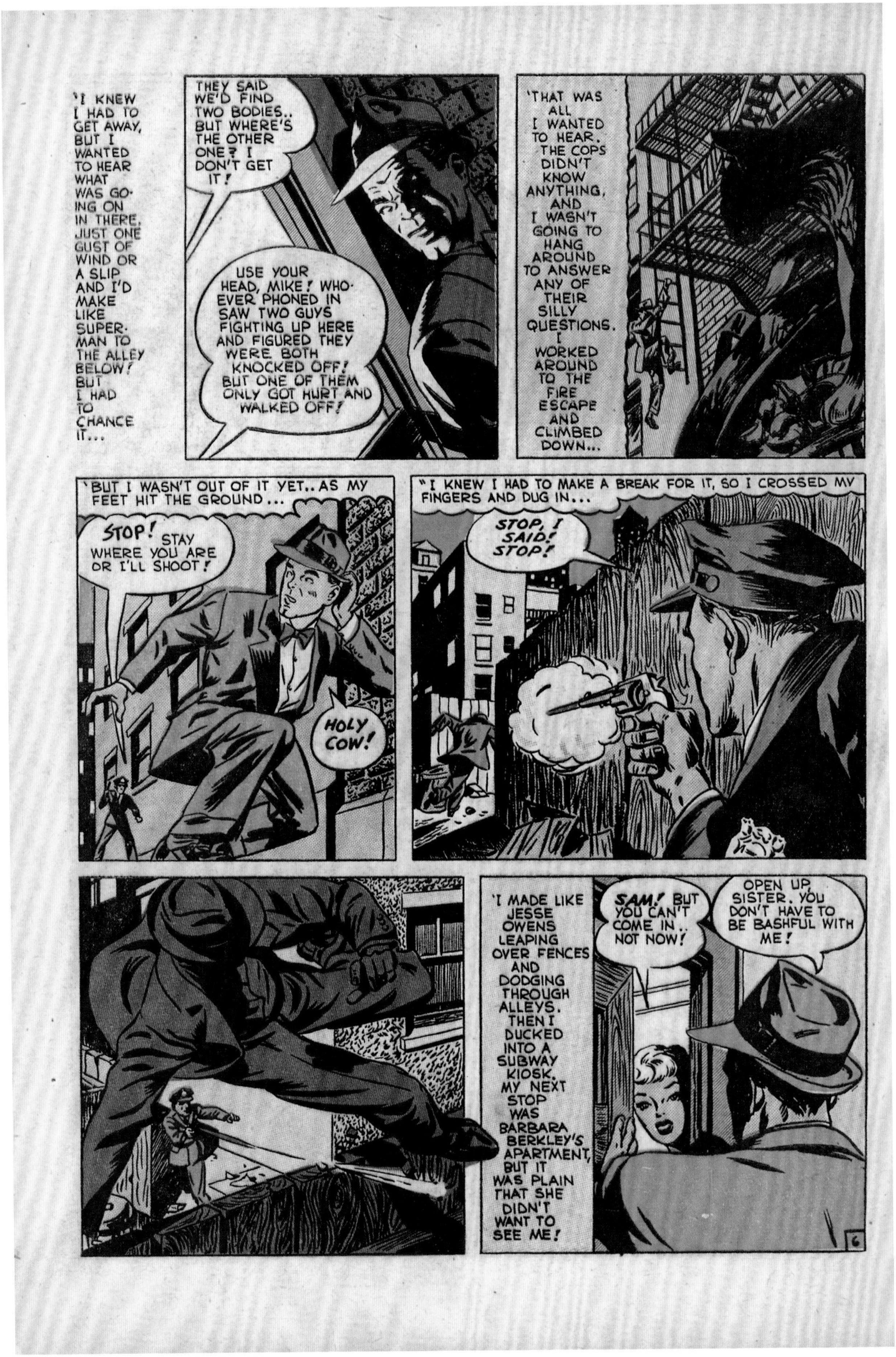
'I KNEW I HAD TO GET AWAY, BUT I WANTED TO HEAR WHAT WAS GOING ON IN THERE. JUST ONE GUST OF WIND OR A SLIP AND I'D MAKE LIKE SUPERMAN TO THE ALLEY BELOW! BUT I HAD TO CHANCE IT...
THEY SAID WE'D FIND TWO BODIES.. BUT WHERE'S THE OTHER ONE? I DON'T GET IT!
USE YOUR HEAD, MIKE! WHOEVER PHONED IN SAW TWO GUYS FIGHTING UP HERE AND FIGURED THEY WERE BOTH KNOCKED OFF! BUT ONE OF THEM ONLY GOT HURT AND WALKED OFF!
'THAT WAS ALL I WANTED TO HEAR. THE COPS DIDN'T KNOW ANYTHING, AND I WASN'T GOING TO HANG AROUND TO ANSWER ANY OF THEIR SILLY QUESTIONS. I WORKED AROUND TO THE FIRE ESCAPE AND CLIMBED DOWN...
'BUT I WASN'T OUT OF IT YET.. AS MY FEET HIT THE GROUND...
STOP! STAY WHERE YOU ARE OR I'LL SHOOT!
HOLY COW!
"I KNEW I HAD TO MAKE A BREAK FOR IT, SO I CROSSED MY FINGERS AND DUG IN...
STOP, I SAID! STOP!
'I MADE LIKE JESSE OWENS LEAPING OVER FENCES AND DODGING THROUGH ALLEYS. THEN I DUCKED INTO A SUBWAY KIOSK. MY NEXT STOP WAS BARBARA BERKLEY'S APARTMENT, BUT IT WAS PLAIN THAT SHE DIDN'T WANT TO SEE ME!
SAM! BUT YOU CAN'T COME IN.. NOT NOW!
OPEN UP, SISTER. YOU DON'T HAVE TO BE BASHFUL WITH ME!
6

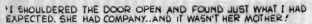

'I SHOULDERED THE DOOR OPEN AND FOUND JUST WHAT I HAD EXPECTED. SHE HAD COMPANY..AND IT WASN'T HER MOTHER!

WELL, YOU DIDN'T HAVE TO PULL THE BULL ACT, SAM! IF I'D KNOWN IT WAS *THAT* IMPORTANT I'D HAVE OPENED THE DOOR...

I'LL BET! NOW HOW'S ABOUT PLAYING HOST AND INTRODUCING YOUR BOY FRIEND?

MY NAME IS MARKS. I'M MRS. BERKLEY'S LAWYER. I DON'T LIKE YOUR TONE OF VOICE, HILL! I SUGGEST YOU KEEP A CIVIL TONGUE IN YOUR HEAD!

STOW IT, MISTER.. AND GIVE ME A.. CIGARETTE!

THANKS, BUD..AND HERE'S SOMETHING FOR YOU, MRS. BERKLEY.. SOMETHING YOUR HUSBAND ASKED ME TO GIVE YOU!

MY BROOCH! AND A PICTURE! BUT I DON'T UNDERSTAND! WHERE ARE THE OTHER JEWELS..AND WHY THE PICTURE?

DON'T BE COY, SISTER! YOUR POOR SUCKER OF A HUSBAND DIDN'T LEAVE YOU FOR ANOTHER DAME..YOU PAID HIM OFF AND THREW HIM OUT!

YOU'VE GOT IT ALL WRONG! WHY, HE EVEN STOLE MY JEWELS! YOU KNOW THAT!

DO I? LISTEN, NO CROOK WOULD PULL A JOB AND KEEP THE STUFF ON HIM. THE ICE WOULD BURN A HOLE THROUGH HIS POCKET! YOUR HUSBAND HAD YOUR PICTURE BECAUSE HE LOVED YOU..AND HE HAD THE BROOCH BECAUSE IT WAS PLANTED ON HIM... *BY YOUR BOY FRIEND!*

NO!

YOU HAVEN'T GOT A SHRED OF PROOF, HILL! YOU.. *HEY!*

SIT DOWN, BIG BOY, AND GET THE DUST OUT OF YOUR EARS! MAYBE YOU'LL THINK DIFFERENTLY!

7

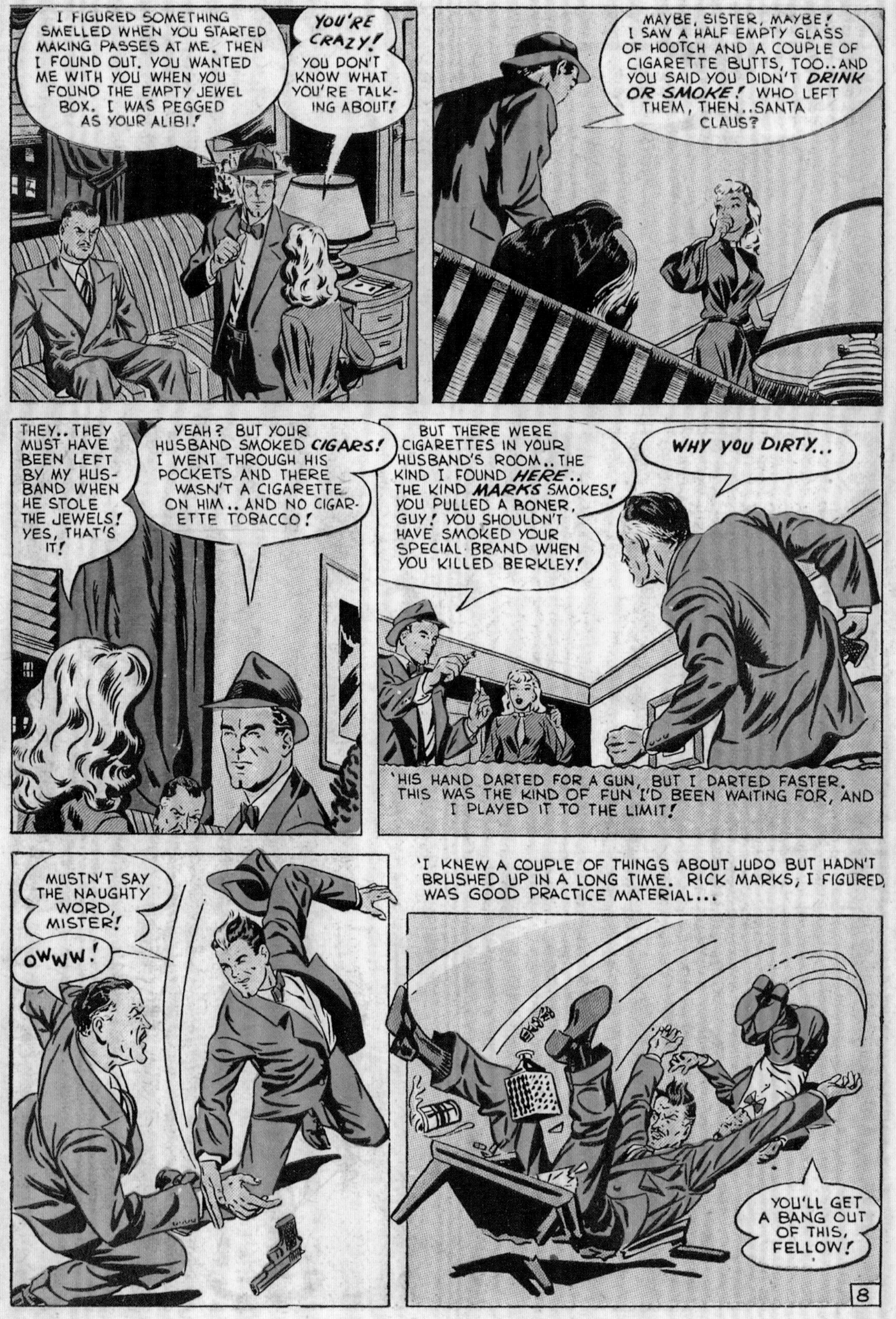
I FIGURED SOMETHING SMELLED WHEN YOU STARTED MAKING PASSES AT ME. THEN I FOUND OUT. YOU WANTED ME WITH YOU WHEN YOU FOUND THE EMPTY JEWEL BOX. I WAS PEGGED AS YOUR ALIBI!
YOU'RE CRAZY! YOU DON'T KNOW WHAT YOU'RE TALKING ABOUT!
MAYBE, SISTER, MAYBE! I SAW A HALF EMPTY GLASS OF HOOTCH AND A COUPLE OF CIGARETTE BUTTS, TOO..AND YOU SAID YOU DIDN'T DRINK OR SMOKE! WHO LEFT THEM, THEN..SANTA CLAUS?
THEY..THEY MUST HAVE BEEN LEFT BY MY HUSBAND WHEN HE STOLE THE JEWELS! YES, THAT'S IT!
YEAH? BUT YOUR HUSBAND SMOKED CIGARS! I WENT THROUGH HIS POCKETS AND THERE WASN'T A CIGARETTE ON HIM..AND NO CIGARETTE TOBACCO!
BUT THERE WERE CIGARETTES IN YOUR HUSBAND'S ROOM..THE KIND I FOUND HERE..THE KIND MARKS SMOKES! YOU PULLED A BONER, GUY! YOU SHOULDN'T HAVE SMOKED YOUR SPECIAL BRAND WHEN YOU KILLED BERKLEY!
WHY YOU DIRTY...
'HIS HAND DARTED FOR A GUN, BUT I DARTED FASTER. THIS WAS THE KIND OF FUN I'D BEEN WAITING FOR, AND I PLAYED IT TO THE LIMIT!
MUSTN'T SAY THE NAUGHTY WORD, MISTER!
OWWW!
'I KNEW A COUPLE OF THINGS ABOUT JUDO BUT HADN'T BRUSHED UP IN A LONG TIME. RICK MARKS, I FIGURED, WAS GOOD PRACTICE MATERIAL...
YOU'LL GET A BANG OUT OF THIS, FELLOW!
8

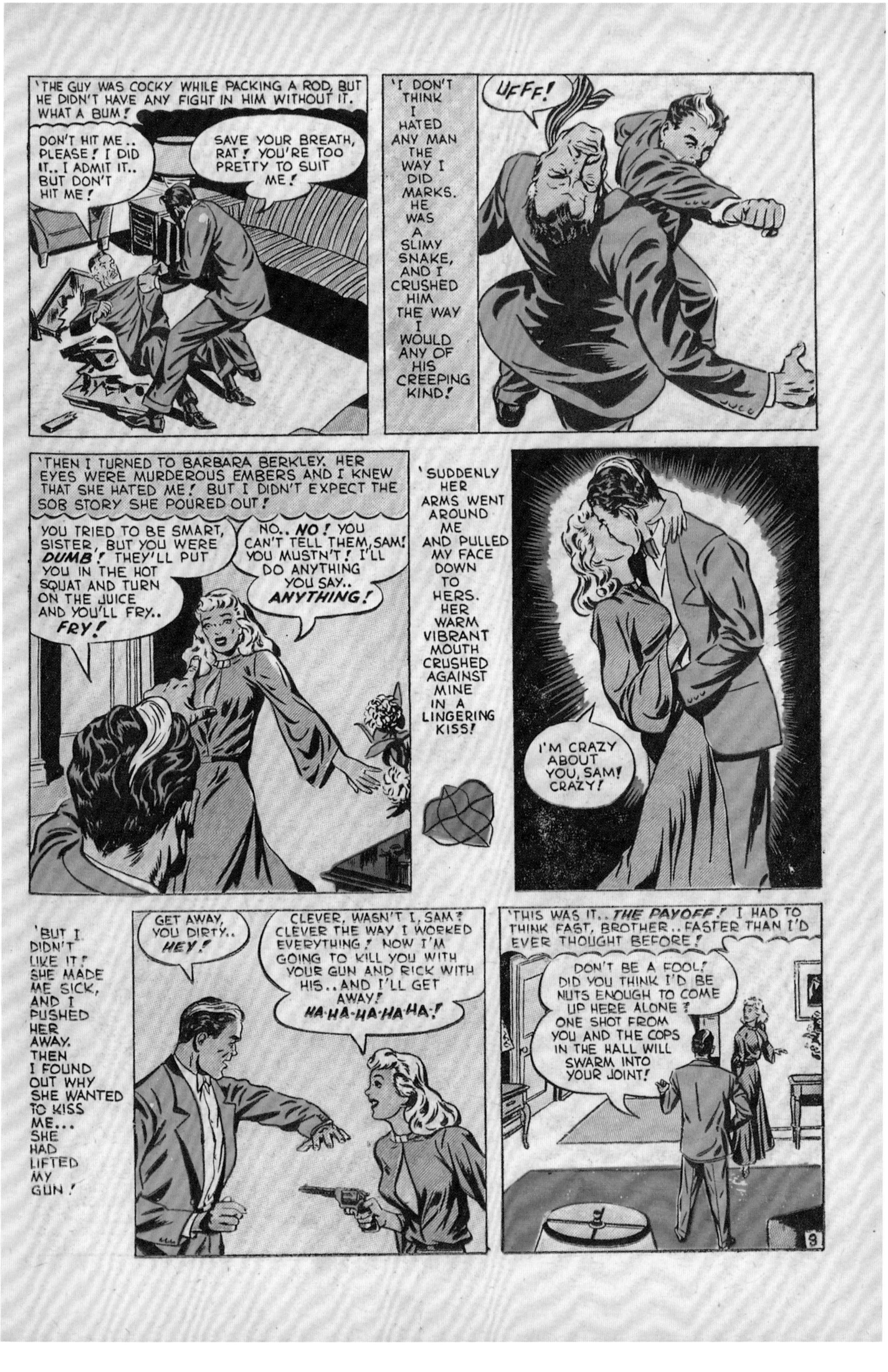
'THE GUY WAS COCKY WHILE PACKING A ROD, BUT HE DIDN'T HAVE ANY FIGHT IN HIM WITHOUT IT. WHAT A BUM!
DON'T HIT ME.. PLEASE! I DID IT.. I ADMIT IT.. BUT DON'T HIT ME!
SAVE YOUR BREATH, RAT! YOU'RE TOO PRETTY TO SUIT ME!
'I DON'T THINK I HATED ANY MAN THE WAY I DID MARKS. HE WAS A SLIMY SNAKE, AND I CRUSHED HIM THE WAY I WOULD ANY OF HIS CREEPING KIND!
UFFF!
'THEN I TURNED TO BARBARA BERKLEY. HER EYES WERE MURDEROUS EMBERS AND I KNEW THAT SHE HATED ME! BUT I DIDN'T EXPECT THE SOB STORY SHE POURED OUT!
YOU TRIED TO BE SMART, SISTER, BUT YOU WERE DUMB! THEY'LL PUT YOU IN THE HOT SQUAT AND TURN ON THE JUICE AND YOU'LL FRY.. FRY!
NO.. NO! YOU CAN'T TELL THEM, SAM! YOU MUSTN'T! I'LL DO ANYTHING YOU SAY.. ANYTHING!
'SUDDENLY HER ARMS WENT AROUND ME AND PULLED MY FACE DOWN TO HERS. HER WARM VIBRANT MOUTH CRUSHED AGAINST MINE IN A LINGERING KISS!
I'M CRAZY ABOUT YOU, SAM! CRAZY!
'BUT I DIDN'T LIKE IT! SHE MADE ME SICK, AND I PUSHED HER AWAY. THEN I FOUND OUT WHY SHE WANTED TO KISS ME... SHE HAD LIFTED MY GUN!
GET AWAY, YOU DIRTY.. HEY!
CLEVER, WASN'T I, SAM? CLEVER THE WAY I WORKED EVERYTHING! NOW I'M GOING TO KILL YOU WITH YOUR GUN AND RICK WITH HIS.. AND I'LL GET AWAY!
HA-HA-HA-HA-HA!
'THIS WAS IT.. THE PAYOFF! I HAD TO THINK FAST, BROTHER.. FASTER THAN I'D EVER THOUGHT BEFORE!
DON'T BE A FOOL! DID YOU THINK I'D BE NUTS ENOUGH TO COME UP HERE ALONE? ONE SHOT FROM YOU AND THE COPS IN THE HALL WILL SWARM INTO YOUR JOINT!
3

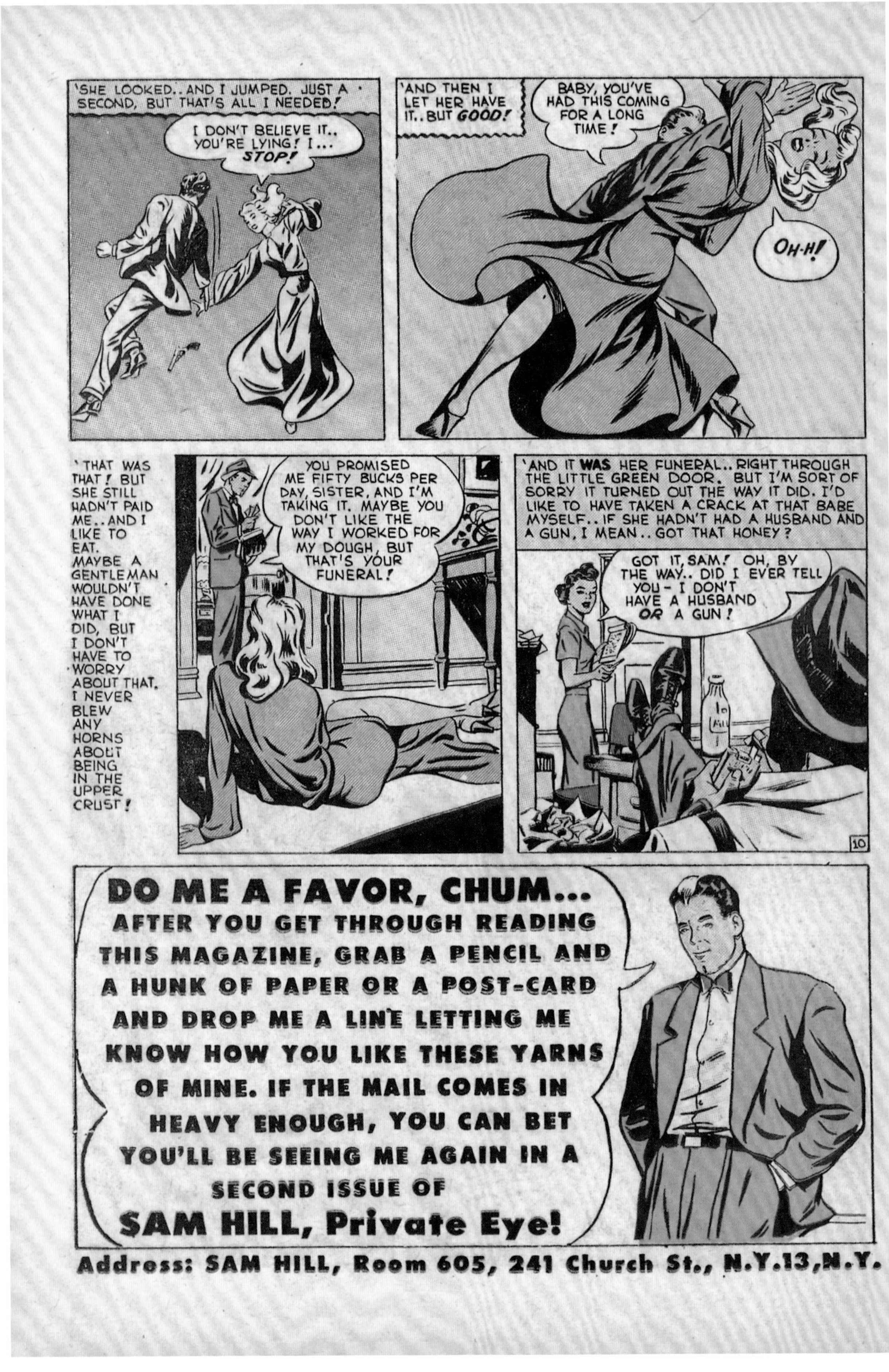
'SHE LOOKED.. AND I JUMPED. JUST A SECOND, BUT THAT'S ALL I NEEDED!
I DON'T BELIEVE IT.. YOU'RE LYING! I... STOP!
'AND THEN I LET HER HAVE IT.. BUT GOOD!
BABY, YOU'VE HAD THIS COMING FOR A LONG TIME!
OH-H!
'THAT WAS THAT! BUT SHE STILL HADN'T PAID ME.. AND I LIKE TO EAT. MAYBE A GENTLEMAN WOULDN'T HAVE DONE WHAT I DID, BUT I DON'T HAVE TO WORRY ABOUT THAT. I NEVER BLEW ANY HORNS ABOUT BEING IN THE UPPER CRUST!
YOU PROMISED ME FIFTY BUCKS PER DAY, SISTER, AND I'M TAKING IT. MAYBE YOU DON'T LIKE THE WAY I WORKED FOR MY DOUGH, BUT THAT'S YOUR FUNERAL!
'AND IT WAS HER FUNERAL.. RIGHT THROUGH THE LITTLE GREEN DOOR. BUT I'M SORT OF SORRY IT TURNED OUT THE WAY IT DID. I'D LIKE TO HAVE TAKEN A CRACK AT THAT BABE MYSELF.. IF SHE HADN'T HAD A HUSBAND AND A GUN, I MEAN.. GOT THAT HONEY?
GOT IT, SAM! OH, BY THE WAY.. DID I EVER TELL YOU - I DON'T HAVE A HUSBAND OR A GUN!
10
DO ME A FAVOR, CHUM... AFTER YOU GET THROUGH READING THIS MAGAZINE, GRAB A PENCIL AND A HUNK OF PAPER OR A POST-CARD AND DROP ME A LINE LETTING ME KNOW HOW YOU LIKE THESE YARNS OF MINE. IF THE MAIL COMES IN HEAVY ENOUGH, YOU CAN BET YOU'LL BE SEEING ME AGAIN IN A SECOND ISSUE OF SAM HILL, Private Eye!
Address: SAM HILL, Room 605, 241 Church St., N.Y.13, N.Y.

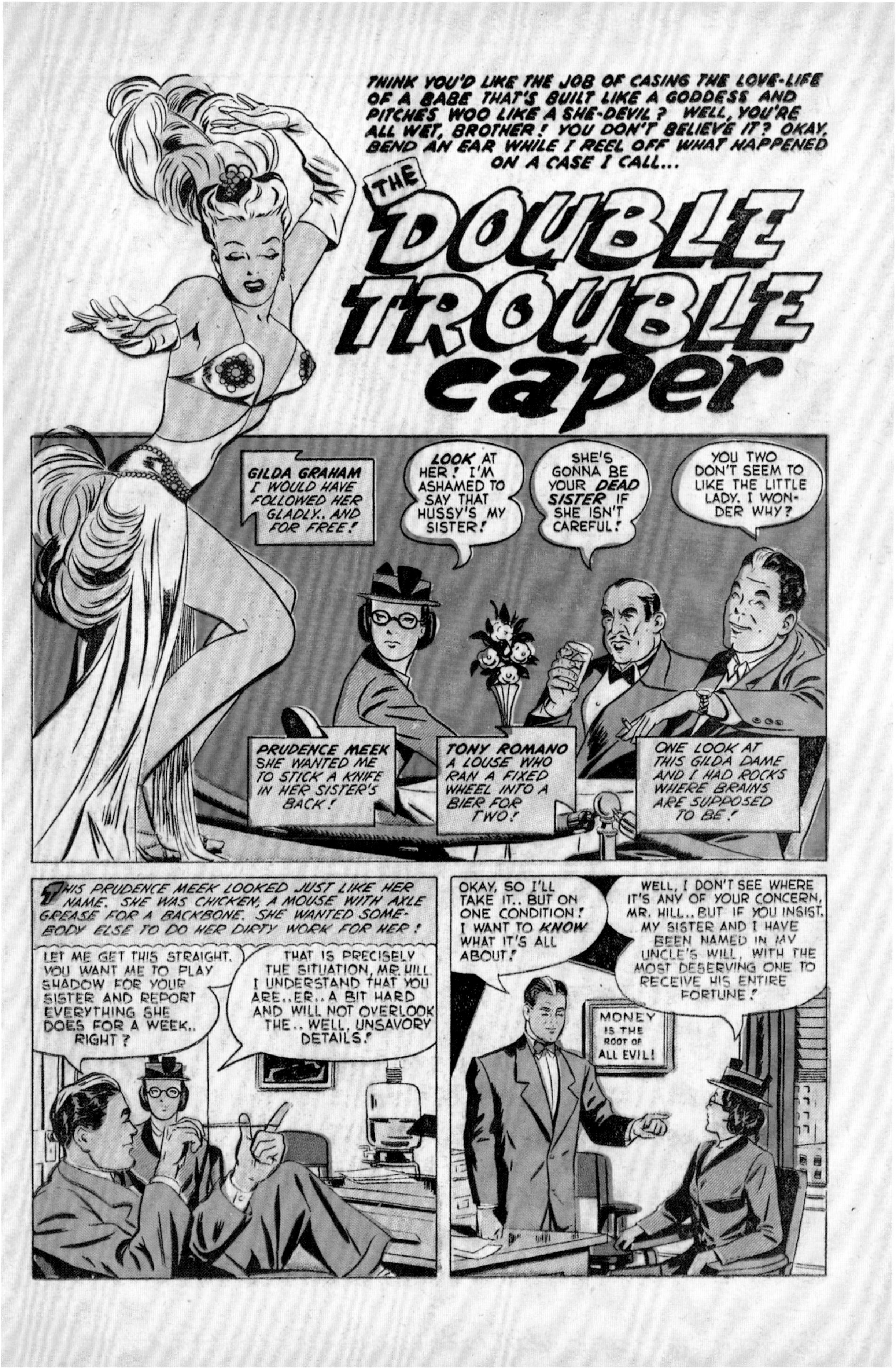
THINK YOU'D LIKE THE JOB OF CASING THE LOVE-LIFE OF A BABE THAT'S BUILT LIKE A GODDESS AND PITCHES WOO LIKE A SHE-DEVIL? WELL, YOU'RE ALL WET, BROTHER! YOU DON'T BELIEVE IT? OKAY, BEND AN EAR WHILE I REEL OFF WHAT HAPPENED ON A CASE I CALL...
THE DOUBLE TROUBLE caper
GILDA GRAHAM I WOULD HAVE FOLLOWED HER GLADLY.. AND FOR FREE!
LOOK AT HER! I'M ASHAMED TO SAY THAT HUSSY'S MY SISTER!
SHE'S GONNA BE YOUR DEAD SISTER IF SHE ISN'T CAREFUL!
YOU TWO DON'T SEEM TO LIKE THE LITTLE LADY. I WONDER WHY?
PRUDENCE MEEK SHE WANTED ME TO STICK A KNIFE IN HER SISTER'S BACK!
TONY ROMANO A LOUSE WHO RAN A FIXED WHEEL INTO A BIER FOR TWO!
ONE LOOK AT THIS GILDA DAME AND I HAD ROCKS WHERE BRAINS ARE SUPPOSED TO BE!
THIS PRUDENCE MEEK LOOKED JUST LIKE HER NAME. SHE WAS CHICKEN, A MOUSE WITH AXLE GREASE FOR A BACKBONE. SHE WANTED SOMEBODY ELSE TO DO HER DIRTY WORK FOR HER!
LET ME GET THIS STRAIGHT. YOU WANT ME TO PLAY SHADOW FOR YOUR SISTER AND REPORT EVERYTHING SHE DOES FOR A WEEK.. RIGHT?
THAT IS PRECISELY THE SITUATION, MR. HILL. I UNDERSTAND THAT YOU ARE..ER..A BIT HARD AND WILL NOT OVERLOOK THE.. WELL, UNSAVORY DETAILS!
OKAY, SO I'LL TAKE IT.. BUT ON ONE CONDITION! I WANT TO KNOW WHAT IT'S ALL ABOUT!
WELL, I DON'T SEE WHERE IT'S ANY OF YOUR CONCERN, MR. HILL.. BUT IF YOU INSIST, MY SISTER AND I HAVE BEEN NAMED IN MY UNCLE'S WILL, WITH THE MOST DESERVING ONE TO RECEIVE HIS ENTIRE FORTUNE!
MONEY IS THE ROOT OF ALL EVIL!

Sam Hill no. 1 (1950)

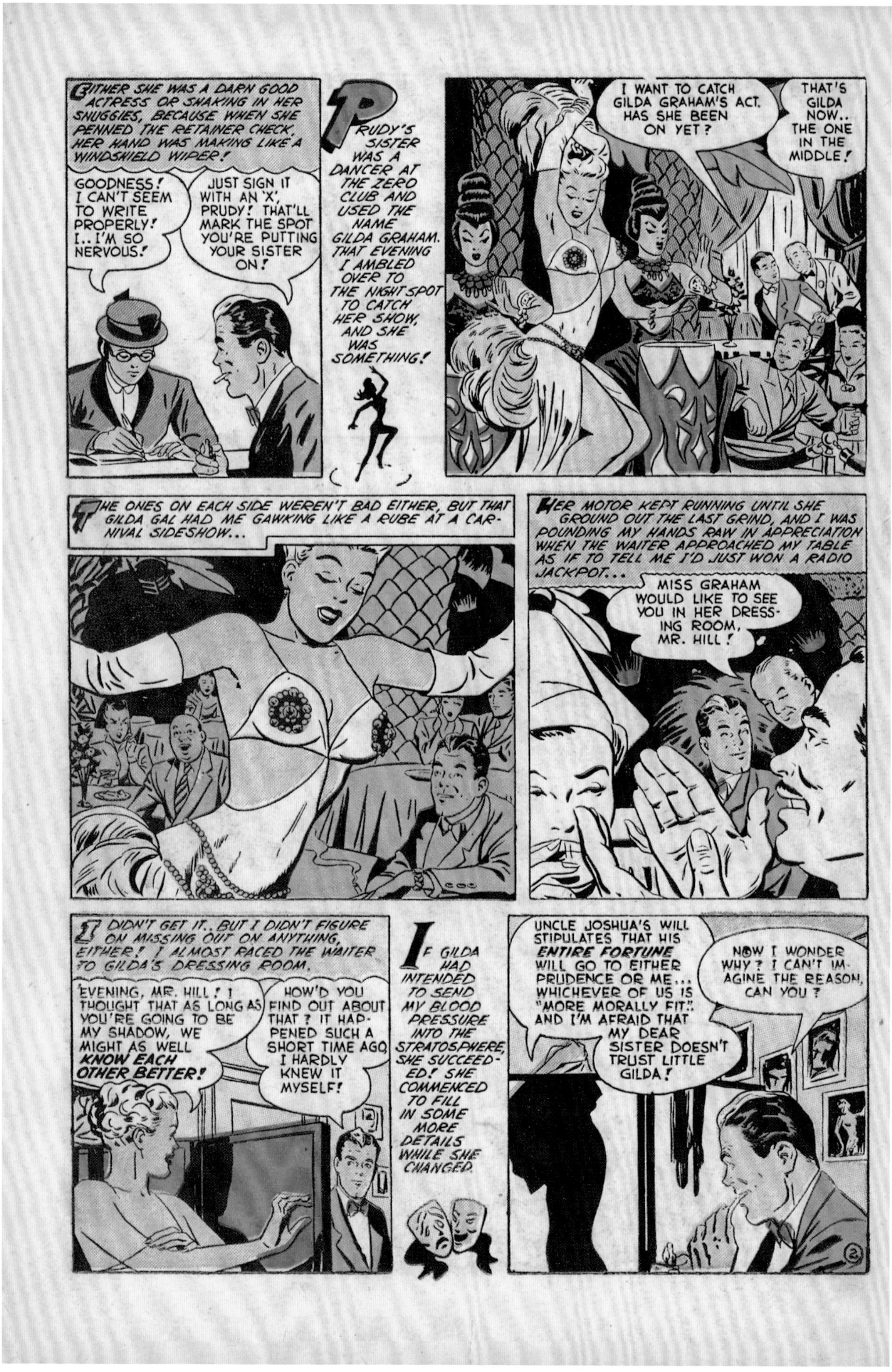
EITHER SHE WAS A DARN GOOD ACTRESS OR SHAKING IN HER SNUGGIES, BECAUSE WHEN SHE PENNED THE RETAINER CHECK, HER HAND WAS MAKING LIKE A WINDSHIELD WIPER!
GOODNESS! I CAN'T SEEM TO WRITE PROPERLY! I.. I'M SO NERVOUS!
JUST SIGN IT WITH AN 'X', PRUDY! THAT'LL MARK THE SPOT YOU'RE PUTTING YOUR SISTER ON!
PRUDY'S SISTER WAS A DANCER AT THE ZERO CLUB AND USED THE NAME GILDA GRAHAM. THAT EVENING I AMBLED OVER TO THE NIGHT SPOT TO CATCH HER SHOW, AND SHE WAS SOMETHING!
I WANT TO CATCH GILDA GRAHAM'S ACT. HAS SHE BEEN ON YET?
THAT'S GILDA NOW.. THE ONE IN THE MIDDLE!
THE ONES ON EACH SIDE WEREN'T BAD EITHER, BUT THAT GILDA GAL HAD ME GAWKING LIKE A RUBE AT A CARNIVAL SIDESHOW...
HER MOTOR KEPT RUNNING UNTIL SHE GROUND OUT THE LAST GRIND, AND I WAS POUNDING MY HANDS RAW IN APPRECIATION WHEN THE WAITER APPROACHED MY TABLE AS IF TO TELL ME I'D JUST WON A RADIO JACKPOT...
MISS GRAHAM WOULD LIKE TO SEE YOU IN HER DRESSING ROOM, MR. HILL!
I DIDN'T GET IT.. BUT I DIDN'T FIGURE ON MISSING OUT ON ANYTHING, EITHER! I ALMOST RACED THE WAITER TO GILDA'S DRESSING ROOM.
'EVENING, MR. HILL! I THOUGHT THAT AS LONG AS YOU'RE GOING TO BE MY SHADOW, WE MIGHT AS WELL KNOW EACH OTHER BETTER!
HOW'D YOU FIND OUT ABOUT THAT? IT HAPPENED SUCH A SHORT TIME AGO, I HARDLY KNEW IT MYSELF!
IF GILDA HAD INTENDED TO SEND MY BLOOD PRESSURE INTO THE STRATOSPHERE, SHE SUCCEEDED! SHE COMMENCED TO FILL IN SOME MORE DETAILS WHILE SHE CHANGED.
UNCLE JOSHUA'S WILL STIPULATES THAT HIS ENTIRE FORTUNE WILL GO TO EITHER PRUDENCE OR ME... WHICHEVER OF US IS "MORE MORALLY FIT." AND I'M AFRAID THAT MY DEAR SISTER DOESN'T TRUST LITTLE GILDA!
NOW I WONDER WHY? I CAN'T IMAGINE THE REASON, CAN YOU?
2

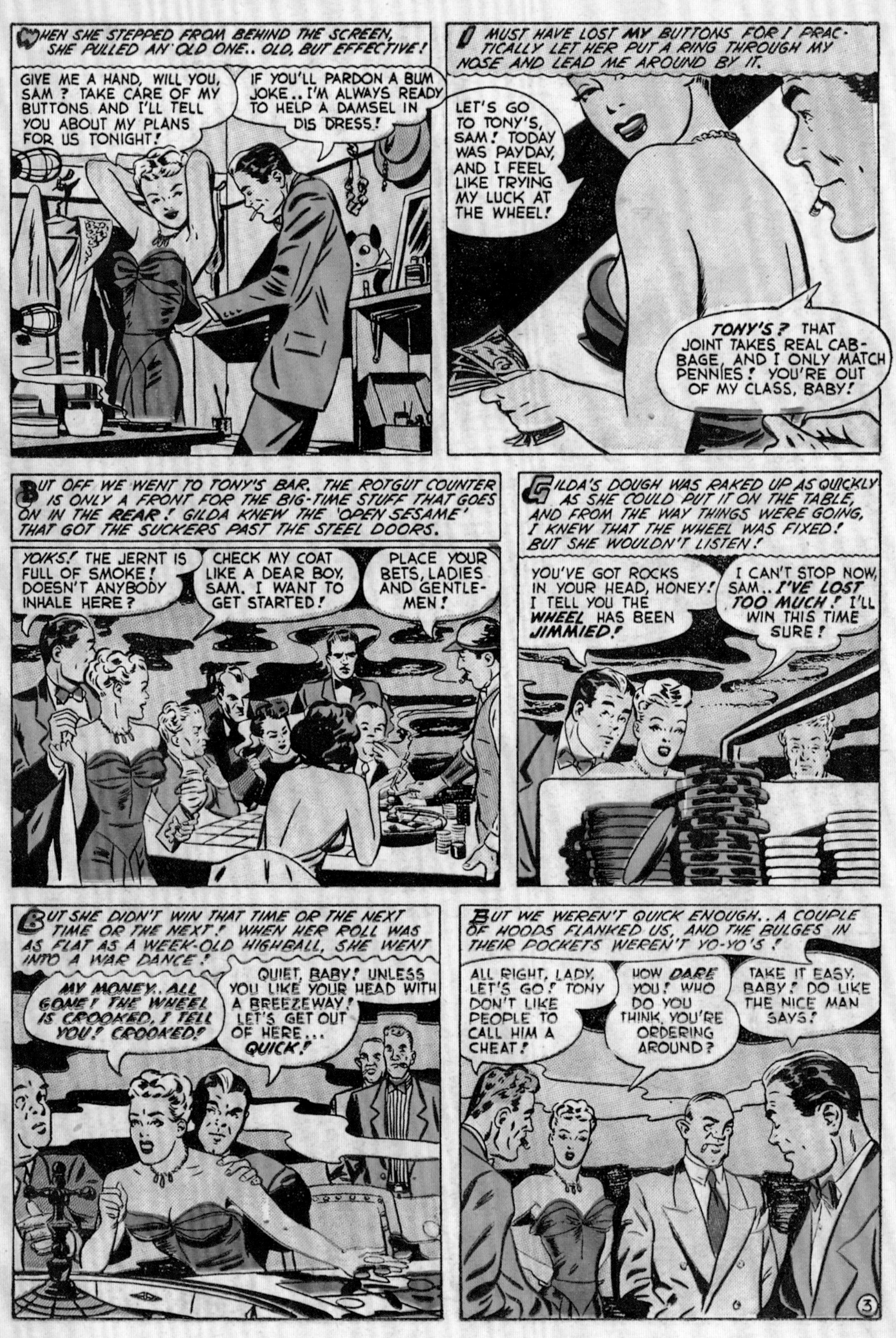
WHEN SHE STEPPED FROM BEHIND THE SCREEN, SHE PULLED AN' OLD ONE.. OLD, BUT EFFECTIVE!
GIVE ME A HAND, WILL YOU, SAM? TAKE CARE OF MY BUTTONS AND I'LL TELL YOU ABOUT MY PLANS FOR US TONIGHT!
IF YOU'LL PARDON A BUM JOKE.. I'M ALWAYS READY TO HELP A DAMSEL IN DIS DRESS!
I MUST HAVE LOST MY BUTTONS FOR I PRACTICALLY LET HER PUT A RING THROUGH MY NOSE AND LEAD ME AROUND BY IT.
LET'S GO TO TONY'S, SAM! TODAY WAS PAYDAY, AND I FEEL LIKE TRYING MY LUCK AT THE WHEEL!
TONY'S? THAT JOINT TAKES REAL CABBAGE, AND I ONLY MATCH PENNIES! YOU'RE OUT OF MY CLASS, BABY!
BUT OFF WE WENT TO TONY'S BAR. THE ROTGUT COUNTER IS ONLY A FRONT FOR THE BIG-TIME STUFF THAT GOES ON IN THE REAR! GILDA KNEW THE 'OPEN SESAME' THAT GOT THE SUCKERS PAST THE STEEL DOORS.
YOIKS! THE JERNT IS FULL OF SMOKE! DOESN'T ANYBODY INHALE HERE?
CHECK MY COAT LIKE A DEAR BOY, SAM. I WANT TO GET STARTED!
PLACE YOUR BETS, LADIES AND GENTLEMEN!
GILDA'S DOUGH WAS RAKED UP AS QUICKLY AS SHE COULD PUT IT ON THE TABLE, AND FROM THE WAY THINGS WERE GOING, I KNEW THAT THE WHEEL WAS FIXED! BUT SHE WOULDN'T LISTEN!
YOU'VE GOT ROCKS IN YOUR HEAD, HONEY! I TELL YOU THE WHEEL HAS BEEN JIMMIED!
I CAN'T STOP NOW, SAM.. I'VE LOST TOO MUCH! I'LL WIN THIS TIME SURE!
BUT SHE DIDN'T WIN THAT TIME OR THE NEXT TIME OR THE NEXT! WHEN HER ROLL WAS AS FLAT AS A WEEK-OLD HIGHBALL, SHE WENT INTO A WAR DANCE!
MY MONEY.. ALL GONE! THE WHEEL IS CROOKED, I TELL YOU! CROOKED!
QUIET, BABY! UNLESS YOU LIKE YOUR HEAD WITH A BREEZEWAY! LET'S GET OUT OF HERE... QUICK!
BUT WE WEREN'T QUICK ENOUGH.. A COUPLE OF HOODS FLANKED US, AND THE BULGES IN THEIR POCKETS WEREN'T YO-YO'S!
ALL RIGHT, LADY, LET'S GO! TONY DON'T LIKE PEOPLE TO CALL HIM A CHEAT!
HOW DARE YOU! WHO DO YOU THINK YOU'RE ORDERING AROUND?
TAKE IT EASY, BABY! DO LIKE THE NICE MAN SAYS!
3

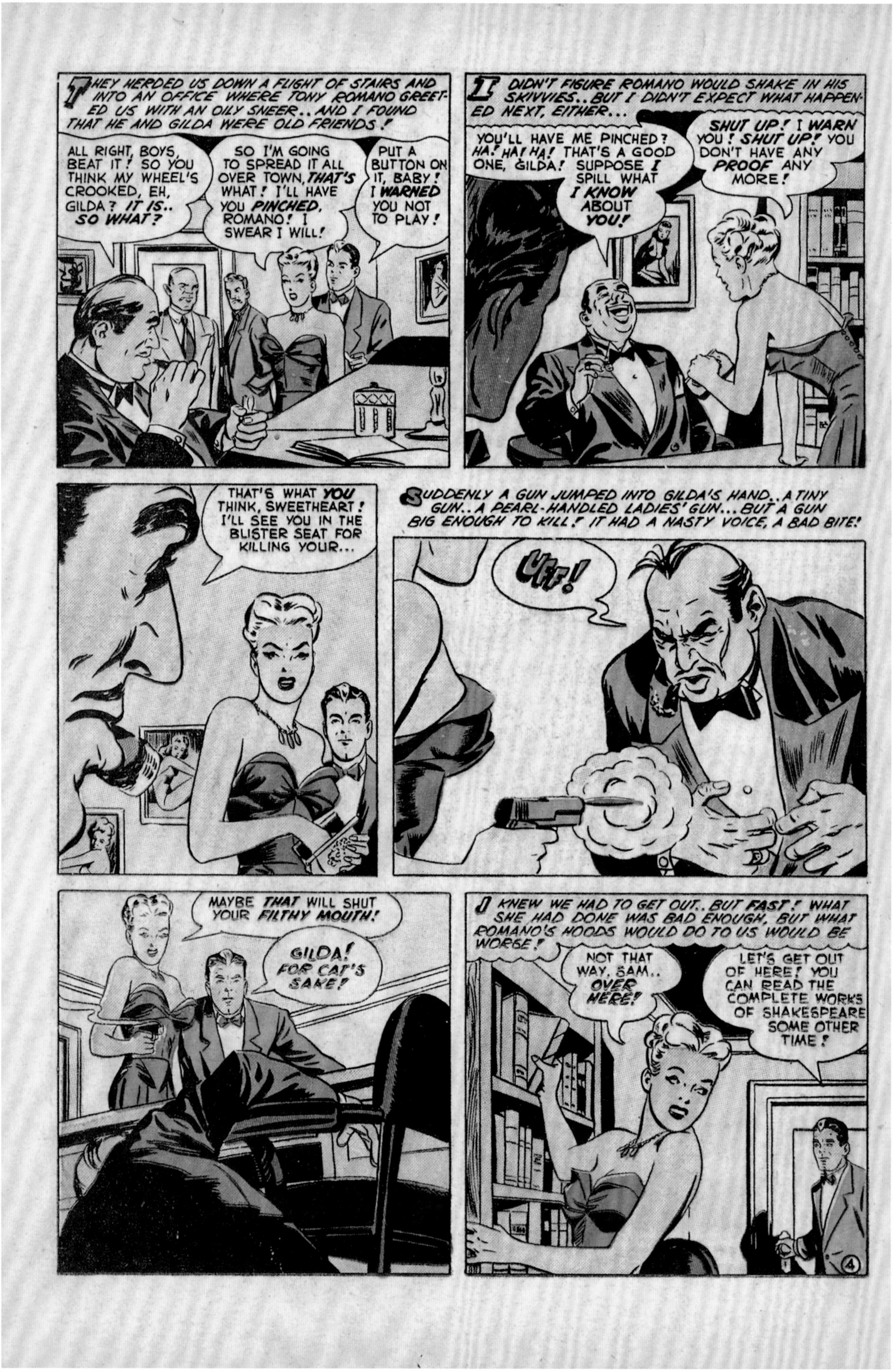
THEY HERDED US DOWN A FLIGHT OF STAIRS AND INTO AN OFFICE WHERE TONY ROMANO GREETED US WITH AN OILY SNEER...AND I FOUND THAT HE AND GILDA WERE OLD FRIENDS!
ALL RIGHT, BOYS, BEAT IT! SO YOU THINK MY WHEEL'S CROOKED, EH, GILDA? IT IS.. SO WHAT?
SO I'M GOING TO SPREAD IT ALL OVER TOWN, THAT'S WHAT! I'LL HAVE YOU PINCHED, ROMANO! I SWEAR I WILL!
PUT A BUTTON ON IT, BABY! I WARNED YOU NOT TO PLAY!
I DIDN'T FIGURE ROMANO WOULD SHAKE IN HIS SKIVVIES..BUT I DIDN'T EXPECT WHAT HAPPENED NEXT, EITHER...
YOU'LL HAVE ME PINCHED? HA! HA! HA! THAT'S A GOOD ONE, GILDA! SUPPOSE I SPILL WHAT I KNOW ABOUT YOU!
SHUT UP! I WARN YOU! SHUT UP! YOU DON'T HAVE ANY PROOF ANY MORE!
THAT'S WHAT YOU THINK, SWEETHEART! I'LL SEE YOU IN THE BLISTER SEAT FOR KILLING YOUR...
SUDDENLY A GUN JUMPED INTO GILDA'S HAND..A TINY GUN..A PEARL-HANDLED LADIES' GUN...BUT A GUN BIG ENOUGH TO KILL! IT HAD A NASTY VOICE, A BAD BITE!
UFF!
MAYBE THAT WILL SHUT YOUR FILTHY MOUTH!
GILDA! FOR CAT'S SAKE!
I KNEW WE HAD TO GET OUT..BUT FAST! WHAT SHE HAD DONE WAS BAD ENOUGH, BUT WHAT ROMANO'S HOODS WOULD DO TO US WOULD BE WORSE!
NOT THAT WAY, SAM.. OVER HERE!
LET'S GET OUT OF HERE! YOU CAN READ THE COMPLETE WORKS OF SHAKESPEARE SOME OTHER TIME!
4

GILDA PULLED A BOOK AND THE WHOLE BOOKCASE SWUNG BACK. A HIDDEN EXIT! JUST LIKE IN THE MOVIES! IT OCCURRED TO ME THAT SHE WAS RUNNING THE SHOW.. BUT SHE WASN'T FINISHED WITH ROMANO. HE STILL HAD ENOUGH LEFT TO PULL OUT A BLASTER AND SQUEEZE A SHOT AT US AS WE DASHED OUT!

HURRY, BABY.. PUMP THOSE PINS!

EE°K! MY ARM!

WE TOOK IT ON THE LAM DOWN AN ALLEY. ROMANO'S HOODS CAME AFTER US.. AND IT LOOKED LIKE A TIGHT SPOT...

C'MON.. MOVE! THEY'LL HANG US IF THEY GET US!

GET 'EM! THEY BUMPED TONY!

I.. CAN'T.. ≥PUFF≥.. GO.. ANY FASTER!

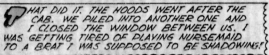

LUCKY FOR US, THERE WAS A CAB WAITING WHEN WE GOT TO THE STREET. WE HOPPED IN AND WHEN THE CABBIE SAW MY HEATER HE REALLY TOOK OFF!

THROW THE COAL TO THIS HEAP, BUDDY! FAST!

YES, SIR!

I TOLD THE DRIVER WHAT TO DO. HE TOOK A CORNER, SLOWED DOWN.. AND WE HOPPED OUT! IT WAS OUR ONLY CHANCE TO KEEP FROM NEEDING CORKS IN OUR HIDES!

THAT DID IT. THE HOODS WENT AFTER THE CAB. WE PILED INTO ANOTHER ONE AND I CLOSED THE WINDOW BETWEEN US. I WAS GETTING TIRED OF PLAYING NURSEMAID TO A BRAT I WAS SUPPOSED TO BE SHADOWING!

OKAY, BABY, LAY IT ON THE LINE! WHY THE FIREWORKS IN ROMANO'S OFFICE?

OH, SAM, I (SOB) I DON'T KNOW WHAT TO SAY! I JUST (SOB) LOST MY HEAD!

IF I WAS SUPPOSED TO SUPPLY THE SHOULDER FOR HER TO CRY ON, I DIDN'T READ THE SCRIPT...

NO, BABY! THAT'S NOT THE WAY I SEE IT! YOU MEANT TO KILL ROMANO TONIGHT.. AND YOU WANTED ME IN ON IT! WHY?

YOU'RE ALL WRONG, SAM, I SWEAR IT! LOOK.. THIS PAPER WILL PROVE IT!

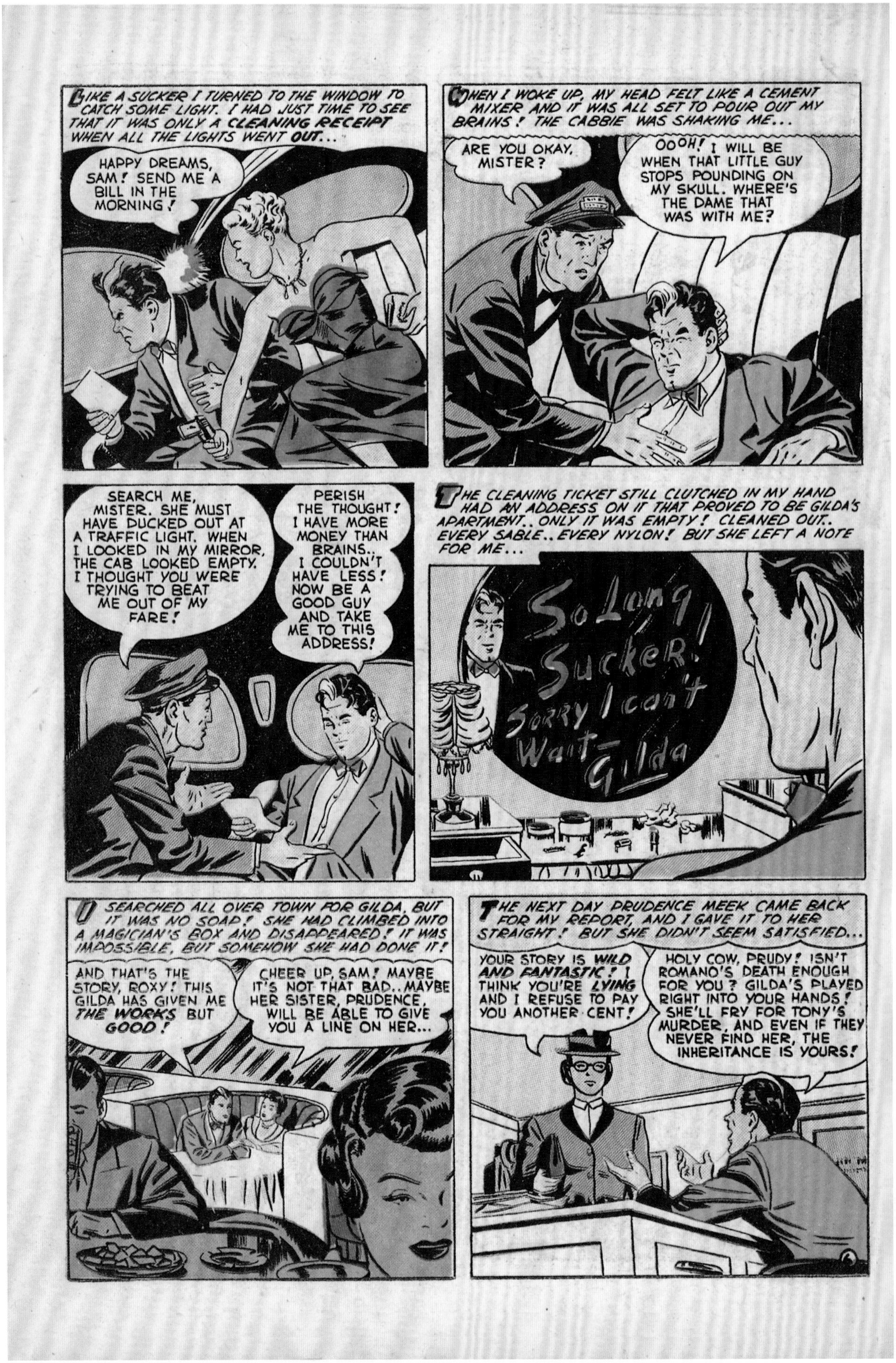
LIKE A SUCKER I TURNED TO THE WINDOW TO CATCH SOME LIGHT. I HAD JUST TIME TO SEE THAT IT WAS ONLY A CLEANING RECEIPT WHEN ALL THE LIGHTS WENT OUT...
HAPPY DREAMS, SAM! SEND ME A BILL IN THE MORNING!
WHEN I WOKE UP, MY HEAD FELT LIKE A CEMENT MIXER AND IT WAS ALL SET TO POUR OUT MY BRAINS! THE CABBIE WAS SHAKING ME...
ARE YOU OKAY, MISTER?
OOOH! I WILL BE WHEN THAT LITTLE GUY STOPS POUNDING ON MY SKULL. WHERE'S THE DAME THAT WAS WITH ME?
SEARCH ME, MISTER. SHE MUST HAVE DUCKED OUT AT A TRAFFIC LIGHT. WHEN I LOOKED IN MY MIRROR, THE CAB LOOKED EMPTY. I THOUGHT YOU WERE TRYING TO BEAT ME OUT OF MY FARE!
PERISH THE THOUGHT! I HAVE MORE MONEY THAN BRAINS.. I COULDN'T HAVE LESS! NOW BE A GOOD GUY AND TAKE ME TO THIS ADDRESS!
THE CLEANING TICKET STILL CLUTCHED IN MY HAND HAD AN ADDRESS ON IT THAT PROVED TO BE GILDA'S APARTMENT.. ONLY IT WAS EMPTY! CLEANED OUT.. EVERY SABLE.. EVERY NYLON! BUT SHE LEFT A NOTE FOR ME...
So Long Sucker! Sorry I can't Wait— Gilda
I SEARCHED ALL OVER TOWN FOR GILDA, BUT IT WAS NO SOAP! SHE HAD CLIMBED INTO A MAGICIAN'S BOX AND DISAPPEARED! IT WAS IMPOSSIBLE, BUT SOMEHOW SHE HAD DONE IT!
AND THAT'S THE STORY, ROXY! THIS GILDA HAS GIVEN ME THE WORKS BUT GOOD!
CHEER UP, SAM! MAYBE IT'S NOT THAT BAD.. MAYBE HER SISTER, PRUDENCE, WILL BE ABLE TO GIVE YOU A LINE ON HER...
THE NEXT DAY PRUDENCE MEEK CAME BACK FOR MY REPORT, AND I GAVE IT TO HER STRAIGHT! BUT SHE DIDN'T SEEM SATISFIED...
YOUR STORY IS WILD AND FANTASTIC! I THINK YOU'RE LYING AND I REFUSE TO PAY YOU ANOTHER CENT!
HOLY COW, PRUDY! ISN'T ROMANO'S DEATH ENOUGH FOR YOU? GILDA'S PLAYED RIGHT INTO YOUR HANDS! SHE'LL FRY FOR TONY'S MURDER, AND EVEN IF THEY NEVER FIND HER, THE INHERITANCE IS YOURS!

IF THEY NEVER FIND HER! A BELL RANG IN THE BACK OF MY HEAD! I THOUGHT I HAD THE ANSWER.. I KNEW I HAD THE ANSWER!

MY ARM, MR. HILL.. YOU'RE HURTING ME!

I HAD FIGURED RIGHT.. AND JUST TO BE POSITIVE I PULLED HER COAT DOWN AND RIPPED THE SLEEVE OFF HER DRESS!

NOT AS MUCH AS TONY ROMANO'S BULLET, I'LL BET!

STOP IT, YOU BEAST!

AND THESE PHONY CHEATERS AND WIG AREN'T VERY BECOMING, EITHER.. GILDA!

NOW I KNOW THE WHOLE STORY, BABY! YOU KILLED YOUR SISTER AND ROMANO KNEW IT! YOU HAD TO KILL HIM, TOO...

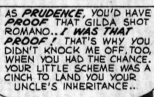

AS PRUDENCE, YOU'D HAVE PROOF THAT GILDA SHOT ROMANO.. I WAS THAT PROOF! THAT'S WHY YOU DIDN'T KNOCK ME OFF, TOO, WHEN YOU HAD THE CHANCE. YOUR LITTLE SCHEME WAS A CINCH TO LAND YOU YOUR UNCLE'S INHERITANCE..

SAM H
PRIVATE INVE

THAT BABE WAS A WILDCAT. SUDDENLY THERE WAS A GUN IN HER HAND.. THAT SAME LITTLE AUTOMATIC.. BUT THIS TIME SHE HAD TO GLOAT A LITTLE.

YES, I KILLED THEM! AND NOW I'LL JUST HAVE TO KILL YOU.. BECAUSE YOU ARE THE ONLY PERSON WHO KNOWS WHO I AM! I'M AFRAID THIS IS GOOD-BY, SAM!

YEAH.. I GUESS IT IS!

MY GAL FRIDAY MOVED FAST, AND I COULD HAVE KISSED HER PRETTY PAINTED LIPS! I NEVER KNEW SHE COULD HEAVE A MILK BOTTLE LIKE THAT!

GOOD-BY, HONEY.. OR SHOULD I SAY GOODNIGHT?

GOOD GIRL, ROXY! REMIND ME TO GIVE YOU A RAISE SOME DAY!

AND THAT WAS THAT! ROXY HAD SAID THAT PRUDENCE MIGHT GIVE ME A LINE ON GILDA.. BUT I DIDN'T REALIZE IT MIGHT BE THAT GOOD A LINE! YES, SIR, YOU'VE GOT TO HAND IT TO ROXY.. SHE'S SOME GAL!

CALL THE PIE WAGON FOR OUR CLIENT, ROXY! THEN HURRY BACK AND I'LL GIVE YOU A KISS!

WHY WAIT, BOSS? WHEN I HIT 'EM THEY STAY HIT.. AND I COULD USE THAT KISS NOW!

H. G. PETER

(?–1958)

H. G. Peter found his way into comic books late in life. Though his early history is largely unknown, he was apparently already working for the *San Francisco Chronicle* by 1906, and as early as 1908 was contributing detailed pen-and-ink tableaus to magazines, including *Judge*. According to Dr. William Moulton Marston, Peter claimed to have worked with Bud Fisher on *Mutt and Jeff*.

By 1940 Peter was living on Staten Island and drawing for the new comic books that were emerging. Marston, the creator of Wonder Woman, employed Peter to draw his new character from her 1941 debut in *All-Star Comics* no. 8 until 1958. Sheldon Mayer, who edited those comics, noted that Peter was considerably older than himself and his peers. Already a veteran illustrator, Peter's sophisticated compositions and assured line work set him apart from the very young men who dominated this new medium. Peter's style, with its roots in turn of the century Victoriana, was ideally suited to the mythological scenarios of Wonder Woman. He often worked in the Marston Art Studio on Madison Avenue and 43rd Street in Manhattan, aided by a number of usually female assistants in cranking out first the comic book and then the daily comic strip.

Man O'Metal debuted in *Heroic Comics* no. 7 in 1941 (sharing space with Bill Everett's Hydroman), and it was in this comic that Peter was able to move away from Wonder Woman's cramped, detail-oriented panels to expansive pulp-style heroics. The Man O'Metal stories chronicled the adventures of Pat Dempsey, a former steel worker whose dousing by molten steel enables him, at the slightest exposure to electricity or fire, to transform into a flaming blue metallic being. Naturally, Dempsey goes to work for the U.S. government as a secret agent. Peter gave Dempsey a near-grotesque, enormous physique perfectly built for gory action sequences. Each panel is crowded with figures rendered in sinewy lines. At times Peter's characters resemble Andreas Vesalius's skinless anatomical renderings of the Renaissance and can also call to mind the haunted skeletal figurations of the nineteenth-century avant-garde painter James Ensor. Occasionally readers can catch a glimpse of other nineteenth-century styles, but these are quickly jarred loose by the shirtless, muscular hero barging across the page. It's partly that push and pull—between the style Peter had worked for decades and the obvious freedom he must have felt in letting a certain amount of chaos onto the page—that makes "Man O'Metal" so compelling. These tumbling pages have an unusually strong visceral presence. Peter's use of the sheer physicality of his renderings was uncommonly developed for that period in comic books, anticipating the 1960s style that Jack Kirby would initiate, with his thick masses of flesh and ultra-kinetic action sequences.

Little is known about Peter's life, and his name has been mostly subsumed underneath Marston's and the Amazon the good doctor created. Peter's Man O'Metal ran until *Heroic Comics* no. 28, usually with multi-issue storylines. Peter devoted most of his time in the late 1940s and throughout the 1950s to Wonder Woman, and died the same year he was let go from the feature.

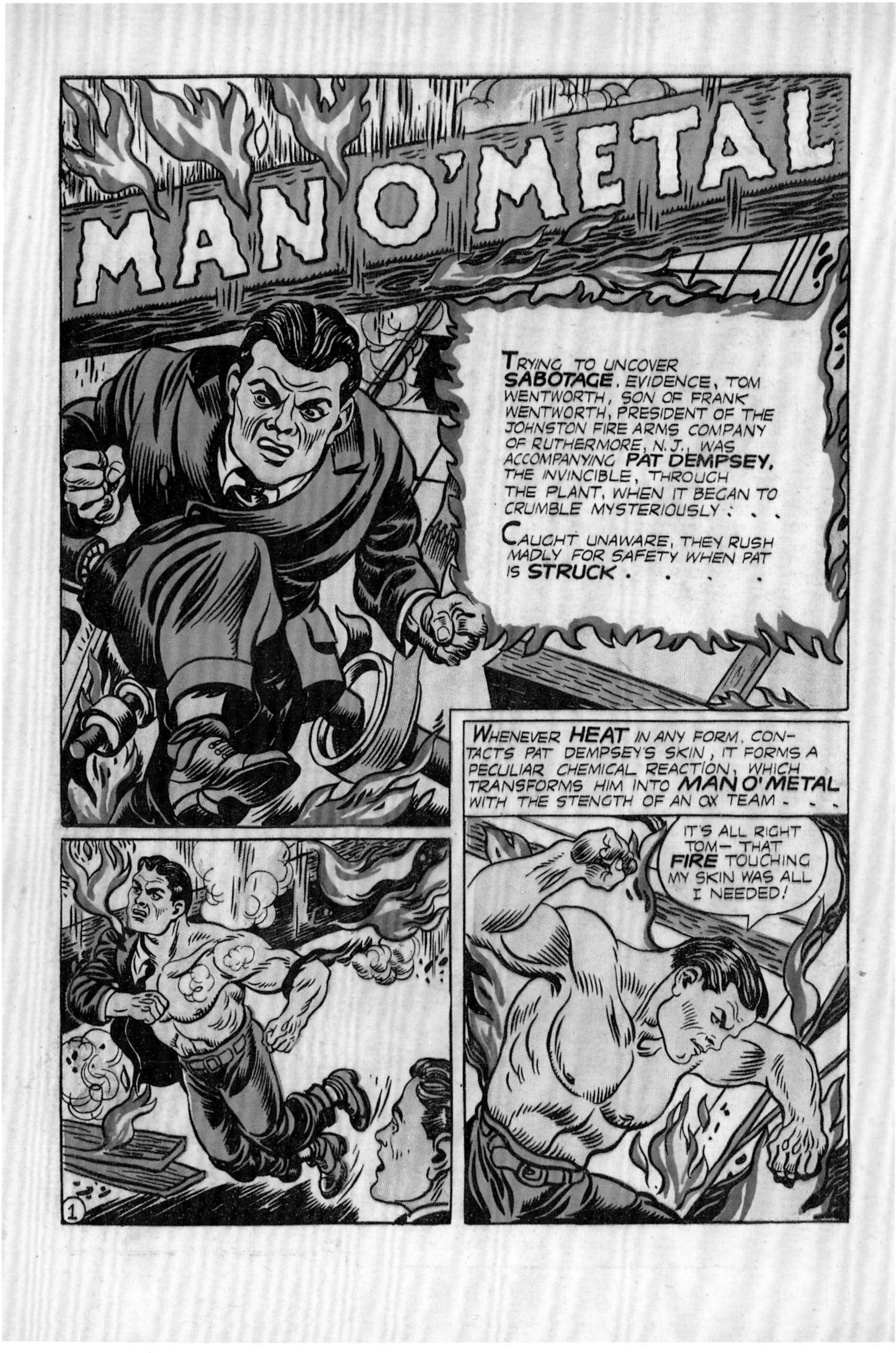
MAN O'METAL
TRYING TO UNCOVER SABOTAGE. EVIDENCE, TOM WENTWORTH, SON OF FRANK WENTWORTH, PRESIDENT OF THE JOHNSTON FIRE ARMS COMPANY OF RUTHERMORE, N.J., WAS ACCOMPANYING PAT DEMPSEY, THE INVINCIBLE, THROUGH THE PLANT, WHEN IT BEGAN TO CRUMBLE MYSTERIOUSLY: . .
CAUGHT UNAWARE, THEY RUSH MADLY FOR SAFETY WHEN PAT IS STRUCK . . . .
WHENEVER HEAT IN ANY FORM, CONTACTS PAT DEMPSEY'S SKIN, IT FORMS A PECULIAR CHEMICAL REACTION, WHICH TRANSFORMS HIM INTO MAN O'METAL WITH THE STENGTH OF AN OX TEAM - . .
IT'S ALL RIGHT TOM— THAT FIRE TOUCHING MY SKIN WAS ALL I NEEDED!
1

Reg'lar Fellers Heroic Comics no. 13 (1942)

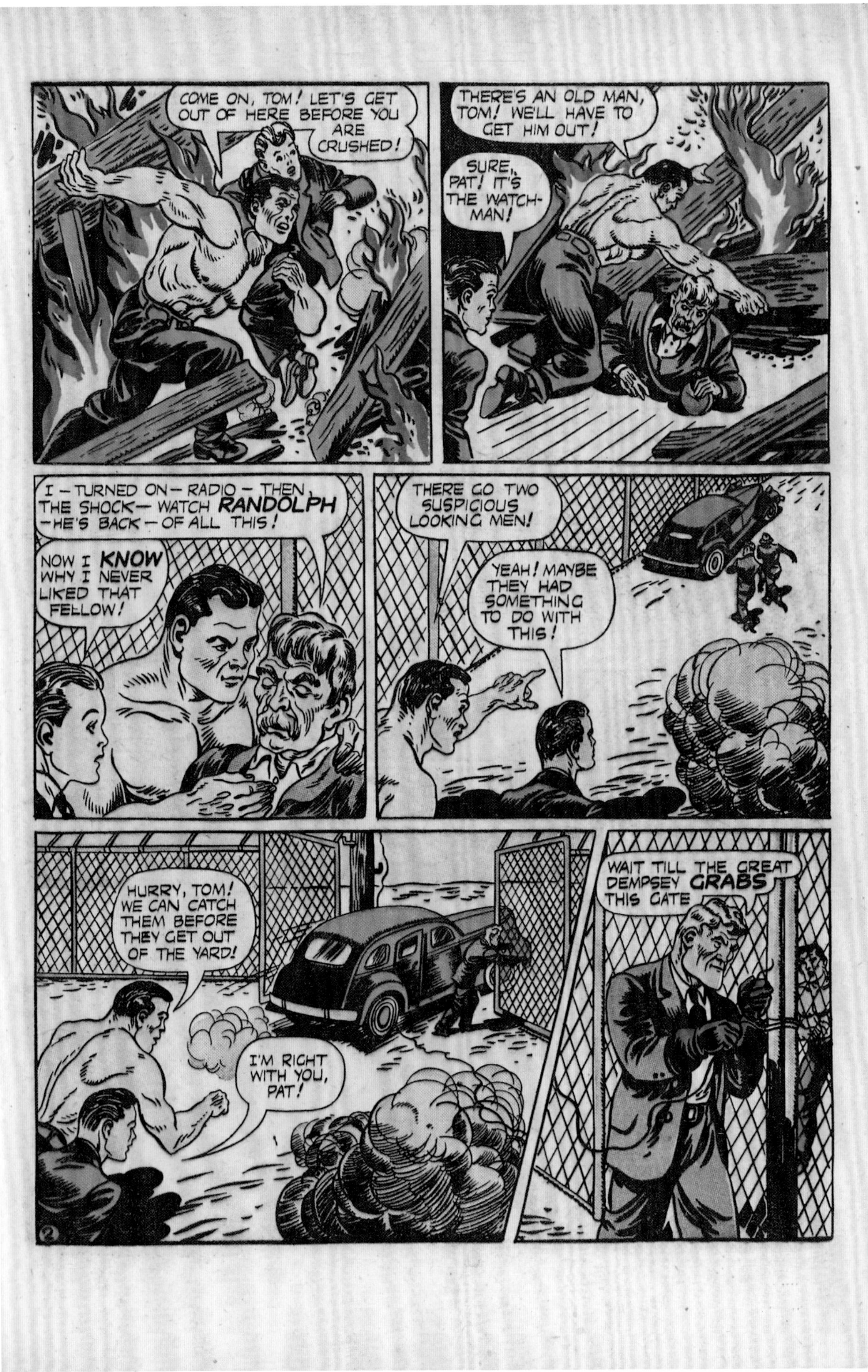
COME ON, TOM! LET'S GET OUT OF HERE BEFORE YOU ARE CRUSHED!
THERE'S AN OLD MAN, TOM! WE'LL HAVE TO GET HIM OUT!
SURE, PAT! IT'S THE WATCH-MAN!
I—TURNED ON—RADIO—THEN, THE SHOCK—WATCH RANDOLPH—HE'S BACK—OF ALL THIS!
NOW I KNOW WHY I NEVER LIKED THAT FELLOW!
THERE GO TWO SUSPICIOUS LOOKING MEN!
YEAH! MAYBE THEY HAD SOMETHING TO DO WITH THIS!
HURRY, TOM! WE CAN CATCH THEM BEFORE THEY GET OUT OF THE YARD!
I'M RIGHT WITH YOU, PAT!
WAIT TILL THE GREAT DEMPSEY GRABS THIS GATE

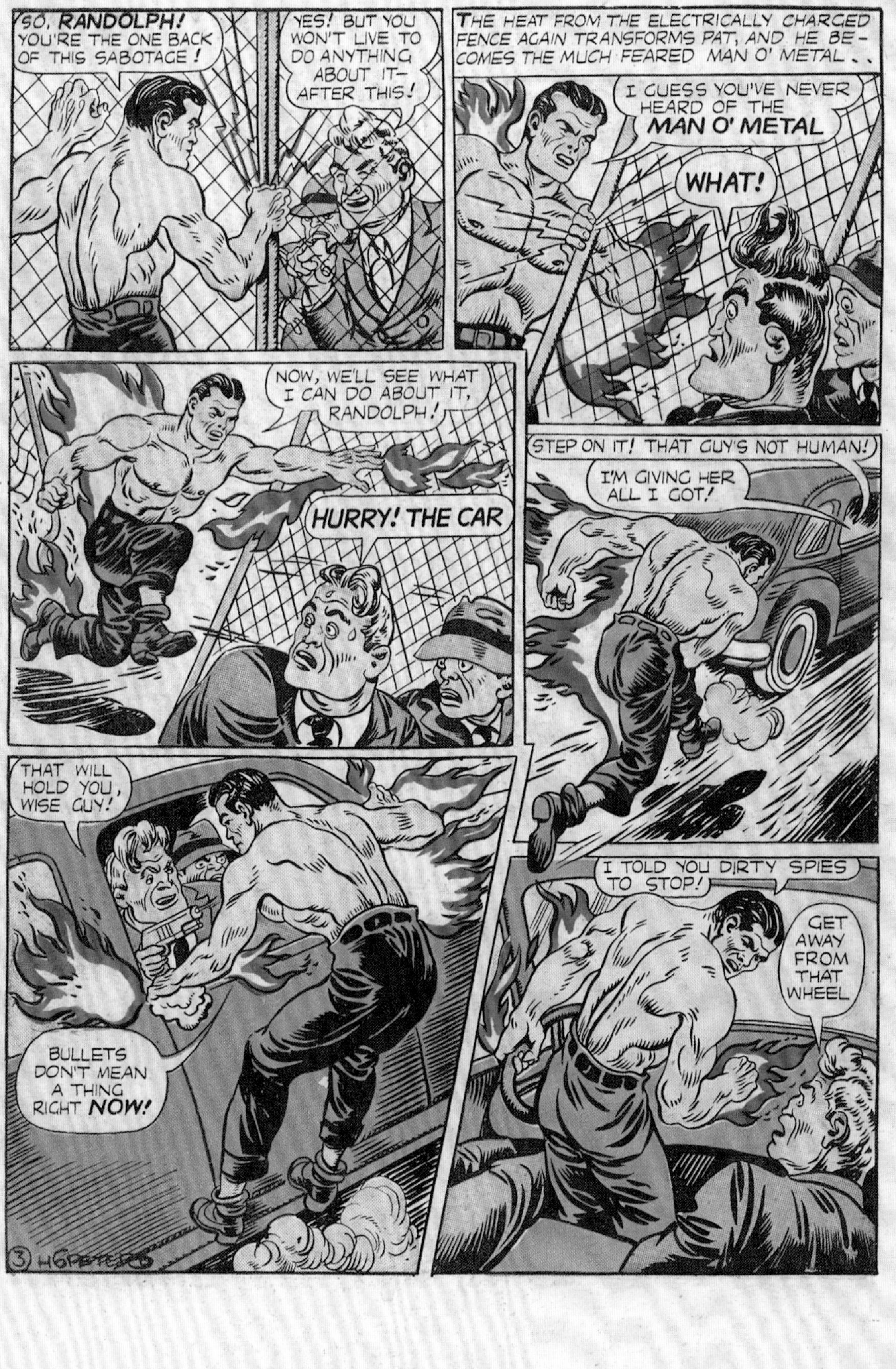
SO, RANDOLPH! YOU'RE THE ONE BACK OF THIS SABOTAGE!
YES! BUT YOU WON'T LIVE TO DO ANYTHING ABOUT IT– AFTER THIS!
THE HEAT FROM THE ELECTRICALLY CHARGED FENCE AGAIN TRANSFORMS PAT, AND HE BECOMES THE MUCH FEARED MAN O' METAL . .
I GUESS YOU'VE NEVER HEARD OF THE MAN O' METAL
WHAT!
NOW, WE'LL SEE WHAT I CAN DO ABOUT IT, RANDOLPH!
HURRY! THE CAR
STEP ON IT! THAT GUY'S NOT HUMAN!
I'M GIVING HER ALL I GOT!
THAT WILL HOLD YOU, WISE GUY!
BULLETS DON'T MEAN A THING RIGHT NOW!
I TOLD YOU DIRTY SPIES TO STOP!
GET AWAY FROM THAT WHEEL
3

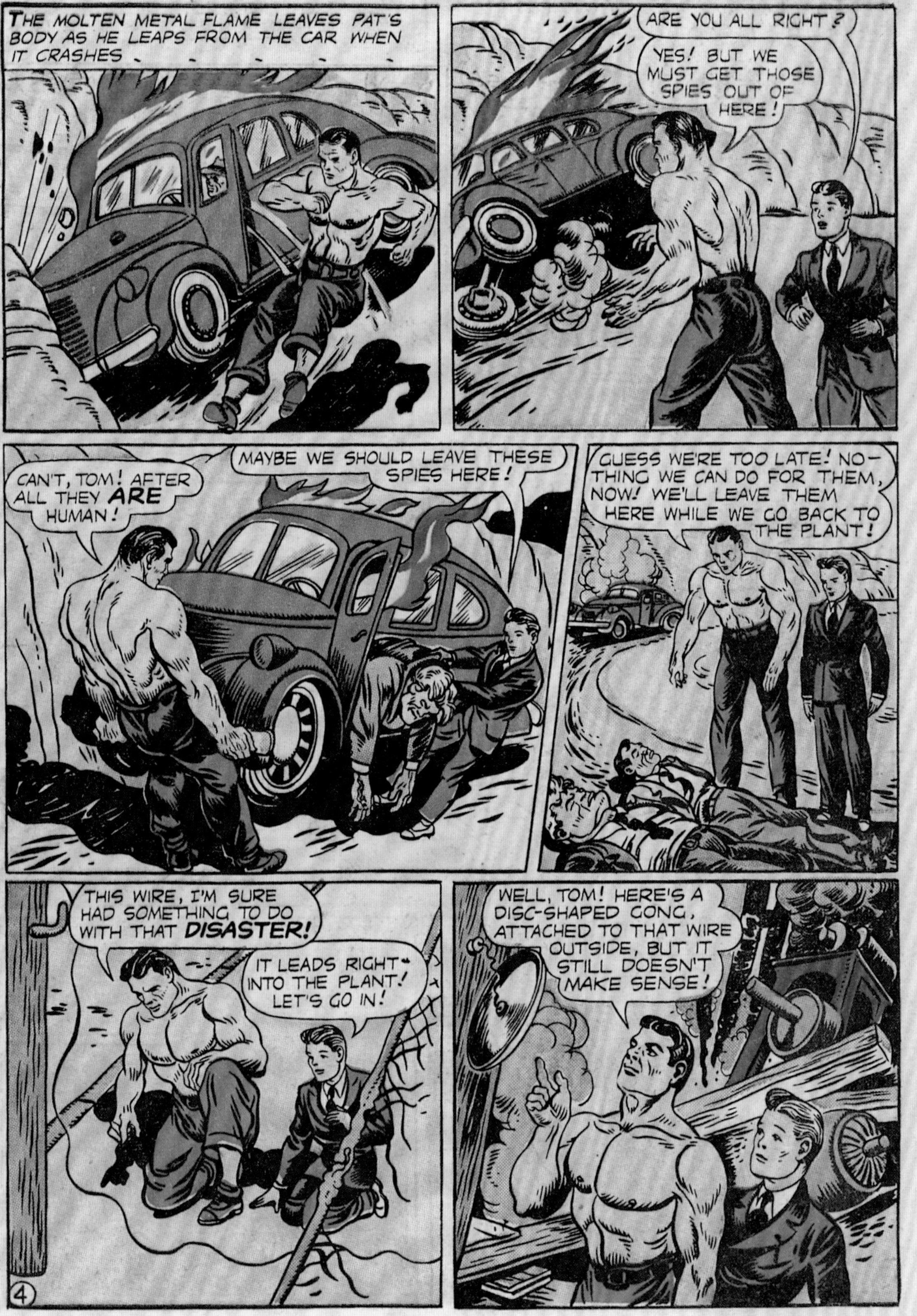
THE MOLTEN METAL FLAME LEAVES PAT'S BODY AS HE LEAPS FROM THE CAR WHEN IT CRASHES . . . . .
ARE YOU ALL RIGHT?
YES! BUT WE MUST GET THOSE SPIES OUT OF HERE!
MAYBE WE SHOULD LEAVE THESE SPIES HERE!
CAN'T, TOM! AFTER ALL THEY ARE HUMAN!
GUESS WE'RE TOO LATE! NOTHING WE CAN DO FOR THEM, NOW! WE'LL LEAVE THEM HERE WHILE WE GO BACK TO THE PLANT!
THIS WIRE, I'M SURE HAD SOMETHING TO DO WITH THAT DISASTER!
IT LEADS RIGHT INTO THE PLANT! LET'S GO IN!
WELL, TOM! HERE'S A DISC-SHAPED GONG, ATTACHED TO THAT WIRE OUTSIDE, BUT IT STILL DOESN'T MAKE SENSE!
4

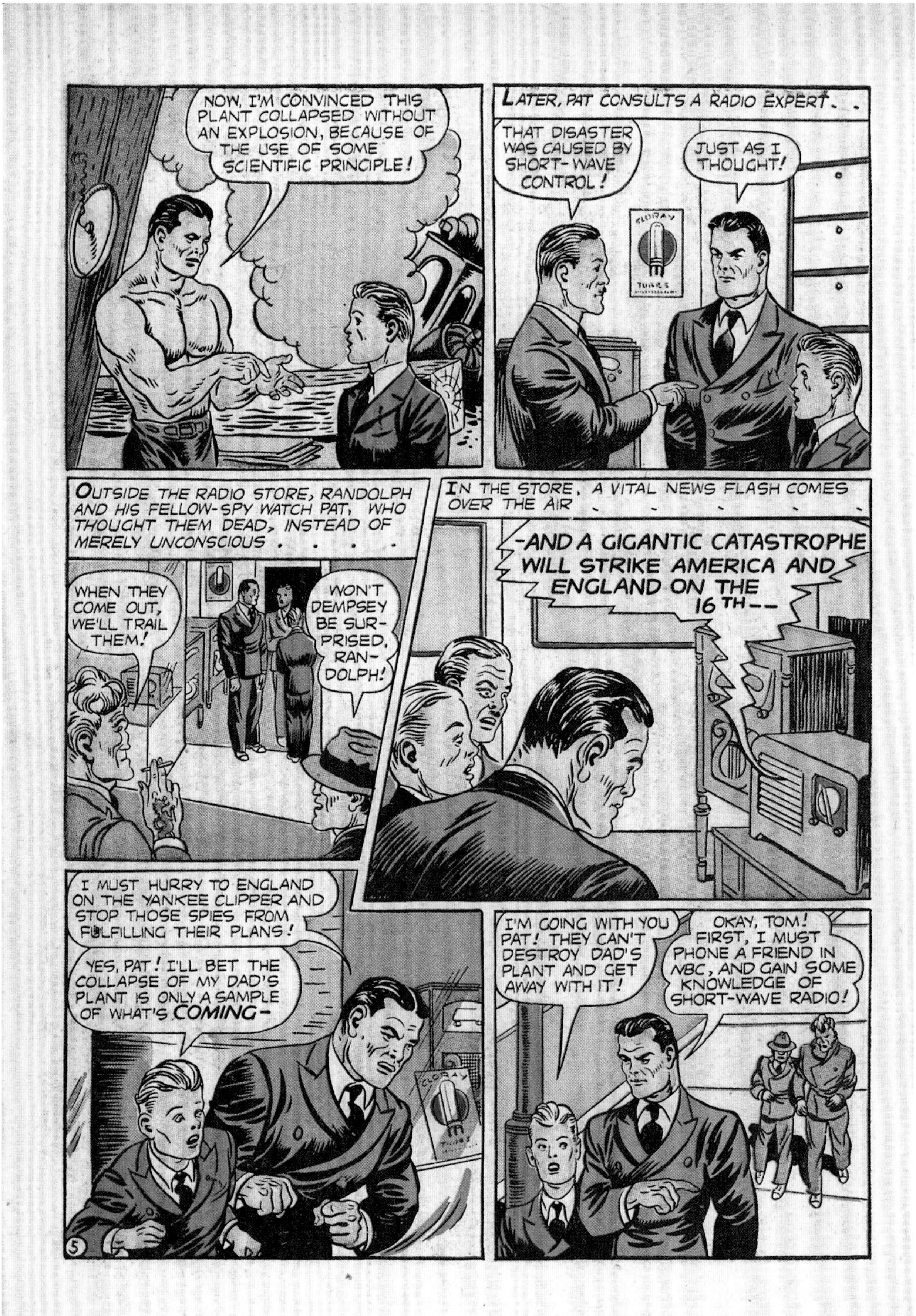
NOW, I'M CONVINCED THIS PLANT COLLAPSED WITHOUT AN EXPLOSION, BECAUSE OF THE USE OF SOME SCIENTIFIC PRINCIPLE!
LATER, PAT CONSULTS A RADIO EXPERT . . .
THAT DISASTER WAS CAUSED BY SHORT-WAVE CONTROL!
JUST AS I THOUGHT!
OUTSIDE THE RADIO STORE, RANDOLPH AND HIS FELLOW-SPY WATCH PAT, WHO THOUGHT THEM DEAD, INSTEAD OF MERELY UNCONSCIOUS . . . .
WHEN THEY COME OUT, WE'LL TRAIL THEM!
WON'T DEMPSEY BE SURPRISED, RANDOLPH!
IN THE STORE, A VITAL NEWS FLASH COMES OVER THE AIR . . . . . .
-AND A GIGANTIC CATASTROPHE WILL STRIKE AMERICA AND ENGLAND ON THE 16TH--
I MUST HURRY TO ENGLAND ON THE YANKEE CLIPPER AND STOP THOSE SPIES FROM FULFILLING THEIR PLANS!
YES, PAT! I'LL BET THE COLLAPSE OF MY DAD'S PLANT IS ONLY A SAMPLE OF WHAT'S COMING-
I'M GOING WITH YOU PAT! THEY CAN'T DESTROY DAD'S PLANT AND GET AWAY WITH IT!
OKAY, TOM! FIRST, I MUST PHONE A FRIEND IN NBC, AND GAIN SOME KNOWLEDGE OF SHORT-WAVE RADIO!
5

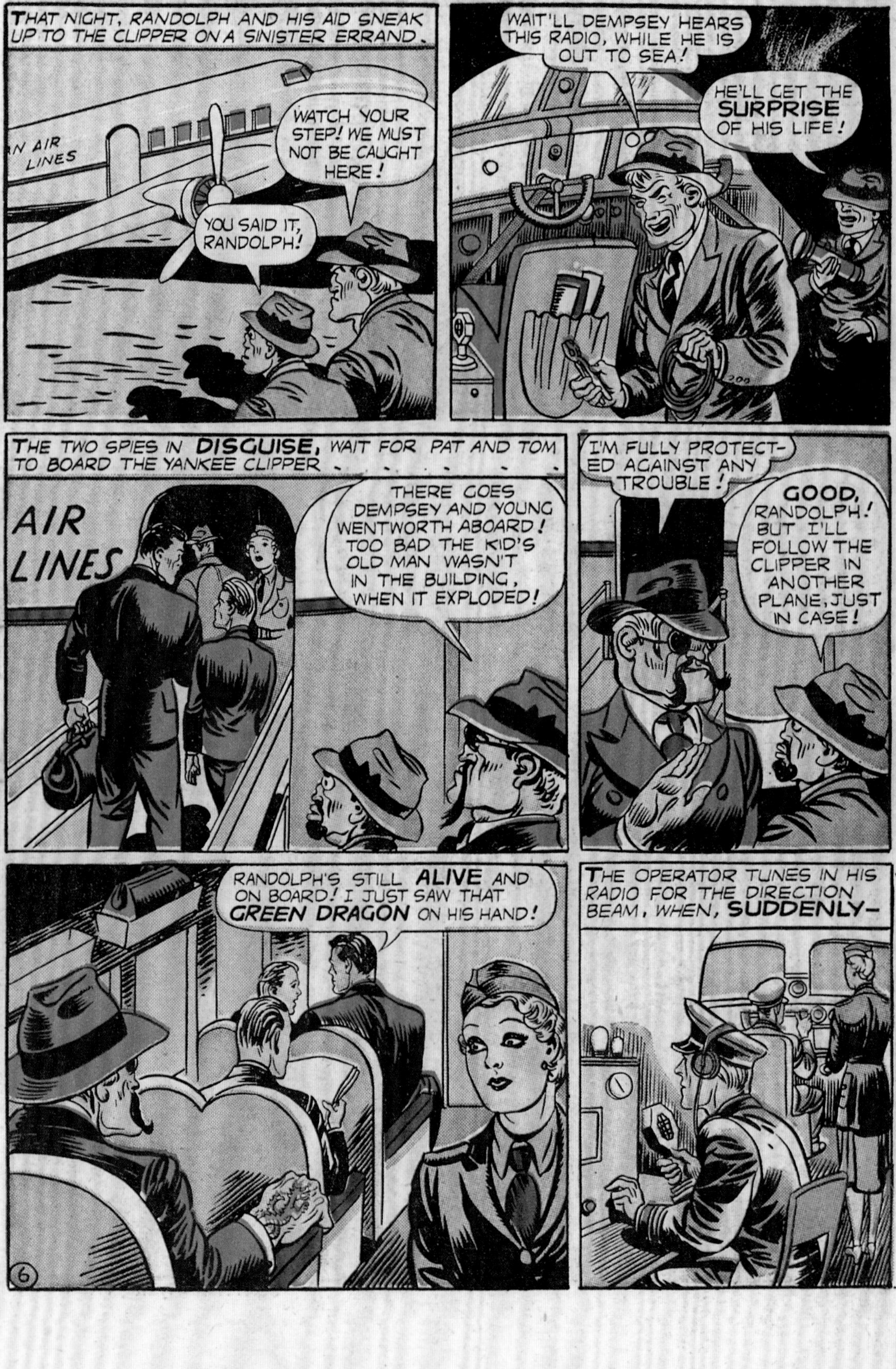
THAT NIGHT, RANDOLPH AND HIS AID SNEAK UP TO THE CLIPPER ON A SINISTER ERRAND.
AIR LINES
WATCH YOUR STEP! WE MUST NOT BE CAUGHT HERE!
YOU SAID IT, RANDOLPH!
WAIT'LL DEMPSEY HEARS THIS RADIO, WHILE HE IS OUT TO SEA!
HE'LL GET THE SURPRISE OF HIS LIFE!
THE TWO SPIES IN DISGUISE, WAIT FOR PAT AND TOM TO BOARD THE YANKEE CLIPPER - - - - - -
AIR LINES
THERE GOES DEMPSEY AND YOUNG WENTWORTH ABOARD! TOO BAD THE KID'S OLD MAN WASN'T IN THE BUILDING, WHEN IT EXPLODED!
I'M FULLY PROTECTED AGAINST ANY TROUBLE!
GOOD, RANDOLPH! BUT I'LL FOLLOW THE CLIPPER IN ANOTHER PLANE, JUST IN CASE!
RANDOLPH'S STILL ALIVE AND ON BOARD! I JUST SAW THAT GREEN DRAGON ON HIS HAND!
6
THE OPERATOR TUNES IN HIS RADIO FOR THE DIRECTION BEAM, WHEN, SUDDENLY—

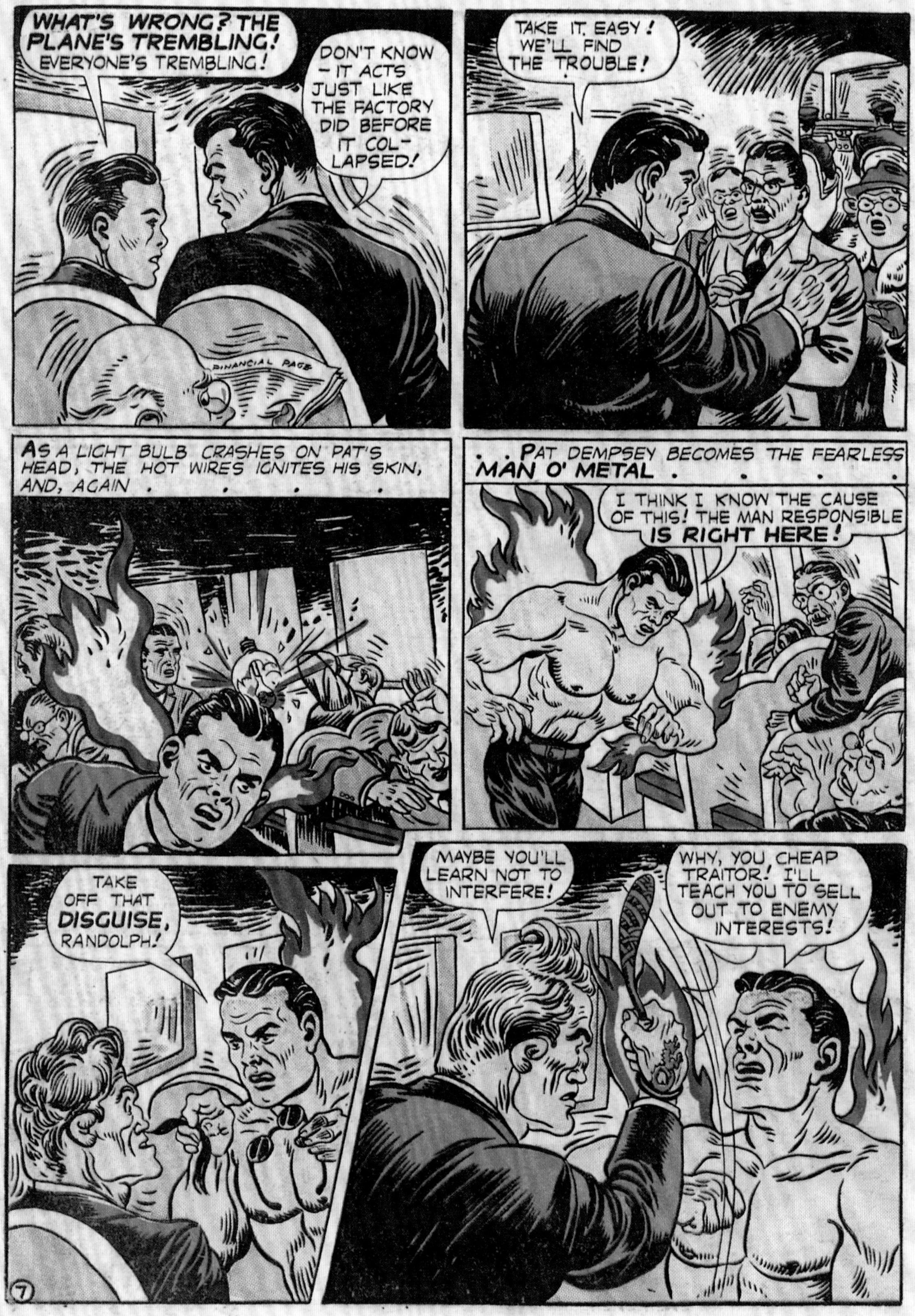
WHAT'S WRONG? THE PLANE'S TREMBLING! EVERYONE'S TREMBLING!
DON'T KNOW – IT ACTS JUST LIKE THE FACTORY DID BEFORE IT COL-LAPSED!
FINANCIAL PAGE
TAKE IT EASY! WE'LL FIND THE TROUBLE!
AS A LIGHT BULB CRASHES ON PAT'S HEAD, THE HOT WIRES IGNITES HIS SKIN, AND, AGAIN . . . .
. . PAT DEMPSEY BECOMES THE FEARLESS MAN O' METAL . . . .
I THINK I KNOW THE CAUSE OF THIS! THE MAN RESPONSIBLE IS RIGHT HERE!
TAKE OFF THAT DISGUISE, RANDOLPH!
MAYBE YOU'LL LEARN NOT TO INTERFERE!
WHY, YOU CHEAP TRAITOR! I'LL TEACH YOU TO SELL OUT TO ENEMY INTERESTS!
7

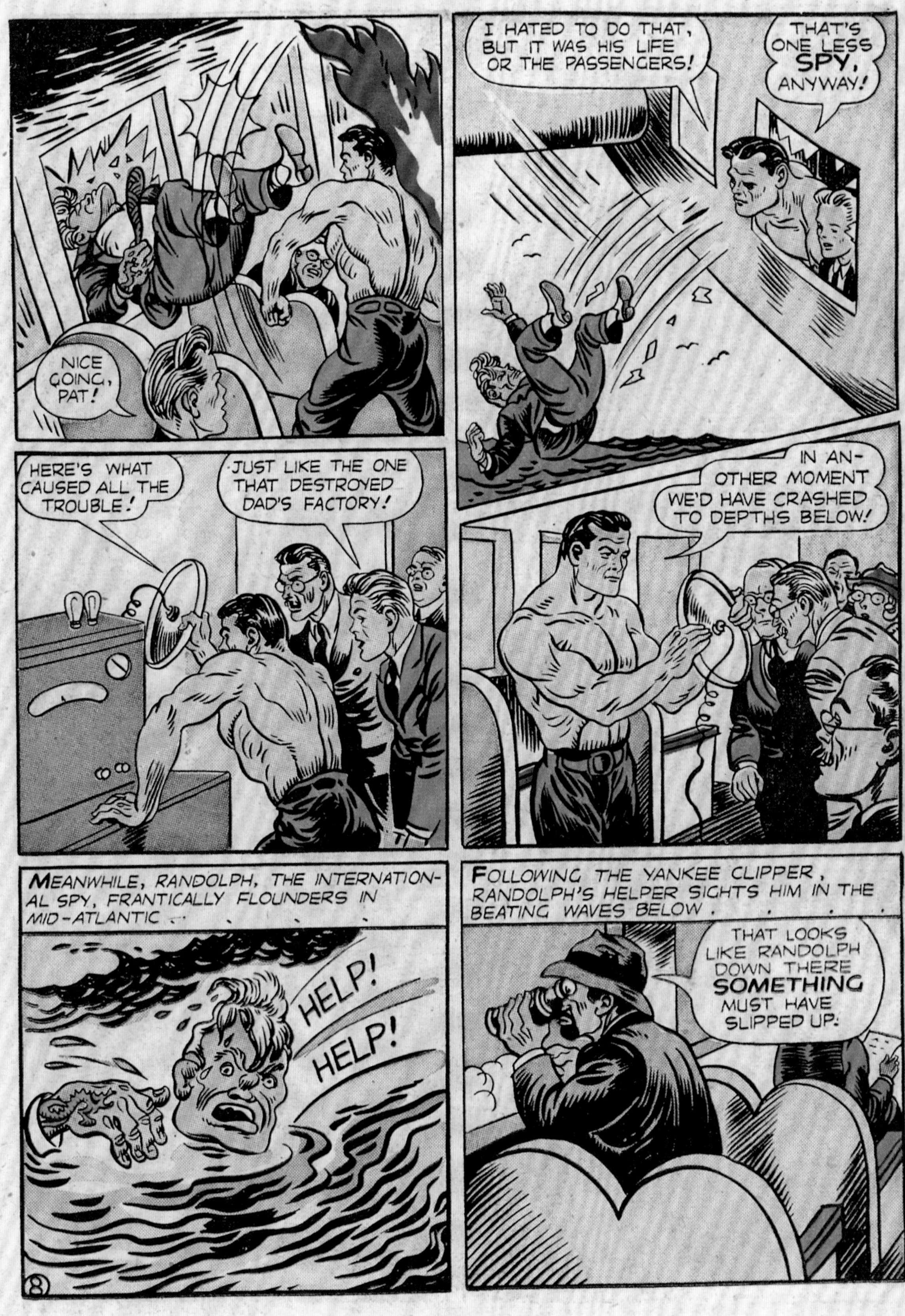
NICE GOING, PAT!
I HATED TO DO THAT, BUT IT WAS HIS LIFE OR THE PASSENGERS!
THAT'S ONE LESS SPY, ANYWAY!
HERE'S WHAT CAUSED ALL THE TROUBLE!
JUST LIKE THE ONE THAT DESTROYED DAD'S FACTORY!
IN ANOTHER MOMENT WE'D HAVE CRASHED TO DEPTHS BELOW!
MEANWHILE, RANDOLPH, THE INTERNATIONAL SPY, FRANTICALLY FLOUNDERS IN MID-ATLANTIC . . .
HELP!
HELP!
8
FOLLOWING THE YANKEE CLIPPER, RANDOLPH'S HELPER SIGHTS HIM IN THE BEATING WAVES BELOW . . . .
THAT LOOKS LIKE RANDOLPH DOWN THERE SOMETHING MUST HAVE SLIPPED UP.

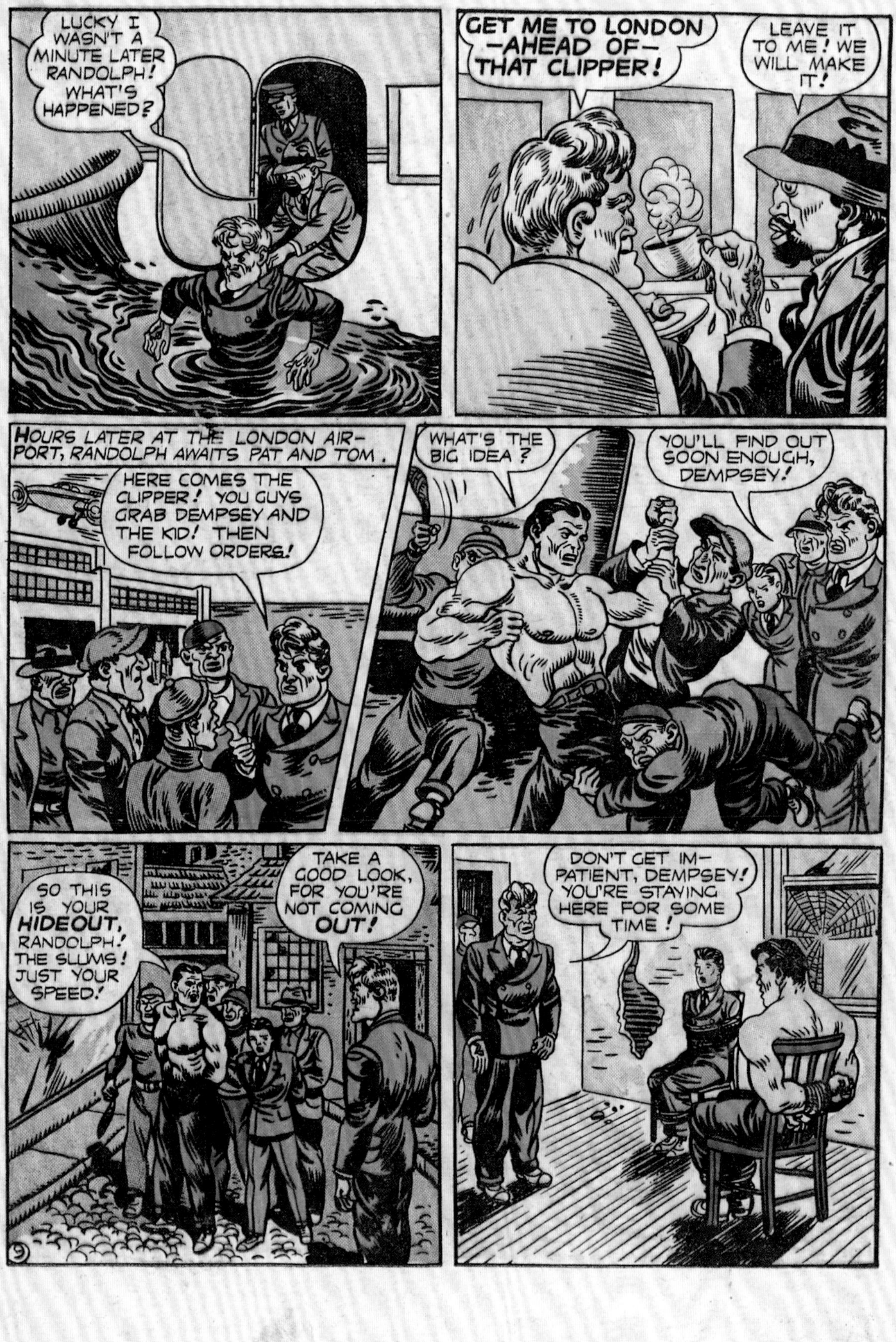
LUCKY I WASN'T A MINUTE LATER RANDOLPH! WHAT'S HAPPENED?
GET ME TO LONDON —AHEAD OF— THAT CLIPPER!
LEAVE IT TO ME! WE WILL MAKE IT!
HOURS LATER AT THE LONDON AIRPORT, RANDOLPH AWAITS PAT AND TOM.
HERE COMES THE CLIPPER! YOU GUYS GRAB DEMPSEY AND THE KID! THEN FOLLOW ORDERS!
WHAT'S THE BIG IDEA?
YOU'LL FIND OUT SOON ENOUGH, DEMPSEY!
SO THIS IS YOUR HIDEOUT, RANDOLPH! THE SLUMS! JUST YOUR SPEED!
TAKE A GOOD LOOK, FOR YOU'RE NOT COMING OUT!
DON'T GET IMPATIENT, DEMPSEY! YOU'RE STAYING HERE FOR SOME TIME!

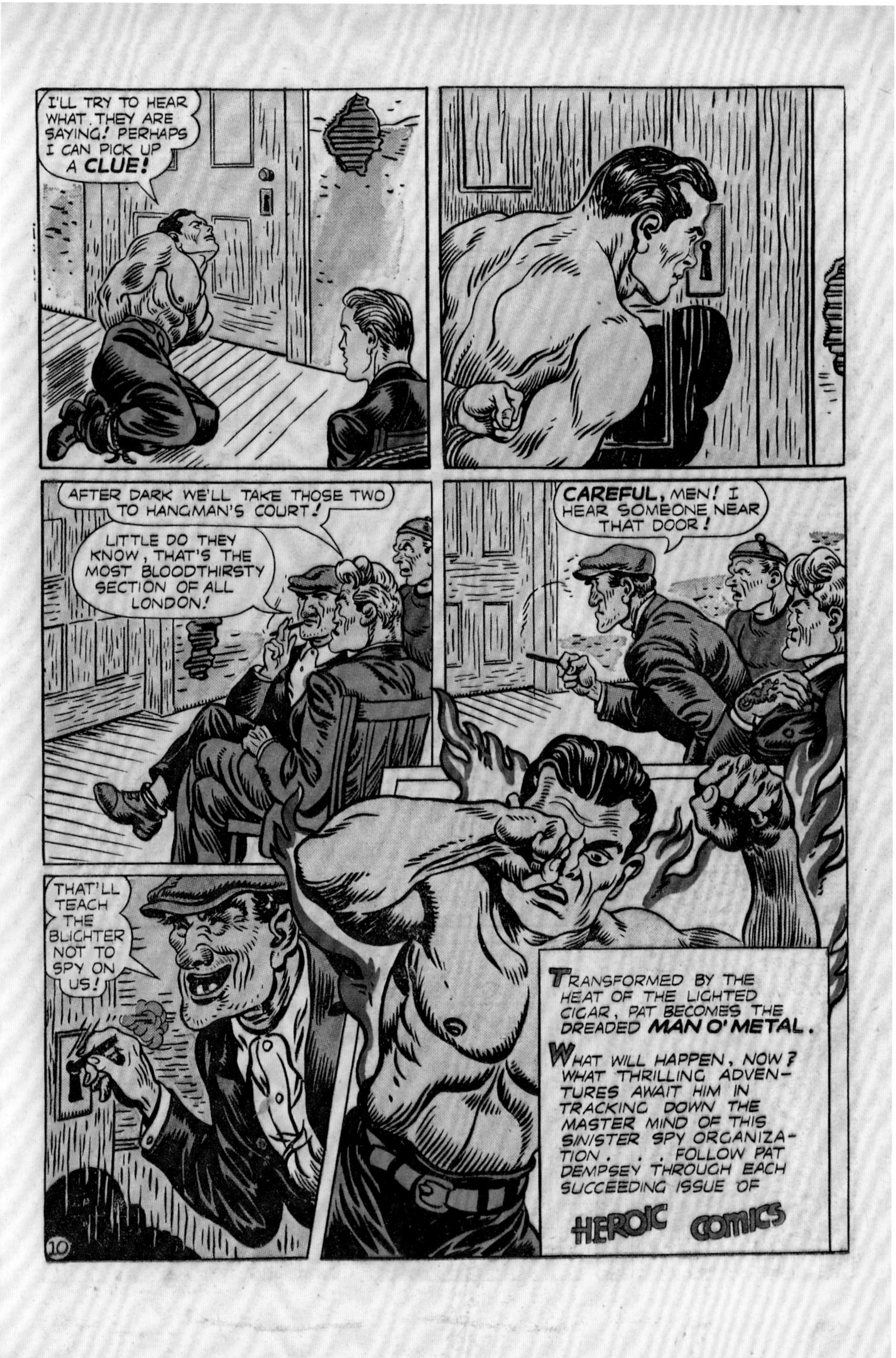
I'LL TRY TO HEAR WHAT THEY ARE SAYING! PERHAPS I CAN PICK UP A CLUE!
AFTER DARK WE'LL TAKE THOSE TWO TO HANGMAN'S COURT!
LITTLE DO THEY KNOW, THAT'S THE MOST BLOODTHIRSTY SECTION OF ALL LONDON!
CAREFUL, MEN! I HEAR SOMEONE NEAR THAT DOOR!
THAT'LL TEACH THE BLIGHTER NOT TO SPY ON US!
TRANSFORMED BY THE HEAT OF THE LIGHTED CIGAR, PAT BECOMES THE DREADED MAN O' METAL.
WHAT WILL HAPPEN, NOW? WHAT THRILLING ADVENTURES AWAIT HIM IN TRACKING DOWN THE MASTER MIND OF THIS SINISTER SPY ORGANIZATION . . . FOLLOW PAT DEMPSEY THROUGH EACH SUCCEEDING ISSUE OF
HEROIC COMICS
10

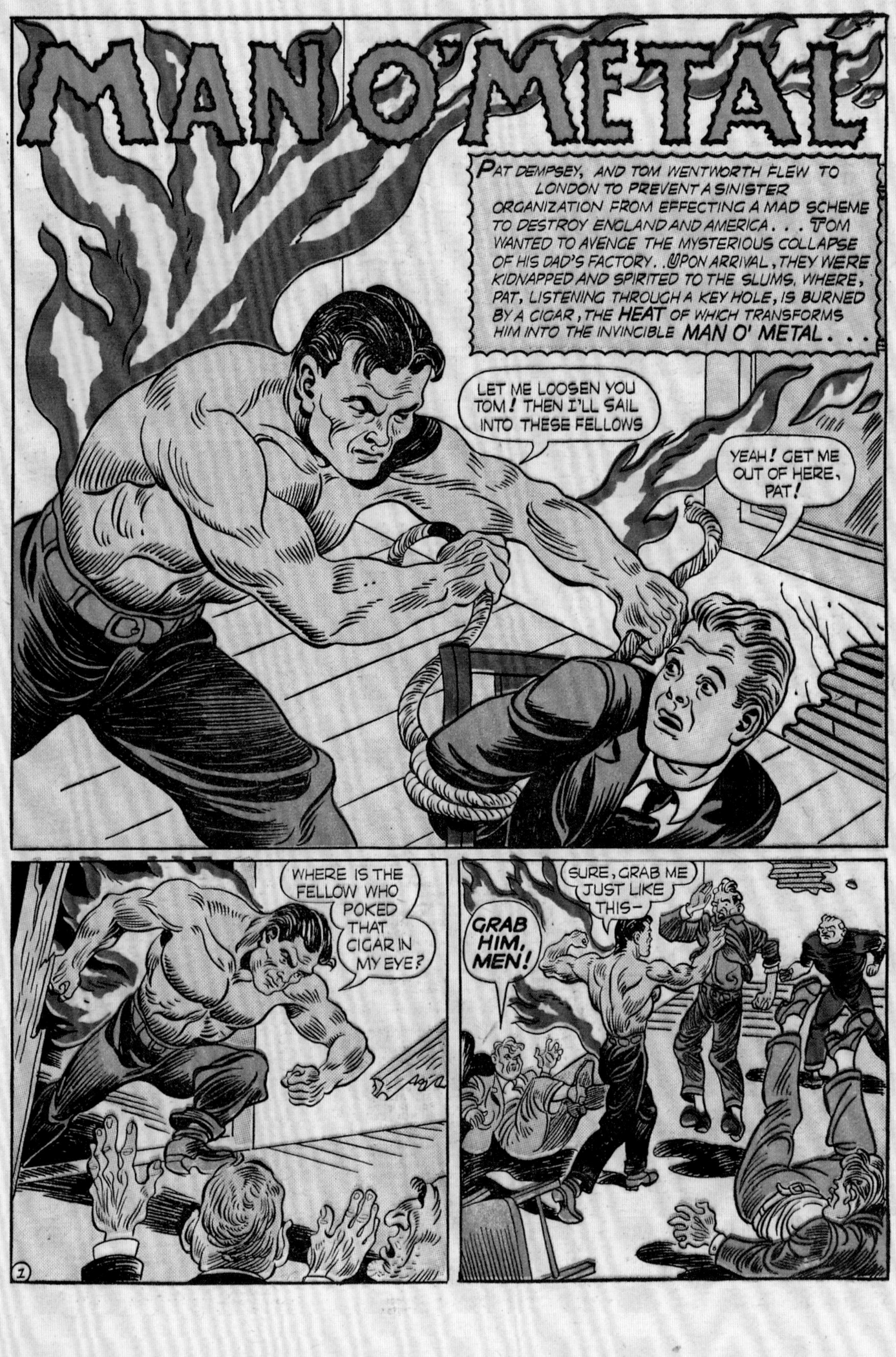
MAN O' METAL
PAT DEMPSEY, AND TOM WENTWORTH FLEW TO LONDON TO PREVENT A SINISTER ORGANIZATION FROM EFFECTING A MAD SCHEME TO DESTROY ENGLAND AND AMERICA. . . TOM WANTED TO AVENGE THE MYSTERIOUS COLLAPSE OF HIS DAD'S FACTORY. . UPON ARRIVAL, THEY WERE KIDNAPPED AND SPIRITED TO THE SLUMS, WHERE, PAT, LISTENING THROUGH A KEY HOLE, IS BURNED BY A CIGAR, THE HEAT OF WHICH TRANSFORMS HIM INTO THE INVINCIBLE MAN O' METAL. . .
LET ME LOOSEN YOU TOM! THEN I'LL SAIL INTO THESE FELLOWS
YEAH! GET ME OUT OF HERE, PAT!
WHERE IS THE FELLOW WHO POKED THAT CIGAR IN MY EYE?
GRAB HIM, MEN!
SURE, GRAB ME JUST LIKE THIS-

Reg'lar Fellers Heroic Comics no. 14 (1942)

LET'S GET OUT OF HERE! I MUST PHONE THE ENGLISH BROADCASTING STUDIOS!
YEAH! BEFORE THESE SPIES COME TO!
YES, MR DEMPSEY, WE'VE BEEN CONTACTED BY YOUR FRIEND IN THE AMERICAN BROADCASTING COMPANY AND WE'RE WORKING OUT A PLAN!
LATER
SO THIS IS HANGMAN'S COURT-
YES! NOW TO TRACK DOWN THOSE SPIES AND RUIN THEIR CROOKED SCHEME!
THIS LOOKS AS THOUGH IT MIGHT LEAD TO THEIR RENDEZVOUS!
TAKE IT EASY PAT!
AS THEY MOVE SLOWLY THROUGH THE DARK TOWARD THE BIG, HEAVY DOOR, PAT DEMPSEY AND TOM ARE UNAWARE OF THE TWO HUGE EYES GLARING OUT AT THEM.
2
THIS IS IT, TOM! FOLLOW ME-

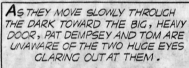

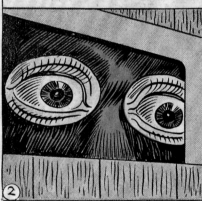

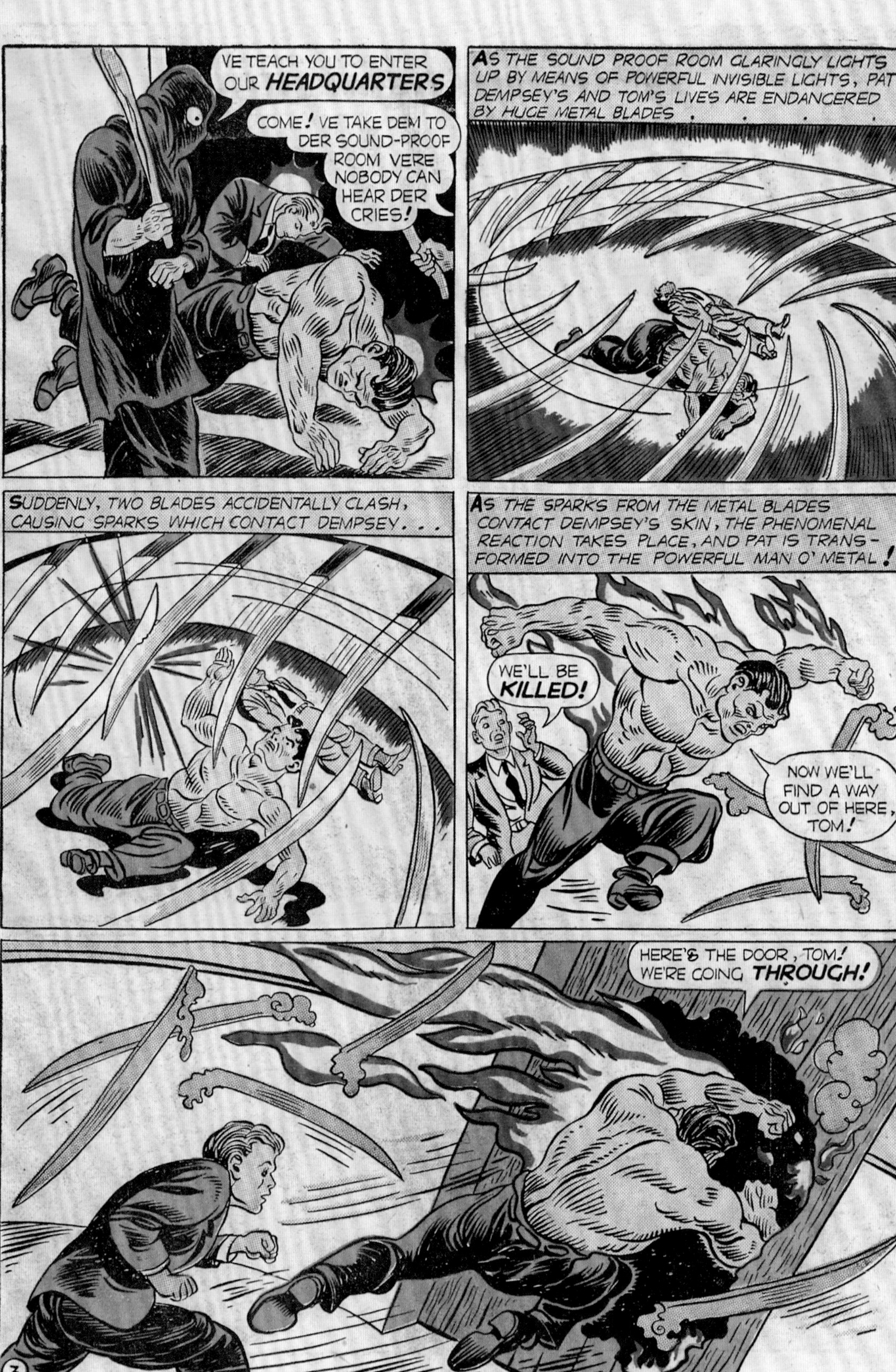
VE TEACH YOU TO ENTER OUR HEADQUARTERS
COME! VE TAKE DEM TO DER SOUND-PROOF ROOM VERE NOBODY CAN HEAR DER CRIES!
AS THE SOUND PROOF ROOM GLARINGLY LIGHTS UP BY MEANS OF POWERFUL INVISIBLE LIGHTS, PAT DEMPSEY'S AND TOM'S LIVES ARE ENDANGERED BY HUGE METAL BLADES . . . .
SUDDENLY, TWO BLADES ACCIDENTALLY CLASH, CAUSING SPARKS WHICH CONTACT DEMPSEY . . .
AS THE SPARKS FROM THE METAL BLADES CONTACT DEMPSEY'S SKIN, THE PHENOMENAL REACTION TAKES PLACE, AND PAT IS TRANSFORMED INTO THE POWERFUL MAN O' METAL!
WE'LL BE KILLED!
NOW WE'LL FIND A WAY OUT OF HERE, TOM!
HERE'S THE DOOR, TOM! WE'RE GOING THROUGH!
3

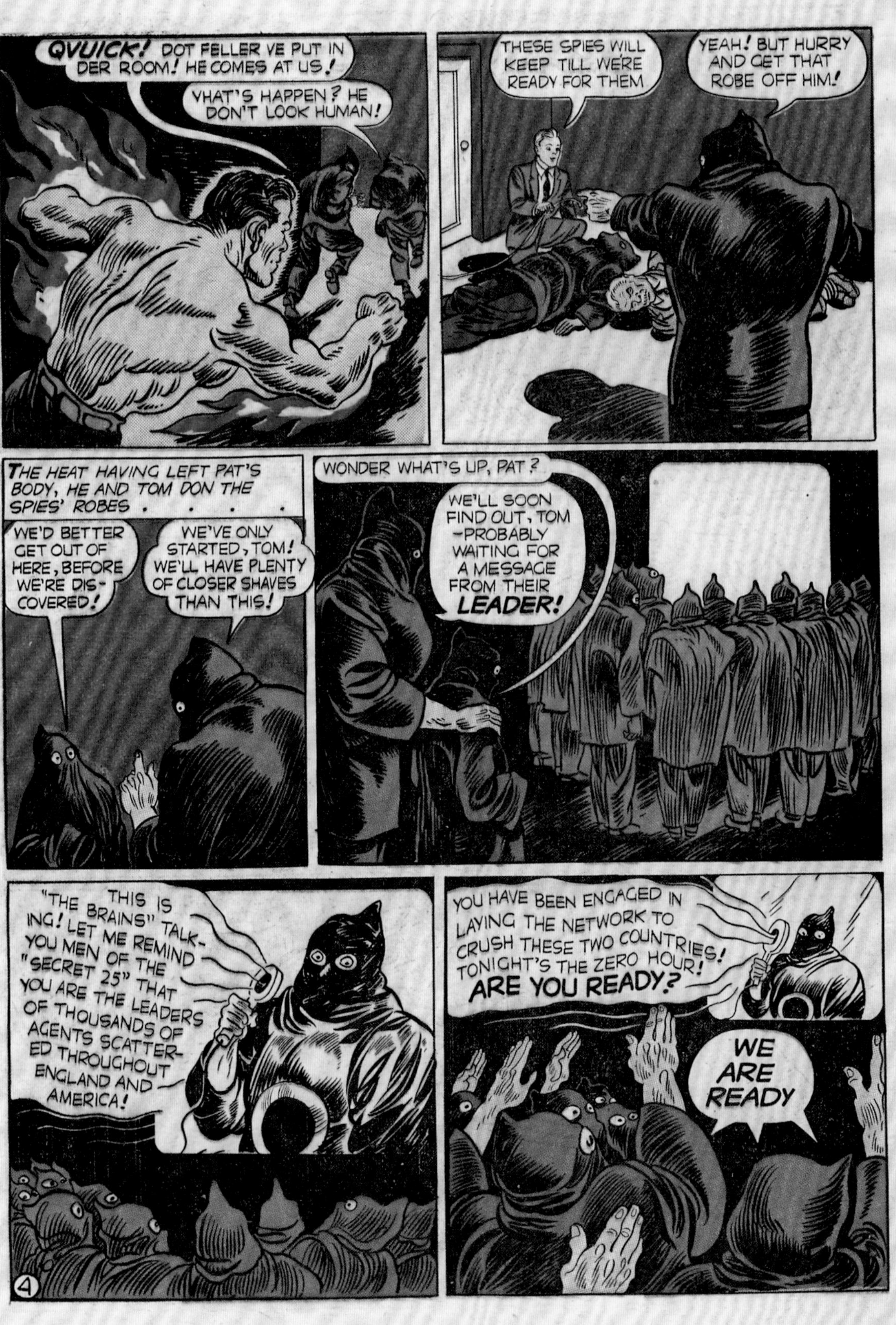
QVUICK! DOT FELLER VE PUT IN DER ROOM! HE COMES AT US!
VHAT'S HAPPEN? HE DON'T LOOK HUMAN!
THESE SPIES WILL KEEP TILL WE'RE READY FOR THEM
YEAH! BUT HURRY AND GET THAT ROBE OFF HIM!
THE HEAT HAVING LEFT PAT'S BODY, HE AND TOM DON THE SPIES' ROBES . . . .
WE'D BETTER GET OUT OF HERE, BEFORE WE'RE DISCOVERED!
WE'VE ONLY STARTED, TOM! WE'LL HAVE PLENTY OF CLOSER SHAVES THAN THIS!
WONDER WHAT'S UP, PAT?
WE'LL SOON FIND OUT, TOM -PROBABLY WAITING FOR A MESSAGE FROM THEIR LEADER!
"THIS IS "THE BRAINS" TALKING! LET ME REMIND YOU MEN OF THE "SECRET 25" THAT YOU ARE THE LEADERS OF THOUSANDS OF AGENTS SCATTERED THROUGHOUT ENGLAND AND AMERICA!
YOU HAVE BEEN ENGAGED IN LAYING THE NETWORK TO CRUSH THESE TWO COUNTRIES! TONIGHT'S THE ZERO HOUR! ARE YOU READY?
WE ARE READY
4

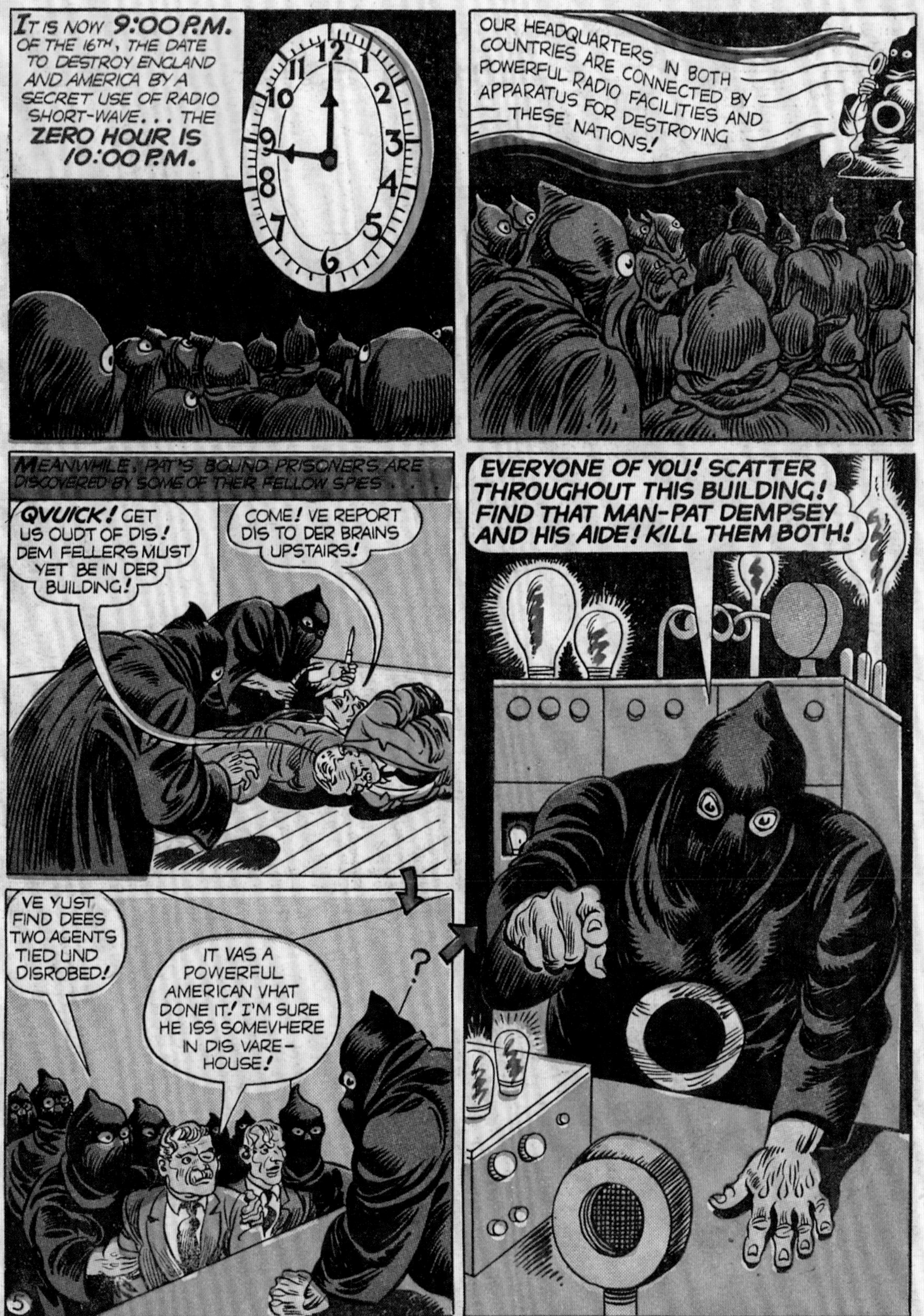
IT IS NOW 9:00 P.M. OF THE 16TH, THE DATE TO DESTROY ENGLAND AND AMERICA BY A SECRET USE OF RADIO SHORT-WAVE . . . THE ZERO HOUR IS 10:00 P.M.
OUR HEADQUARTERS IN BOTH COUNTRIES ARE CONNECTED BY POWERFUL RADIO FACILITIES AND APPARATUS FOR DESTROYING THESE NATIONS!
MEANWHILE, PAT'S BOUND PRISONERS ARE DISCOVERED BY SOME OF THEIR FELLOW SPIES . . .
QVUICK! GET US OUDT OF DIS! DEM FELLERS MUST YET BE IN DER BUILDING!
COME! VE REPORT DIS TO DER BRAINS UPSTAIRS!
VE YUST FIND DEES TWO AGENTS TIED UND DISROBED!
IT VAS A POWERFUL AMERICAN VHAT DONE IT! I'M SURE HE ISS SOMEVHERE IN DIS VARE-HOUSE!
?
EVERYONE OF YOU! SCATTER THROUGHOUT THIS BUILDING! FIND THAT MAN-PAT DEMPSEY AND HIS AIDE! KILL THEM BOTH!

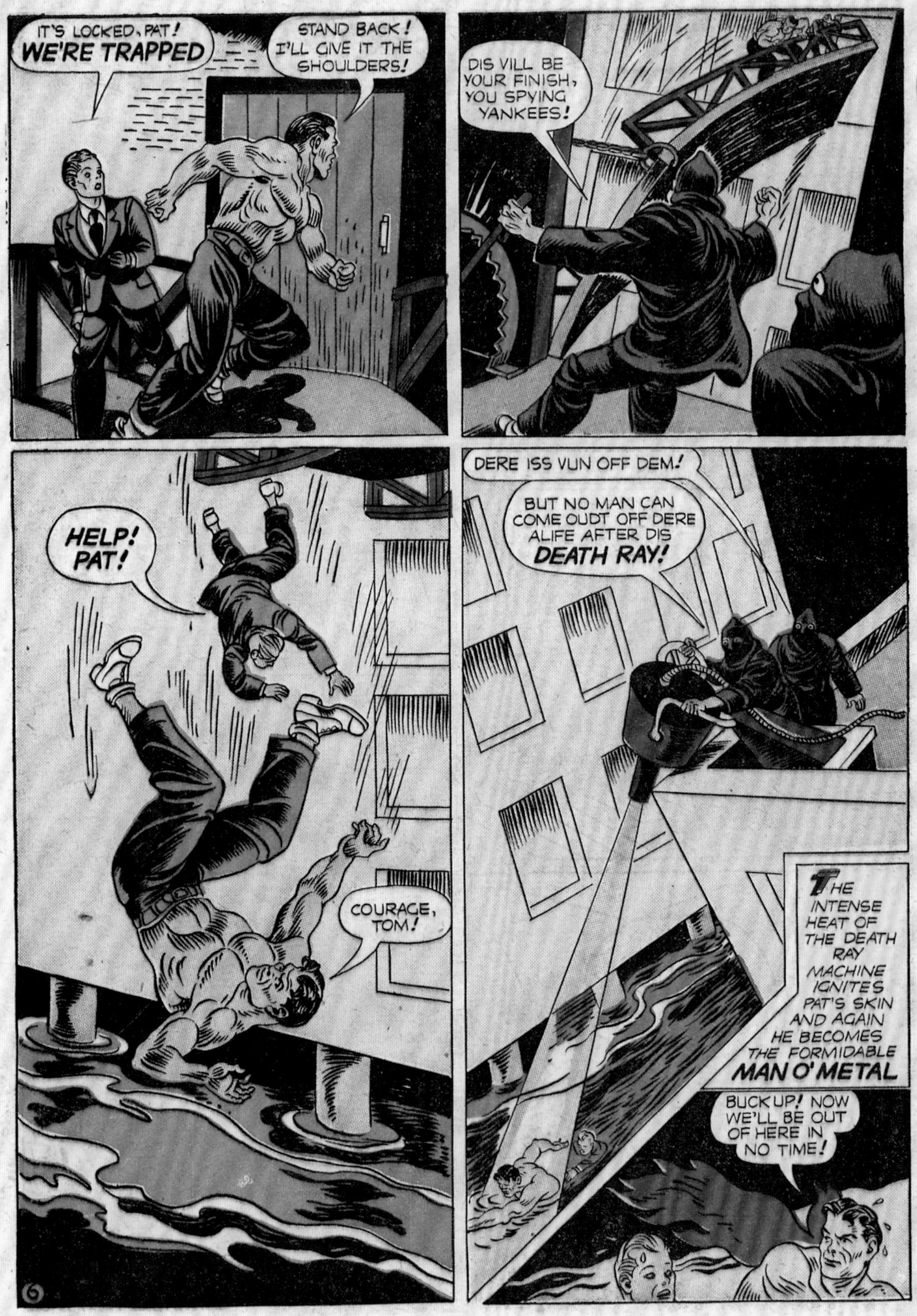
IT'S LOCKED, PAT! WE'RE TRAPPED
STAND BACK! I'LL GIVE IT THE SHOULDERS!
DIS VILL BE YOUR FINISH, YOU SPYING YANKEES!
HELP! PAT!
COURAGE, TOM!
DERE ISS VUN OFF DEM!
BUT NO MAN CAN COME OUDT OFF DERE ALIFE AFTER DIS DEATH RAY!
THE INTENSE HEAT OF THE DEATH RAY MACHINE IGNITES PAT'S SKIN AND AGAIN HE BECOMES THE FORMIDABLE MAN O'METAL
BUCK UP! NOW WE'LL BE OUT OF HERE IN NO TIME!
6

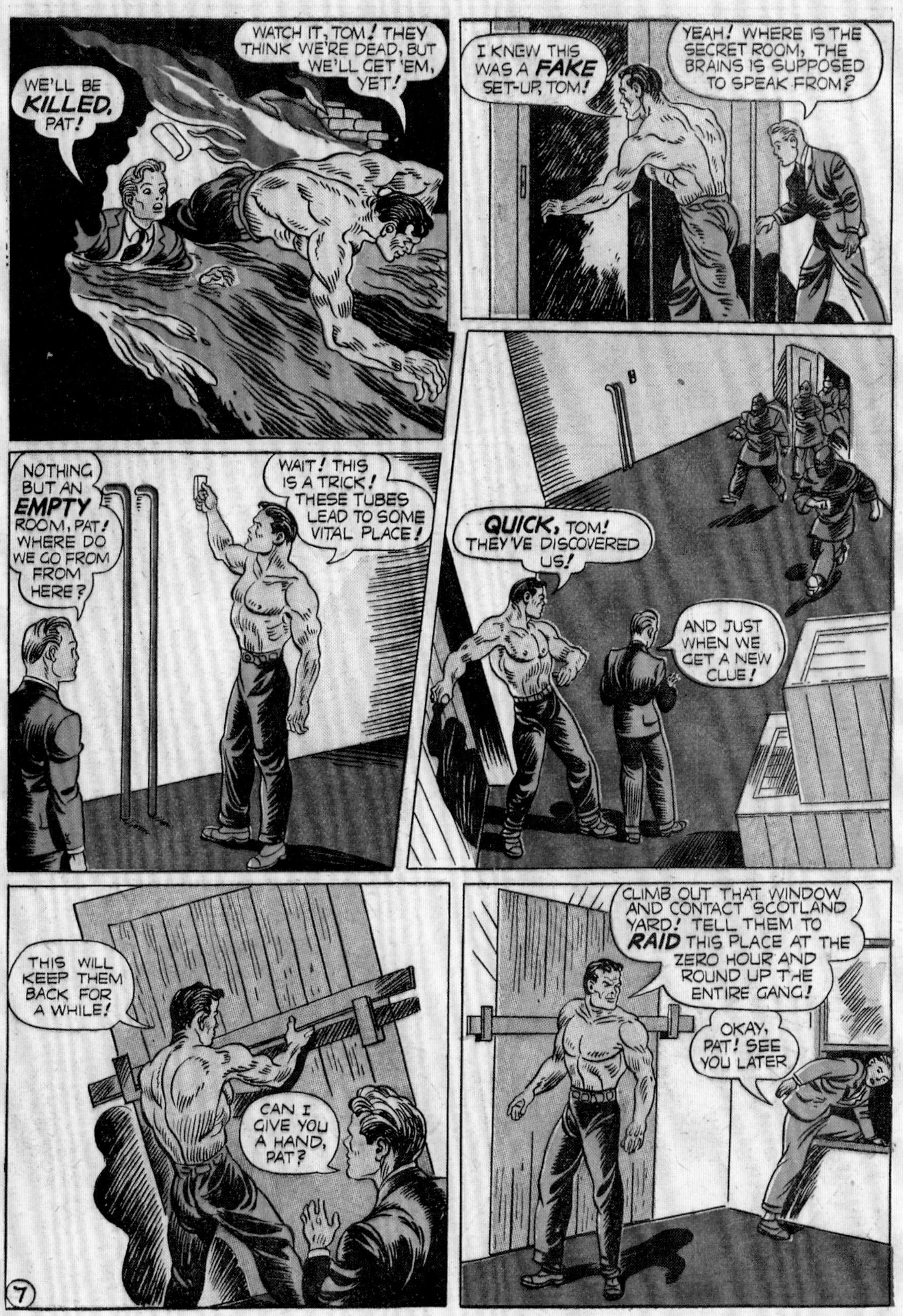
WE'LL BE KILLED, PAT!
WATCH IT, TOM! THEY THINK WE'RE DEAD, BUT WE'LL GET 'EM, YET!
I KNEW THIS WAS A FAKE SET-UP, TOM!
YEAH! WHERE IS THE SECRET ROOM, THE BRAINS IS SUPPOSED TO SPEAK FROM?
NOTHING BUT AN EMPTY ROOM, PAT! WHERE DO WE GO FROM FROM HERE?
WAIT! THIS IS A TRICK! THESE TUBES LEAD TO SOME VITAL PLACE!
QUICK, TOM! THEY'VE DISCOVERED US!
AND JUST WHEN WE GET A NEW CLUE!
THIS WILL KEEP THEM BACK FOR A WHILE!
CAN I GIVE YOU A HAND, PAT?
7
CLIMB OUT THAT WINDOW AND CONTACT SCOTLAND YARD! TELL THEM TO RAID THIS PLACE AT THE ZERO HOUR AND ROUND UP THE ENTIRE GANG!
OKAY, PAT! SEE YOU LATER

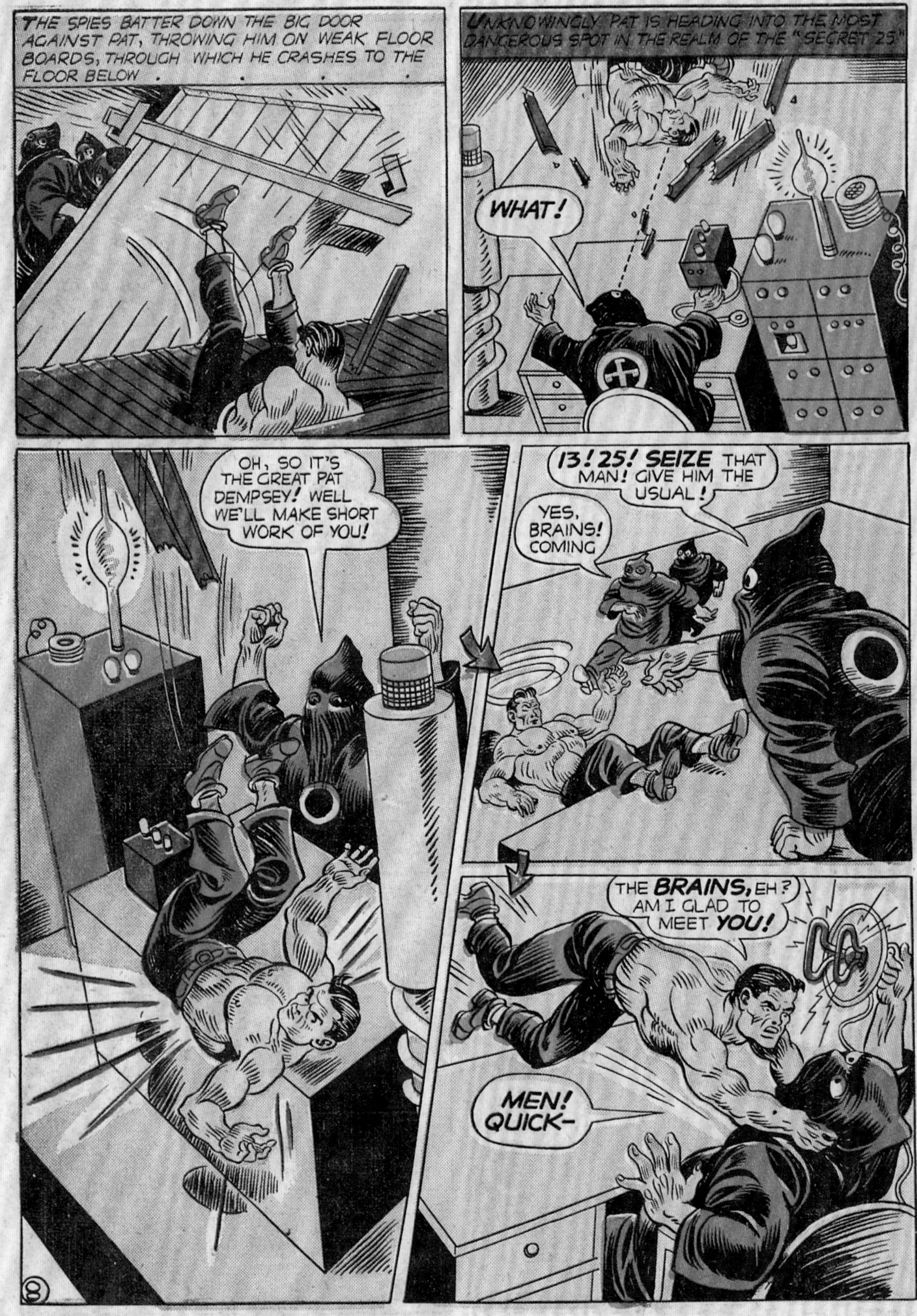
THE SPIES BATTER DOWN THE BIG DOOR AGAINST PAT, THROWING HIM ON WEAK FLOOR BOARDS, THROUGH WHICH HE CRASHES TO THE FLOOR BELOW . . . .
UNKNOWINGLY PAT IS HEADING INTO THE MOST DANGEROUS SPOT IN THE REALM OF THE "SECRET 25"
WHAT!
OH, SO IT'S THE GREAT PAT DEMPSEY! WELL WE'LL MAKE SHORT WORK OF YOU!
13! 25! SEIZE THAT MAN! GIVE HIM THE USUAL!
YES, BRAINS! COMING
THE BRAINS, EH? AM I GLAD TO MEET YOU!
MEN! QUICK-
8

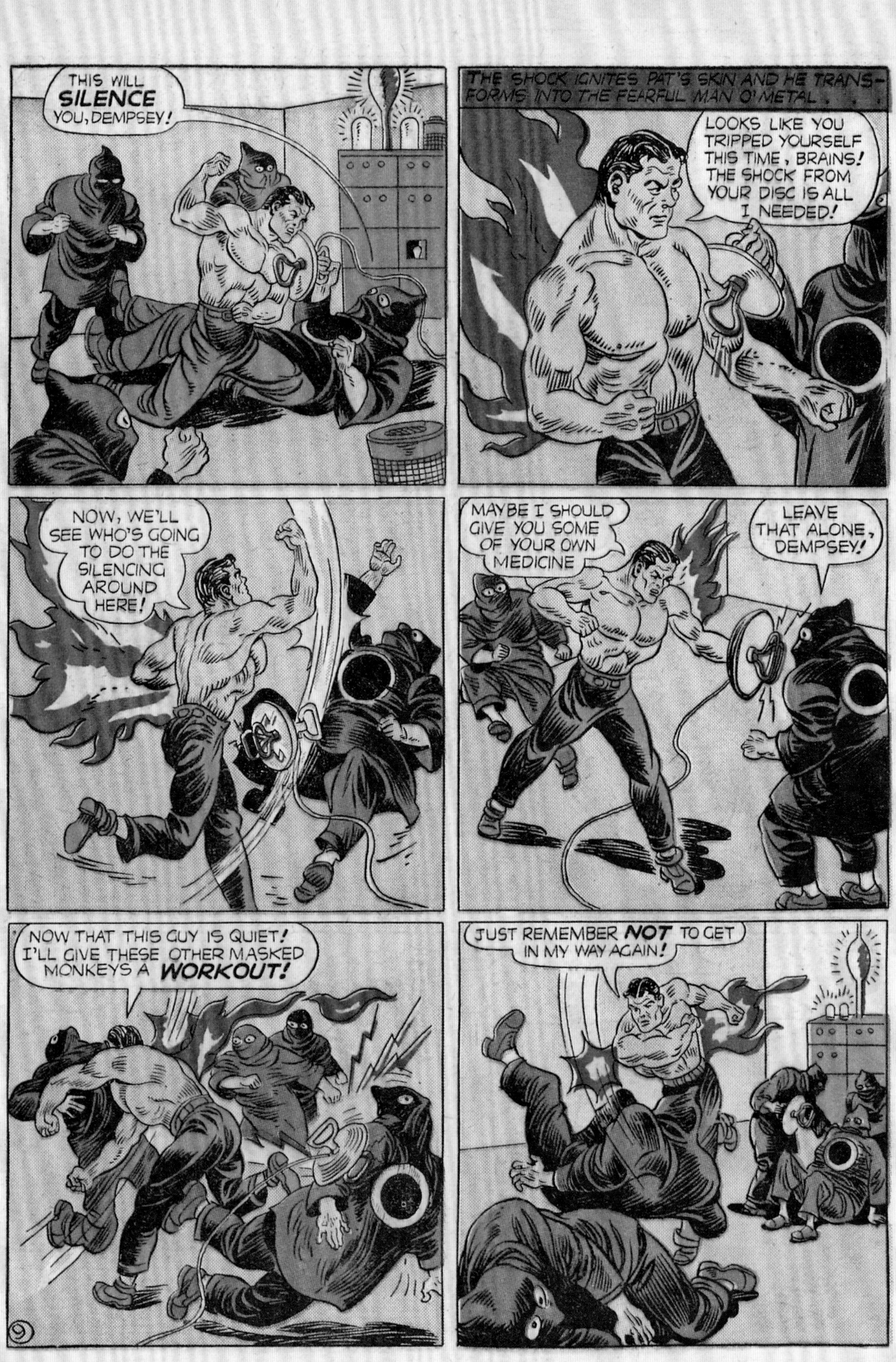
THIS WILL SILENCE YOU, DEMPSEY!
THE SHOCK IGNITES PAT'S SKIN AND HE TRANSFORMS INTO THE FEARFUL MAN O' METAL . . .
LOOKS LIKE YOU TRIPPED YOURSELF THIS TIME, BRAINS! THE SHOCK FROM YOUR DISC IS ALL I NEEDED!
NOW, WE'LL SEE WHO'S GOING TO DO THE SILENCING AROUND HERE!
MAYBE I SHOULD GIVE YOU SOME OF YOUR OWN MEDICINE
LEAVE THAT ALONE, DEMPSEY!
NOW THAT THIS GUY IS QUIET! I'LL GIVE THESE OTHER MASKED MONKEYS A WORKOUT!
9
JUST REMEMBER NOT TO GET IN MY WAY AGAIN!

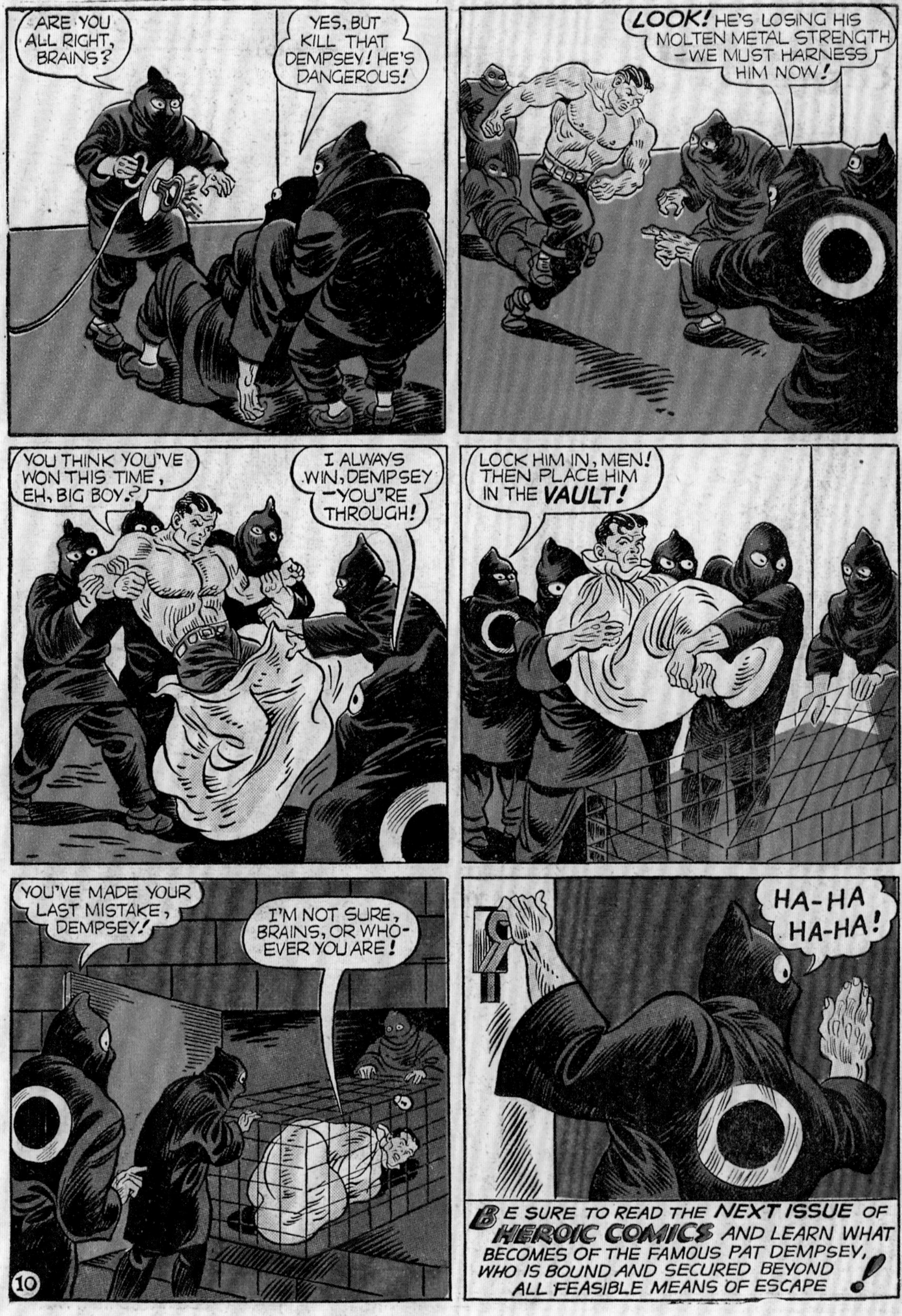
ARE YOU ALL RIGHT, BRAINS?
YES, BUT KILL THAT DEMPSEY! HE'S DANGEROUS!
LOOK! HE'S LOSING HIS MOLTEN METAL STRENGTH —WE MUST HARNESS HIM NOW!
YOU THINK YOU'VE WON THIS TIME, EH, BIG BOY?
I ALWAYS WIN, DEMPSEY —YOU'RE THROUGH!
LOCK HIM IN, MEN! THEN PLACE HIM IN THE VAULT!
YOU'VE MADE YOUR LAST MISTAKE, DEMPSEY!
I'M NOT SURE, BRAINS, OR WHO-EVER YOU ARE!
10
HA-HA HA-HA!
BE SURE TO READ THE NEXT ISSUE OF HEROIC COMICS AND LEARN WHAT BECOMES OF THE FAMOUS PAT DEMPSEY, WHO IS BOUND AND SECURED BEYOND ALL FEASIBLE MEANS OF ESCAPE!

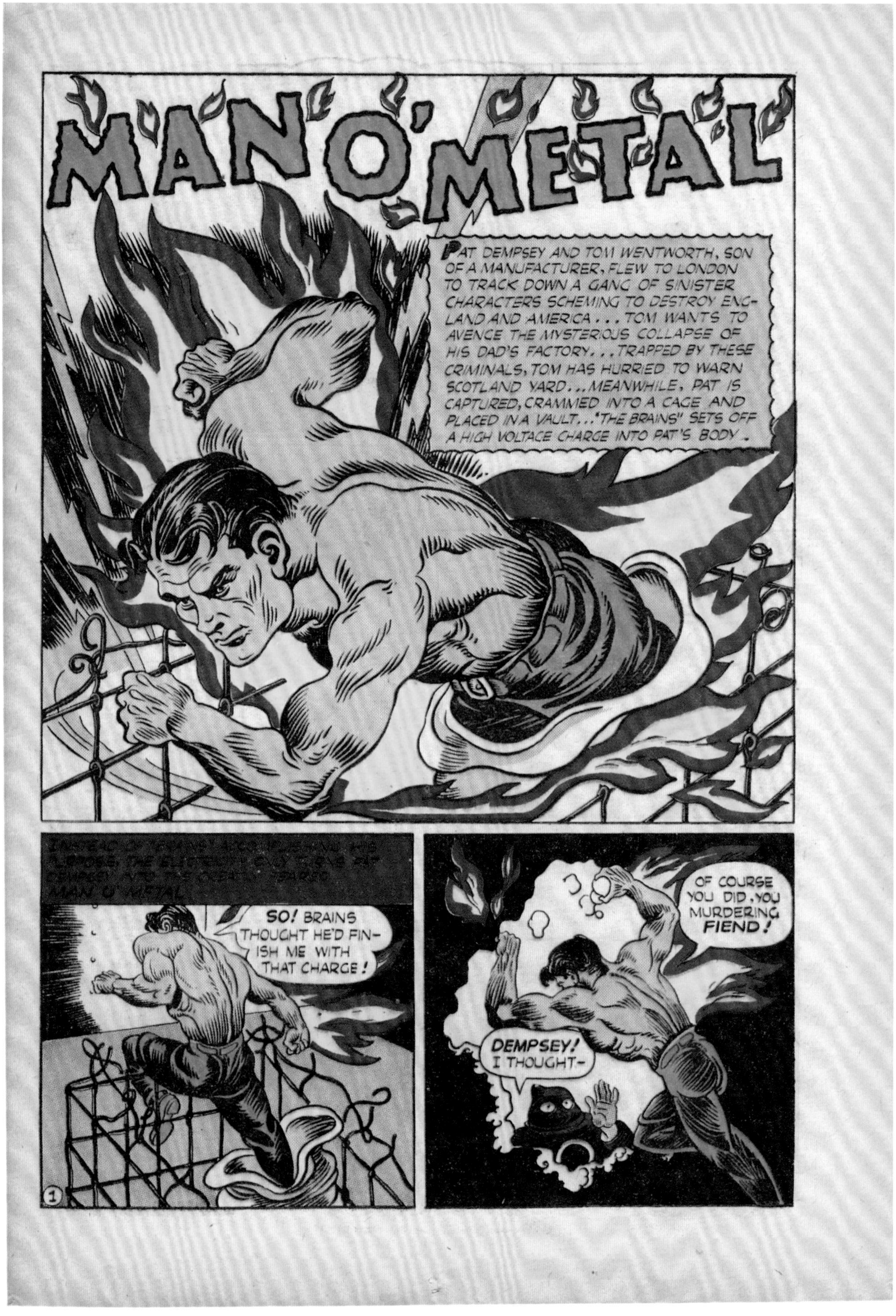
MAN O' METAL
PAT DEMPSEY AND TOM WENTWORTH, SON OF A MANUFACTURER, FLEW TO LONDON TO TRACK DOWN A GANG OF SINISTER CHARACTERS SCHEMING TO DESTROY ENGLAND AND AMERICA . . . TOM WANTS TO AVENGE THE MYSTERIOUS COLLAPSE OF HIS DAD'S FACTORY . . . TRAPPED BY THESE CRIMINALS, TOM HAS HURRIED TO WARN SCOTLAND YARD . . . MEANWHILE, PAT IS CAPTURED, CRAMMED INTO A CAGE AND PLACED IN A VAULT . . . "THE BRAINS" SETS OFF A HIGH VOLTAGE CHARGE INTO PAT'S BODY .
SO! BRAINS THOUGHT HE'D FINISH ME WITH THAT CHARGE!
DEMPSEY! I THOUGHT-
OF COURSE YOU DID, YOU MURDERING FIEND!

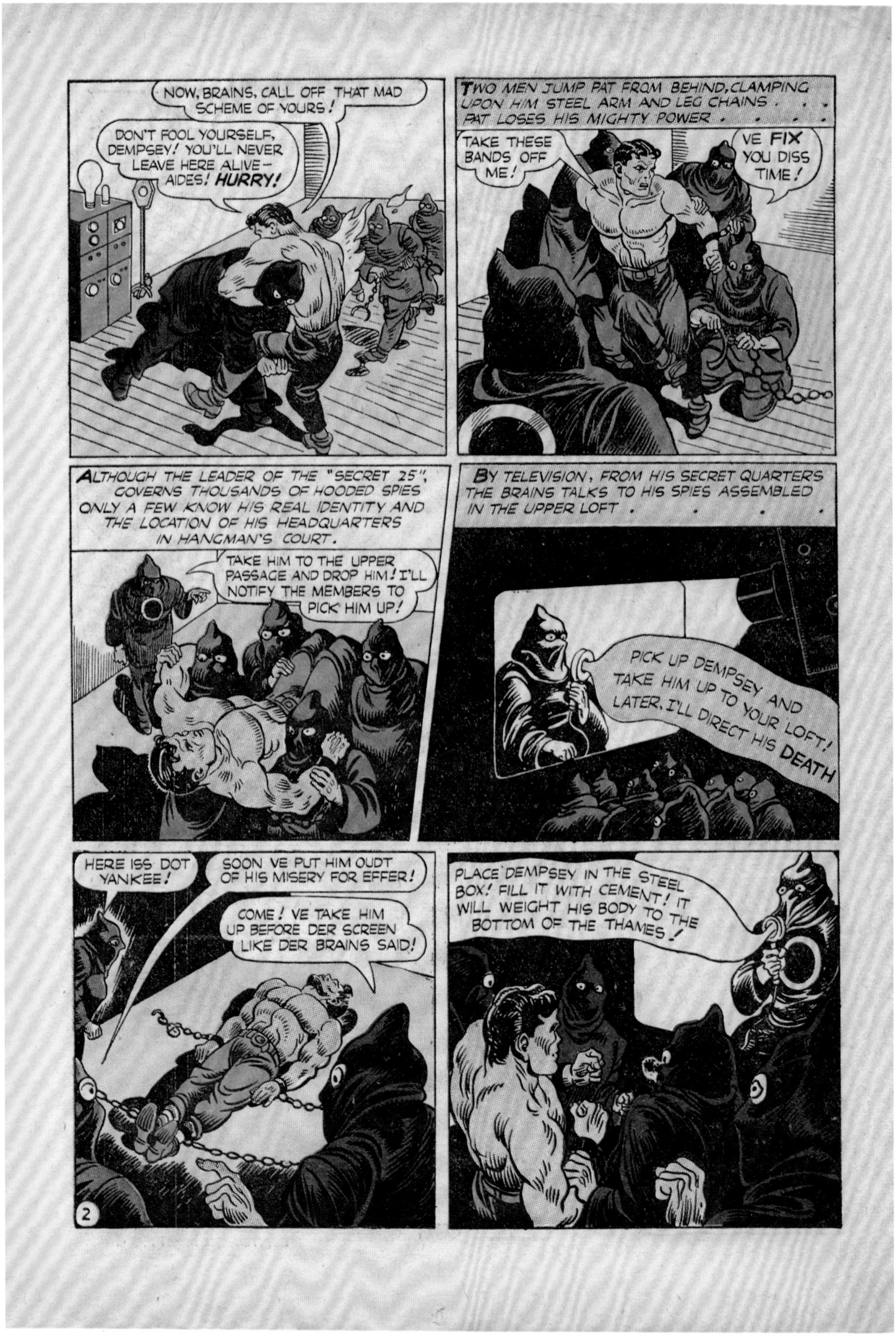
NOW, BRAINS, CALL OFF THAT MAD SCHEME OF YOURS!
DON'T FOOL YOURSELF, DEMPSEY! YOU'LL NEVER LEAVE HERE ALIVE-AIDES! HURRY!
TWO MEN JUMP PAT FROM BEHIND, CLAMPING UPON HIM STEEL ARM AND LEG CHAINS . . . PAT LOSES HIS MIGHTY POWER . . . .
TAKE THESE BANDS OFF ME!
VE FIX YOU DISS TIME!
ALTHOUGH THE LEADER OF THE "SECRET 25", GOVERNS THOUSANDS OF HOODED SPIES ONLY A FEW KNOW HIS REAL IDENTITY AND THE LOCATION OF HIS HEADQUARTERS IN HANGMAN'S COURT.
TAKE HIM TO THE UPPER PASSAGE AND DROP HIM! I'LL NOTIFY THE MEMBERS TO PICK HIM UP!
BY TELEVISION, FROM HIS SECRET QUARTERS THE BRAINS TALKS TO HIS SPIES ASSEMBLED IN THE UPPER LOFT . . . .
PICK UP DEMPSEY AND TAKE HIM UP TO YOUR LOFT! LATER, I'LL DIRECT HIS DEATH
HERE ISS DOT YANKEE!
SOON VE PUT HIM OUDT OF HIS MISERY FOR EFFER!
COME! VE TAKE HIM UP BEFORE DER SCREEN LIKE DER BRAINS SAID!
2
PLACE DEMPSEY IN THE STEEL BOX! FILL IT WITH CEMENT! IT WILL WEIGHT HIS BODY TO THE BOTTOM OF THE THAMES!

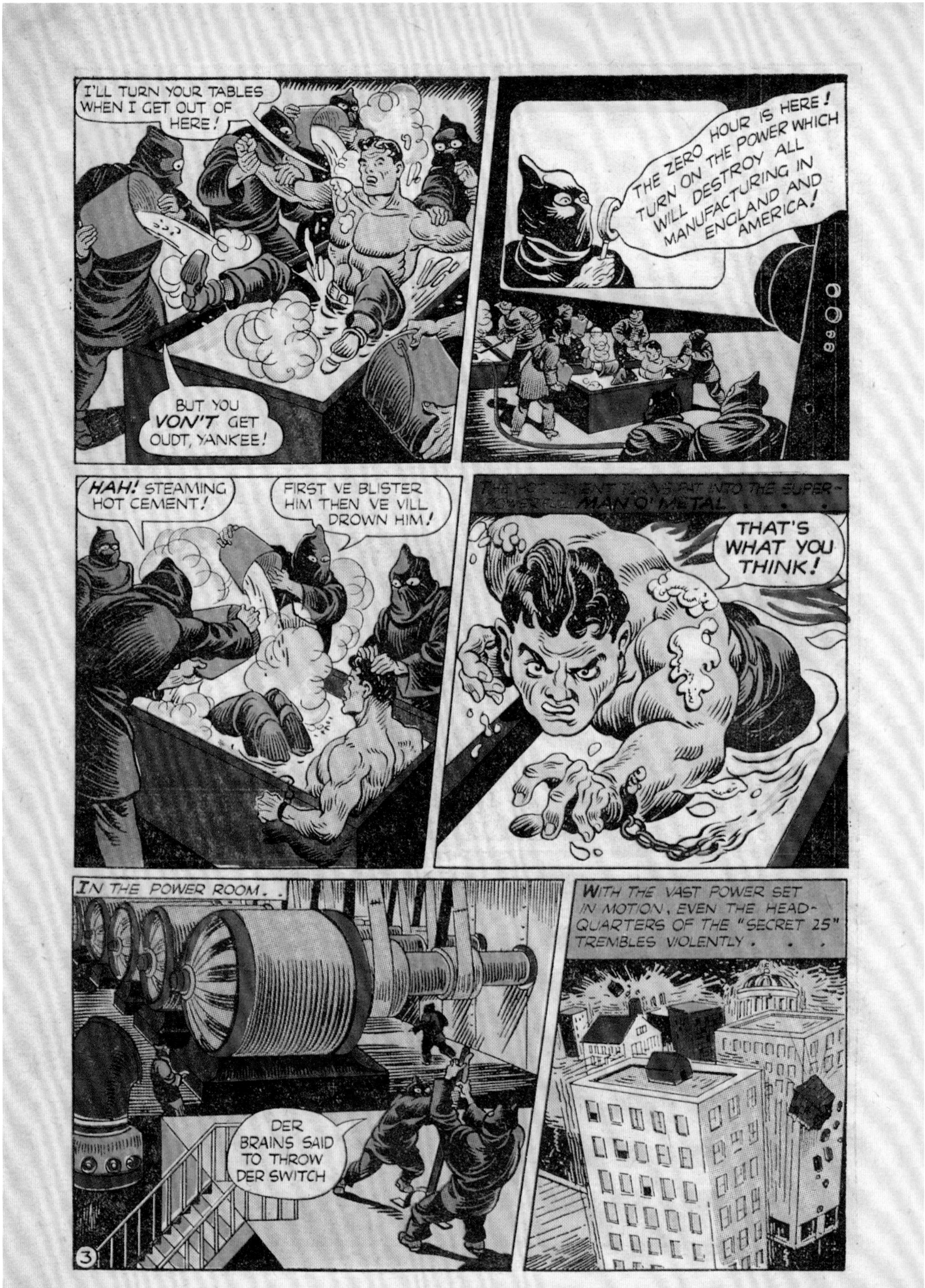
I'LL TURN YOUR TABLES WHEN I GET OUT OF HERE!
BUT YOU VON'T GET OUDT, YANKEE!
THE ZERO HOUR IS HERE! TURN ON THE POWER WHICH WILL DESTROY ALL MANUFACTURING IN ENGLAND AND AMERICA!
HAH! STEAMING HOT CEMENT!
FIRST VE BLISTER HIM THEN VE VILL DROWN HIM!
MAN O' METAL . . .
THAT'S WHAT YOU THINK!
IN THE POWER ROOM. . .
DER BRAINS SAID TO THROW DER SWITCH
3
WITH THE VAST POWER SET IN MOTION, EVEN THE HEAD-QUARTERS OF THE "SECRET 25" TREMBLES VIOLENTLY . . .

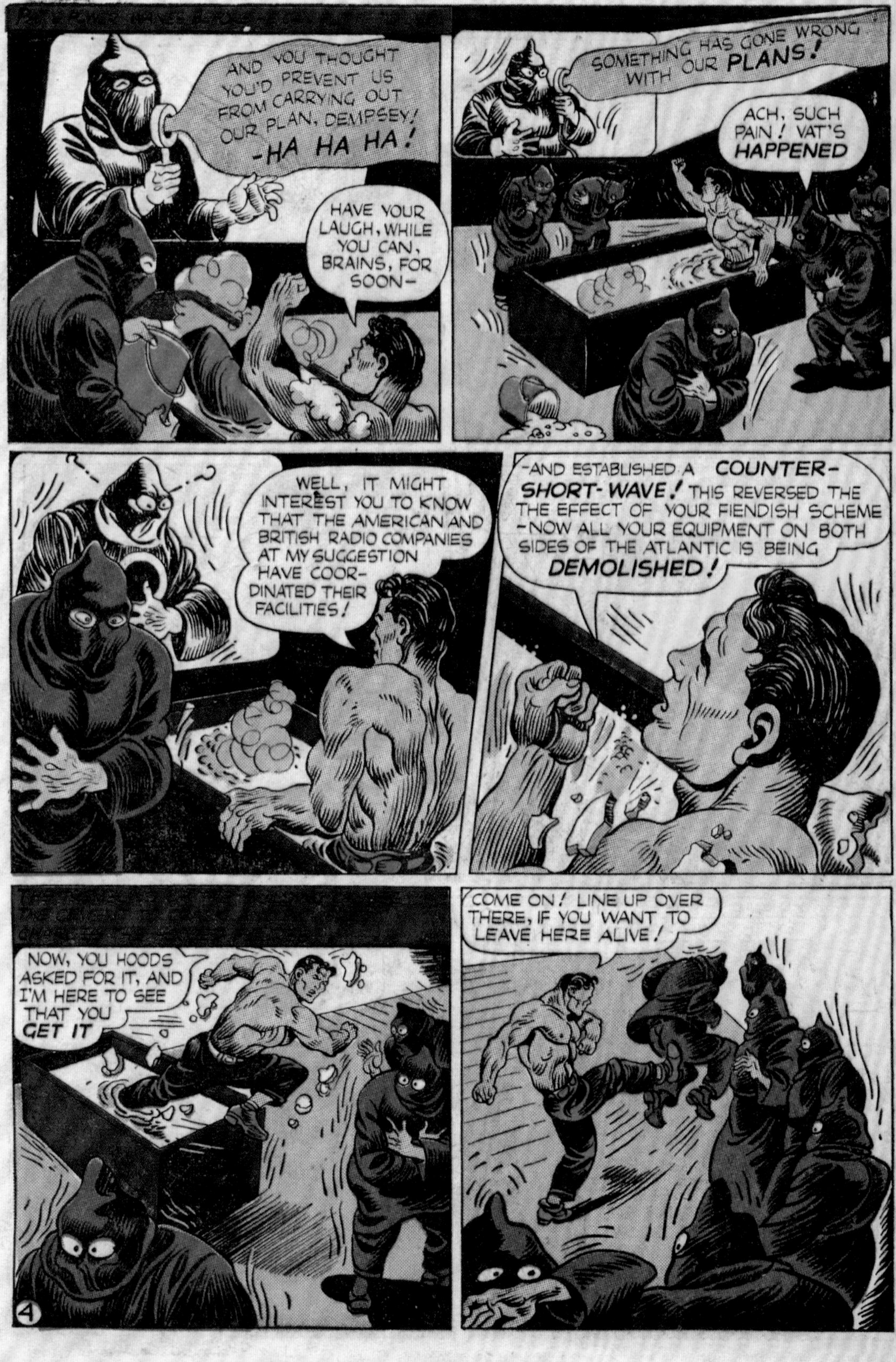
AND YOU THOUGHT YOU'D PREVENT US FROM CARRYING OUT OUR PLAN, DEMPSEY! -HA HA HA!
HAVE YOUR LAUGH, WHILE YOU CAN, BRAINS, FOR SOON-
SOMETHING HAS GONE WRONG WITH OUR PLANS!
ACH, SUCH PAIN! VAT'S HAPPENED
WELL, IT MIGHT INTEREST YOU TO KNOW THAT THE AMERICAN AND BRITISH RADIO COMPANIES AT MY SUGGESTION HAVE COORDINATED THEIR FACILITIES!
-AND ESTABLISHED A COUNTER-SHORT-WAVE! THIS REVERSED THE THE EFFECT OF YOUR FIENDISH SCHEME -NOW ALL YOUR EQUIPMENT ON BOTH SIDES OF THE ATLANTIC IS BEING DEMOLISHED!
NOW, YOU HOODS ASKED FOR IT, AND I'M HERE TO SEE THAT YOU GET IT
COME ON! LINE UP OVER THERE, IF YOU WANT TO LEAVE HERE ALIVE!
4

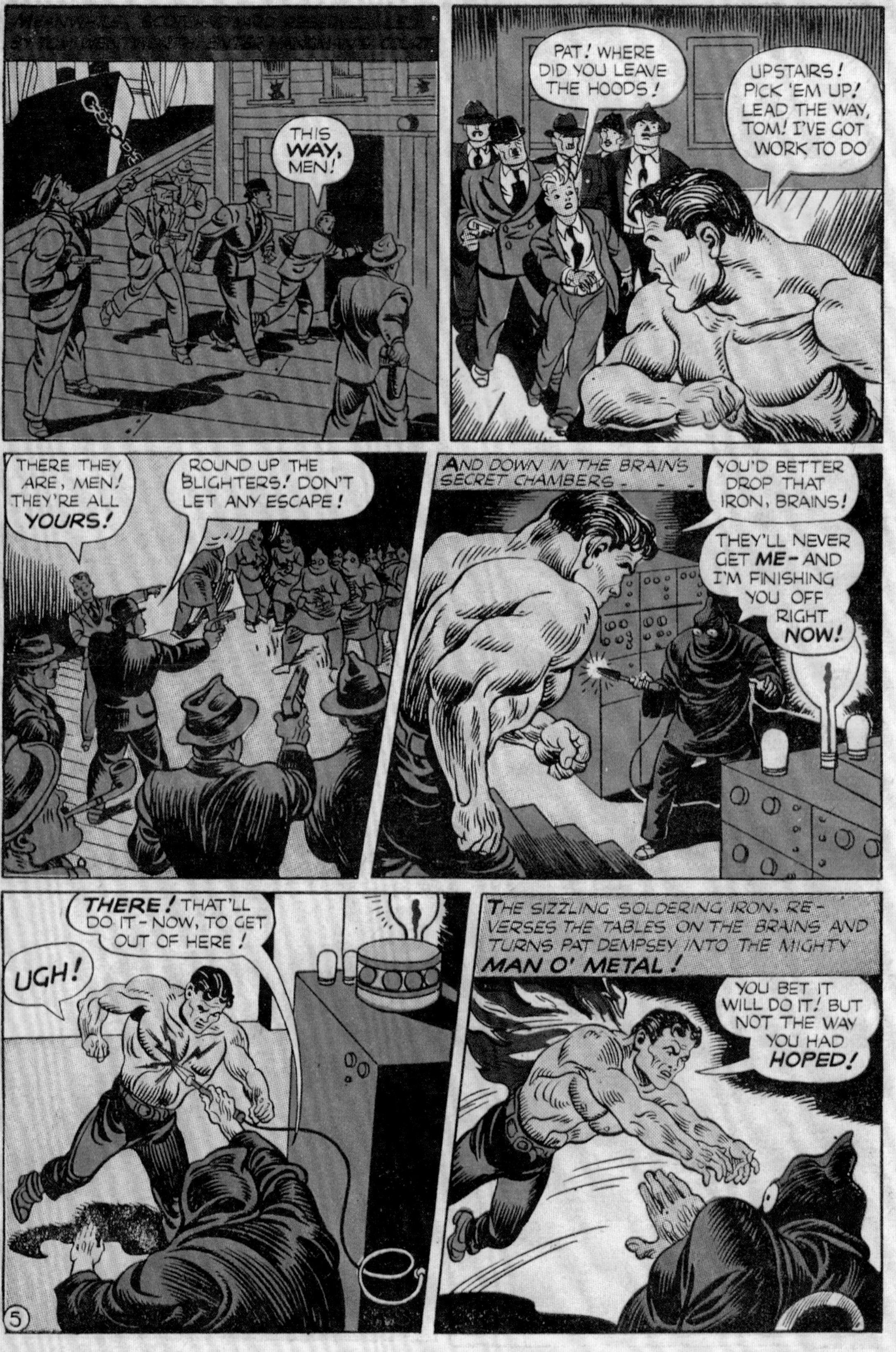
THIS WAY, MEN!
PAT! WHERE DID YOU LEAVE THE HOODS!
UPSTAIRS! PICK 'EM UP! LEAD THE WAY, TOM! I'VE GOT WORK TO DO
THERE THEY ARE, MEN! THEY'RE ALL YOURS!
ROUND UP THE BLIGHTERS! DON'T LET ANY ESCAPE!
AND DOWN IN THE BRAINS SECRET CHAMBERS - - -
YOU'D BETTER DROP THAT IRON, BRAINS!
THEY'LL NEVER GET ME- AND I'M FINISHING YOU OFF RIGHT NOW!
THERE! THAT'LL DO IT - NOW, TO GET OUT OF HERE!
UGH!
5
THE SIZZLING SOLDERING IRON, RE-VERSES THE TABLES ON THE BRAINS AND TURNS PAT DEMPSEY INTO THE MIGHTY MAN O' METAL!
YOU BET IT WILL DO IT! BUT NOT THE WAY YOU HAD HOPED!

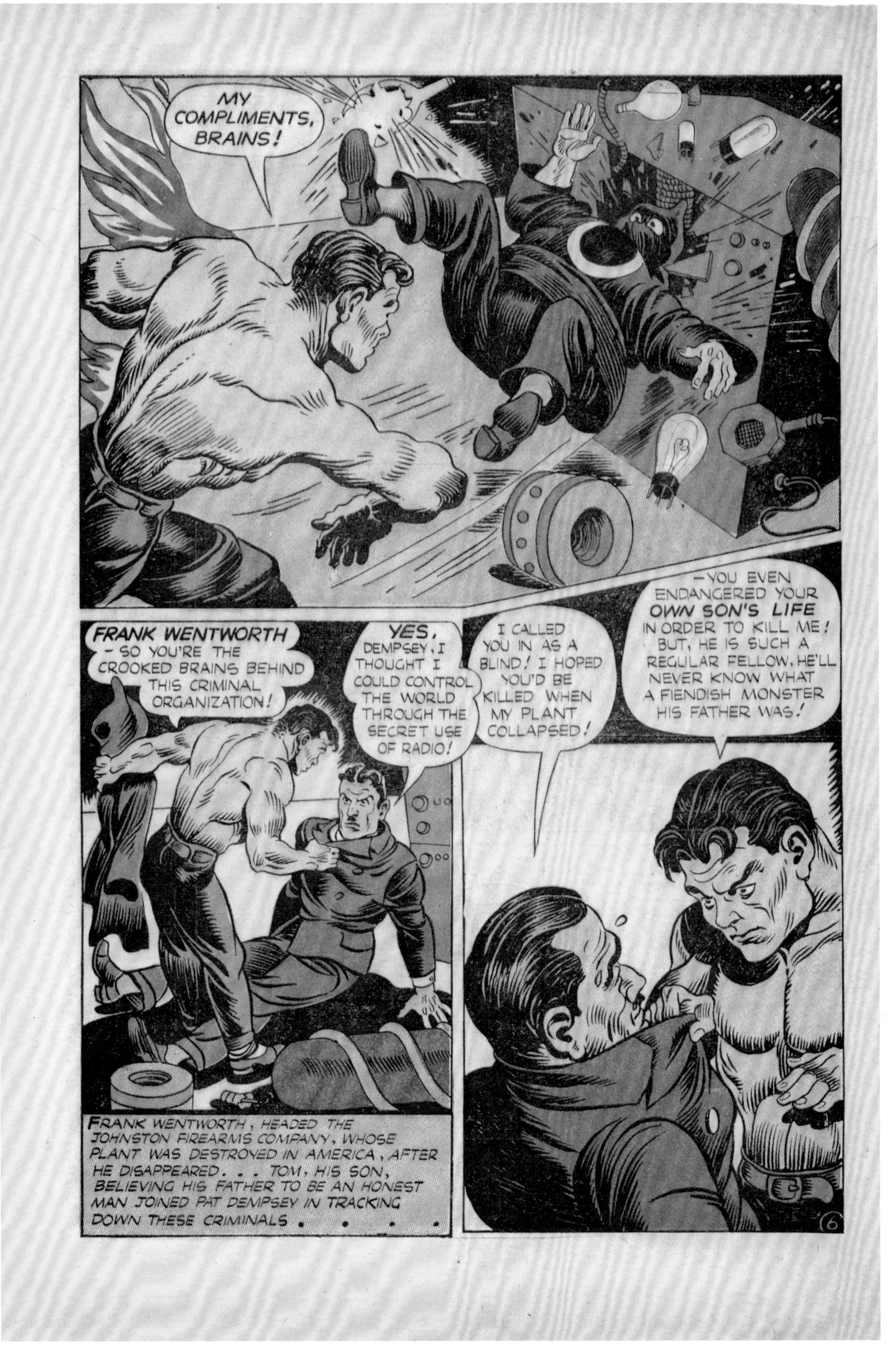
MY COMPLIMENTS, BRAINS!
FRANK WENTWORTH - SO YOU'RE THE CROOKED BRAINS BEHIND THIS CRIMINAL ORGANIZATION!
YES, DEMPSEY, I THOUGHT I COULD CONTROL THE WORLD THROUGH THE SECRET USE OF RADIO!
I CALLED YOU IN AS A BLIND! I HOPED YOU'D BE KILLED WHEN MY PLANT COLLAPSED!
-YOU EVEN ENDANGERED YOUR OWN SON'S LIFE IN ORDER TO KILL ME! BUT, HE IS SUCH A REGULAR FELLOW, HE'LL NEVER KNOW WHAT A FIENDISH MONSTER HIS FATHER WAS!
FRANK WENTWORTH, HEADED THE JOHNSTON FIREARMS COMPANY, WHOSE PLANT WAS DESTROYED IN AMERICA, AFTER HE DISAPPEARED. . . TOM, HIS SON, BELIEVING HIS FATHER TO BE AN HONEST MAN JOINED PAT DEMPSEY IN TRACKING DOWN THESE CRIMINALS . . . .
6

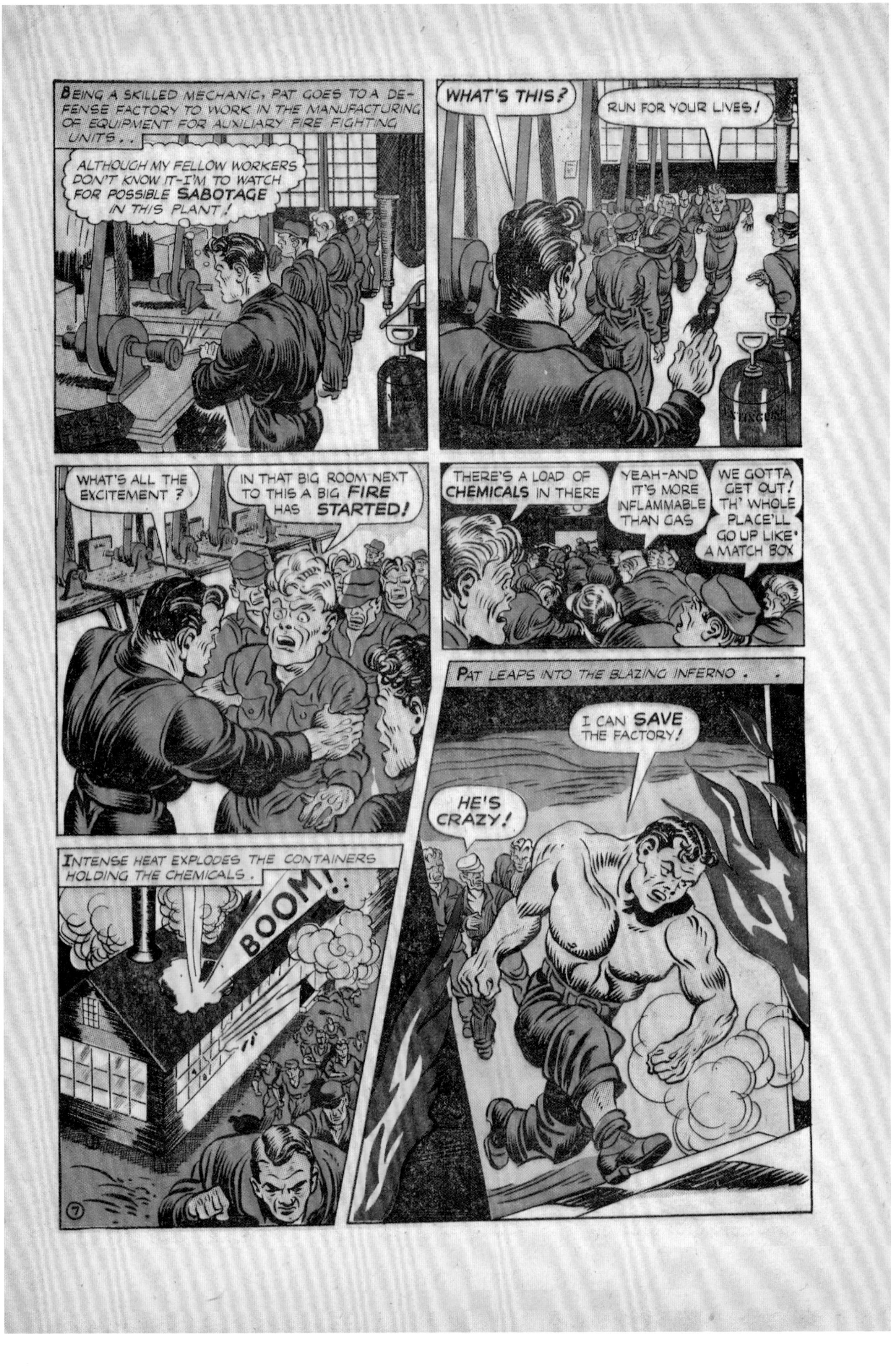
BEING A SKILLED MECHANIC, PAT GOES TO A DEFENSE FACTORY TO WORK IN THE MANUFACTURING OF EQUIPMENT FOR AUXILIARY FIRE FIGHTING UNITS..
ALTHOUGH MY FELLOW WORKERS DON'T KNOW IT-I'M TO WATCH FOR POSSIBLE SABOTAGE IN THIS PLANT!
WHAT'S THIS?
RUN FOR YOUR LIVES!
WHAT'S ALL THE EXCITEMENT ?
IN THAT BIG ROOM NEXT TO THIS A BIG FIRE HAS STARTED!
THERE'S A LOAD OF CHEMICALS IN THERE
YEAH-AND IT'S MORE INFLAMMABLE THAN GAS
WE GOTTA GET OUT! TH' WHOLE PLACE'LL GO UP LIKE A MATCH BOX
PAT LEAPS INTO THE BLAZING INFERNO . .
I CAN SAVE THE FACTORY!
HE'S CRAZY!
INTENSE HEAT EXPLODES THE CONTAINERS HOLDING THE CHEMICALS .
BOOM!
7

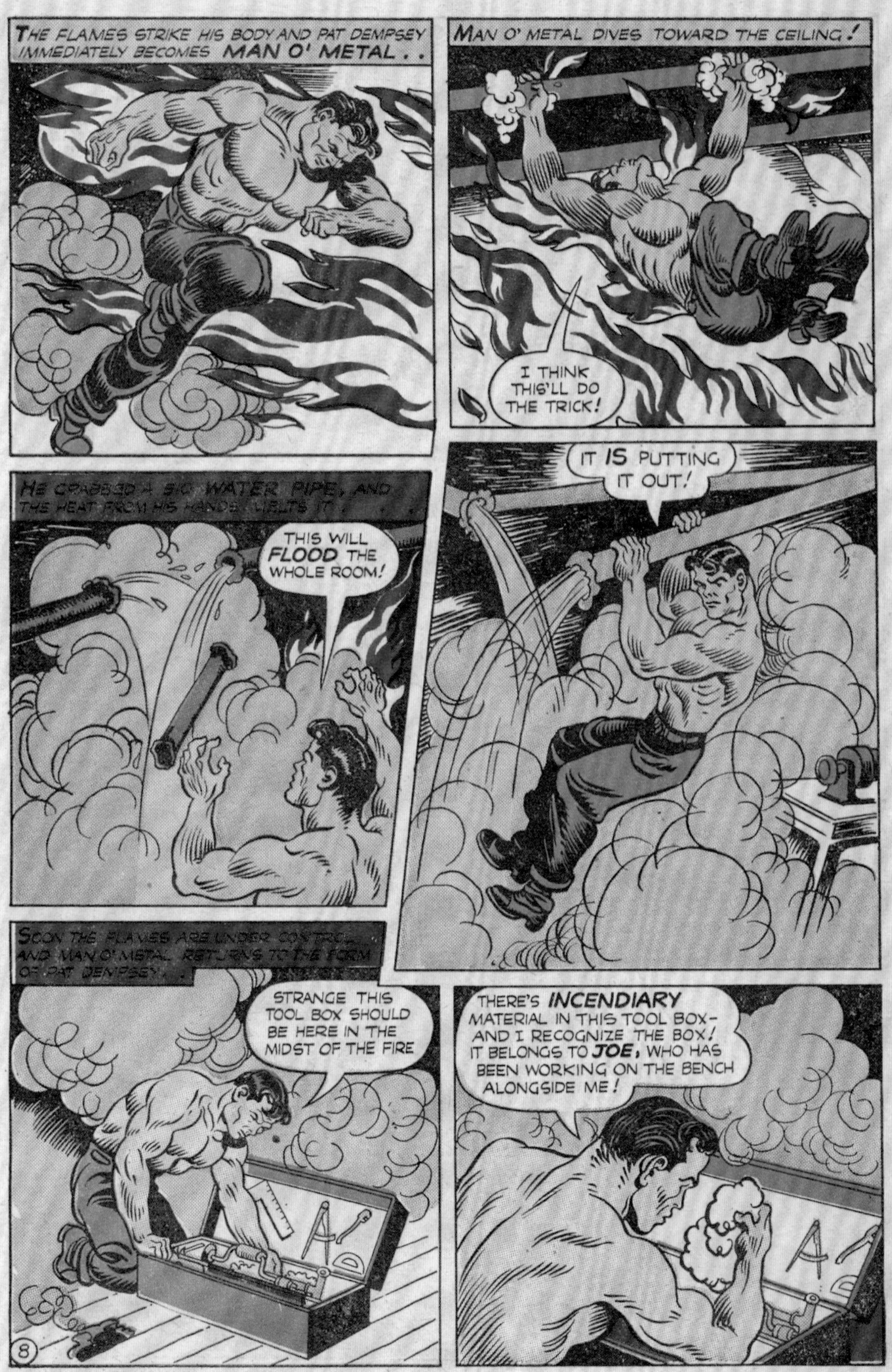
THE FLAMES STRIKE HIS BODY AND PAT DEMPSEY IMMEDIATELY BECOMES MAN O' METAL . .
MAN O' METAL DIVES TOWARD THE CEILING!
I THINK THIS'LL DO THE TRICK!
HE GRABBED A BIG WATER PIPE, AND THE HEAT FROM HIS HANDS MELTS IT . . .
THIS WILL FLOOD THE WHOLE ROOM!
IT IS PUTTING IT OUT!
SOON THE FLAMES ARE UNDER CONTROL, AND MAN O' METAL RETURNS TO THE FORM OF PAT DEMPSEY . .
STRANGE THIS TOOL BOX SHOULD BE HERE IN THE MIDST OF THE FIRE
THERE'S INCENDIARY MATERIAL IN THIS TOOL BOX- AND I RECOGNIZE THE BOX! IT BELONGS TO JOE, WHO HAS BEEN WORKING ON THE BENCH ALONGSIDE ME!
8

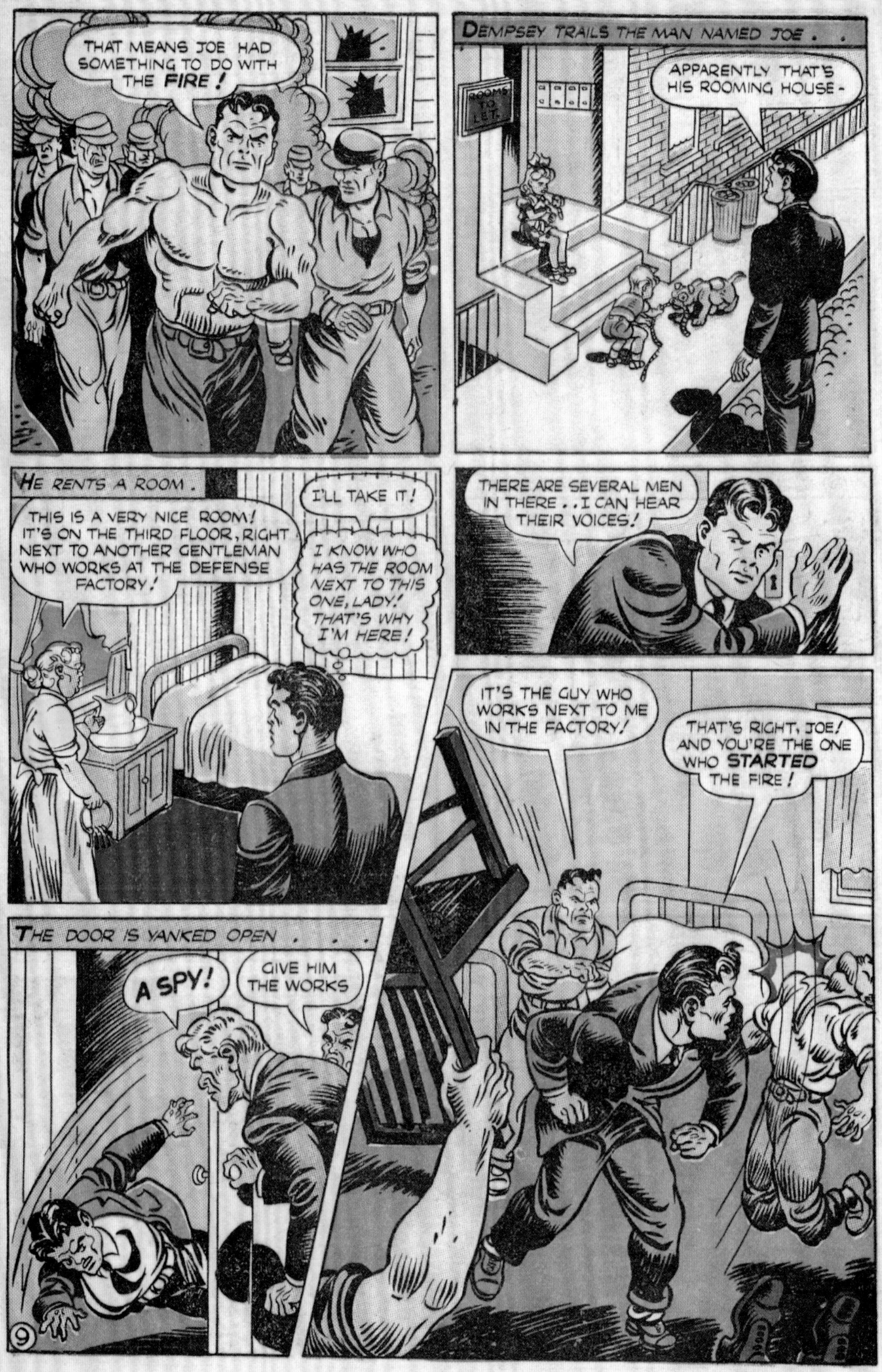
THAT MEANS JOE HAD SOMETHING TO DO WITH THE FIRE!
DEMPSEY TRAILS THE MAN NAMED JOE . . .
APPARENTLY THAT'S HIS ROOMING HOUSE-
ROOMS TO LET.
HE RENTS A ROOM.
THIS IS A VERY NICE ROOM! IT'S ON THE THIRD FLOOR, RIGHT NEXT TO ANOTHER GENTLEMAN WHO WORKS AT THE DEFENSE FACTORY!
I'LL TAKE IT!
I KNOW WHO HAS THE ROOM NEXT TO THIS ONE, LADY! THAT'S WHY I'M HERE!
THERE ARE SEVERAL MEN IN THERE . . I CAN HEAR THEIR VOICES!
THE DOOR IS YANKED OPEN . . .
A SPY!
GIVE HIM THE WORKS
IT'S THE GUY WHO WORKS NEXT TO ME IN THE FACTORY!
THAT'S RIGHT, JOE! AND YOU'RE THE ONE WHO STARTED THE FIRE!
9

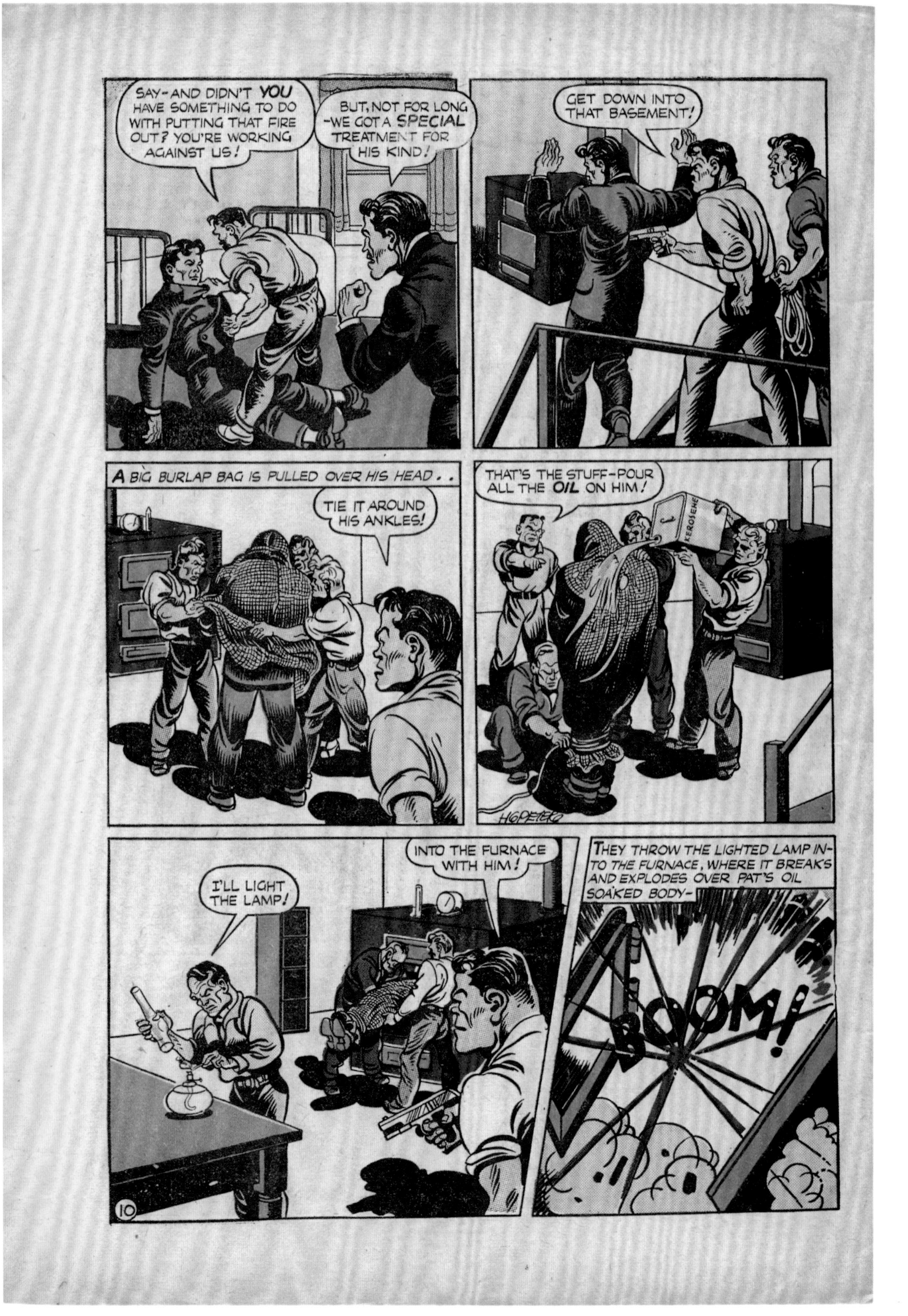
SAY-AND DIDN'T YOU HAVE SOMETHING TO DO WITH PUTTING THAT FIRE OUT? YOU'RE WORKING AGAINST US!
BUT, NOT FOR LONG -WE GOT A SPECIAL TREATMENT FOR HIS KIND!
GET DOWN INTO THAT BASEMENT!
A BIG BURLAP BAG IS PULLED OVER HIS HEAD . .
TIE IT AROUND HIS ANKLES!
THAT'S THE STUFF-POUR ALL THE OIL ON HIM!
KEROSENE
H.G. PETER
I'LL LIGHT THE LAMP!
INTO THE FURNACE WITH HIM!
THEY THROW THE LIGHTED LAMP INTO THE FURNACE, WHERE IT BREAKS AND EXPLODES OVER PAT'S OIL SOAKED BODY-
BOOM!
10

Where They Were Drawing From

Some artists, such as Mort Meskin, Sam J. Glanzman, Michael McMillan, and Peter Morisi, start out seemingly in thrall to a certain visual style—whether it's early Simon and Kirby heroics, chiaroscuro noir, pulp pen-and-ink drawings, or the linear grotesques of the Chicago artists group the Hairy Who—but then gradually move into their own languages as they find their footing in comics. As a result of the frantic need to produce new material and the corresponding speed at which the material is consumed, this developmental process moves along rather quickly.

The style lineages that run through comics are fruitful pathways by which to navigate their history. Meskin comes from the playful lights and darks of Milton Caniff and Noel Sickles as much as the dynamic figuration of Simon and Kirby. Meskin's work then leads to artists like Alex Toth and, later, David Mazzucchelli. An outgrowth of these same influences also underlies the work of Pete Morisi, who added a literal cinema-style presentation to the mix. Glanzman is an idiosyncratic craftsman who seems to come from the flamboyant linear stylings of Joseph Clement Coll and whose work parallels fellow comics artist Joe Kubert's in its fearless emphasis on figuration and bodies in motion rather than discernible set pieces.

McMillan anticipates the contemporary zines and underground comics in his seamless blend of comic book sources like the generic superheroics of the 1940s, with the artwork and wordplay of the Chicago artists like Jim Nutt and Karl Wirsum.

All of these artists, of course, are most successful when their talents are applied to a worthy story, which is always the difficulty of comics.

SHARON RUDAHL

(b. 1947)

Sharon Rudahl's masterpiece, *The Adventures of Crystal Night*, was released just a little too early to have the impact it deserved. Published in 1980, just before the alternative comics boom and quite a few years after the underground had wound down, it contains as many visual and literary ideas as Rudahl could cram into thirty-five pages. A story of class stratification, rebellion, and identity in a far-flung Jewish future, one can only imagine the bewilderment it engendered more than two decades ago. But its mix of gender politics, religion, sociology, sexuality, and science fiction anticipated much of contemporary small press comics.

Prior to *Crystal Night*, Rudahl had drawn only a handful of comics which primarily appeared in a few anthologies. More than twenty-five years after *Crystal Night*, she resurfaced with her recent *The Dangerous Woman: The Graphic Biography of Emma Goldman* (2007). Her sporadic publishing belies an unusually full life.

Rudahl was born in Arlington, Virginia, and raised in suburban Maryland. She became politically active at a young age, and attended college at Cooper Union in New York. As a twenty-year-old, she paid some of her living expenses by writing a now-infamous hippie sex fantasia novel for Olympia Press titled *Acid Temple Ball*, under the pseudonym "Mary Sativa." Rudahl was always interested in narrative art, like Käthe Kollwitz and Thomas Hart Benton, but it was her discovery of underground cartoonists, particularly Justin Green and Spain (Manuel Rodriguez), that pushed her to make her own comics. Rudahl moved to San Francisco and worked on a few issues of *Wimmen's Comix*, then moved on again as the underground began to falter, first to Yugoslavia and then back to California.

Crystal Night evolved out of Rudahl's work in comics, her political travels in the 1970s, and, as she noted in correspondence, from: "Being a newly arrived pedestrian in L.A.; science news about organ transplants and fertility treatments; a mild interest in my Jewish ethnic heritage—the words 'Crystal Night' seemed too transcendently beautiful to only refer to an atrocity." Drawn in an intricate style that fluidly mixes futuristic visions with grounded, earthy characterizations, *Crystal Night* is an unusually self-assured comic. Part of what makes this comic so extraordinary is that it was perhaps the only underground comic book to mine the same advanced territory as the science fiction of the 1970s, rather than the more commonly employed retro pulp material. Rudahl has long maintained an interest in genre literature, dating back to her adolescence, and notes that, "When state sponsored, elite, taught-in-school, serious art becomes absolutely useless at providing what people need from art, something bubbles up from despised popular forms . . . underground comics, natch, but also consider how much better Raymond Chandler and Philip K. Dick were than the 'serious' literary writers of their generations. What no one would dare say in 'literature' can be said in science fiction or porn."

Rudahl spoke volumes with *Crystal Night*, and then took a long break. Since completing *The Dangerous Woman*, she has drawn a number of other history-based comics and still lives and works in Los Angeles.

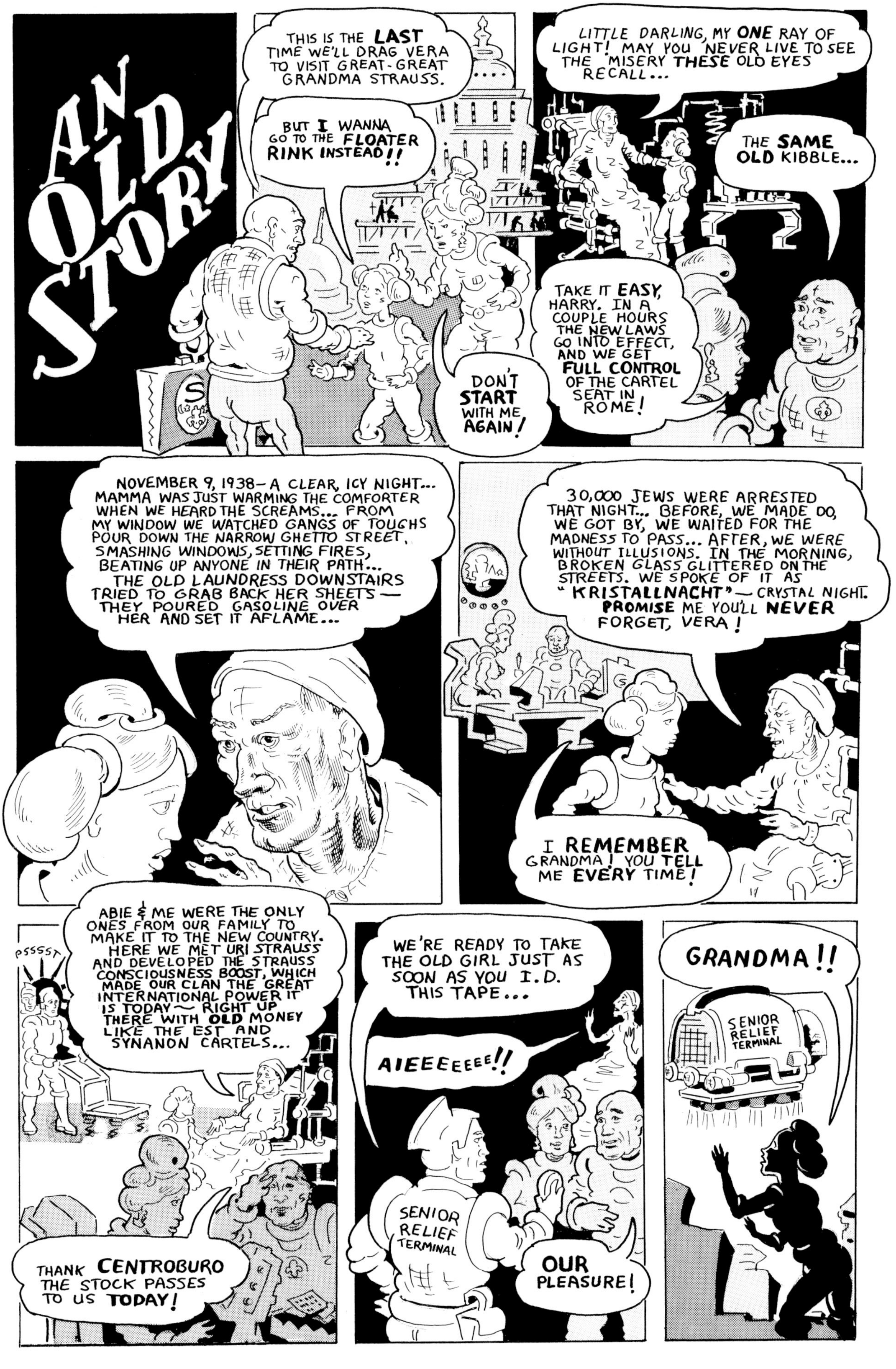
AN OLD STORY
THIS IS THE LAST TIME WE'LL DRAG VERA TO VISIT GREAT-GREAT GRANDMA STRAUSS.
BUT I WANNA GO TO THE FLOATER RINK INSTEAD!!
DON'T START WITH ME AGAIN!
LITTLE DARLING, MY ONE RAY OF LIGHT! MAY YOU NEVER LIVE TO SEE THE MISERY THESE OLD EYES RECALL...
THE SAME OLD KIBBLE...
TAKE IT EASY, HARRY. IN A COUPLE HOURS THE NEW LAWS GO INTO EFFECT, AND WE GET FULL CONTROL OF THE CARTEL SEAT IN ROME!
NOVEMBER 9, 1938 – A CLEAR, ICY NIGHT... MAMMA WAS JUST WARMING THE COMFORTER WHEN WE HEARD THE SCREAMS... FROM MY WINDOW WE WATCHED GANGS OF TOUGHS POUR DOWN THE NARROW GHETTO STREET, SMASHING WINDOWS, SETTING FIRES, BEATING UP ANYONE IN THEIR PATH... THE OLD LAUNDRESS DOWNSTAIRS TRIED TO GRAB BACK HER SHEETS — THEY POURED GASOLINE OVER HER AND SET IT AFLAME...
30,000 JEWS WERE ARRESTED THAT NIGHT... BEFORE, WE MADE DO, WE GOT BY, WE WAITED FOR THE MADNESS TO PASS... AFTER, WE WERE WITHOUT ILLUSIONS. IN THE MORNING, BROKEN GLASS GLITTERED ON THE STREETS. WE SPOKE OF IT AS "KRISTALLNACHT" — CRYSTAL NIGHT. PROMISE ME YOU'LL NEVER FORGET, VERA!
I REMEMBER GRANDMA! YOU TELL ME EVERY TIME!
ABIE & ME WERE THE ONLY ONES FROM OUR FAMILY TO MAKE IT TO THE NEW COUNTRY. HERE WE MET URI STRAUSS AND DEVELOPED THE STRAUSS CONSCIOUSNESS BOOST, WHICH MADE OUR CLAN THE GREAT INTERNATIONAL POWER IT IS TODAY — RIGHT UP THERE WITH OLD MONEY LIKE THE EST AND SYNANON CARTELS...
PSSSST
THANK CENTROBURO THE STOCK PASSES TO US TODAY!
WE'RE READY TO TAKE THE OLD GIRL JUST AS SOON AS YOU I.D. THIS TAPE...
AIEEEEEEE!!
SENIOR RELIEF TERMINAL
OUR PLEASURE!
GRANDMA!!
SENIOR RELIEF TERMINAL

The Adventures of Crystal Night (1980)

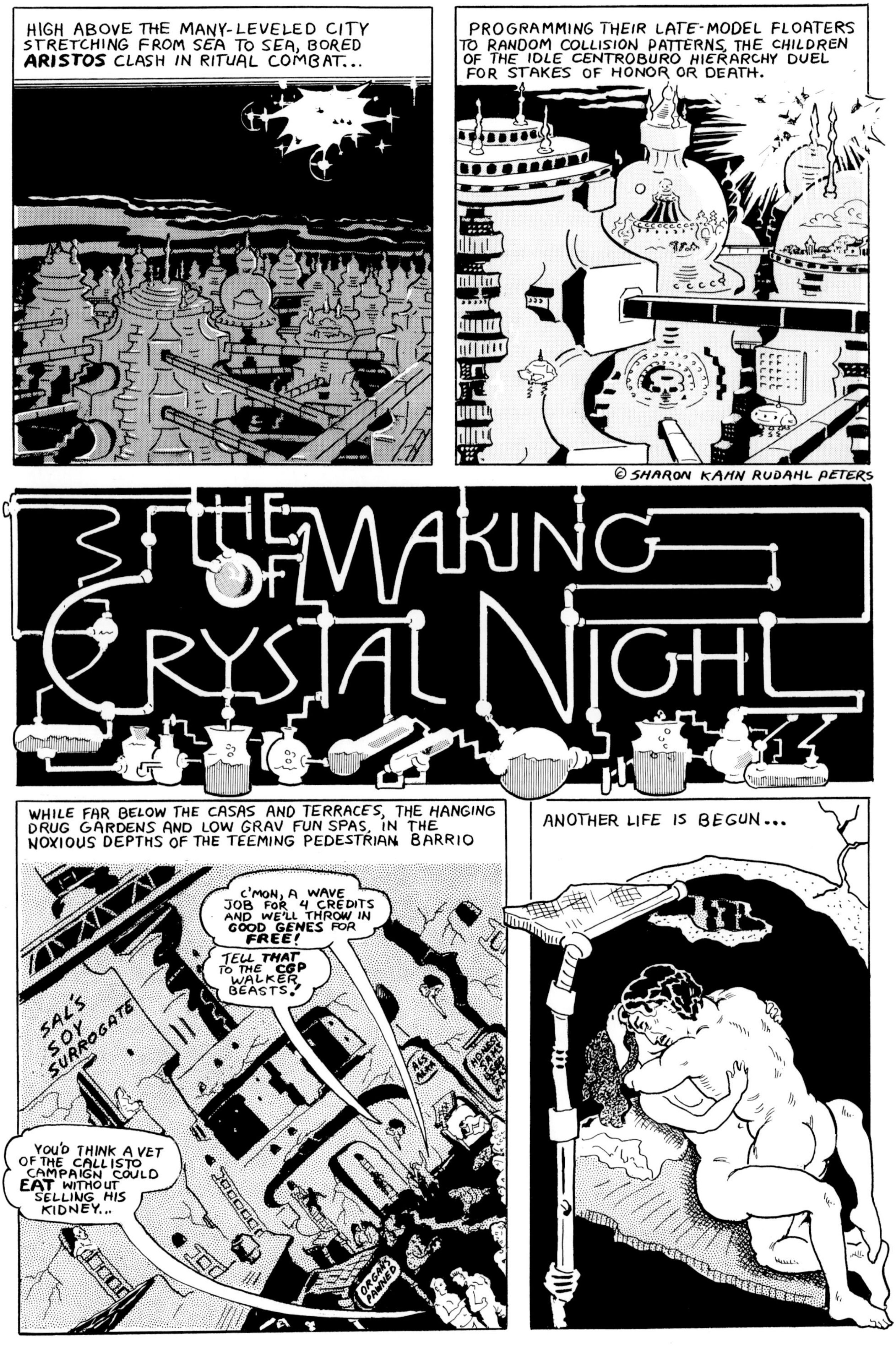
HIGH ABOVE THE MANY-LEVELED CITY STRETCHING FROM SEA TO SEA, BORED **ARISTOS** CLASH IN RITUAL COMBAT...
PROGRAMMING THEIR LATE-MODEL FLOATERS TO RANDOM COLLISION PATTERNS, THE CHILDREN OF THE IDLE CENTROBURO HIERARCHY DUEL FOR STAKES OF HONOR OR DEATH.
© SHARON KAHN RUDAHL PETERS
THE MAKING OF CRYSTAL NIGHT
WHILE FAR BELOW THE CASAS AND TERRACES, THE HANGING DRUG GARDENS AND LOW GRAV FUN SPAS, IN THE NOXIOUS DEPTHS OF THE TEEMING PEDESTRIAN BARRIO
C'MON, A WAVE JOB FOR 4 CREDITS AND WE'LL THROW IN **GOOD GENES** FOR **FREE!**
TELL **THAT** TO THE **CGP** WALKER BEASTS!
SAL'S SOY SURROGATE
YOU'D THINK A VET OF THE CALLISTO CAMPAIGN COULD **EAT** WITHOUT SELLING HIS KIDNEY...
ORGANS PAWNED
ANOTHER LIFE IS BEGUN...

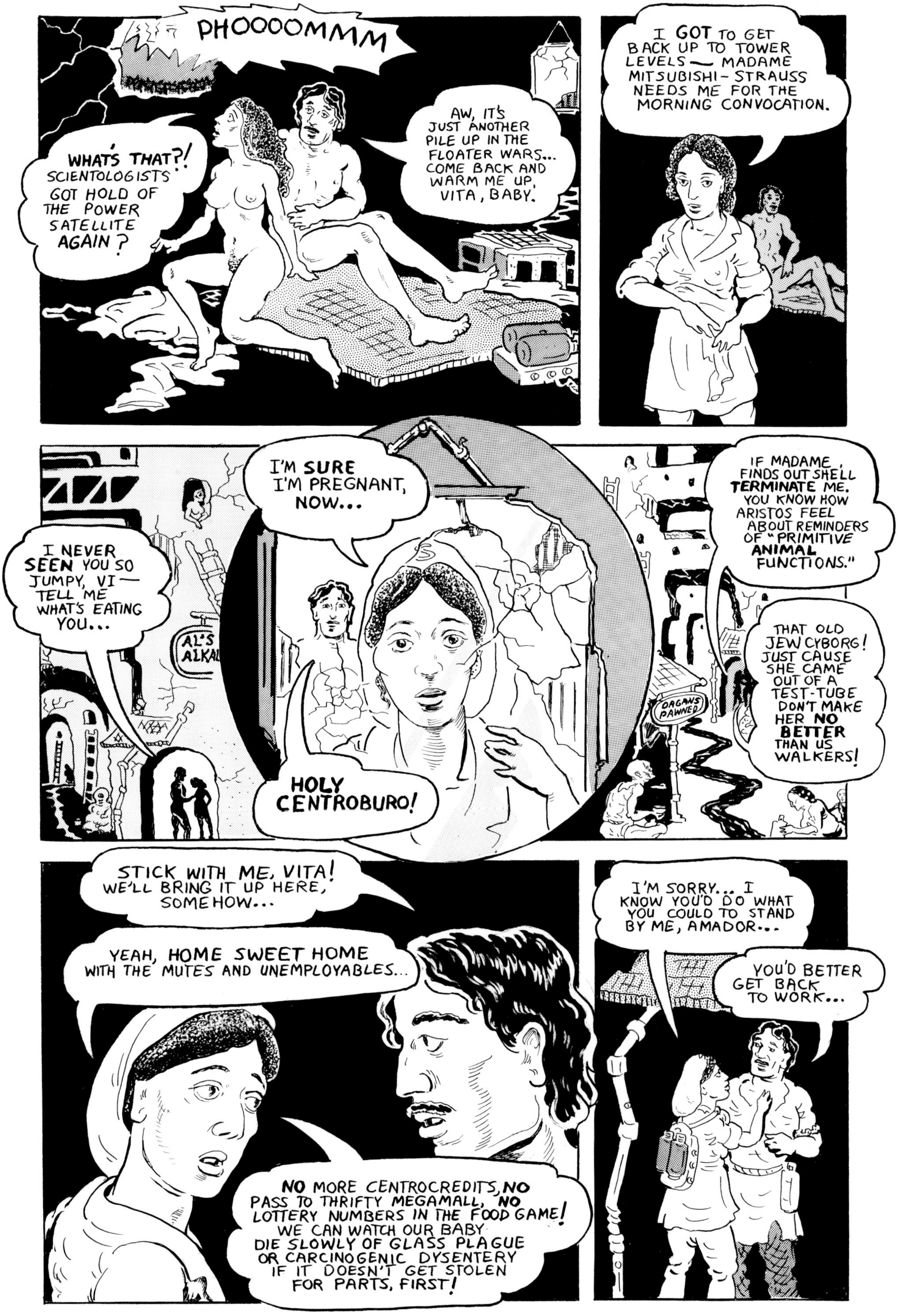
PHOOOOMMM
WHAT'S THAT?! SCIENTOLOGISTS GOT HOLD OF THE POWER SATELLITE AGAIN?
AW, IT'S JUST ANOTHER PILE UP IN THE FLOATER WARS... COME BACK AND WARM ME UP, VITA, BABY.
I GOT TO GET BACK UP TO TOWER LEVELS — MADAME MITSUBISHI-STRAUSS NEEDS ME FOR THE MORNING CONVOCATION.
I NEVER SEEN YOU SO JUMPY, VI — TELL ME WHAT'S EATING YOU...
I'M SURE I'M PREGNANT, NOW...
HOLY CENTROBURO!
IF MADAME FINDS OUT SHE'LL TERMINATE ME. YOU KNOW HOW ARISTOS FEEL ABOUT REMINDERS OF "PRIMITIVE ANIMAL FUNCTIONS."
THAT OLD JEW CYBORG! JUST CAUSE SHE CAME OUT OF A TEST-TUBE DON'T MAKE HER NO BETTER THAN US WALKERS!
ORGANS PAWNED
STICK WITH ME, VITA! WE'LL BRING IT UP HERE, SOMEHOW...
YEAH, HOME SWEET HOME WITH THE MUTES AND UNEMPLOYABLES...
NO MORE CENTROCREDITS, NO PASS TO THRIFTY MEGAMALL, NO LOTTERY NUMBERS IN THE FOOD GAME! WE CAN WATCH OUR BABY DIE SLOWLY OF GLASS PLAGUE OR CARCINOGENIC DYSENTERY IF IT DOESN'T GET STOLEN FOR PARTS, FIRST!
I'M SORRY... I KNOW YOU'D DO WHAT YOU COULD TO STAND BY ME, AMADOR...
YOU'D BETTER GET BACK TO WORK...

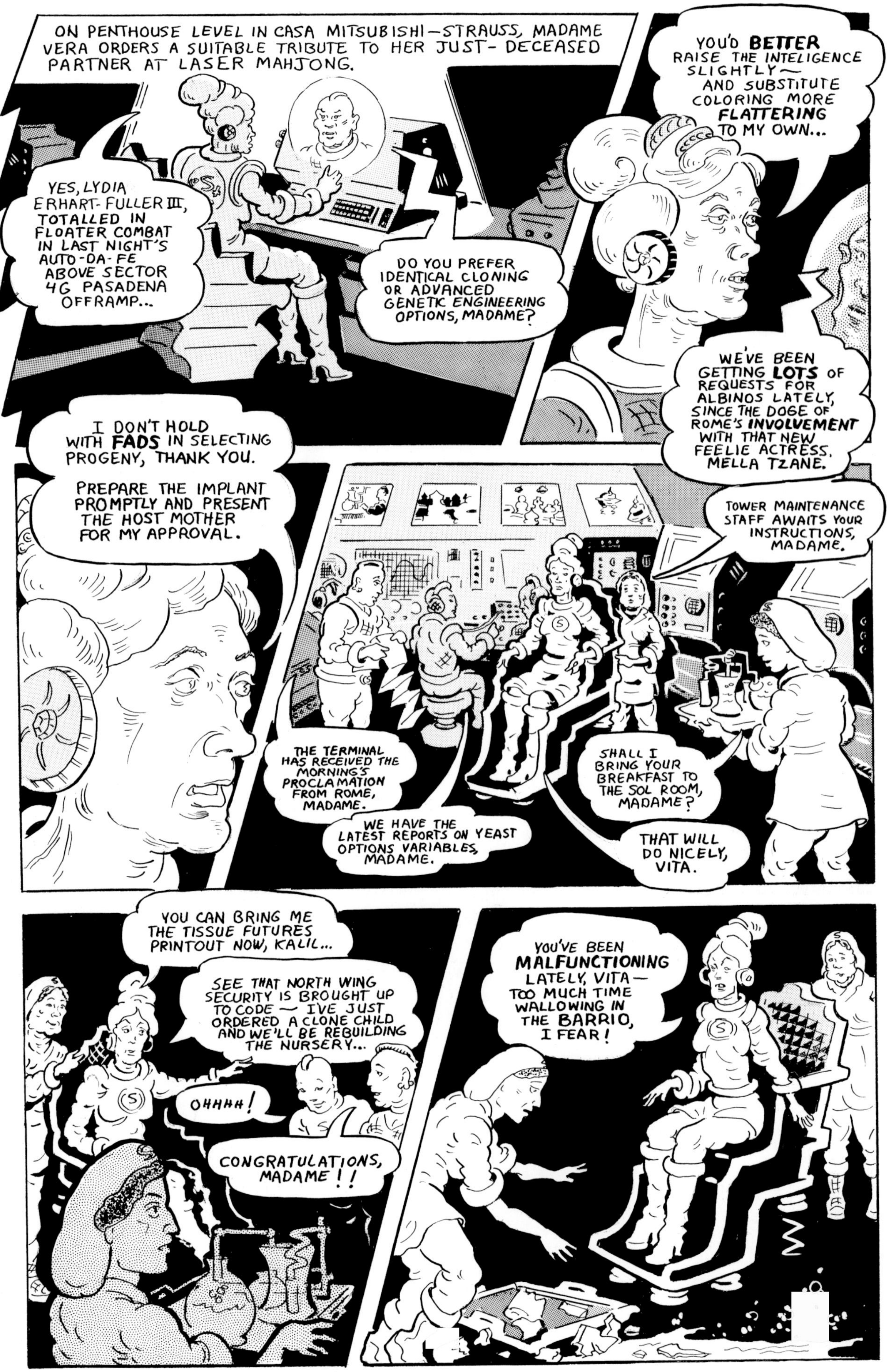
ON PENTHOUSE LEVEL IN CASA MITSUBISHI—STRAUSS, MADAME VERA ORDERS A SUITABLE TRIBUTE TO HER JUST-DECEASED PARTNER AT LASER MAHJONG.
YES, LYDIA ERHART-FULLER III, TOTALLED IN FLOATER COMBAT IN LAST NIGHT'S AUTO-DA-FE ABOVE SECTOR 4G PASADENA OFFRAMP...
DO YOU PREFER IDENTICAL CLONING OR ADVANCED GENETIC ENGINEERING OPTIONS, MADAME?
YOU'D BETTER RAISE THE INTELIGENCE SLIGHTLY— AND SUBSTITUTE COLORING MORE FLATTERING TO MY OWN...
WE'VE BEEN GETTING LOTS OF REQUESTS FOR ALBINOS LATELY, SINCE THE DOGE OF ROME'S INVOLVEMENT WITH THAT NEW FEELIE ACTRESS, MELLA TZANE.
I DON'T HOLD WITH FADS IN SELECTING PROGENY, THANK YOU.
PREPARE THE IMPLANT PROMPTLY AND PRESENT THE HOST MOTHER FOR MY APPROVAL.
TOWER MAINTENANCE STAFF AWAITS YOUR INSTRUCTIONS, MADAME.
THE TERMINAL HAS RECEIVED THE MORNING'S PROCLAMATION FROM ROME, MADAME.
WE HAVE THE LATEST REPORTS ON YEAST OPTIONS VARIABLES, MADAME.
SHALL I BRING YOUR BREAKFAST TO THE SOL ROOM, MADAME?
THAT WILL DO NICELY, VITA.
YOU CAN BRING ME THE TISSUE FUTURES PRINTOUT NOW, KALIL...
SEE THAT NORTH WING SECURITY IS BROUGHT UP TO CODE— I'VE JUST ORDERED A CLONE CHILD AND WE'LL BE REBUILDING THE NURSERY...
OHHHH!
CONGRATULATIONS, MADAME!!
YOU'VE BEEN MALFUNCTIONING LATELY, VITA— TOO MUCH TIME WALLOWING IN THE BARRIO, I FEAR!

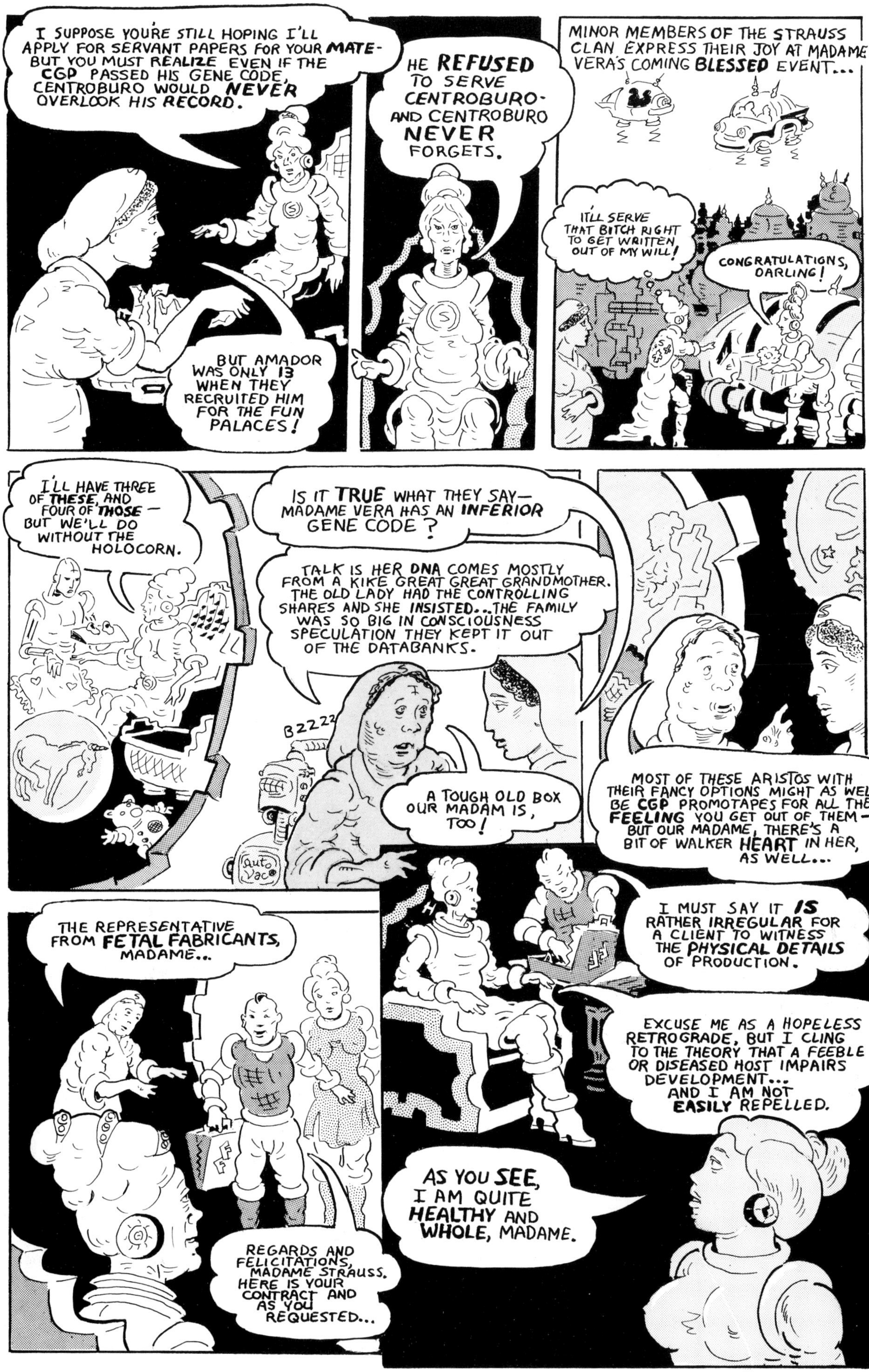
I SUPPOSE YOU'RE STILL HOPING I'LL APPLY FOR SERVANT PAPERS FOR YOUR MATE-BUT YOU MUST REALIZE EVEN IF THE CGP PASSED HIS GENE CODE, CENTROBURO WOULD NEVER OVERLOOK HIS RECORD.
BUT AMADOR WAS ONLY 13 WHEN THEY RECRUITED HIM FOR THE FUN PALACES!
HE REFUSED TO SERVE CENTROBURO-AND CENTROBURO NEVER FORGETS.
MINOR MEMBERS OF THE STRAUSS CLAN EXPRESS THEIR JOY AT MADAME VERA'S COMING BLESSED EVENT...
IT'LL SERVE THAT BITCH RIGHT TO GET WRITTEN OUT OF MY WILL!
CONGRATULATIONS, DARLING!
I'LL HAVE THREE OF THESE, AND FOUR OF THOSE - BUT WE'LL DO WITHOUT THE HOLOCORN.
IS IT TRUE WHAT THEY SAY-MADAME VERA HAS AN INFERIOR GENE CODE?
TALK IS HER DNA COMES MOSTLY FROM A KIKE GREAT GREAT GRANDMOTHER. THE OLD LADY HAD THE CONTROLLING SHARES AND SHE INSISTED...THE FAMILY WAS SO BIG IN CONSCIOUSNESS SPECULATION THEY KEPT IT OUT OF THE DATABANKS.
BZZZZ
A TOUGH OLD BOX OUR MADAM IS, TOO!
AUTO VAC
MOST OF THESE ARISTOS WITH THEIR FANCY OPTIONS MIGHT AS WELL BE CGP PROMOTAPES FOR ALL THE FEELING YOU GET OUT OF THEM-BUT OUR MADAME, THERE'S A BIT OF WALKER HEART IN HER, AS WELL...
THE REPRESENTATIVE FROM FETAL FABRICANTS, MADAME...
REGARDS AND FELICITATIONS, MADAME STRAUSS. HERE IS YOUR CONTRACT AND AS YOU REQUESTED...
I MUST SAY IT IS RATHER IRREGULAR FOR A CLIENT TO WITNESS THE PHYSICAL DETAILS OF PRODUCTION.
EXCUSE ME AS A HOPELESS RETROGRADE, BUT I CLING TO THE THEORY THAT A FEEBLE OR DISEASED HOST IMPAIRS DEVELOPMENT... AND I AM NOT EASILY REPELLED.
AS YOU SEE, I AM QUITE HEALTHY AND WHOLE, MADAME.

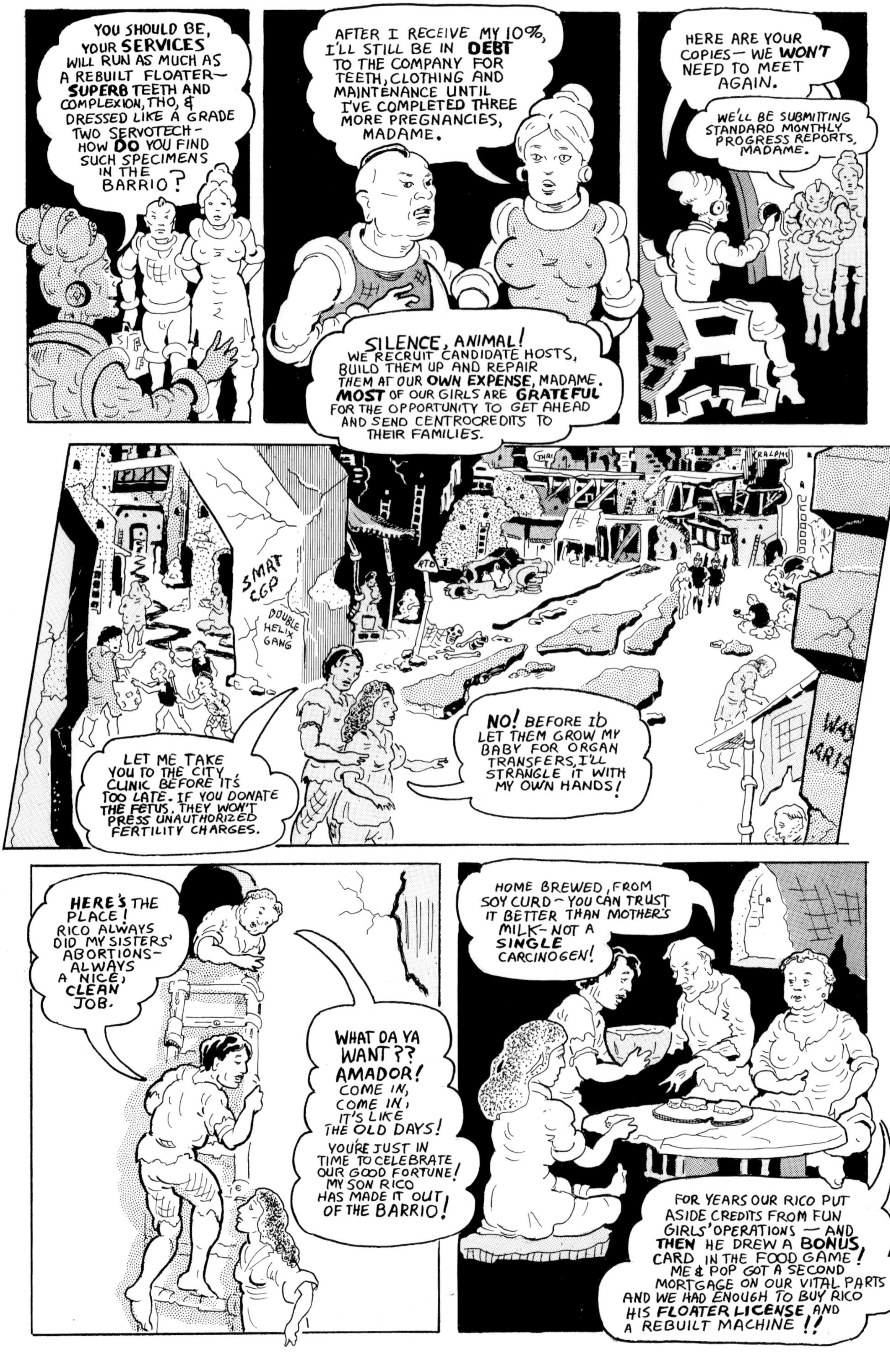
YOU SHOULD BE, YOUR SERVICES WILL RUN AS MUCH AS A REBUILT FLOATER— SUPERB TEETH AND COMPLEXION, THO, & DRESSED LIKE A GRADE TWO SERVOTECH— HOW DO YOU FIND SUCH SPECIMENS IN THE BARRIO?
AFTER I RECEIVE MY 10%, I'LL STILL BE IN DEBT TO THE COMPANY FOR TEETH, CLOTHING AND MAINTENANCE UNTIL I'VE COMPLETED THREE MORE PREGNANCIES, MADAME.
SILENCE, ANIMAL! WE RECRUIT CANDIDATE HOSTS, BUILD THEM UP AND REPAIR THEM AT OUR OWN EXPENSE, MADAME. MOST OF OUR GIRLS ARE GRATEFUL FOR THE OPPORTUNITY TO GET AHEAD AND SEND CENTROCREDITS TO THEIR FAMILIES.
HERE ARE YOUR COPIES— WE WON'T NEED TO MEET AGAIN.
WE'LL BE SUBMITTING STANDARD MONTHLY PROGRESS REPORTS, MADAME.
RALPHS
SMAT CGP
DOUBLE HELIX GANG
LET ME TAKE YOU TO THE CITY CLINIC BEFORE IT'S TOO LATE. IF YOU DONATE THE FETUS, THEY WON'T PRESS UNAUTHORIZED FERTILITY CHARGES.
NO! BEFORE I'D LET THEM GROW MY BABY FOR ORGAN TRANSFERS, I'LL STRANGLE IT WITH MY OWN HANDS!
HERE'S THE PLACE! RICO ALWAYS DID MY SISTERS' ABORTIONS— ALWAYS A NICE, CLEAN JOB.
WHAT DA YA WANT?? AMADOR! COME IN, COME IN, IT'S LIKE THE OLD DAYS!
YOU'RE JUST IN TIME TO CELEBRATE OUR GOOD FORTUNE! MY SON RICO HAS MADE IT OUT OF THE BARRIO!
HOME BREWED, FROM SOY CURD— YOU CAN TRUST IT BETTER THAN MOTHER'S MILK— NOT A SINGLE CARCINOGEN!
FOR YEARS OUR RICO PUT ASIDE CREDITS FROM FUN GIRLS' OPERATIONS — AND THEN HE DREW A BONUS CARD IN THE FOOD GAME! ME & POP GOT A SECOND MORTGAGE ON OUR VITAL PARTS AND WE HAD ENOUGH TO BUY RICO HIS FLOATER LICENSE AND A REBUILT MACHINE!!

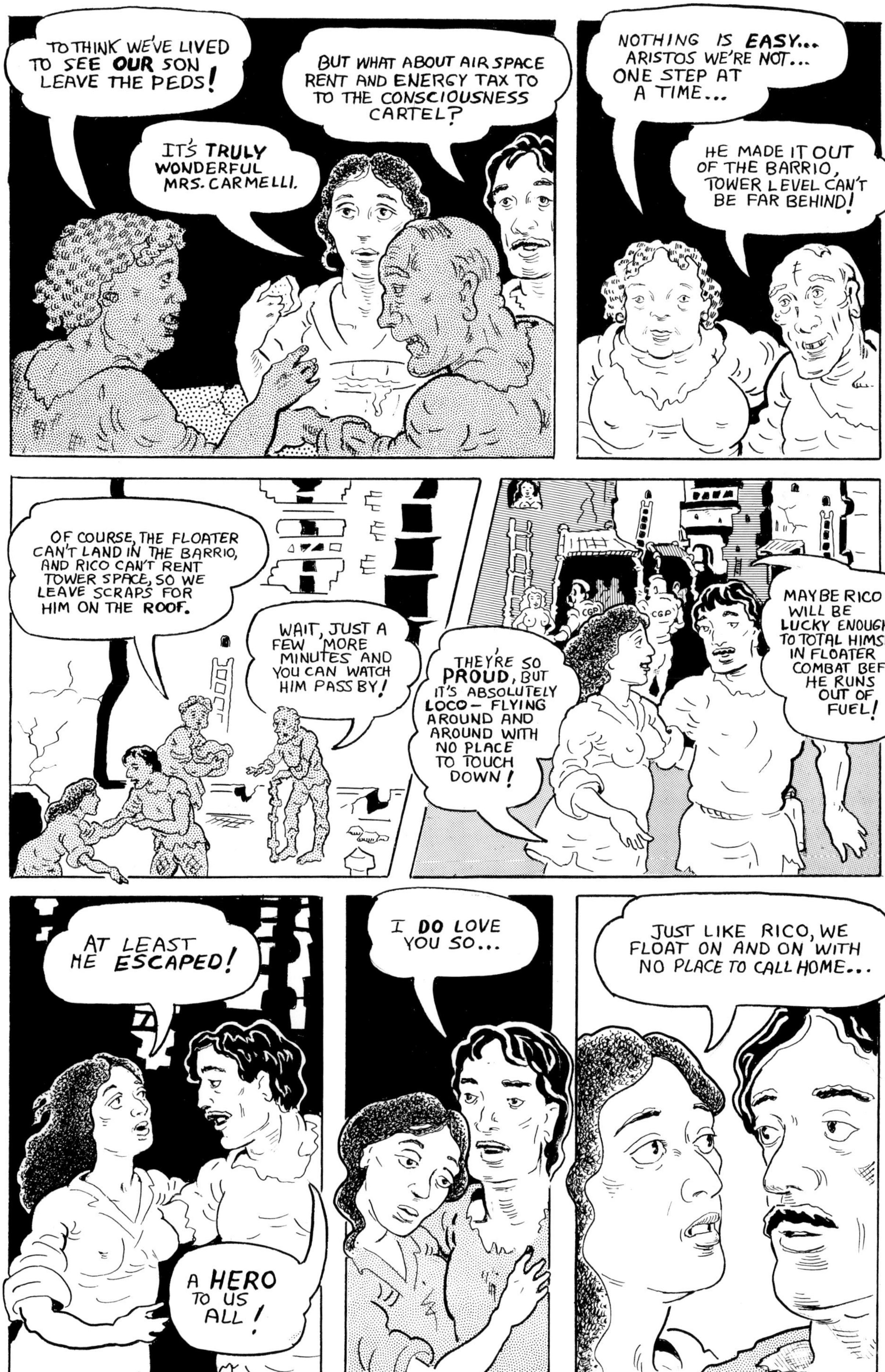
TO THINK WE'VE LIVED TO SEE OUR SON LEAVE THE PEDS!
IT'S TRULY WONDERFUL MRS. CARMELLI.
BUT WHAT ABOUT AIR SPACE RENT AND ENERGY TAX TO TO THE CONSCIOUSNESS CARTEL?
NOTHING IS EASY... ARISTOS WE'RE NOT... ONE STEP AT A TIME...
HE MADE IT OUT OF THE BARRIO, TOWER LEVEL CAN'T BE FAR BEHIND!
OF COURSE, THE FLOATER CAN'T LAND IN THE BARRIO, AND RICO CAN'T RENT TOWER SPACE, SO WE LEAVE SCRAPS FOR HIM ON THE ROOF.
WAIT, JUST A FEW MORE MINUTES AND YOU CAN WATCH HIM PASS BY!
THEY'RE SO PROUD, BUT IT'S ABSOLUTELY LOCO- FLYING AROUND AND AROUND WITH NO PLACE TO TOUCH DOWN!
MAYBE RICO WILL BE LUCKY ENOUGH TO TOTAL HIMSELF IN FLOATER COMBAT BEFORE HE RUNS OUT OF FUEL!
AT LEAST HE ESCAPED!
A HERO TO US ALL!
I DO LOVE YOU SO...
JUST LIKE RICO, WE FLOAT ON AND ON WITH NO PLACE TO CALL HOME...

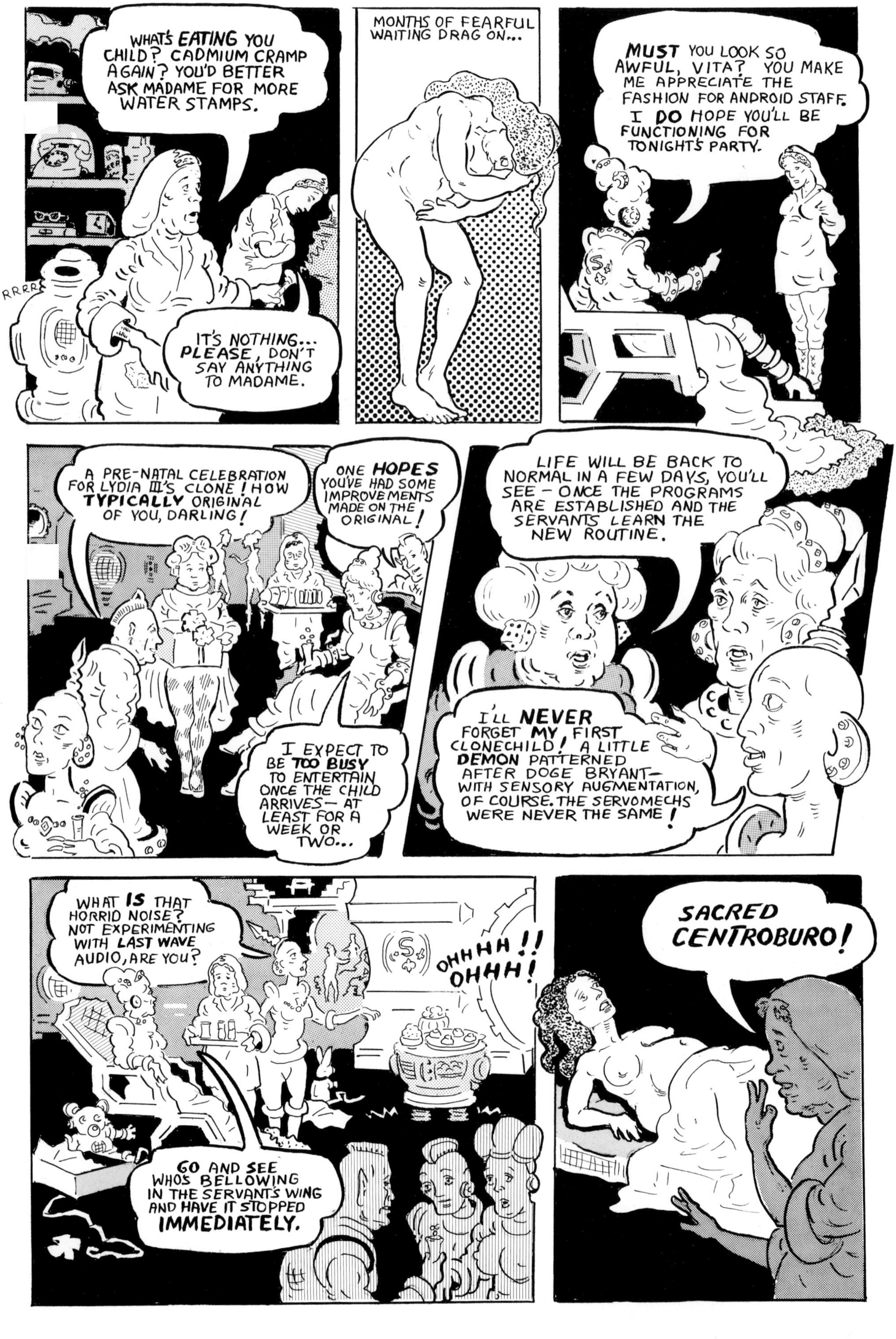
WHAT'S EATING YOU CHILD? CADMIUM CRAMP AGAIN? YOU'D BETTER ASK MADAME FOR MORE WATER STAMPS.
RRRR
IT'S NOTHING... PLEASE, DON'T SAY ANYTHING TO MADAME.
MONTHS OF FEARFUL WAITING DRAG ON...
MUST YOU LOOK SO AWFUL, VITA? YOU MAKE ME APPRECIATE THE FASHION FOR ANDROID STAFF. I DO HOPE YOU'LL BE FUNCTIONING FOR TONIGHT'S PARTY.
A PRE-NATAL CELEBRATION FOR LYDIA III'S CLONE! HOW TYPICALLY ORIGINAL OF YOU, DARLING!
ONE HOPES YOU'VE HAD SOME IMPROVEMENTS MADE ON THE ORIGINAL!
I EXPECT TO BE TOO BUSY TO ENTERTAIN ONCE THE CHILD ARRIVES— AT LEAST FOR A WEEK OR TWO...
LIFE WILL BE BACK TO NORMAL IN A FEW DAYS, YOU'LL SEE — ONCE THE PROGRAMS ARE ESTABLISHED AND THE SERVANTS LEARN THE NEW ROUTINE.
I'LL NEVER FORGET MY FIRST CLONECHILD! A LITTLE DEMON PATTERNED AFTER DOGE BRYANT— WITH SENSORY AUGMENTATION, OF COURSE. THE SERVOMECHS WERE NEVER THE SAME!
WHAT IS THAT HORRID NOISE? NOT EXPERIMENTING WITH LAST WAVE AUDIO, ARE YOU?
OHHHH!! OHHH!
GO AND SEE WHO'S BELLOWING IN THE SERVANT'S WING AND HAVE IT STOPPED IMMEDIATELY.
SACRED CENTROBURO!

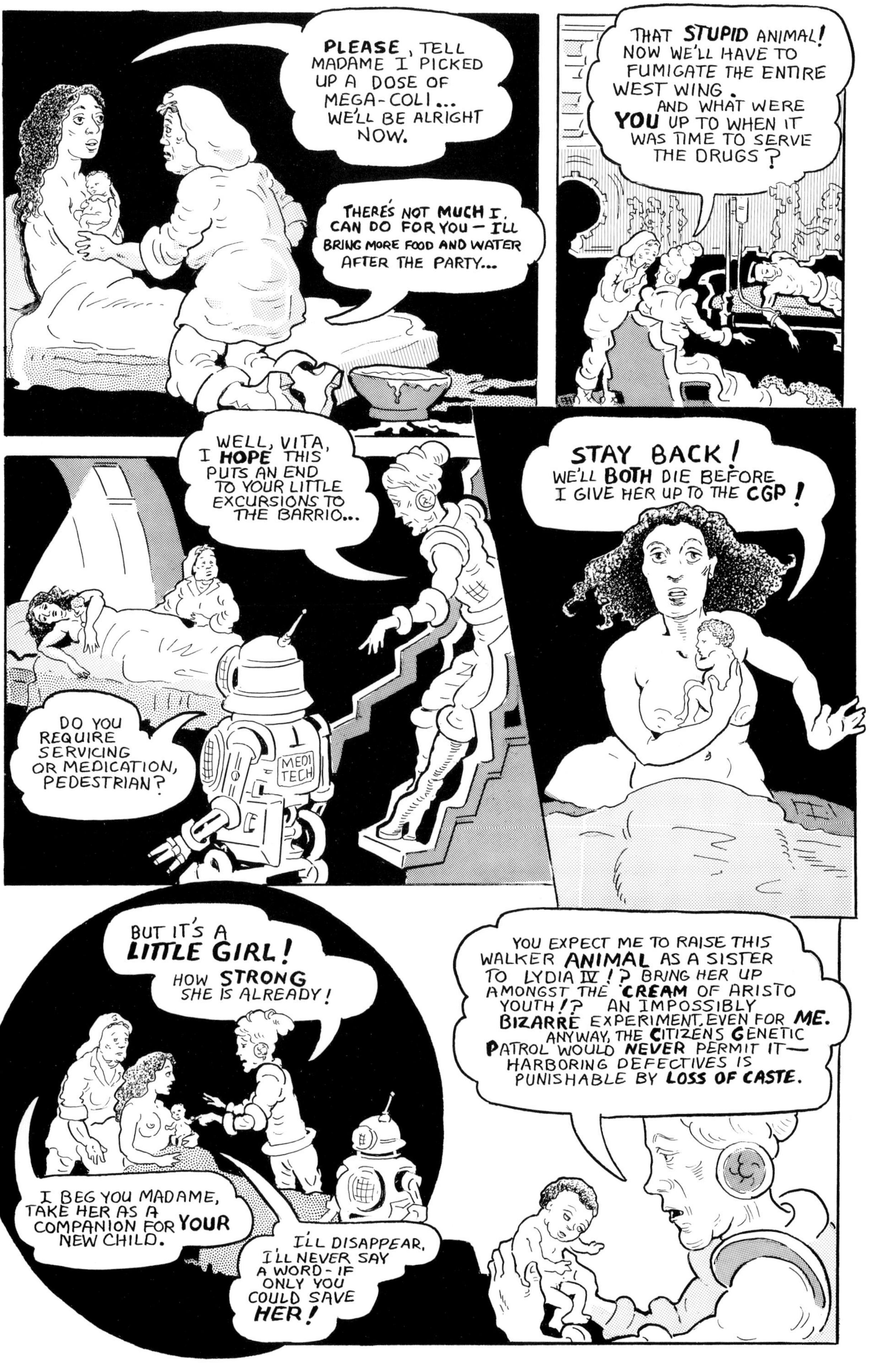
PLEASE, TELL MADAME I PICKED UP A DOSE OF MEGA-COLI... WE'LL BE ALRIGHT NOW.
THERE'S NOT MUCH I CAN DO FOR YOU — I'LL BRING MORE FOOD AND WATER AFTER THE PARTY...
THAT STUPID ANIMAL! NOW WE'LL HAVE TO FUMIGATE THE ENTIRE WEST WING.
AND WHAT WERE YOU UP TO WHEN IT WAS TIME TO SERVE THE DRUGS?
WELL, VITA, I HOPE THIS PUTS AN END TO YOUR LITTLE EXCURSIONS TO THE BARRIO...
DO YOU REQUIRE SERVICING OR MEDICATION, PEDESTRIAN?
MEDI TECH
STAY BACK! WE'LL BOTH DIE BEFORE I GIVE HER UP TO THE CGP!
BUT IT'S A LITTLE GIRL! HOW STRONG SHE IS ALREADY!
I BEG YOU MADAME, TAKE HER AS A COMPANION FOR YOUR NEW CHILD.
I'LL DISAPPEAR, I'LL NEVER SAY A WORD - IF ONLY YOU COULD SAVE HER!
YOU EXPECT ME TO RAISE THIS WALKER ANIMAL AS A SISTER TO LYDIA IV!? BRING HER UP AMONGST THE 'CREAM OF ARISTO YOUTH!? AN IMPOSSIBLY BIZARRE EXPERIMENT, EVEN FOR ME.
ANYWAY, THE CITIZENS GENETIC PATROL WOULD NEVER PERMIT IT — HARBORING DEFECTIVES IS PUNISHABLE BY LOSS OF CASTE.

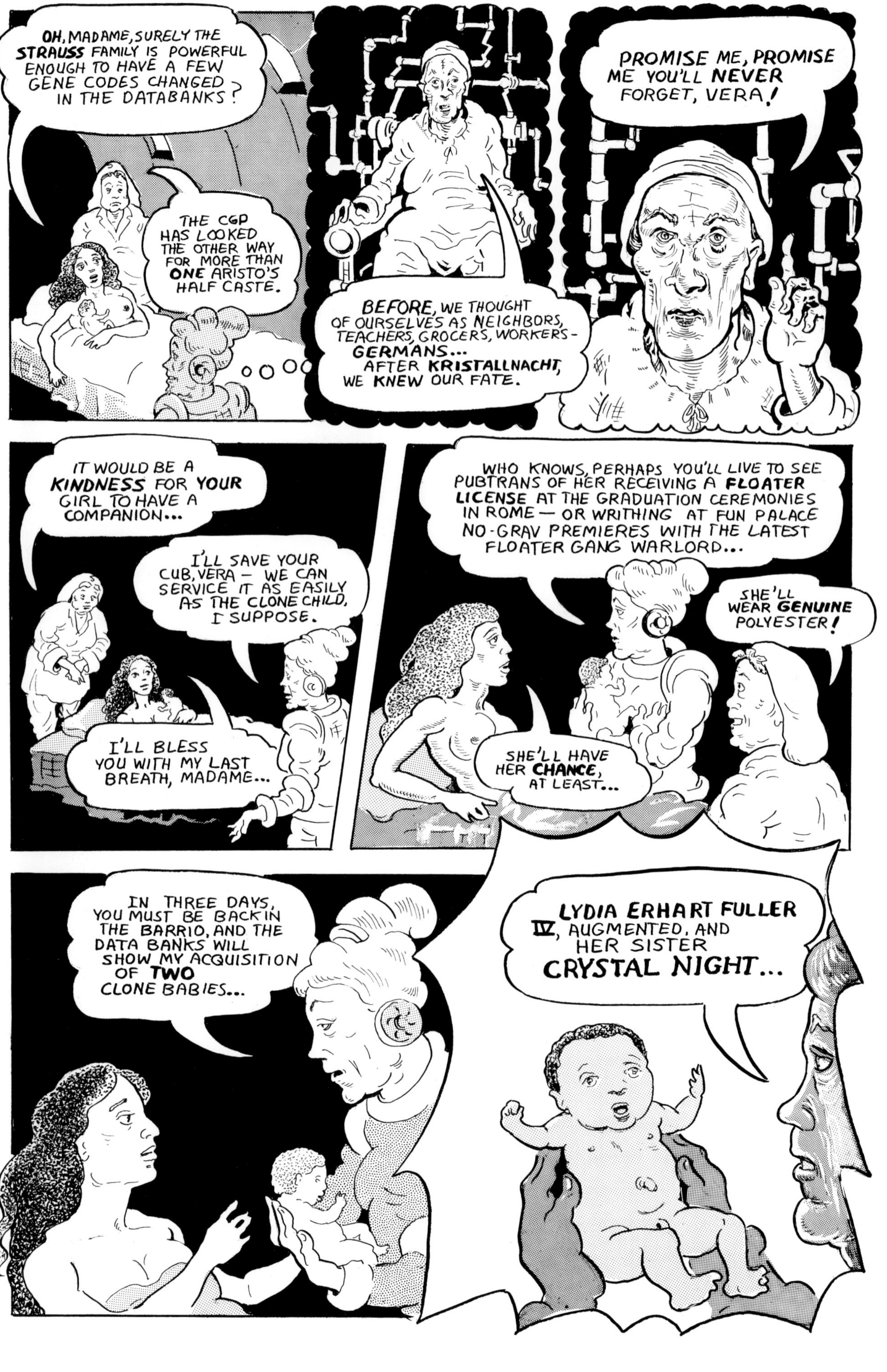
OH, MADAME, SURELY THE STRAUSS FAMILY IS POWERFUL ENOUGH TO HAVE A FEW GENE CODES CHANGED IN THE DATABANKS?
THE CGP HAS LOOKED THE OTHER WAY FOR MORE THAN ONE ARISTO'S HALF CASTE.
BEFORE, WE THOUGHT OF OURSELVES AS NEIGHBORS, TEACHERS, GROCERS, WORKERS- GERMANS... AFTER KRISTALLNACHT, WE KNEW OUR FATE.
PROMISE ME, PROMISE ME YOU'LL NEVER FORGET, VERA!
IT WOULD BE A KINDNESS FOR YOUR GIRL TO HAVE A COMPANION...
I'LL SAVE YOUR CUB, VERA — WE CAN SERVICE IT AS EASILY AS THE CLONE CHILD, I SUPPOSE.
I'LL BLESS YOU WITH MY LAST BREATH, MADAME...
WHO KNOWS, PERHAPS YOU'LL LIVE TO SEE PUBTRANS OF HER RECEIVING A FLOATER LICENSE AT THE GRADUATION CEREMONIES IN ROME — OR WRITHING AT FUN PALACE NO-GRAV PREMIERES WITH THE LATEST FLOATER GANG WARLORD...
SHE'LL WEAR GENUINE POLYESTER!
SHE'LL HAVE HER CHANCE, AT LEAST...
IN THREE DAYS, YOU MUST BE BACK IN THE BARRIO, AND THE DATA BANKS WILL SHOW MY ACQUISITION OF TWO CLONE BABIES...
LYDIA ERHART FULLER IV, AUGMENTED, AND HER SISTER CRYSTAL NIGHT...

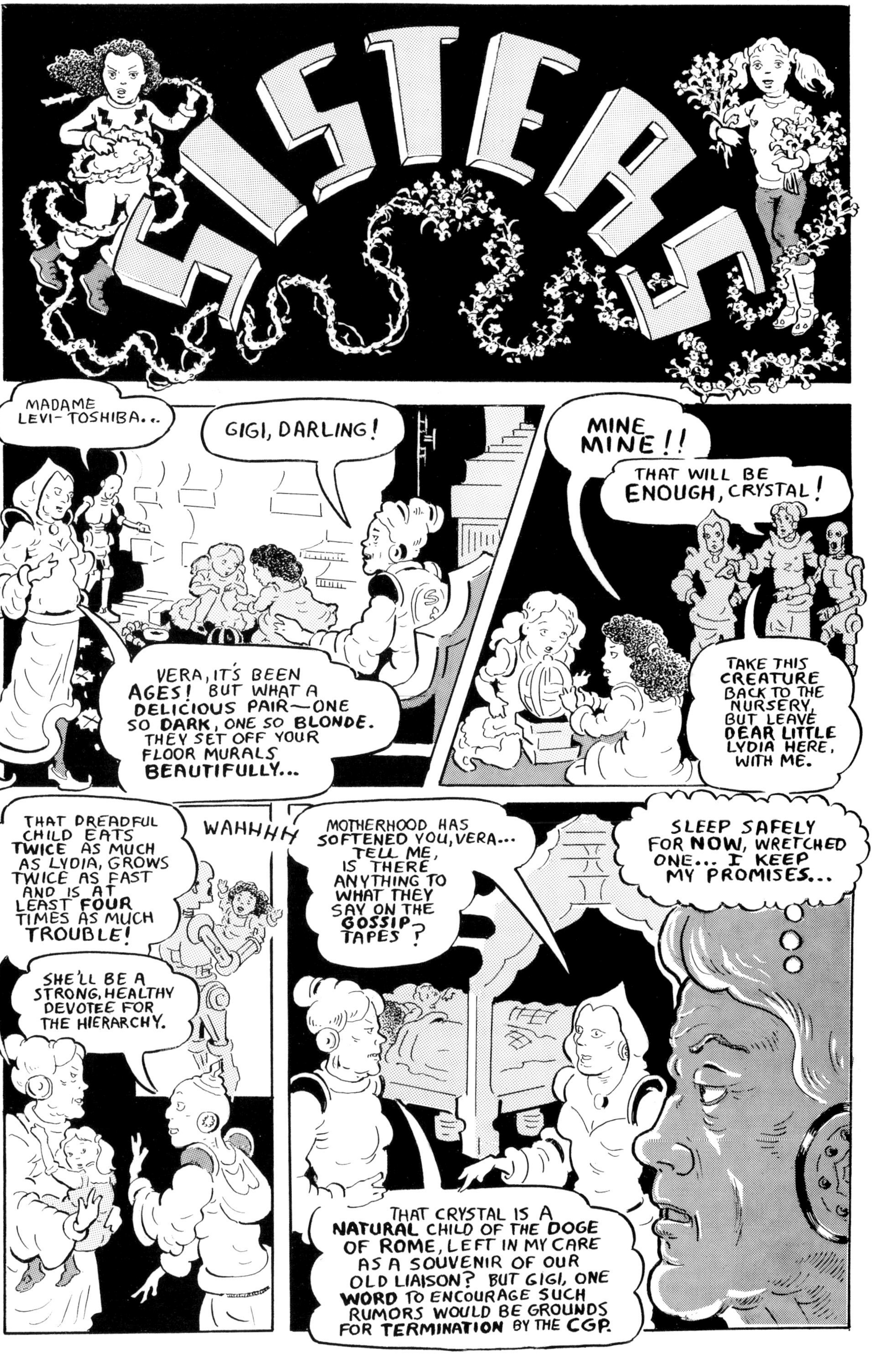
SISTERS
MADAME LEVI-TOSHIBA...
GIGI, DARLING!
VERA, IT'S BEEN AGES! BUT WHAT A DELICIOUS PAIR—ONE SO DARK, ONE SO BLONDE. THEY SET OFF YOUR FLOOR MURALS BEAUTIFULLY...
MINE MINE!!
THAT WILL BE ENOUGH, CRYSTAL!
TAKE THIS CREATURE BACK TO THE NURSERY, BUT LEAVE DEAR LITTLE LYDIA HERE, WITH ME.
THAT DREADFUL CHILD EATS TWICE AS MUCH AS LYDIA, GROWS TWICE AS FAST AND IS AT LEAST FOUR TIMES AS MUCH TROUBLE!
WAHHHH
SHE'LL BE A STRONG, HEALTHY DEVOTEE FOR THE HIERARCHY.
MOTHERHOOD HAS SOFTENED YOU, VERA... TELL ME, IS THERE ANYTHING TO WHAT THEY SAY ON THE GOSSIP TAPES?
SLEEP SAFELY FOR NOW, WRETCHED ONE... I KEEP MY PROMISES...
THAT CRYSTAL IS A NATURAL CHILD OF THE DOGE OF ROME, LEFT IN MY CARE AS A SOUVENIR OF OUR OLD LIAISON? BUT GIGI, ONE WORD TO ENCOURAGE SUCH RUMORS WOULD BE GROUNDS FOR TERMINATION BY THE CGP.

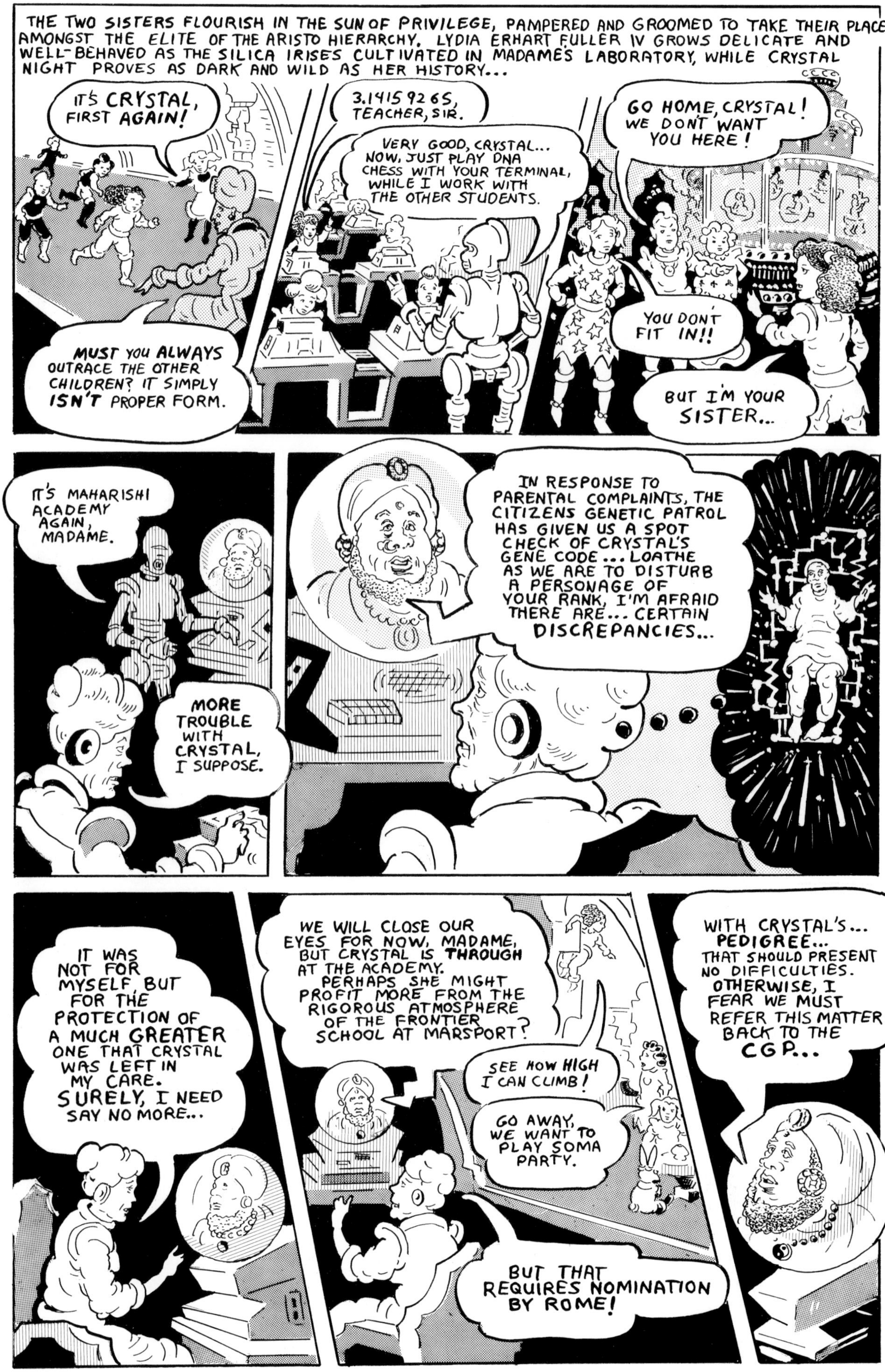
THE TWO SISTERS FLOURISH IN THE SUN OF PRIVILEGE, PAMPERED AND GROOMED TO TAKE THEIR PLACE AMONGST THE ELITE OF THE ARISTO HIERARCHY. LYDIA ERHART FULLER IV GROWS DELICATE AND WELL-BEHAVED AS THE SILICA IRISES CULTIVATED IN MADAME'S LABORATORY, WHILE CRYSTAL NIGHT PROVES AS DARK AND WILD AS HER HISTORY...
IT'S CRYSTAL, FIRST AGAIN!
MUST YOU ALWAYS OUTRACE THE OTHER CHILDREN? IT SIMPLY ISN'T PROPER FORM.
3.1415 9265, TEACHER, SIR.
VERY GOOD, CRYSTAL... NOW, JUST PLAY DNA CHESS WITH YOUR TERMINAL, WHILE I WORK WITH THE OTHER STUDENTS.
GO HOME, CRYSTAL! WE DON'T WANT YOU HERE!
YOU DON'T FIT IN!!
BUT I'M YOUR SISTER...
IT'S MAHARISHI ACADEMY AGAIN, MADAME.
MORE TROUBLE WITH CRYSTAL, I SUPPOSE.
IN RESPONSE TO PARENTAL COMPLAINTS, THE CITIZENS GENETIC PATROL HAS GIVEN US A SPOT CHECK OF CRYSTAL'S GENE CODE... LOATHE AS WE ARE TO DISTURB A PERSONAGE OF YOUR RANK, I'M AFRAID THERE ARE... CERTAIN DISCREPANCIES...
IT WAS NOT FOR MYSELF BUT FOR THE PROTECTION OF A MUCH GREATER ONE THAT CRYSTAL WAS LEFT IN MY CARE. SURELY, I NEED SAY NO MORE...
WE WILL CLOSE OUR EYES FOR NOW, MADAME, BUT CRYSTAL IS THROUGH AT THE ACADEMY. PERHAPS SHE MIGHT PROFIT MORE FROM THE RIGOROUS ATMOSPHERE OF THE FRONTIER SCHOOL AT MARSPORT?
SEE HOW HIGH I CAN CLIMB!
GO AWAY, WE WANT TO PLAY SOMA PARTY.
BUT THAT REQUIRES NOMINATION BY ROME!
WITH CRYSTAL'S... PEDIGREE... THAT SHOULD PRESENT NO DIFFICULTIES. OTHERWISE, I FEAR WE MUST REFER THIS MATTER BACK TO THE CGP...

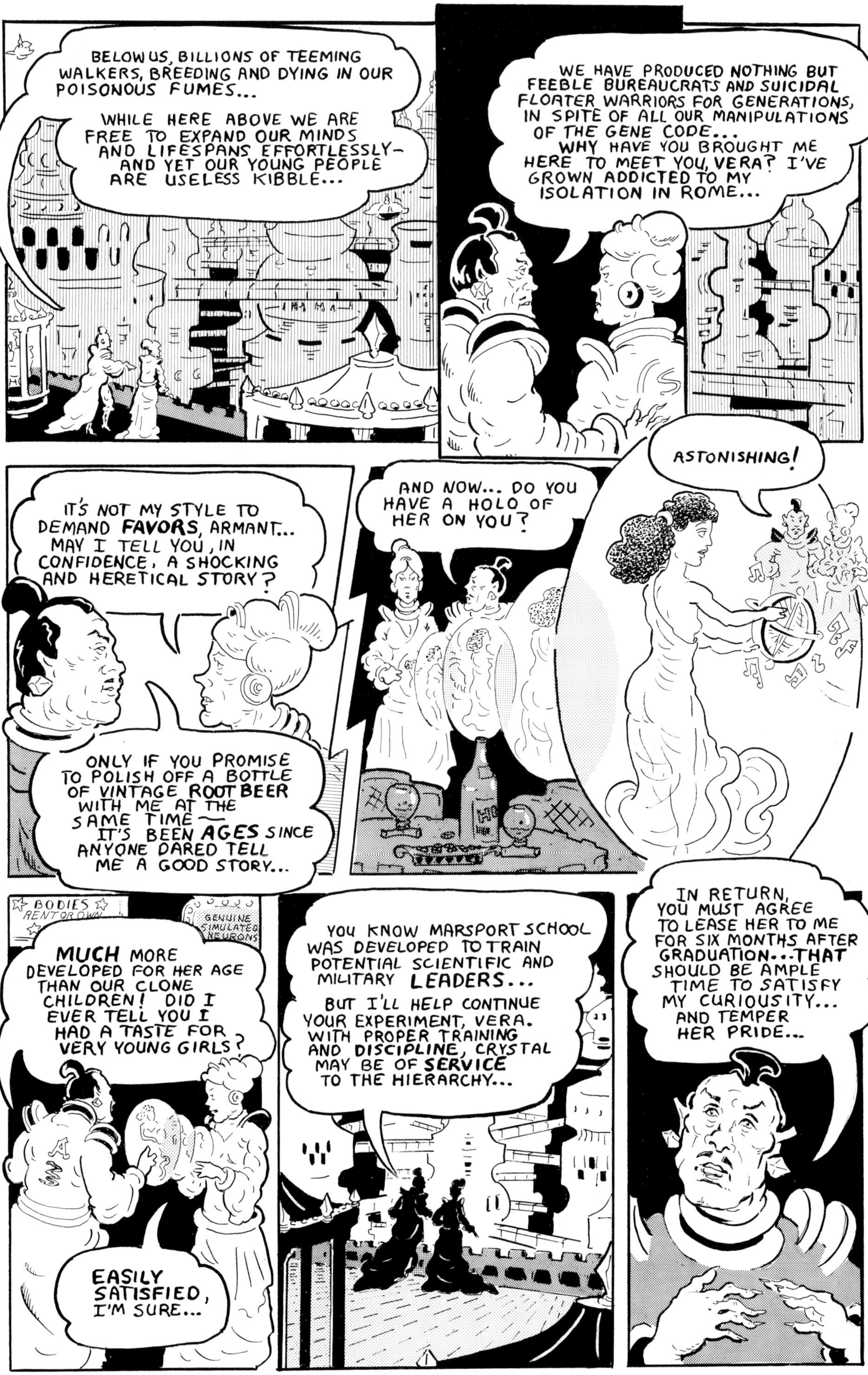
BELOW US, BILLIONS OF TEEMING WALKERS, BREEDING AND DYING IN OUR POISONOUS FUMES... WHILE HERE ABOVE WE ARE FREE TO EXPAND OUR MINDS AND LIFESPANS EFFORTLESSLY— AND YET OUR YOUNG PEOPLE ARE USELESS KIBBLE...
WE HAVE PRODUCED NOTHING BUT FEEBLE BUREAUCRATS AND SUICIDAL FLOATER WARRIORS FOR GENERATIONS, IN SPITE OF ALL OUR MANIPULATIONS OF THE GENE CODE... WHY HAVE YOU BROUGHT ME HERE TO MEET YOU, VERA? I'VE GROWN ADDICTED TO MY ISOLATION IN ROME...
IT'S NOT MY STYLE TO DEMAND FAVORS, ARMANT... MAY I TELL YOU, IN CONFIDENCE, A SHOCKING AND HERETICAL STORY?
ONLY IF YOU PROMISE TO POLISH OFF A BOTTLE OF VINTAGE ROOT BEER WITH ME AT THE SAME TIME— IT'S BEEN AGES SINCE ANYONE DARED TELL ME A GOOD STORY...
AND NOW... DO YOU HAVE A HOLO OF HER ON YOU?
ASTONISHING!
BODIES RENT OR OWN
GENUINE SIMULATED NEURONS
MUCH MORE DEVELOPED FOR HER AGE THAN OUR CLONE CHILDREN! DID I EVER TELL YOU I HAD A TASTE FOR VERY YOUNG GIRLS?
EASILY SATISFIED, I'M SURE...
YOU KNOW MARSPORT SCHOOL WAS DEVELOPED TO TRAIN POTENTIAL SCIENTIFIC AND MILITARY LEADERS... BUT I'LL HELP CONTINUE YOUR EXPERIMENT, VERA. WITH PROPER TRAINING AND DISCIPLINE, CRYSTAL MAY BE OF SERVICE TO THE HIERARCHY...
IN RETURN, YOU MUST AGREE TO LEASE HER TO ME FOR SIX MONTHS AFTER GRADUATION...THAT SHOULD BE AMPLE TIME TO SATISFY MY CURIOUSITY... AND TEMPER HER PRIDE...

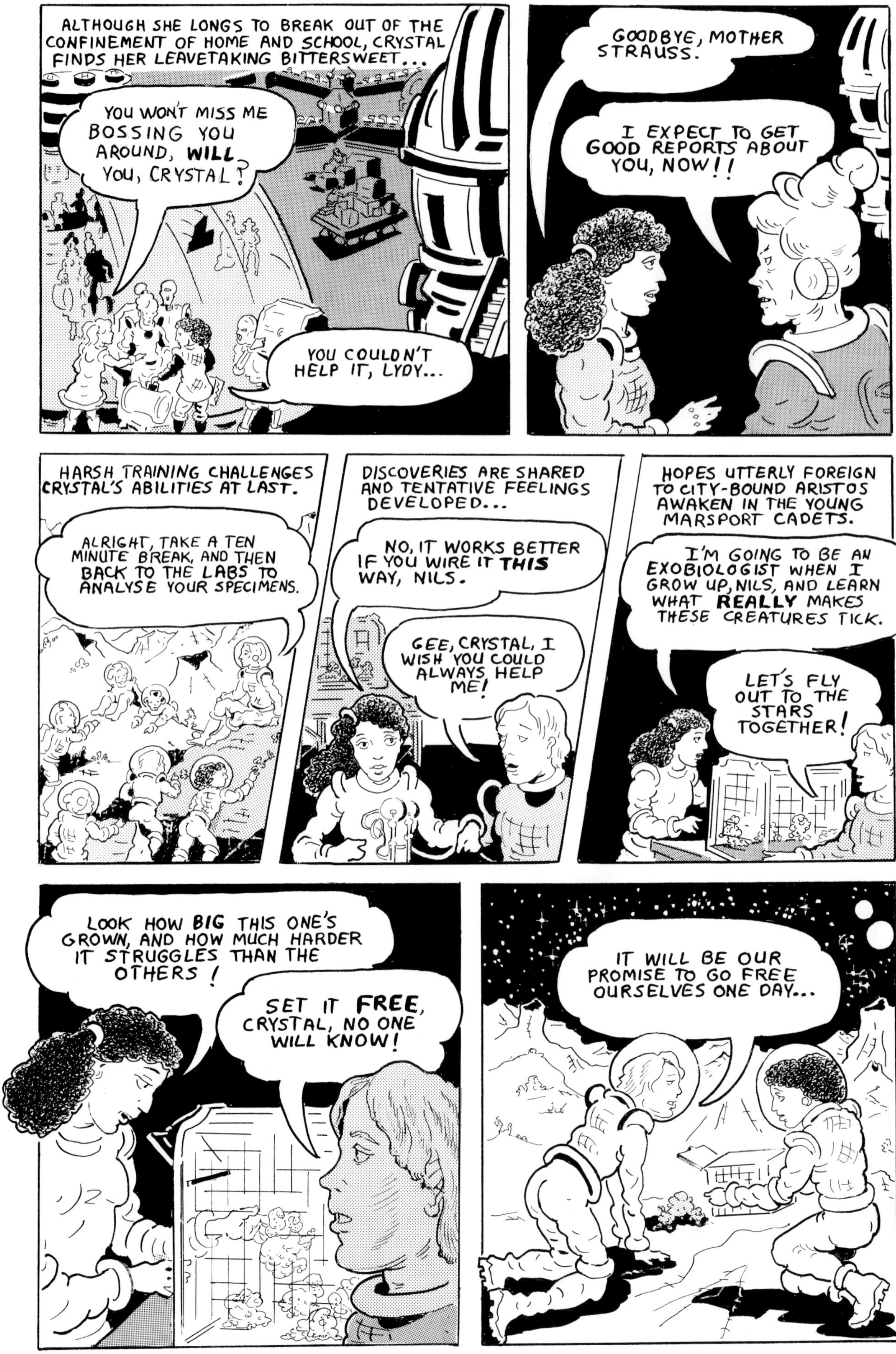
ALTHOUGH SHE LONGS TO BREAK OUT OF THE CONFINEMENT OF HOME AND SCHOOL, CRYSTAL FINDS HER LEAVETAKING BITTERSWEET...
YOU WON'T MISS ME BOSSING YOU AROUND, WILL YOU, CRYSTAL?
YOU COULDN'T HELP IT, LYDY...
GOODBYE, MOTHER STRAUSS.
I EXPECT TO GET GOOD REPORTS ABOUT YOU, NOW!!
HARSH TRAINING CHALLENGES CRYSTAL'S ABILITIES AT LAST.
ALRIGHT, TAKE A TEN MINUTE BREAK, AND THEN BACK TO THE LABS TO ANALYSE YOUR SPECIMENS.
DISCOVERIES ARE SHARED AND TENTATIVE FEELINGS DEVELOPED...
NO, IT WORKS BETTER IF YOU WIRE IT THIS WAY, NILS.
GEE, CRYSTAL, I WISH YOU COULD ALWAYS HELP ME!
HOPES UTTERLY FOREIGN TO CITY-BOUND ARISTOS AWAKEN IN THE YOUNG MARSPORT CADETS.
I'M GOING TO BE AN EXOBIOLOGIST WHEN I GROW UP, NILS, AND LEARN WHAT REALLY MAKES THESE CREATURES TICK.
LET'S FLY OUT TO THE STARS TOGETHER!
LOOK HOW BIG THIS ONE'S GROWN, AND HOW MUCH HARDER IT STRUGGLES THAN THE OTHERS!
SET IT FREE, CRYSTAL, NO ONE WILL KNOW!
IT WILL BE OUR PROMISE TO GO FREE OURSELVES ONE DAY...

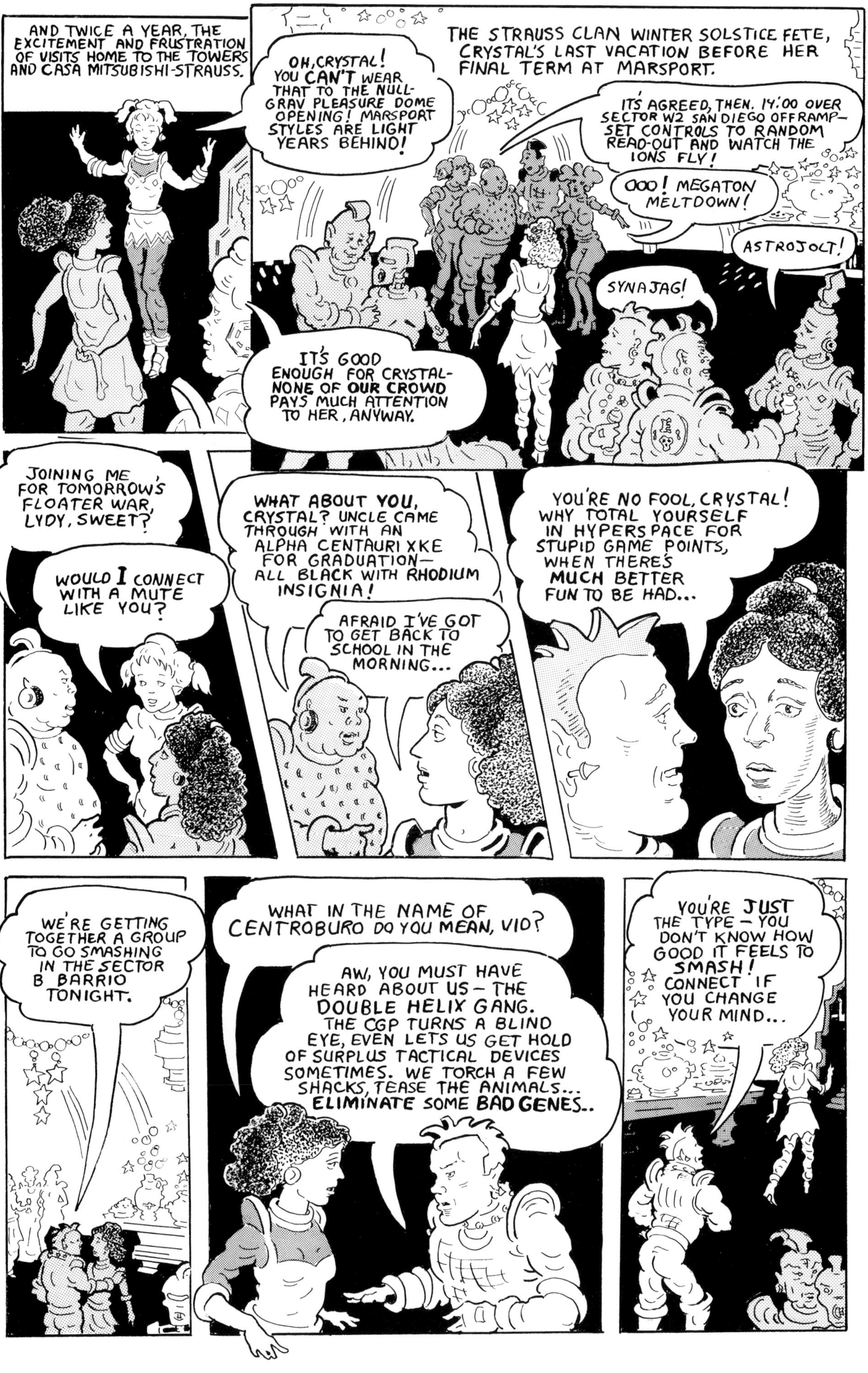
AND TWICE A YEAR, THE EXCITEMENT AND FRUSTRATION OF VISITS HOME TO THE TOWERS AND CASA MITSUBISHI-STRAUSS.
OH, CRYSTAL! YOU CAN'T WEAR THAT TO THE NULL-GRAV PLEASURE DOME OPENING! MARSPORT STYLES ARE LIGHT YEARS BEHIND!
THE STRAUSS CLAN WINTER SOLSTICE FETE, CRYSTAL'S LAST VACATION BEFORE HER FINAL TERM AT MARSPORT.
IT'S AGREED, THEN. 14:00 OVER SECTOR W2 SAN DIEGO OFFRAMP-SET CONTROLS TO RANDOM READ-OUT AND WATCH THE IONS FLY!
OOO! MEGATON MELTDOWN!
ASTROJOLT!
SYNAJAG!
IT'S GOOD ENOUGH FOR CRYSTAL-NONE OF OUR CROWD PAYS MUCH ATTENTION TO HER, ANYWAY.
JOINING ME FOR TOMORROW'S FLOATER WAR, LYDY, SWEET?
WOULD I CONNECT WITH A MUTE LIKE YOU?
WHAT ABOUT YOU, CRYSTAL? UNCLE CAME THROUGH WITH AN ALPHA CENTAURI XKE FOR GRADUATION—ALL BLACK WITH RHODIUM INSIGNIA!
AFRAID I'VE GOT TO GET BACK TO SCHOOL IN THE MORNING...
YOU'RE NO FOOL, CRYSTAL! WHY TOTAL YOURSELF IN HYPERSPACE FOR STUPID GAME POINTS, WHEN THERE'S MUCH BETTER FUN TO BE HAD...
WE'RE GETTING TOGETHER A GROUP TO GO SMASHING IN THE SECTOR B BARRIO TONIGHT.
WHAT IN THE NAME OF CENTROBURO DO YOU MEAN, VIO?
AW, YOU MUST HAVE HEARD ABOUT US – THE DOUBLE HELIX GANG. THE CGP TURNS A BLIND EYE, EVEN LETS US GET HOLD OF SURPLUS TACTICAL DEVICES SOMETIMES. WE TORCH A FEW SHACKS, TEASE THE ANIMALS... ELIMINATE SOME BAD GENES..
YOU'RE JUST THE TYPE – YOU DON'T KNOW HOW GOOD IT FEELS TO SMASH! CONNECT IF YOU CHANGE YOUR MIND...

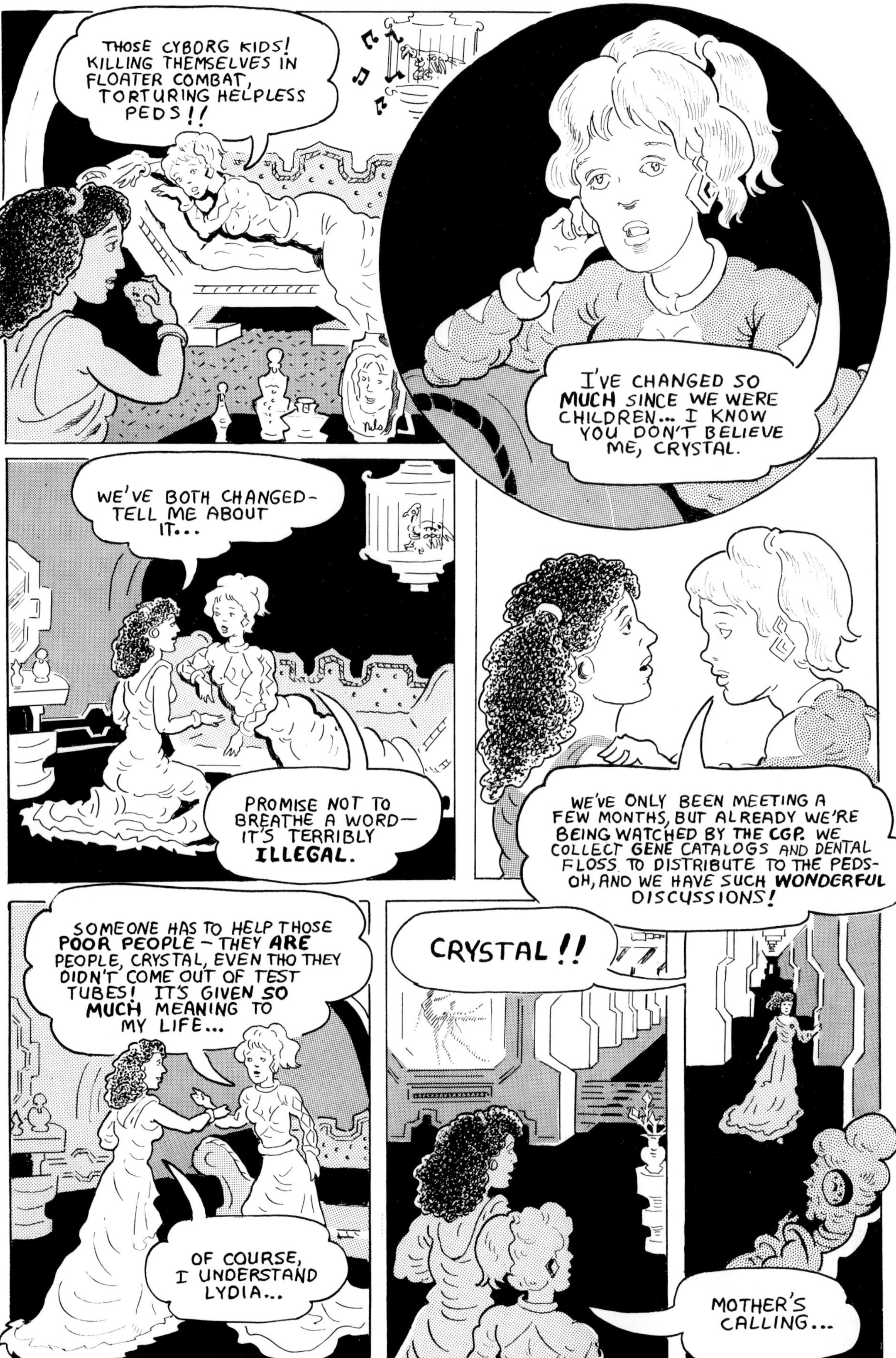
THOSE CYBORG KIDS! KILLING THEMSELVES IN FLOATER COMBAT, TORTURING HELPLESS PEDS!!
I'VE CHANGED SO MUCH SINCE WE WERE CHILDREN... I KNOW YOU DON'T BELIEVE ME, CRYSTAL.
WE'VE BOTH CHANGED- TELL ME ABOUT IT...
PROMISE NOT TO BREATHE A WORD— IT'S TERRIBLY ILLEGAL.
WE'VE ONLY BEEN MEETING A FEW MONTHS, BUT ALREADY WE'RE BEING WATCHED BY THE CGP. WE COLLECT GENE CATALOGS AND DENTAL FLOSS TO DISTRIBUTE TO THE PEDS- OH, AND WE HAVE SUCH WONDERFUL DISCUSSIONS!
SOMEONE HAS TO HELP THOSE POOR PEOPLE — THEY ARE PEOPLE, CRYSTAL, EVEN THO THEY DIDN'T COME OUT OF TEST TUBES! IT'S GIVEN SO MUCH MEANING TO MY LIFE...
OF COURSE, I UNDERSTAND LYDIA...
CRYSTAL!!
MOTHER'S CALLING...

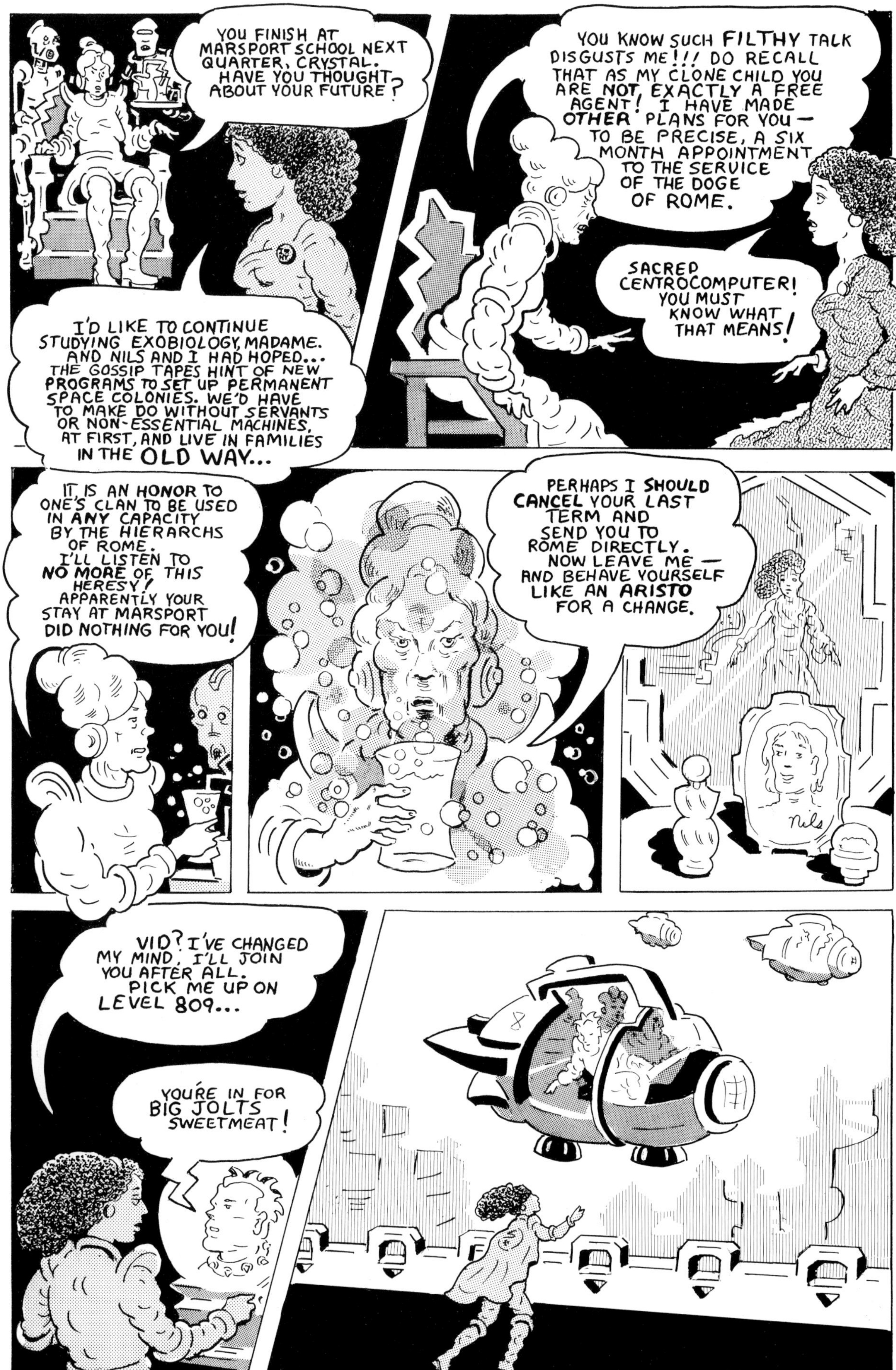
YOU FINISH AT MARSPORT SCHOOL NEXT QUARTER, CRYSTAL. HAVE YOU THOUGHT ABOUT YOUR FUTURE?
I'D LIKE TO CONTINUE STUDYING EXOBIOLOGY, MADAME. AND NILS AND I HAD HOPED... THE GOSSIP TAPES HINT OF NEW PROGRAMS TO SET UP PERMANENT SPACE COLONIES. WE'D HAVE TO MAKE DO WITHOUT SERVANTS OR NON-ESSENTIAL MACHINES, AT FIRST, AND LIVE IN FAMILIES IN THE OLD WAY...
YOU KNOW SUCH FILTHY TALK DISGUSTS ME!!! DO RECALL THAT AS MY CLONE CHILD YOU ARE NOT, EXACTLY A FREE AGENT! I HAVE MADE OTHER PLANS FOR YOU — TO BE PRECISE, A SIX MONTH APPOINTMENT TO THE SERVICE OF THE DOGE OF ROME.
SACRED CENTROCOMPUTER! YOU MUST KNOW WHAT THAT MEANS!
IT IS AN HONOR TO ONE'S CLAN TO BE USED IN ANY CAPACITY BY THE HIERARCHS OF ROME. I'LL LISTEN TO NO MORE OF THIS HERESY! APPARENTLY YOUR STAY AT MARSPORT DID NOTHING FOR YOU!
PERHAPS I SHOULD CANCEL YOUR LAST TERM AND SEND YOU TO ROME DIRECTLY. NOW LEAVE ME — AND BEHAVE YOURSELF LIKE AN ARISTO FOR A CHANGE.
Nils
VID? I'VE CHANGED MY MIND, I'LL JOIN YOU AFTER ALL. PICK ME UP ON LEVEL 809...
YOU'RE IN FOR BIG JOLTS SWEETMEAT!

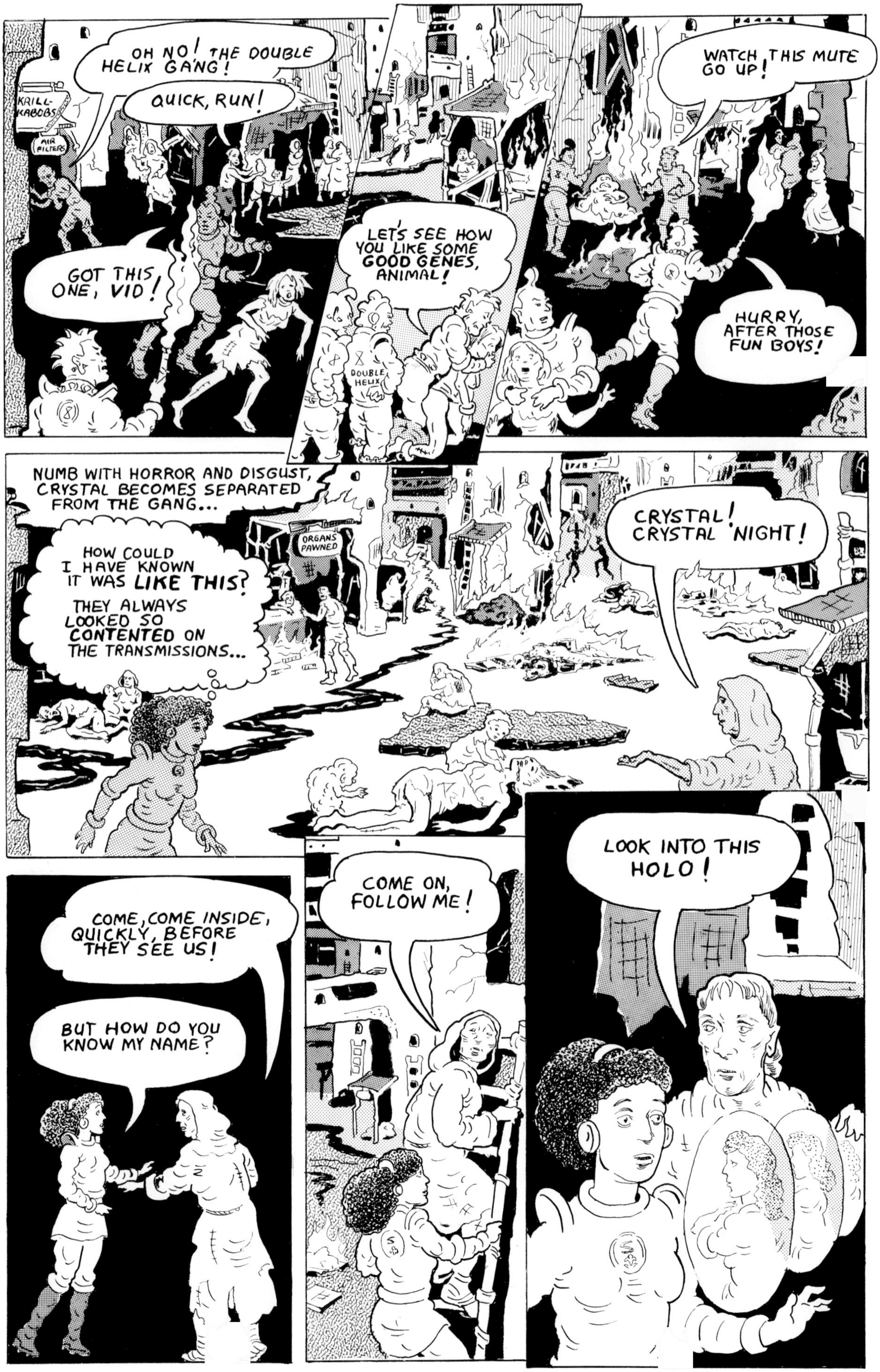
OH NO! THE DOUBLE HELIX GANG!
QUICK, RUN!
KRILL-KABOBS
AIR FILTERS
GOT THIS ONE, VID!
LET'S SEE HOW YOU LIKE SOME GOOD GENES, ANIMAL!
DOUBLE HELIX
WATCH THIS MUTE GO UP!
HURRY, AFTER THOSE FUN BOYS!
NUMB WITH HORROR AND DISGUST, CRYSTAL BECOMES SEPARATED FROM THE GANG...
ORGANS PAWNED
HOW COULD I HAVE KNOWN IT WAS LIKE THIS? THEY ALWAYS LOOKED SO CONTENTED ON THE TRANSMISSIONS...
CRYSTAL! CRYSTAL NIGHT!
COME, COME INSIDE, QUICKLY, BEFORE THEY SEE US!
BUT HOW DO YOU KNOW MY NAME?
COME ON, FOLLOW ME!
LOOK INTO THIS HOLO!

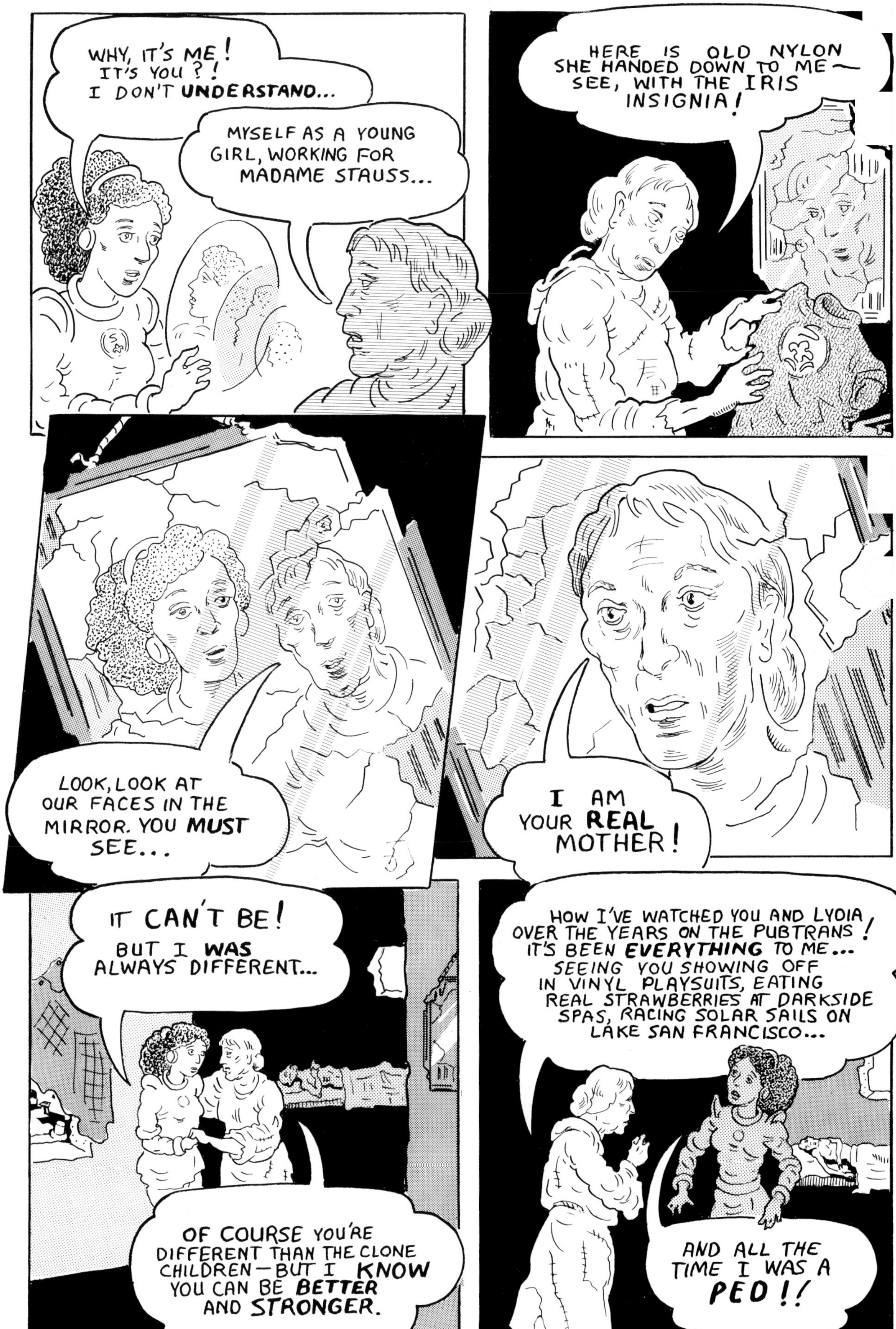
WHY, IT'S ME! IT'S YOU?! I DON'T UNDERSTAND...
MYSELF AS A YOUNG GIRL, WORKING FOR MADAME STAUSS...
HERE IS OLD NYLON SHE HANDED DOWN TO ME— SEE, WITH THE IRIS INSIGNIA!
LOOK, LOOK AT OUR FACES IN THE MIRROR. YOU MUST SEE...
I AM YOUR REAL MOTHER!
IT CAN'T BE! BUT I WAS ALWAYS DIFFERENT...
OF COURSE YOU'RE DIFFERENT THAN THE CLONE CHILDREN—BUT I KNOW YOU CAN BE BETTER AND STRONGER.
HOW I'VE WATCHED YOU AND LYDIA OVER THE YEARS ON THE PUBTRANS! IT'S BEEN EVERYTHING TO ME... SEEING YOU SHOWING OFF IN VINYL PLAYSUITS, EATING REAL STRAWBERRIES AT DARKSIDE SPAS, RACING SOLAR SAILS ON LAKE SAN FRANCISCO...
AND ALL THE TIME I WAS A PED!!

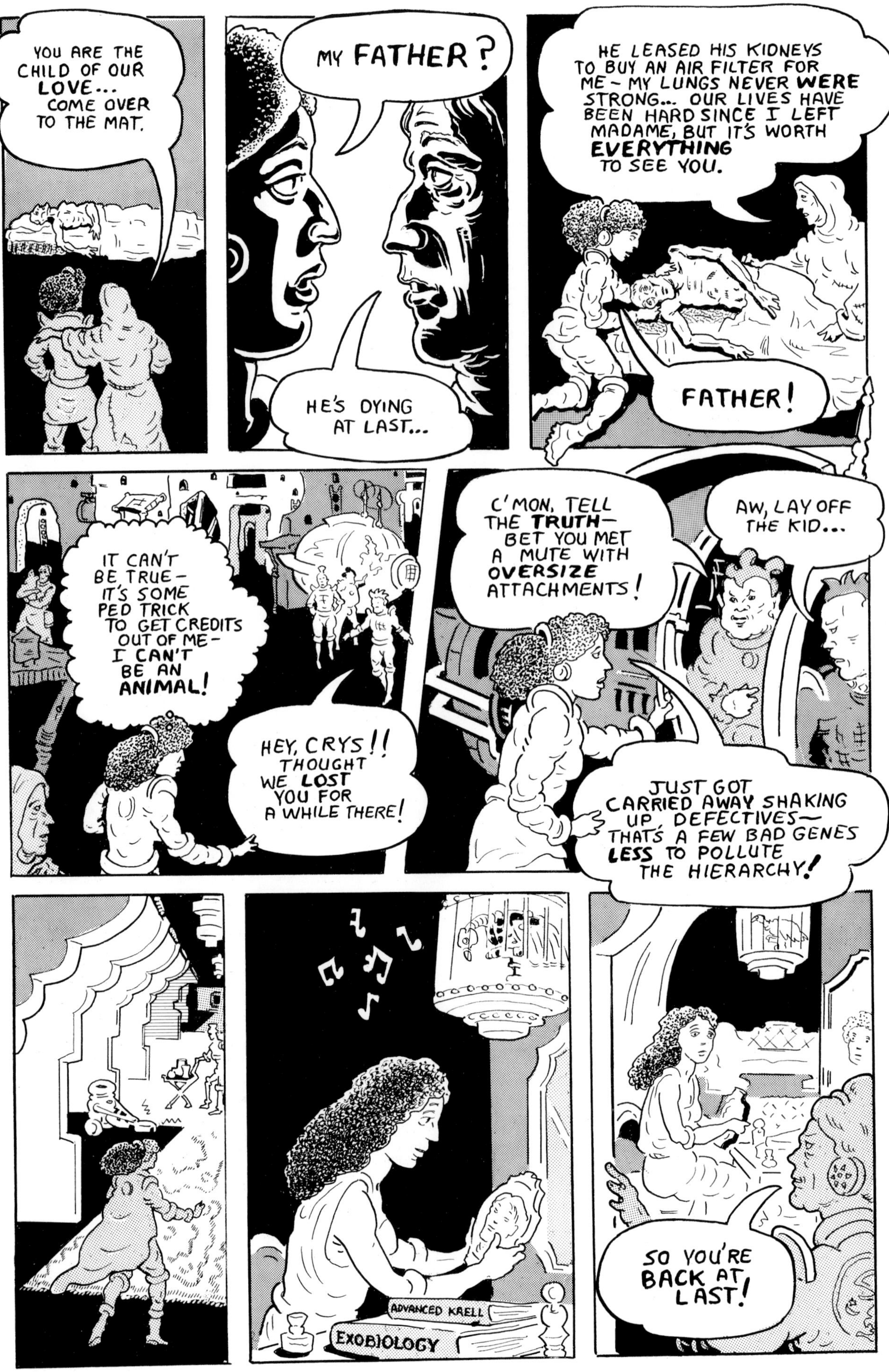
YOU ARE THE CHILD OF OUR LOVE... COME OVER TO THE MAT.
MY FATHER?
HE'S DYING AT LAST...
HE LEASED HIS KIDNEYS TO BUY AN AIR FILTER FOR ME - MY LUNGS NEVER WERE STRONG... OUR LIVES HAVE BEEN HARD SINCE I LEFT MADAME, BUT IT'S WORTH EVERYTHING TO SEE YOU.
FATHER!
IT CAN'T BE TRUE- IT'S SOME PED TRICK TO GET CREDITS OUT OF ME- I CAN'T BE AN ANIMAL!
HEY, CRYS!! THOUGHT WE LOST YOU FOR A WHILE THERE!
C'MON, TELL THE TRUTH- BET YOU MET A MUTE WITH OVERSIZE ATTACHMENTS!
AW, LAY OFF THE KID...
JUST GOT CARRIED AWAY SHAKING UP DEFECTIVES— THAT'S A FEW BAD GENES LESS TO POLLUTE THE HIERARCHY!
ADVANCED KRELL
EXOBIOLOGY
SO YOU'RE BACK AT LAST!

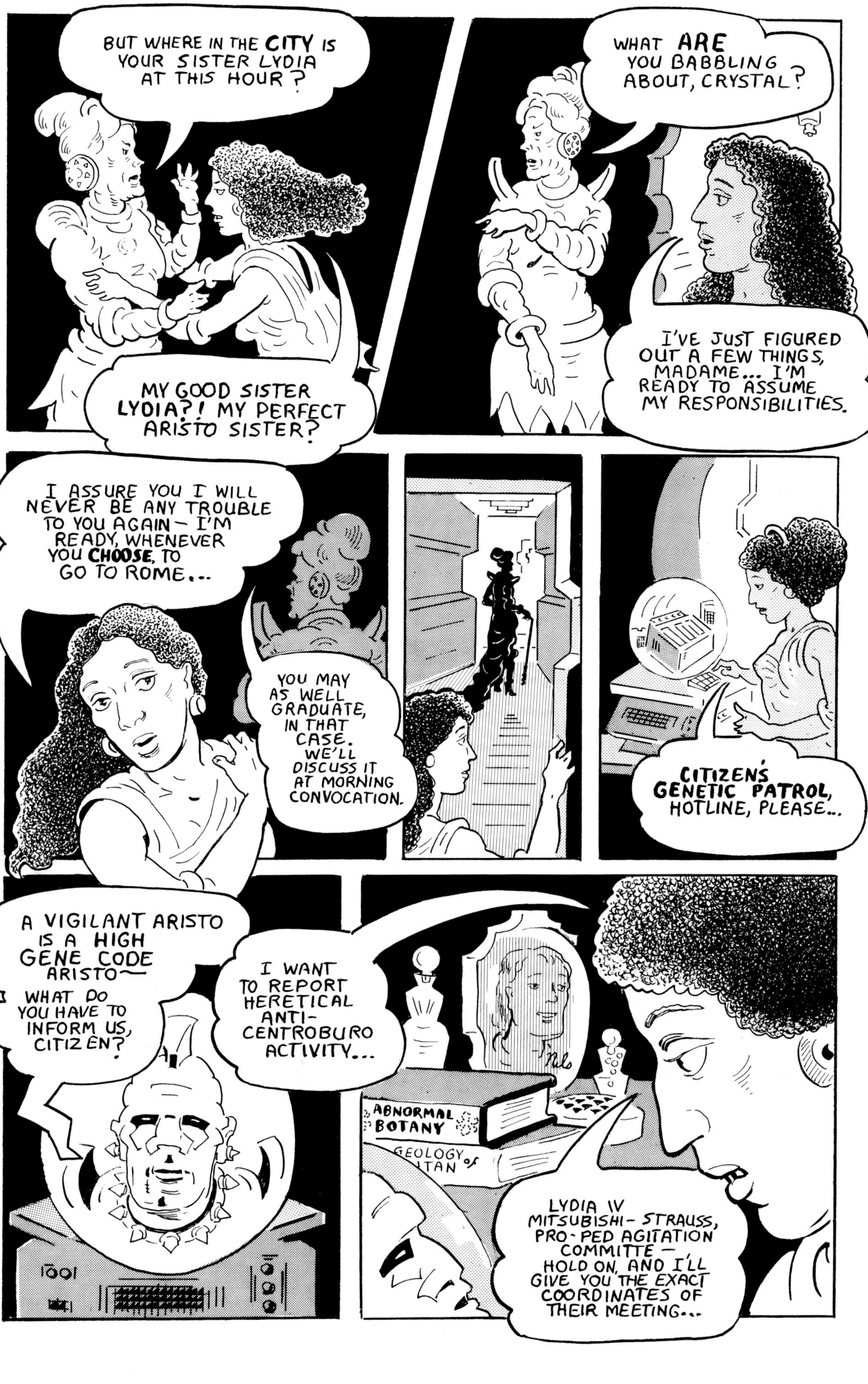
BUT WHERE IN THE CITY IS YOUR SISTER LYDIA AT THIS HOUR?
MY GOOD SISTER LYDIA?! MY PERFECT ARISTO SISTER?
WHAT ARE YOU BABBLING ABOUT, CRYSTAL?
I'VE JUST FIGURED OUT A FEW THINGS, MADAME... I'M READY TO ASSUME MY RESPONSIBILITIES.
I ASSURE YOU I WILL NEVER BE ANY TROUBLE TO YOU AGAIN– I'M READY, WHENEVER YOU CHOOSE, TO GO TO ROME...
YOU MAY AS WELL GRADUATE, IN THAT CASE. WE'LL DISCUSS IT AT MORNING CONVOCATION.
CITIZEN'S GENETIC PATROL, HOTLINE, PLEASE...
A VIGILANT ARISTO IS A HIGH GENE CODE ARISTO~
WHAT DO YOU HAVE TO INFORM US, CITIZEN?
I WANT TO REPORT HERETICAL ANTI-CENTROBURO ACTIVITY...
ABNORMAL BOTANY
GEOLOGY of TITAN
LYDIA IV MITSUBISHI-STRAUSS, PRO-PED AGITATION COMMITTE– HOLD ON, AND I'LL GIVE YOU THE EXACT COORDINATES OF THEIR MEETING...

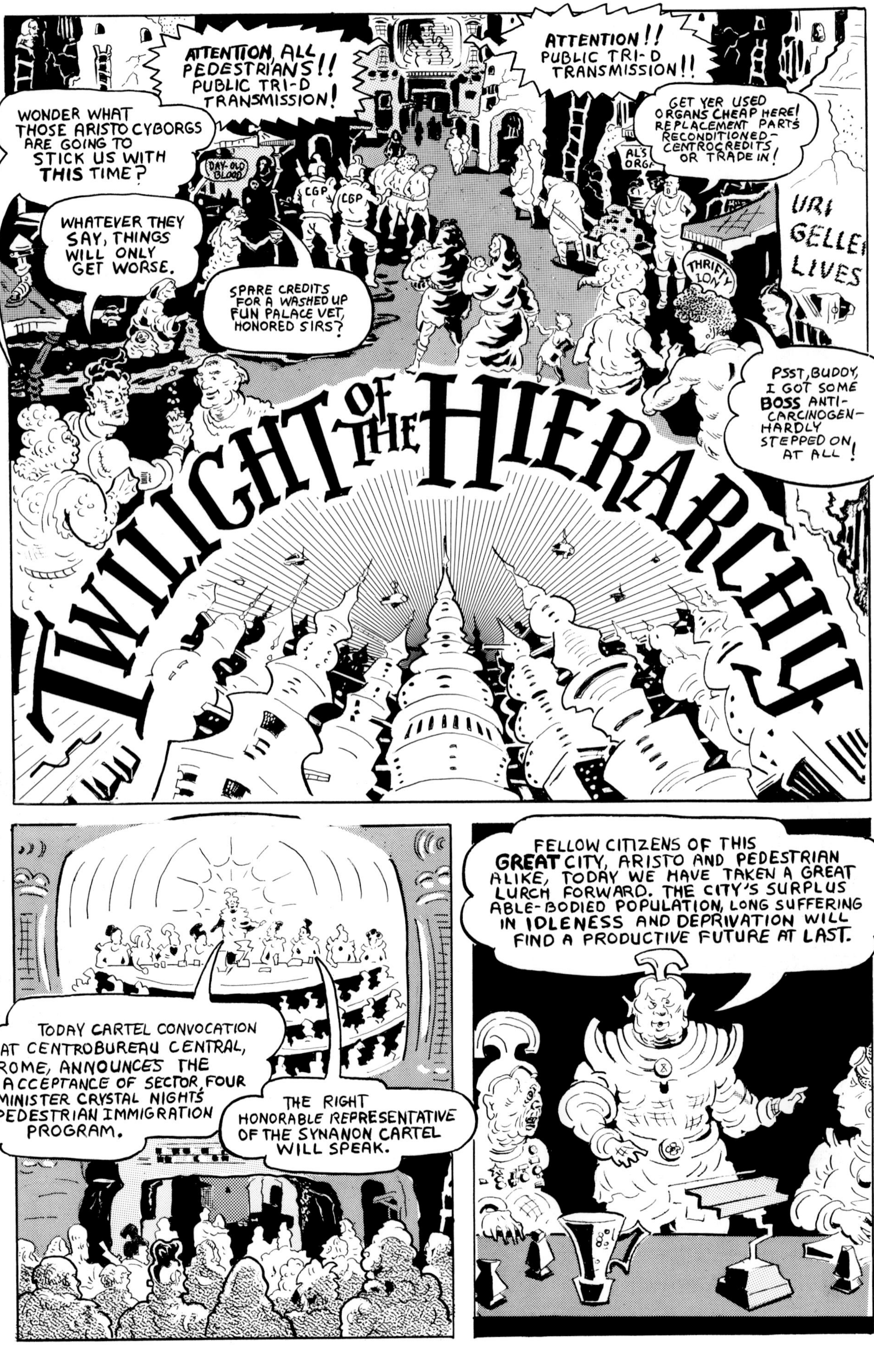
ATTENTION, ALL PEDESTRIANS!! PUBLIC TRI-D TRANSMISSION!
ATTENTION!! PUBLIC TRI-D TRANSMISSION!!
WONDER WHAT THOSE ARISTO CYBORGS ARE GOING TO STICK US WITH THIS TIME?
GET YER USED ORGANS CHEAP HERE! REPLACEMENT PARTS RECONDITIONED- CENTROCREDITS OR TRADE IN!
DAY-OLD BLOOD
CGP
CGP
WHATEVER THEY SAY, THINGS WILL ONLY GET WORSE.
SPARE CREDITS FOR A WASHED UP FUN PALACE VET, HONORED SIRS?
THRIFTY LON
URI GELLER LIVES
PSST, BUDDY, I GOT SOME BOSS ANTI-CARCINOGEN- HARDLY STEPPED ON AT ALL!
TWILIGHT OF THE HIERARCHY
TODAY CARTEL CONVOCATION AT CENTROBUREAU CENTRAL, ROME, ANNOUNCES THE ACCEPTANCE OF SECTOR FOUR MINISTER CRYSTAL NIGHT'S PEDESTRIAN IMMIGRATION PROGRAM.
THE RIGHT HONORABLE REPRESENTATIVE OF THE SYNANON CARTEL WILL SPEAK.
FELLOW CITIZENS OF THIS GREAT CITY, ARISTO AND PEDESTRIAN ALIKE, TODAY WE HAVE TAKEN A GREAT LURCH FORWARD. THE CITY'S SURPLUS ABLE-BODIED POPULATION, LONG SUFFERING IN IDLENESS AND DEPRIVATION WILL FIND A PRODUCTIVE FUTURE AT LAST.

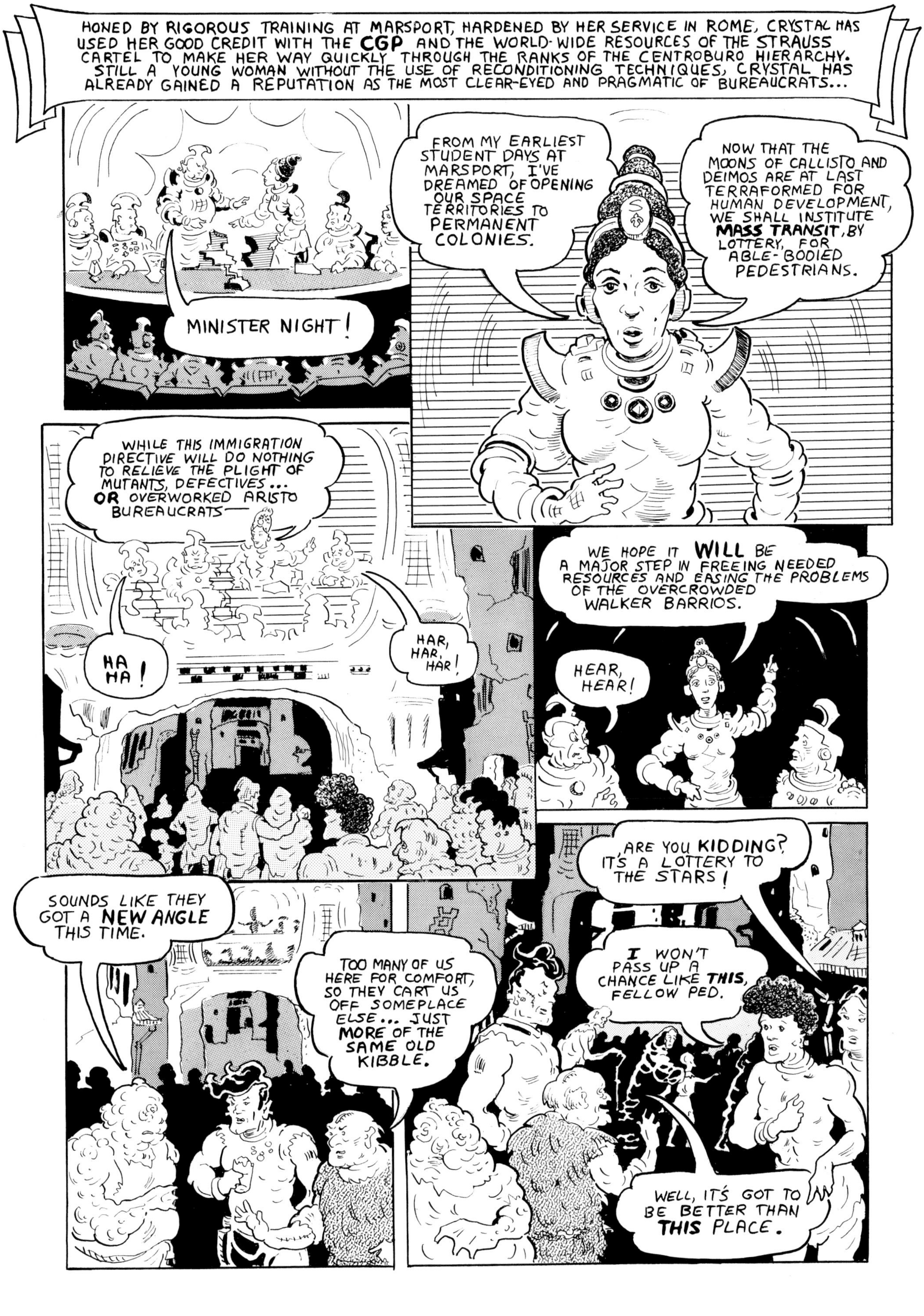
HONED BY RIGOROUS TRAINING AT MARSPORT, HARDENED BY HER SERVICE IN ROME, CRYSTAL HAS USED HER GOOD CREDIT WITH THE CGP AND THE WORLD-WIDE RESOURCES OF THE STRAUSS CARTEL TO MAKE HER WAY QUICKLY THROUGH THE RANKS OF THE CENTROBURO HIERARCHY. STILL A YOUNG WOMAN WITHOUT THE USE OF RECONDITIONING TECHNIQUES, CRYSTAL HAS ALREADY GAINED A REPUTATION AS THE MOST CLEAR-EYED AND PRAGMATIC OF BUREAUCRATS...
MINISTER NIGHT!
FROM MY EARLIEST STUDENT DAYS AT MARSPORT, I'VE DREAMED OF OPENING OUR SPACE TERRITORIES TO PERMANENT COLONIES.
NOW THAT THE MOONS OF CALLISTO AND DEIMOS ARE AT LAST TERRAFORMED FOR HUMAN DEVELOPMENT, WE SHALL INSTITUTE MASS TRANSIT, BY LOTTERY, FOR ABLE-BODIED PEDESTRIANS.
WHILE THIS IMMIGRATION DIRECTIVE WILL DO NOTHING TO RELIEVE THE PLIGHT OF MUTANTS, DEFECTIVES... OR OVERWORKED ARISTO BUREAUCRATS—
HA HA!
HAR, HAR, HAR!
WE HOPE IT WILL BE A MAJOR STEP IN FREEING NEEDED RESOURCES AND EASING THE PROBLEMS OF THE OVERCROWDED WALKER BARRIOS.
HEAR, HEAR!
SOUNDS LIKE THEY GOT A NEW ANGLE THIS TIME.
TOO MANY OF US HERE FOR COMFORT, SO THEY CART US OFF SOMEPLACE ELSE... JUST MORE OF THE SAME OLD KIBBLE.
ARE YOU KIDDING? IT'S A LOTTERY TO THE STARS!
I WON'T PASS UP A CHANCE LIKE THIS, FELLOW PED.
WELL, IT'S GOT TO BE BETTER THAN THIS PLACE.

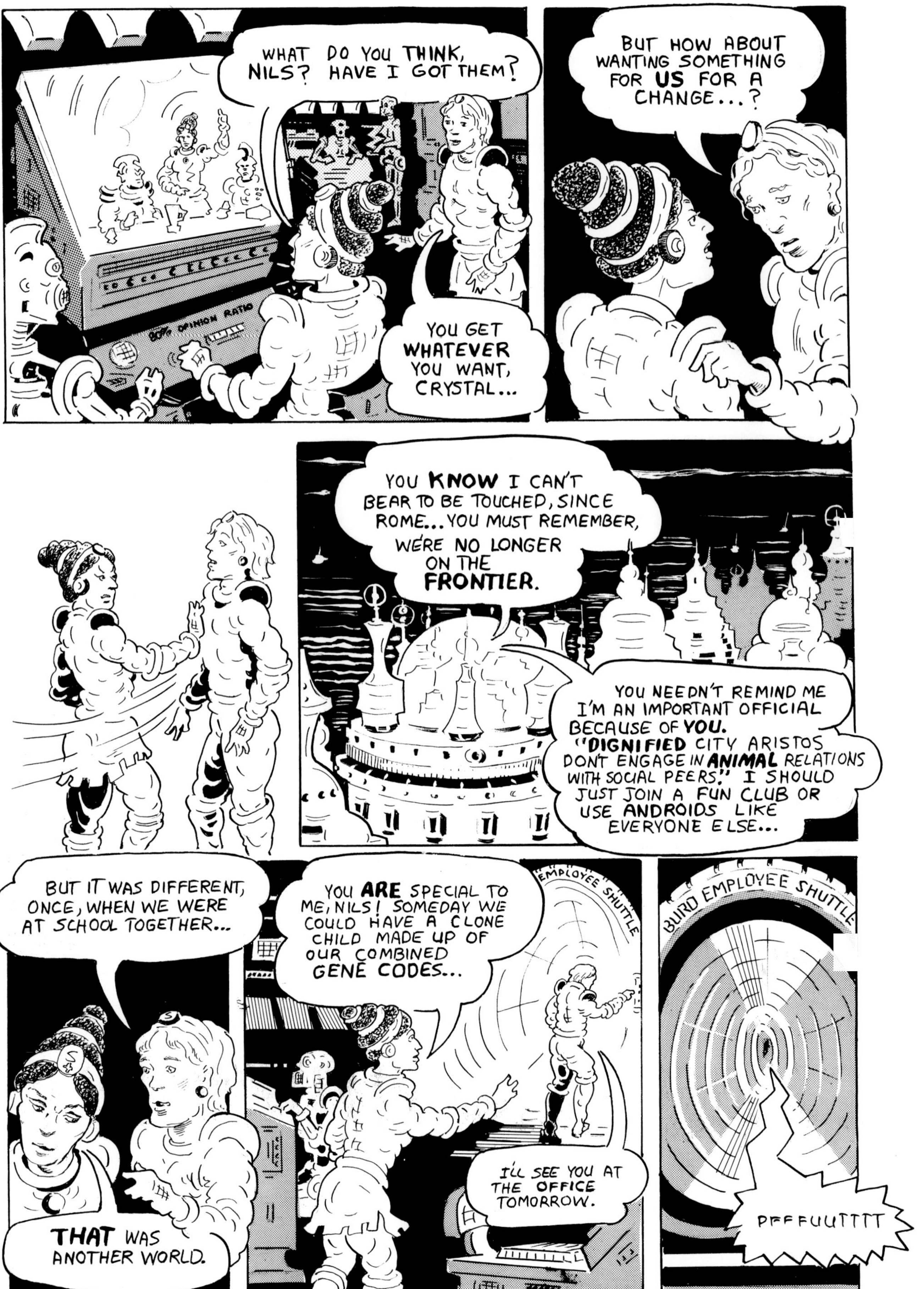
WHAT DO YOU THINK, NILS? HAVE I GOT THEM?
80% OPINION RATIO
YOU GET WHATEVER YOU WANT, CRYSTAL...
BUT HOW ABOUT WANTING SOMETHING FOR US FOR A CHANGE...?
YOU KNOW I CAN'T BEAR TO BE TOUCHED, SINCE ROME... YOU MUST REMEMBER, WE'RE NO LONGER ON THE FRONTIER.
YOU NEEDN'T REMIND ME I'M AN IMPORTANT OFFICIAL BECAUSE OF YOU. "DIGNIFIED CITY ARISTOS DON'T ENGAGE IN ANIMAL RELATIONS WITH SOCIAL PEERS." I SHOULD JUST JOIN A FUN CLUB OR USE ANDROIDS LIKE EVERYONE ELSE...
BUT IT WAS DIFFERENT, ONCE, WHEN WE WERE AT SCHOOL TOGETHER...
THAT WAS ANOTHER WORLD.
YOU ARE SPECIAL TO ME, NILS! SOMEDAY WE COULD HAVE A CLONE CHILD MADE UP OF OUR COMBINED GENE CODES...
EMPLOYEE SHUTTLE
I'LL SEE YOU AT THE OFFICE TOMORROW.
BURD EMPLOYEE SHUTTLE
PFFFUUTTTT

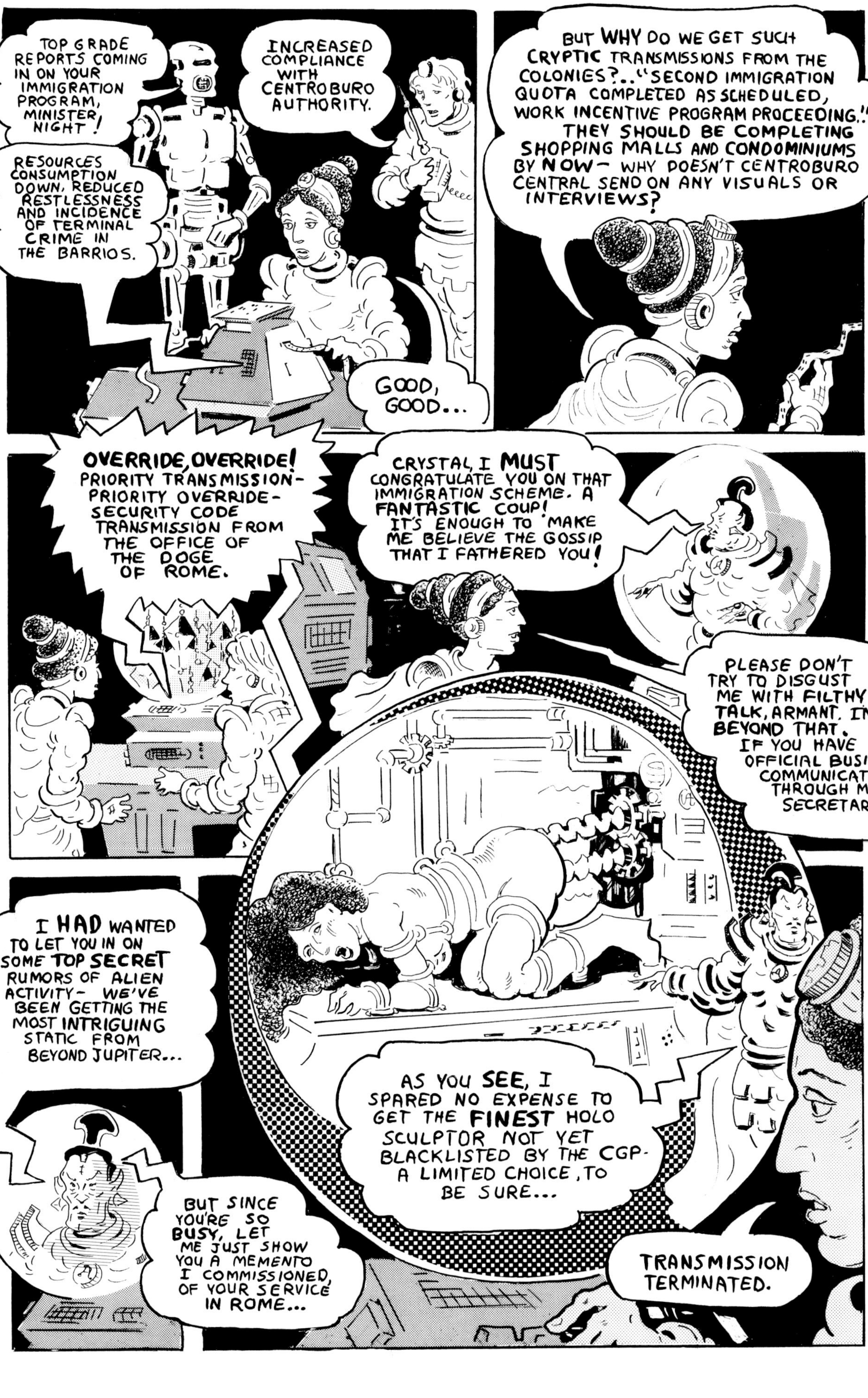
TOP GRADE REPORTS COMING IN ON YOUR IMMIGRATION PROGRAM, MINISTER NIGHT!
INCREASED COMPLIANCE WITH CENTROBURO AUTHORITY.
RESOURCES CONSUMPTION DOWN, REDUCED RESTLESSNESS AND INCIDENCE OF TERMINAL CRIME IN THE BARRIOS.
GOOD, GOOD...
BUT WHY DO WE GET SUCH CRYPTIC TRANSMISSIONS FROM THE COLONIES?.."SECOND IMMIGRATION QUOTA COMPLETED AS SCHEDULED, WORK INCENTIVE PROGRAM PROCEEDING.".. THEY SHOULD BE COMPLETING SHOPPING MALLS AND CONDOMINIUMS BY NOW— WHY DOESN'T CENTROBURO CENTRAL SEND ON ANY VISUALS OR INTERVIEWS?
OVERRIDE, OVERRIDE! PRIORITY TRANSMISSION- PRIORITY OVERRIDE- SECURITY CODE TRANSMISSION FROM THE OFFICE OF THE DOGE OF ROME.
CRYSTAL, I MUST CONGRATULATE YOU ON THAT IMMIGRATION SCHEME. A FANTASTIC COUP! IT'S ENOUGH TO MAKE ME BELIEVE THE GOSSIP THAT I FATHERED YOU!
PLEASE DON'T TRY TO DISGUST ME WITH FILTHY TALK, ARMANT. I'M BEYOND THAT. IF YOU HAVE OFFICIAL BUSINESS, COMMUNICATE THROUGH MY SECRETARY.
I HAD WANTED TO LET YOU IN ON SOME TOP SECRET RUMORS OF ALIEN ACTIVITY- WE'VE BEEN GETTING THE MOST INTRIGUING STATIC FROM BEYOND JUPITER...
BUT SINCE YOU'RE SO BUSY, LET ME JUST SHOW YOU A MEMENTO I COMMISSIONED, OF YOUR SERVICE IN ROME...
AS YOU SEE, I SPARED NO EXPENSE TO GET THE FINEST HOLO SCULPTOR NOT YET BLACKLISTED BY THE CGP- A LIMITED CHOICE, TO BE SURE...
TRANSMISSION TERMINATED.

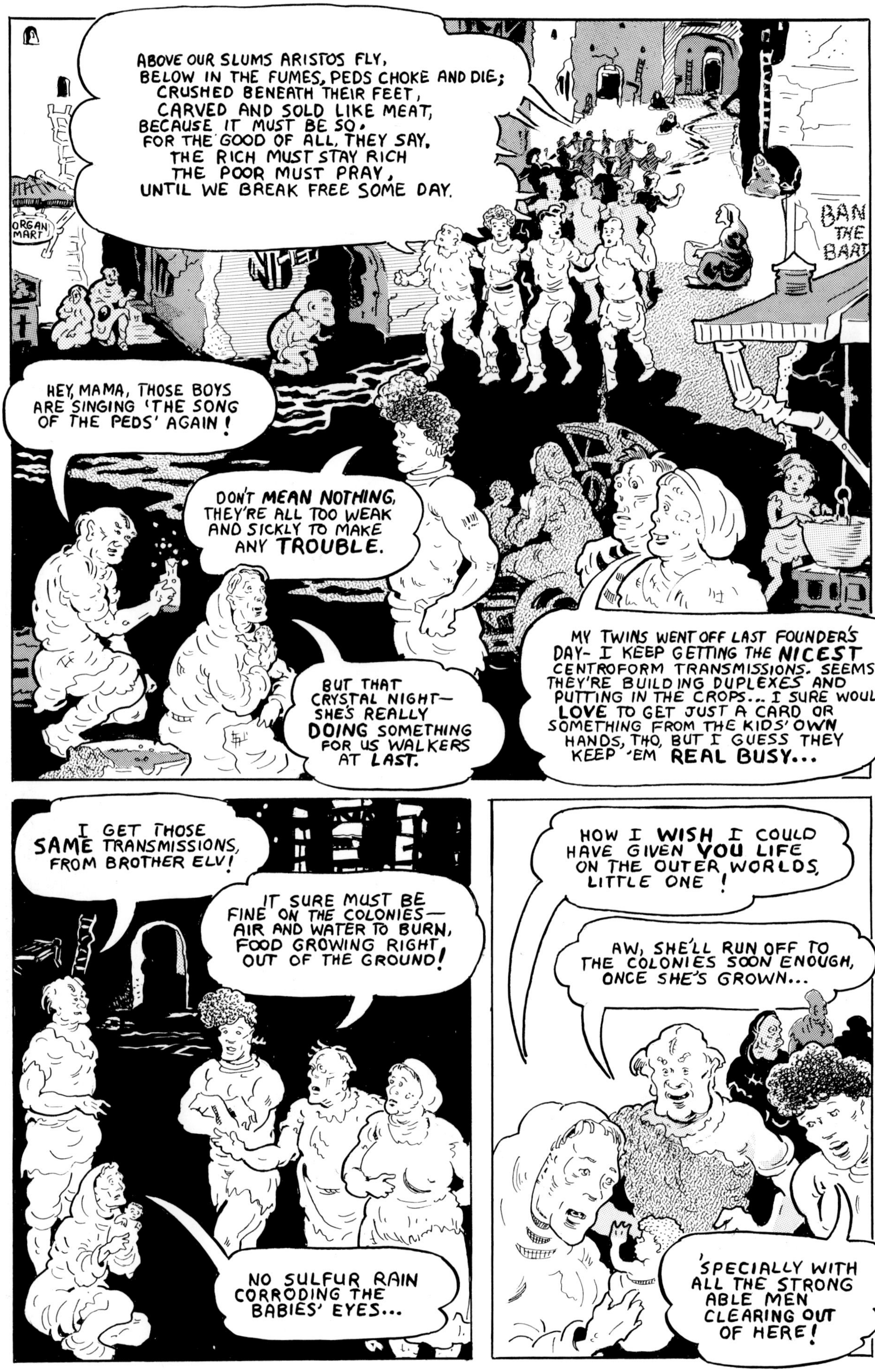
ABOVE OUR SLUMS ARISTOS FLY,
BELOW IN THE FUMES, PEDS CHOKE AND DIE;
CRUSHED BENEATH THEIR FEET,
CARVED AND SOLD LIKE MEAT,
BECAUSE IT MUST BE SO.
FOR THE GOOD OF ALL, THEY SAY.
THE RICH MUST STAY RICH
THE POOR MUST PRAY,
UNTIL WE BREAK FREE SOME DAY.
ORGAN MART
BAN THE BART
HEY, MAMA, THOSE BOYS ARE SINGING 'THE SONG OF THE PEDS' AGAIN!
DON'T MEAN NOTHING, THEY'RE ALL TOO WEAK AND SICKLY TO MAKE ANY TROUBLE.
BUT THAT CRYSTAL NIGHT— SHE'S REALLY DOING SOMETHING FOR US WALKERS AT LAST.
MY TWINS WENT OFF LAST FOUNDER'S DAY- I KEEP GETTING THE NICEST CENTROFORM TRANSMISSIONS. SEEMS THEY'RE BUILDING DUPLEXES AND PUTTING IN THE CROPS... I SURE WOULD LOVE TO GET JUST A CARD OR SOMETHING FROM THE KIDS' OWN HANDS, THO, BUT I GUESS THEY KEEP 'EM REAL BUSY...
I GET THOSE SAME TRANSMISSIONS, FROM BROTHER ELV!
IT SURE MUST BE FINE ON THE COLONIES— AIR AND WATER TO BURN, FOOD GROWING RIGHT OUT OF THE GROUND!
NO SULFUR RAIN CORRODING THE BABIES' EYES...
HOW I WISH I COULD HAVE GIVEN YOU LIFE ON THE OUTER WORLDS, LITTLE ONE!
AW, SHE'LL RUN OFF TO THE COLONIES SOON ENOUGH, ONCE SHE'S GROWN...
'SPECIALLY WITH ALL THE STRONG ABLE MEN CLEARING OUT OF HERE!

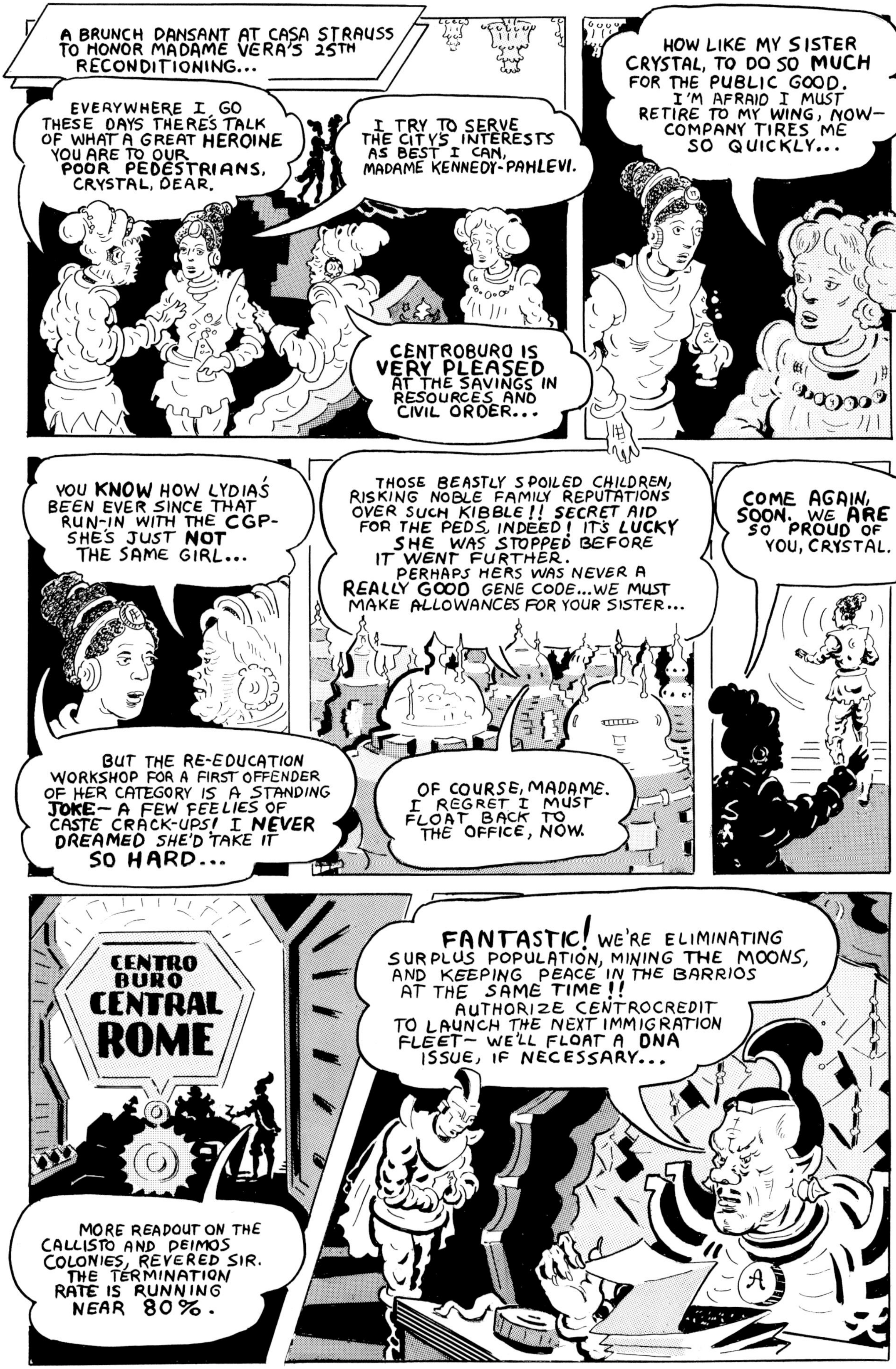
A BRUNCH DANSANT AT CASA STRAUSS TO HONOR MADAME VERA'S 25TH RECONDITIONING...
EVERYWHERE I GO THESE DAYS THERE'S TALK OF WHAT A GREAT HEROINE YOU ARE TO OUR POOR PEDESTRIANS, CRYSTAL, DEAR.
I TRY TO SERVE THE CITY'S INTERESTS AS BEST I CAN, MADAME KENNEDY-PAHLEVI.
CENTROBURO IS VERY PLEASED AT THE SAVINGS IN RESOURCES AND CIVIL ORDER...
HOW LIKE MY SISTER CRYSTAL, TO DO SO MUCH FOR THE PUBLIC GOOD. I'M AFRAID I MUST RETIRE TO MY WING, NOW— COMPANY TIRES ME SO QUICKLY...
YOU KNOW HOW LYDIA'S BEEN EVER SINCE THAT RUN-IN WITH THE CGP- SHE'S JUST NOT THE SAME GIRL...
BUT THE RE-EDUCATION WORKSHOP FOR A FIRST OFFENDER OF HER CATEGORY IS A STANDING JOKE— A FEW FEELIES OF CASTE CRACK-UPS! I NEVER DREAMED SHE'D TAKE IT SO HARD...
THOSE BEASTLY SPOILED CHILDREN, RISKING NOBLE FAMILY REPUTATIONS OVER SUCH KIBBLE!! SECRET AID FOR THE PEDS, INDEED! IT'S LUCKY SHE WAS STOPPED BEFORE IT WENT FURTHER. PERHAPS HERS WAS NEVER A REALLY GOOD GENE CODE...WE MUST MAKE ALLOWANCES FOR YOUR SISTER...
OF COURSE, MADAME. I REGRET I MUST FLOAT BACK TO THE OFFICE, NOW.
COME AGAIN, SOON. WE ARE SO PROUD OF YOU, CRYSTAL.
CENTRO BURO CENTRAL ROME
FANTASTIC! WE'RE ELIMINATING SURPLUS POPULATION, MINING THE MOONS, AND KEEPING PEACE IN THE BARRIOS AT THE SAME TIME!! AUTHORIZE CENTROCREDIT TO LAUNCH THE NEXT IMMIGRATION FLEET— WE'LL FLOAT A DNA ISSUE, IF NECESSARY...
MORE READOUT ON THE CALLISTO AND DEIMOS COLONIES, REVERED SIR. THE TERMINATION RATE IS RUNNING NEAR 80%.

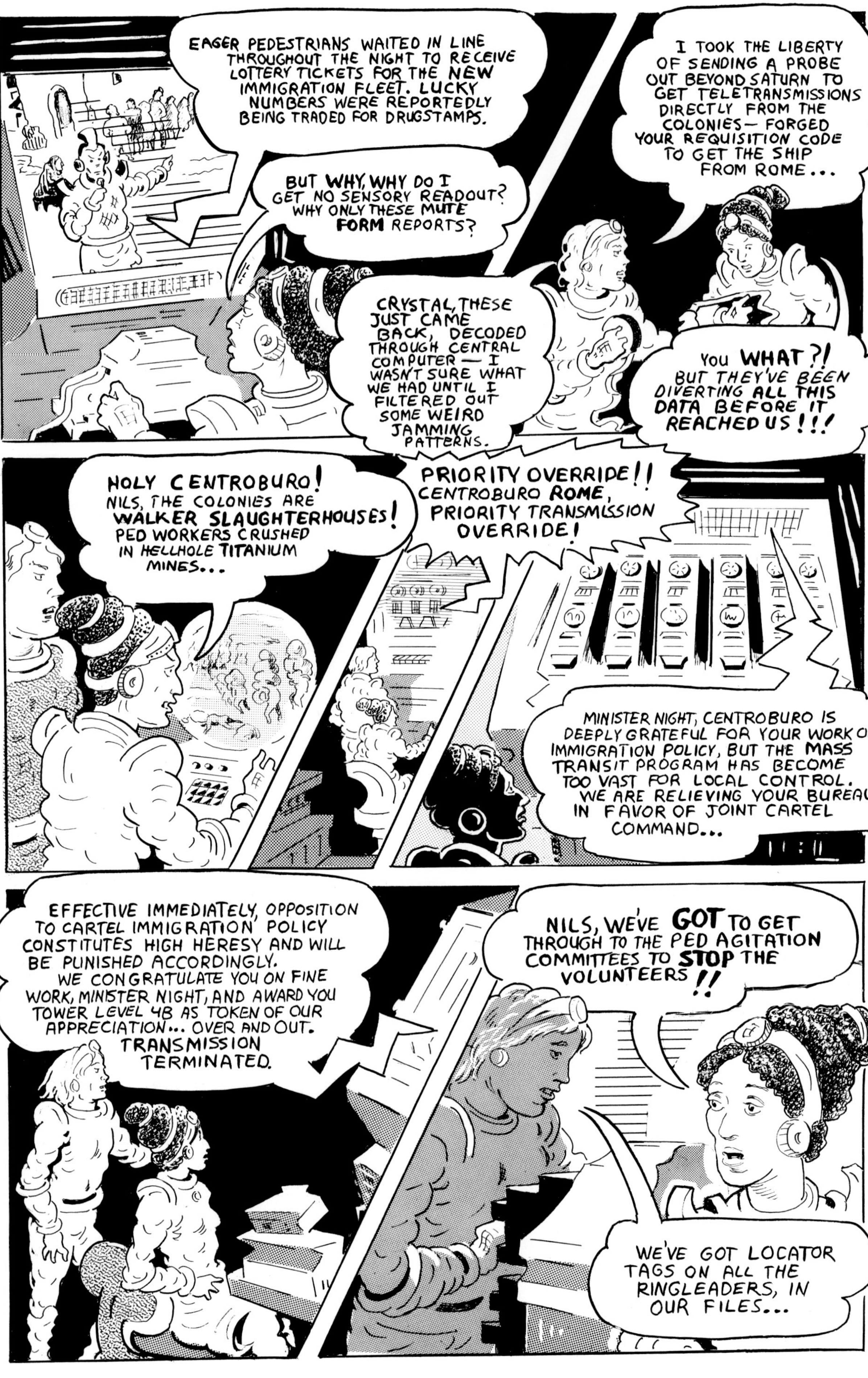
EAGER PEDESTRIANS WAITED IN LINE THROUGHOUT THE NIGHT TO RECEIVE LOTTERY TICKETS FOR THE NEW IMMIGRATION FLEET. LUCKY NUMBERS WERE REPORTEDLY BEING TRADED FOR DRUGSTAMPS.
BUT WHY, WHY DO I GET NO SENSORY READOUT? WHY ONLY THESE MUTE FORM REPORTS?
CRYSTAL, THESE JUST CAME BACK, DECODED THROUGH CENTRAL COMPUTER — I WASN'T SURE WHAT WE HAD UNTIL I FILTERED OUT SOME WEIRD JAMMING PATTERNS.
I TOOK THE LIBERTY OF SENDING A PROBE OUT BEYOND SATURN TO GET TELETRANSMISSIONS DIRECTLY FROM THE COLONIES — FORGED YOUR REQUISITION CODE TO GET THE SHIP FROM ROME...
YOU WHAT?! BUT THEY'VE BEEN DIVERTING ALL THIS DATA BEFORE IT REACHED US!!!
HOLY CENTROBURO! NILS, THE COLONIES ARE WALKER SLAUGHTERHOUSES! PED WORKERS CRUSHED IN HELLHOLE TITANIUM MINES...
PRIORITY OVERRIDE!! CENTROBURO ROME, PRIORITY TRANSMISSION OVERRIDE!
MINISTER NIGHT, CENTROBURO IS DEEPLY GRATEFUL FOR YOUR WORK ON IMMIGRATION POLICY, BUT THE MASS TRANSIT PROGRAM HAS BECOME TOO VAST FOR LOCAL CONTROL. WE ARE RELIEVING YOUR BUREAU IN FAVOR OF JOINT CARTEL COMMAND...
EFFECTIVE IMMEDIATELY, OPPOSITION TO CARTEL IMMIGRATION POLICY CONSTITUTES HIGH HERESY AND WILL BE PUNISHED ACCORDINGLY. WE CONGRATULATE YOU ON FINE WORK, MINISTER NIGHT, AND AWARD YOU TOWER LEVEL 4B AS TOKEN OF OUR APPRECIATION... OVER AND OUT. TRANSMISSION TERMINATED.
NILS, WE'VE GOT TO GET THROUGH TO THE PED AGITATION COMMITTEES TO STOP THE VOLUNTEERS!!
WE'VE GOT LOCATOR TAGS ON ALL THE RINGLEADERS, IN OUR FILES...

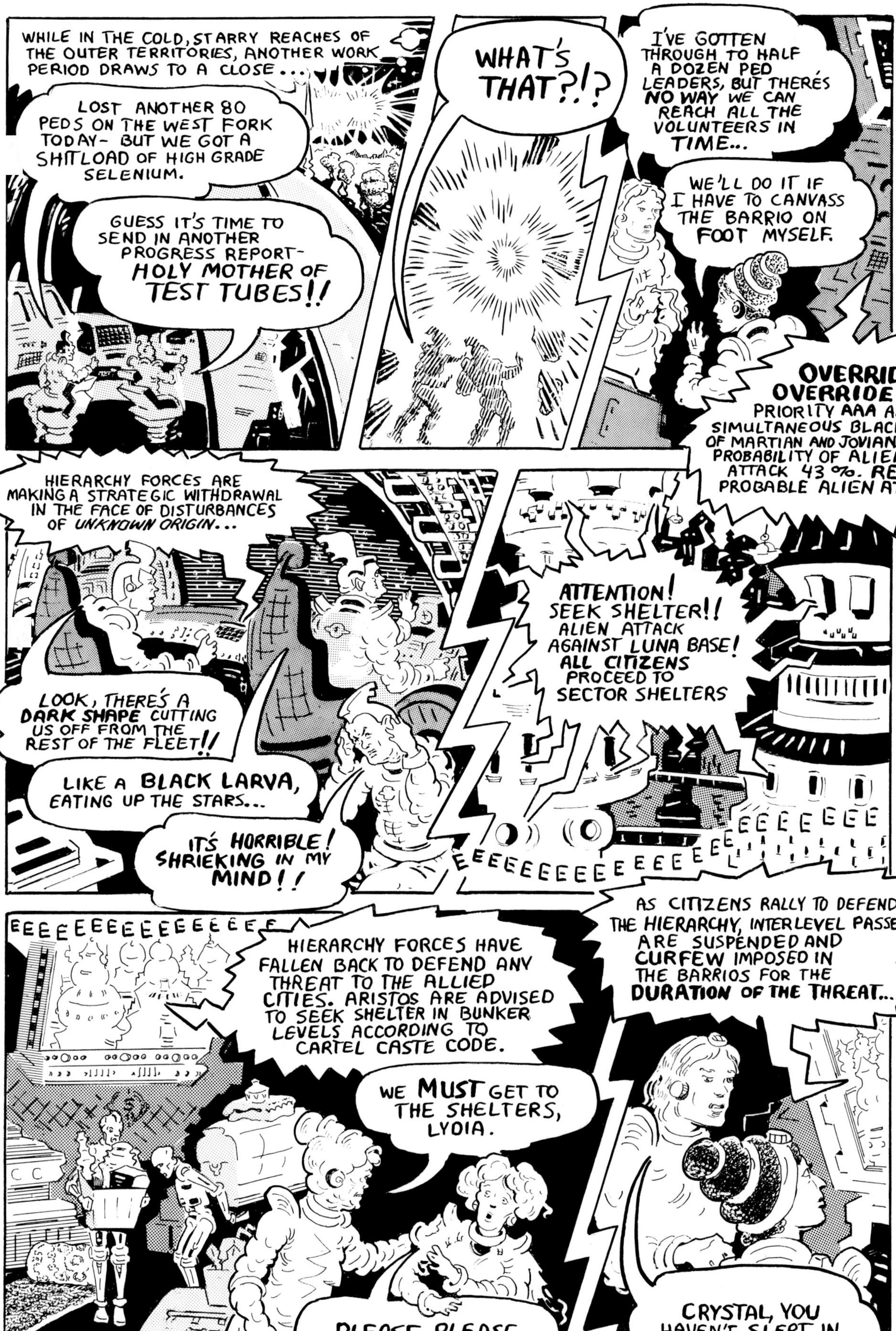
WHILE IN THE COLD, STARRY REACHES OF THE OUTER TERRITORIES, ANOTHER WORK PERIOD DRAWS TO A CLOSE...
LOST ANOTHER 80 PEDS ON THE WEST FORK TODAY- BUT WE GOT A SHITLOAD OF HIGH GRADE SELENIUM.
GUESS IT'S TIME TO SEND IN ANOTHER PROGRESS REPORT- HOLY MOTHER OF TEST TUBES!!
WHAT'S THAT?!?
I'VE GOTTEN THROUGH TO HALF A DOZEN PED LEADERS, BUT THERE'S NO WAY WE CAN REACH ALL THE VOLUNTEERS IN TIME...
WE'LL DO IT IF I HAVE TO CANVASS THE BARRIO ON FOOT MYSELF.
OVERRIDE!! OVERRIDE!! PRIORITY AAA ALERT! SIMULTANEOUS BLACKOUT OF MARTIAN AND JOVIAN BASES- PROBABILITY OF ALIEN ATTACK 43%. REPEAT: PROBABLE ALIEN ATTACK!
HIERARCHY FORCES ARE MAKING A STRATEGIC WITHDRAWAL IN THE FACE OF DISTURBANCES OF UNKNOWN ORIGIN...
LOOK, THERE'S A DARK SHAPE CUTTING US OFF FROM THE REST OF THE FLEET!!
LIKE A BLACK LARVA, EATING UP THE STARS...
IT'S HORRIBLE! SHRIEKING IN MY MIND!!
ATTENTION! SEEK SHELTER!! ALIEN ATTACK AGAINST LUNA BASE! ALL CITIZENS PROCEED TO SECTOR SHELTERS
EEEEEEEEEEEEEEEEEEEEEEEEE
EEEEEEEEEEEEEEEEEE
HIERARCHY FORCES HAVE FALLEN BACK TO DEFEND ANY THREAT TO THE ALLIED CITIES. ARISTOS ARE ADVISED TO SEEK SHELTER IN BUNKER LEVELS ACCORDING TO CARTEL CASTE CODE.
WE MUST GET TO THE SHELTERS, LYDIA.
PLEASE, PLEASE, DON'T MAKE ME LEAVE HOME!
AS CITIZENS RALLY TO DEFEND THE HIERARCHY, INTERLEVEL PASSES ARE SUSPENDED AND CURFEW IMPOSED IN THE BARRIOS FOR THE DURATION OF THE THREAT...
CRYSTAL, YOU HAVEN'T SLEPT IN FOUR NIGHTS...

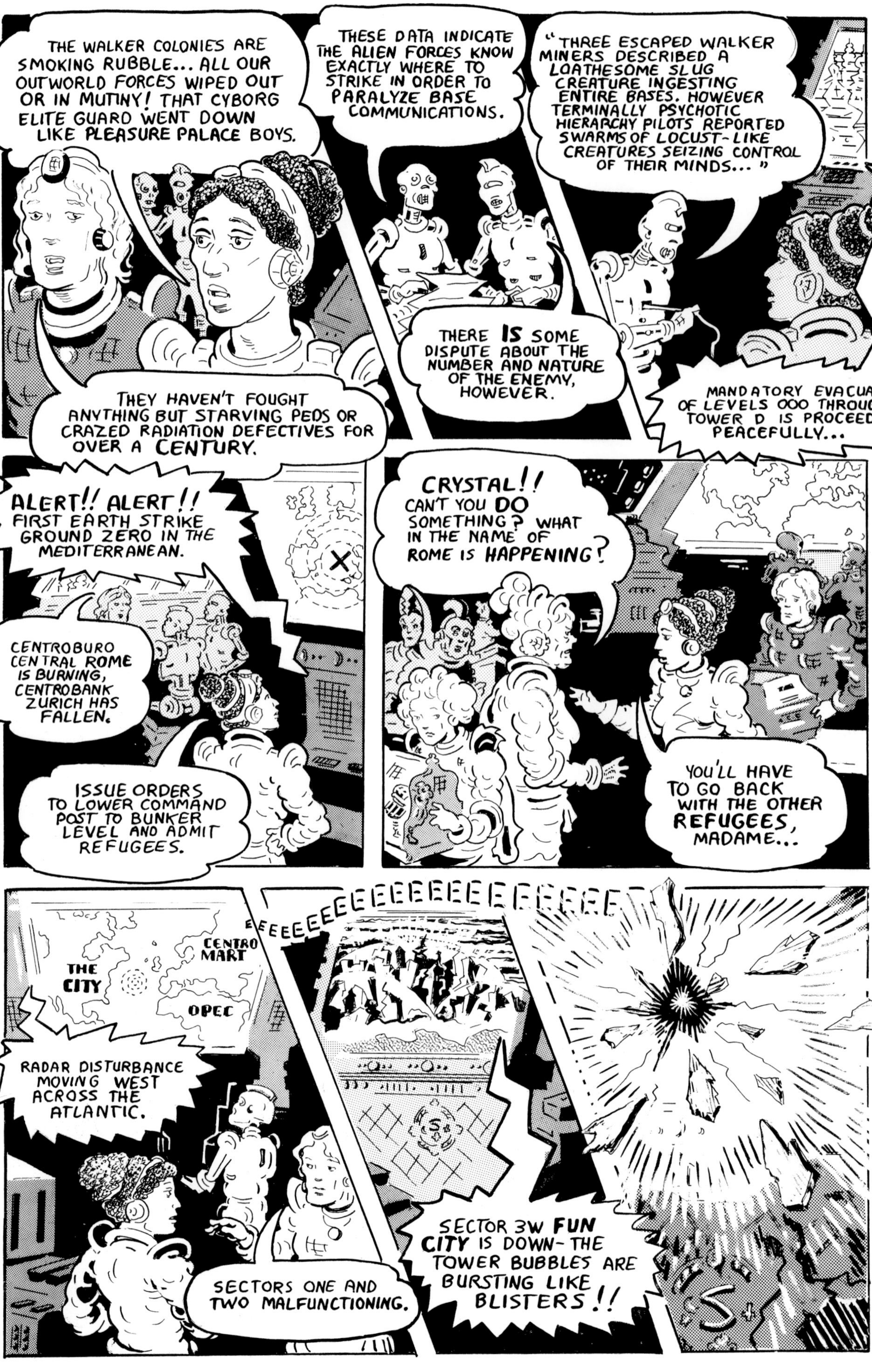
THE WALKER COLONIES ARE SMOKING RUBBLE... ALL OUR OUTWORLD FORCES WIPED OUT OR IN MUTINY! THAT CYBORG ELITE GUARD WENT DOWN LIKE PLEASURE PALACE BOYS.
THEY HAVEN'T FOUGHT ANYTHING BUT STARVING PEDS OR CRAZED RADIATION DEFECTIVES FOR OVER A CENTURY.
THESE DATA INDICATE THE ALIEN FORCES KNOW EXACTLY WHERE TO STRIKE IN ORDER TO PARALYZE BASE COMMUNICATIONS.
THERE IS SOME DISPUTE ABOUT THE NUMBER AND NATURE OF THE ENEMY, HOWEVER.
"THREE ESCAPED WALKER MINERS DESCRIBED A LOATHESOME SLUG CREATURE INGESTING ENTIRE BASES. HOWEVER TERMINALLY PSYCHOTIC HIERARCHY PILOTS REPORTED SWARMS OF LOCUST-LIKE CREATURES SEIZING CONTROL OF THEIR MINDS..."
MANDATORY EVACUATION OF LEVELS 000 THROUGH TOWER D IS PROCEEDING PEACEFULLY...
ALERT!! ALERT!! FIRST EARTH STRIKE GROUND ZERO IN THE MEDITERRANEAN.
CENTROBURO CENTRAL ROME IS BURNING, CENTROBANK ZURICH HAS FALLEN.
ISSUE ORDERS TO LOWER COMMAND POST TO BUNKER LEVEL AND ADMIT REFUGEES.
CRYSTAL!! CAN'T YOU DO SOMETHING? WHAT IN THE NAME OF ROME IS HAPPENING?
YOU'LL HAVE TO GO BACK WITH THE OTHER REFUGEES, MADAME...
THE CITY
CENTRO MART
OPEC
RADAR DISTURBANCE MOVING WEST ACROSS THE ATLANTIC.
SECTORS ONE AND TWO MALFUNCTIONING.
EEEEEEEEEEEEEEEEEEEEEEEEEEEE
SECTOR 3W FUN CITY IS DOWN- THE TOWER BUBBLES ARE BURSTING LIKE BLISTERS!!

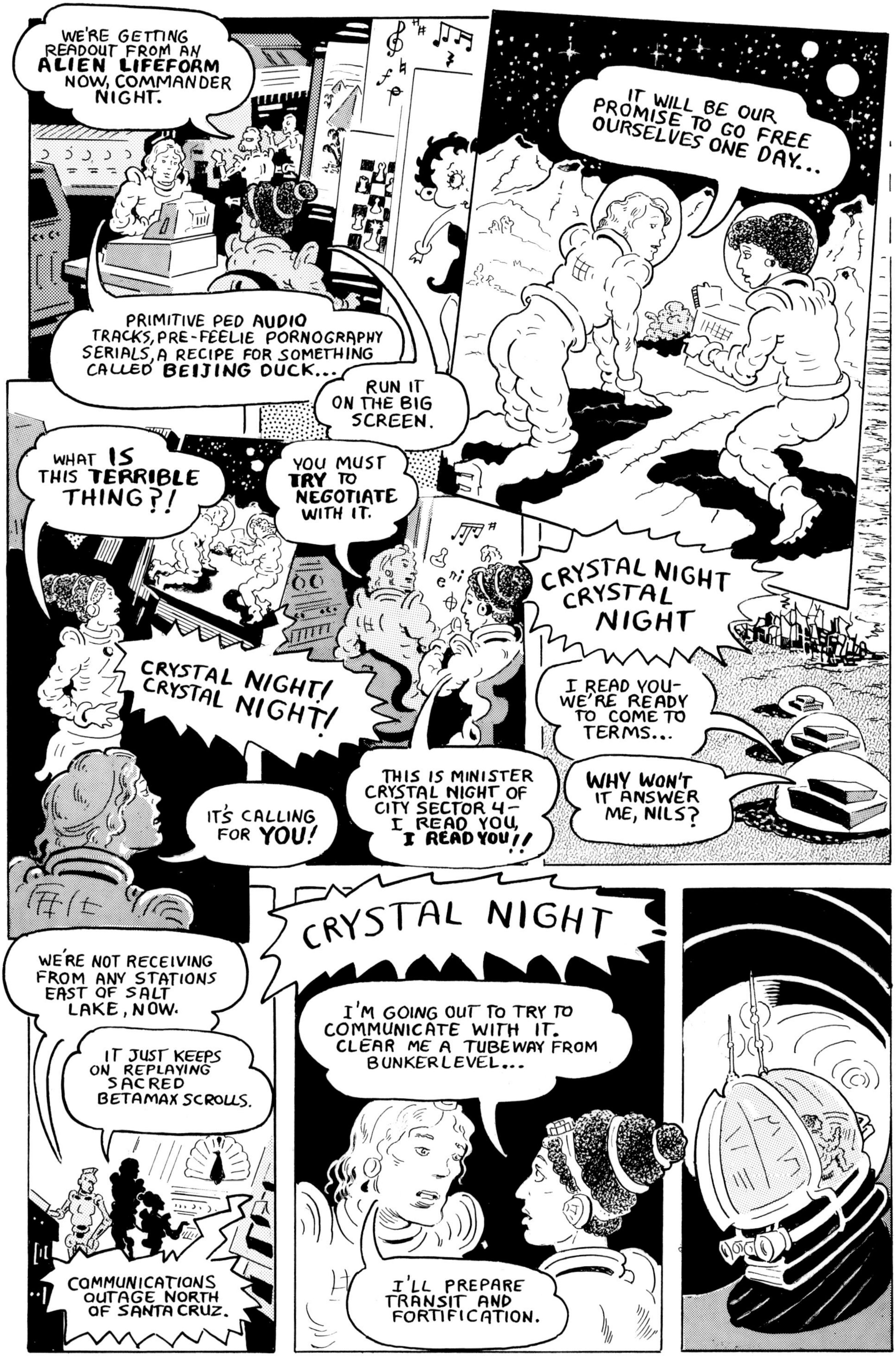
WE'RE GETTING READOUT FROM AN ALIEN LIFEFORM NOW, COMMANDER NIGHT.
PRIMITIVE PED AUDIO TRACKS, PRE-FEELIE PORNOGRAPHY SERIALS, A RECIPE FOR SOMETHING CALLED BEIJING DUCK...
RUN IT ON THE BIG SCREEN.
IT WILL BE OUR PROMISE TO GO FREE OURSELVES ONE DAY...
WHAT IS THIS TERRIBLE THING?!
YOU MUST TRY TO NEGOTIATE WITH IT.
CRYSTAL NIGHT! CRYSTAL NIGHT!
IT'S CALLING FOR YOU!
THIS IS MINISTER CRYSTAL NIGHT OF CITY SECTOR 4— I READ YOU, I READ YOU!!
CRYSTAL NIGHT CRYSTAL NIGHT
I READ YOU— WE'RE READY TO COME TO TERMS...
WHY WON'T IT ANSWER ME, NILS?
CRYSTAL NIGHT
WE'RE NOT RECEIVING FROM ANY STATIONS EAST OF SALT LAKE, NOW.
IT JUST KEEPS ON REPLAYING SACRED BETAMAX SCROLLS.
COMMUNICATIONS OUTAGE NORTH OF SANTA CRUZ.
I'M GOING OUT TO TRY TO COMMUNICATE WITH IT. CLEAR ME A TUBEWAY FROM BUNKERLEVEL...
I'LL PREPARE TRANSIT AND FORTIFICATION.

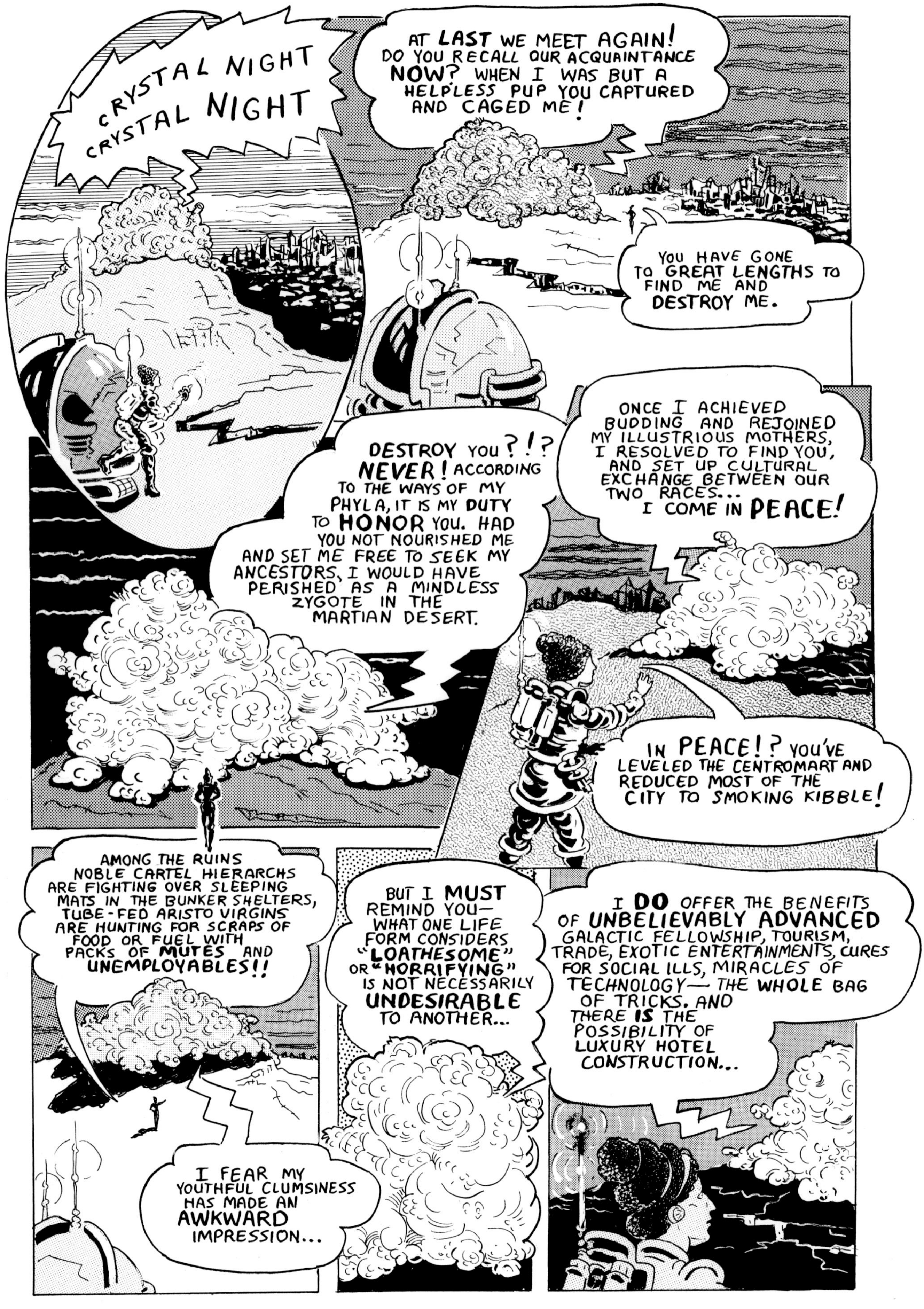
CRYSTAL NIGHT CRYSTAL NIGHT
AT LAST WE MEET AGAIN! DO YOU RECALL OUR ACQUAINTANCE NOW? WHEN I WAS BUT A HELPLESS PUP YOU CAPTURED AND CAGED ME!
YOU HAVE GONE TO GREAT LENGTHS TO FIND ME AND DESTROY ME.
DESTROY YOU?!? NEVER! ACCORDING TO THE WAYS OF MY PHYLA, IT IS MY DUTY TO HONOR YOU. HAD YOU NOT NOURISHED ME AND SET ME FREE TO SEEK MY ANCESTORS, I WOULD HAVE PERISHED AS A MINDLESS ZYGOTE IN THE MARTIAN DESERT.
ONCE I ACHIEVED BUDDING AND REJOINED MY ILLUSTRIOUS MOTHERS, I RESOLVED TO FIND YOU, AND SET UP CULTURAL EXCHANGE BETWEEN OUR TWO RACES... I COME IN PEACE!
IN PEACE!? YOU'VE LEVELED THE CENTROMART AND REDUCED MOST OF THE CITY TO SMOKING KIBBLE!
AMONG THE RUINS NOBLE CARTEL HIERARCHS ARE FIGHTING OVER SLEEPING MATS IN THE BUNKER SHELTERS, TUBE-FED ARISTO VIRGINS ARE HUNTING FOR SCRAPS OF FOOD OR FUEL WITH PACKS OF MUTES AND UNEMPLOYABLES!!
I FEAR MY YOUTHFUL CLUMSINESS HAS MADE AN AWKWARD IMPRESSION...
BUT I MUST REMIND YOU— WHAT ONE LIFE FORM CONSIDERS "LOATHESOME" OR "HORRIFYING" IS NOT NECESSARILY UNDESIRABLE TO ANOTHER...
I DO OFFER THE BENEFITS OF UNBELIEVABLY ADVANCED GALACTIC FELLOWSHIP, TOURISM, TRADE, EXOTIC ENTERTAINMENTS, CURES FOR SOCIAL ILLS, MIRACLES OF TECHNOLOGY— THE WHOLE BAG OF TRICKS. AND THERE IS THE POSSIBILITY OF LUXURY HOTEL CONSTRUCTION...

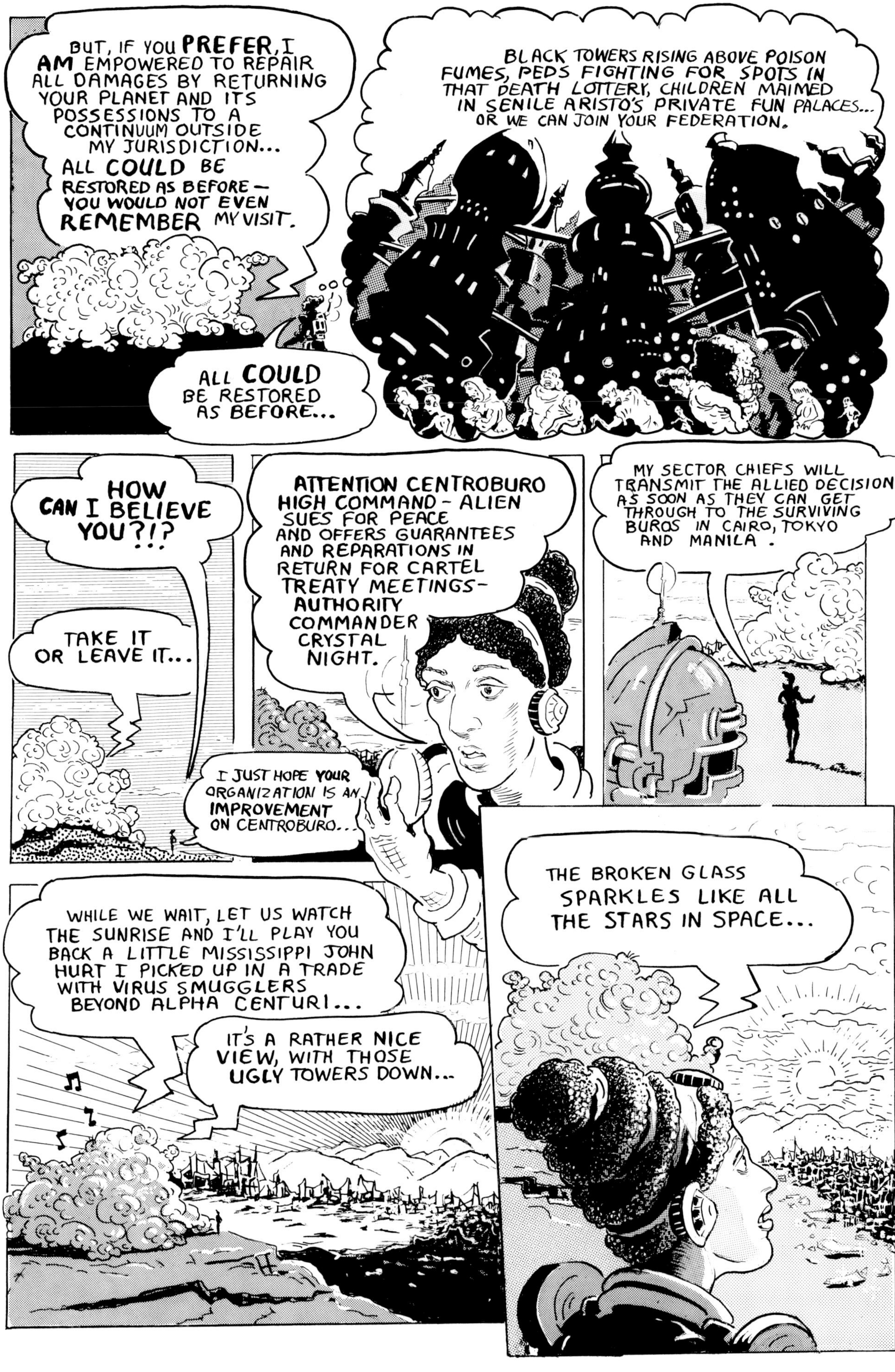
BUT, IF YOU PREFER, I AM EMPOWERED TO REPAIR ALL DAMAGES BY RETURNING YOUR PLANET AND ITS POSSESSIONS TO A CONTINUUM OUTSIDE MY JURISDICTION... ALL COULD BE RESTORED AS BEFORE — YOU WOULD NOT EVEN REMEMBER MY VISIT.
ALL COULD BE RESTORED AS BEFORE...
BLACK TOWERS RISING ABOVE POISON FUMES, PEDS FIGHTING FOR SPOTS IN THAT DEATH LOTTERY, CHILDREN MAIMED IN SENILE ARISTO'S PRIVATE FUN PALACES... OR WE CAN JOIN YOUR FEDERATION.
HOW CAN I BELIEVE YOU?!?...
TAKE IT OR LEAVE IT...
ATTENTION CENTROBURO HIGH COMMAND - ALIEN SUES FOR PEACE AND OFFERS GUARANTEES AND REPARATIONS IN RETURN FOR CARTEL TREATY MEETINGS- AUTHORITY COMMANDER CRYSTAL NIGHT.
I JUST HOPE YOUR ORGANIZATION IS AN IMPROVEMENT ON CENTROBURO...
MY SECTOR CHIEFS WILL TRANSMIT THE ALLIED DECISION AS SOON AS THEY CAN GET THROUGH TO THE SURVIVING BUROS IN CAIRO, TOKYO AND MANILA.
WHILE WE WAIT, LET US WATCH THE SUNRISE AND I'LL PLAY YOU BACK A LITTLE MISSISSIPPI JOHN HURT I PICKED UP IN A TRADE WITH VIRUS SMUGGLERS BEYOND ALPHA CENTURI...
IT'S A RATHER NICE VIEW, WITH THOSE UGLY TOWERS DOWN...
THE BROKEN GLASS SPARKLES LIKE ALL THE STARS IN SPACE...

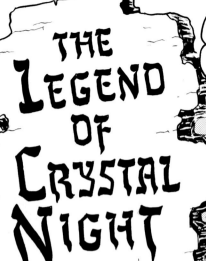

THE LEGEND OF CRYSTAL NIGHT

AND THAT IS THE STORY YOUR GRANDMOTHER'S GRANDMOTHER ALWAYS TOLD — HOW CRYSTAL NIGHT AND HER ALIEN FRIEND BROUGHT DOWN THE TOWERS OF THE EVIL ARISTOS.

AND THEN WE JOINED THE GREAT INTERGALACTIC FEDERATION, AND EVERYONE HAD ENOUGH TO EAT AND NO MORE PRISONS OR ANYTHING?

NO ONE KNOWS FOR SURE, BUT IT WASN'T **EXACTLY** LIKE THAT...

IN FACT, I CAN'T RECALL A SINGLE **OTHER** STORY ABOUT THE ALIEN FEDERATION...

BUT I GUESS THINGS **ARE** A **LOT BETTER** NOW THAN IN THE DAYS OF THE ARISTOS.

LOOK, HERE COMES PA WITH THE ALGAE BLOCKS FROM THE RIVER!!

TIME TO GET TO WORK HELPING YOUR MA, NOW, BEFORE YOUR BROTHERS GET BACK FROM THE FIELDS...

BUT PROMISE TOMORROW YOU'LL TELL ME ANOTHER STORY!

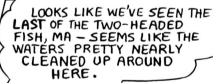

LOOKS LIKE WE'VE SEEN THE **LAST** OF THE TWO-HEADED FISH, MA — SEEMS LIKE THE WATERS PRETTY NEARLY CLEANED UP AROUND HERE.

MY VEGETABLES ARE COMING UP FINE TOO, BUT I'M WORRIED ABOUT THOSE HERDERS FROM THE VALLEY — THERE'S **TALK** OF A NEW BORDER FIGHT.

END

CREDITS FOR **INSPIRATION** ~ TO EMILE ZOLA, PHILIP K. DICK, LOYAL PUBLISHER DENIS KITCHEN, AND **THE PROFESSIONAL CHESS** ASSOCIATION

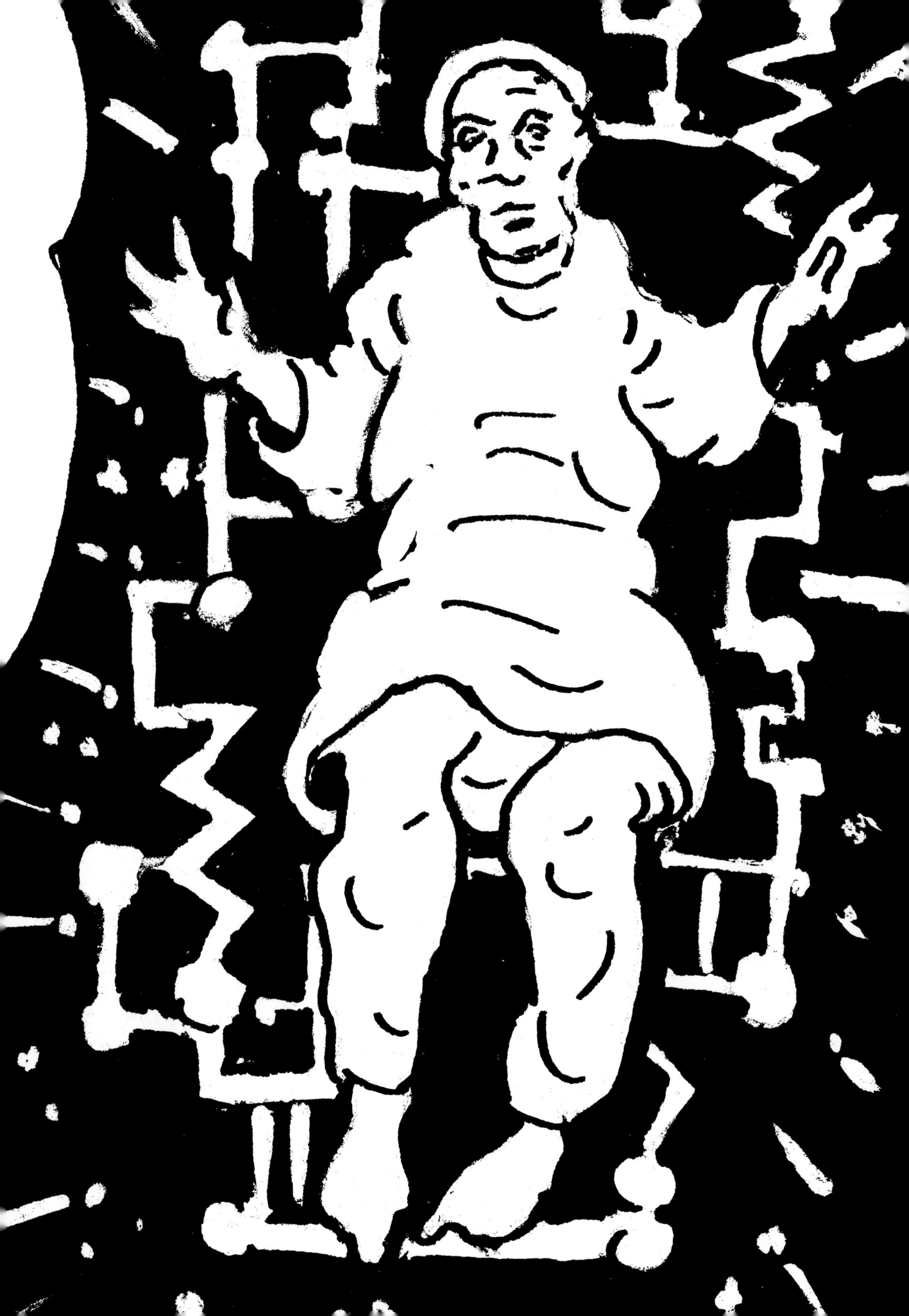

MORT MESKIN

(1916–95)

Mort Meskin was a tremendous influence on the first and second generation of American cartoonists—his expert staging and lively drawing inspired and generated competition from his colleagues throughout the 1940s.

Meskin was born in Brooklyn in 1916. He graduated from the Pratt Institute and went to work in the comic book industry in 1938, drawing all sorts of features, and swiftly carving out his own style in the crowded field. In 1941 he went to work for National Allied Publications (which later became DC Comics), where he drew the Vigilante and Johnny Quick, among other characters. During this time Meskin became friends with the artists Jerry Robinson and George Roussos, and in 1945 Meskin and Robinson formed their own studio, creating comics for multiple publishers, including Spark Publications, for which Meskin created Golden Lad.

Golden Lad is a fairly generic boy super hero—Tommy Preston touches a "magic talisman," transforms into Golden Lad, and fights crime—but Meskin took the premise and imbued each panel with life. A student of film, he was reputed to have gone to see *Citizen Kane* fifteen times, the lighting and camera angles of which influenced a generation of cartoonists. Meskin also studied the illustrative comics of Noel Sickles, and became an early master of panel design in comic books. Never too crowded, always open and airy, Meskin's panels are practically studies in minimal design. He used basic geometric shapes to indicate backgrounds, thrusting figures into the foreground of the action. Meskin wasn't going for realism—he instead insinuated a lively figure through a collection of sparse lines and prudent blacks. When Meskin used his formidable compositional gifts to depict multiple characters in a panel, as he does throughout "The Menace of the Minstrel!" he inspires a certain amount of awe in the reader. His groups are raucous, fascinating collections of faces, limbs, and expressions. All of this work would be a bit static if it wasn't for his linework. His brushy inking has a casual quality to it; whether through necessary haste or stylistic choice, the well-placed, offhand strokes add to up compelling marks. These drawings, his superlative design, off-kilter perspectives, and wonky figures influenced cartoonists from Steve Ditko to Alex Toth, both of whom looked to him as an artist's artist.

Meskin suffered from an unspecified mental illness in the mid-to-late 1940s, though once recovered he was back in comics, this time working for Joe Simon and Jack Kirby's studio creating gnarled images and psychologically fraught comics, including a wonderful title he created called *The Strange World of Your Dreams*. When Simon and Kirby shuttered their operation in 1954, Meskin returned to DC Comics and, in a far more unassuming, economical style, drew scores of stories for the company. He finally left comics in 1965, working in advertising for the rest of his commercial career. He left behind a body of work rich with visual possibilities: line, design, form, and characterization. Meskin did it all, and he did it with grace.

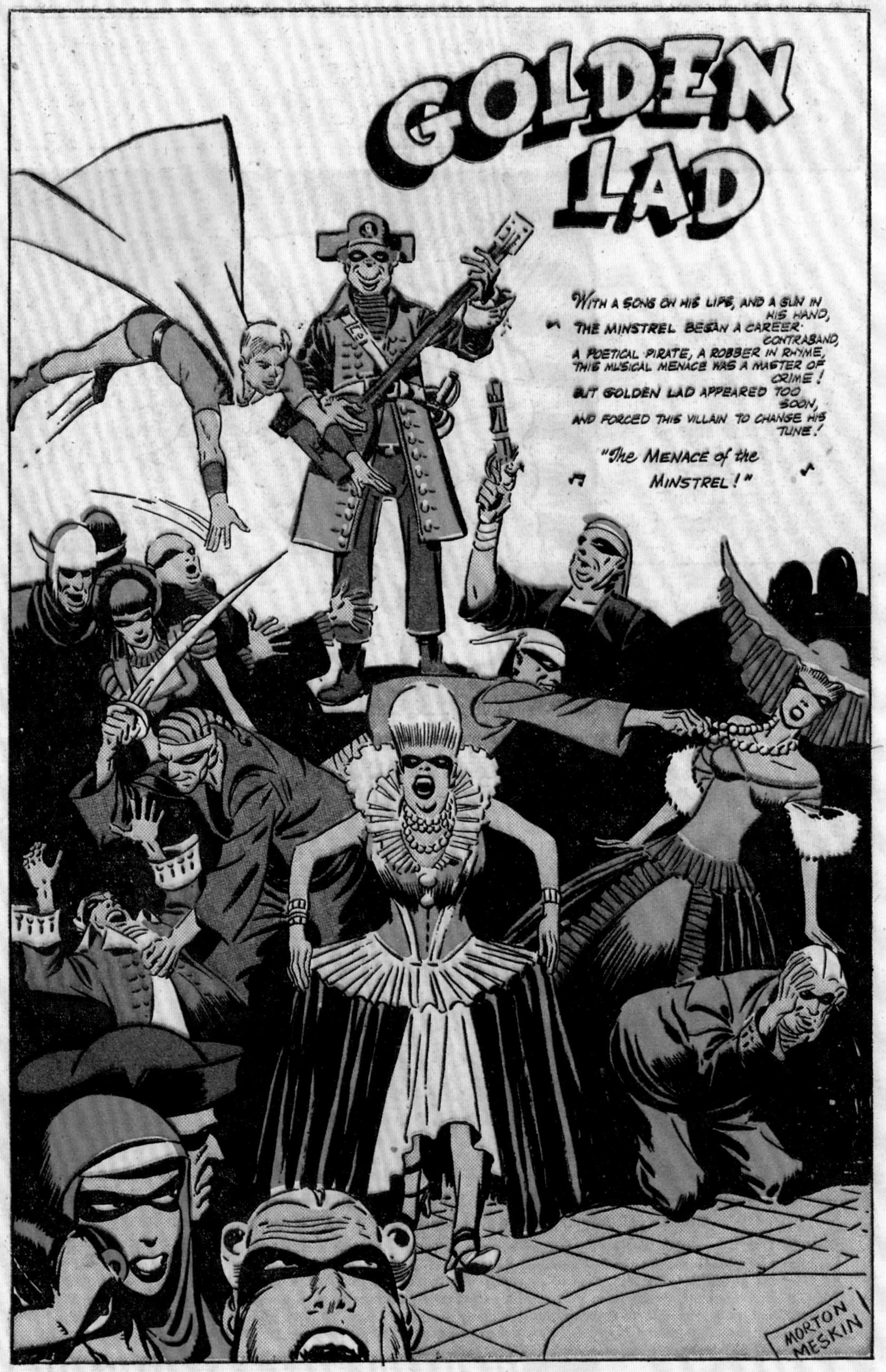
GOLDEN LAD
WITH A SONG ON HIS LIPS, AND A GUN IN HIS HAND,
THE MINSTREL BEGAN A CAREER CONTRABAND,
A POETICAL PIRATE, A ROBBER IN RHYME,
THIS MUSICAL MENACE WAS A MASTER OF CRIME!
BUT GOLDEN LAD APPEARED TOO SOON,
AND FORCED THIS VILLAIN TO CHANGE HIS TUNE!
"The MENACE of the MINSTREL!"
MORTON MESKIN

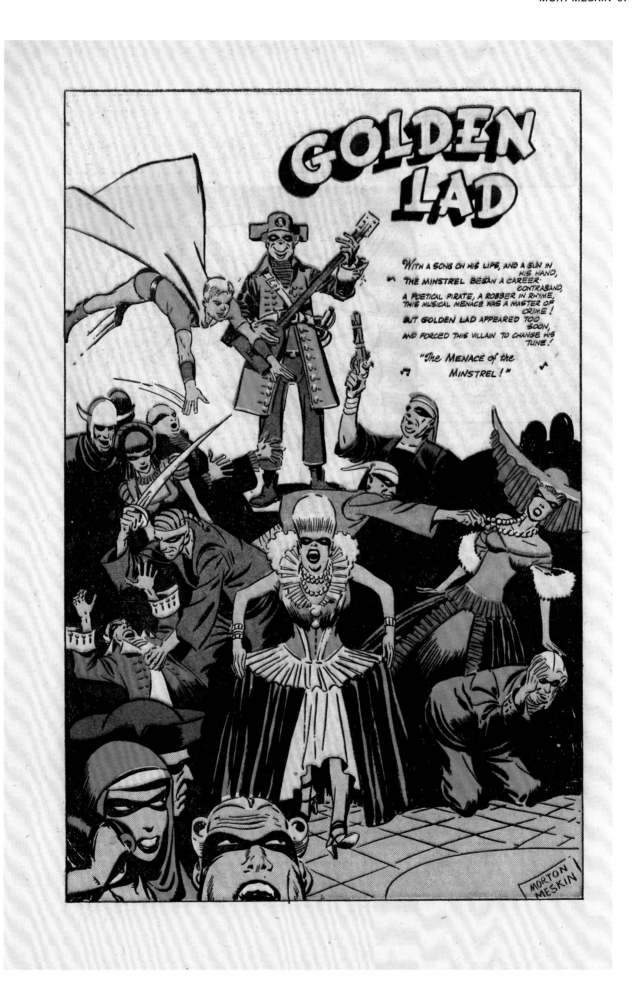

Golden Lad no. 4 (1946)

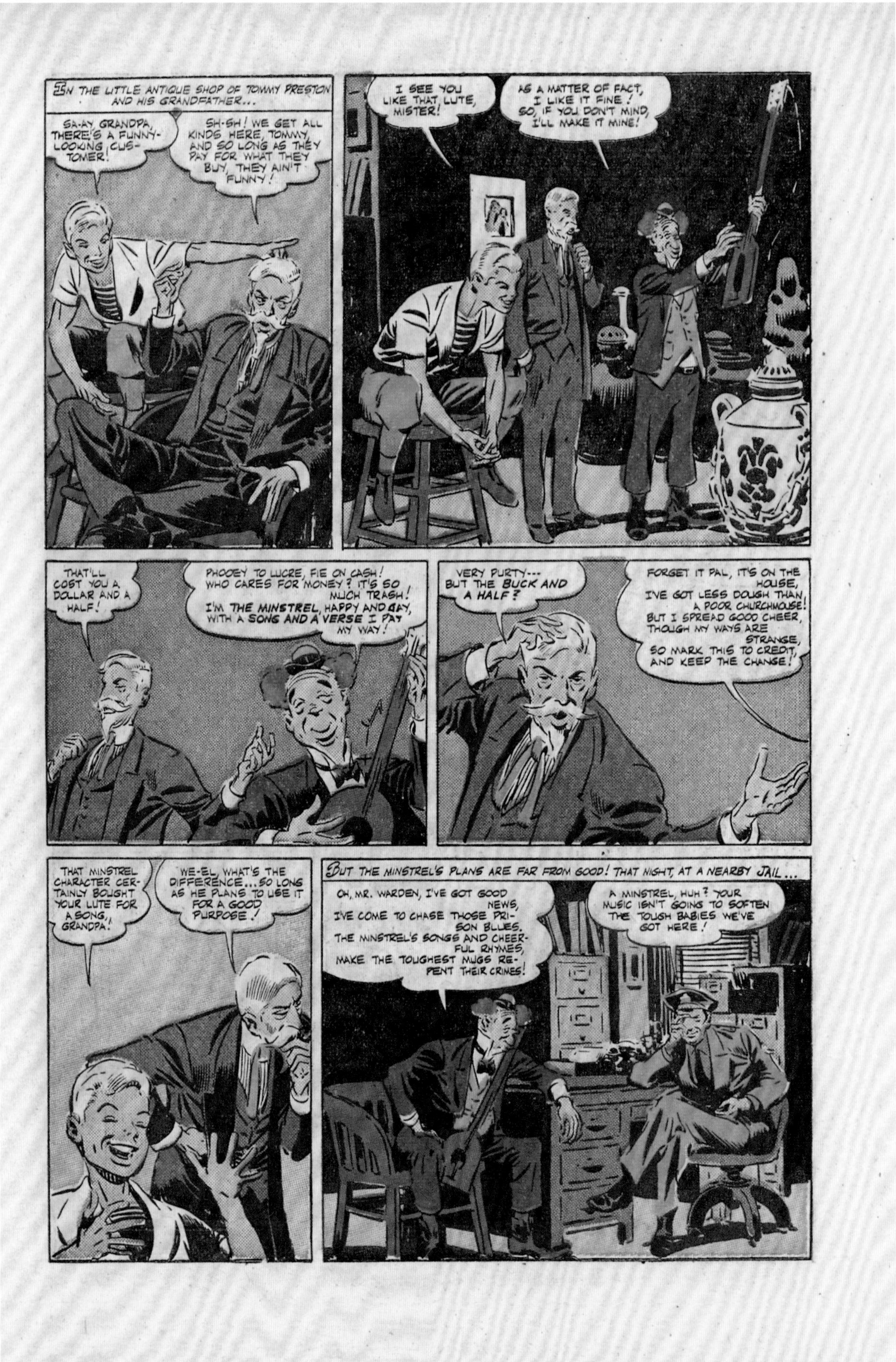
IN THE LITTLE ANTIQUE SHOP OF TOMMY PRESTON AND HIS GRANDFATHER...
SA-AY, GRANDPA, THERE'S A FUNNY-LOOKING CUS-TOMER!
SH-SH! WE GET ALL KINDS HERE, TOMMY, AND SO LONG AS THEY PAY FOR WHAT THEY BUY, THEY AIN'T FUNNY!
I SEE YOU LIKE THAT LUTE, MISTER!
AS A MATTER OF FACT, I LIKE IT FINE! SO, IF YOU DON'T MIND, I'LL MAKE IT MINE!
THAT'LL COST YOU A DOLLAR AND A HALF!
PHOOEY TO LUCRE, FIE ON CASH! WHO CARES FOR MONEY? IT'S SO MUCH TRASH! I'M THE MINSTREL, HAPPY AND GAY, WITH A SONG AND A VERSE I PAY MY WAY!
VERY PURTY--- BUT THE BUCK AND A HALF?
FORGET IT PAL, IT'S ON THE HOUSE, I'VE GOT LESS DOUGH THAN A POOR CHURCHMOUSE! BUT I SPREAD GOOD CHEER, THOUGH MY WAYS ARE STRANGE, SO MARK THIS TO CREDIT, AND KEEP THE CHANGE!
THAT MINSTREL CHARACTER CER-TAINLY BOUGHT YOUR LUTE FOR A SONG, GRANDPA!
WE-EL, WHAT'S THE DIFFERENCE...SO LONG AS HE PLANS TO USE IT FOR A GOOD PURPOSE!
BUT THE MINSTREL'S PLANS ARE FAR FROM GOOD! THAT NIGHT, AT A NEARBY JAIL...
OH, MR. WARDEN, I'VE GOT GOOD NEWS, I'VE COME TO CHASE THOSE PRI-SON BLUES. THE MINSTREL'S SONGS AND CHEER-FUL RHYMES, MAKE THE TOUGHEST MUGS RE-PENT THEIR CRIMES!
A MINSTREL, HUH? YOUR MUSIC ISN'T GOING TO SOFTEN THE TOUGH BABIES WE'VE GOT HERE!

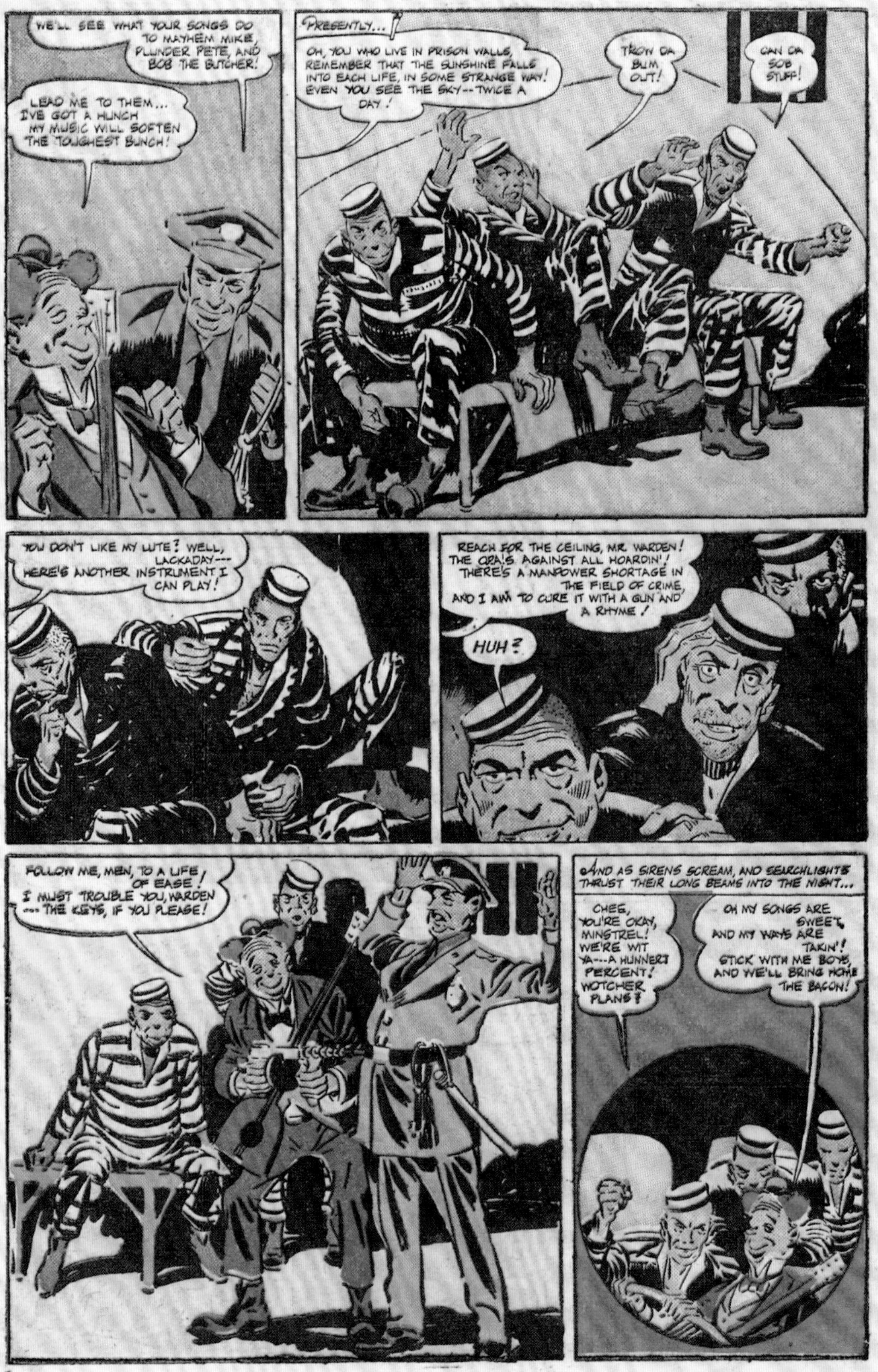
WE'LL SEE WHAT YOUR SONGS DO TO MAYHEM MIKE, PLUNDER PETE, AND BOB THE BUTCHER!
LEAD ME TO THEM... I'VE GOT A HUNCH MY MUSIC WILL SOFTEN THE TOUGHEST BUNCH!
PRESENTLY...
OH, YOU WHO LIVE IN PRISON WALLS, REMEMBER THAT THE SUNSHINE FALLS INTO EACH LIFE, IN SOME STRANGE WAY! EVEN YOU SEE THE SKY--TWICE A DAY!
TROW DA BUM OUT!
CAN DA SOB STUFF!
YOU DON'T LIKE MY LUTE? WELL, LACKADAY--- HERE'S ANOTHER INSTRUMENT I CAN PLAY!
REACH FOR THE CEILING, MR. WARDEN! THE OPA'S AGAINST ALL HOARDIN'! THERE'S A MANPOWER SHORTAGE IN THE FIELD OF CRIME, AND I AIM TO CURE IT WITH A GUN AND A RHYME!
HUH?
FOLLOW ME, MEN, TO A LIFE OF EASE! I MUST TROUBLE YOU, WARDEN --- THE KEYS, IF YOU PLEASE!
AND AS SIRENS SCREAM, AND SEARCHLIGHTS THRUST THEIR LONG BEAMS INTO THE NIGHT...
CHEE, YOU'RE OKAY, MINSTREL! WE'RE WIT YA---A HUNNERT PERCENT! WOTCHER PLANS?
OH MY SONGS ARE SWEET, AND MY WAYS ARE TAKIN'! STICK WITH ME BOYS, AND WE'LL BRING HOME THE BACON!

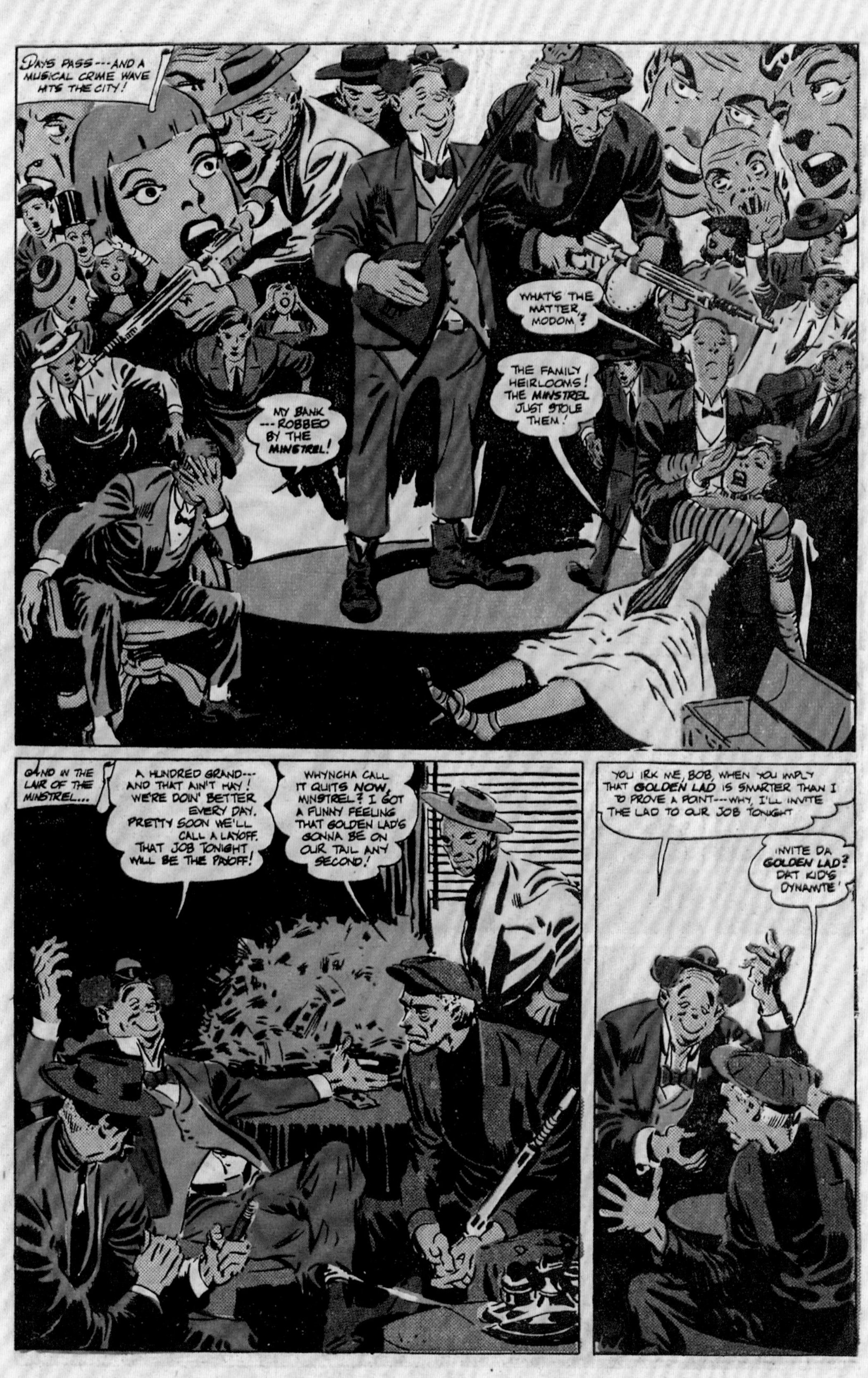
DAYS PASS---AND A MUSICAL CRIME WAVE HITS THE CITY!
WHAT'S THE MATTER, MODOM?
THE FAMILY HEIRLOOMS! THE MINSTREL JUST STOLE THEM!
MY BANK---ROBBED BY THE MINSTREL!
AND IN THE LAIR OF THE MINSTREL...
A HUNDRED GRAND---AND THAT AIN'T HAY! WE'RE DOIN' BETTER EVERY DAY. PRETTY SOON WE'LL CALL A LAYOFF. THAT JOB TONIGHT WILL BE THE PAYOFF!
WHYNCHA CALL IT QUITS NOW, MINSTREL? I GOT A FUNNY FEELING THAT GOLDEN LAD'S GONNA BE ON OUR TAIL ANY SECOND!
YOU IRK ME, BOB, WHEN YOU IMPLY THAT GOLDEN LAD IS SMARTER THAN I TO PROVE A POINT---WHY, I'LL INVITE THE LAD TO OUR JOB TONIGHT
INVITE DA GOLDEN LAD? DAT KID'S DYNAMITE!

HELLO--- DAILY SCOOP? WELL, LISTEN, MATES, AND TAKE THIS AD AT YOUR REGULAR RATES! BZBZBZBZ...
WOW! DAT'S A HOT ONE!
DA MINSTREL SURE IS A CARD! SOME INVITATION! HAW!
That NIGHT---AT GRANDPA PRESTON'S ANTIQUE SHOP...
SAY, TOMMY, DID YOU SEE THIS? THE MINSTREL HAS A MESSAGE TO GOLDEN LAD HERE!
A MESSAGE? READ IT TO ME, GRANDPA!
"TO GOLDEN LAD: TO WHERE EACH IS ANOTHER, THE MINSTREL'S EN ROUTE, BROTHER WON'T KNOW BROTHER BUT I'LL GET MY LOOT!" ... NOW WHAT IN TARNATION CAN HE MEAN BY THAT?
TO WHERE EACH IS ANOTHER...
TAKE CARE OF THE STORE, TOMMY. I'M GOIN' OUT FOR A WALK IN THE NIGHT AIR, TO SEE IF I CAN MAKE SOME SENSE OUT OF THAT RIDDLE!
OKAY, GRAND-PA!
I CAN'T FIGURE THIS OUT, BUT MAYBE GOLDEN LAD CAN!

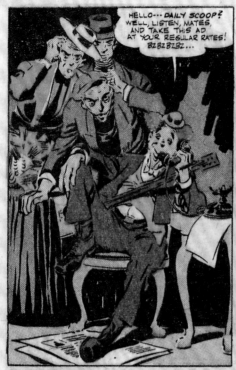

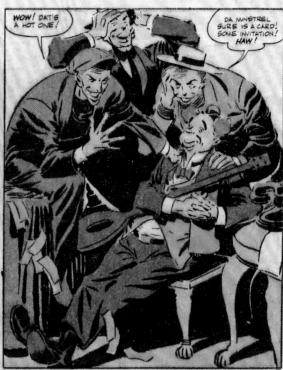

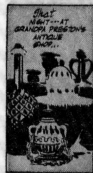

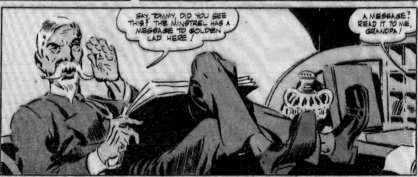

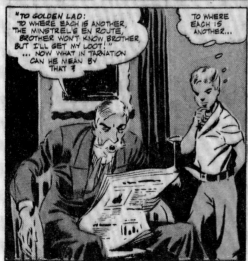

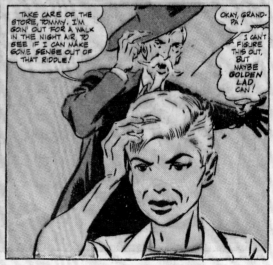

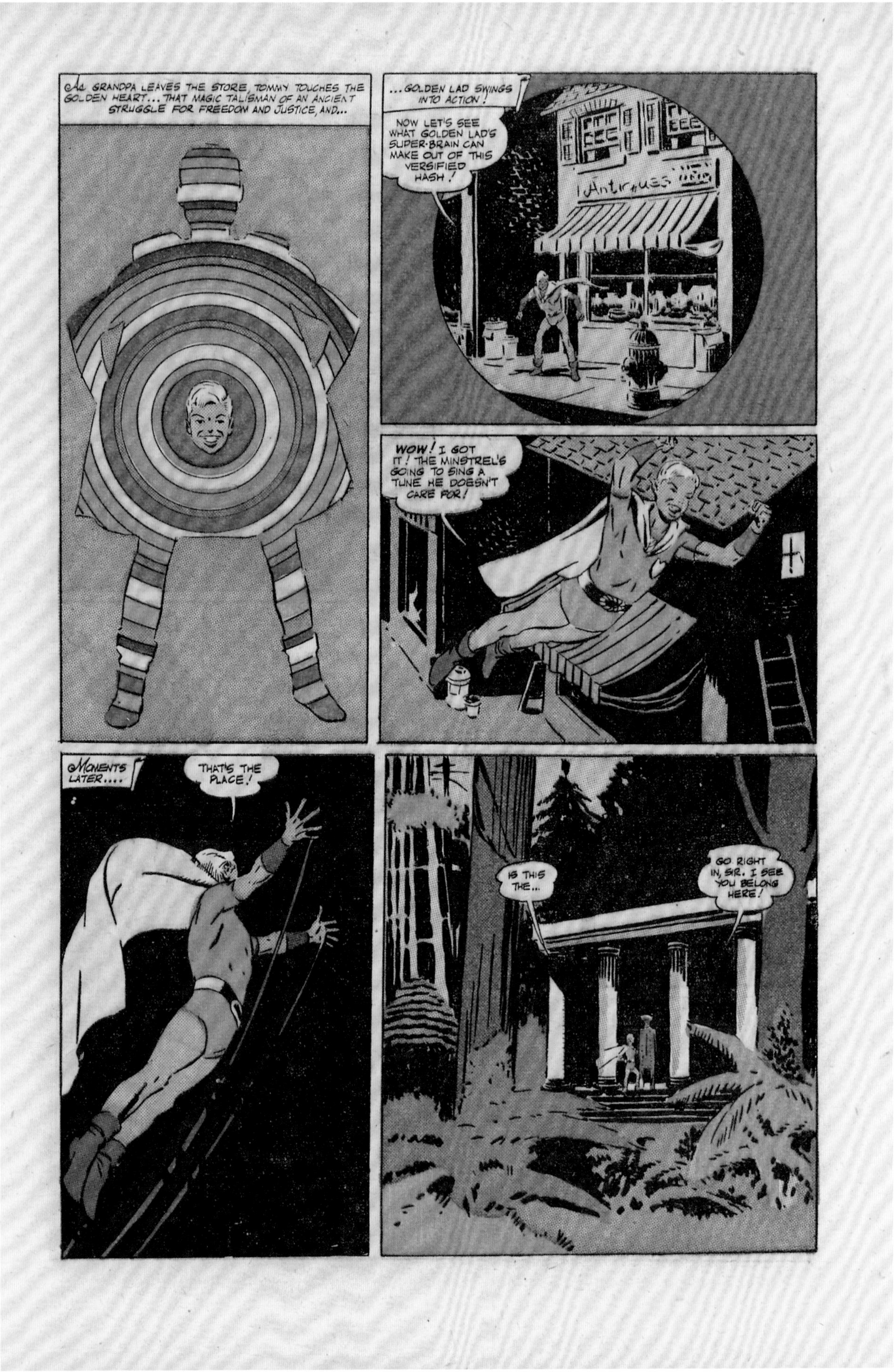
As GRANDPA LEAVES THE STORE, TOMMY TOUCHES THE GOLDEN HEART... THAT MAGIC TALISMAN OF AN ANCIENT STRUGGLE FOR FREEDOM AND JUSTICE, AND...
...GOLDEN LAD SWINGS INTO ACTION!
NOW LET'S SEE WHAT GOLDEN LAD'S SUPER-BRAIN CAN MAKE OUT OF THIS VERSIFIED HASH!
WOW! I GOT IT! THE MINSTREL'S GOING TO SING A TUNE HE DOESN'T CARE FOR!
MOMENTS LATER....
THAT'S THE PLACE!
IS THIS THE...
GO RIGHT IN, SIR. I SEE YOU BELONG HERE!

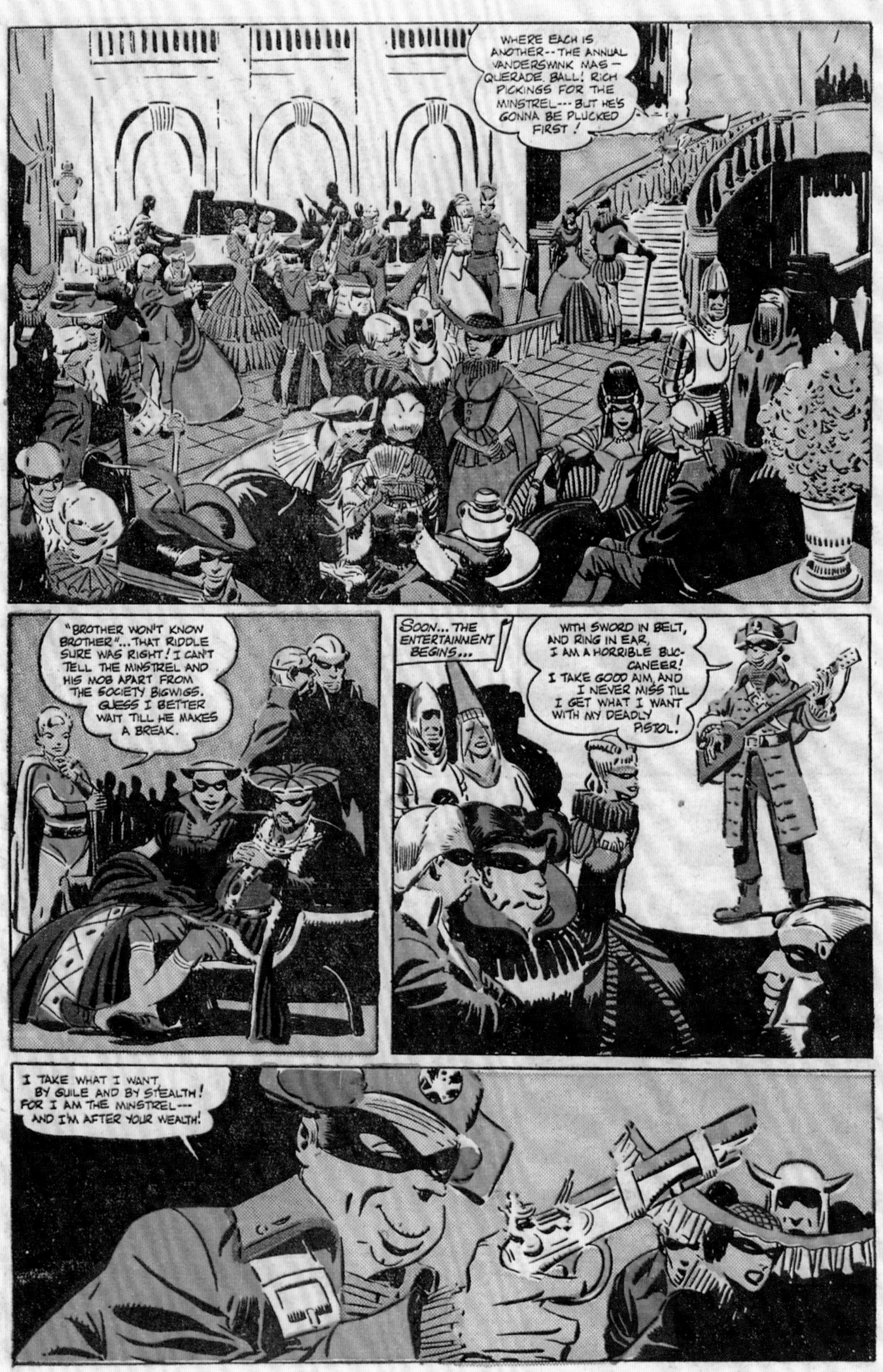
WHERE EACH IS ANOTHER-- THE ANNUAL VANDERSWINK MAS-QUERADE BALL! RICH PICKINGS FOR THE MINSTREL--- BUT HE'S GONNA BE PLUCKED FIRST!
"BROTHER WON'T KNOW BROTHER"... THAT RIDDLE SURE WAS RIGHT! I CAN'T TELL THE MINSTREL AND HIS MOB APART FROM THE SOCIETY BIGWIGS. GUESS I BETTER WAIT TILL HE MAKES A BREAK.
SOON... THE ENTERTAINMENT BEGINS...
WITH SWORD IN BELT, AND RING IN EAR, I AM A HORRIBLE BUC-CANEER! I TAKE GOOD AIM, AND I NEVER MISS TILL I GET WHAT I WANT WITH MY DEADLY PISTOL!
I TAKE WHAT I WANT, BY GUILE AND BY STEALTH! FOR I AM THE MINSTREL--- AND I'M AFTER YOUR WEALTH!

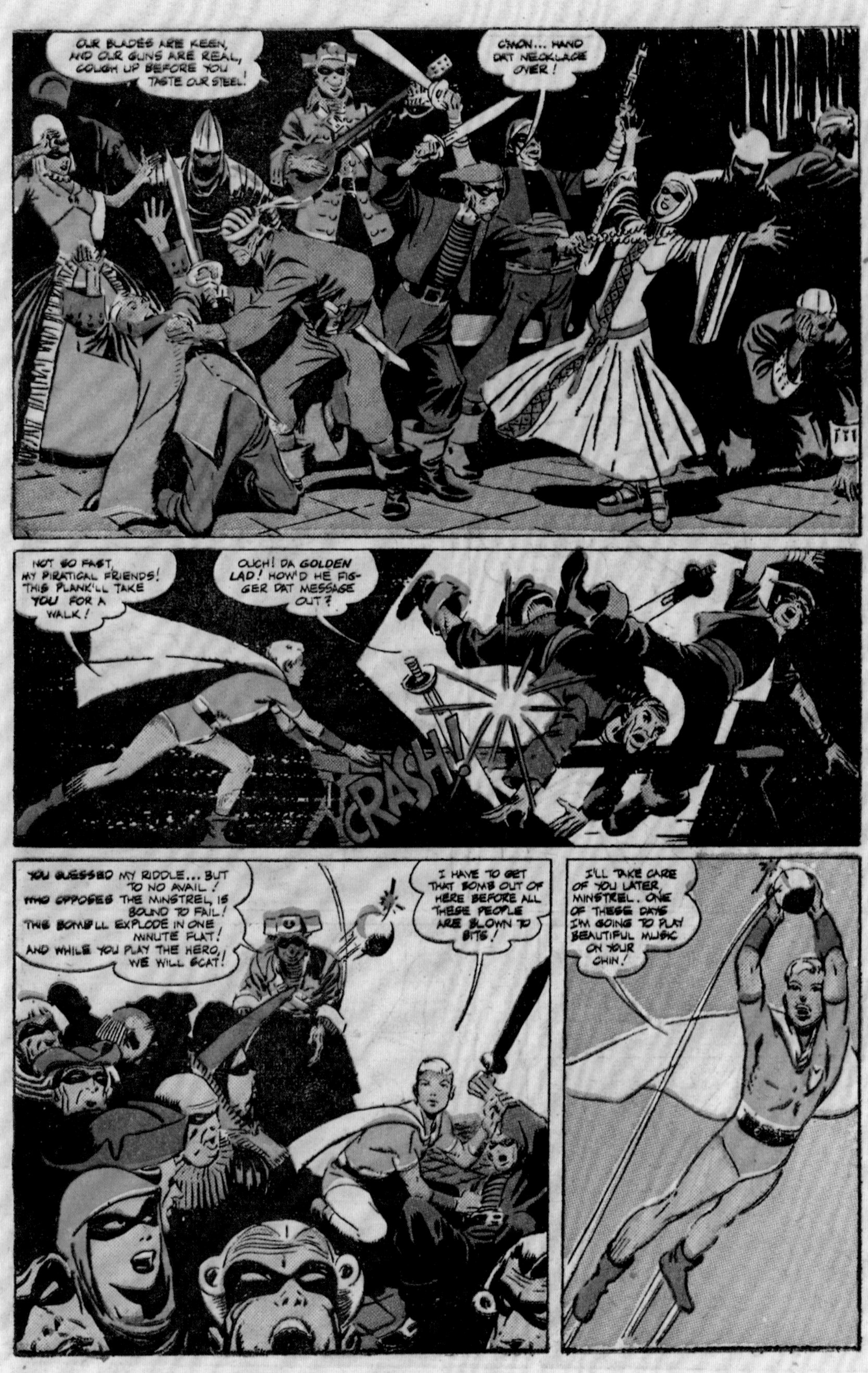
OUR BLADES ARE KEEN, AND OUR GUNS ARE REAL, COUGH UP BEFORE YOU TASTE OUR STEEL!
C'MON... HAND DAT NECKLACE OVER!
NOT SO FAST, MY PIRATICAL FRIENDS! THIS PLANK'LL TAKE YOU FOR A WALK!
OUCH! DA GOLDEN LAD! HOW'D HE FIGGER DAT MESSAGE OUT?
CRASH!
YOU GUESSED MY RIDDLE... BUT TO NO AVAIL! WHO OPPOSES THE MINSTREL, IS BOUND TO FAIL! THIS BOMB'LL EXPLODE IN ONE MINUTE FLAT! AND WHILE YOU PLAY THE HERO, WE WILL SCAT!
I HAVE TO GET THAT BOMB OUT OF HERE BEFORE ALL THESE PEOPLE ARE BLOWN TO BITS!
I'LL TAKE CARE OF YOU LATER, MINSTREL. ONE OF THESE DAYS I'M GOING TO PLAY BEAUTIFUL MUSIC ON YOUR CHIN!

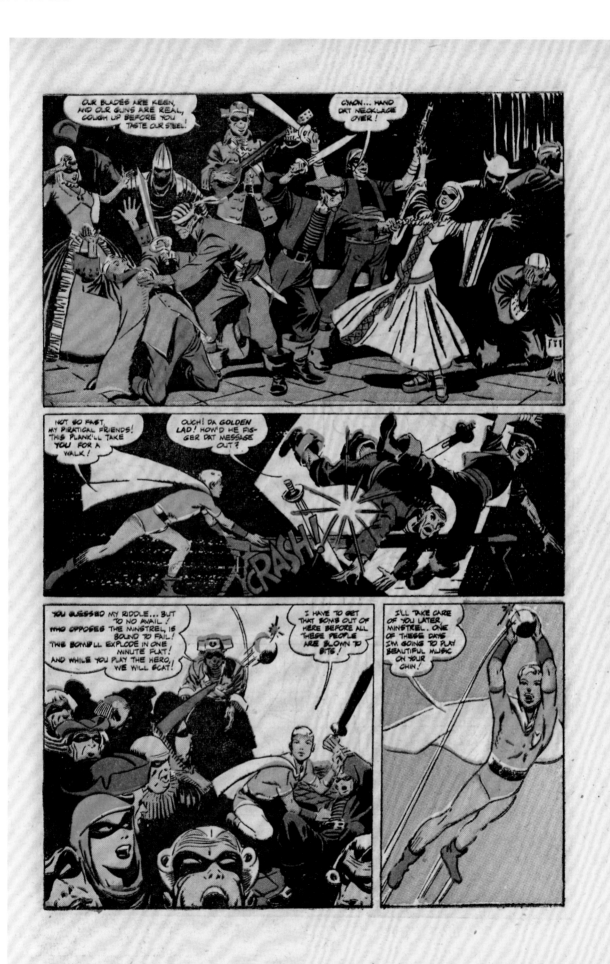

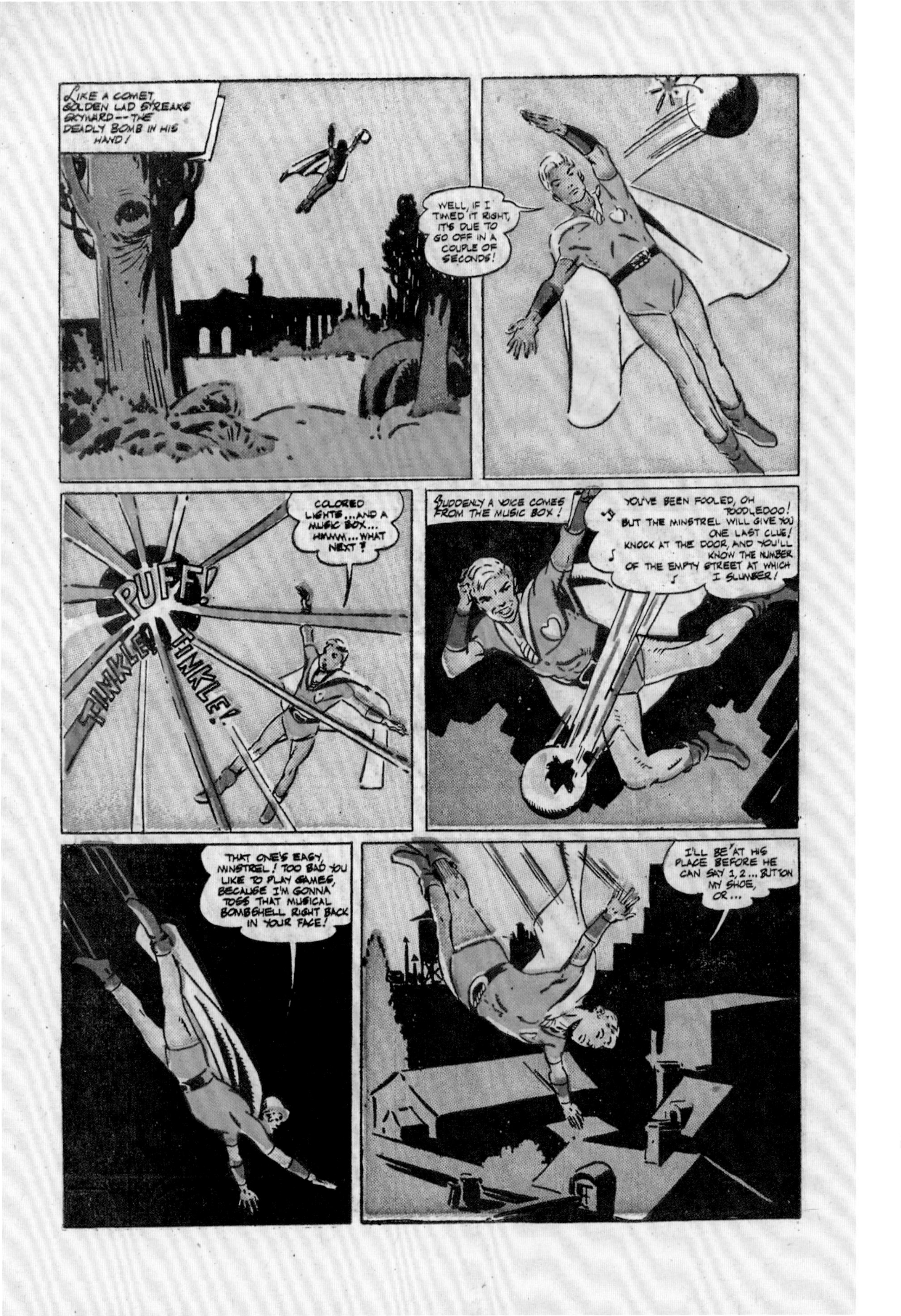
LIKE A COMET GOLDEN LAD STREAKS SKYWARD--THE DEADLY BOMB IN HIS HAND!
WELL, IF I TIMED IT RIGHT, IT'S DUE TO GO OFF IN A COUPLE OF SECONDS!
COLORED LIGHTS...AND A MUSIC BOX... HMMM...WHAT NEXT?
PUFF!
TINKLE! TINKLE!
SUDDENLY A VOICE COMES FROM THE MUSIC BOX!
YOU'VE BEEN FOOLED, OH TOODLEDOO! BUT THE MINSTREL WILL GIVE YOU ONE LAST CLUE! KNOCK AT THE DOOR, AND YOU'LL KNOW THE NUMBER OF THE EMPTY STREET AT WHICH I SLUMBER!
THAT ONE'S EASY, MINSTREL! TOO BAD YOU LIKE TO PLAY GAMES, BECAUSE I'M GONNA TOSS THAT MUSICAL BOMBSHELL RIGHT BACK IN YOUR FACE!
I'LL BE AT HIS PLACE BEFORE HE CAN SAY 1, 2... BUTTON MY SHOE, OR...

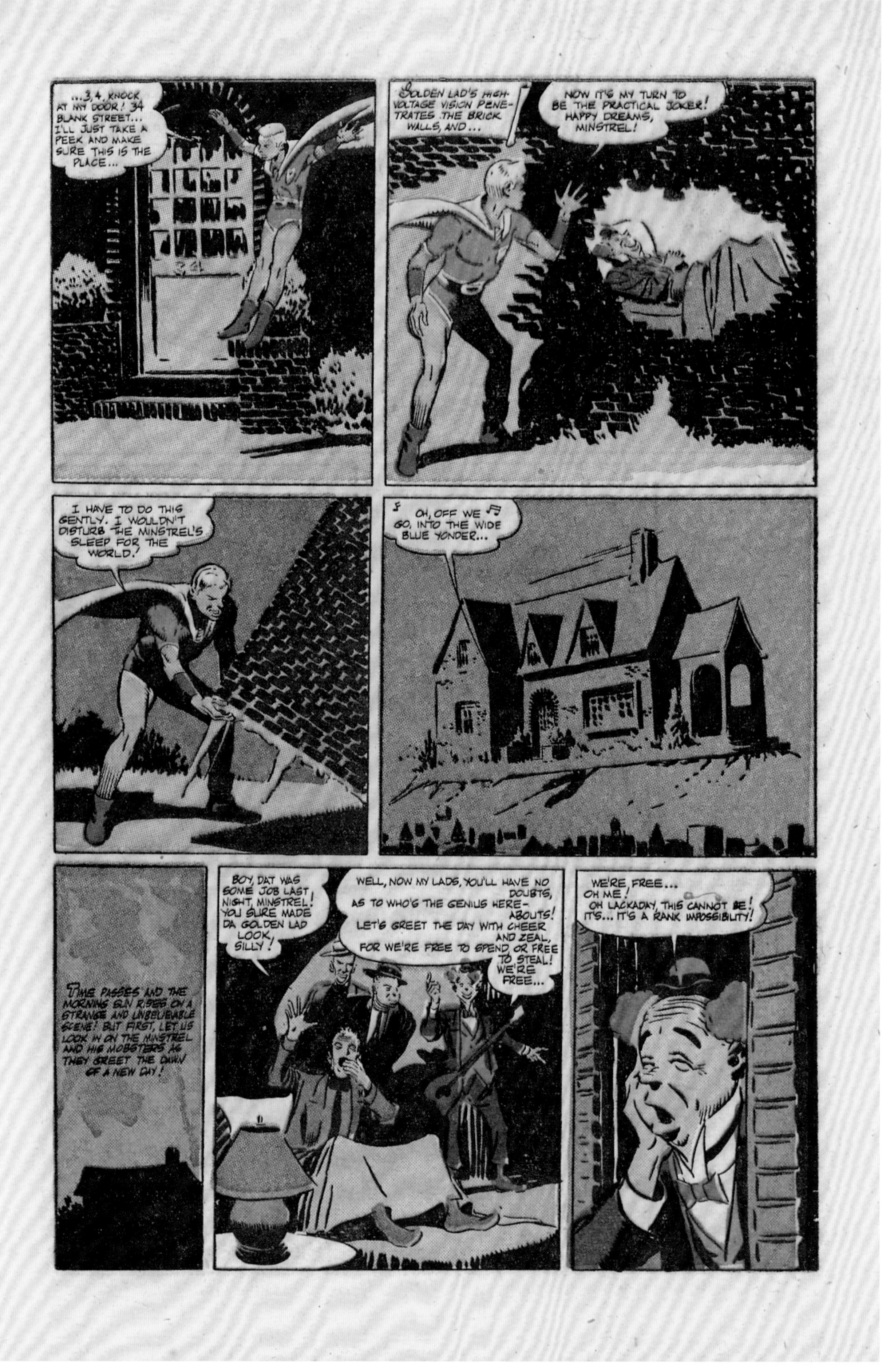
...3, 4, KNOCK AT MY DOOR! 34 BLANK STREET... I'LL JUST TAKE A PEEK AND MAKE SURE THIS IS THE PLACE...
GOLDEN LAD'S HIGH-VOLTAGE VISION PENE-TRATES THE BRICK WALLS, AND...
NOW IT'S MY TURN TO BE THE PRACTICAL JOKER! HAPPY DREAMS, MINSTREL!
I HAVE TO DO THIS GENTLY. I WOULDN'T DISTURB THE MINSTREL'S SLEEP FOR THE WORLD!
OH, OFF WE GO, INTO THE WIDE BLUE YONDER...
TIME PASSES AND THE MORNING SUN RISES ON A STRANGE AND UNBELIEVABLE SCENE! BUT FIRST, LET US LOOK IN ON THE MINSTREL AND HIS MOBSTERS AS THEY GREET THE DAWN OF A NEW DAY!
BOY, DAT WAS SOME JOB LAST NIGHT, MINSTREL! YOU SURE MADE DA GOLDEN LAD LOOK SILLY!
WELL, NOW MY LADS, YOU'LL HAVE NO DOUBTS, AS TO WHO'S THE GENIUS HERE-ABOUTS! LET'S GREET THE DAY WITH CHEER AND ZEAL, FOR WE'RE FREE TO SPEND OR FREE TO STEAL! WE'RE FREE...
WE'RE FREE... OH ME! OH LACKADAY, THIS CANNOT BE! IT'S... IT'S A RANK IMPOSSIBILITY!

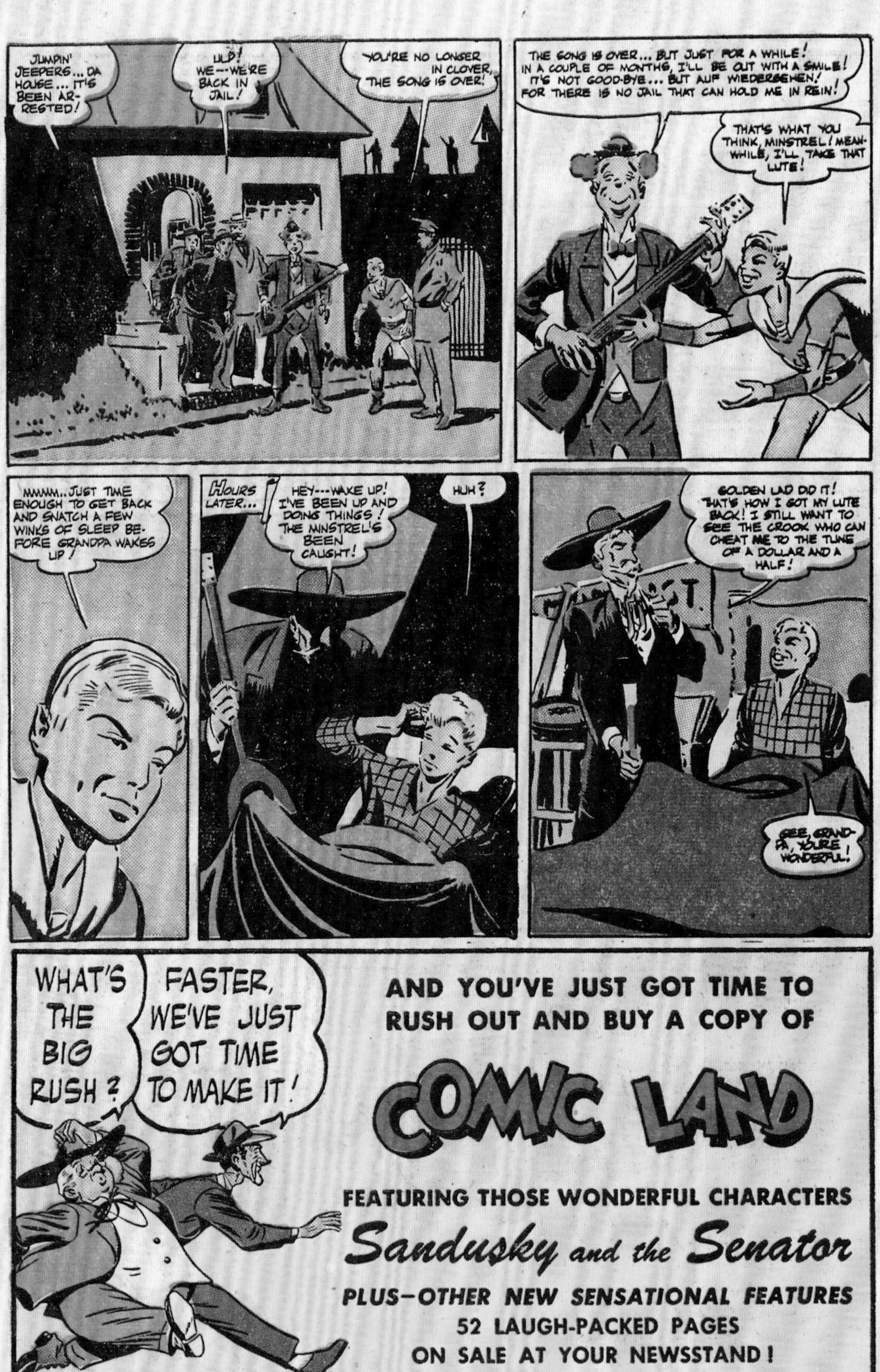
JUMPIN' JEEPERS... DA HOUSE... IT'S BEEN AR-RESTED!
ULP! WE--WE'RE BACK IN JAIL!
YOU'RE NO LONGER IN CLOVER, THE SONG IS OVER!
THE SONG IS OVER... BUT JUST FOR A WHILE! IN A COUPLE OF MONTHS, I'LL BE OUT WITH A SMILE! IT'S NOT GOOD-BYE... BUT AUF WIEDERSEHEN! FOR THERE IS NO JAIL THAT CAN HOLD ME IN REIN!
THAT'S WHAT YOU THINK, MINSTREL! MEAN-WHILE, I'LL TAKE THAT LUTE!
MMMM.. JUST TIME ENOUGH TO GET BACK AND SNATCH A FEW WINKS OF SLEEP BE-FORE GRANDPA WAKES UP!
HOURS LATER...
HEY---WAKE UP! I'VE BEEN UP AND DOING THINGS! THE MINSTREL'S BEEN CAUGHT!
HUH?
GOLDEN LAD DID IT! THAT'S HOW I GOT MY LUTE BACK! I STILL WANT TO SEE THE CROOK WHO CAN CHEAT ME TO THE TUNE OF A DOLLAR AND A HALF!
GEE, GRAND-PA, YOU'RE WONDERFUL!
WHAT'S THE BIG RUSH?
FASTER, WE'VE JUST GOT TIME TO MAKE IT!
AND YOU'VE JUST GOT TIME TO RUSH OUT AND BUY A COPY OF
COMIC LAND
FEATURING THOSE WONDERFUL CHARACTERS
Sandusky and the Senator
PLUS—OTHER NEW SENSATIONAL FEATURES
52 LAUGH-PACKED PAGES
ON SALE AT YOUR NEWSSTAND!

SAM J. GLANZMAN

(b. 1924)

Kona, first published in 1962, was part of a spate of jungle-themed hero comics that appeared, loincloth at the ready, in the early 1960s. Written at first by Don Segall and soon after by Sam Glanzman, *Kona* had an extra layer of angst and near-psychedelic visuals that set it apart from the rest of the jungle men.

When *Kona* was published, Sam Glanzman was already a longtime comic book artist and illustrator. Born in Baltimore and raised in Virginia and Long Island, he began drawing comic books in 1941 with the obscure *Fly-Man* for Harvey Comics. Glanzman bounced around between a few other publishers until enlisting in the army in 1942. Upon his return he bartended and worked in a factory for Republic Aviation, installing machine guns. He returned to comics in the late 1950s and landed at Dell on a variety of different titles. The standout remains *Kona*.

Ostensibly the story of a family—Dr. Henry Dodd, his daughter, Mary, and her two children—who are marooned on a fantastic island, in Glanzman's hands the title turned into a study of the white-haired Kona, a somewhat anguished and highly moral Neanderthal. Working first with writer Don Segall and then with his editor, the artist L. B. Cole (who also edited John Stanley's *Tales from the Tomb)*, Glanzman created visceral, gripping stories of near constant danger marked by Kona's attempts to protect the Dodds from the mythical beasts that ruled the island. Glanzman created pages, he noted, "that would hold the reader's eye as single compositions; I didn't want the reader to ever glance off the page." This translated into page designs that usually neglected a panel grid in favor of panels or scenarios inset in larger drawings. Glanzman's figures are in constant motion, running, fighting, falling—there is hardly room for a reader to take a breath. Working from "stick figure" pencils, Glanzman rendered his illustrations mostly in ink, which further increased the urgency of the imagery. Glanzman's dialogue here and in his later war stories is marked by lyrical passages such as "Nobody wins wars . . .

like these!" and "What guarantee do we have that to the animal kingdom . . . 'Man' is not regarded as the most hideous of all forms? The most bestial?" This pulp philosophizing in concert with frequent full-page drawings amplifies the drama, making the action and danger palpable. With *Kona*, Glanzman imbued a hackneyed genre with real life, and gave comics an unforgettable protagonist.

Kona ran twenty-one issues before being cancelled in 1967. Glanzman then moved on to DC Comics, for which he began a long run of war comics acclaimed for their emotional content, hard-edged realism, and highly personal insights. These stories made Glanzman a hero to a generation of comics enthusiasts. He published four graphic novels in the 1980s and continued drawing comics into the 1990s. Now retired, he lives in upstate New York with his wife. On his life as a cartoonist, Glanzman noted, "It isn't much different than when I worked at Republic Aviation, except that I can sleep late and take as many days off as I want."

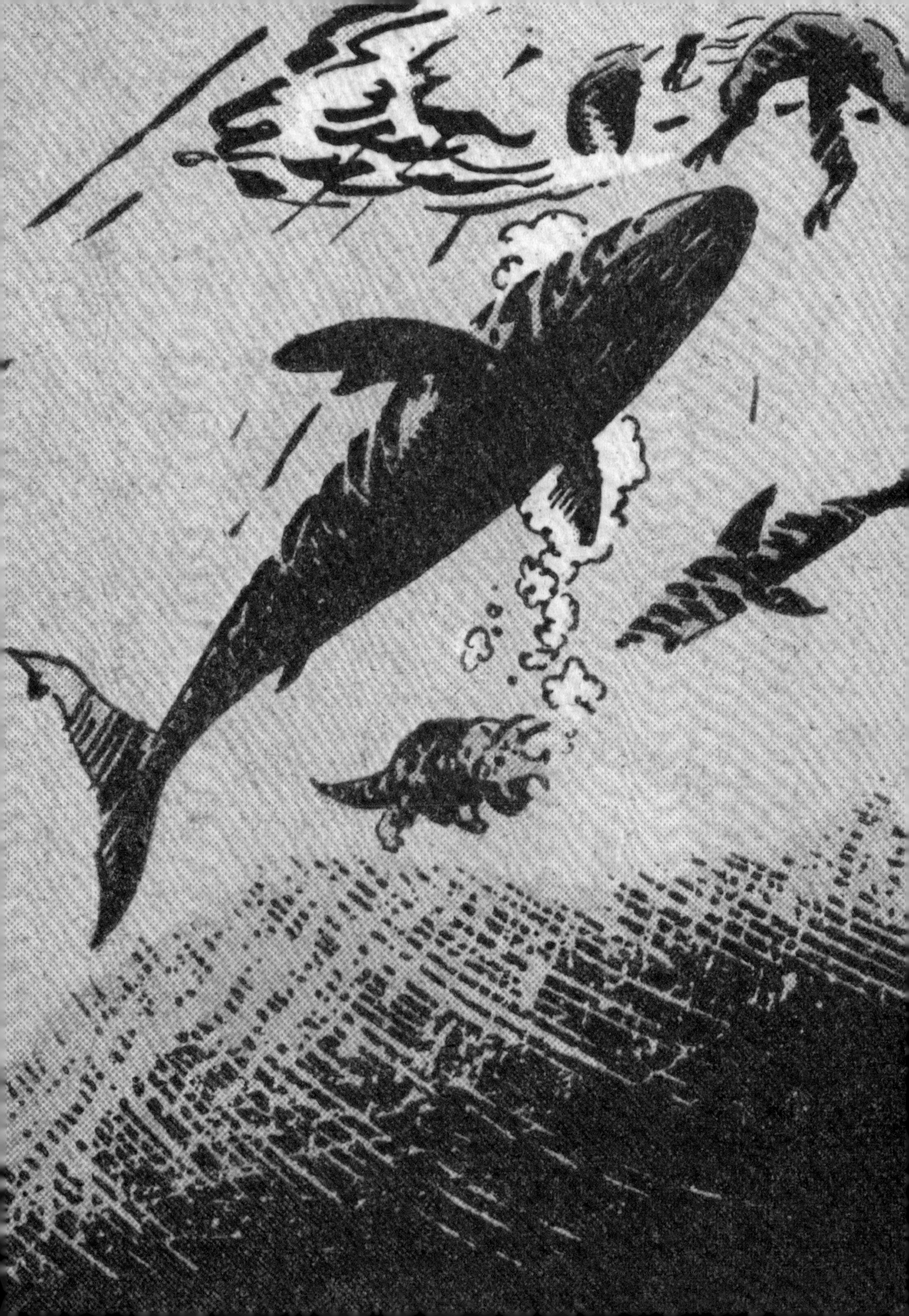

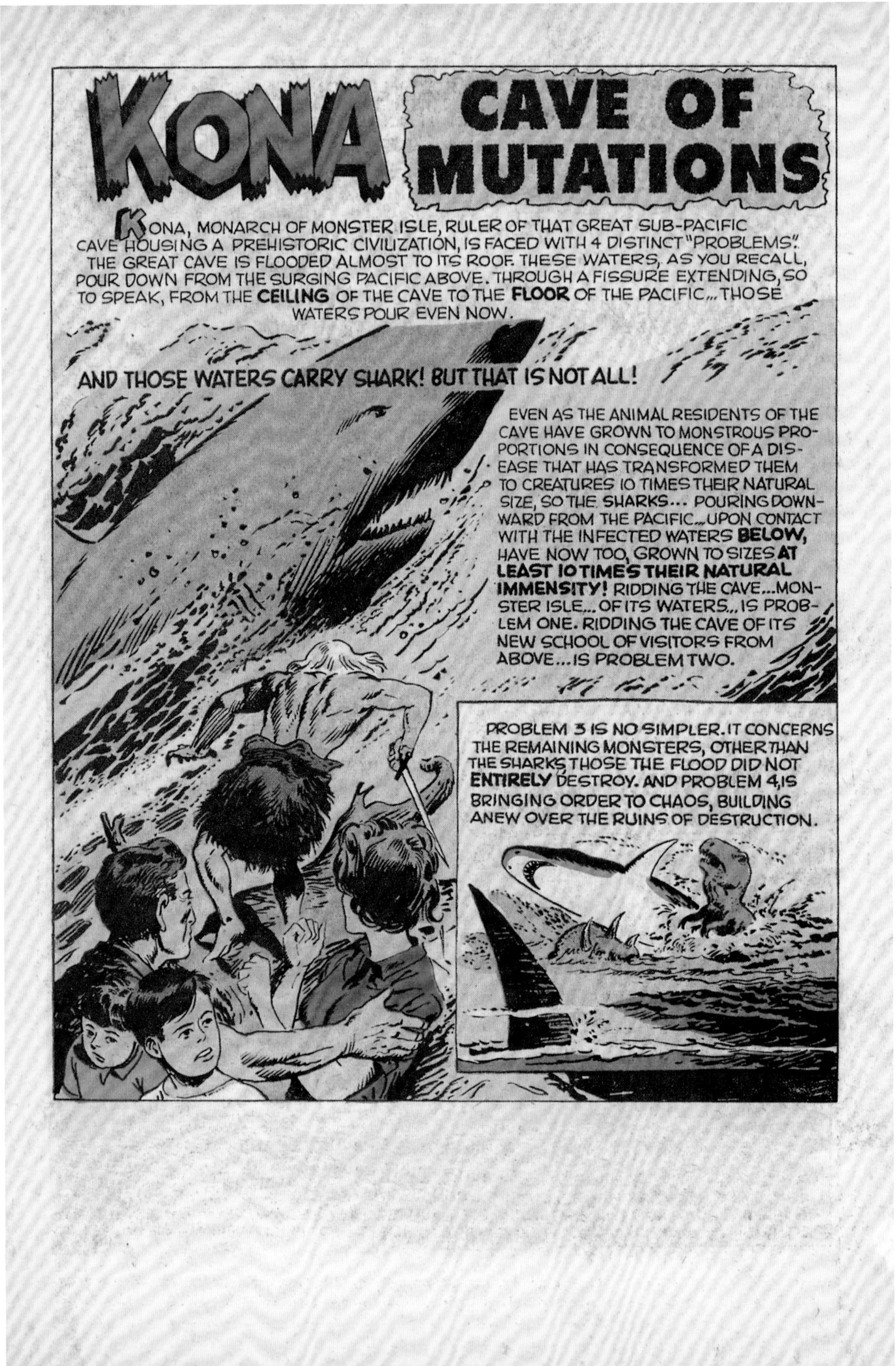
KONA
CAVE OF MUTATIONS
KONA, MONARCH OF MONSTER ISLE, RULER OF THAT GREAT SUB-PACIFIC CAVE HOUSING A PREHISTORIC CIVILIZATION, IS FACED WITH 4 DISTINCT "PROBLEMS". THE GREAT CAVE IS FLOODED ALMOST TO ITS ROOF. THESE WATERS, AS YOU RECALL, POUR DOWN FROM THE SURGING PACIFIC ABOVE. THROUGH A FISSURE EXTENDING, SO TO SPEAK, FROM THE CEILING OF THE CAVE TO THE FLOOR OF THE PACIFIC... THOSE WATERS POUR EVEN NOW.
AND THOSE WATERS CARRY SHARK! BUT THAT IS NOT ALL!
EVEN AS THE ANIMAL RESIDENTS OF THE CAVE HAVE GROWN TO MONSTROUS PROPORTIONS IN CONSEQUENCE OF A DISEASE THAT HAS TRANSFORMED THEM TO CREATURES 10 TIMES THEIR NATURAL SIZE, SO THE SHARKS... POURING DOWNWARD FROM THE PACIFIC... UPON CONTACT WITH THE INFECTED WATERS BELOW, HAVE NOW TOO, GROWN TO SIZES AT LEAST 10 TIMES THEIR NATURAL IMMENSITY! RIDDING THE CAVE... MONSTER ISLE... OF ITS WATERS... IS PROBLEM ONE. RIDDING THE CAVE OF ITS NEW SCHOOL OF VISITORS FROM ABOVE... IS PROBLEM TWO.
PROBLEM 3 IS NO SIMPLER. IT CONCERNS THE REMAINING MONSTERS, OTHER THAN THE SHARKS, THOSE THE FLOOD DID NOT ENTIRELY DESTROY. AND PROBLEM 4, IS BRINGING ORDER TO CHAOS, BUILDING ANEW OVER THE RUINS OF DESTRUCTION.

Kona no. 3 (1962)

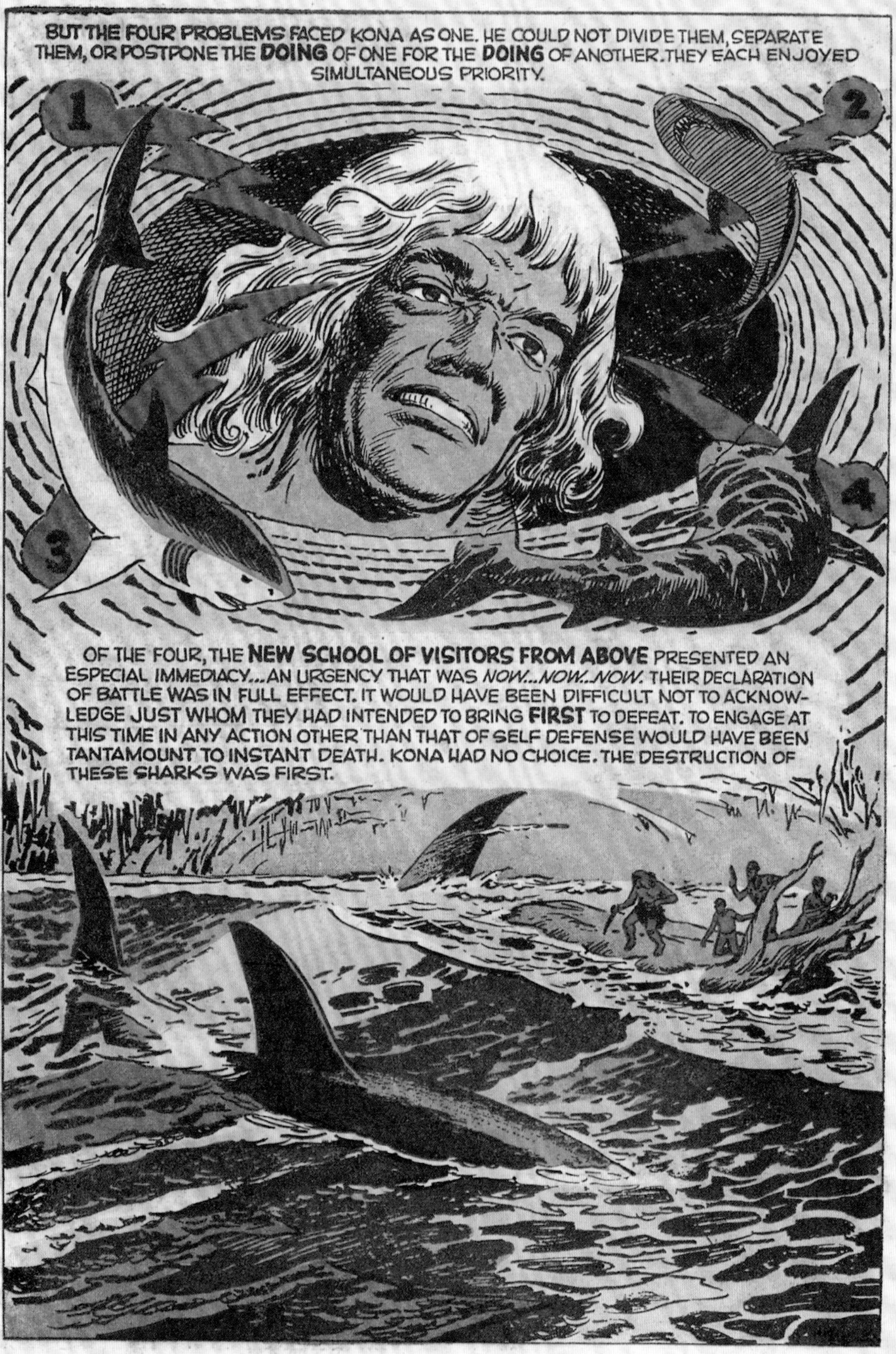
BUT THE FOUR PROBLEMS FACED KONA AS ONE. HE COULD NOT DIVIDE THEM, SEPARATE THEM, OR POSTPONE THE DOING OF ONE FOR THE DOING OF ANOTHER. THEY EACH ENJOYED SIMULTANEOUS PRIORITY.
1
2
3
4
OF THE FOUR, THE NEW SCHOOL OF VISITORS FROM ABOVE PRESENTED AN ESPECIAL IMMEDIACY... AN URGENCY THAT WAS NOW...NOW...NOW. THEIR DECLARATION OF BATTLE WAS IN FULL EFFECT. IT WOULD HAVE BEEN DIFFICULT NOT TO ACKNOWLEDGE JUST WHOM THEY HAD INTENDED TO BRING FIRST TO DEFEAT. TO ENGAGE AT THIS TIME IN ANY ACTION OTHER THAN THAT OF SELF DEFENSE WOULD HAVE BEEN TANTAMOUNT TO INSTANT DEATH. KONA HAD NO CHOICE. THE DESTRUCTION OF THESE SHARKS WAS FIRST.

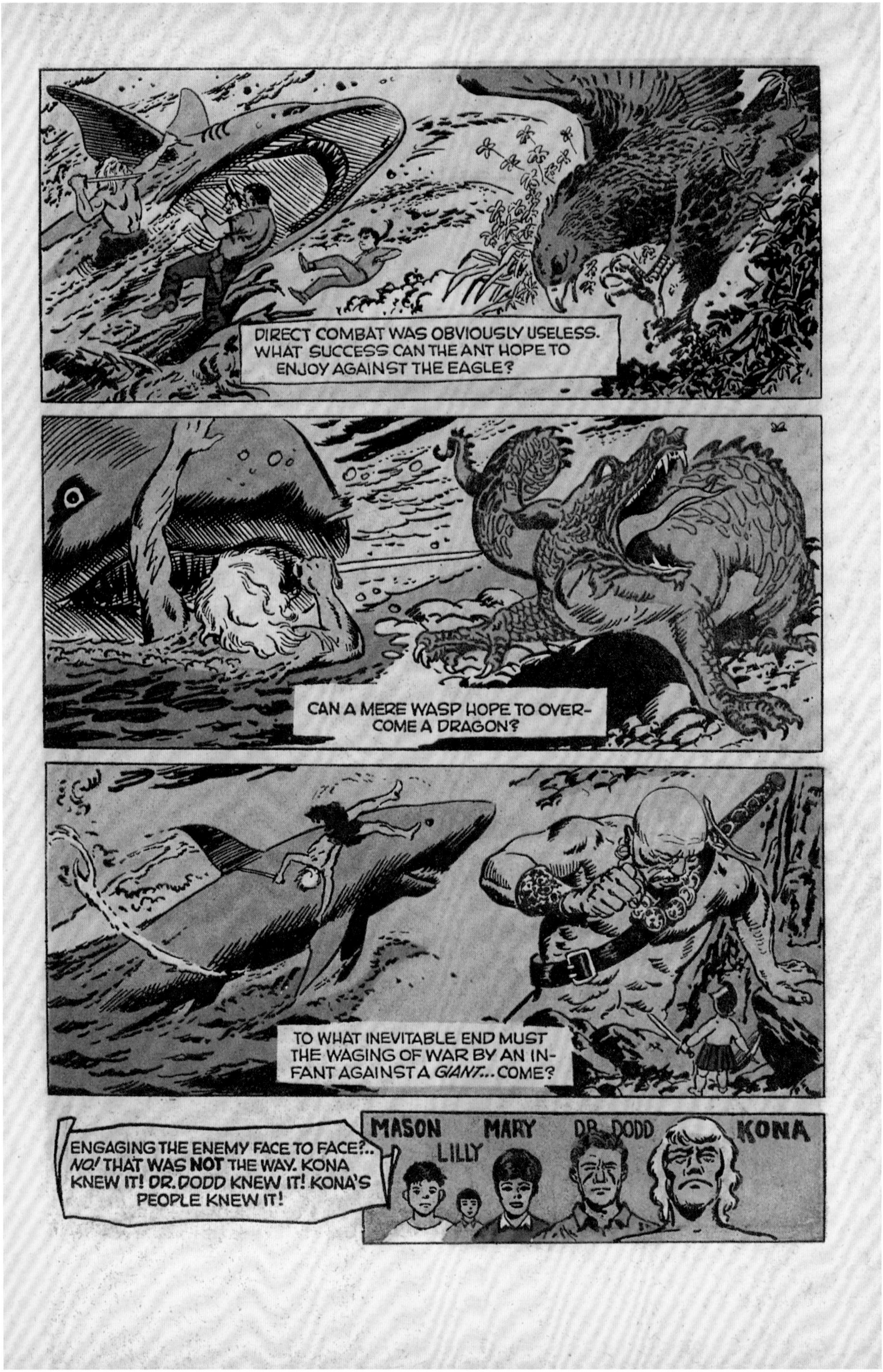
DIRECT COMBAT WAS OBVIOUSLY USELESS. WHAT SUCCESS CAN THE ANT HOPE TO ENJOY AGAINST THE EAGLE?
CAN A MERE WASP HOPE TO OVER-COME A DRAGON?
TO WHAT INEVITABLE END MUST THE WAGING OF WAR BY AN IN-FANT AGAINST A *GIANT*... COME?
ENGAGING THE ENEMY FACE TO FACE?.. *NO!* THAT WAS **NOT** THE WAY. KONA KNEW IT! DR. DODD KNEW IT! KONA'S PEOPLE KNEW IT!
MASON
LILLY
MARY
DR. DODD
KONA

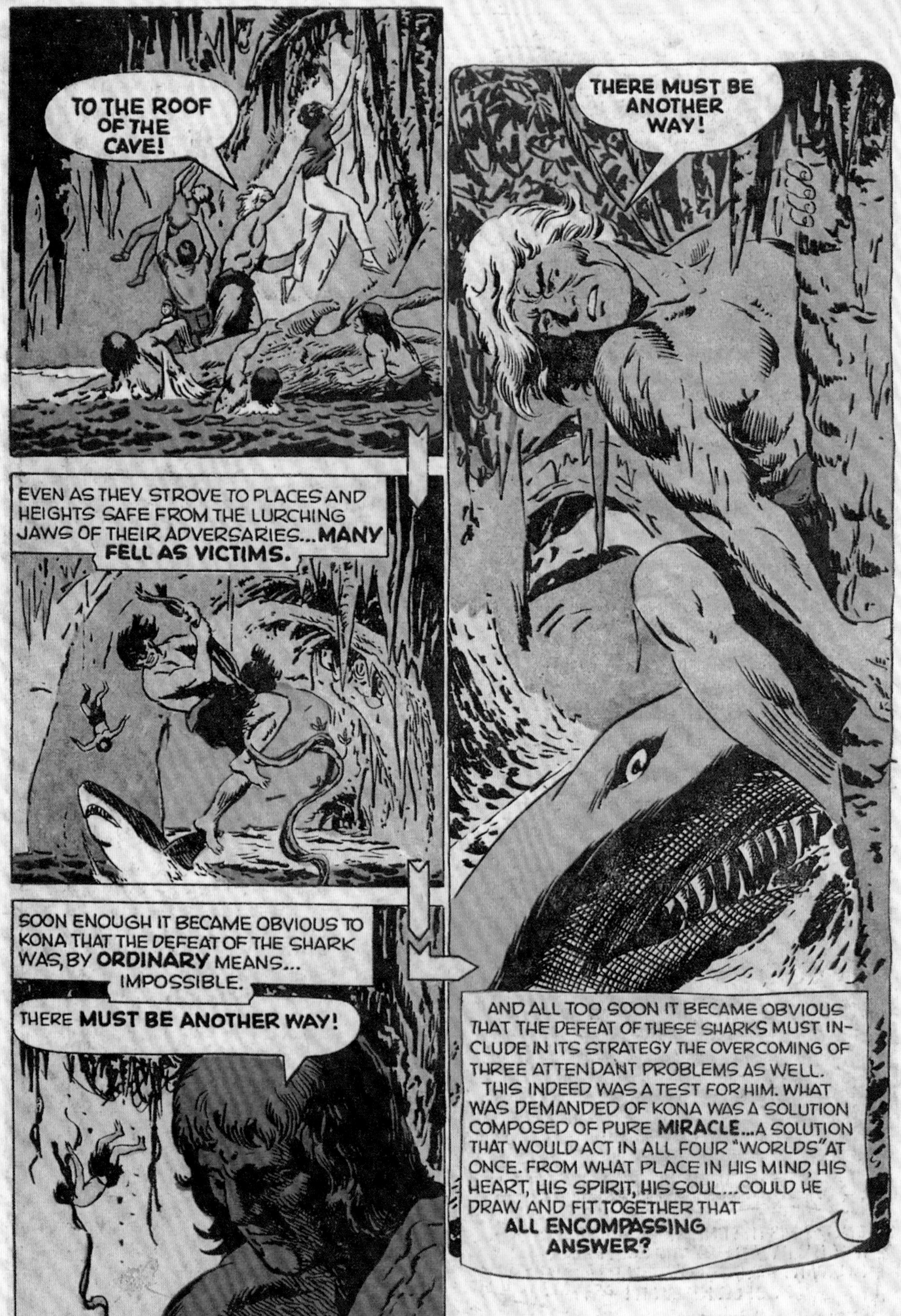
TO THE ROOF OF THE CAVE!
EVEN AS THEY STROVE TO PLACES AND HEIGHTS SAFE FROM THE LURCHING JAWS OF THEIR ADVERSARIES... MANY FELL AS VICTIMS.
SOON ENOUGH IT BECAME OBVIOUS TO KONA THAT THE DEFEAT OF THE SHARK WAS, BY ORDINARY MEANS... IMPOSSIBLE.
THERE MUST BE ANOTHER WAY!
THERE MUST BE ANOTHER WAY!
AND ALL TOO SOON IT BECAME OBVIOUS THAT THE DEFEAT OF THESE SHARKS MUST INCLUDE IN ITS STRATEGY THE OVERCOMING OF THREE ATTENDANT PROBLEMS AS WELL.
THIS INDEED WAS A TEST FOR HIM. WHAT WAS DEMANDED OF KONA WAS A SOLUTION COMPOSED OF PURE MIRACLE... A SOLUTION THAT WOULD ACT IN ALL FOUR "WORLDS" AT ONCE. FROM WHAT PLACE IN HIS MIND, HIS HEART, HIS SPIRIT, HIS SOUL... COULD HE DRAW AND FIT TOGETHER THAT ALL ENCOMPASSING ANSWER?

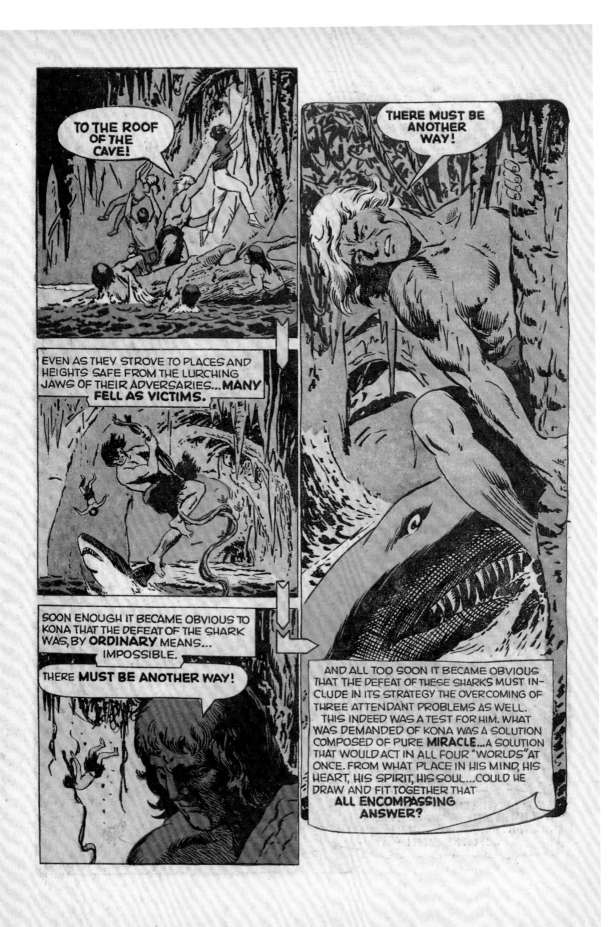

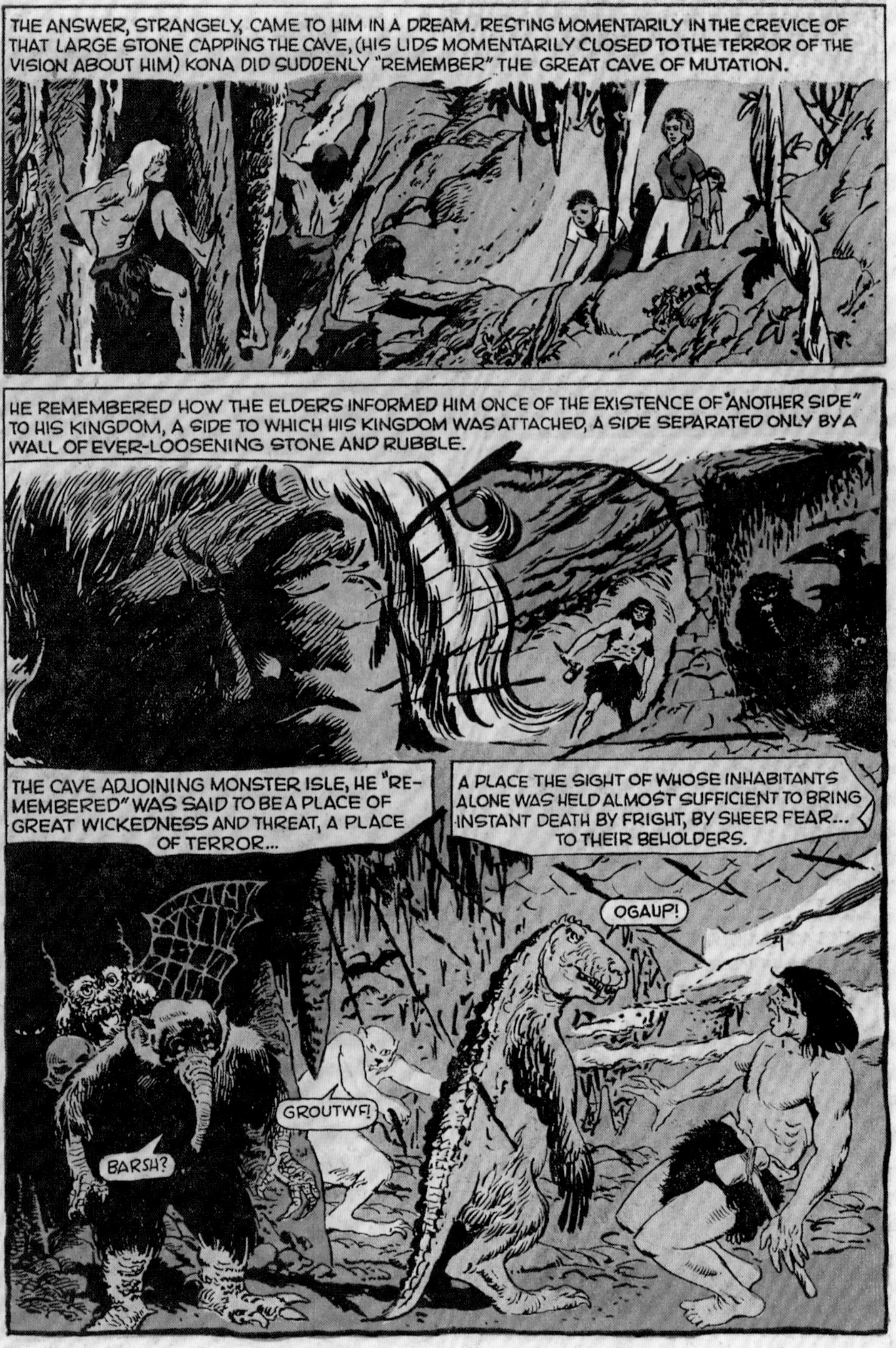
THE ANSWER, STRANGELY, CAME TO HIM IN A DREAM. RESTING MOMENTARILY IN THE CREVICE OF THAT LARGE STONE CAPPING THE CAVE, (HIS LIDS MOMENTARILY CLOSED TO THE TERROR OF THE VISION ABOUT HIM) KONA DID SUDDENLY "REMEMBER" THE GREAT CAVE OF MUTATION.
HE REMEMBERED HOW THE ELDERS INFORMED HIM ONCE OF THE EXISTENCE OF "ANOTHER SIDE" TO HIS KINGDOM, A SIDE TO WHICH HIS KINGDOM WAS ATTACHED, A SIDE SEPARATED ONLY BY A WALL OF EVER-LOOSENING STONE AND RUBBLE.
THE CAVE ADJOINING MONSTER ISLE, HE "REMEMBERED" WAS SAID TO BE A PLACE OF GREAT WICKEDNESS AND THREAT, A PLACE OF TERROR...
A PLACE THE SIGHT OF WHOSE INHABITANTS ALONE WAS HELD ALMOST SUFFICIENT TO BRING INSTANT DEATH BY FRIGHT, BY SHEER FEAR... TO THEIR BEHOLDERS.
OGAUP!
GROUTWF!
BARSH?

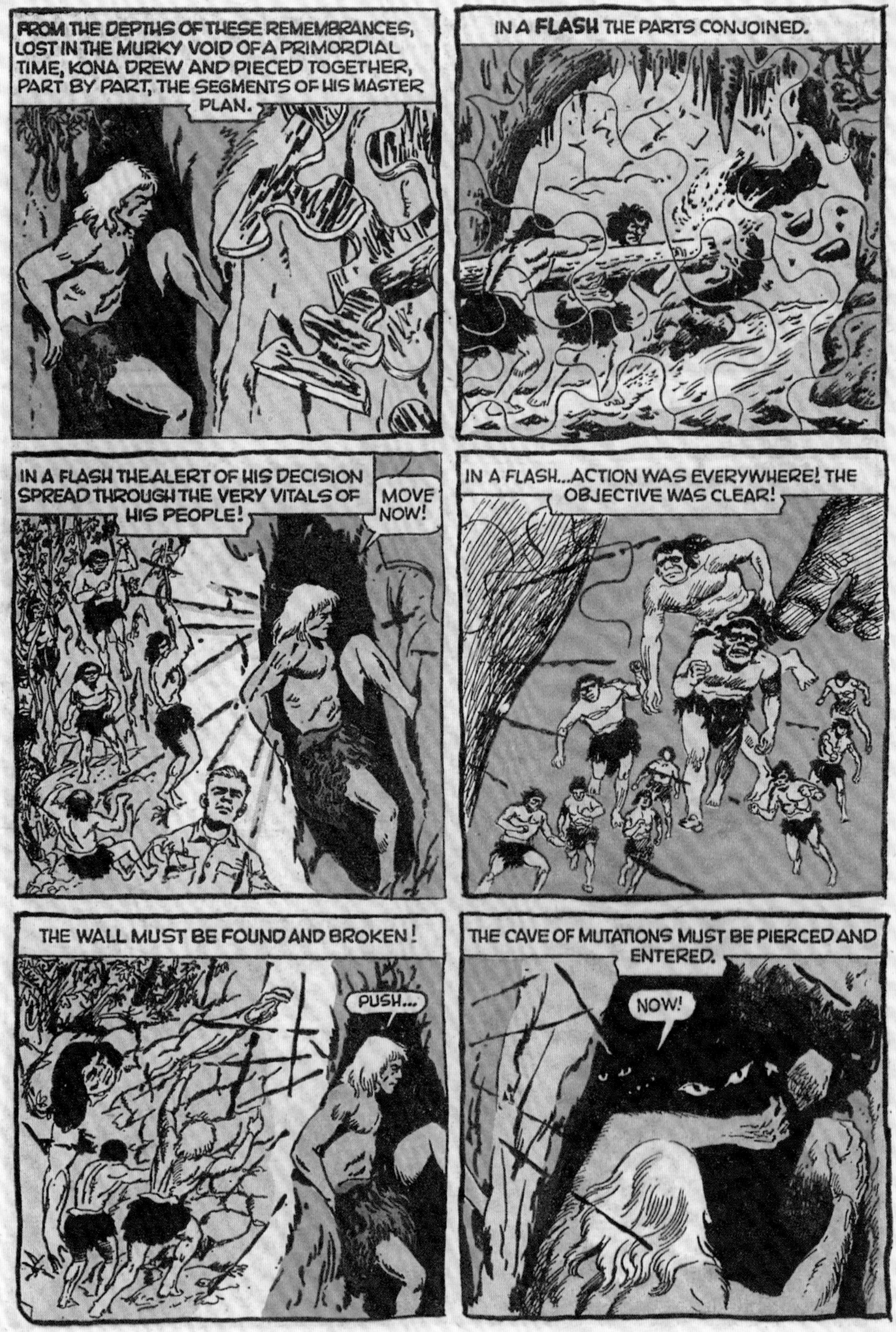
FROM THE DEPTHS OF THESE REMEMBRANCES, LOST IN THE MURKY VOID OF A PRIMORDIAL TIME, KONA DREW AND PIECED TOGETHER, PART BY PART, THE SEGMENTS OF HIS MASTER PLAN.
IN A FLASH THE PARTS CONJOINED.
IN A FLASH THE ALERT OF HIS DECISION SPREAD THROUGH THE VERY VITALS OF HIS PEOPLE!
MOVE NOW!
IN A FLASH...ACTION WAS EVERYWHERE! THE OBJECTIVE WAS CLEAR!
THE WALL MUST BE FOUND AND BROKEN!
PUSH...
THE CAVE OF MUTATIONS MUST BE PIERCED AND ENTERED.
NOW!

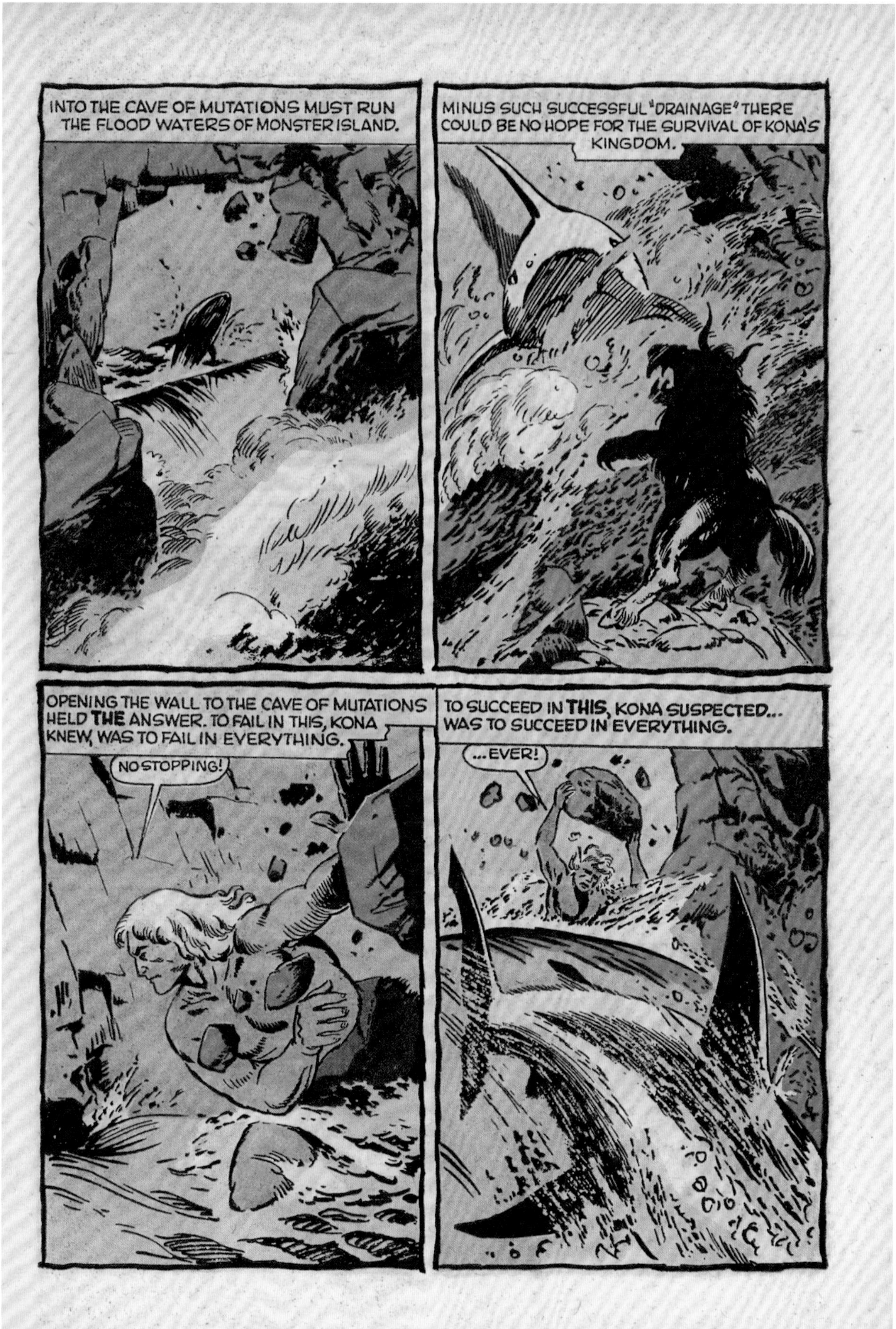
INTO THE CAVE OF MUTATIONS MUST RUN THE FLOOD WATERS OF MONSTER ISLAND.
MINUS SUCH SUCCESSFUL "DRAINAGE" THERE COULD BE NO HOPE FOR THE SURVIVAL OF KONA'S KINGDOM.
OPENING THE WALL TO THE CAVE OF MUTATIONS HELD THE ANSWER. TO FAIL IN THIS, KONA KNEW, WAS TO FAIL IN EVERYTHING.
NO STOPPING!
TO SUCCEED IN THIS, KONA SUSPECTED... WAS TO SUCCEED IN EVERYTHING.
...EVER!

NOT ONLY WOULD THE BREAKING OF THAT WALL EFFECT THE DRAINAGE OF THE FLOOD WATERS...
BUT IT MIGHT BRING RIDDANCE TO THE SCHOOL OF VISITORS FROM ABOVE.

FORCE EXIT..

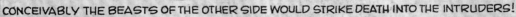

CONCEIVABLY THE BEASTS OF THE OTHER SIDE WOULD STRIKE DEATH INTO THE INTRUDERS!

...WIDE OPEN!

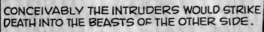

CONCEIVABLY THE INTRUDERS WOULD STRIKE DEATH INTO THE BEASTS OF THE OTHER SIDE.

CONCEIVABLY EACH WOULD DESTROY EACH.

SCALES OF DEATH IN BALANCE!

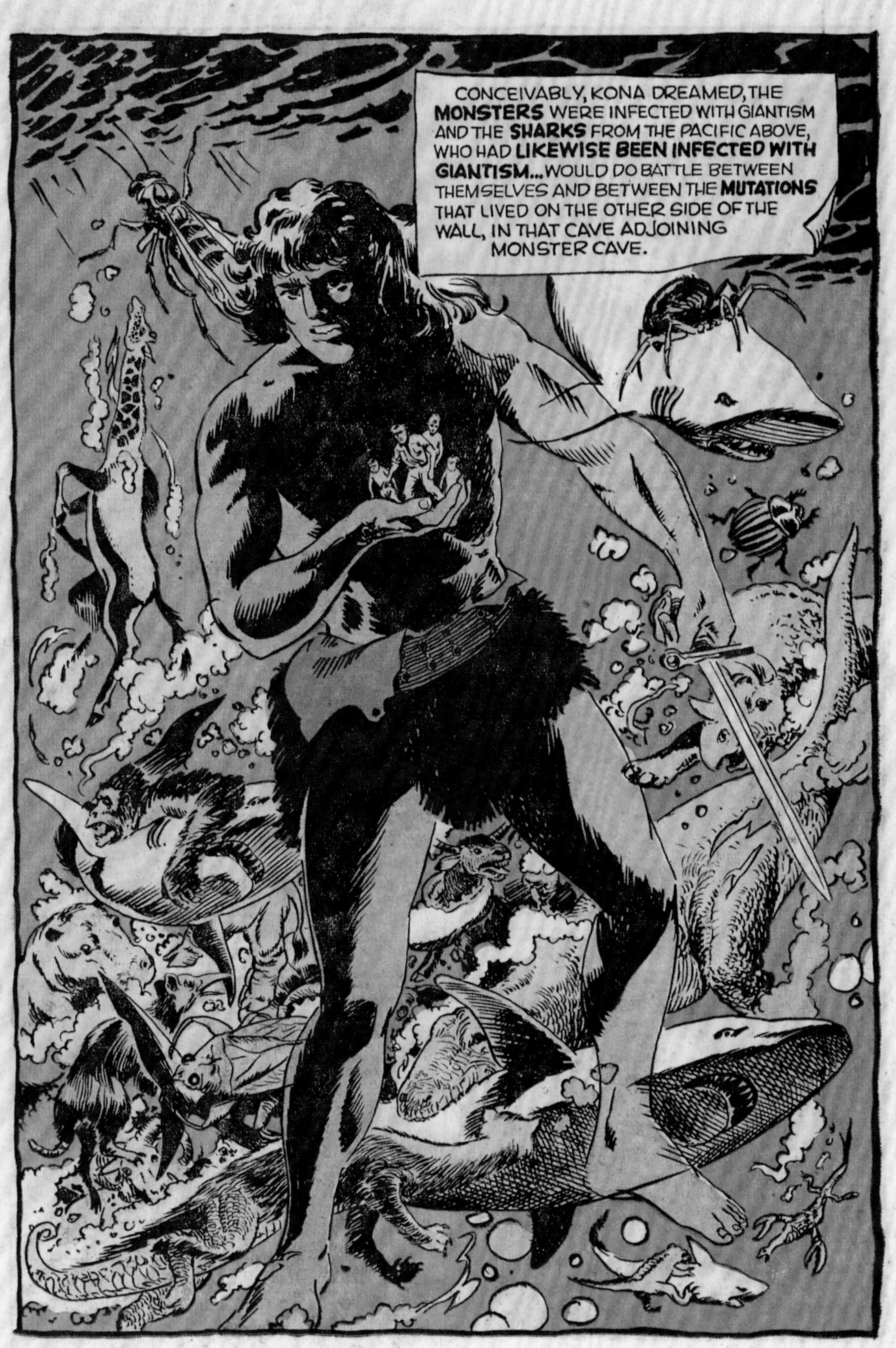
CONCEIVABLY, KONA DREAMED, THE MONSTERS WERE INFECTED WITH GIANTISM AND THE SHARKS FROM THE PACIFIC ABOVE, WHO HAD LIKEWISE BEEN INFECTED WITH GIANTISM... WOULD DO BATTLE BETWEEN THEMSELVES AND BETWEEN THE MUTATIONS THAT LIVED ON THE OTHER SIDE OF THE WALL, IN THAT CAVE ADJOINING MONSTER CAVE.

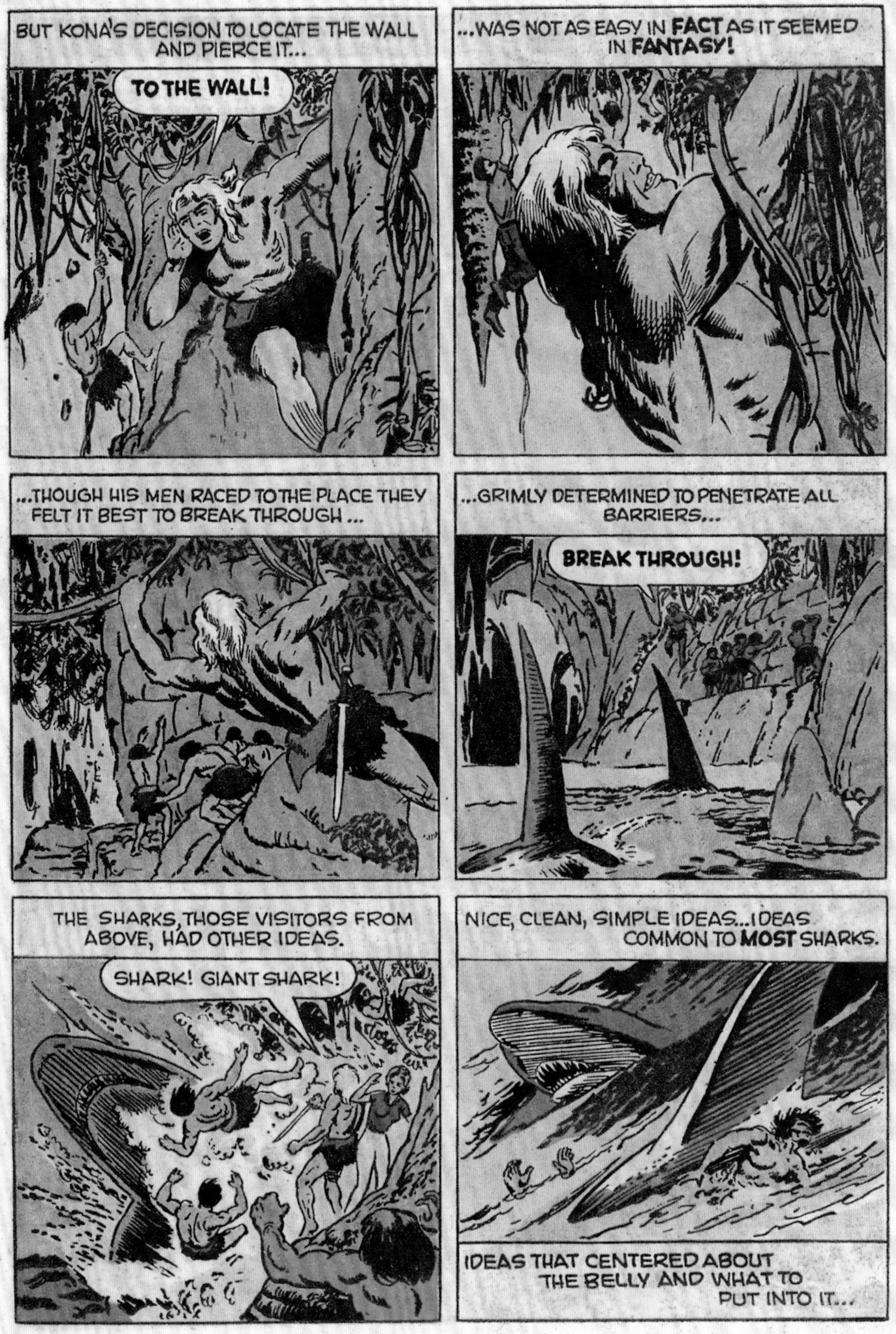
BUT KONA'S DECISION TO LOCATE THE WALL AND PIERCE IT...
TO THE WALL!
...WAS NOT AS EASY IN **FACT** AS IT SEEMED IN **FANTASY!**
...THOUGH HIS MEN RACED TO THE PLACE THEY FELT IT BEST TO BREAK THROUGH ...
...GRIMLY DETERMINED TO PENETRATE ALL BARRIERS...
BREAK THROUGH!
THE SHARKS, THOSE VISITORS FROM ABOVE, HAD OTHER IDEAS.
SHARK! GIANT SHARK!
NICE, CLEAN, SIMPLE IDEAS...IDEAS COMMON TO **MOST** SHARKS.
IDEAS THAT CENTERED ABOUT THE BELLY AND WHAT TO PUT INTO IT...

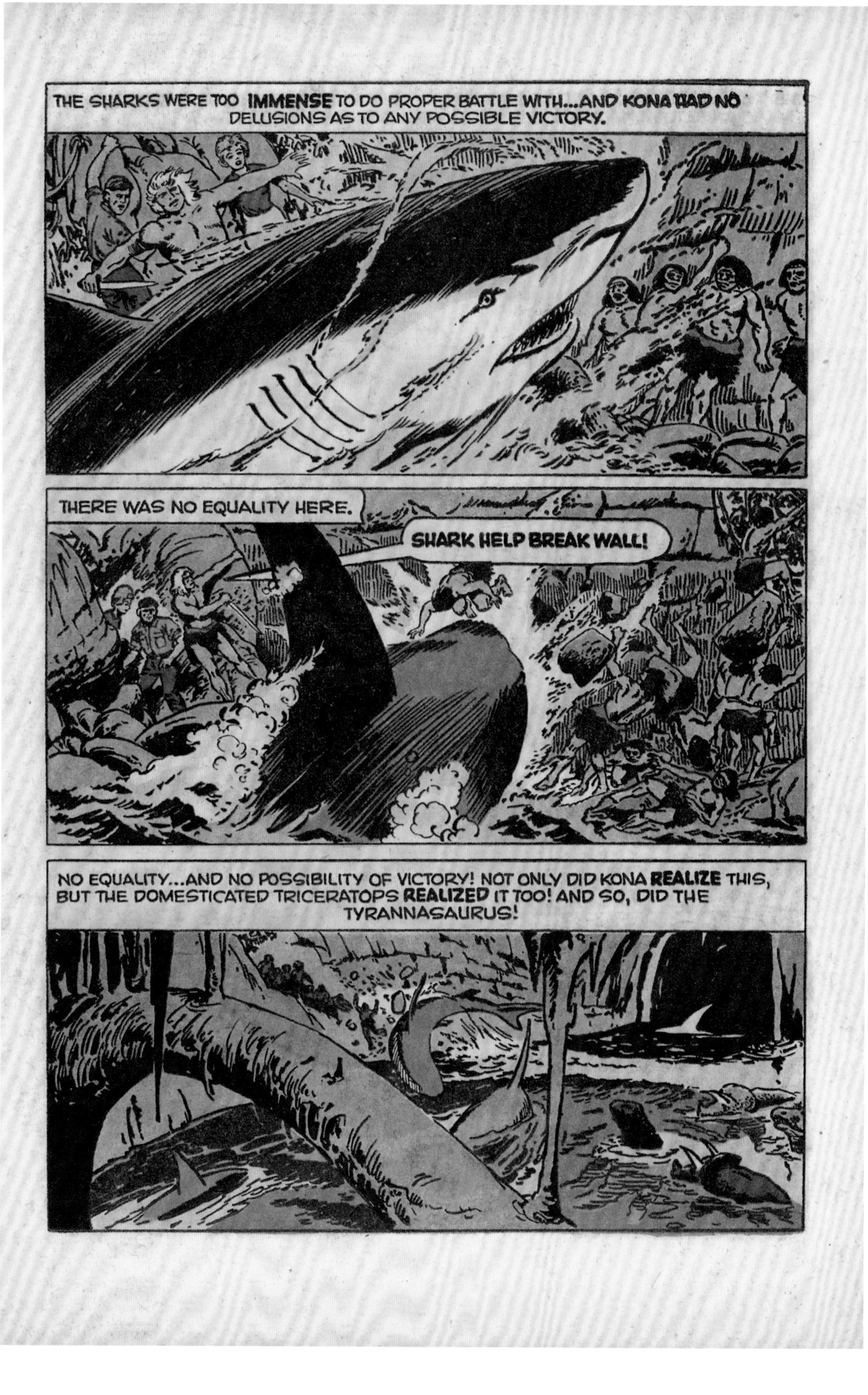
THE SHARKS WERE TOO IMMENSE TO DO PROPER BATTLE WITH...AND KONA HAD NO DELUSIONS AS TO ANY POSSIBLE VICTORY.
THERE WAS NO EQUALITY HERE.
SHARK HELP BREAK WALL!
NO EQUALITY...AND NO POSSIBILITY OF VICTORY! NOT ONLY DID KONA REALIZE THIS, BUT THE DOMESTICATED TRICERATOPS REALIZED IT TOO! AND SO, DID THE TYRANNASAURUS!

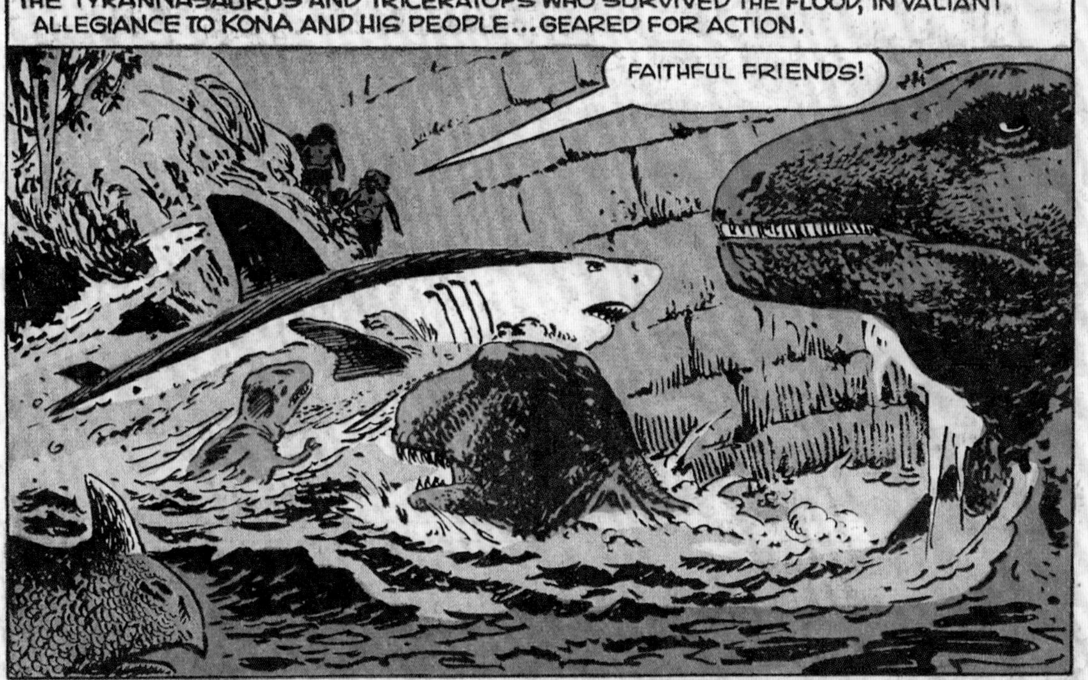
THE TYRANNASAURUS AND TRICERATOPS WHO SURVIVED THE FLOOD, IN VALIANT ALLEGIANCE TO KONA AND HIS PEOPLE...GEARED FOR ACTION.
FAITHFUL FRIENDS!

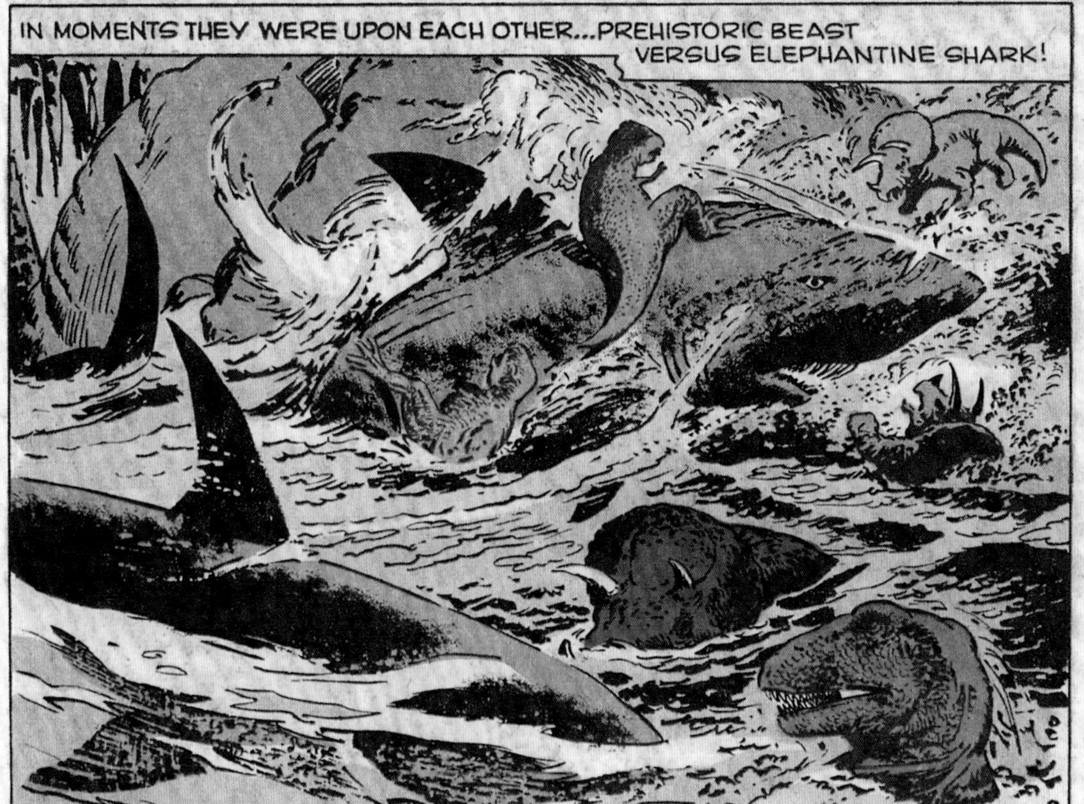
IN MOMENTS THEY WERE UPON EACH OTHER...PREHISTORIC BEAST VERSUS ELEPHANTINE SHARK!

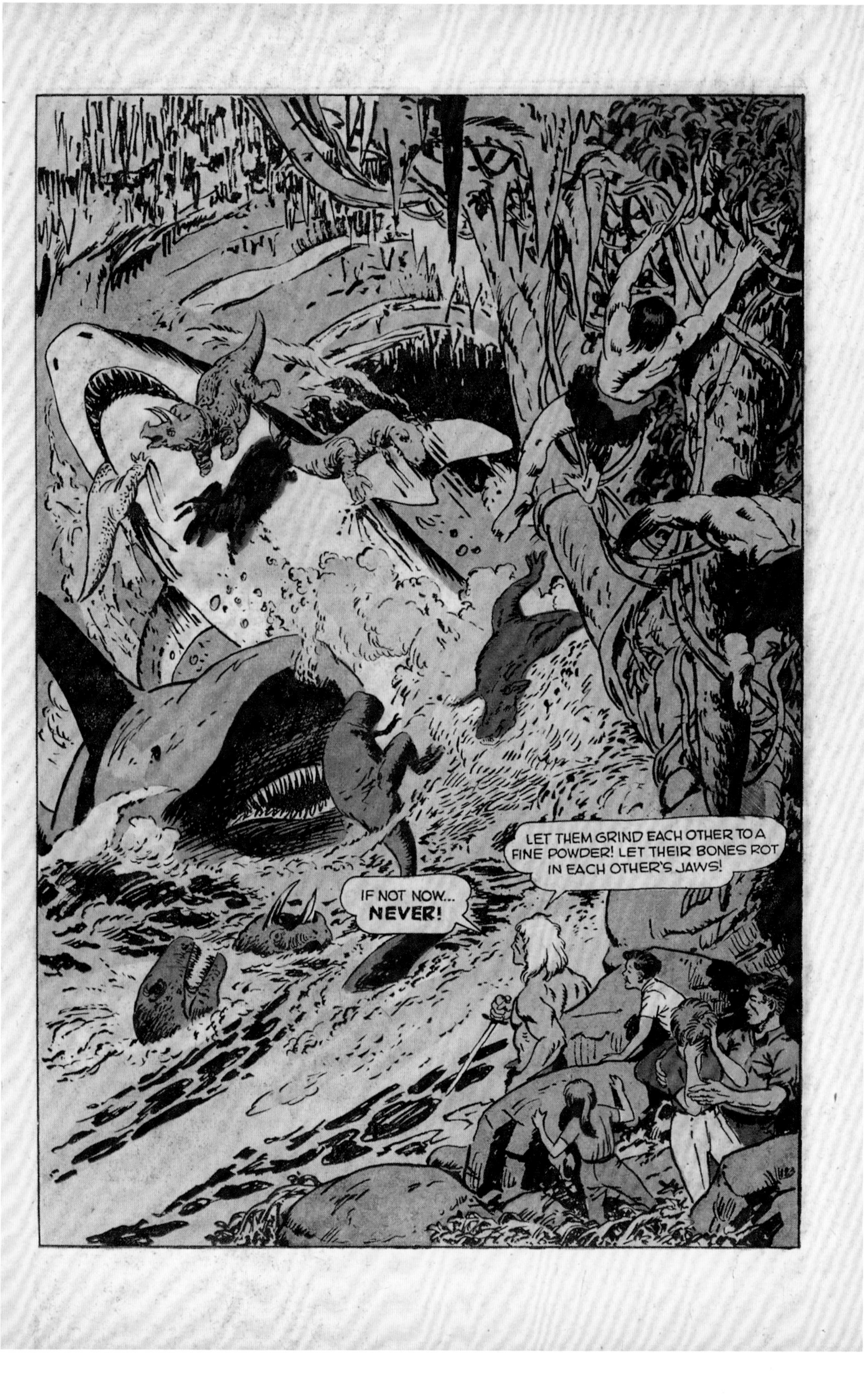
LET THEM GRIND EACH OTHER TO A FINE POWDER! LET THEIR BONES ROT IN EACH OTHER'S JAWS!
IF NOT NOW... NEVER!

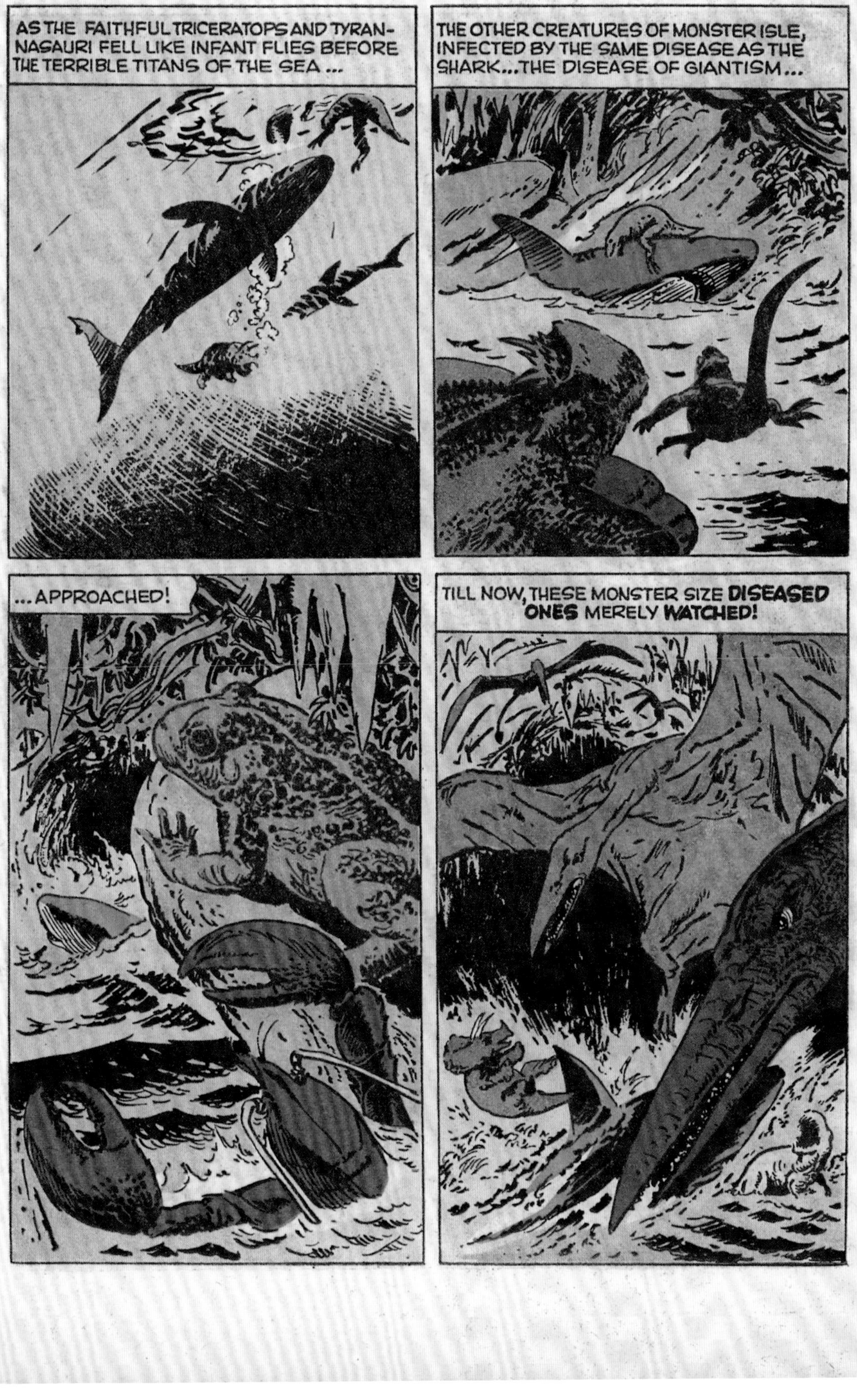
AS THE FAITHFUL TRICERATOPS AND TYRANNASAURI FELL LIKE INFANT FLIES BEFORE THE TERRIBLE TITANS OF THE SEA ...
THE OTHER CREATURES OF MONSTER ISLE, INFECTED BY THE SAME DISEASE AS THE SHARK...THE DISEASE OF GIANTISM...
...APPROACHED!
TILL NOW, THESE MONSTER SIZE DISEASED ONES MERELY WATCHED!

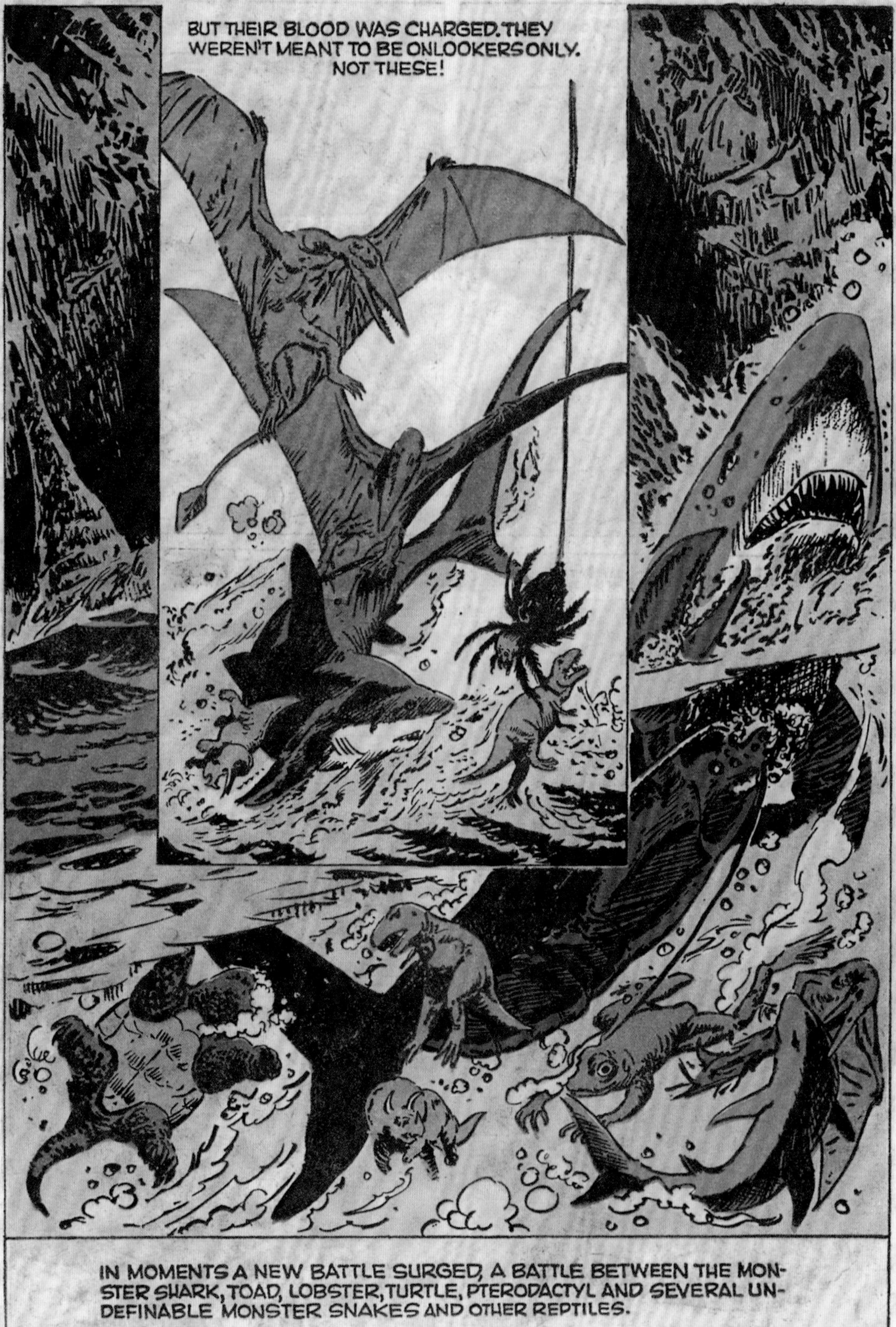
BUT THEIR BLOOD WAS CHARGED. THEY WEREN'T MEANT TO BE ONLOOKERS ONLY. NOT THESE!
IN MOMENTS A NEW BATTLE SURGED, A BATTLE BETWEEN THE MONSTER SHARK, TOAD, LOBSTER, TURTLE, PTERODACTYL AND SEVERAL UNDEFINABLE MONSTER SNAKES AND OTHER REPTILES.

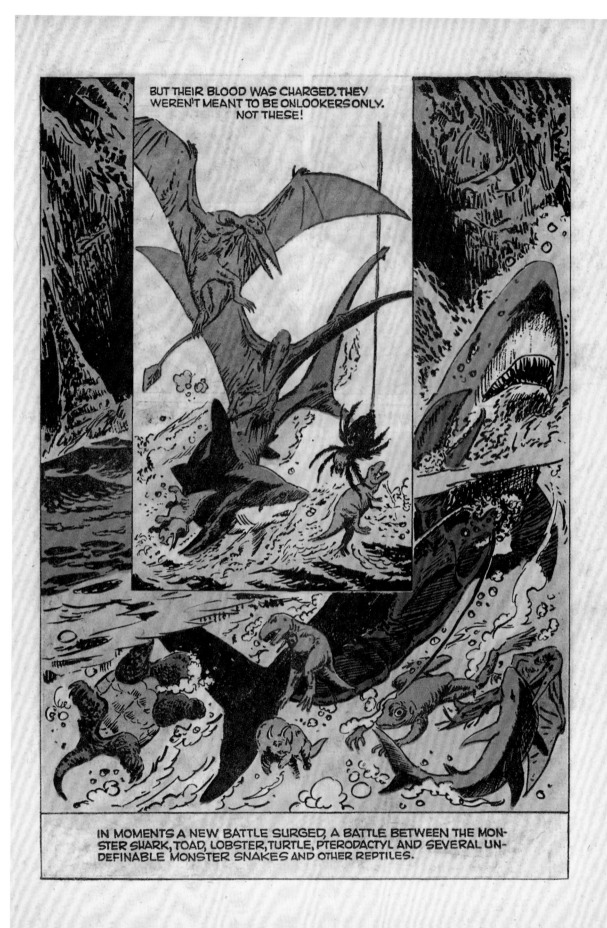

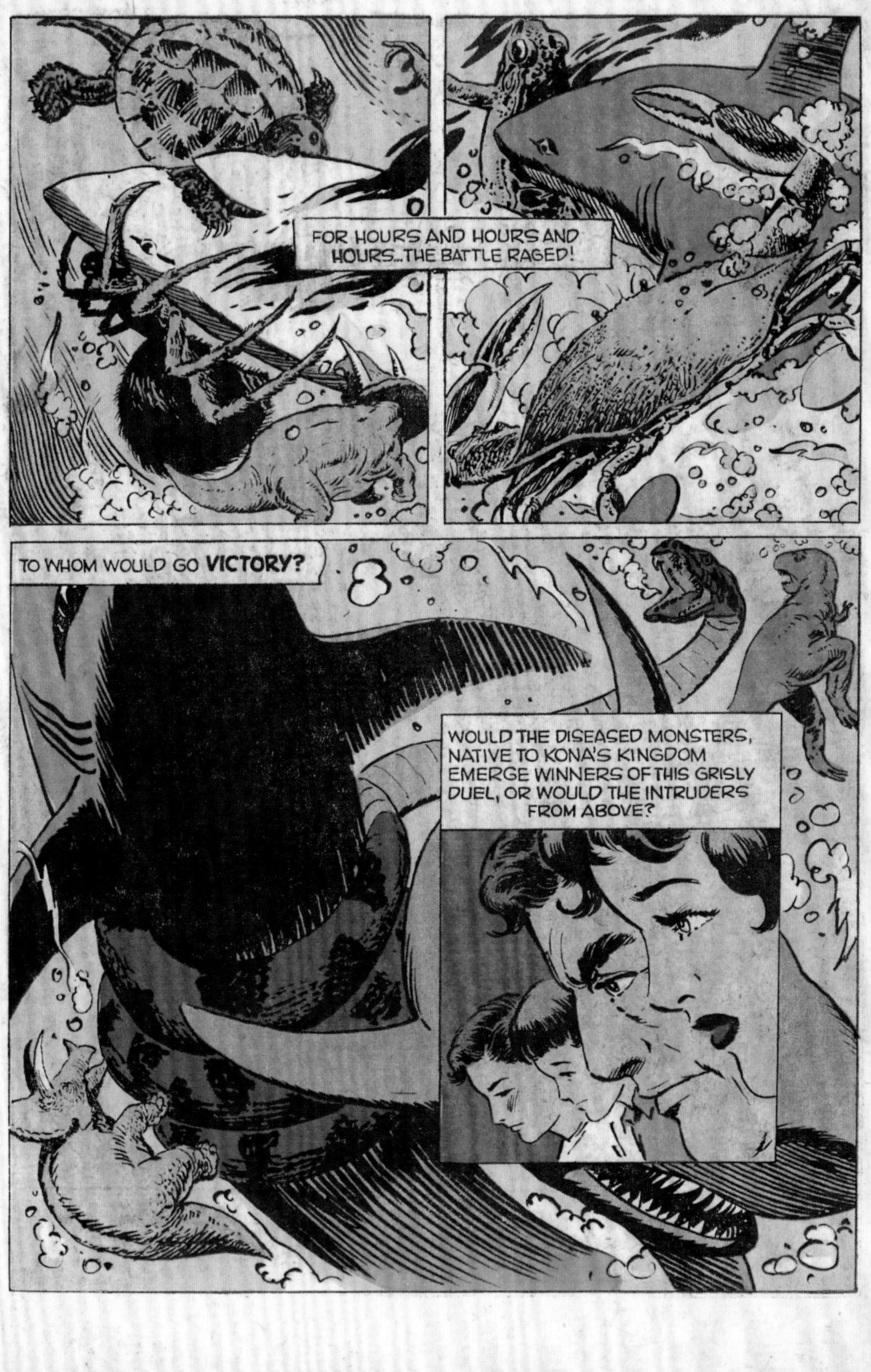
FOR HOURS AND HOURS AND HOURS...THE BATTLE RAGED!
TO WHOM WOULD GO VICTORY?
WOULD THE DISEASED MONSTERS, NATIVE TO KONA'S KINGDOM EMERGE WINNERS OF THIS GRISLY DUEL, OR WOULD THE INTRUDERS FROM ABOVE?

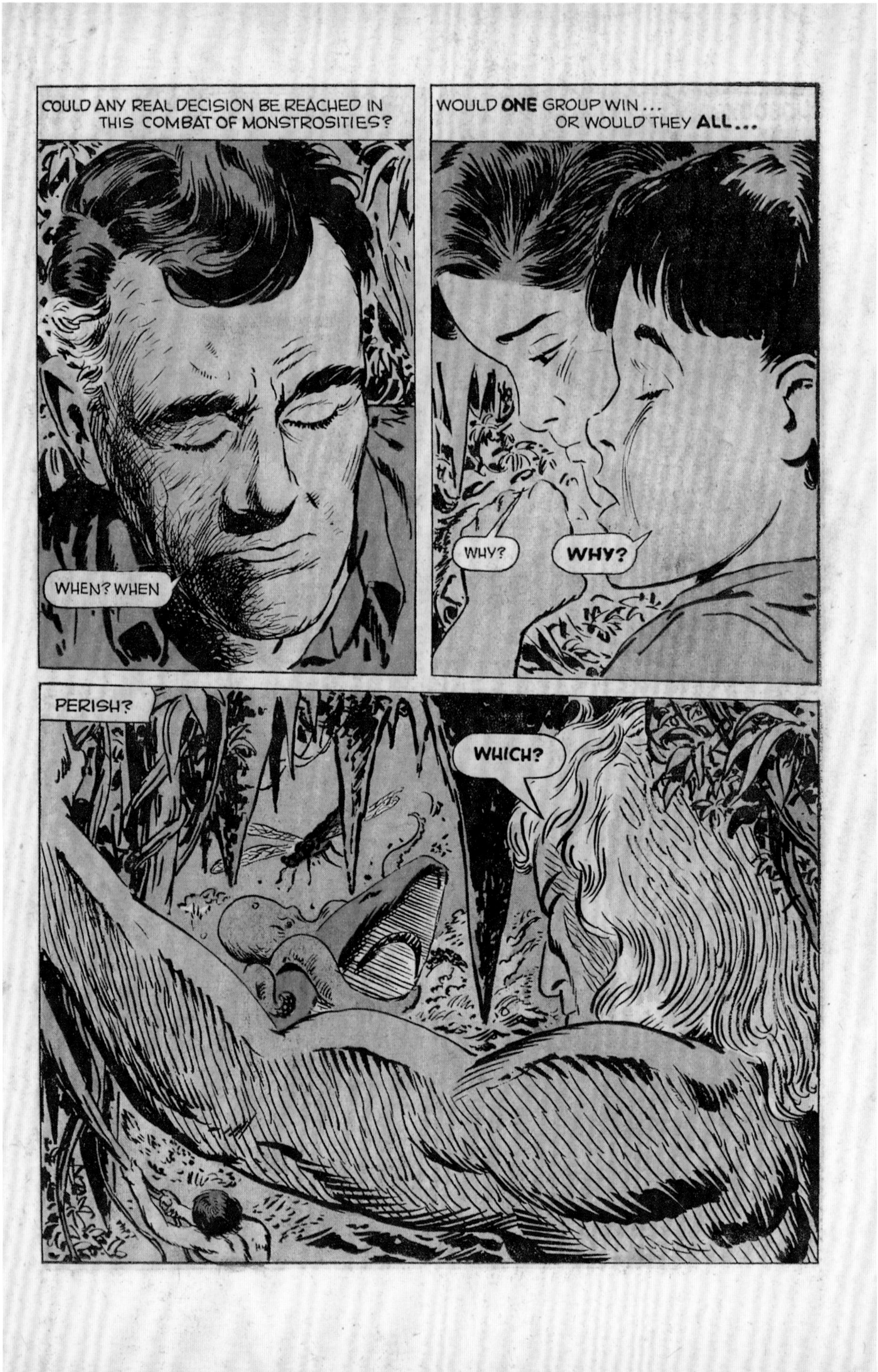
COULD ANY REAL DECISION BE REACHED IN THIS COMBAT OF MONSTROSITIES?
WHEN? WHEN
WOULD ONE GROUP WIN ... OR WOULD THEY ALL...
WHY?
WHY?
PERISH?
WHICH?

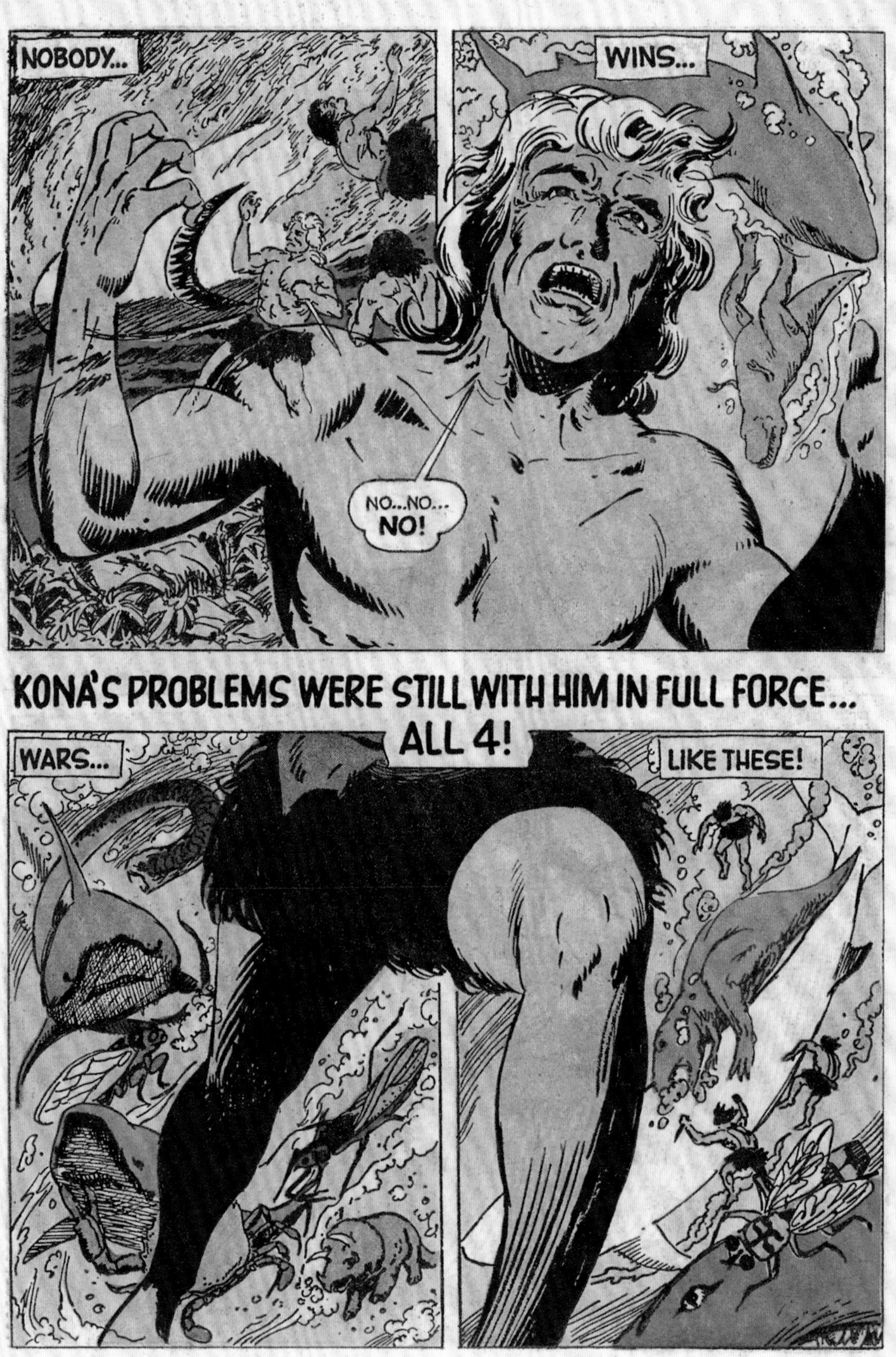
NOBODY...
WINS...
NO...NO... NO!
KONA'S PROBLEMS WERE STILL WITH HIM IN FULL FORCE... ALL 4!
WARS...
LIKE THESE!

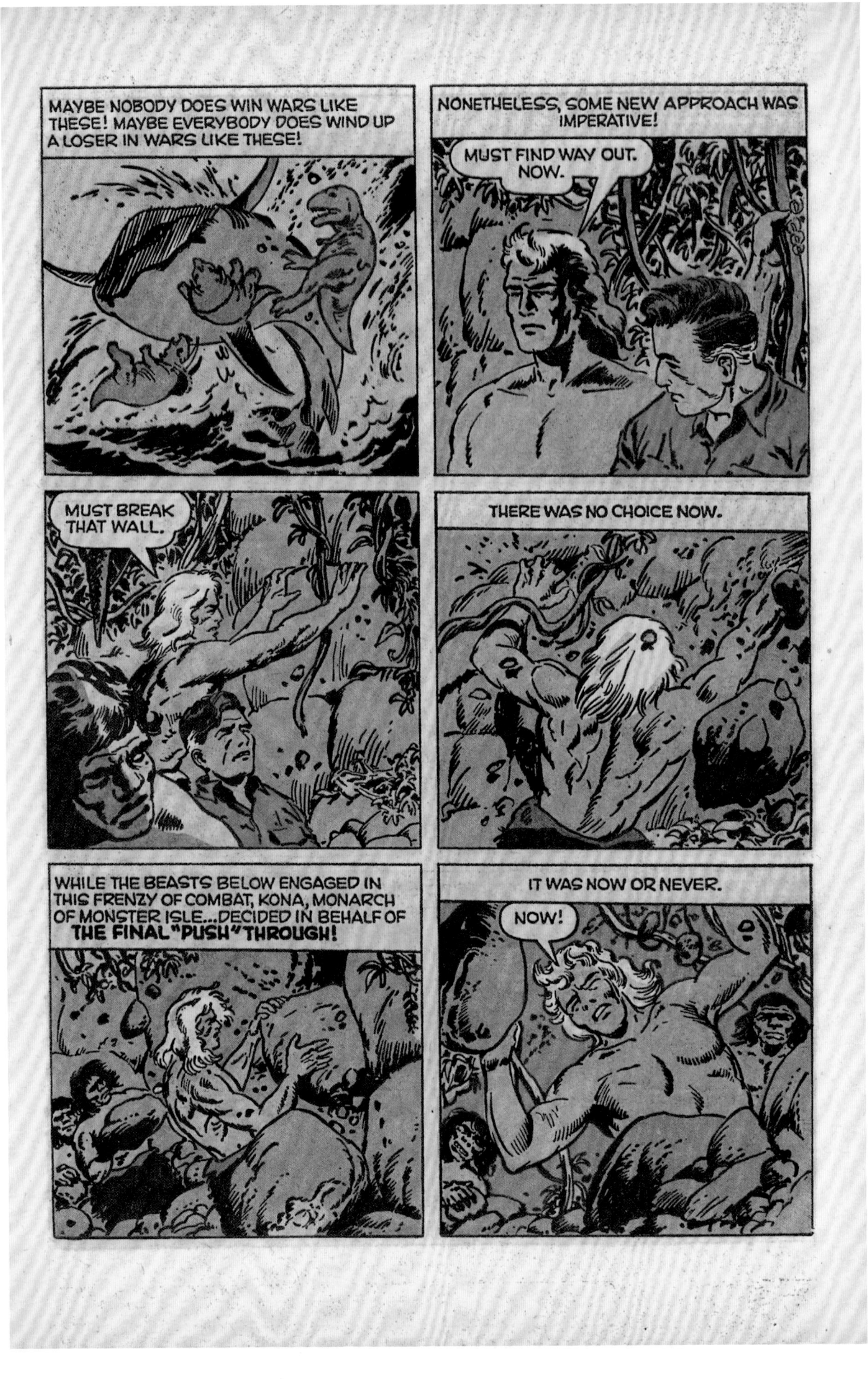
MAYBE NOBODY DOES WIN WARS LIKE THESE! MAYBE EVERYBODY DOES WIND UP A LOSER IN WARS LIKE THESE!
NONETHELESS, SOME NEW APPROACH WAS IMPERATIVE!
MUST FIND WAY OUT. NOW.
MUST BREAK THAT WALL.
THERE WAS NO CHOICE NOW.
WHILE THE BEASTS BELOW ENGAGED IN THIS FRENZY OF COMBAT, KONA, MONARCH OF MONSTER ISLE...DECIDED IN BEHALF OF THE FINAL "PUSH" THROUGH!
IT WAS NOW OR NEVER.
NOW!

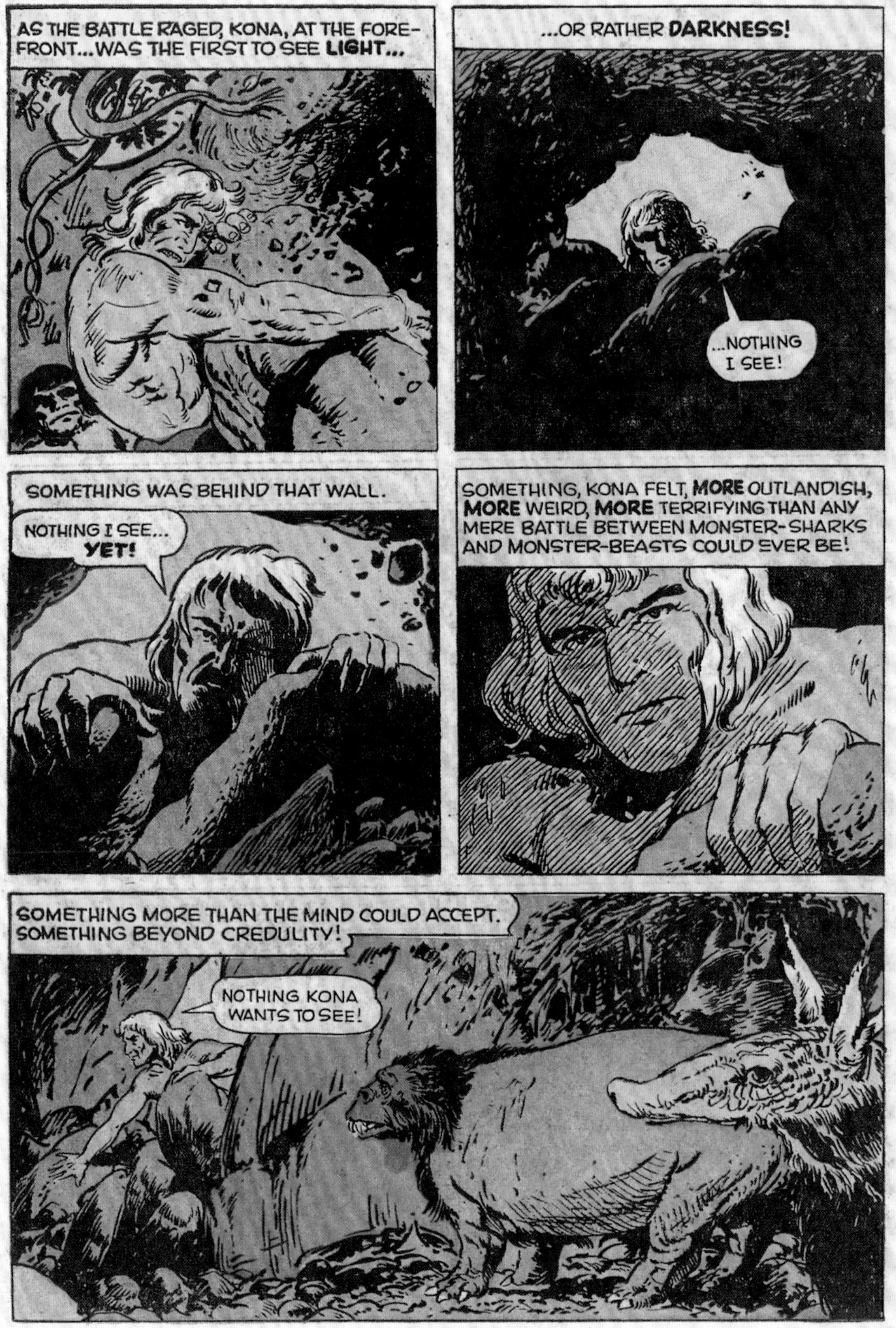
AS THE BATTLE RAGED, KONA, AT THE FORE-FRONT...WAS THE FIRST TO SEE LIGHT...
...OR RATHER DARKNESS!
...NOTHING I SEE!
SOMETHING WAS BEHIND THAT WALL.
NOTHING I SEE... YET!
SOMETHING, KONA FELT, MORE OUTLANDISH, MORE WEIRD, MORE TERRIFYING THAN ANY MERE BATTLE BETWEEN MONSTER-SHARKS AND MONSTER-BEASTS COULD EVER BE!
SOMETHING MORE THAN THE MIND COULD ACCEPT. SOMETHING BEYOND CREDULITY!
NOTHING KONA WANTS TO SEE!

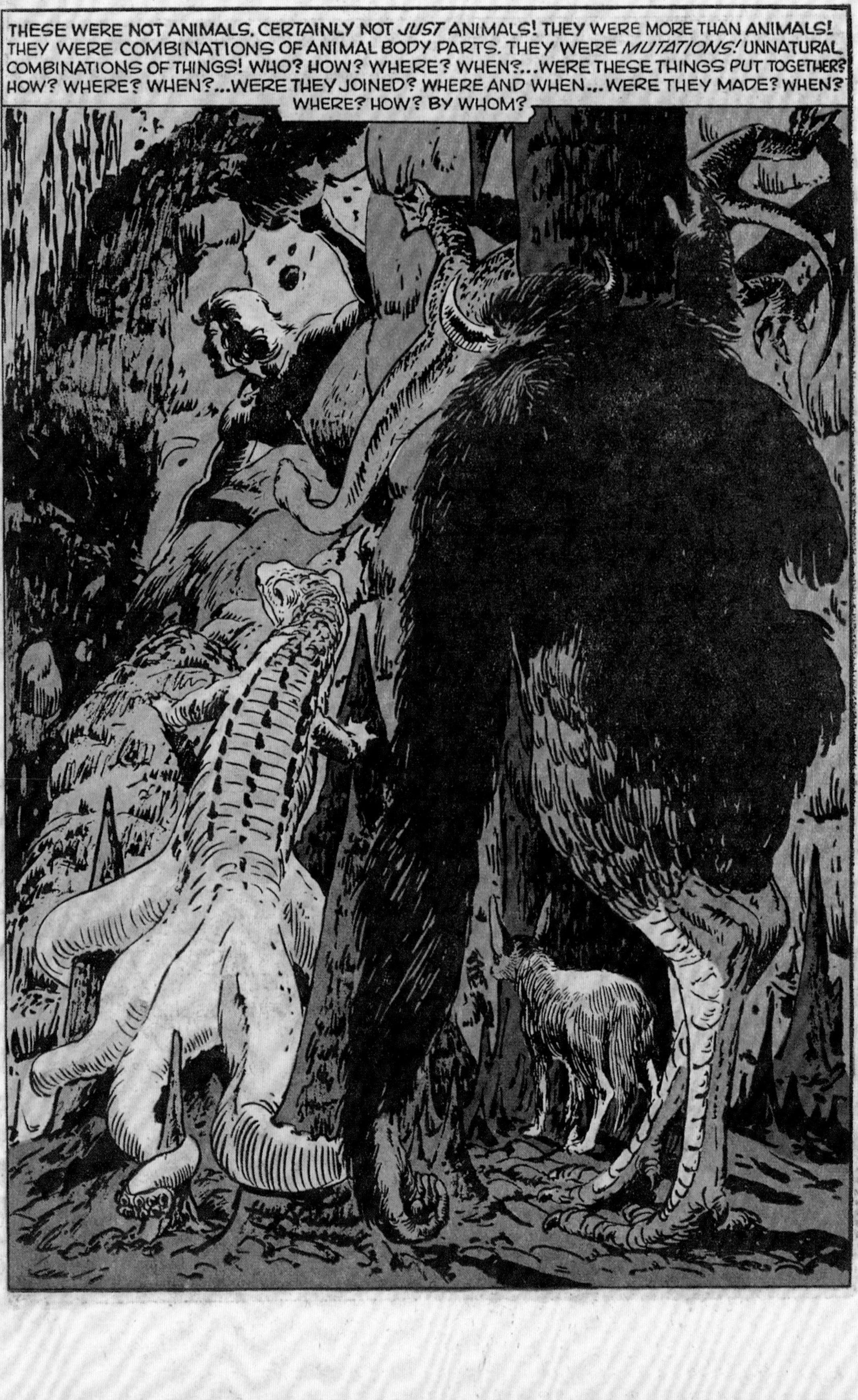
THESE WERE NOT ANIMALS, CERTAINLY NOT JUST ANIMALS! THEY WERE MORE THAN ANIMALS! THEY WERE COMBINATIONS OF ANIMAL BODY PARTS. THEY WERE MUTATIONS! UNNATURAL COMBINATIONS OF THINGS! WHO? HOW? WHERE? WHEN?...WERE THESE THINGS PUT TOGETHER? HOW? WHERE? WHEN?...WERE THEY JOINED? WHERE AND WHEN...WERE THEY MADE? WHEN? WHERE? HOW? BY WHOM?

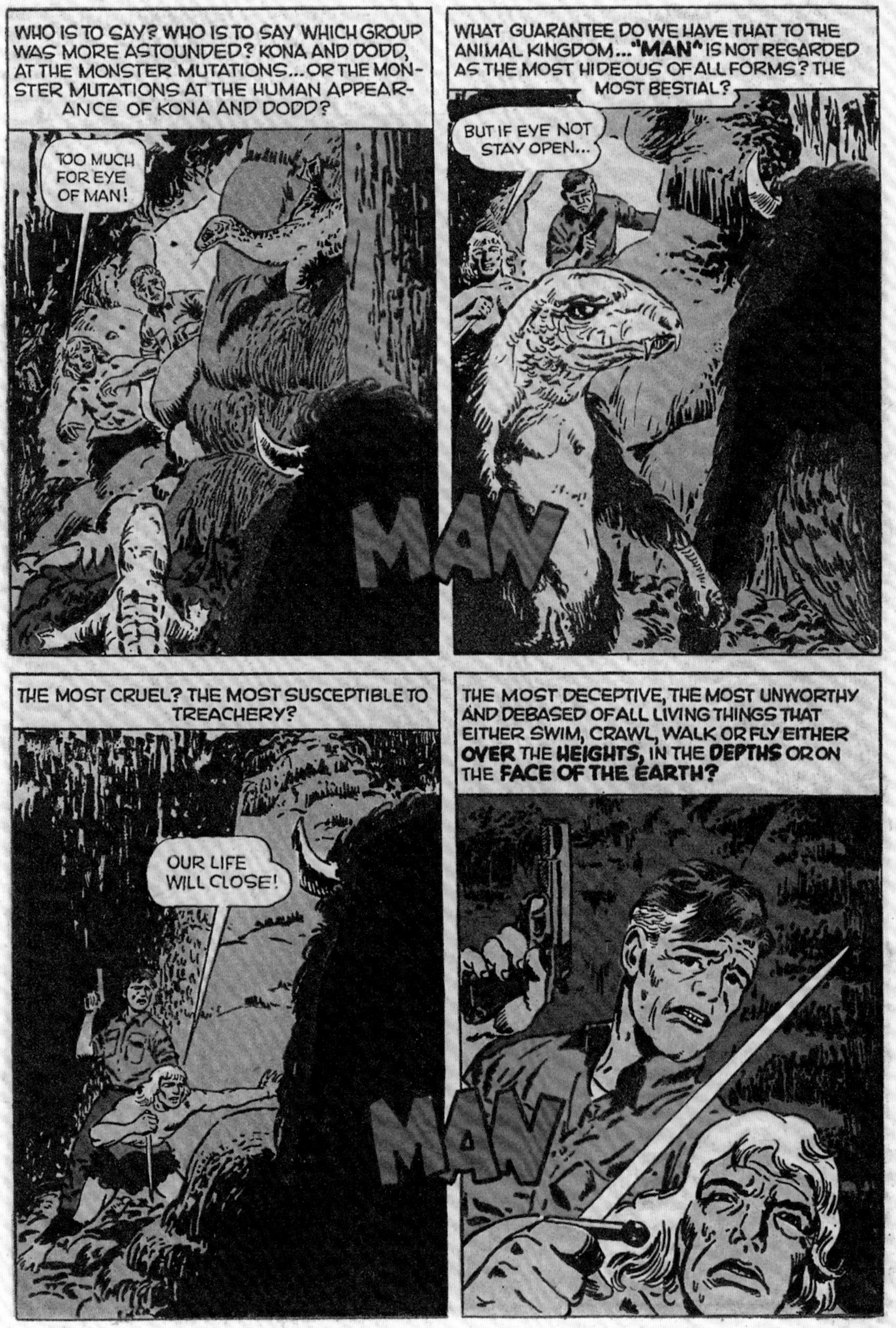
WHO IS TO SAY? WHO IS TO SAY WHICH GROUP WAS MORE ASTOUNDED? KONA AND DODD, AT THE MONSTER MUTATIONS...OR THE MONSTER MUTATIONS AT THE HUMAN APPEARANCE OF KONA AND DODD?
TOO MUCH FOR EYE OF MAN!
WHAT GUARANTEE DO WE HAVE THAT TO THE ANIMAL KINGDOM..."MAN" IS NOT REGARDED AS THE MOST HIDEOUS OF ALL FORMS? THE MOST BESTIAL?
BUT IF EYE NOT STAY OPEN...
MAN
THE MOST CRUEL? THE MOST SUSCEPTIBLE TO TREACHERY?
OUR LIFE WILL CLOSE!
THE MOST DECEPTIVE, THE MOST UNWORTHY AND DEBASED OF ALL LIVING THINGS THAT EITHER SWIM, CRAWL, WALK OR FLY EITHER OVER THE HEIGHTS, IN THE DEPTHS OR ON THE FACE OF THE EARTH?
MAN

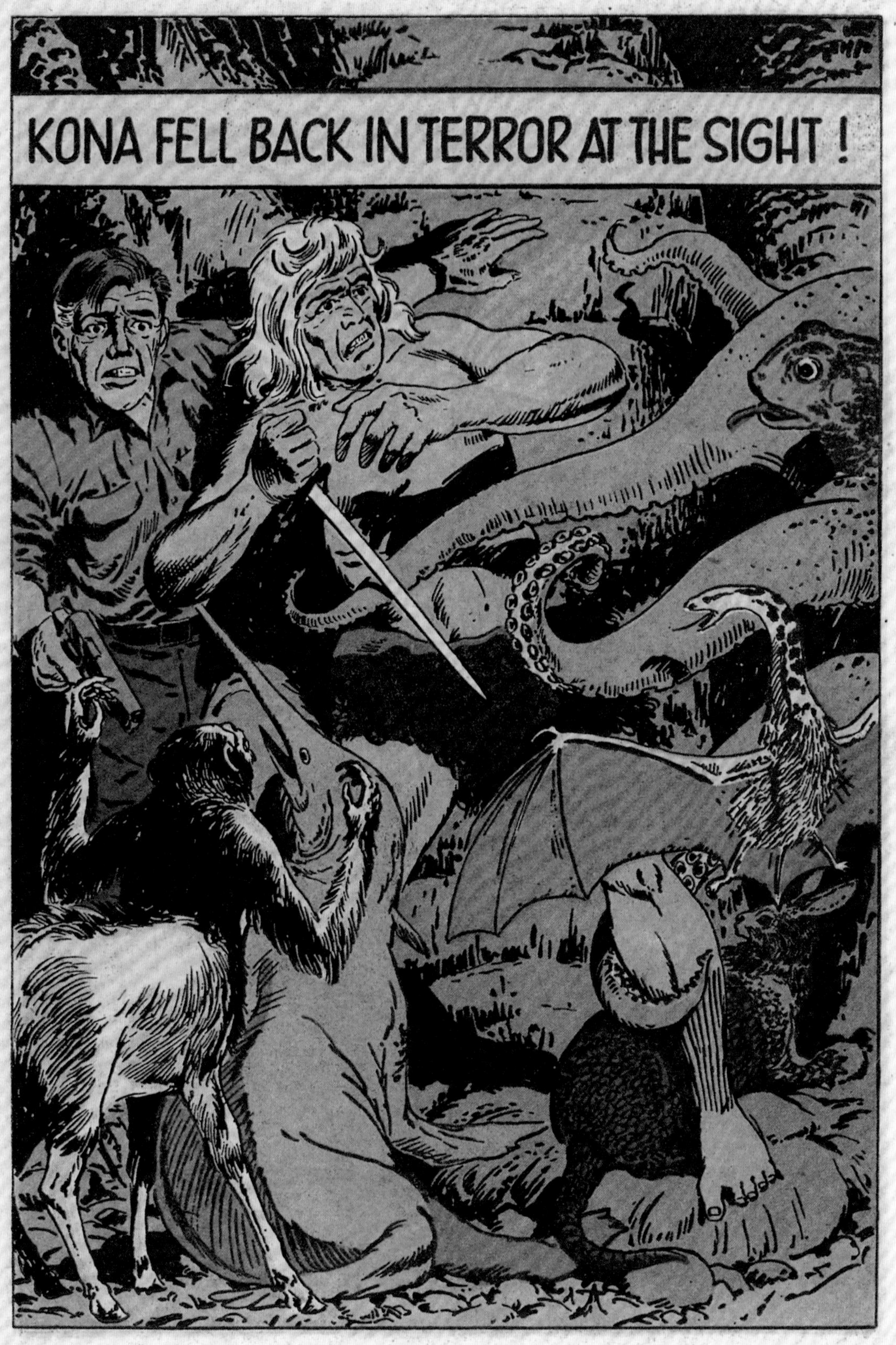
KONA FELL BACK IN TERROR AT THE SIGHT !

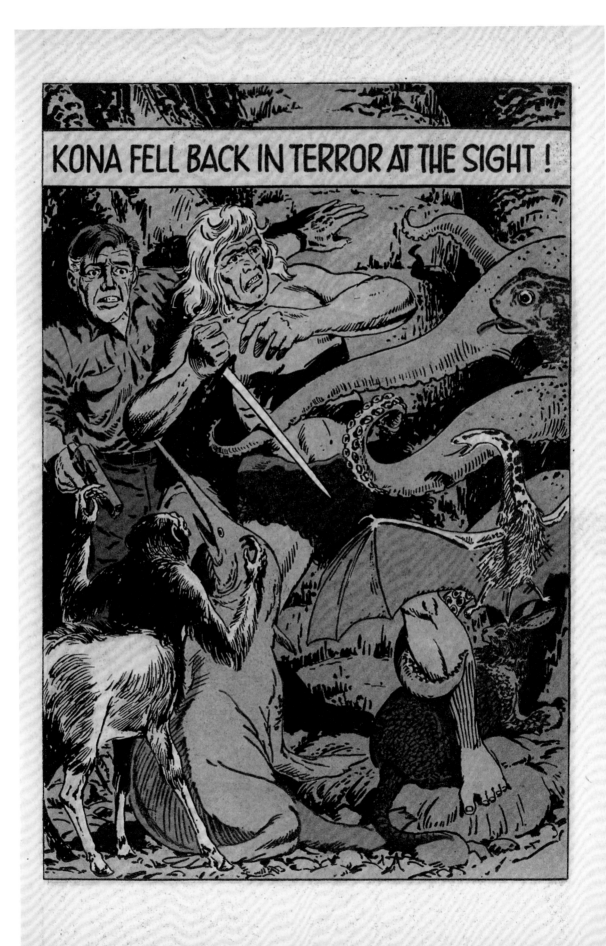

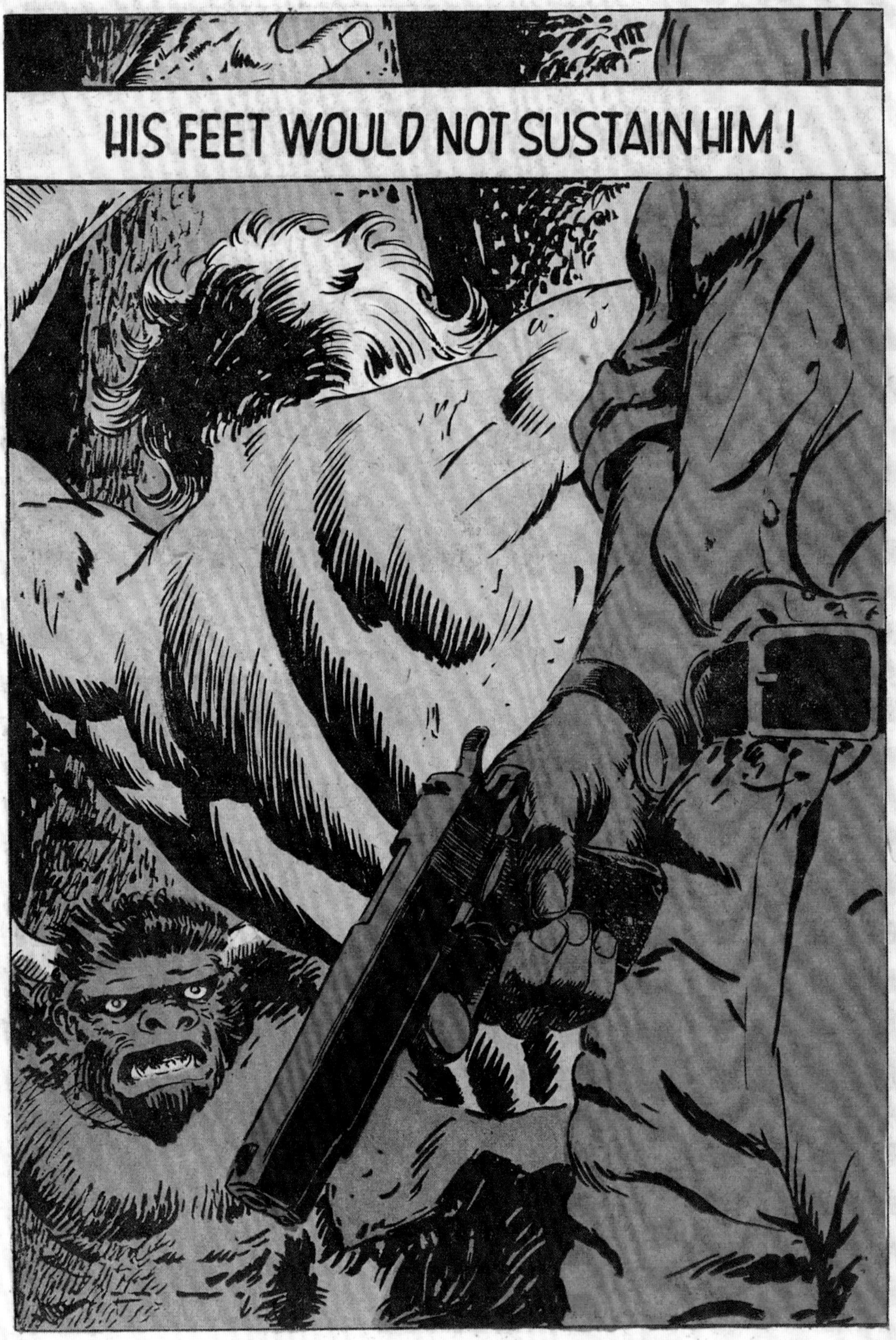
HIS FEET WOULD NOT SUSTAIN HIM!

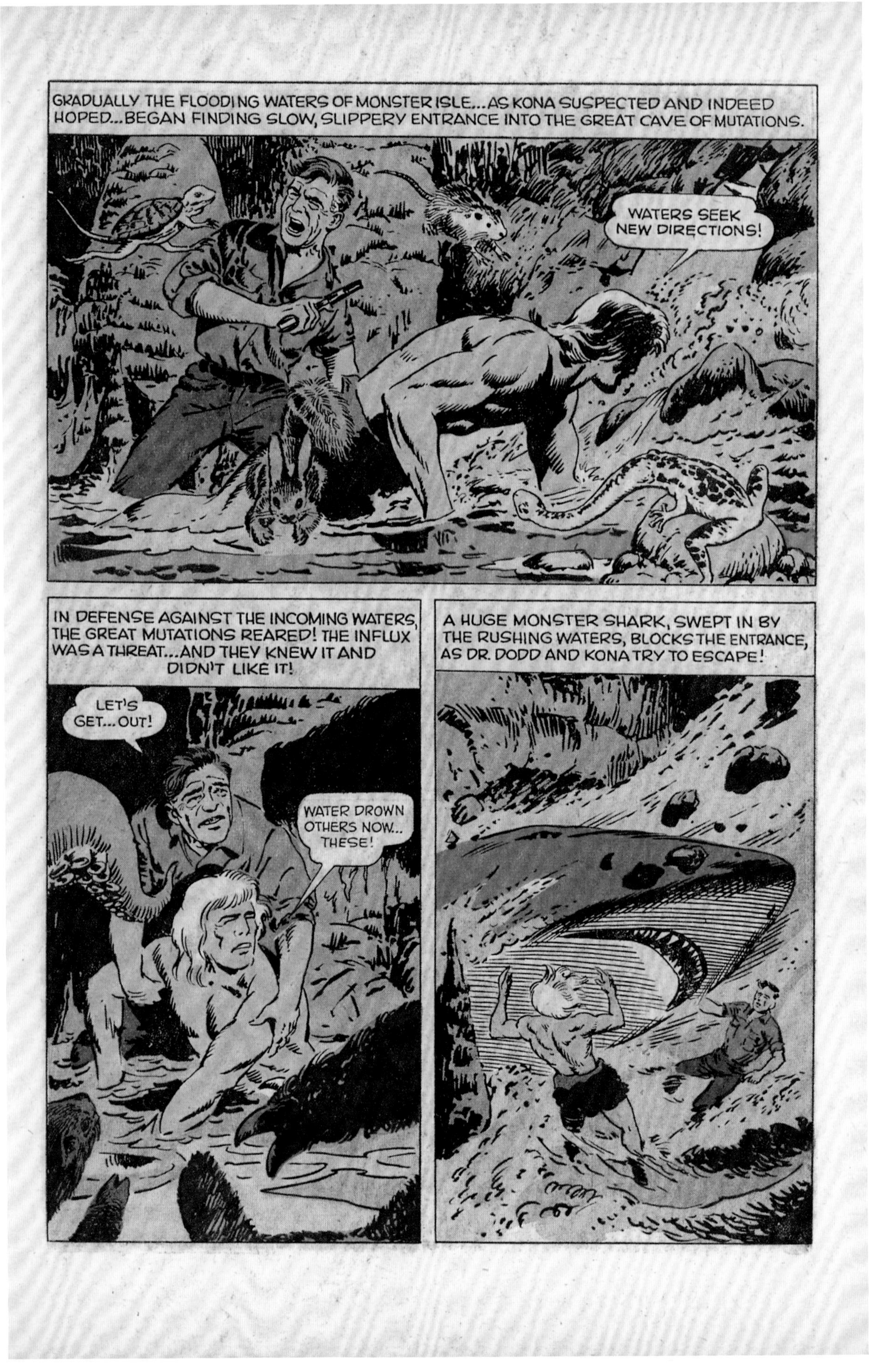
GRADUALLY THE FLOODING WATERS OF MONSTER ISLE...AS KONA SUSPECTED AND INDEED HOPED...BEGAN FINDING SLOW, SLIPPERY ENTRANCE INTO THE GREAT CAVE OF MUTATIONS.
WATERS SEEK NEW DIRECTIONS!
IN DEFENSE AGAINST THE INCOMING WATERS, THE GREAT MUTATIONS REARED! THE INFLUX WAS A THREAT...AND THEY KNEW IT AND DIDN'T LIKE IT!
LET'S GET...OUT!
WATER DROWN OTHERS NOW... THESE!
A HUGE MONSTER SHARK, SWEPT IN BY THE RUSHING WATERS, BLOCKS THE ENTRANCE, AS DR. DODD AND KONA TRY TO ESCAPE!

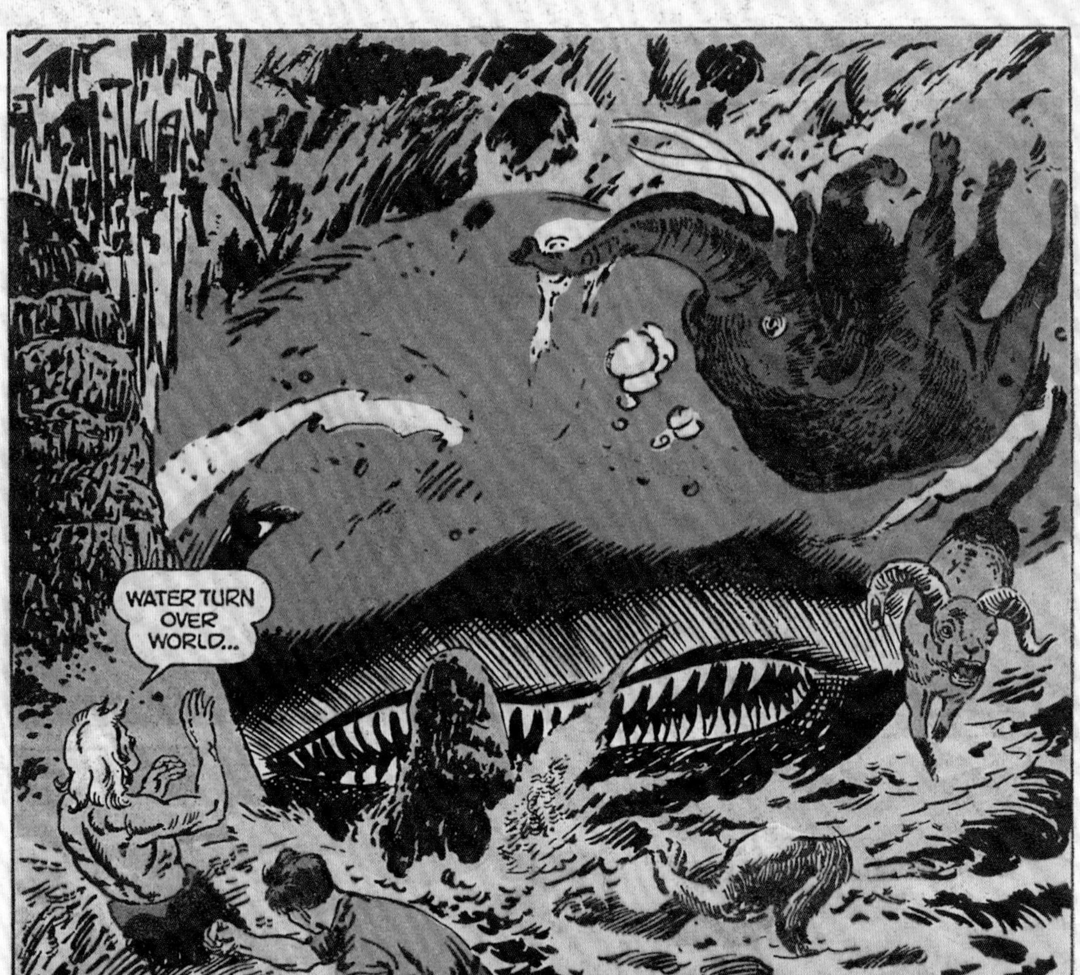
WATER TURN OVER WORLD...

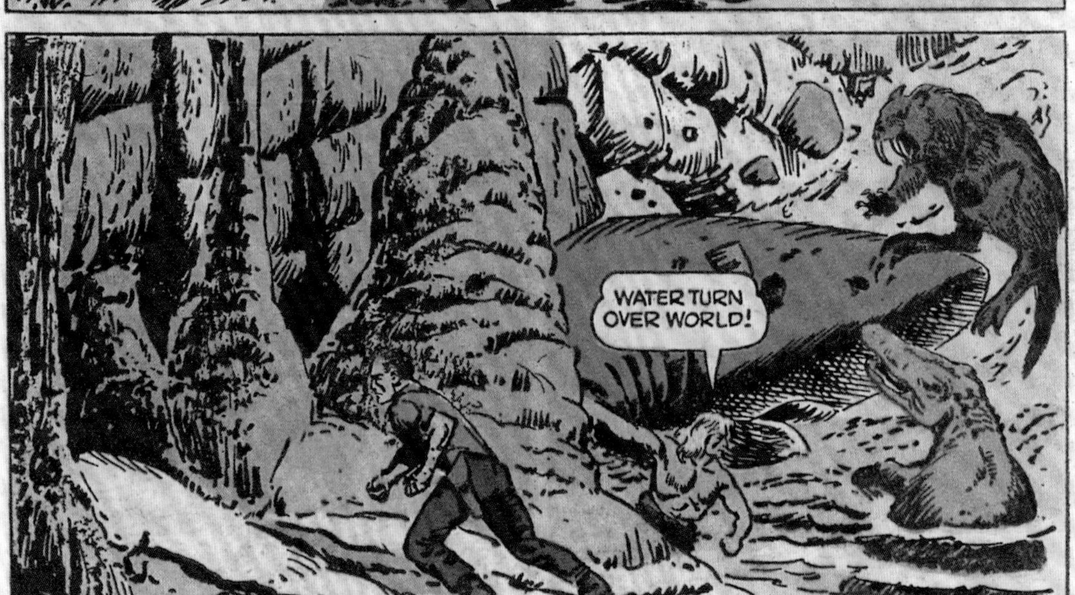
WATER TURN OVER WORLD!

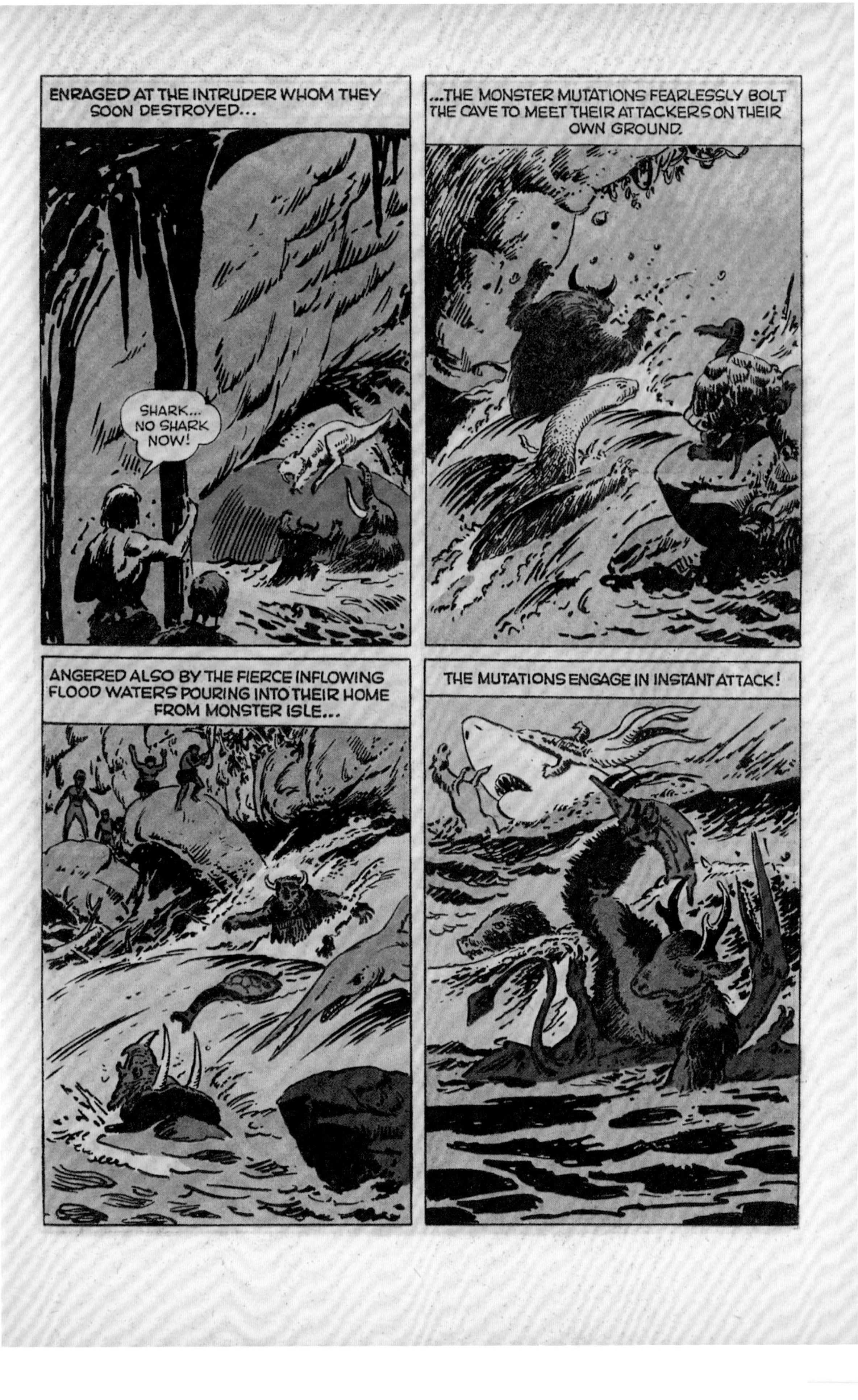
ENRAGED AT THE INTRUDER WHOM THEY SOON DESTROYED...
SHARK... NO SHARK NOW!
...THE MONSTER MUTATIONS FEARLESSLY BOLT THE CAVE TO MEET THEIR ATTACKERS ON THEIR OWN GROUND.
ANGERED ALSO BY THE FIERCE INFLOWING FLOOD WATERS POURING INTO THEIR HOME FROM MONSTER ISLE...
THE MUTATIONS ENGAGE IN INSTANT ATTACK!

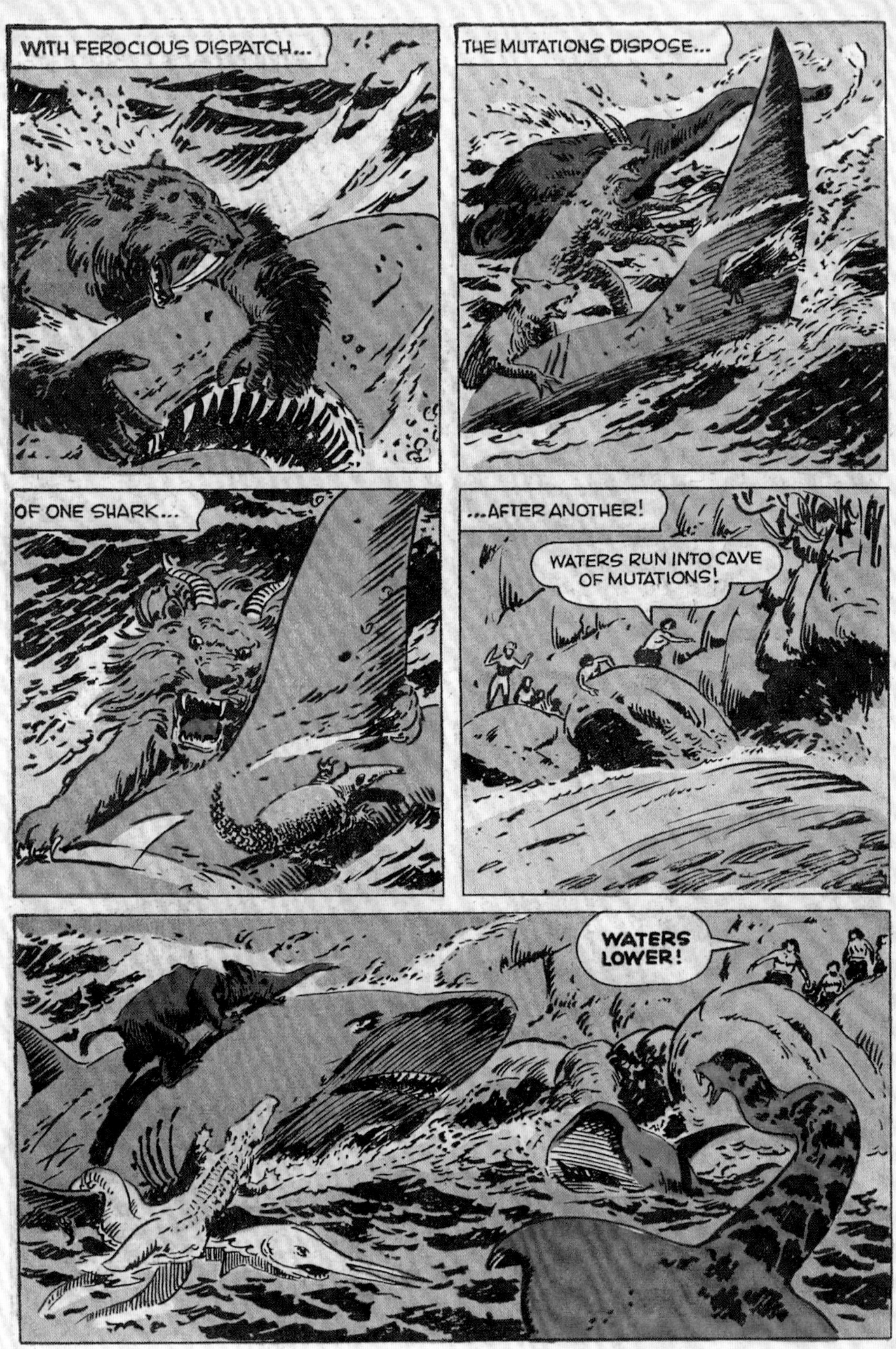
WITH FEROCIOUS DISPATCH...
THE MUTATIONS DISPOSE...
OF ONE SHARK...
...AFTER ANOTHER!
WATERS RUN INTO CAVE OF MUTATIONS!
WATERS LOWER!

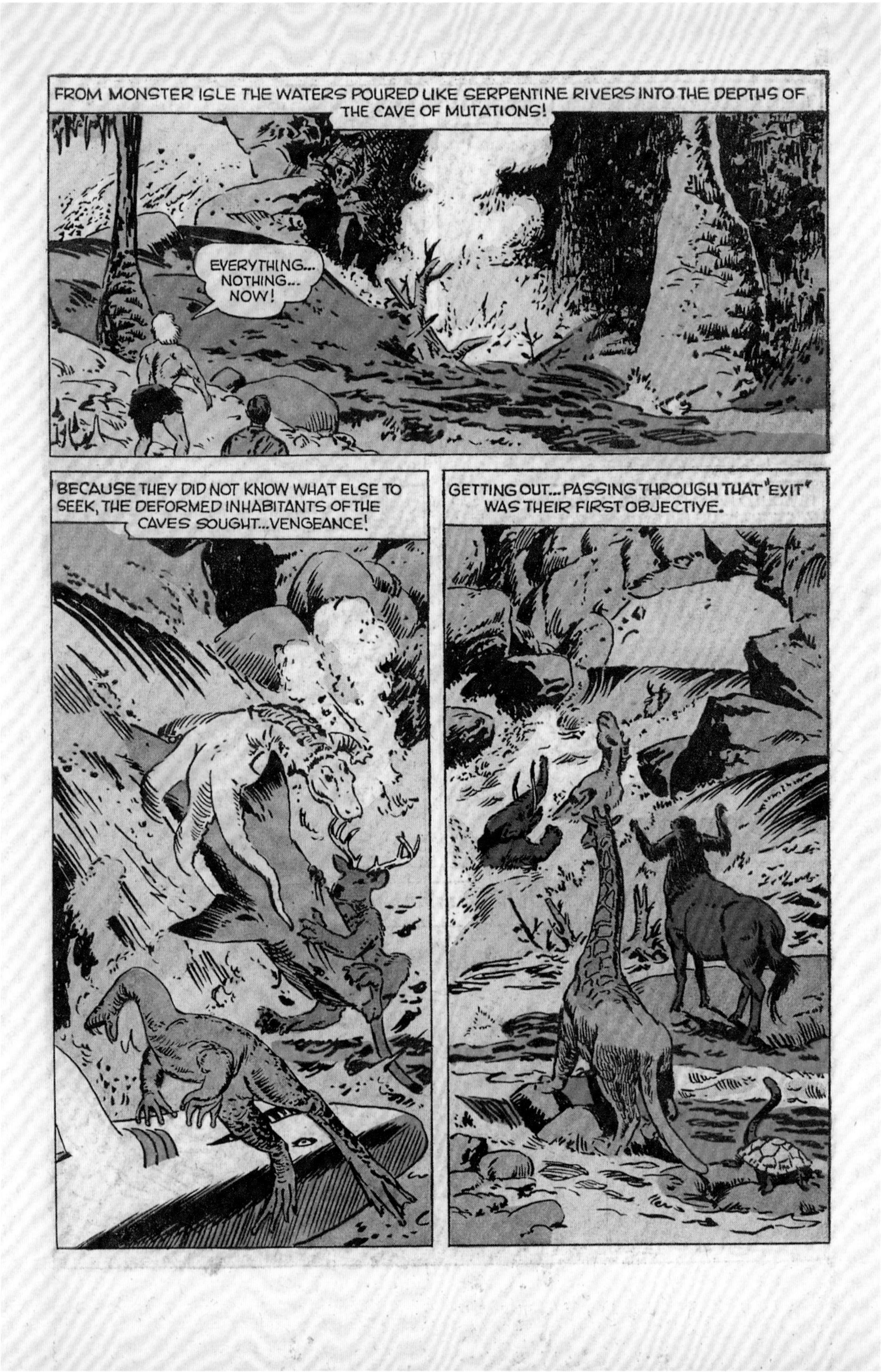
FROM MONSTER ISLE THE WATERS POURED LIKE SERPENTINE RIVERS INTO THE DEPTHS OF THE CAVE OF MUTATIONS!
EVERYTHING... NOTHING... NOW!
BECAUSE THEY DID NOT KNOW WHAT ELSE TO SEEK, THE DEFORMED INHABITANTS OF THE CAVES SOUGHT...VENGEANCE!
GETTING OUT... PASSING THROUGH THAT "EXIT" WAS THEIR FIRST OBJECTIVE.

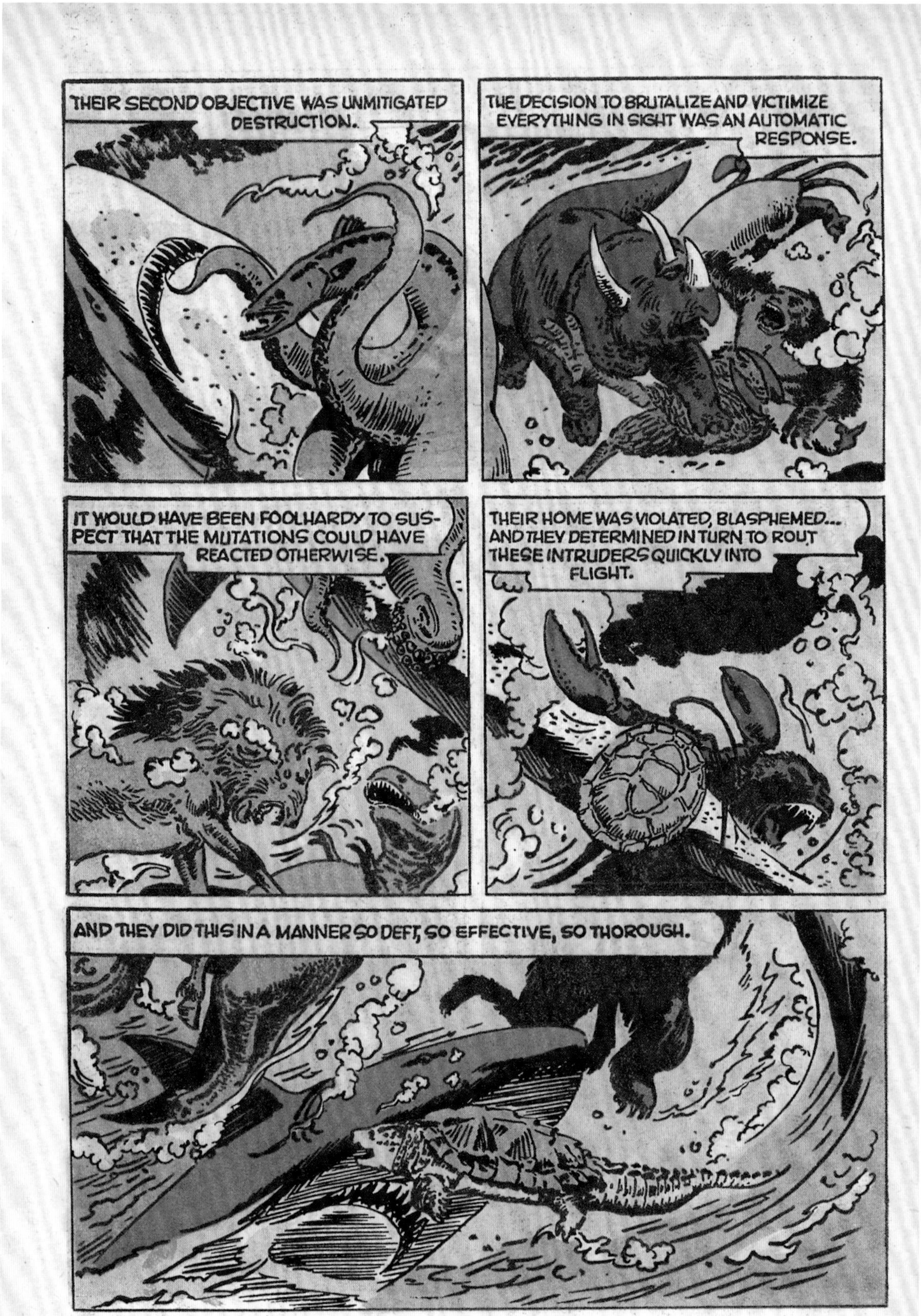
THEIR SECOND OBJECTIVE WAS UNMITIGATED DESTRUCTION.
THE DECISION TO BRUTALIZE AND VICTIMIZE EVERYTHING IN SIGHT WAS AN AUTOMATIC RESPONSE.
IT WOULD HAVE BEEN FOOLHARDY TO SUSPECT THAT THE MUTATIONS COULD HAVE REACTED OTHERWISE.
THEIR HOME WAS VIOLATED, BLASPHEMED... AND THEY DETERMINED IN TURN TO ROUT THESE INTRUDERS QUICKLY INTO FLIGHT.
AND THEY DID THIS IN A MANNER SO DEFT, SO EFFECTIVE, SO THOROUGH.

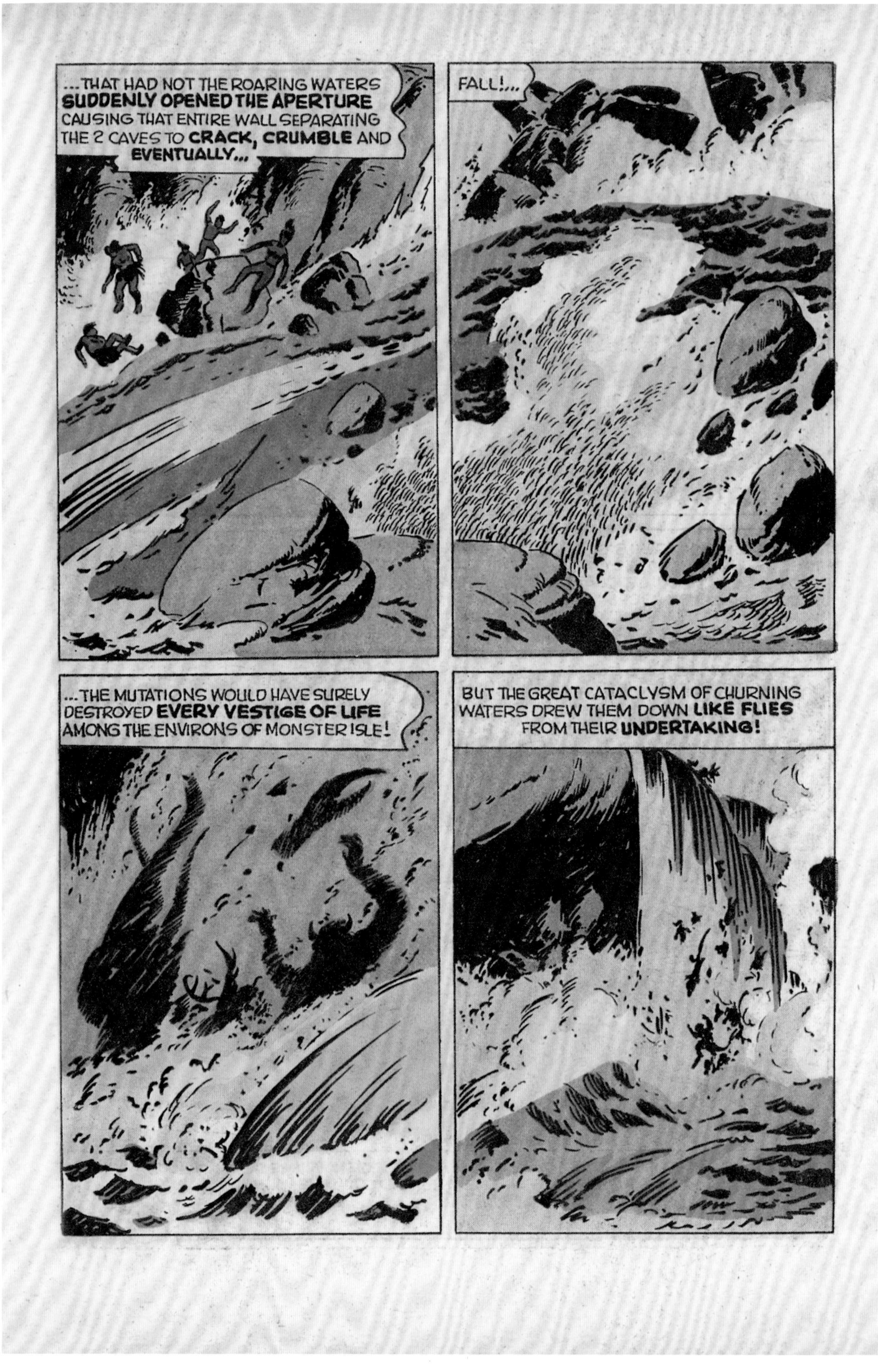
...THAT HAD NOT THE ROARING WATERS SUDDENLY OPENED THE APERTURE CAUSING THAT ENTIRE WALL SEPARATING THE 2 CAVES TO CRACK, CRUMBLE AND EVENTUALLY...
FALL!...
...THE MUTATIONS WOULD HAVE SURELY DESTROYED EVERY VESTIGE OF LIFE AMONG THE ENVIRONS OF MONSTER ISLE!
BUT THE GREAT CATACLYSM OF CHURNING WATERS DREW THEM DOWN LIKE FLIES FROM THEIR UNDERTAKING!

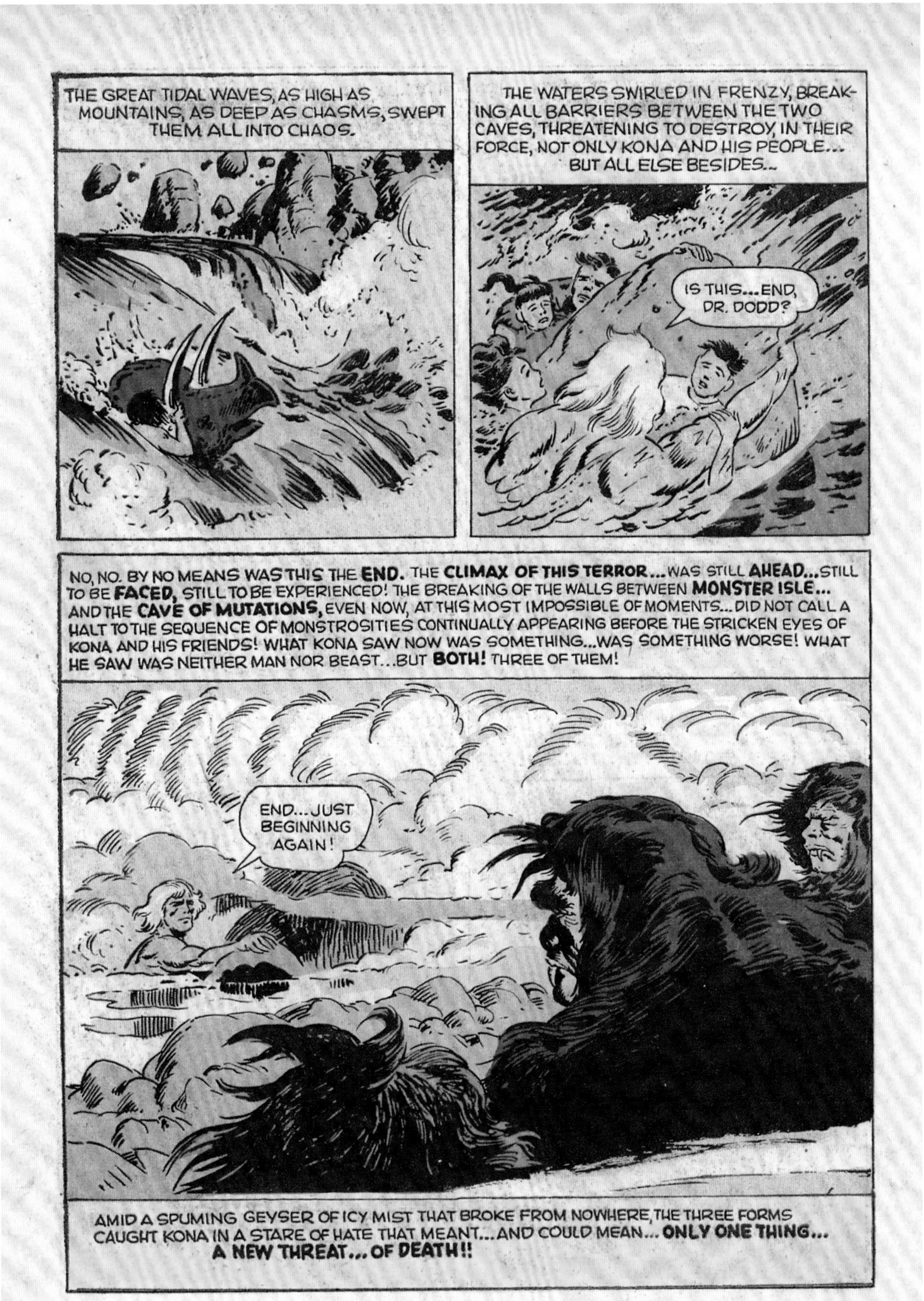
THE GREAT TIDAL WAVES, AS HIGH AS MOUNTAINS, AS DEEP AS CHASMS, SWEPT THEM ALL INTO CHAOS.
THE WATERS SWIRLED IN FRENZY, BREAKING ALL BARRIERS BETWEEN THE TWO CAVES, THREATENING TO DESTROY, IN THEIR FORCE, NOT ONLY KONA AND HIS PEOPLE... BUT ALL ELSE BESIDES...
IS THIS...END, DR. DODD?
NO, NO. BY NO MEANS WAS THIS THE END. THE CLIMAX OF THIS TERROR...WAS STILL AHEAD...STILL TO BE FACED, STILL TO BE EXPERIENCED! THE BREAKING OF THE WALLS BETWEEN MONSTER ISLE... AND THE CAVE OF MUTATIONS, EVEN NOW, AT THIS MOST IMPOSSIBLE OF MOMENTS...DID NOT CALL A HALT TO THE SEQUENCE OF MONSTROSITIES CONTINUALLY APPEARING BEFORE THE STRICKEN EYES OF KONA AND HIS FRIENDS! WHAT KONA SAW NOW WAS SOMETHING...WAS SOMETHING WORSE! WHAT HE SAW WAS NEITHER MAN NOR BEAST...BUT BOTH! THREE OF THEM!
END...JUST BEGINNING AGAIN!
AMID A SPUMING GEYSER OF ICY MIST THAT BROKE FROM NOWHERE, THE THREE FORMS CAUGHT KONA IN A STARE OF HATE THAT MEANT...AND COULD MEAN... ONLY ONE THING... A NEW THREAT... OF DEATH!!

MICHAEL McMILLAN

(b. 1933)

Michael McMillan had one of those brief but influential careers in comic books possible only in the boom times of the 1940s super-hero craze and the late 1960s-to-early-1970s underground comics flood, when unusual talents were drawn into the mix for a short, fruitful period.

Born in Pasadena, California, McMillan studied architecture and industrial design at the University of Southern California and spent the 1950s and 1960s working in architecture and product design while painting on the side. In 1968, McMillan completed a master's degree in sculpture at San Francisco State, and a year later saw an exhibition by the Chicago art group the Hairy Who at the Art Institute of San Francisco. Fascinated by their graphic panache and punning wordplay, McMillan found himself then inspired by the artists' cartoon imagery and clever witticisms. Around the same heady time, he found *Zap* no. 1 at City Lights Books and thought, "Why not try this." He drew some pages and took them over to the publisher of *Zap*, Don Donahue, and, to McMillan's surprise, Donahue offered to publish the work. And so *Terminal Comics* no. 1 (1971) would be McMillan's comics debut. He describes creating his comics as a "more or less intuitive act. I was getting tired of fine art approaches and I was raised on comics, especially *Classics Illustrated* and pre-Code material." His primary drawing influences were, of course, the Hairy Who, but within comics, the solid, rounded forms of Harold Gray (Little Orphan Annie) and harsh geometries of Chester Gould (Dick Tracy), as well as the naïve early Batman and Superman comics before the art became slick and modeled.

In correspondence, McMillan modestly describes his limited comics output in the context of his approach to all his creative activities: "The real story is: I'm not really a cartoonist. My industrial design background has set me up as a *problem solver*. To avoid being a dilettante I would immerse myself for a number of years, like a method actor, in each phase of activity: elevator design; electronic component packaging; abstract expressionism; neo-Dada; sculpture; comix; animation; poster design; printmaking. In a sense, I have always been an outsider . . . a cartoon carpetbagger."

McMillan published his works in anthologies, including *Arcade*, *Young Lust*, and *Short Order Comix*. By inventing his own 1940s-type characters, such as Comet Ray Man and Captain Flashlight, McMillan was able to explore the medium as a space in which to design costumes, machinery, and landscapes that both satisfied his own artistic interests and created entertaining narratives. Wordplay, plot turns, and a love of nonsense infect the work: his "Time Warp Rendezvous" combines sly sexual humor with pulp plotting and immaculately designed scenarios, while his "Kelvin the Human Fly" is a simultaneous tribute to old-time superheroics and parody of contemporaneous hippie culture. All of his stories are marked by his unique combination of traditional comic book storytelling with highly detailed imagery, giving readers a wonky perspectival space to inhabit for a while, before moving to the next one. McMillan's design background and professional draftsmanship give his comics a lively polish rare in the underground.

McMillan also made his own films, designed posters for the de Young Museum in San Francisco, and, in the late 1970s, worked on a series of animations with underground comics artist Victor Moscoso. McMillan continued drawing (largely unpublished) comics sporadically in the 1980s and early 1990s. An avid rock climber and former cyclist, he now lives in the Bay Area, pursuing printmaking full time.

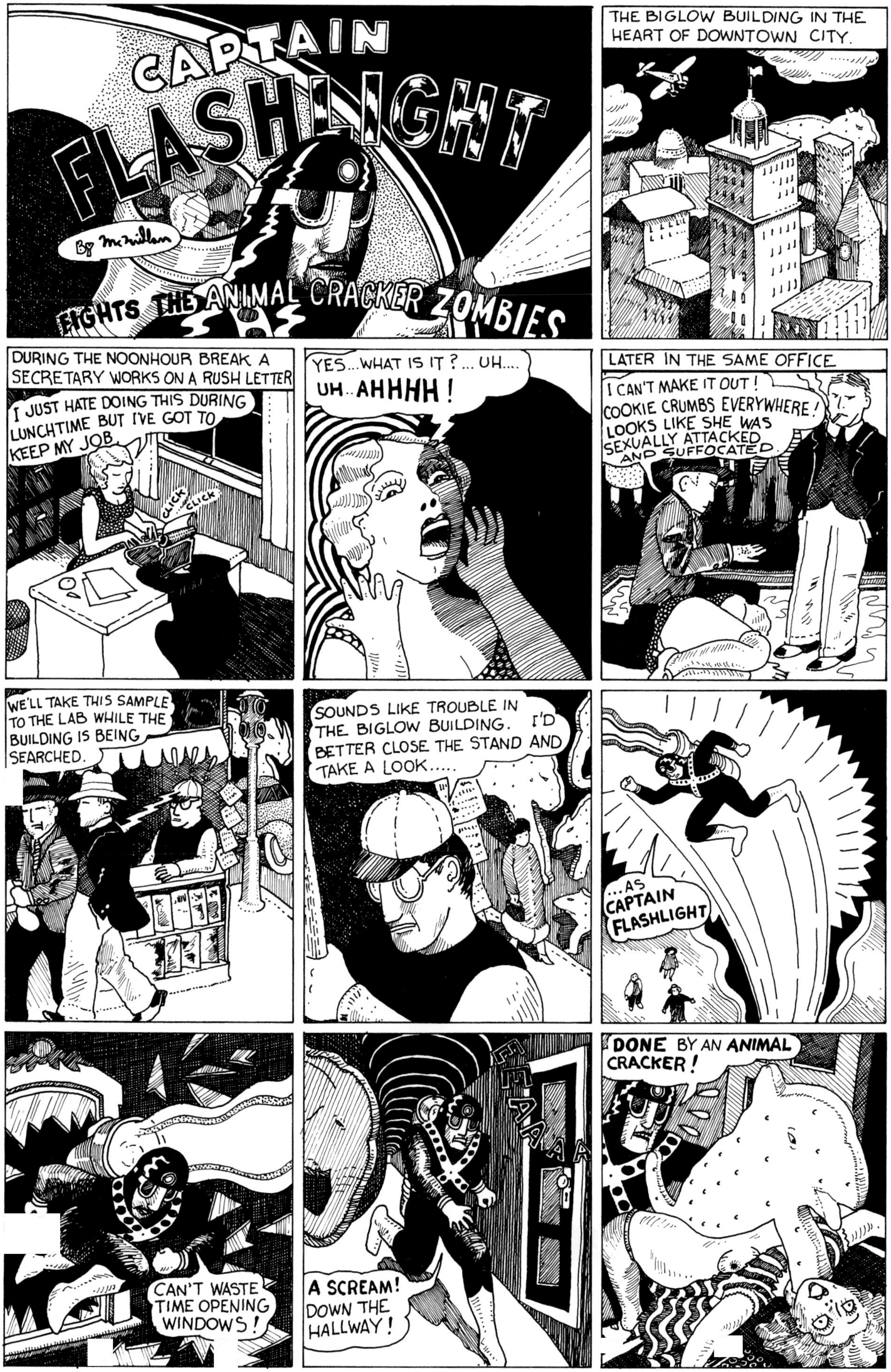
CAPTAIN FLASHLIGHT
By McMillan
FIGHTS THE ANIMAL CRACKER ZOMBIES
THE BIGLOW BUILDING IN THE HEART OF DOWNTOWN CITY.
DURING THE NOONHOUR BREAK A SECRETARY WORKS ON A RUSH LETTER
I JUST HATE DOING THIS DURING LUNCHTIME BUT I'VE GOT TO KEEP MY JOB.
CLICK CLICK
YES...WHAT IS IT?...UH.... UH..AHHHH!
LATER IN THE SAME OFFICE
I CAN'T MAKE IT OUT! COOKIE CRUMBS EVERYWHERE! LOOKS LIKE SHE WAS SEXUALLY ATTACKED AND SUFFOCATED.
WE'LL TAKE THIS SAMPLE TO THE LAB WHILE THE BUILDING IS BEING SEARCHED.
SOUNDS LIKE TROUBLE IN THE BIGLOW BUILDING. I'D BETTER CLOSE THE STAND AND TAKE A LOOK.....
...AS CAPTAIN FLASHLIGHT
CAN'T WASTE TIME OPENING WINDOWS!
EEAAAAA
A SCREAM! DOWN THE HALLWAY!
DONE BY AN ANIMAL CRACKER!

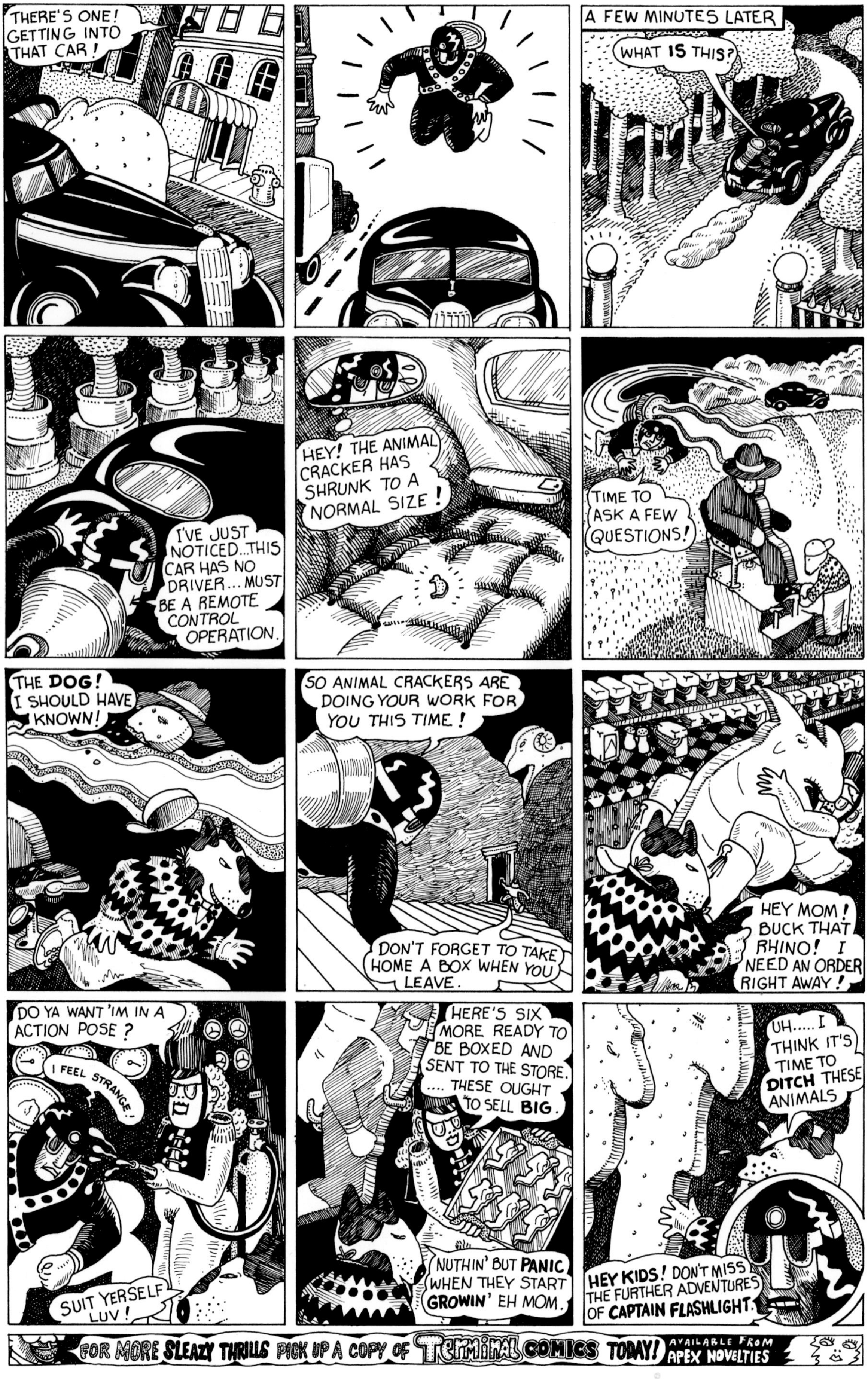
THERE'S ONE! GETTING INTO THAT CAR!
A FEW MINUTES LATER
WHAT IS THIS?
I'VE JUST NOTICED...THIS CAR HAS NO DRIVER... MUST BE A REMOTE CONTROL OPERATION.
HEY! THE ANIMAL CRACKER HAS SHRUNK TO A NORMAL SIZE!
TIME TO ASK A FEW QUESTIONS!
THE DOG! I SHOULD HAVE KNOWN!
SO ANIMAL CRACKERS ARE DOING YOUR WORK FOR YOU THIS TIME!
DON'T FORGET TO TAKE HOME A BOX WHEN YOU LEAVE.
HEY MOM! BUCK THAT RHINO! I NEED AN ORDER RIGHT AWAY!
DO YA WANT 'IM IN A ACTION POSE?
I FEEL STRANGE
SUIT YERSELF LUV!
HERE'S SIX MORE READY TO BE BOXED AND SENT TO THE STORE. .... THESE OUGHT TO SELL BIG.
NUTHIN' BUT PANIC WHEN THEY START GROWIN' EH MOM.
UH..... I THINK IT'S TIME TO DITCH THESE ANIMALS
HEY KIDS! DON'T MISS THE FURTHER ADVENTURES OF CAPTAIN FLASHLIGHT.
FOR MORE SLEAZY THRILLS PICK UP A COPY OF TERMINAL COMICS TODAY! AVAILABLE FROM APEX NOVELTIES

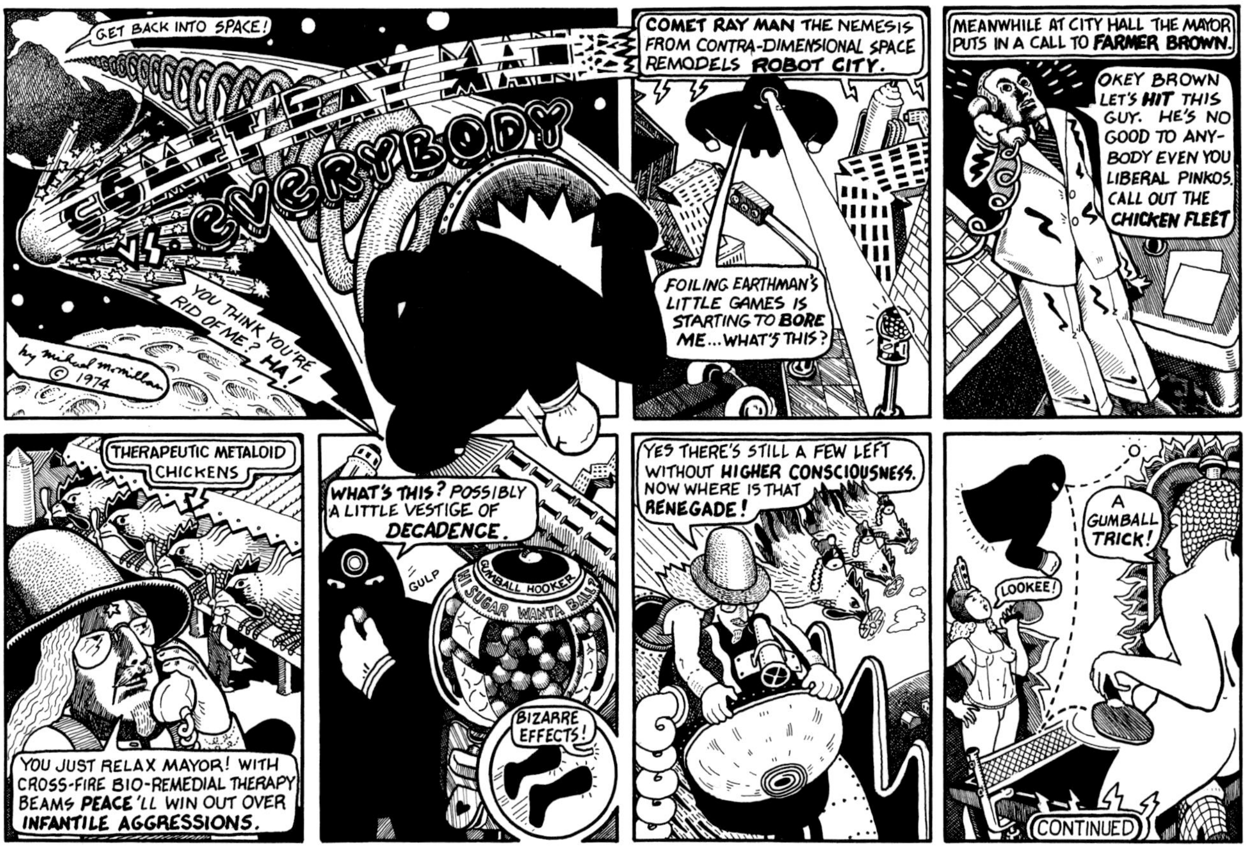
GET BACK INTO SPACE!
vs. EVERYBODY
YOU THINK YOU'RE RID OF ME? HA!
by michael mcmillan © 1974
COMET RAY MAN THE NEMESIS FROM CONTRA-DIMENSIONAL SPACE REMODELS ROBOT CITY.
FOILING EARTHMAN'S LITTLE GAMES IS STARTING TO BORE ME...WHAT'S THIS?
MEANWHILE AT CITY HALL THE MAYOR PUTS IN A CALL TO FARMER BROWN.
OKEY BROWN LET'S HIT THIS GUY. HE'S NO GOOD TO ANYBODY EVEN YOU LIBERAL PINKOS. CALL OUT THE CHICKEN FLEET
THERAPEUTIC METALOID CHICKENS
YOU JUST RELAX MAYOR! WITH CROSS-FIRE BIO-REMEDIAL THERAPY BEAMS PEACE'LL WIN OUT OVER INFANTILE AGGRESSIONS.
WHAT'S THIS? POSSIBLY A LITTLE VESTIGE OF DECADENCE.
GULP
GUMBALL HOOKER
HI SUGAR WANTA BALL
BIZARRE EFFECTS!
YES THERE'S STILL A FEW LEFT WITHOUT HIGHER CONSCIOUSNESS. NOW WHERE IS THAT RENEGADE!
A GUMBALL TRICK!
LOOKEE!
CONTINUED

Unpublished (1975)

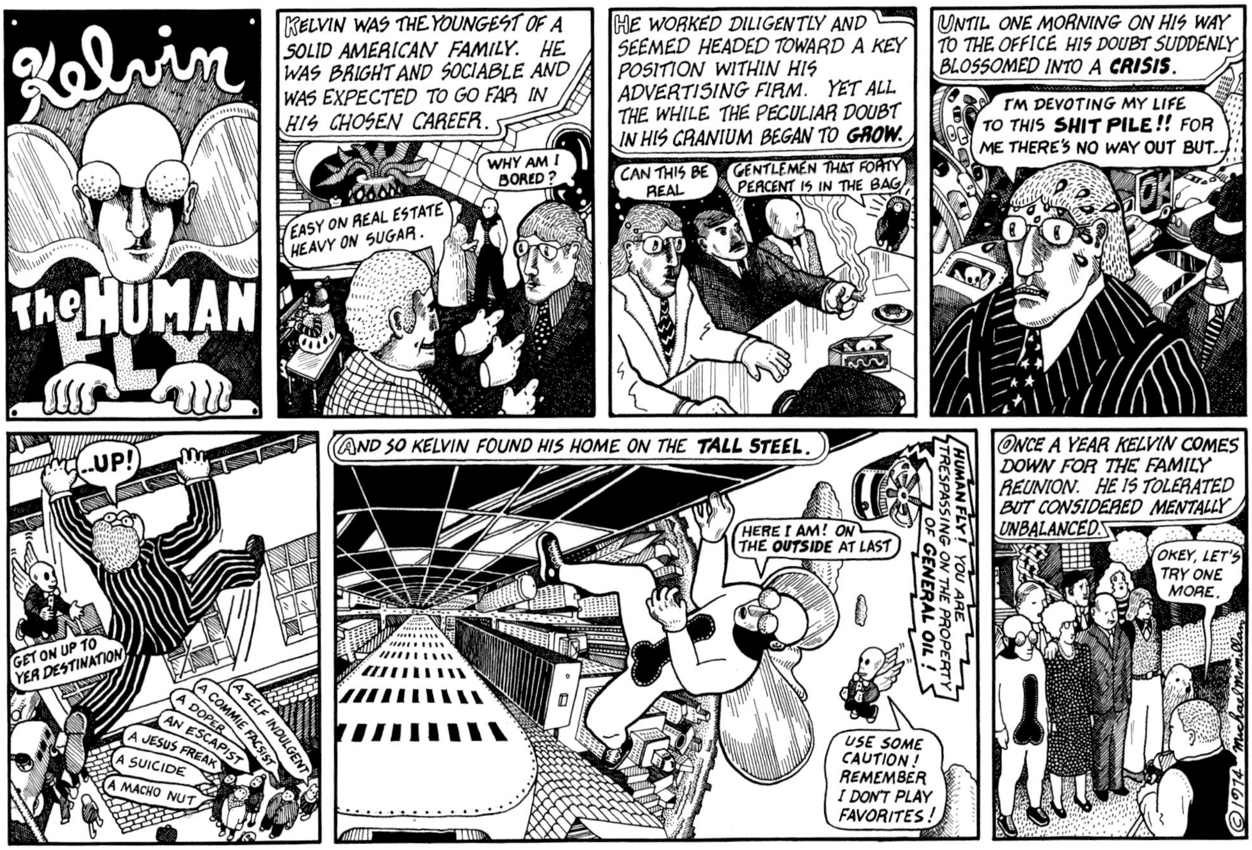
Kelvin The HUMAN FLY
KELVIN WAS THE YOUNGEST OF A SOLID AMERICAN FAMILY. HE WAS BRIGHT AND SOCIABLE AND WAS EXPECTED TO GO FAR IN HIS CHOSEN CAREER.
WHY AM I BORED?
EASY ON REAL ESTATE HEAVY ON SUGAR.
HE WORKED DILIGENTLY AND SEEMED HEADED TOWARD A KEY POSITION WITHIN HIS ADVERTISING FIRM. YET ALL THE WHILE THE PECULIAR DOUBT IN HIS CRANIUM BEGAN TO GROW.
CAN THIS BE REAL
GENTLEMEN THAT FORTY PERCENT IS IN THE BAG
UNTIL ONE MORNING ON HIS WAY TO THE OFFICE HIS DOUBT SUDDENLY BLOSSOMED INTO A CRISIS.
I'M DEVOTING MY LIFE TO THIS SHIT PILE!! FOR ME THERE'S NO WAY OUT BUT..
..UP!
GET ON UP TO YER DESTINATION
A SELF INDULGENT
A COMMIE FACSIST
A DOPER
AN ESCAPIST
A JESUS FREAK
A SUICIDE
A MACHO NUT
AND SO KELVIN FOUND HIS HOME ON THE TALL STEEL.
HUMAN FLY! YOU ARE TRESPASSING ON THE PROPERTY OF GENERAL OIL!
HERE I AM! ON THE OUTSIDE AT LAST
USE SOME CAUTION! REMEMBER I DON'T PLAY FAVORITES!
ONCE A YEAR KELVIN COMES DOWN FOR THE FAMILY REUNION. HE IS TOLERATED BUT CONSIDERED MENTALLY UNBALANCED.
OKEY, LET'S TRY ONE MORE.
© 1974 michael mcmillan

Arcade no. 1 (1975)

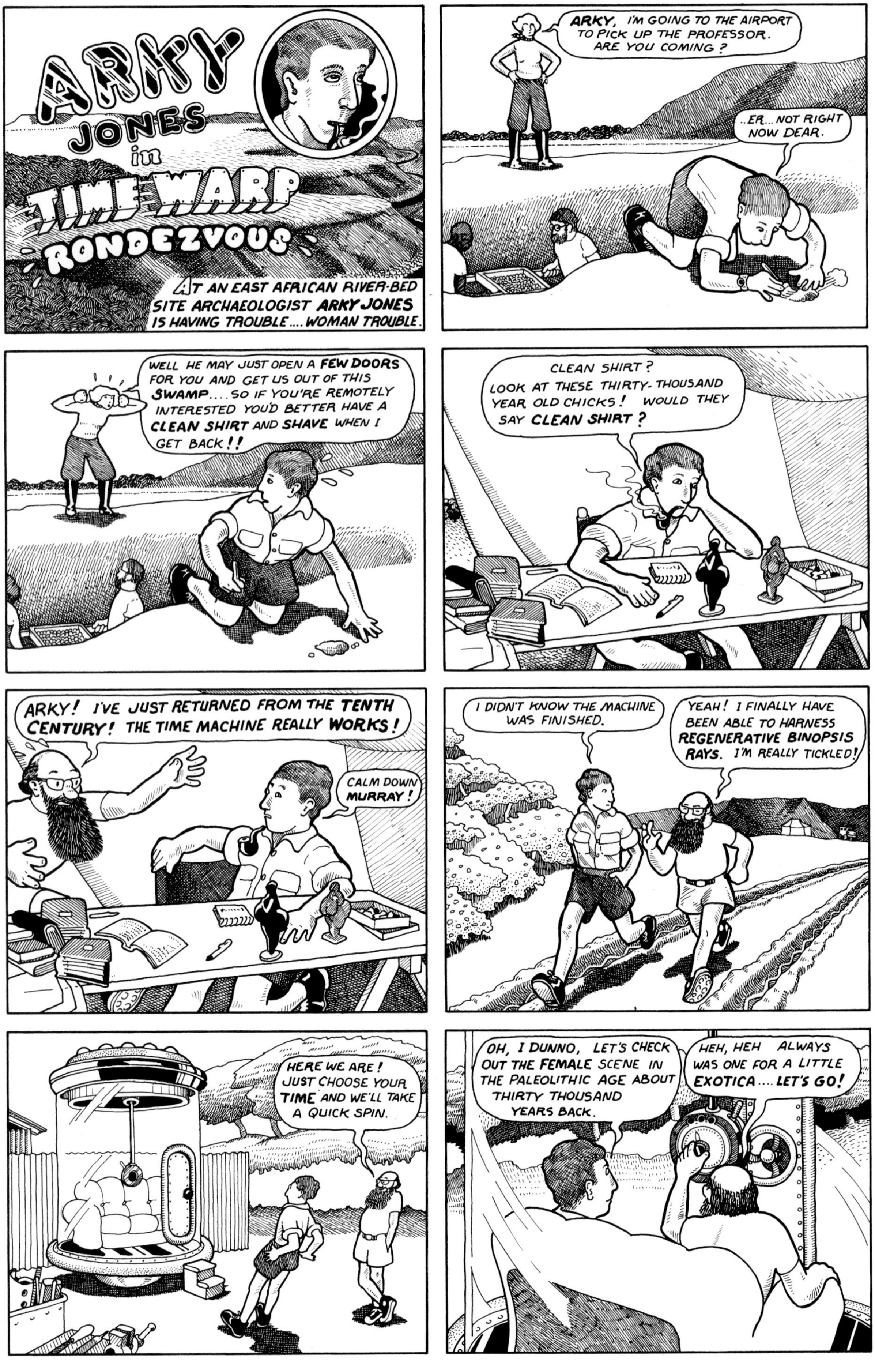
ARKY JONES in TIME WARP RONDEZVOUS
AT AN EAST AFRICAN RIVER-BED SITE ARCHAEOLOGIST ARKY JONES IS HAVING TROUBLE.... WOMAN TROUBLE.
ARKY, I'M GOING TO THE AIRPORT TO PICK UP THE PROFESSOR. ARE YOU COMING ?
..ER... NOT RIGHT NOW DEAR.
WELL HE MAY JUST OPEN A FEW DOORS FOR YOU AND GET US OUT OF THIS SWAMP.... SO IF YOU'RE REMOTELY INTERESTED YOU'D BETTER HAVE A CLEAN SHIRT AND SHAVE WHEN I GET BACK!!
CLEAN SHIRT ? LOOK AT THESE THIRTY-THOUSAND YEAR OLD CHICKS! WOULD THEY SAY CLEAN SHIRT ?
ARKY! I'VE JUST RETURNED FROM THE TENTH CENTURY! THE TIME MACHINE REALLY WORKS!
CALM DOWN MURRAY!
I DIDN'T KNOW THE MACHINE WAS FINISHED.
YEAH! I FINALLY HAVE BEEN ABLE TO HARNESS REGENERATIVE BINOPSIS RAYS. I'M REALLY TICKLED!
HERE WE ARE! JUST CHOOSE YOUR TIME AND WE'LL TAKE A QUICK SPIN.
OH, I DUNNO, LET'S CHECK OUT THE FEMALE SCENE IN THE PALEOLITHIC AGE ABOUT THIRTY THOUSAND YEARS BACK.
HEH, HEH ALWAYS WAS ONE FOR A LITTLE EXOTICA.... LET'S GO!

Young Lust no. 5 (1977)

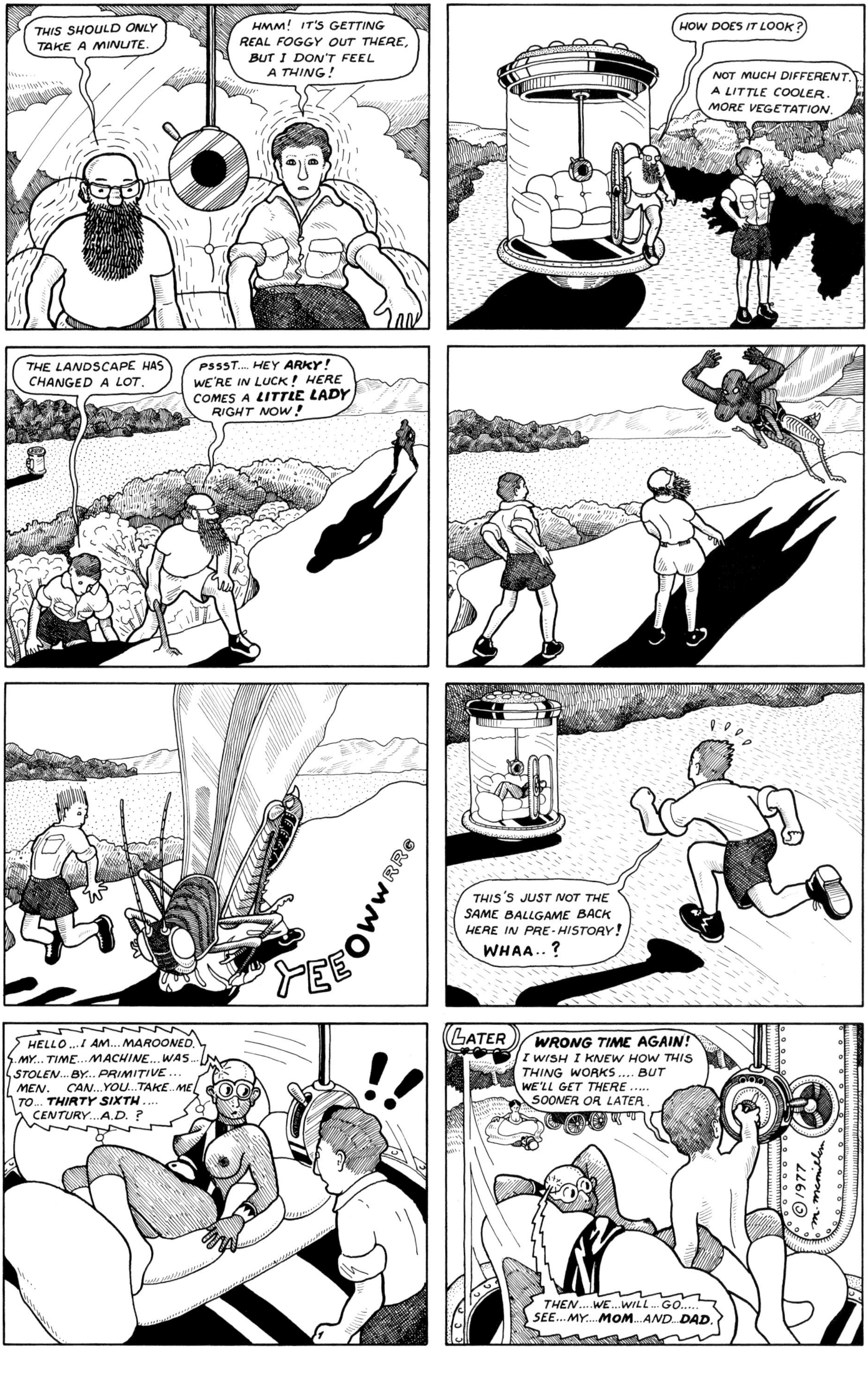
THIS SHOULD ONLY TAKE A MINUTE.
HMM! IT'S GETTING REAL FOGGY OUT THERE, BUT I DON'T FEEL A THING!
HOW DOES IT LOOK?
NOT MUCH DIFFERENT. A LITTLE COOLER. MORE VEGETATION.
THE LANDSCAPE HAS CHANGED A LOT.
PSSST.... HEY ARKY! WE'RE IN LUCK! HERE COMES A LITTLE LADY RIGHT NOW!
YEEOWWRRG
THIS'S JUST NOT THE SAME BALLGAME BACK HERE IN PRE-HISTORY!
WHAA..?
HELLO...I AM...MAROONED. MY...TIME...MACHINE...WAS...STOLEN...BY...PRIMITIVE... MEN. CAN...YOU...TAKE...ME TO... THIRTY SIXTH.... CENTURY...A.D. ?
!!
LATER
WRONG TIME AGAIN! I WISH I KNEW HOW THIS THING WORKS.... BUT WE'LL GET THERE..... SOONER OR LATER.
THEN....WE...WILL...GO.... SEE...MY....MOM...AND...DAD.
© 1977 m. mcmillan

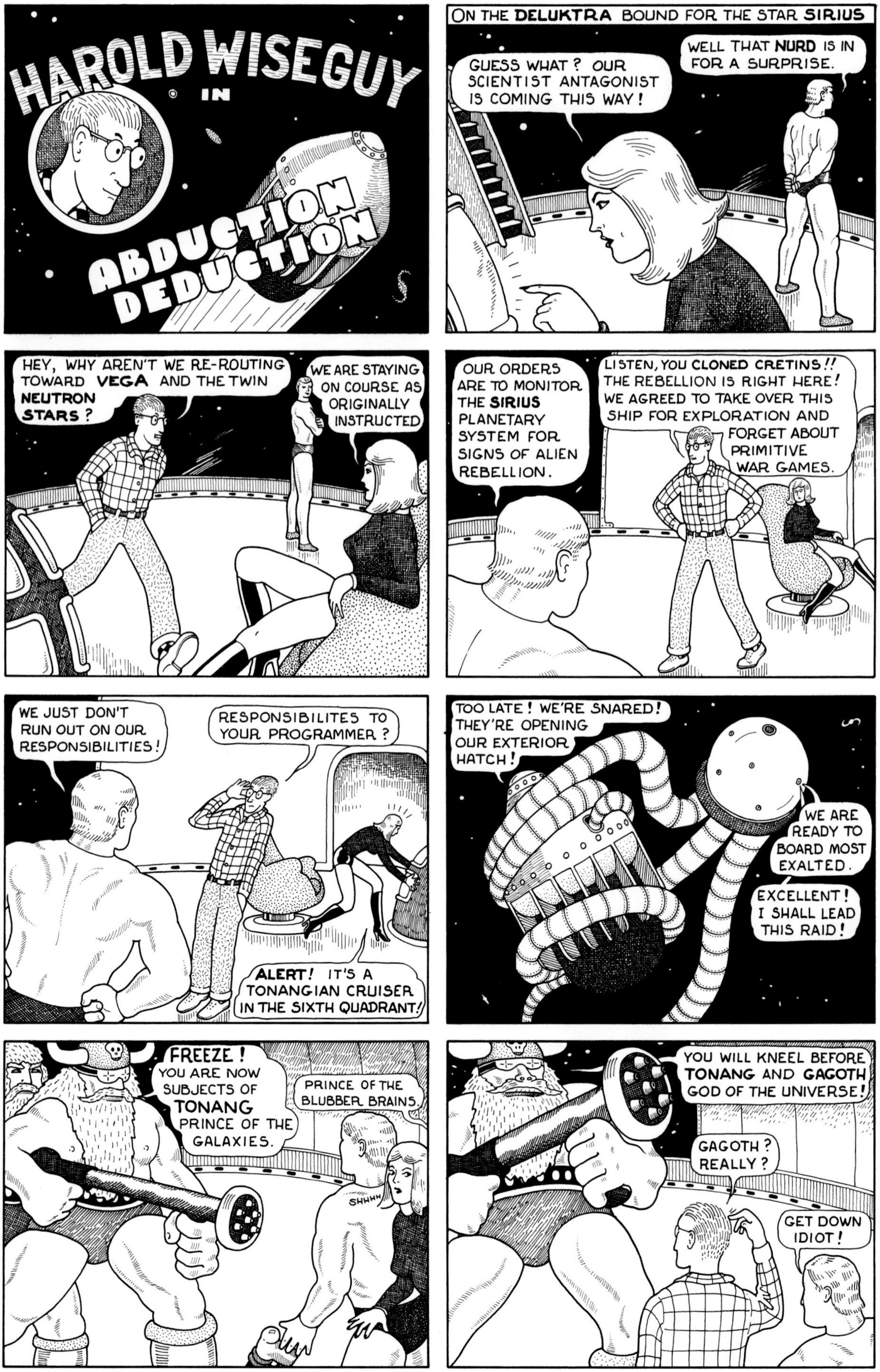
HAROLD WISEGUY IN
ABDUCTION DEDUCTION
ON THE DELUKTRA BOUND FOR THE STAR SIRIUS
GUESS WHAT? OUR SCIENTIST ANTAGONIST IS COMING THIS WAY!
WELL THAT NURD IS IN FOR A SURPRISE.
HEY, WHY AREN'T WE RE-ROUTING TOWARD VEGA AND THE TWIN NEUTRON STARS?
WE ARE STAYING ON COURSE AS ORIGINALLY INSTRUCTED
OUR ORDERS ARE TO MONITOR THE SIRIUS PLANETARY SYSTEM FOR SIGNS OF ALIEN REBELLION.
LISTEN, YOU CLONED CRETINS!! THE REBELLION IS RIGHT HERE! WE AGREED TO TAKE OVER THIS SHIP FOR EXPLORATION AND FORGET ABOUT PRIMITIVE WAR GAMES.
WE JUST DON'T RUN OUT ON OUR RESPONSIBILITIES!
RESPONSIBILITES TO YOUR PROGRAMMER?
ALERT! IT'S A TONANGIAN CRUISER IN THE SIXTH QUADRANT!
TOO LATE! WE'RE SNARED! THEY'RE OPENING OUR EXTERIOR HATCH!
WE ARE READY TO BOARD MOST EXALTED.
EXCELLENT! I SHALL LEAD THIS RAID!
FREEZE! YOU ARE NOW SUBJECTS OF TONANG PRINCE OF THE GALAXIES.
PRINCE OF THE BLUBBER BRAINS.
SHHHH
YOU WILL KNEEL BEFORE TONANG AND GAGOTH GOD OF THE UNIVERSE!
GAGOTH? REALLY?
GET DOWN IDIOT!

Young Lust no. 6 (1980)

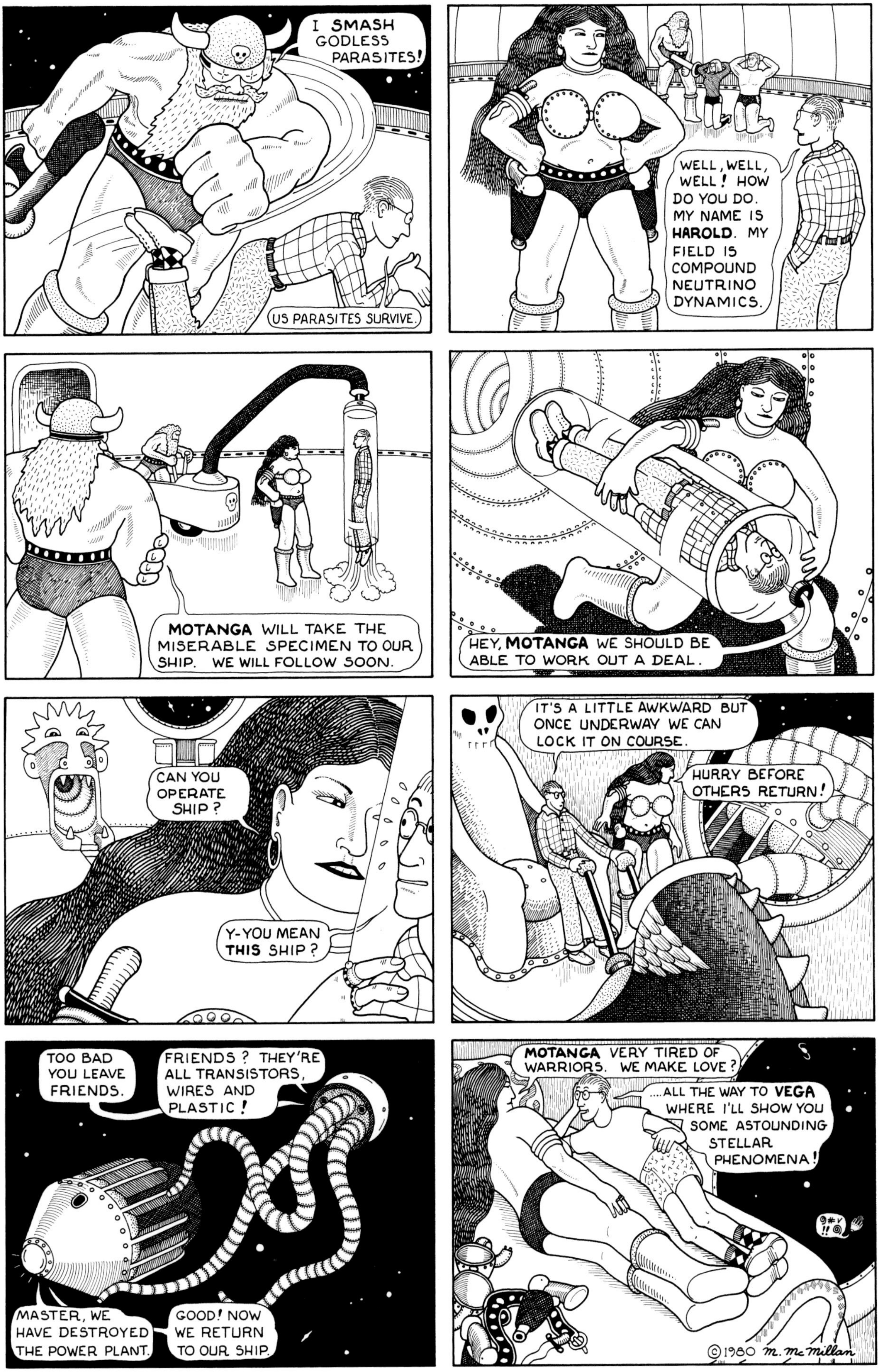
I SMASH GODLESS PARASITES!
US PARASITES SURVIVE.
WELL, WELL, WELL! HOW DO YOU DO. MY NAME IS HAROLD. MY FIELD IS COMPOUND NEUTRINO DYNAMICS.
MOTANGA WILL TAKE THE MISERABLE SPECIMEN TO OUR SHIP. WE WILL FOLLOW SOON.
HEY, MOTANGA WE SHOULD BE ABLE TO WORK OUT A DEAL.
CAN YOU OPERATE SHIP?
Y-YOU MEAN THIS SHIP?
IT'S A LITTLE AWKWARD BUT ONCE UNDERWAY WE CAN LOCK IT ON COURSE.
HURRY BEFORE OTHERS RETURN!
TOO BAD YOU LEAVE FRIENDS.
FRIENDS? THEY'RE ALL TRANSISTORS, WIRES AND PLASTIC!
MASTER, WE HAVE DESTROYED THE POWER PLANT.
GOOD! NOW WE RETURN TO OUR SHIP.
MOTANGA VERY TIRED OF WARRIORS. WE MAKE LOVE?
...ALL THE WAY TO VEGA WHERE I'LL SHOW YOU SOME ASTOUNDING STELLAR PHENOMENA!
©1980 m. mcmillan

PETE MORISI

(1928–2003)

Pete Morisi led a double life for much of his career. An NYPD police officer by day and comic book artist by night, he had perhaps the most unusual "day job" of any cartoonist.

Born and raised in Brooklyn, Morisi's first published work appeared in 1946, and by 1948 he was regularly freelancing for a number of publishers on all the genres he could handle. In 1953 Morisi created Johnny Dynamite for Comic Media. Admittedly influenced by the success of Mike Hammer and other noir PIs running through American film and literature (just like Sam Hill), Morisi created the character and then wrote and drew the majority of Johnny Dynamite's violent romps through the Chicago area. The stories are wonderfully pulpy, derivative stuff, but Morisi was drawing his finest artwork and his striking visuals lifted the material to unusual heights. He was a master of moment-to-moment storytelling. Each action, each pose, was fondly defined and crisply rendered so that a reader can't help but be immersed in his spaces. Morisi told his stories through a series of still images using every camera angle and filmic device he could think of. As if to accentuate the "screen" effect, the panels all have rounded corners and there is nary a speed line, sound effect, or any of the other trappings of comics pages in sight. This method is highly economical, and even refined, comic book storytelling. Yet Morisi was not making storyboards on paper. His panels are crowded compositions full of close-ups on his hero's invariably agonized or beat-up face. And then there is a rare "setup" panel; it too is crowded with shapes, objects, and color. Morisi, one supposes, drew it as he lived it: The sheer crowded claustrophobia of a teeming city is always at the fore, and characters are always right up against something, surrounded by buildings, trapped in rooms. Morisi renders all of this with a graceful, minimal line. Though he was influenced by Milton Caniff and claimed a major influence by artist George Tuska, Morisi seems more related to the "clear line" school of European cartooning. There

are no expressionist effects in this noir—just an eerie dead-of-night stillness, which makes it all the more effective.

Johnny Dynamite ran first in *Dynamite* and then as his own title from 1953 to 1954, with brief revivals in 1955 and 1956. By 1954 the comics industry was in a downward slide, and Morisi jumped to Charlton Comics, where he drew a bit more *Dynamite* and a few other titles. Due to the ongoing comics slump, in 1956 Morisi had to move on—there just wasn't enough work to sustain him and his family. Having always wanted to be a policeman, he joined the force in 1956 and continued on the job until 1976.

But something wouldn't quite let Pete Morisi give up comics altogether. Though the police department forbade any extracurricular work, Morisi continued drawing comics for Charlton Comics when he was off duty, signing the work "PAM" and keeping his true identity a closely guarded secret. He drew Westerns for a while, and then, in 1965, brought his ever more streamlined style to the super-hero craze with his creation of the character Thunderbolt, a mystical crime fighter. Morisi continued drawing for Charlton until 1976, producing more than one hundred stories in all. When Charlton finally closed down the same year he retired from the force, Morisi found himself a bit at loose ends. His style out of fashion and, thanks to his pseudonym, his name largely unknown, he never quite made it back into comics. Fully retired by the late 1980s, he lived on Staten Island until his death in 2003.

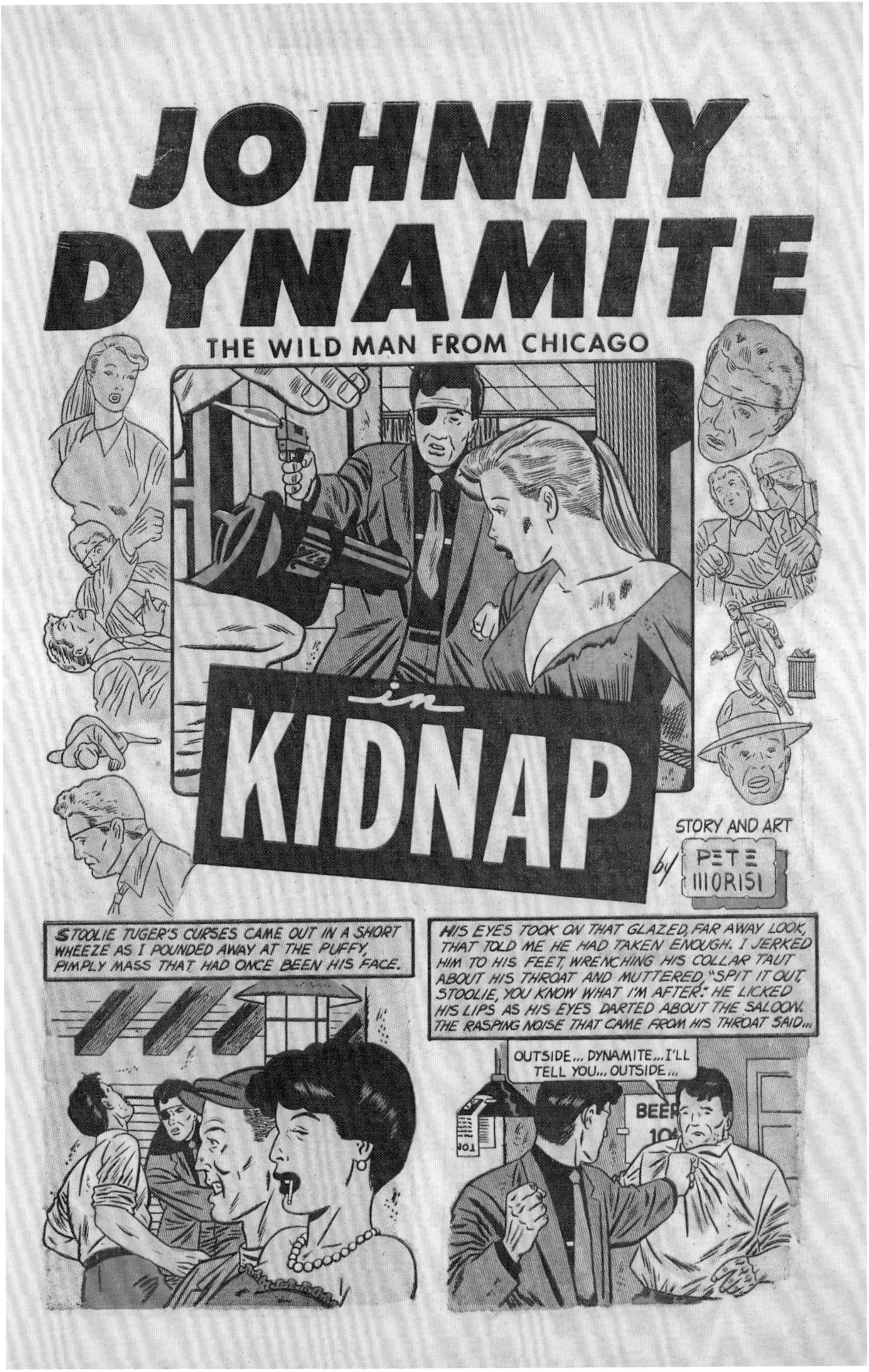
JOHNNY DYNAMITE
THE WILD MAN FROM CHICAGO
in
KIDNAP
STORY AND ART
by PETE MORISI
STOOLIE TUGER'S CURSES CAME OUT IN A SHORT WHEEZE AS I POUNDED AWAY AT THE PUFFY, PIMPLY MASS THAT HAD ONCE BEEN HIS FACE.
HIS EYES TOOK ON THAT GLAZED, FAR AWAY LOOK, THAT TOLD ME HE HAD TAKEN ENOUGH. I JERKED HIM TO HIS FEET, WRENCHING HIS COLLAR TAUT ABOUT HIS THROAT AND MUTTERED, "SPIT IT OUT, STOOLIE, YOU KNOW WHAT I'M AFTER." HE LICKED HIS LIPS AS HIS EYES DARTED ABOUT THE SALOON. THE RASPING NOISE THAT CAME FROM HIS THROAT SAID...
OUTSIDE... DYNAMITE... I'LL TELL YOU... OUTSIDE...
BEER

Dynamite no. 6 (1954)

I SHOVED TUGER THROUGH THE BACK DOOR OF THE SALOON INTO A DARKENED ALLEY...
COUGH IT UP, STOOLIE! YOU'VE BEEN AROUND THE UNDERWORLD LONG ENOUGH TO KNOW WHAT GOES ON. WHO PUT THE GRAB ON MY SECRETARY, JUDY KANE?
TAWNY ADAM IS THE ONE YOU WANT. S...SHE'S GOT YOUR BROAD. I DON'T KNOW THE DEAL...HONEST. JUST THAT SHE KIDNAPPED YOUR BROAD TO GET TO YOU.
IF YOU'RE GIVING ME A WRONG WORD, STOOLIE, YOU CAN START LOOKING FOR A SIX BY SIX RIGHT NOW. I'M NOT PLAYING GAMES!
HONEST JOHNNY, I'M LEVELIN'. CHECK IT YOURSELF. THIS TAWNY BABE IS STASHED OUT AT 612 LAKE DRIVE. THAT'S ALL I KNOW... HONEST.
I LEFT TUGER LAYING IN THE ALLEY WITH THE REST OF THE GARBAGE, AND HOPPED INTO THE RENTED CAR. TAWNY ADAM, EH? I HAD HEARD OF HER. SHE HAD MADE THE BIG JUMP FROM SMALL TIME VICE GIRL TO BIG TIME JEWEL PEDDLER. BUT THIS KIDNAP DEAL DIDN'T FIGURE. WHAT DID SHE WANT OF JUDY? WHAT DID SHE WANT OF ME?
WITH
MARILYN MONROE
I MADE LAKE DRIVE IN TWENTY MINUTES FLAT. I PARKED THE BUS AND CHECKED MY SHOULDER SLING. IF TAWNY ADAM HAD HARMED JUDY IN ANY WAY, SHE'D GET A DUM-DUM IN HER BELLY FOR HER TROUBLE.
YEAH? WHATCHA WANT?
JUDY KANE, PUNK!
I RAMMED MY FIST ACROSS HIS CHEEK WITH A CRACK THAT MADE HIS TEETH GIVE WAY. HE STAGGERED BACK, DROOLING BLOOD FROM HIS LIPS, AS I FOLLOWED THROUGH WITH ONE ROUNDHOUSE AFTER ANOTHER. I WAS ABOUT READY TO PUT HIM AWAY WHEN...
WELL, MR. DYNAMITE, I SEE YOU'VE SAVED US THE TROUBLE OF CONTACTING YOU.

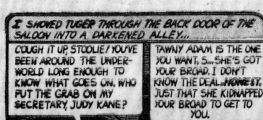

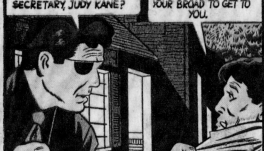

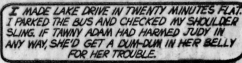

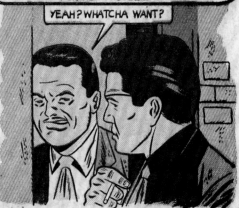

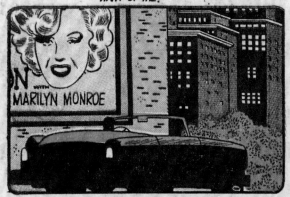

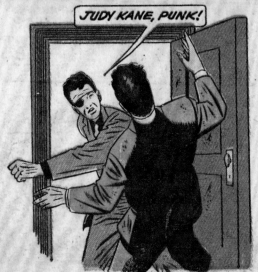

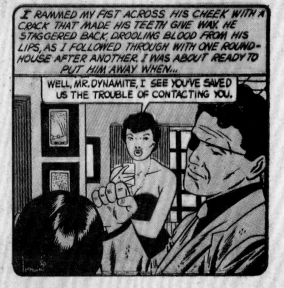

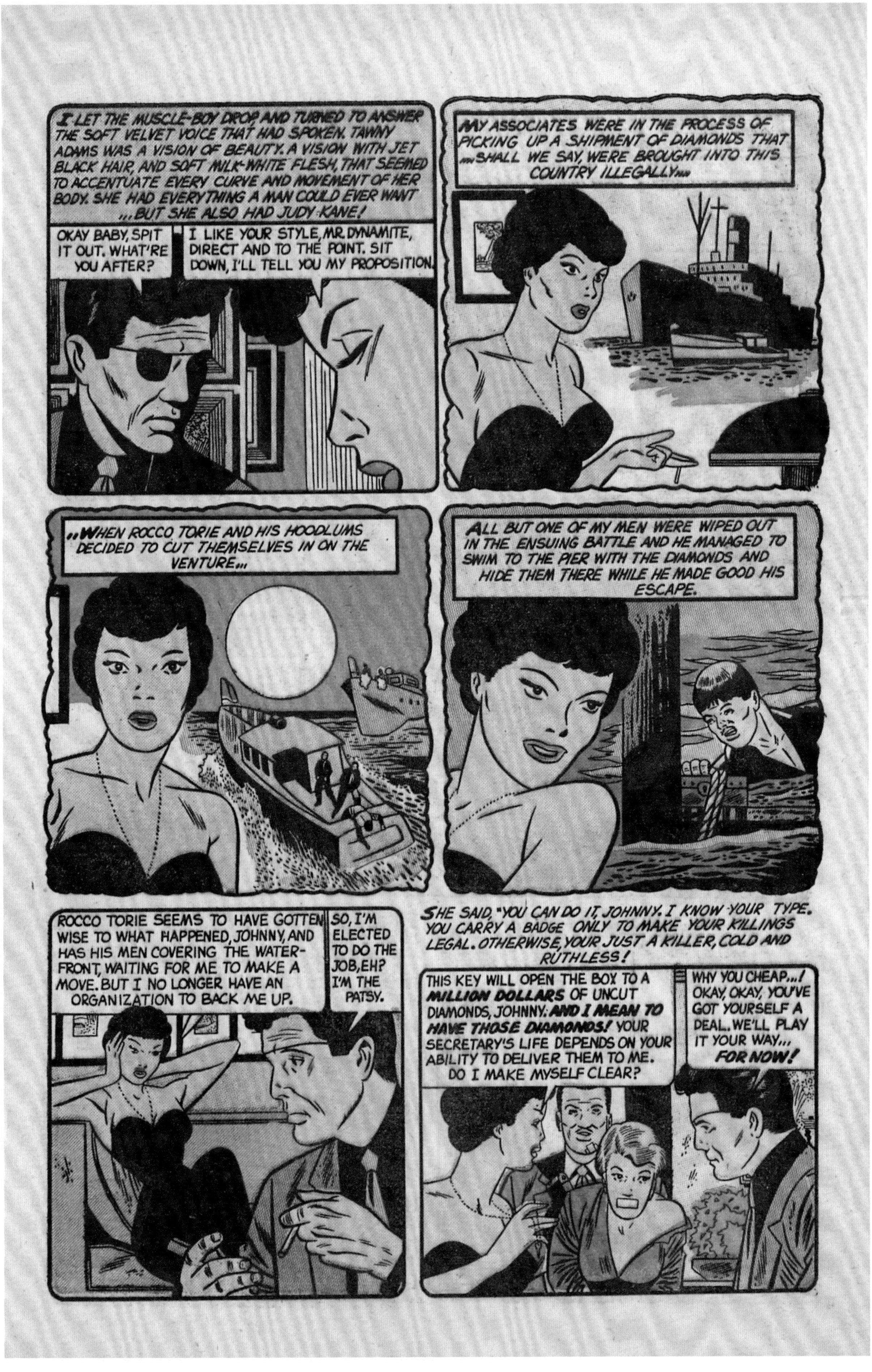
I LET THE MUSCLE-BOY DROP AND TURNED TO ANSWER THE SOFT VELVET VOICE THAT HAD SPOKEN. TAWNY ADAMS WAS A VISION OF BEAUTY. A VISION WITH JET BLACK HAIR, AND SOFT MILK-WHITE FLESH, THAT SEEMED TO ACCENTUATE EVERY CURVE AND MOVEMENT OF HER BODY. SHE HAD EVERYTHING A MAN COULD EVER WANT ...BUT SHE ALSO HAD JUDY KANE!
OKAY BABY, SPIT IT OUT. WHAT'RE YOU AFTER?
I LIKE YOUR STYLE, MR. DYNAMITE, DIRECT AND TO THE POINT. SIT DOWN, I'LL TELL YOU MY PROPOSITION.
MY ASSOCIATES WERE IN THE PROCESS OF PICKING UP A SHIPMENT OF DIAMONDS THAT ...SHALL WE SAY, WERE BROUGHT INTO THIS COUNTRY ILLEGALLY...
...WHEN ROCCO TORIE AND HIS HOODLUMS DECIDED TO CUT THEMSELVES IN ON THE VENTURE...
ALL BUT ONE OF MY MEN WERE WIPED OUT IN THE ENSUING BATTLE AND HE MANAGED TO SWIM TO THE PIER WITH THE DIAMONDS AND HIDE THEM THERE WHILE HE MADE GOOD HIS ESCAPE.
ROCCO TORIE SEEMS TO HAVE GOTTEN WISE TO WHAT HAPPENED, JOHNNY, AND HAS HIS MEN COVERING THE WATER-FRONT, WAITING FOR ME TO MAKE A MOVE. BUT I NO LONGER HAVE AN ORGANIZATION TO BACK ME UP.
SO, I'M ELECTED TO DO THE JOB, EH? I'M THE PATSY.
SHE SAID, "YOU CAN DO IT, JOHNNY. I KNOW YOUR TYPE. YOU CARRY A BADGE ONLY TO MAKE YOUR KILLINGS LEGAL. OTHERWISE, YOUR JUST A KILLER, COLD AND RUTHLESS!
THIS KEY WILL OPEN THE BOX TO A MILLION DOLLARS OF UNCUT DIAMONDS, JOHNNY. AND I MEAN TO HAVE THOSE DIAMONDS! YOUR SECRETARY'S LIFE DEPENDS ON YOUR ABILITY TO DELIVER THEM TO ME. DO I MAKE MYSELF CLEAR?
WHY YOU CHEAP...! OKAY, OKAY, YOU'VE GOT YOURSELF A DEAL. WE'LL PLAY IT YOUR WAY... FOR NOW!

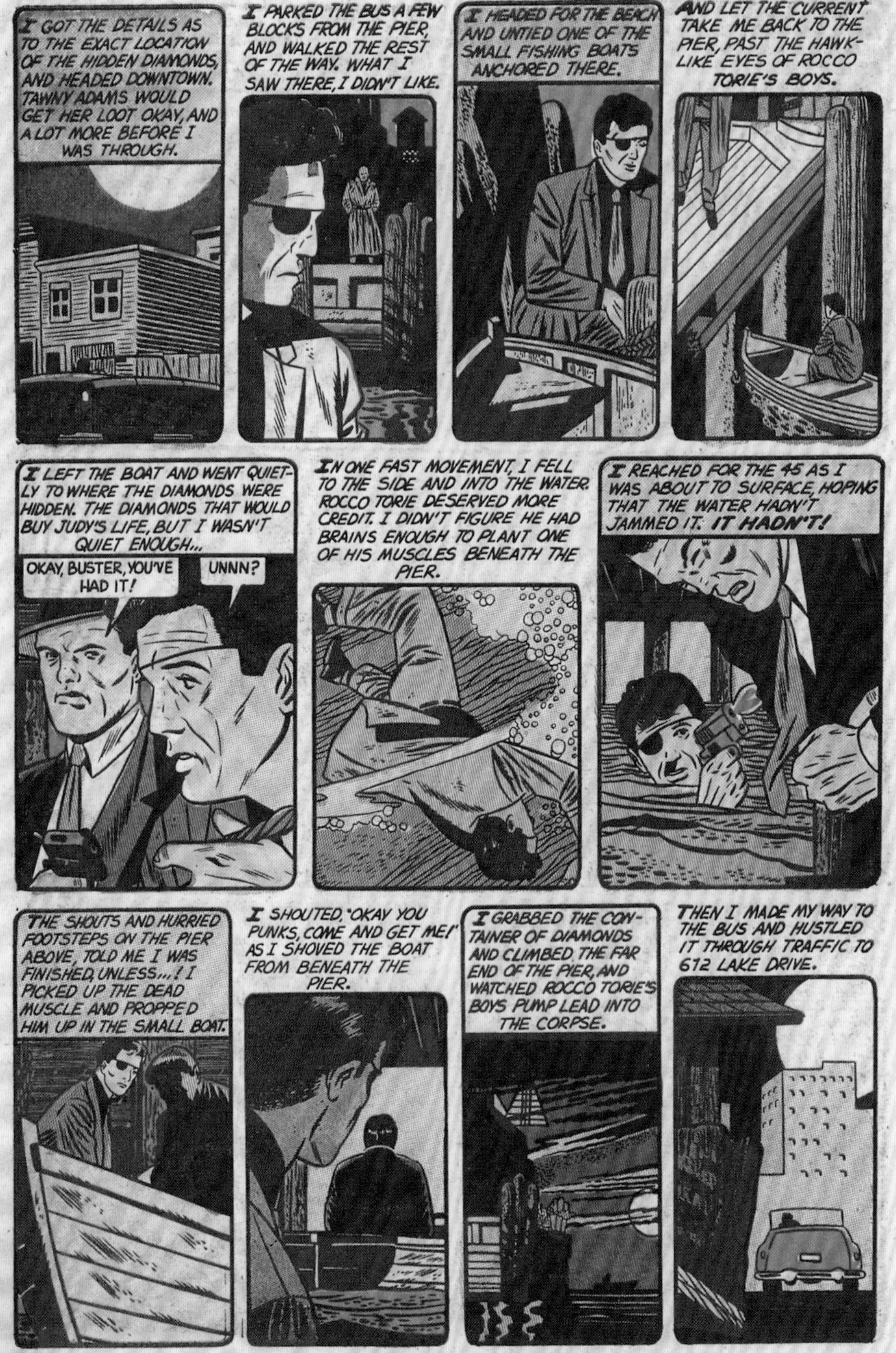
I GOT THE DETAILS AS TO THE EXACT LOCATION OF THE HIDDEN DIAMONDS, AND HEADED DOWNTOWN. TAWNY ADAMS WOULD GET HER LOOT OKAY, AND A LOT MORE BEFORE I WAS THROUGH.
I PARKED THE BUS A FEW BLOCKS FROM THE PIER, AND WALKED THE REST OF THE WAY. WHAT I SAW THERE, I DIDN'T LIKE.
I HEADED FOR THE BEACH AND UNTIED ONE OF THE SMALL FISHING BOATS ANCHORED THERE.
AND LET THE CURRENT TAKE ME BACK TO THE PIER, PAST THE HAWK-LIKE EYES OF ROCCO TORIE'S BOYS.
I LEFT THE BOAT AND WENT QUIETLY TO WHERE THE DIAMONDS WERE HIDDEN. THE DIAMONDS THAT WOULD BUY JUDY'S LIFE, BUT I WASN'T QUIET ENOUGH...
OKAY, BUSTER, YOU'VE HAD IT!
UNNN?
IN ONE FAST MOVEMENT, I FELL TO THE SIDE AND INTO THE WATER. ROCCO TORIE DESERVED MORE CREDIT. I DIDN'T FIGURE HE HAD BRAINS ENOUGH TO PLANT ONE OF HIS MUSCLES BENEATH THE PIER.
I REACHED FOR THE 45 AS I WAS ABOUT TO SURFACE, HOPING THAT THE WATER HADN'T JAMMED IT. IT HADN'T!
THE SHOUTS AND HURRIED FOOTSTEPS ON THE PIER ABOVE, TOLD ME I WAS FINISHED, UNLESS...! I PICKED UP THE DEAD MUSCLE AND PROPPED HIM UP IN THE SMALL BOAT.
I SHOUTED, "OKAY YOU PUNKS, COME AND GET ME!" AS I SHOVED THE BOAT FROM BENEATH THE PIER.
I GRABBED THE CONTAINER OF DIAMONDS AND CLIMBED THE FAR END OF THE PIER, AND WATCHED ROCCO TORIE'S BOYS PUMP LEAD INTO THE CORPSE.
THEN I MADE MY WAY TO THE BUS AND HUSTLED IT THROUGH TRAFFIC TO 612 LAKE DRIVE.

WHEN I REACHED THERE, I FOUND TAWNY, HER MUSCLE BOY AND JUDY READY TO LEAVE. TAWNY WALKED TOWARD ME AND TOOK THE METAL BOX OF DIAMONDS FROM MY HANDS.

THANK YOU, JOHNNY. I KNEW YOU WERE THE MAN FOR THE JOB.

SKIP THE ORCHIDS, BABY. JUST UNTIE JUDY KANE.

SHE SAID, "I HAVE A PLANE READY, JOHNNY, WAITING TO TAKE HARRY OUT OF THE COUNTRY. TAKE US TO THAT PLANE, AND THEN YOU SHALL HAVE YOUR JUDY KANE."

I SWORE UNDER MY BREATH AND SAID, "LET'S GET MOVING." TWENTY MINUTES LATER, WE WERE AT A SMALL DESERTED AIRFIELD ON THE OUTSKIRTS OF CHICAGO. TAWNY, ADAMS, HARRY AND MYSELF HEADED FOR THE PLANE, WHILE JUDY REMAINED IN THE CAR. SITTING TARGET...IN CASE I TRIED GETTING CUTE.

YOU HANDLED YOUR END OF THE DEAL VERY NICELY, JOHNNY. IT'S TOO BAD WE'RE ON OPPOSITE SIDES OF THE FENCE. WE COULD MAKE A GOOD TEAM.

WE'LL MEET AGAIN, BABY. AND WHEN WE DO, THINGS'LL BE DIFFERENT... *A LOT DIFFERENT!*

SHE CAME UP CLOSE AND SAID, "I'LL TAKE THAT CHANCE, JOHNNY!"

SHE BROKE THE CLINCH, AND STEPPED BACK SAYING, "SO LONG, JOHNNY-BOY!" THEN COBWEBS SEEMED TO SPIN AROUND IN MY HEAD.

THE DRONE OF THE PLANE'S ENGINES CUT INTO THE CRAZY HAZE OF WIRES, THAT WAS PLAYING TRICKS WITH MY MIND. I STAGGERED TO MY FEET AND MADE MY WAY TO THE BUS. JUDY KANE SAT THERE HELPLESS, WITH A PLEADING LOOK IN HER EYES. I UNTIED HER AND HUSTLED THE BUS BACK TO THE CITY.

JOHNNY... THAT LOOK ON YOUR FACE... WHAT'RE YOU GOING TO DO?

THAT RAP ON THE HEAD DID IT BABY. NOW TAWNY ADAMS IS GOING TO PAY THROUGH THE NOSE. SHE'S PUSHING HER LUCK *TOO FAR*.

I PARKED A FEW BLOCKS FROM 612 LAKE DRIVE AND WALKED TO TAWNY'S PLACE WITH JUDY KANE. THEN WE WAITED. I WENT THROUGH A PACK OF CHESTIES, UNTIL....

TAWNY ADAMS WALKED IN FIRST... AND INTO A ROUND-HOUSE THAT CAUGHT HER FLUSH ON THE JAW. SHE WOULDN'T SMILE FOR A LONG TIME.

HARRY PLAYED IT CUTE, AND DUCKED OUT OF MY REACH, TOSSING THE BOX OF DIAMONDS AT ME TO KNOCK ME OFF STRIDE.

YOU LOUSY #!!@#!!

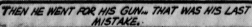

THEN HE WENT FOR HIS GUN... THAT WAS HIS LAST MISTAKE.

HENNESSY CAME DOWN IN ANSWER TO MY CALL AND PICKED UP THE PIECES. NOW IT WAS OVER... TAWNY ADAMS WOULDN'T BOTHER ANYBODY FOR A LONG, LONG TIME.

BUT JOHNNY, WHY DID TAWNY ADAMS, COME BACK HERE? SHE HAD HER DIAMONDS AND...

YEAH. BUT SHE DIDN'T HAVE THE KEY TO THE BOX, JUDY. I HAD THAT. TAWNY THOUGHT SHE HAD FORGOTTEN IT, AND CAME BACK TO PICK IT UP.

I SAID, "SHE COULDN'T TAKE A CHANCE ON BREAKING THE BOX OPEN, FOR FEAR OF RUINING THE UNCUT DIAMONDS. JUDY STARTED TO SAY, "BUT HOW DID YOU GET... AND THEN BLUSHED, AS SHE FIGURED IT OUT. YEAH, TAWNY ADAMS WAS A REAL CUTE BABE, ALL RIGHT. A CUTE BABE WHO LIKED TO SNUGGLE REAL CLOSE WHEN SHE KISSED.

THE END.

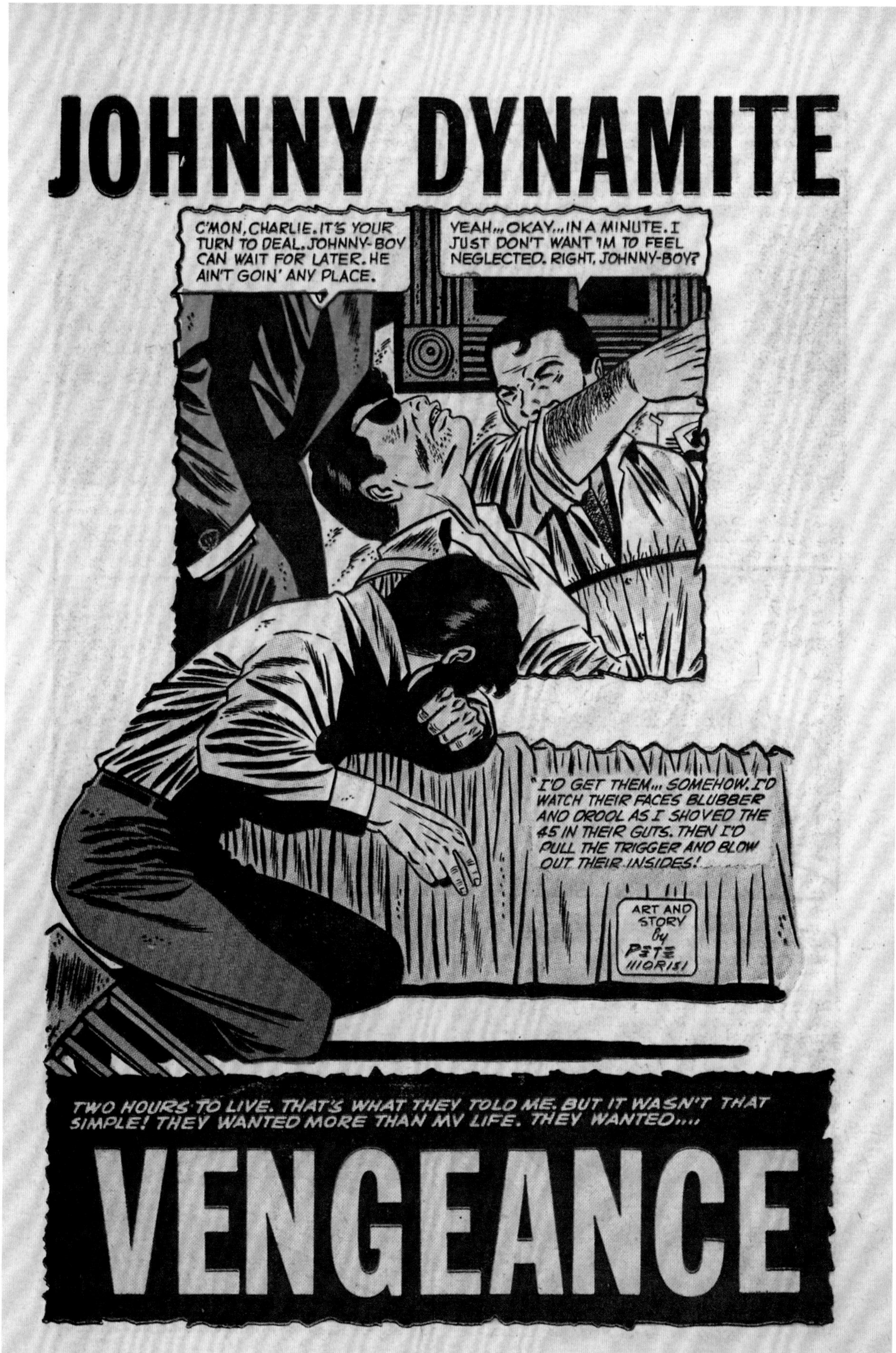
JOHNNY DYNAMITE
C'MON, CHARLIE. IT'S YOUR TURN TO DEAL. JOHNNY-BOY CAN WAIT FOR LATER. HE AIN'T GOIN' ANY PLACE.
YEAH... OKAY... IN A MINUTE. I JUST DON'T WANT 'IM TO FEEL NEGLECTED. RIGHT, JOHNNY-BOY?
I'D GET THEM... SOMEHOW. I'D WATCH THEIR FACES BLUBBER AND DROOL AS I SHOVED THE 45 IN THEIR GUTS. THEN I'D PULL THE TRIGGER AND BLOW OUT THEIR INSIDES!
ART AND STORY by PETE MORISI
TWO HOURS TO LIVE. THAT'S WHAT THEY TOLD ME. BUT IT WASN'T THAT SIMPLE! THEY WANTED MORE THAN MY LIFE. THEY WANTED....
VENGEANCE

Dynamite no. 6 (1954)

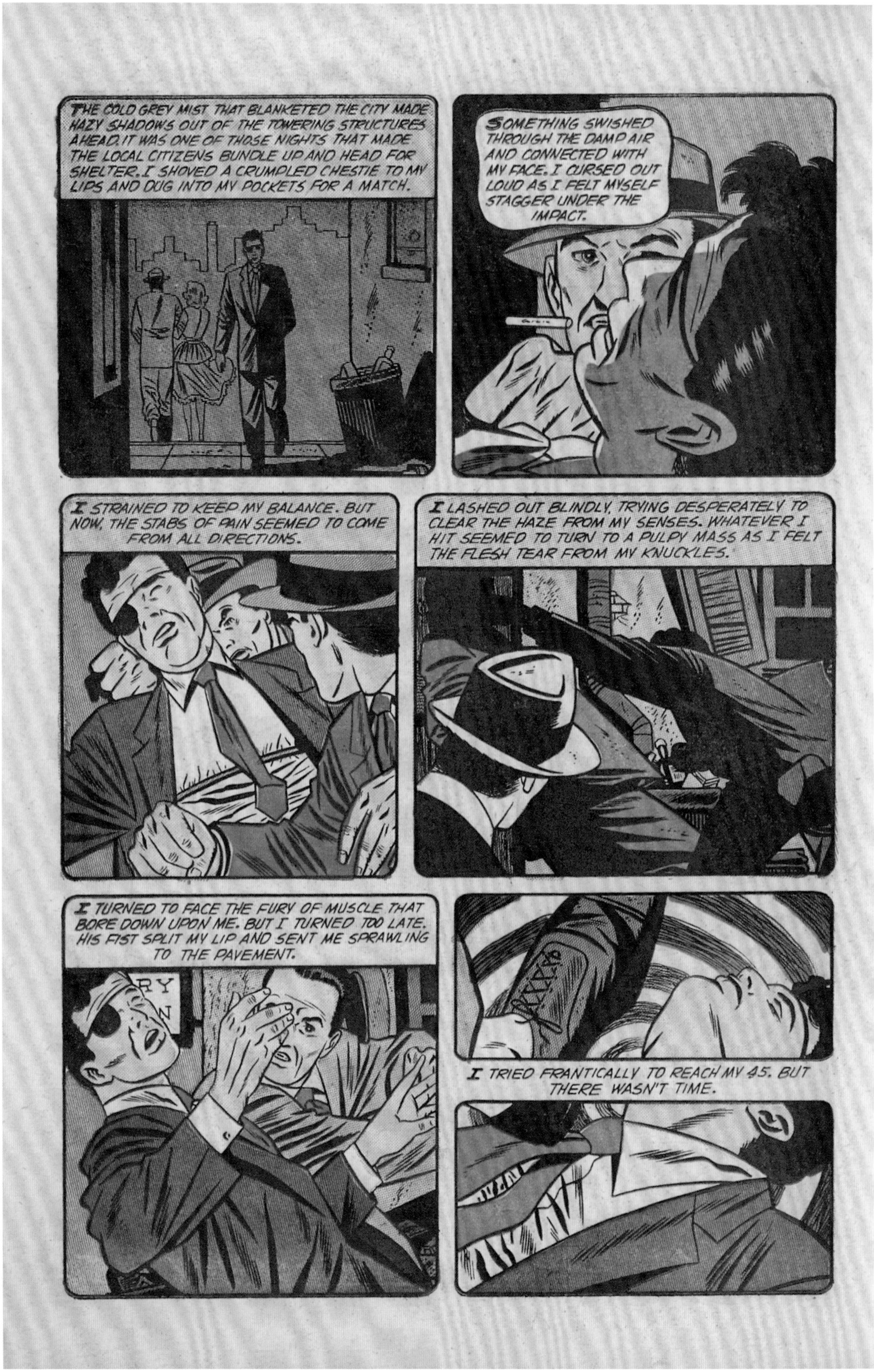
THE COLD GREY MIST THAT BLANKETED THE CITY MADE HAZY SHADOWS OUT OF THE TOWERING STRUCTURES AHEAD. IT WAS ONE OF THOSE NIGHTS THAT MADE THE LOCAL CITIZENS BUNDLE UP AND HEAD FOR SHELTER. I SHOVED A CRUMPLED CHESTIE TO MY LIPS AND DUG INTO MY POCKETS FOR A MATCH.
SOMETHING SWISHED THROUGH THE DAMP AIR AND CONNECTED WITH MY FACE. I CURSED OUT LOUD AS I FELT MYSELF STAGGER UNDER THE IMPACT.
I STRAINED TO KEEP MY BALANCE. BUT NOW, THE STABS OF PAIN SEEMED TO COME FROM ALL DIRECTIONS.
I LASHED OUT BLINDLY, TRYING DESPERATELY TO CLEAR THE HAZE FROM MY SENSES. WHATEVER I HIT SEEMED TO TURN TO A PULPY MASS AS I FELT THE FLESH TEAR FROM MY KNUCKLES.
I TURNED TO FACE THE FURY OF MUSCLE THAT BORE DOWN UPON ME. BUT I TURNED TOO LATE. HIS FIST SPLIT MY LIP AND SENT ME SPRAWLING TO THE PAVEMENT.
I TRIED FRANTICALLY TO REACH MY 45. BUT THERE WASN'T TIME.

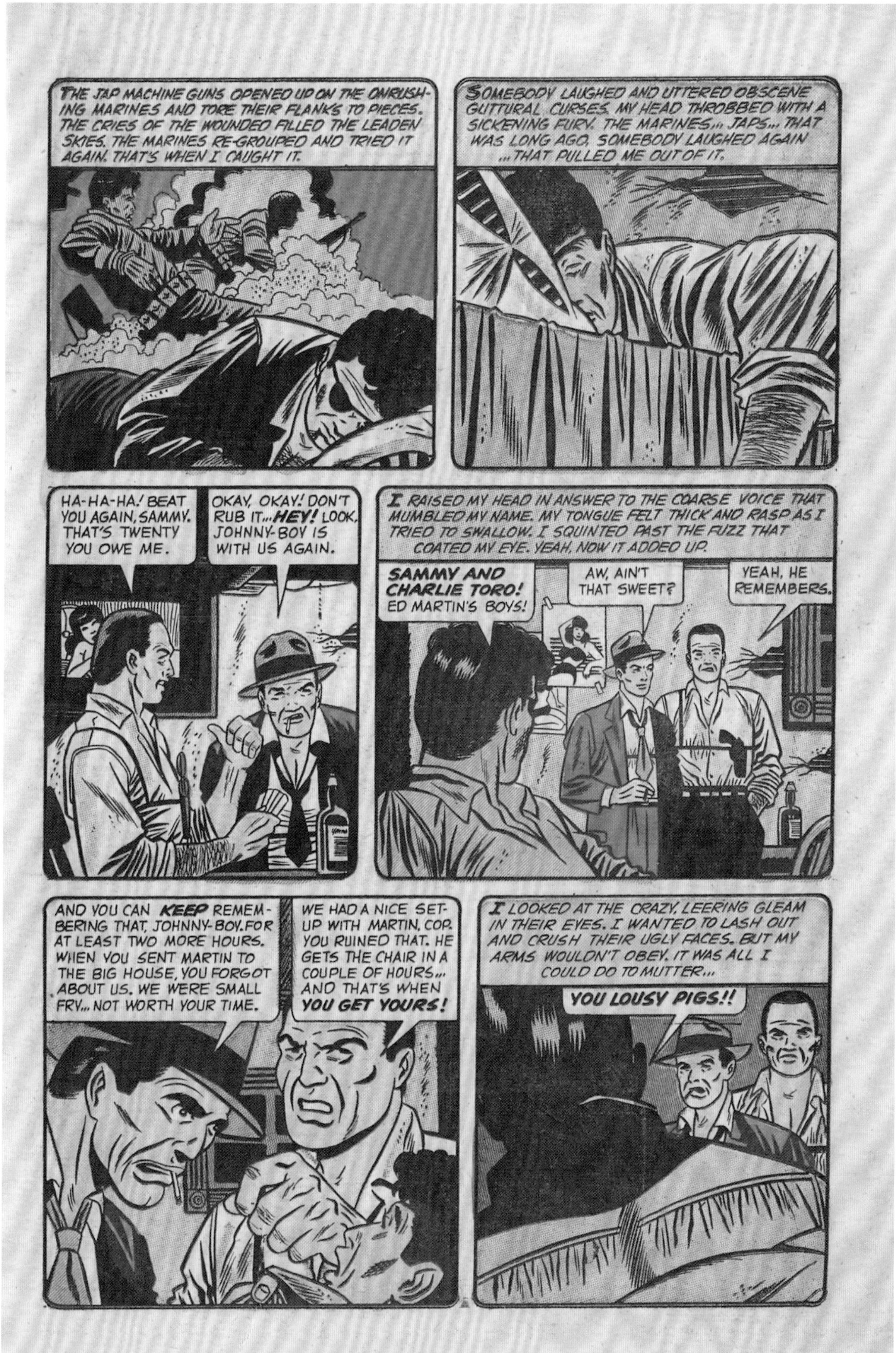
THE JAP MACHINE GUNS OPENED UP ON THE ONRUSHING MARINES AND TORE THEIR FLANKS TO PIECES. THE CRIES OF THE WOUNDED FILLED THE LEADEN SKIES. THE MARINES RE-GROUPED AND TRIED IT AGAIN. THAT'S WHEN I CAUGHT IT.
SOMEBODY LAUGHED AND UTTERED OBSCENE GUTTURAL CURSES. MY HEAD THROBBED WITH A SICKENING FURY. THE MARINES... JAPS... THAT WAS LONG AGO. SOMEBODY LAUGHED AGAIN ...THAT PULLED ME OUT OF IT.
HA-HA-HA! BEAT YOU AGAIN, SAMMY. THAT'S TWENTY YOU OWE ME.
OKAY, OKAY! DON'T RUB IT... HEY! LOOK. JOHNNY-BOY IS WITH US AGAIN.
I RAISED MY HEAD IN ANSWER TO THE COARSE VOICE THAT MUMBLED MY NAME. MY TONGUE FELT THICK AND RASP AS I TRIED TO SWALLOW. I SQUINTED PAST THE FUZZ THAT COATED MY EYE. YEAH, NOW IT ADDED UP.
SAMMY AND CHARLIE TORO! ED MARTIN'S BOYS!
AW, AIN'T THAT SWEET?
YEAH, HE REMEMBERS.
AND YOU CAN KEEP REMEMBERING THAT, JOHNNY-BOY, FOR AT LEAST TWO MORE HOURS. WHEN YOU SENT MARTIN TO THE BIG HOUSE, YOU FORGOT ABOUT US. WE WERE SMALL FRY... NOT WORTH YOUR TIME.
WE HAD A NICE SET-UP WITH MARTIN, COP. YOU RUINED THAT. HE GETS THE CHAIR IN A COUPLE OF HOURS... AND THAT'S WHEN YOU GET YOURS!
I LOOKED AT THE CRAZY, LEERING GLEAM IN THEIR EYES. I WANTED TO LASH OUT AND CRUSH THEIR UGLY FACES. BUT MY ARMS WOULDN'T OBEY. IT WAS ALL I COULD DO TO MUTTER...
YOU LOUSY PIGS!!

CHARLIE CAME AT ME IN A RAGE. "TOUGH GUY" HE SAID, AND POUNDED AWAY AT WAS LEFT OF MY FACE. HE WAS GOOD AT HIS WORK,,, YEAH,,, REAL GOOD.

THE GNAWING IN MY BODY STARTED, AGAIN AND AGAIN THE PAIN WOULD COME, THE PAIN THAT WOULD BURST IN MY BRAIN WITH A TORTUROUS ROAR.

AND THEN IT STOPPED. ALL THAT WAS LEFT WAS THE INKY BLACKNESS AND THE SWIRLING HAZE IN MY MIND THAT MADE IT GO BACK,,, BACK,,, BACK,,,

ED MARTIN AND BLACKIE ADAMS WERE A COUPLE OF CHEAP THUGS WHO HAD POOLED THEIR TALENTS TO GO INTO THE PROTECTION RACKET BACK IN THE OLD DAYS.

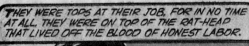

THEY WERE TOPS AT THEIR JOB, FOR IN NO TIME AT ALL, THEY WERE ON TOP OF THE RAT-HEAD THAT LIVED OFF THE BLOOD OF HONEST LABOR.

BUT MARTIN AND ADAMS WEREN'T SATISFIED, THEY HAD TO EXPAND,,, **THEY WANTED MORE!** THE PROHIBITION ACT WAS PASSED, AND OPENED THE DOOR FOR A NEW VENTURE.

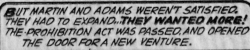

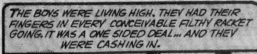

THE BOYS WERE LIVING HIGH. THEY HAD THEIR FINGERS IN EVERY CONCEIVABLE FILTHY RACKET GOING. IT WAS A ONE SIDED DEAL... AND THEY WERE CASHING IN.

BUT THEN THE LAW BEGAN TO MOVE. ONE BY ONE THE HOODLUM EMPIRES TOPPLED. THE UNDERWORLD SHUDDERED IN FEAR AT THE CRACK-DOWN.

BUT ED MARTIN AND BLACKIE ADAMS WERE SHREWD IN THEIR OWN MORONIC WAY. THEY WERE ARMED WITH A BATTERY OF LAWYERS WHEN THE LAW CAME CALLING.

"...AND THEREFORE, YOUR HONOR, I MUST ASK THE COURT TO RULE THIS A MISTRIAL.

THEY DROPPED OUT OF EXISTENCE AFTER THAT. FOR A WHILE THEY LED A QUIET SECLUDED LIFE, OR SO IT SEEMED.

THE YEARS PASSED AND THE BOYS GREW RESTLESS. EASY MONEY BECKONED THEM ONCE AGAIN. AND THEY HURRIED TO ANSWER THE CALL. THIS TIME THE CALL WAS... *NARCOTICS!*

ONCE AGAIN THEY ORGANIZED. ADDING SAMMY AND CHARLIE TORO TO THEIR STAFF. NOW THEY WERE SET TO ROLL.

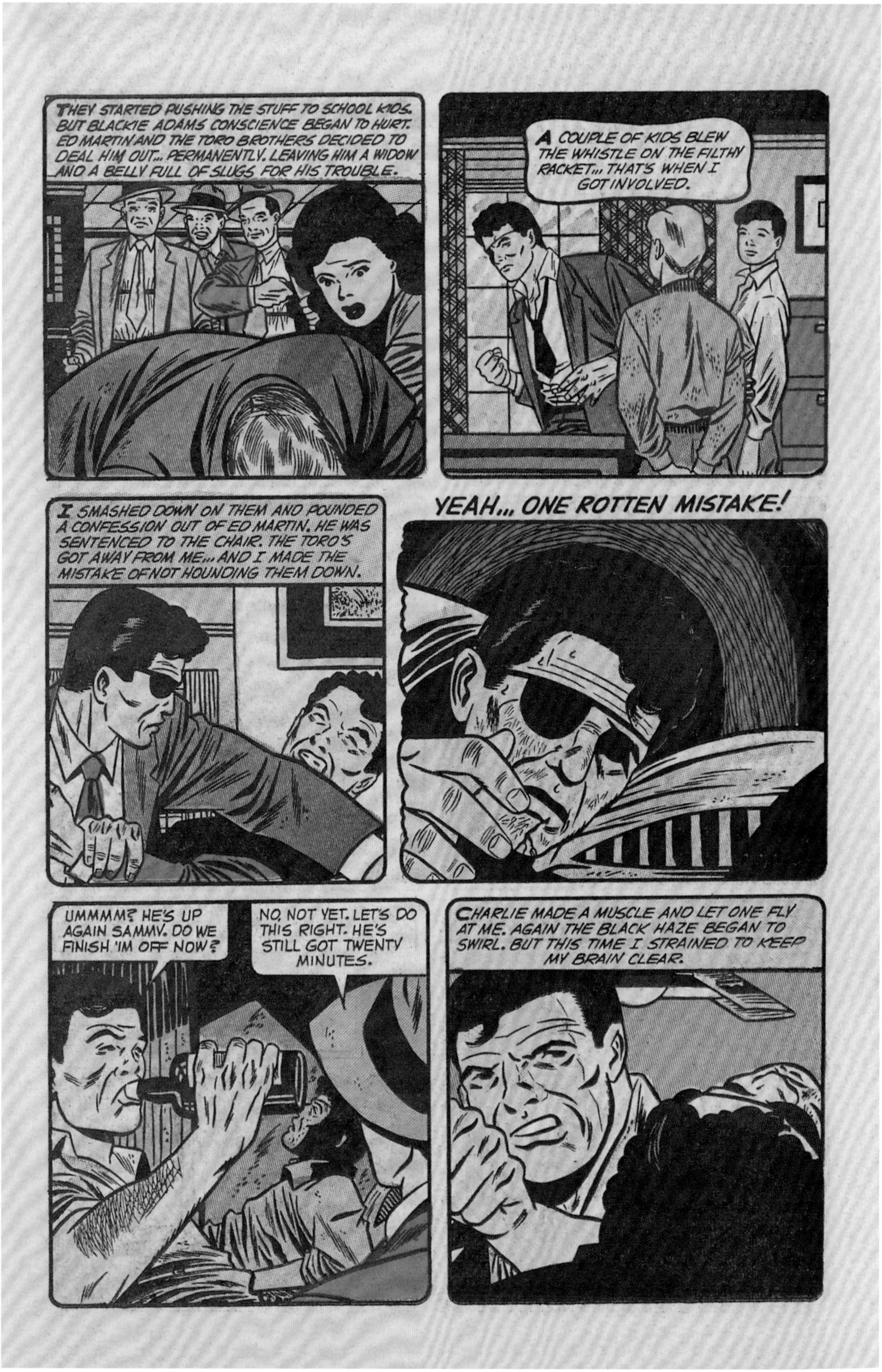
THEY STARTED PUSHING THE STUFF TO SCHOOL KIDS. BUT BLACKIE ADAMS CONSCIENCE BEGAN TO HURT. ED MARTIN AND THE TORO BROTHERS DECIDED TO DEAL HIM OUT... PERMANENTLY. LEAVING HIM A WIDOW AND A BELLY FULL OF SLUGS FOR HIS TROUBLE.
A COUPLE OF KIDS BLEW THE WHISTLE ON THE FILTHY RACKET... THAT'S WHEN I GOT INVOLVED.
I SMASHED DOWN ON THEM AND POUNDED A CONFESSION OUT OF ED MARTIN. HE WAS SENTENCED TO THE CHAIR. THE TORO'S GOT AWAY FROM ME... AND I MADE THE MISTAKE OF NOT HOUNDING THEM DOWN.
YEAH... ONE ROTTEN MISTAKE!
UMMMM? HE'S UP AGAIN SAMMY. DO WE FINISH 'IM OFF NOW?
NO, NOT YET. LET'S DO THIS RIGHT. HE'S STILL GOT TWENTY MINUTES.
CHARLIE MADE A MUSCLE AND LET ONE FLY AT ME. AGAIN THE BLACK HAZE BEGAN TO SWIRL. BUT THIS TIME I STRAINED TO KEEP MY BRAIN CLEAR.

CHARLIE AND SAMMY LET ME LAY THERE AND WENT BACK TO THEIR CARD GAME. I HAD TO PLAN... TO THINK. BUT MY BRAIN WAS A SHADOW, HAZED WITH THE FIRES OF PAIN. THEN I SAW IT.

I MOVED SLOWLY, DELIBERATELY, AND GOT MY HANDS ON THE BOTTLE.

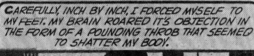

CAREFULLY, INCH BY INCH, I FORCED MYSELF TO MY FEET. MY BRAIN ROARED IT'S OBJECTION IN THE FORM OF A POUNDING THROB THAT SEEMED TO SHATTER MY BODY.

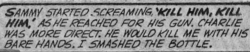

SAMMY STARTED SCREAMING, "KILL HIM, KILL HIM," AS HE REACHED FOR HIS GUN. CHARLIE WAS MORE DIRECT. HE WOULD KILL ME WITH HIS BARE HANDS. I SMASHED THE BOTTLE.

CHARLIE WOULD NEVER KILL AGAIN!

HE FELL INTO A SCREAMING BUNDLE OF PAIN. HE TWISTED AND GROANED... THEN LAY STILL. THE POUNDING IN MY BRAIN BECAME UNBEARABLE. AND I KNEW THEN, THAT I WAS FINISHED.

YOU LOUSY #!@☆#!!

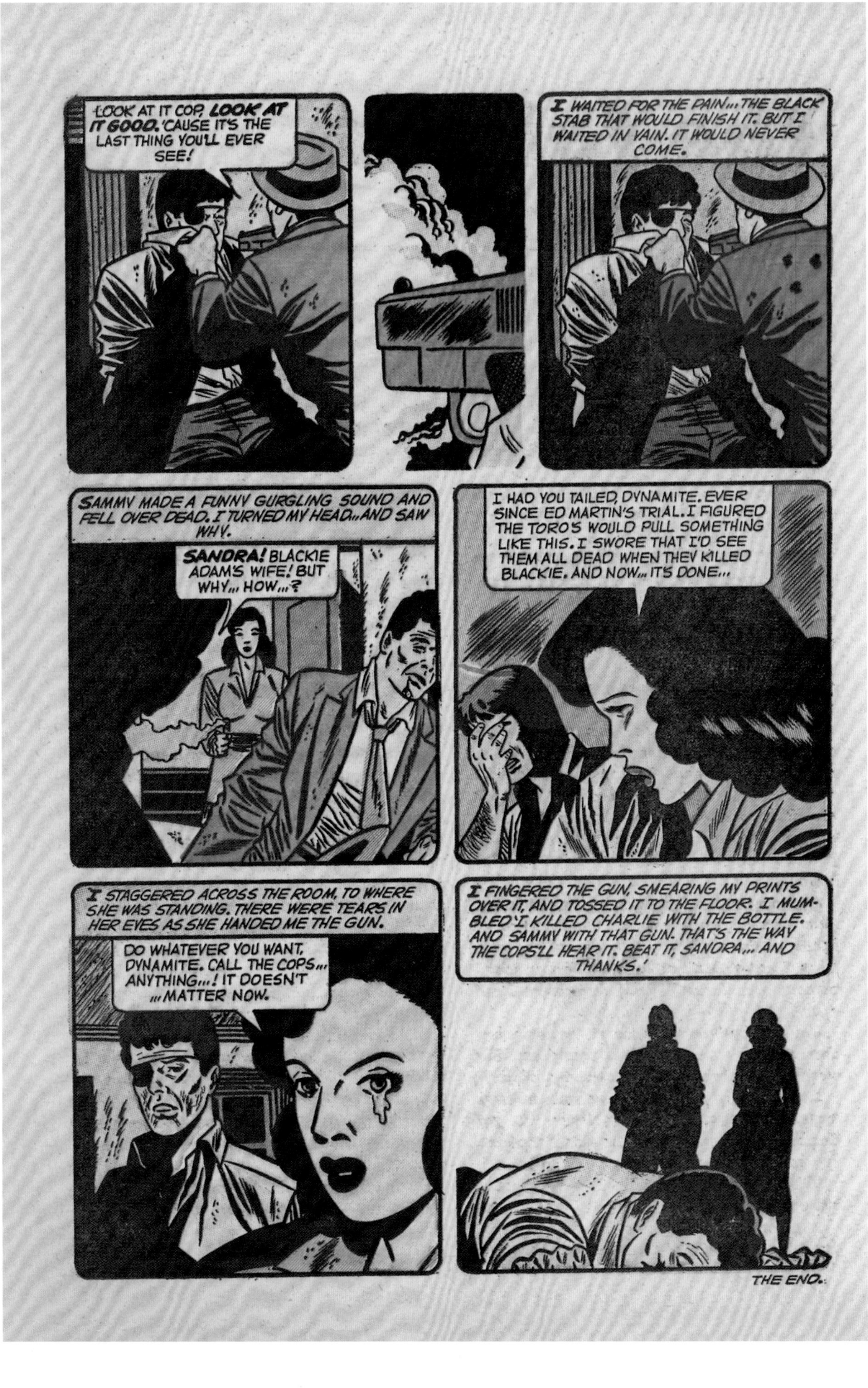
LOOK AT IT COP, LOOK AT IT GOOD. 'CAUSE IT'S THE LAST THING YOU'LL EVER SEE!
I WAITED FOR THE PAIN... THE BLACK STAB THAT WOULD FINISH IT. BUT I WAITED IN VAIN. IT WOULD NEVER COME.
SAMMY MADE A FUNNY GURGLING SOUND AND FELL OVER DEAD. I TURNED MY HEAD... AND SAW WHY.
SANDRA! BLACKIE ADAM'S WIFE! BUT WHY... HOW...?
I HAD YOU TAILED, DYNAMITE. EVER SINCE ED MARTIN'S TRIAL. I FIGURED THE TORO'S WOULD PULL SOMETHING LIKE THIS. I SWORE THAT I'D SEE THEM ALL DEAD WHEN THEY KILLED BLACKIE. AND NOW... IT'S DONE...
I STAGGERED ACROSS THE ROOM, TO WHERE SHE WAS STANDING. THERE WERE TEARS IN HER EYES AS SHE HANDED ME THE GUN.
DO WHATEVER YOU WANT, DYNAMITE. CALL THE COPS... ANYTHING...! IT DOESN'T ...MATTER NOW.
I FINGERED THE GUN, SMEARING MY PRINTS OVER IT, AND TOSSED IT TO THE FLOOR. I MUMBLED 'I KILLED CHARLIE WITH THE BOTTLE. AND SAMMY WITH THAT GUN. THAT'S THE WAY THE COPS'LL HEAR IT. BEAT IT, SANDRA... AND THANKS.'
THE END.

It's All in the Routine

Every comics genre has its rote storytelling forms: Horror happens to embrace the "shock" ending. Used most famously in E.C. Comics to add the occasional moral to an otherwise sordid story, this type of ending tends to flatten out the pacing. Read more than one and the shock becomes just another page turn. Both stories by Matt Fox, while carrying extraordinary artwork, are a bit deflated by their endings. John Stanley's stories, on the other hand, cleverly combine the shock with a shift in layout, allowing the story to manifest itself visually, rather than just shoehorning it into a regular panel grid. One of the curious features of underground comics is their use of the formal constraints of E.C. and other 1950s comics publishers. Even in Thompson's exploratory visions, he adheres to a panel format not dissimilar to a standard 1950s comic book, and his cover hilariously resembles an E.C. cover. No matter how far afield a cartoonist goes, there are always roots back into the medium.

JOHN STANLEY

(1914–93)

John Stanley spent a lifetime in comics, creating some of the best stories in the history of the medium. Born and raised in New York, Stanley worked variously for Max Fleischer's animation studio, Disney's merchandise wing, and, on a freelance basis, the *New Yorker*, among other humor magazines. By the late 1930s Stanley had landed at Western Publishing, scripting and doing layouts for the company's children's publications. In 1945 he received the assignment that would define his career: *Little Lulu*. Stanley would write and lay out *Lulu* for the next fifteen years, perfecting crisp, clear comic book storytelling with absolutely solid narrative structure and classic comedic timing that has had a profound impact on artists including underground comics artist R. Crumb and the Hernandez Brothers (*Love and Rockets*). Stanley of course remained anonymous, but he imbued the mischievous little girl with a full-blown personality and a mythology that made the comic hugely popular.

When Stanley left *Lulu* in 1959, he continued working for Western, and then, when it split with Dell, he remained with the latter, producing more excellent work, including writing and drawing the teen comic book *Thirteen* (*Going on Eighteen*) from 1961 to 1967, and the funny monster feature *Melvin Monster* from 1965 to 1969. Among all these humor comics, Stanley took two ventures into horror in 1962 with *Ghost Stories* no. 1 and *Tales from the Tomb* no. 1. Edited and with a painted cover by L. B. Cole (who also served as Sam Glanzman's editor on *Kona*), *Tomb* has all of Stanley's inventiveness and flair for layout, which is lavished on "realistic," heavily rendered drawing, and grisly subject matter.

"Two for the Price of One" follows Walter, a cad, and his wife, Paula. Stanley methodically takes his time setting up the story, as Walter prepares an elaborate ruse that slowly goes terribly wrong. As with all of his work, Stanley's characters, no matter how cartoony, have an interior life—Paula seems at first cruel but then vulnerable, and Walter's mistress seems genuinely desperate. This is not just an eight-page morality play, like so many other horror comics; Stanley makes the reader actually care about the characters.

"Crazy Quilt," illustrated by Tony Tallarico, is a masterful study of a young woman slowly unraveling. Stanley makes a four-page monologue compelling by varying the expressions, positions, and views of poor Miss Birkley. Both stories build to spectacular finishes that are not so much twist endings as logical outcomes of Stanley's slow narrative build, making them all the more horrific: By the time the end comes, the reader is completely drawn into Stanley's psychological world. Maybe it was just a bit too horrific. There was, according to Stanley, an avalanche of letters complaining about *Tales from the Tomb*, and it was summarily cancelled.

Increasingly dissatisfied with his treatment by his publishers, Stanley left comics for good in 1971. In the 1970s and 1980s he worked first for a silkscreen company and then in advertising before his eventual retirement. He left behind an enormous and multifaceted legacy in comics that is just now being rediscovered.

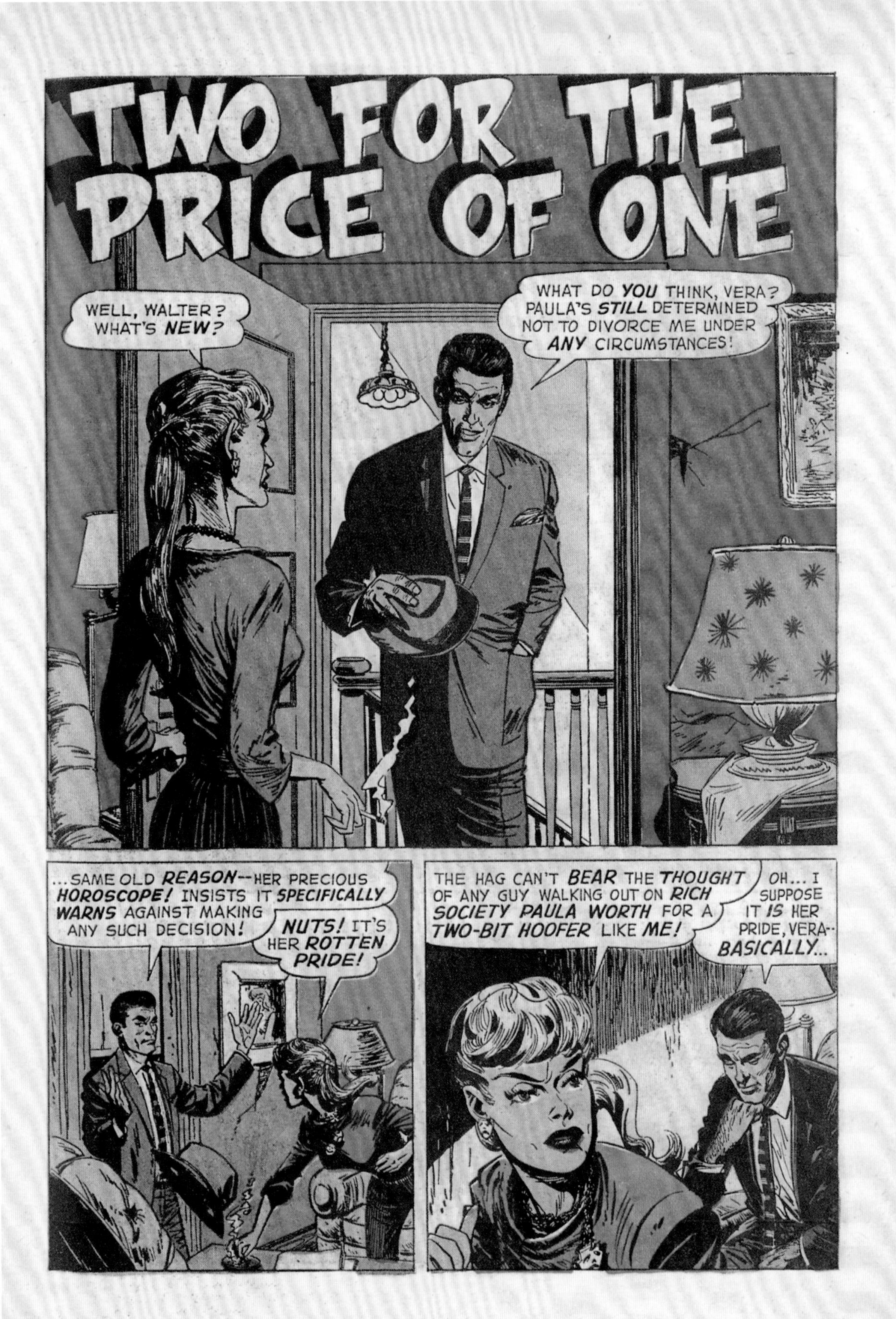
TWO FOR THE PRICE OF ONE
WELL, WALTER? WHAT'S NEW?
WHAT DO YOU THINK, VERA? PAULA'S STILL DETERMINED NOT TO DIVORCE ME UNDER ANY CIRCUMSTANCES!
...SAME OLD REASON--HER PRECIOUS HOROSCOPE! INSISTS IT SPECIFICALLY WARNS AGAINST MAKING ANY SUCH DECISION!
NUTS! IT'S HER ROTTEN PRIDE!
THE HAG CAN'T BEAR THE THOUGHT OF ANY GUY WALKING OUT ON RICH SOCIETY PAULA WORTH FOR A TWO-BIT HOOFER LIKE ME!
OH... I SUPPOSE IT IS HER PRIDE, VERA-- BASICALLY...

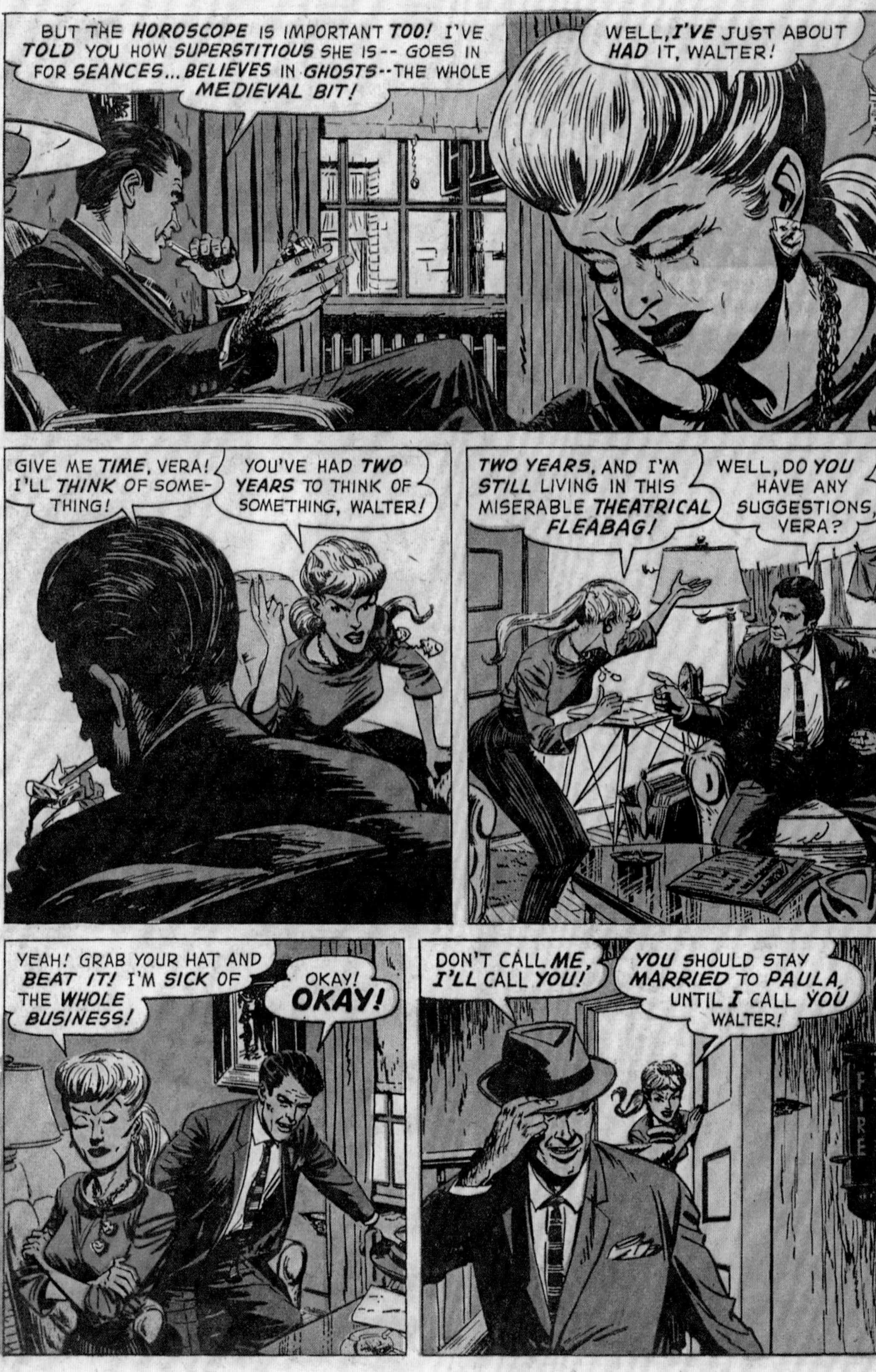
BUT THE HOROSCOPE IS IMPORTANT TOO! I'VE TOLD YOU HOW SUPERSTITIOUS SHE IS-- GOES IN FOR SEANCES... BELIEVES IN GHOSTS--THE WHOLE MEDIEVAL BIT!
WELL, I'VE JUST ABOUT HAD IT, WALTER!
GIVE ME TIME, VERA! I'LL THINK OF SOME-THING!
YOU'VE HAD TWO YEARS TO THINK OF SOMETHING, WALTER!
TWO YEARS, AND I'M STILL LIVING IN THIS MISERABLE THEATRICAL FLEABAG!
WELL, DO YOU HAVE ANY SUGGESTIONS, VERA?
YEAH! GRAB YOUR HAT AND BEAT IT! I'M SICK OF THE WHOLE BUSINESS!
OKAY! OKAY!
DON'T CALL ME, I'LL CALL YOU!
YOU SHOULD STAY MARRIED TO PAULA UNTIL I CALL YOU WALTER!
FIRE

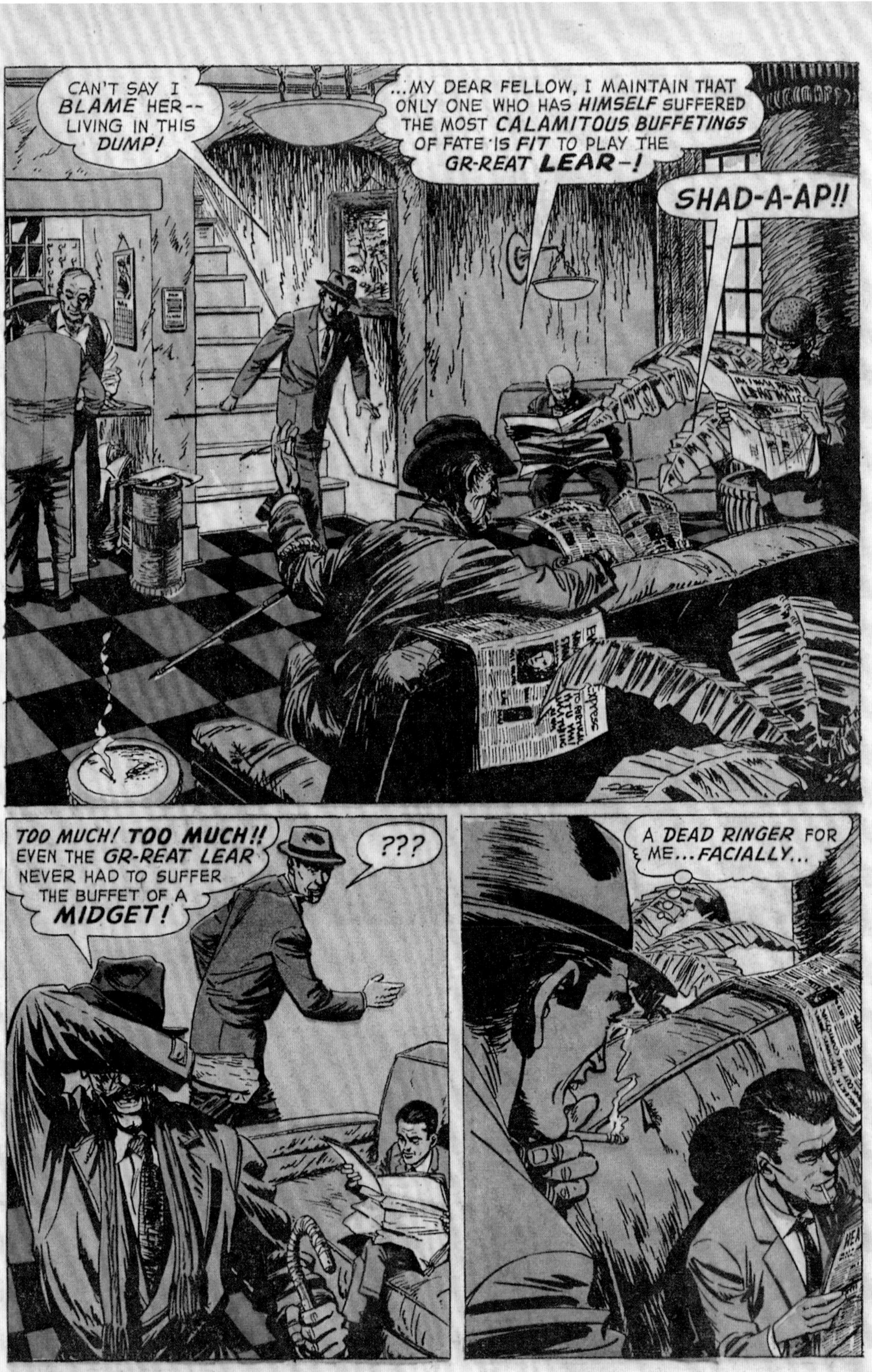
CAN'T SAY I BLAME HER-- LIVING IN THIS DUMP!
...MY DEAR FELLOW, I MAINTAIN THAT ONLY ONE WHO HAS HIMSELF SUFFERED THE MOST CALAMITOUS BUFFETINGS OF FATE IS FIT TO PLAY THE GR-REAT LEAR-!
SHAD-A-AP!!
TOO MUCH! TOO MUCH!! EVEN THE GR-REAT LEAR NEVER HAD TO SUFFER THE BUFFET OF A MIDGET!
???
A DEAD RINGER FOR ME...FACIALLY...

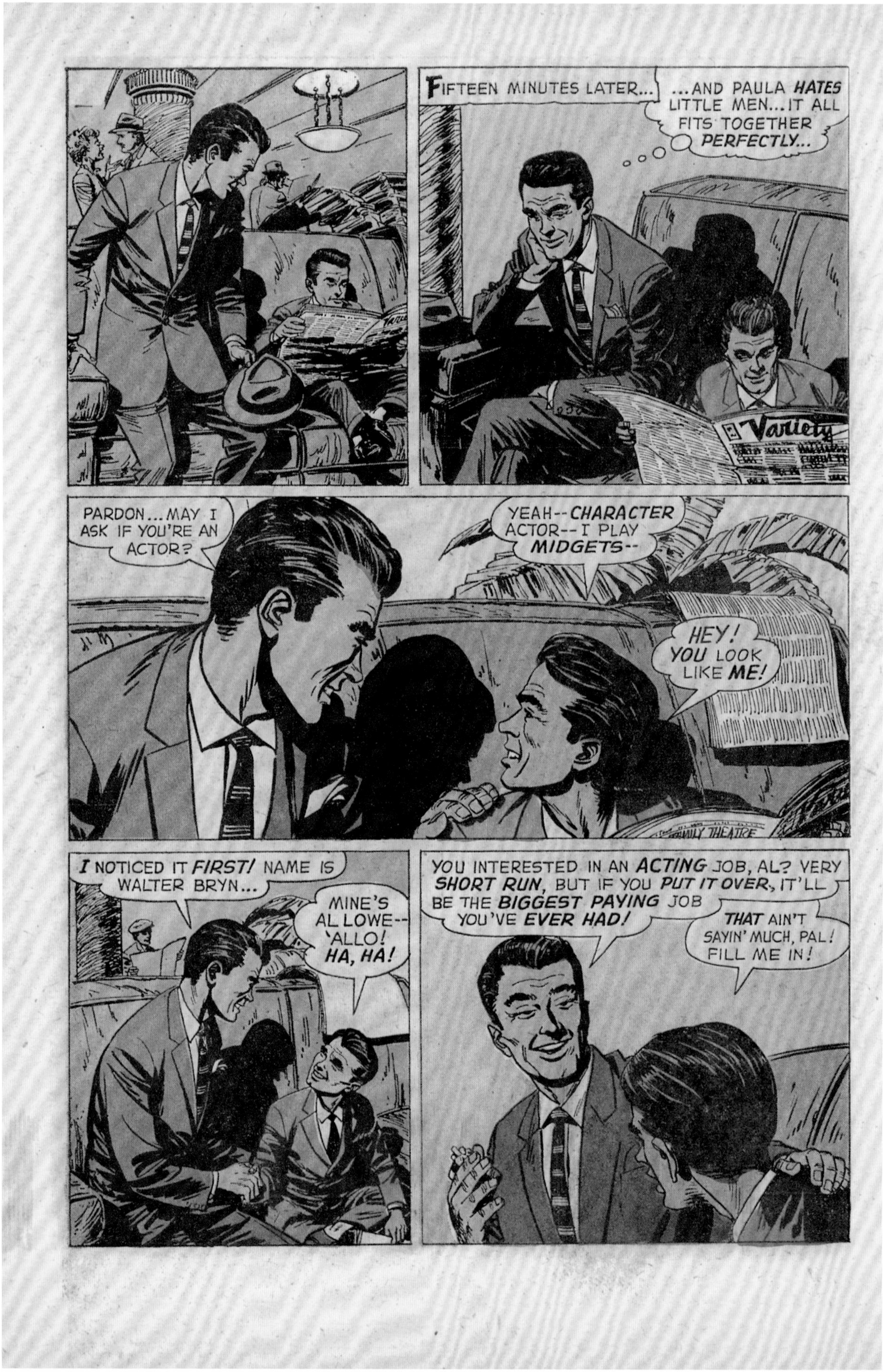
FIFTEEN MINUTES LATER...
...AND PAULA HATES LITTLE MEN...IT ALL FITS TOGETHER PERFECTLY...
Variety
PARDON...MAY I ASK IF YOU'RE AN ACTOR?
YEAH--CHARACTER ACTOR--I PLAY MIDGETS--
HEY! YOU LOOK LIKE ME!
FAMILY THEATRE
I NOTICED IT FIRST! NAME IS WALTER BRYN...
MINE'S AL LOWE--'ALLO! HA, HA!
YOU INTERESTED IN AN ACTING JOB, AL? VERY SHORT RUN, BUT IF YOU PUT IT OVER, IT'LL BE THE BIGGEST PAYING JOB YOU'VE EVER HAD!
THAT AIN'T SAYIN' MUCH, PAL! FILL ME IN!

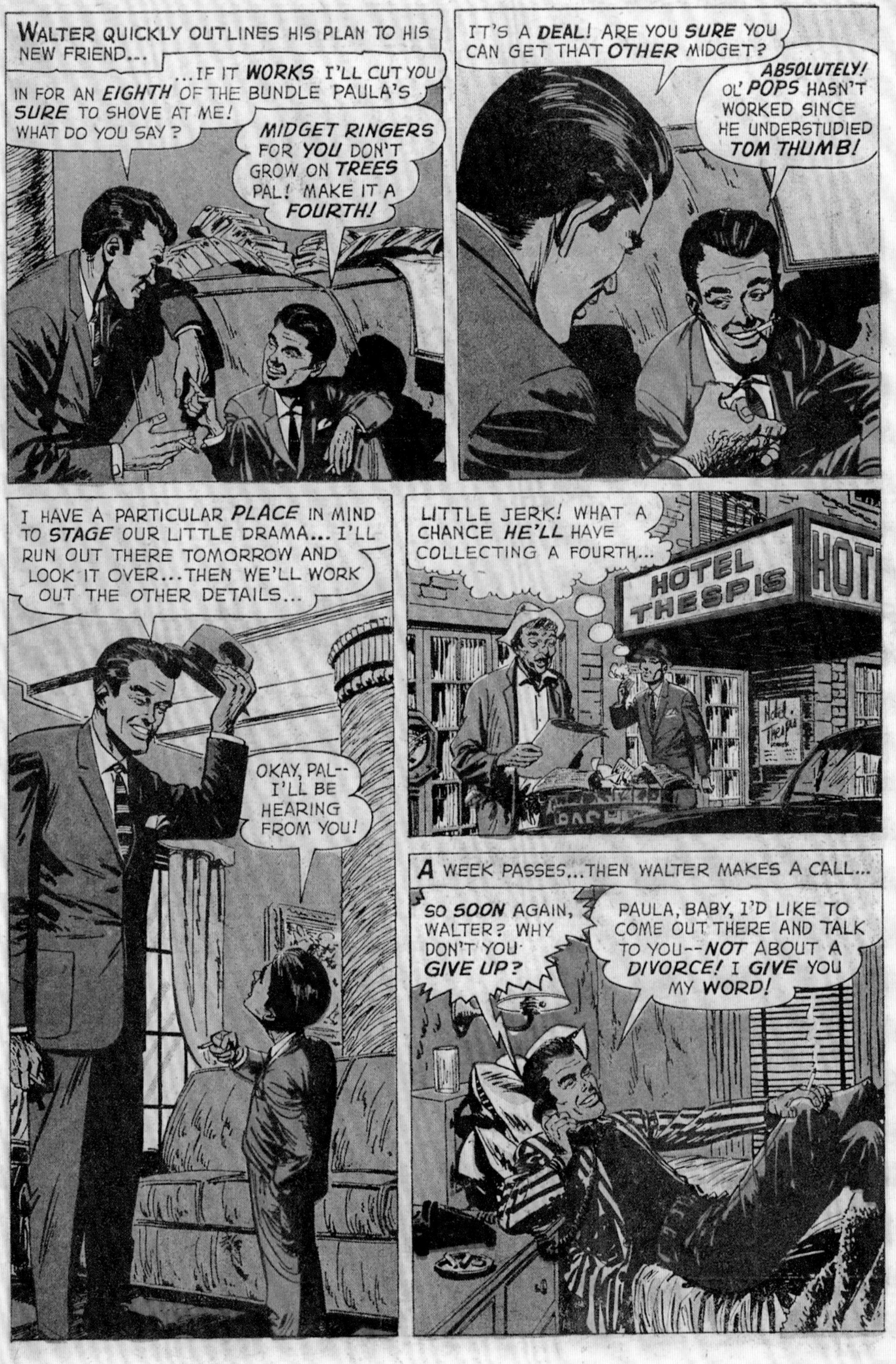
WALTER QUICKLY OUTLINES HIS PLAN TO HIS NEW FRIEND...
...IF IT WORKS I'LL CUT YOU IN FOR AN EIGHTH OF THE BUNDLE PAULA'S SURE TO SHOVE AT ME! WHAT DO YOU SAY?
MIDGET RINGERS FOR YOU DON'T GROW ON TREES PAL! MAKE IT A FOURTH!
IT'S A DEAL! ARE YOU SURE YOU CAN GET THAT OTHER MIDGET?
ABSOLUTELY! OL' POPS HASN'T WORKED SINCE HE UNDERSTUDIED TOM THUMB!
I HAVE A PARTICULAR PLACE IN MIND TO STAGE OUR LITTLE DRAMA... I'LL RUN OUT THERE TOMORROW AND LOOK IT OVER... THEN WE'LL WORK OUT THE OTHER DETAILS...
OKAY, PAL-- I'LL BE HEARING FROM YOU!
LITTLE JERK! WHAT A CHANCE HE'LL HAVE COLLECTING A FOURTH...
HOTEL THESPIS
A WEEK PASSES...THEN WALTER MAKES A CALL...
SO SOON AGAIN, WALTER? WHY DON'T YOU GIVE UP?
PAULA, BABY, I'D LIKE TO COME OUT THERE AND TALK TO YOU--NOT ABOUT A DIVORCE! I GIVE YOU MY WORD!

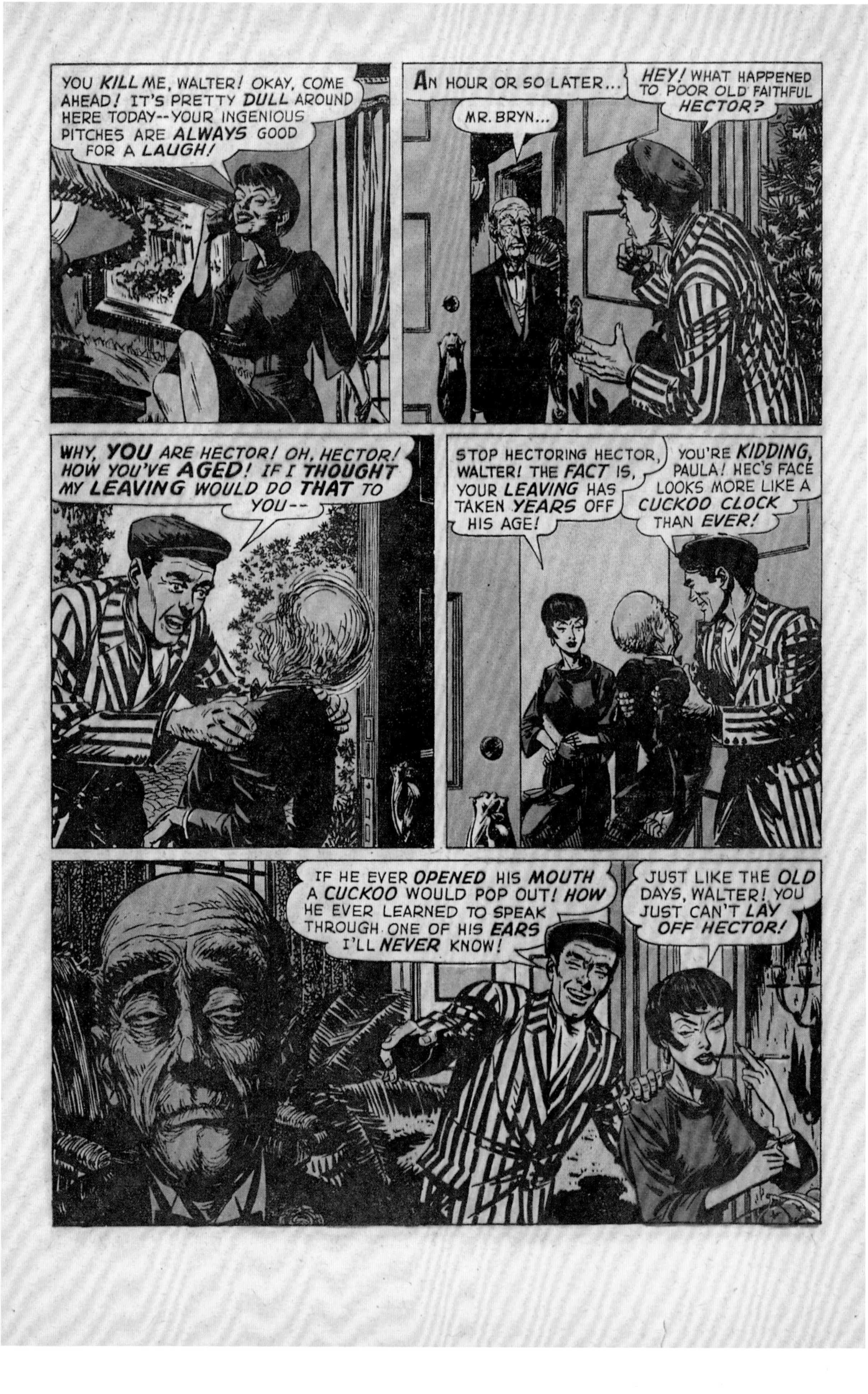
YOU KILL ME, WALTER! OKAY, COME AHEAD! IT'S PRETTY DULL AROUND HERE TODAY--YOUR INGENIOUS PITCHES ARE ALWAYS GOOD FOR A LAUGH!
AN HOUR OR SO LATER...
MR. BRYN...
HEY! WHAT HAPPENED TO POOR OLD FAITHFUL HECTOR?
WHY, YOU ARE HECTOR! OH, HECTOR! HOW YOU'VE AGED! IF I THOUGHT MY LEAVING WOULD DO THAT TO YOU--
STOP HECTORING HECTOR, WALTER! THE FACT IS, YOUR LEAVING HAS TAKEN YEARS OFF HIS AGE!
YOU'RE KIDDING, PAULA! HEC'S FACE LOOKS MORE LIKE A CUCKOO CLOCK THAN EVER!
IF HE EVER OPENED HIS MOUTH A CUCKOO WOULD POP OUT! HOW HE EVER LEARNED TO SPEAK THROUGH ONE OF HIS EARS I'LL NEVER KNOW!
JUST LIKE THE OLD DAYS, WALTER! YOU JUST CAN'T LAY OFF HECTOR!

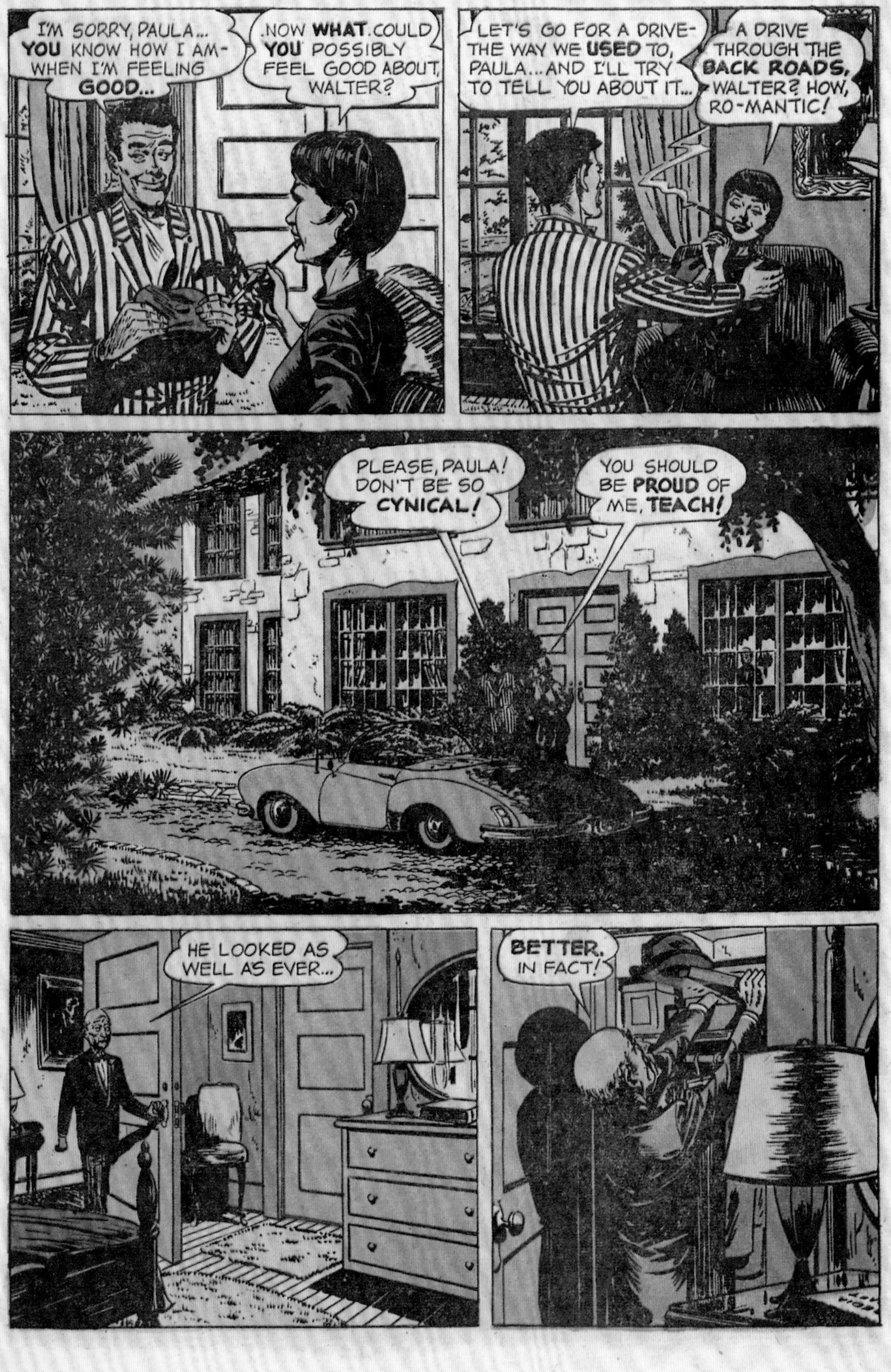
I'M SORRY, PAULA... YOU KNOW HOW I AM-WHEN I'M FEELING GOOD...
..NOW WHAT COULD YOU POSSIBLY FEEL GOOD ABOUT, WALTER?
LET'S GO FOR A DRIVE-THE WAY WE USED TO, PAULA...AND I'LL TRY TO TELL YOU ABOUT IT...
A DRIVE THROUGH THE BACK ROADS, WALTER? HOW, RO-MANTIC!
PLEASE, PAULA! DON'T BE SO CYNICAL!
YOU SHOULD BE PROUD OF ME, TEACH!
HE LOOKED AS WELL AS EVER...
BETTER, IN FACT!

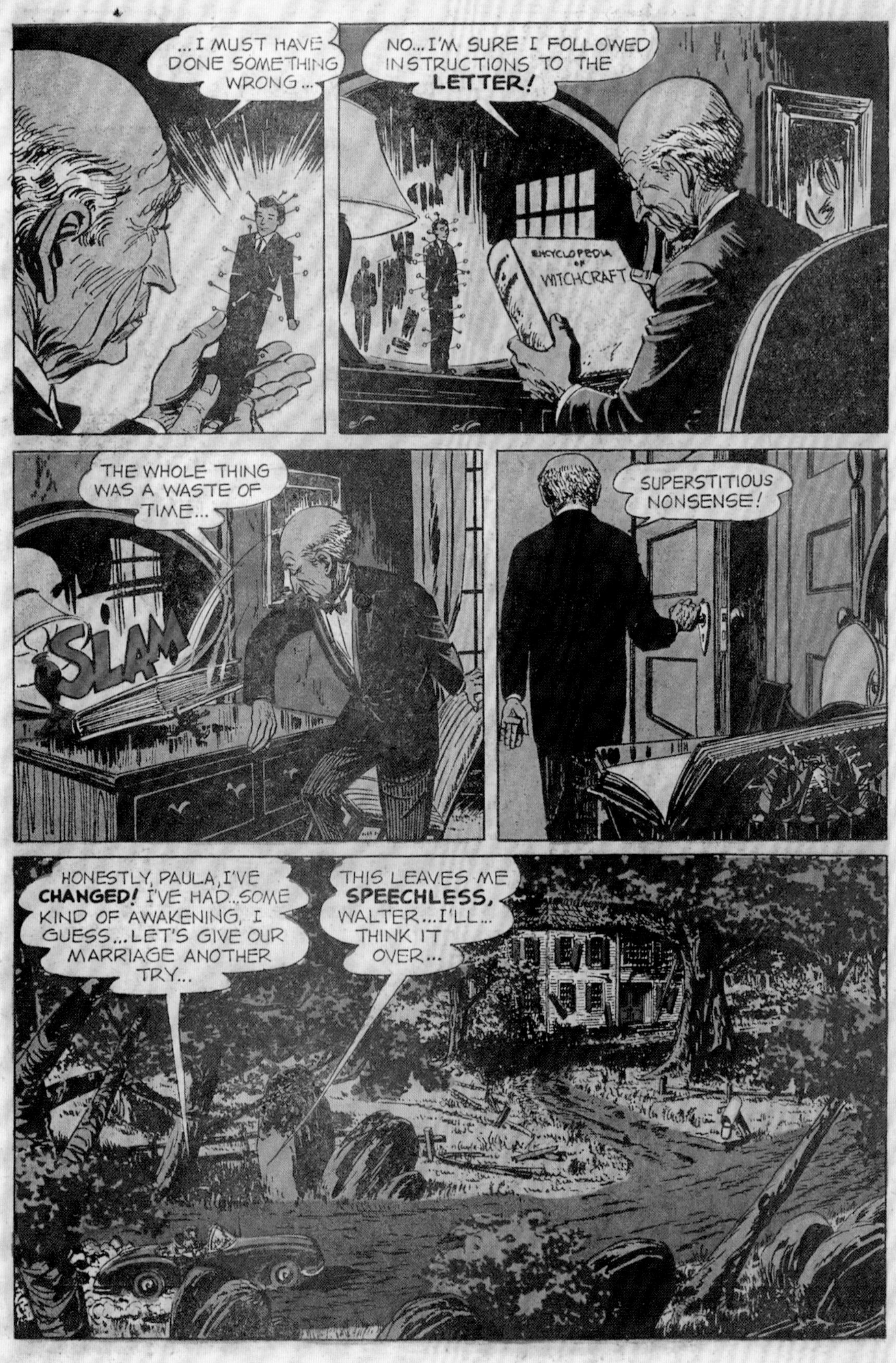
...I MUST HAVE DONE SOMETHING WRONG...
NO...I'M SURE I FOLLOWED INSTRUCTIONS TO THE **LETTER!**
ENCYCLOPEDIA OF WITCHCRAFT
THE WHOLE THING WAS A WASTE OF TIME...
SLAM
SUPERSTITIOUS NONSENSE!
HONESTLY, PAULA, I'VE **CHANGED!** I'VE HAD...SOME KIND OF AWAKENING, I GUESS...LET'S GIVE OUR MARRIAGE ANOTHER TRY...
THIS LEAVES ME **SPEECHLESS,** WALTER...I'LL... THINK IT OVER...

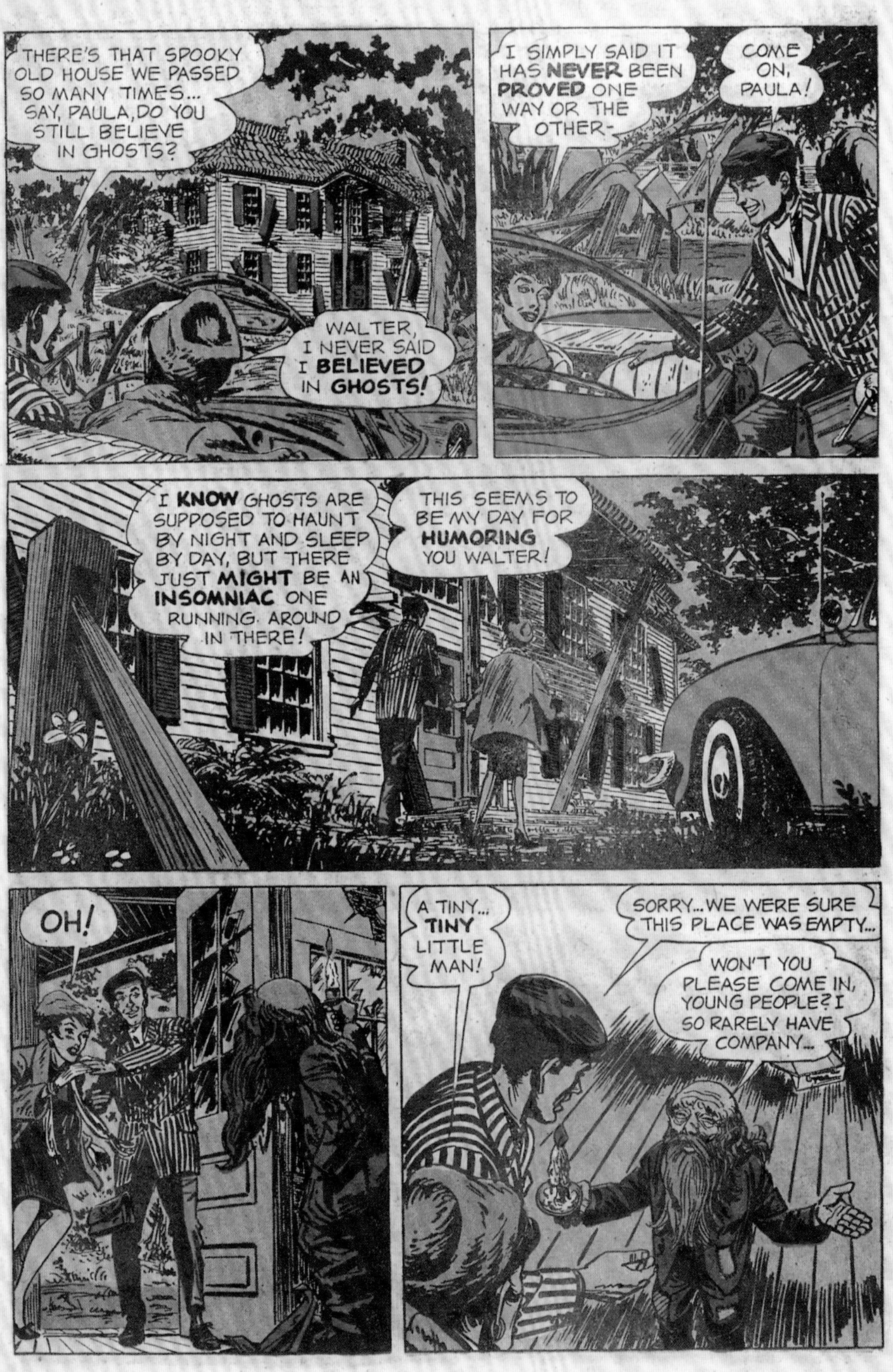
THERE'S THAT SPOOKY OLD HOUSE WE PASSED SO MANY TIMES... SAY, PAULA, DO YOU STILL BELIEVE IN GHOSTS?
WALTER, I NEVER SAID I BELIEVED IN GHOSTS!
I SIMPLY SAID IT HAS NEVER BEEN PROVED ONE WAY OR THE OTHER-
COME ON, PAULA!
I KNOW GHOSTS ARE SUPPOSED TO HAUNT BY NIGHT AND SLEEP BY DAY, BUT THERE JUST MIGHT BE AN INSOMNIAC ONE RUNNING AROUND IN THERE!
THIS SEEMS TO BE MY DAY FOR HUMORING YOU WALTER!
OH!
A TINY... TINY LITTLE MAN!
SORRY... WE WERE SURE THIS PLACE WAS EMPTY...
WON'T YOU PLEASE COME IN, YOUNG PEOPLE? I SO RARELY HAVE COMPANY...

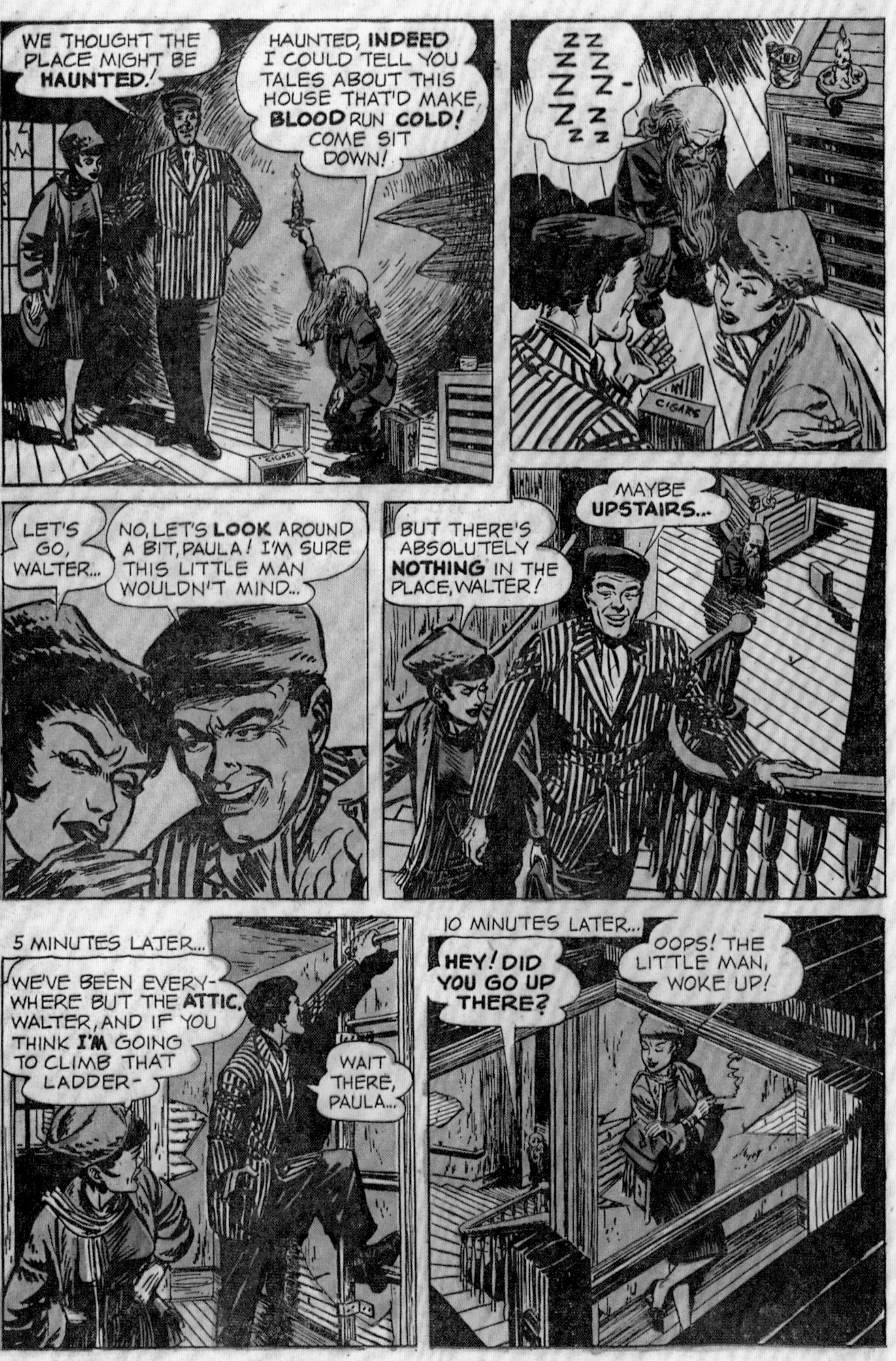
WE THOUGHT THE PLACE MIGHT BE HAUNTED!
HAUNTED, INDEED I COULD TELL YOU TALES ABOUT THIS HOUSE THAT'D MAKE BLOOD RUN COLD! COME SIT DOWN!
CIGARS
Z Z Z Z Z Z - Z Z Z Z
CIGARS
LET'S GO, WALTER...
NO, LET'S LOOK AROUND A BIT, PAULA! I'M SURE THIS LITTLE MAN WOULDN'T MIND...
BUT THERE'S ABSOLUTELY NOTHING IN THE PLACE, WALTER!
MAYBE UPSTAIRS...
5 MINUTES LATER...
WE'VE BEEN EVERYWHERE BUT THE ATTIC, WALTER, AND IF YOU THINK I'M GOING TO CLIMB THAT LADDER-
WAIT THERE, PAULA...
10 MINUTES LATER...
HEY! DID YOU GO UP THERE?
OOPS! THE LITTLE MAN, WOKE UP!

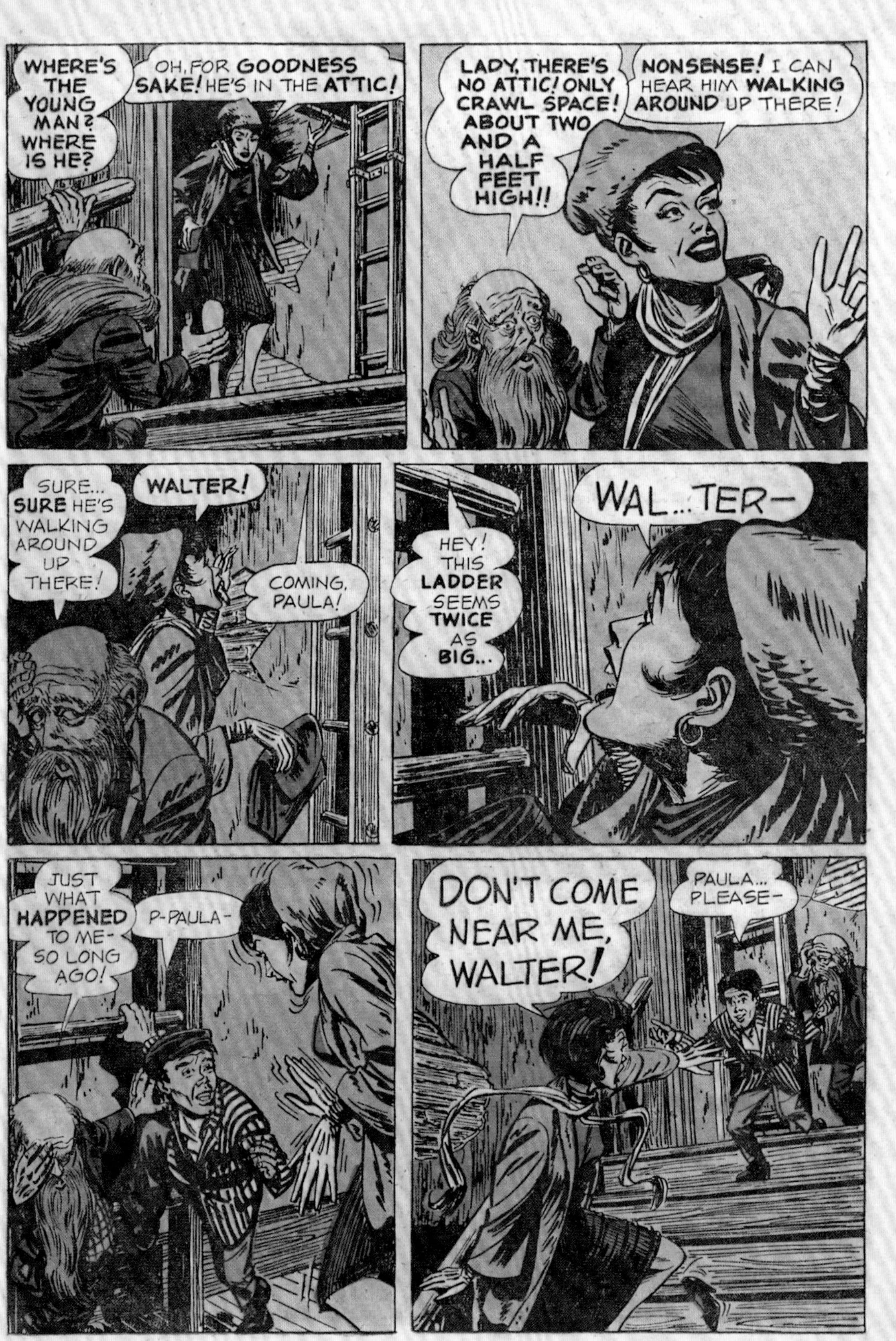
WHERE'S THE YOUNG MAN? WHERE IS HE?
OH, FOR GOODNESS SAKE! HE'S IN THE ATTIC!
LADY, THERE'S NO ATTIC! ONLY CRAWL SPACE! ABOUT TWO AND A HALF FEET HIGH!!
NONSENSE! I CAN HEAR HIM WALKING AROUND UP THERE!
SURE... SURE HE'S WALKING AROUND UP THERE!
WALTER!
COMING, PAULA!
WAL... TER-
HEY! THIS LADDER SEEMS TWICE AS BIG...
JUST WHAT HAPPENED TO ME- SO LONG AGO!
P-PAULA-
DON'T COME NEAR ME, WALTER!
PAULA... PLEASE-

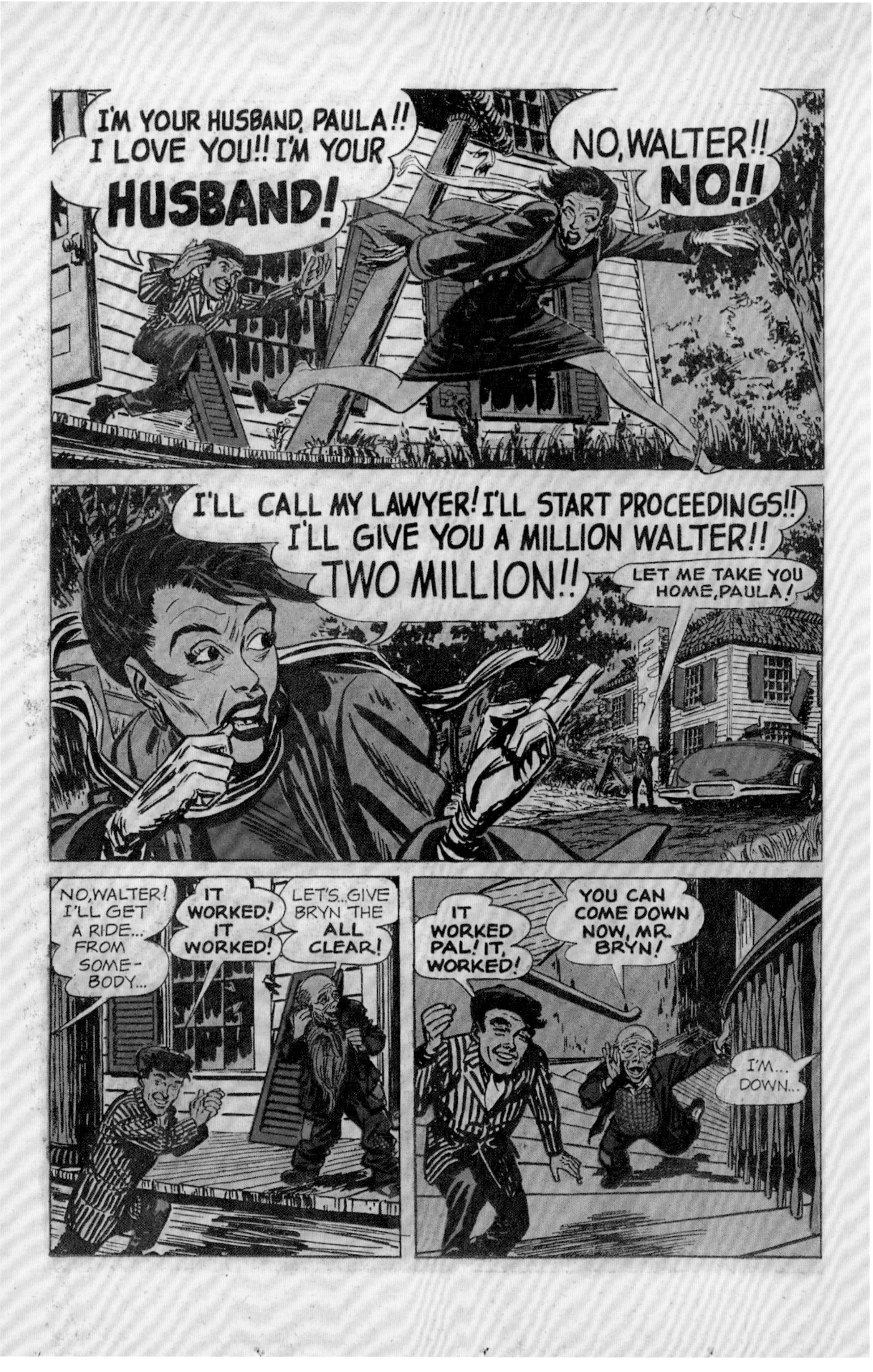
I'M YOUR HUSBAND, PAULA!! I LOVE YOU!! I'M YOUR HUSBAND!
NO, WALTER!! NO!!
I'LL CALL MY LAWYER! I'LL START PROCEEDINGS!! I'LL GIVE YOU A MILLION WALTER!! TWO MILLION!!
LET ME TAKE YOU HOME, PAULA!
NO, WALTER! I'LL GET A RIDE... FROM SOME-BODY...
IT WORKED! IT WORKED!
LET'S...GIVE BRYN THE ALL CLEAR!
IT WORKED PAL! IT, WORKED!
YOU CAN COME DOWN NOW, MR. BRYN!
I'M... DOWN...

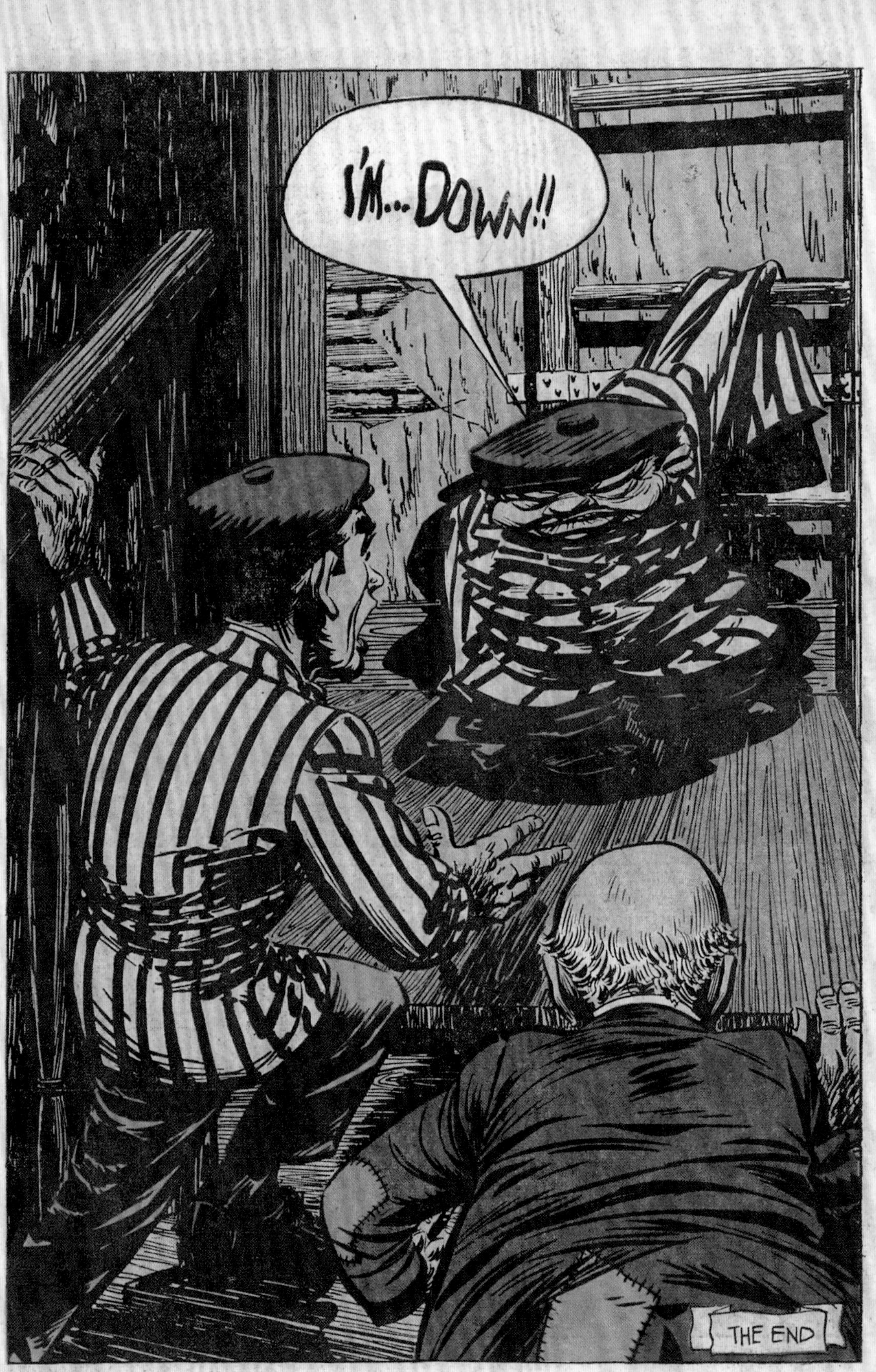
I'M...DOWN!!
THE END

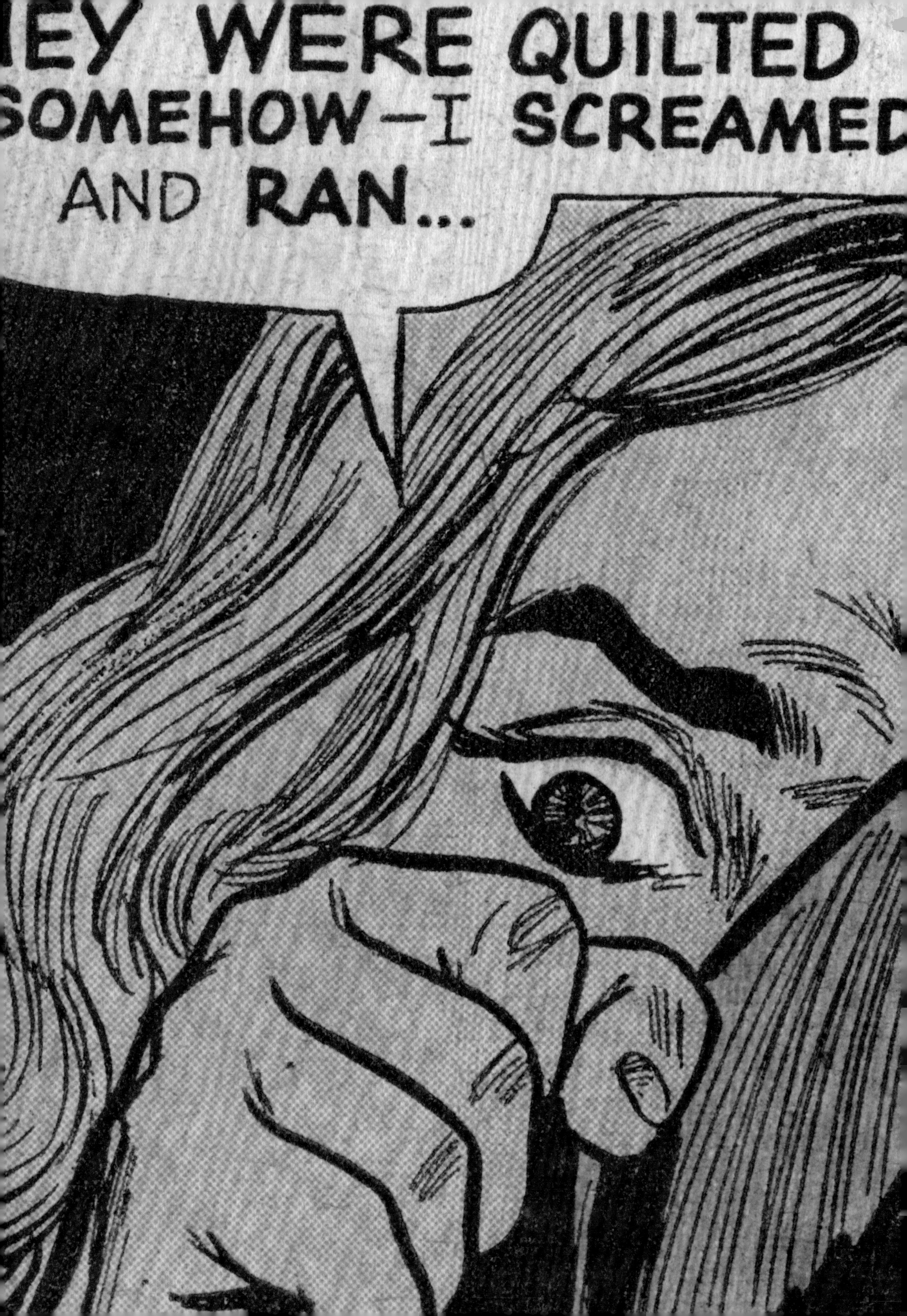
IEY WERE QUILTED
SOMEHOW—I SCREAMED
AND RAN...

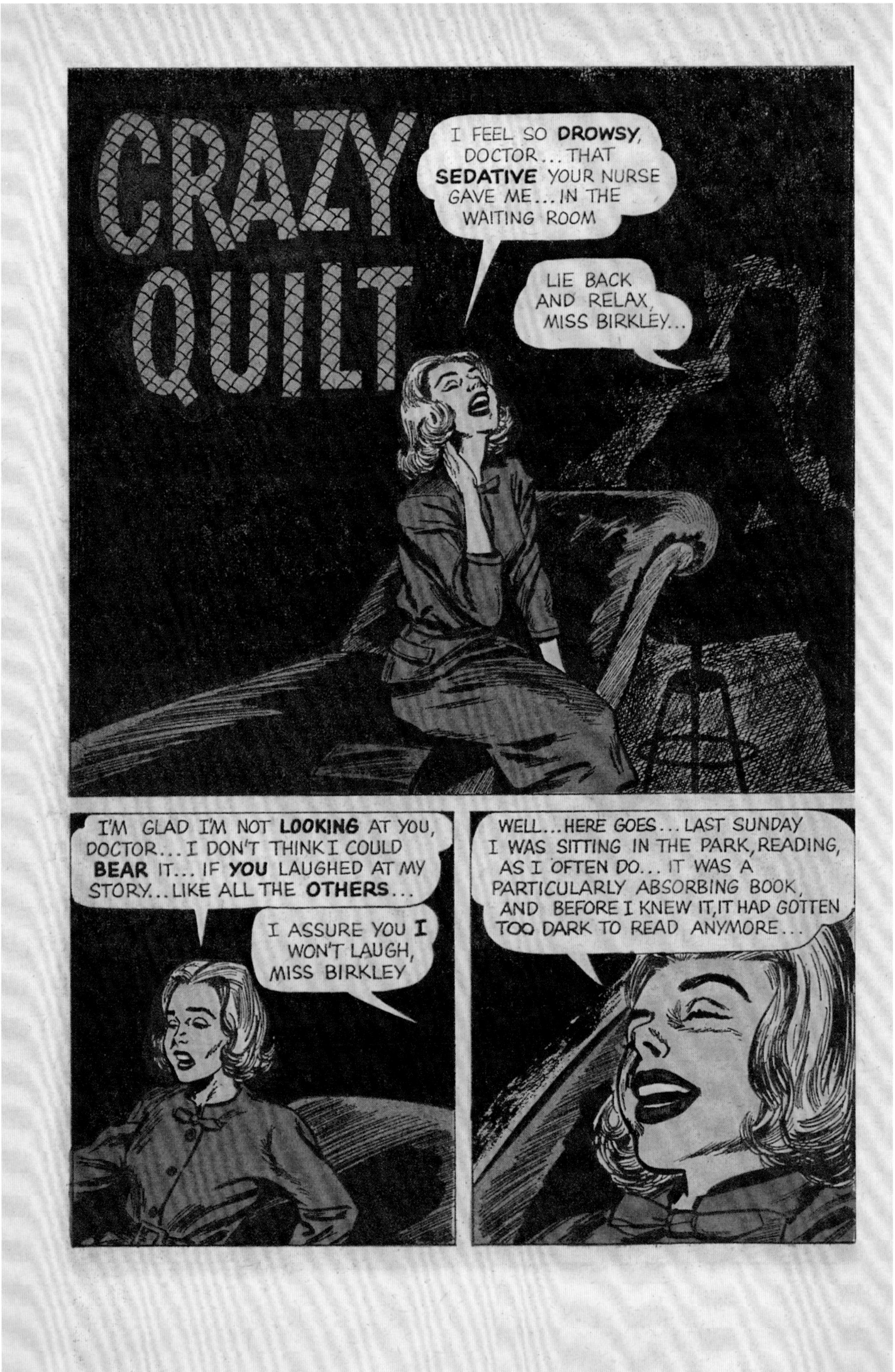
CRAZY QUILT
I FEEL SO DROWSY, DOCTOR... THAT SEDATIVE YOUR NURSE GAVE ME... IN THE WAITING ROOM
LIE BACK AND RELAX, MISS BIRKLEY...
I'M GLAD I'M NOT LOOKING AT YOU, DOCTOR... I DON'T THINK I COULD BEAR IT... IF YOU LAUGHED AT MY STORY... LIKE ALL THE OTHERS...
I ASSURE YOU I WON'T LAUGH, MISS BIRKLEY
WELL... HERE GOES... LAST SUNDAY I WAS SITTING IN THE PARK, READING, AS I OFTEN DO... IT WAS A PARTICULARLY ABSORBING BOOK, AND BEFORE I KNEW IT, IT HAD GOTTEN TOO DARK TO READ ANYMORE...

Tales From The Tomb no. 1 (1962)

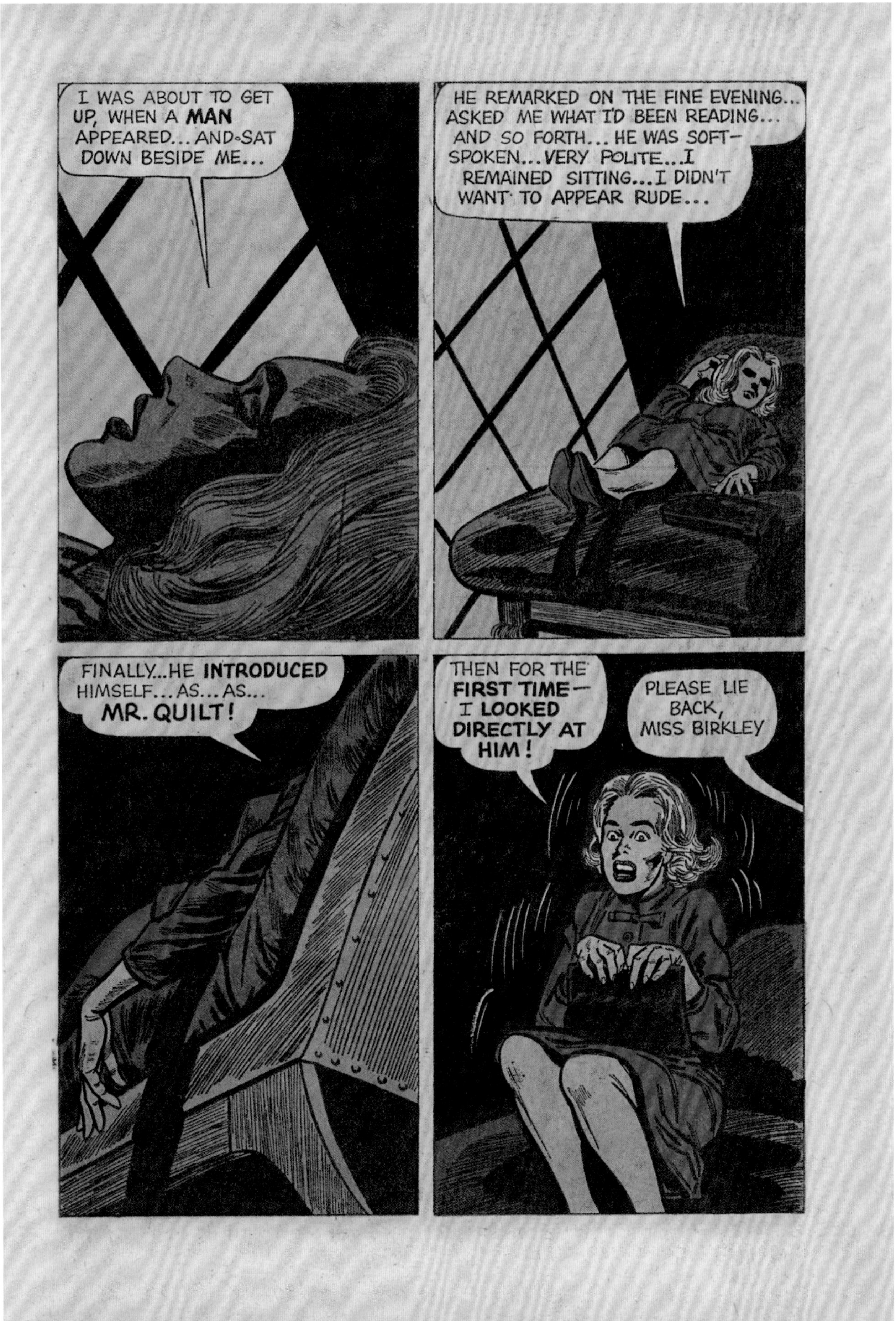
I WAS ABOUT TO GET UP, WHEN A MAN APPEARED... AND SAT DOWN BESIDE ME...
HE REMARKED ON THE FINE EVENING... ASKED ME WHAT I'D BEEN READING... AND SO FORTH... HE WAS SOFT-SPOKEN... VERY POLITE... I REMAINED SITTING... I DIDN'T WANT TO APPEAR RUDE...
FINALLY... HE INTRODUCED HIMSELF... AS... AS... MR. QUILT!
THEN FOR THE FIRST TIME— I LOOKED DIRECTLY AT HIM!
PLEASE LIE BACK, MISS BIRKLEY

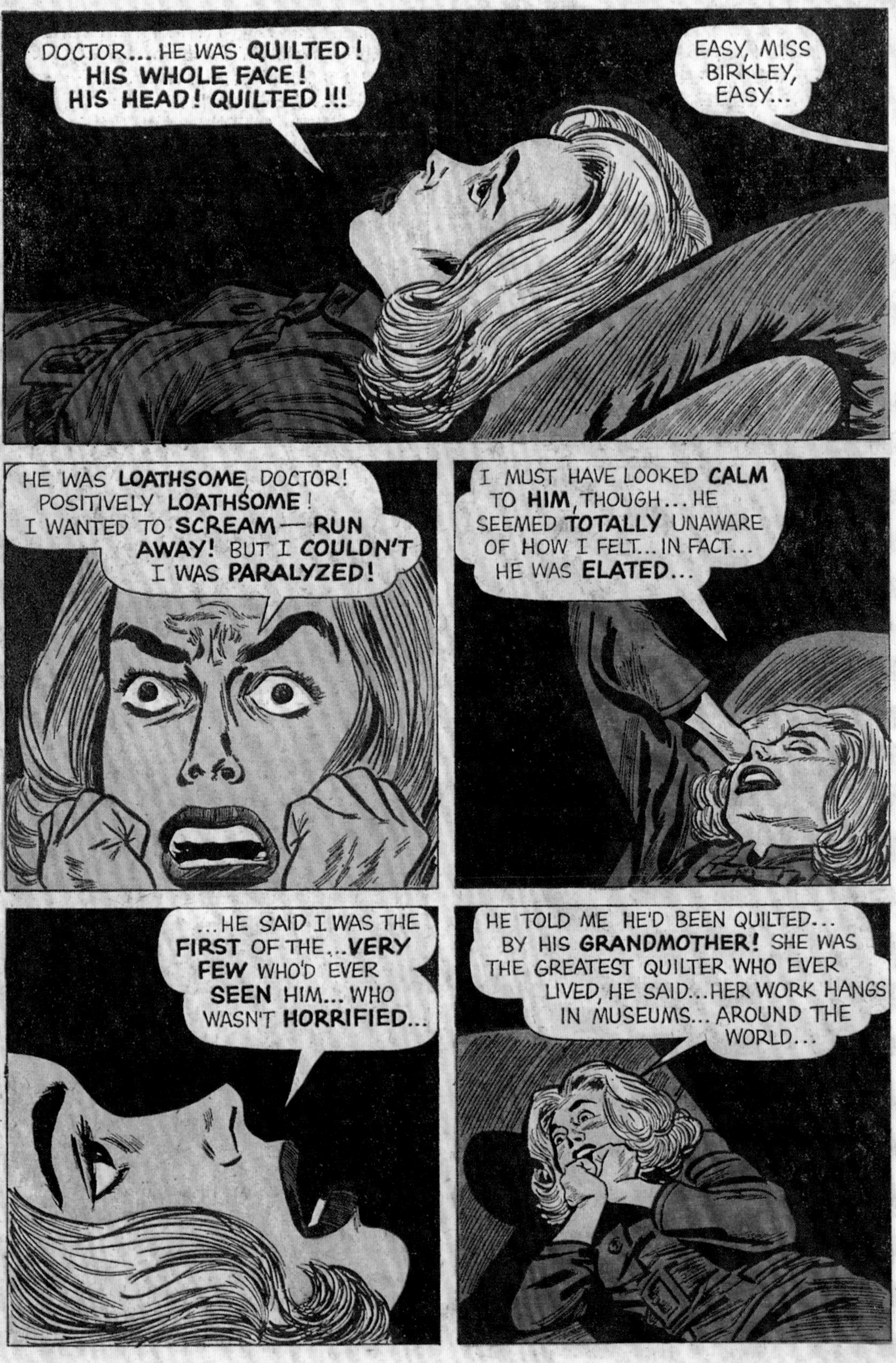
DOCTOR... HE WAS QUILTED! HIS WHOLE FACE! HIS HEAD! QUILTED!!!
EASY, MISS BIRKLEY, EASY...
HE WAS LOATHSOME, DOCTOR! POSITIVELY LOATHSOME! I WANTED TO SCREAM— RUN AWAY! BUT I COULDN'T I WAS PARALYZED!
I MUST HAVE LOOKED CALM TO HIM, THOUGH... HE SEEMED TOTALLY UNAWARE OF HOW I FELT... IN FACT... HE WAS ELATED...
...HE SAID I WAS THE FIRST OF THE...VERY FEW WHO'D EVER SEEN HIM... WHO WASN'T HORRIFIED...
HE TOLD ME HE'D BEEN QUILTED... BY HIS GRANDMOTHER! SHE WAS THE GREATEST QUILTER WHO EVER LIVED, HE SAID...HER WORK HANGS IN MUSEUMS... AROUND THE WORLD...

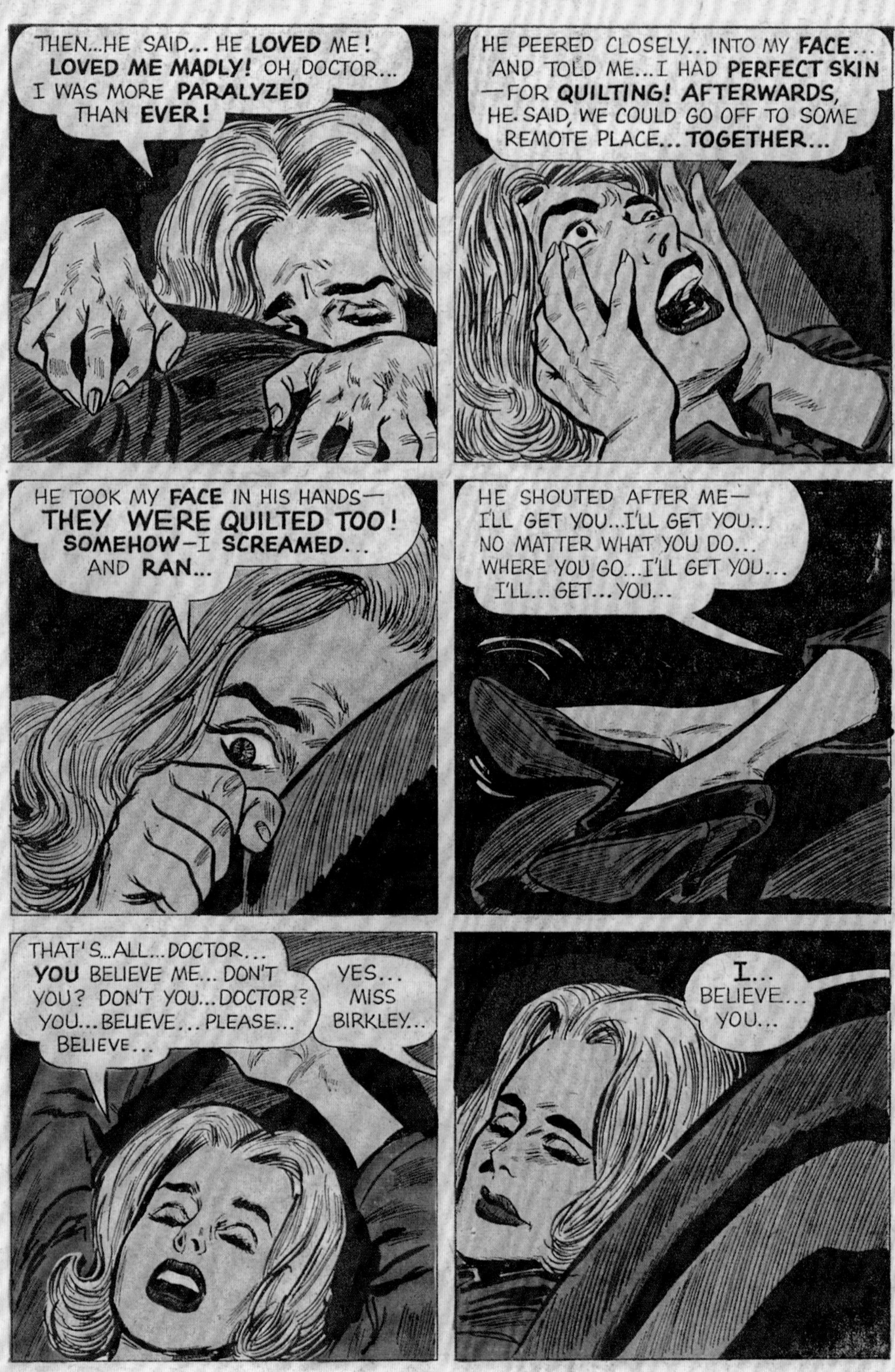
THEN...HE SAID... HE LOVED ME! LOVED ME MADLY! OH, DOCTOR... I WAS MORE PARALYZED THAN EVER!
HE PEERED CLOSELY... INTO MY FACE... AND TOLD ME... I HAD PERFECT SKIN —FOR QUILTING! AFTERWARDS, HE SAID, WE COULD GO OFF TO SOME REMOTE PLACE... TOGETHER...
HE TOOK MY FACE IN HIS HANDS— THEY WERE QUILTED TOO! SOMEHOW—I SCREAMED... AND RAN...
HE SHOUTED AFTER ME— I'LL GET YOU...I'LL GET YOU... NO MATTER WHAT YOU DO... WHERE YOU GO...I'LL GET YOU... I'LL... GET... YOU...
THAT'S...ALL...DOCTOR... YOU BELIEVE ME... DON'T YOU? DON'T YOU...DOCTOR? YOU...BELIEVE... PLEASE... BELIEVE...
YES... MISS BIRKLEY...
I... BELIEVE... YOU...

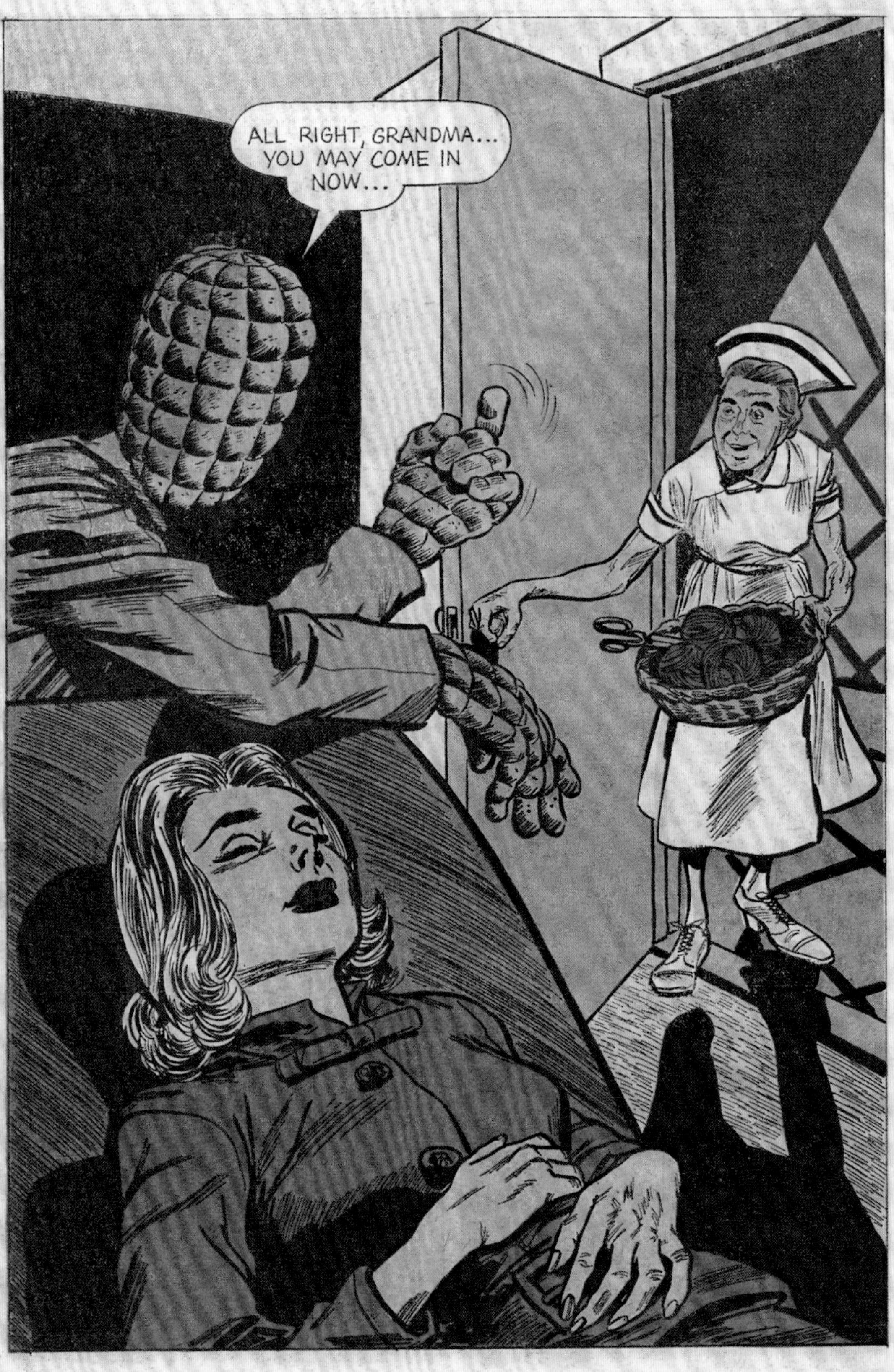
ALL RIGHT, GRANDMA... YOU MAY COME IN NOW...

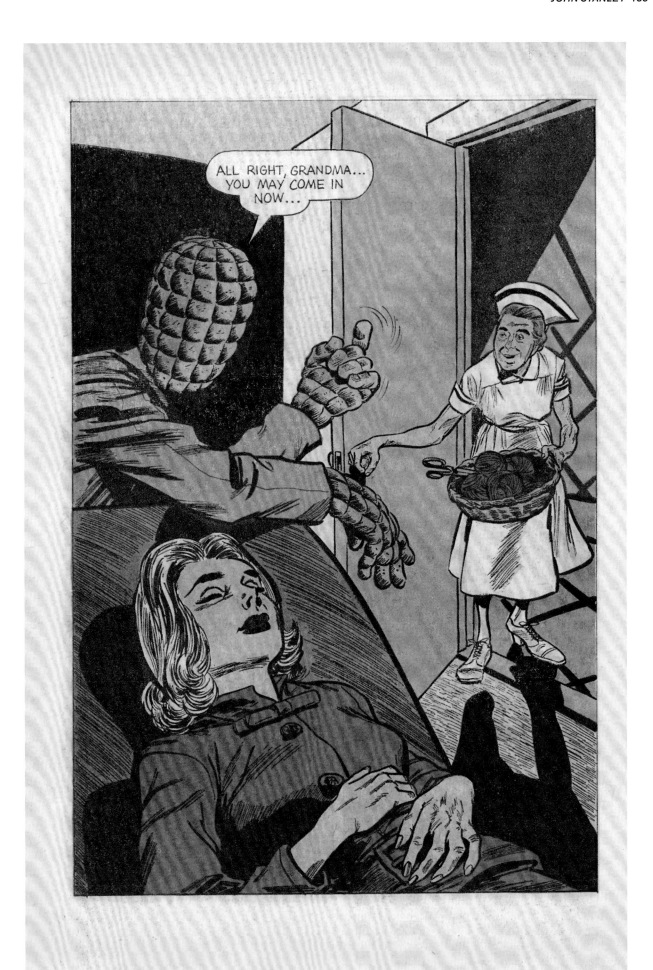

MATT FOX

(1906–88)

Matt Fox drew comics like they were carved out of stone. Each panel of his claustrophobic pages is crammed with details made of multiple discreet pen marks. Not the curvaceous marks of his only admitted influence, Alex Raymond, but rather piles of smaller lines building up forms on the page. There's no grace here, but there is an unmistakable power to the work—everything in a Matt Fox panel is, in its solidity and seemingly nineteenth-century design, uniquely his own. His panels are so fully drawn as to make color almost an afterthought in the comics-making process. Each drawing seems to want to say, "This is what I see. I will make an indelible impression on this page, and this impression will never leave your mind."

There's very little information extant on Fox. He never gave an interview, and his only public statement was for the 1973 *Who's Who of American Comics*. He drew covers and interiors for pulps, most famously a remarkable 1944–50 run of *Weird Tales* covers that, in their sheer visionary design and figuration, hearken back to nineteenth-century engravings. They are truly demonic looking, with none of the showy paint techniques or clichéd looking monsters of most pulp magazine imagery. Fox seemed to invent his imagery out of whole cloth. In his *Who's Who* biography he lists "lithographs, watercolors, color woodcuts, oils, and etchings" as his other artistic activities.

Fox's comics seem out of place in the 1950s horror comic glut. He was much older than his colleagues, his sensibility more rooted in Victorian woodcuts and silent film than anything else. His style mostly neglects the modern filmic narrative techniques then in vogue, and Fox spent what must have been an exorbitant amount of time rendering every detail in each panel (which resemble theatrical stages) with foreground and background collapsed into each other. His characters are always posed and static in the frame, never dynamic or trying to break out of his panels. Instead Fox lets viewers come to him to engage with his tableaus. He was especially effective at depicting characters in agonized terror: their bodies contorted and faces frozen with fear.

Fox drew only a handful of stunning comics, primarily for Atlas in the 1950s and then, later, as an inker for Marvel in the early 1960s. His final published work appears to be a 1967 advertisement for a series of glow-in-the-dark posters he was selling via mail order. There's no trace of work by Fox after that. He, like others before him, seemed to simply vanish.

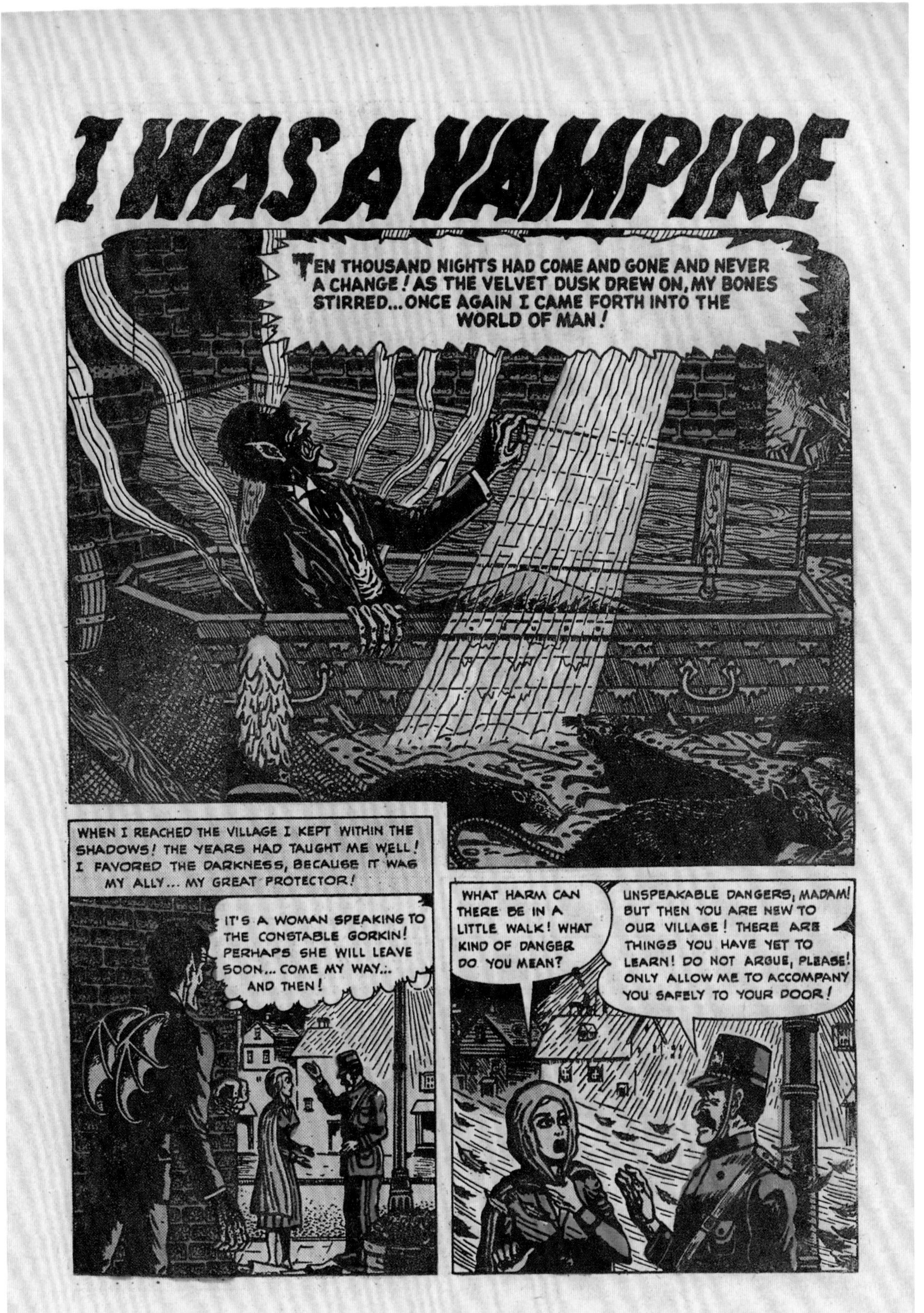
I WAS A VAMPIRE
TEN THOUSAND NIGHTS HAD COME AND GONE AND NEVER A CHANGE! AS THE VELVET DUSK DREW ON, MY BONES STIRRED... ONCE AGAIN I CAME FORTH INTO THE WORLD OF MAN!
WHEN I REACHED THE VILLAGE I KEPT WITHIN THE SHADOWS! THE YEARS HAD TAUGHT ME WELL! I FAVORED THE DARKNESS, BECAUSE IT WAS MY ALLY... MY GREAT PROTECTOR!
IT'S A WOMAN SPEAKING TO THE CONSTABLE GORKIN! PERHAPS SHE WILL LEAVE SOON... COME MY WAY... AND THEN!
WHAT HARM CAN THERE BE IN A LITTLE WALK! WHAT KIND OF DANGER DO YOU MEAN?
UNSPEAKABLE DANGERS, MADAM! BUT THEN YOU ARE NEW TO OUR VILLAGE! THERE ARE THINGS YOU HAVE YET TO LEARN! DO NOT ARGUE, PLEASE! ONLY ALLOW ME TO ACCOMPANY YOU SAFELY TO YOUR DOOR!

Adventures Into Terror no. 19 (1953)

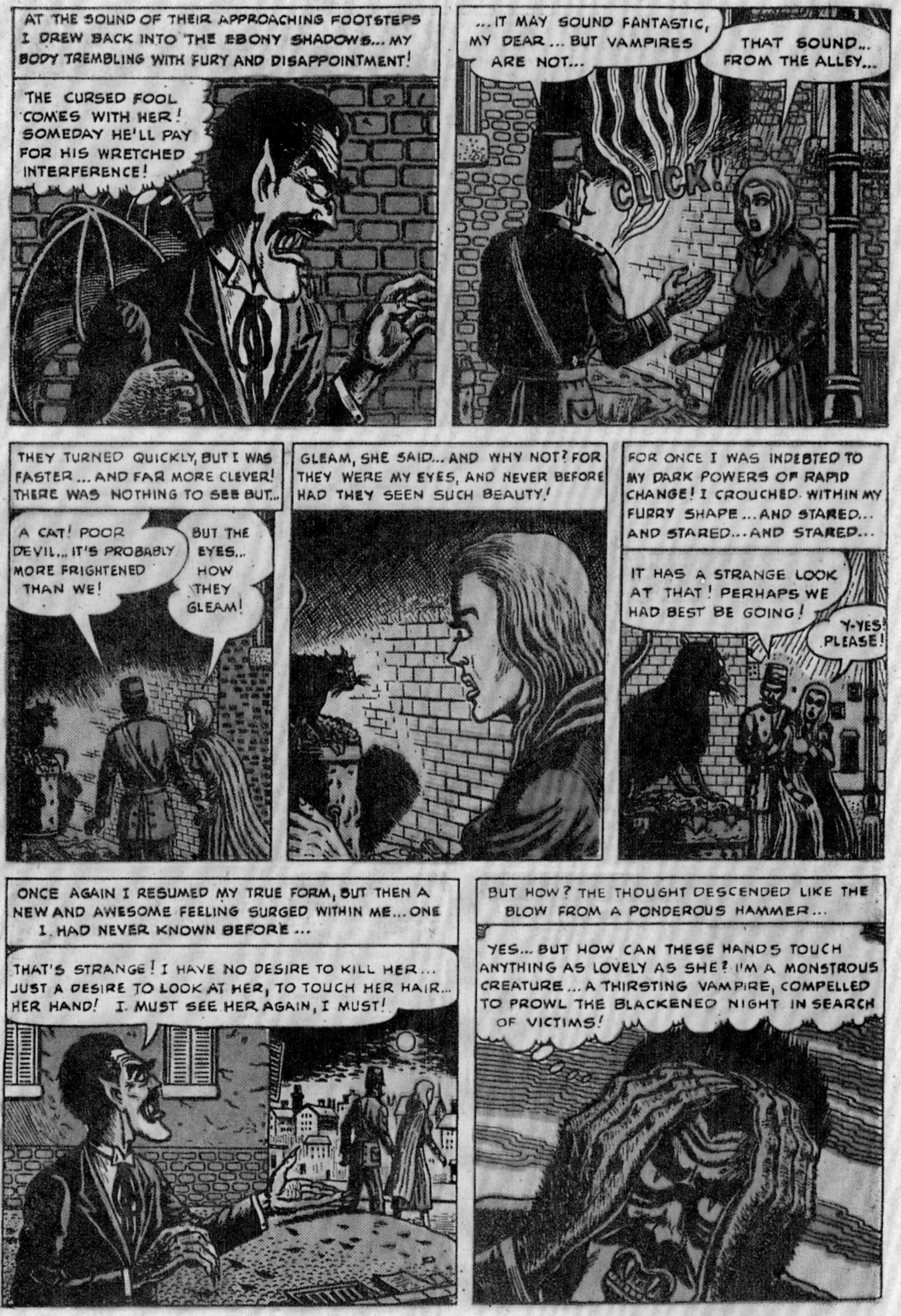
AT THE SOUND OF THEIR APPROACHING FOOTSTEPS I DREW BACK INTO THE EBONY SHADOWS... MY BODY TREMBLING WITH FURY AND DISAPPOINTMENT!
THE CURSED FOOL COMES WITH HER! SOMEDAY HE'LL PAY FOR HIS WRETCHED INTERFERENCE!
...IT MAY SOUND FANTASTIC, MY DEAR ... BUT VAMPIRES ARE NOT...
THAT SOUND... FROM THE ALLEY...
CLICK!
THEY TURNED QUICKLY, BUT I WAS FASTER ... AND FAR MORE CLEVER! THERE WAS NOTHING TO SEE BUT...
A CAT! POOR DEVIL... IT'S PROBABLY MORE FRIGHTENED THAN WE!
BUT THE EYES... HOW THEY GLEAM!
GLEAM, SHE SAID... AND WHY NOT? FOR THEY WERE MY EYES, AND NEVER BEFORE HAD THEY SEEN SUCH BEAUTY!
FOR ONCE I WAS INDEBTED TO MY DARK POWERS OF RAPID CHANGE! I CROUCHED WITHIN MY FURRY SHAPE ... AND STARED... AND STARED... AND STARED...
IT HAS A STRANGE LOOK AT THAT! PERHAPS WE HAD BEST BE GOING!
Y-YES! PLEASE!
ONCE AGAIN I RESUMED MY TRUE FORM, BUT THEN A NEW AND AWESOME FEELING SURGED WITHIN ME... ONE I HAD NEVER KNOWN BEFORE ...
THAT'S STRANGE! I HAVE NO DESIRE TO KILL HER... JUST A DESIRE TO LOOK AT HER, TO TOUCH HER HAIR... HER HAND! I MUST SEE HER AGAIN, I MUST!
BUT HOW? THE THOUGHT DESCENDED LIKE THE BLOW FROM A PONDEROUS HAMMER...
YES... BUT HOW CAN THESE HANDS TOUCH ANYTHING AS LOVELY AS SHE? I'M A MONSTROUS CREATURE ... A THIRSTING VAMPIRE, COMPELLED TO PROWL THE BLACKENED NIGHT IN SEARCH OF VICTIMS!

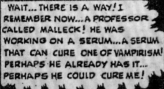

WAIT... THERE IS A WAY! I REMEMBER NOW... A PROFESSOR CALLED MALLECK! HE WAS WORKING ON A SERUM... A SERUM THAT CAN CURE ONE OF VAMPIRISM! PERHAPS HE ALREADY HAS IT... PERHAPS HE COULD CURE ME!

QUICKLY I RETURNED TO MY HIDDEN VAULT TO FIND THE CLIPPING I SO URGENTLY NEEDED! THE HOURS FLEW BY, AND THEN...

I FOUND IT! IT GIVES HIS ADDRESS AND ALL THE FACTS I NEED! TOMORROW NIGHT I WILL VISIT HERR MALLECK AND HE WILL DO AS I SAY! HE MUSTN'T REFUSE ME!

THE FOLLOWING NIGHT, IN THE GUISE OF AN ORDINARY MORTAL, I PRESENTED MYSELF TO HERR MALLECK! I PRETENDED TO BE A SCIENTIST FROM PRAGUE, BUT THE OLD MAN PROVED DIFFERENT!

I HAVE THE SERUM, HERR KRONIN... BUT I CAN SPARE NONE OF IT! IT TAKES SIX MONTHS TO PRODUCE A SINGLE BATCH!

THEN GIVE ME WHAT YOU HAVE! I'LL PAY YOU WELL!

IT'S NOT A MATTER OF MONEY, MY FRIEND! COME BACK IN SIX MONTHS!

NO, HERR MALLECK, I'LL TAKE WHAT YOU HAVE NOW!

ARE YOU THREATENING ME? YOU CAN'T BE... OH, NO, NO!

ARGGHHH!

IT WAS OVER IN A MOMENT, AND IN MY HAND I HELD THE KEY TO A NEW LIFE!

IT WILL WORK, I KNOW IT WILL! SOON I WILL BE A MAN LIKE OTHERS... FREE... FREE TO MEET THE LOVELY CREATURE AND TELL HER OF MY LOVE!

IN A SINGLE MOMENT I THREW BACK MY HEAD AND DRAINED THE CONTENTS OF THE FLASK!

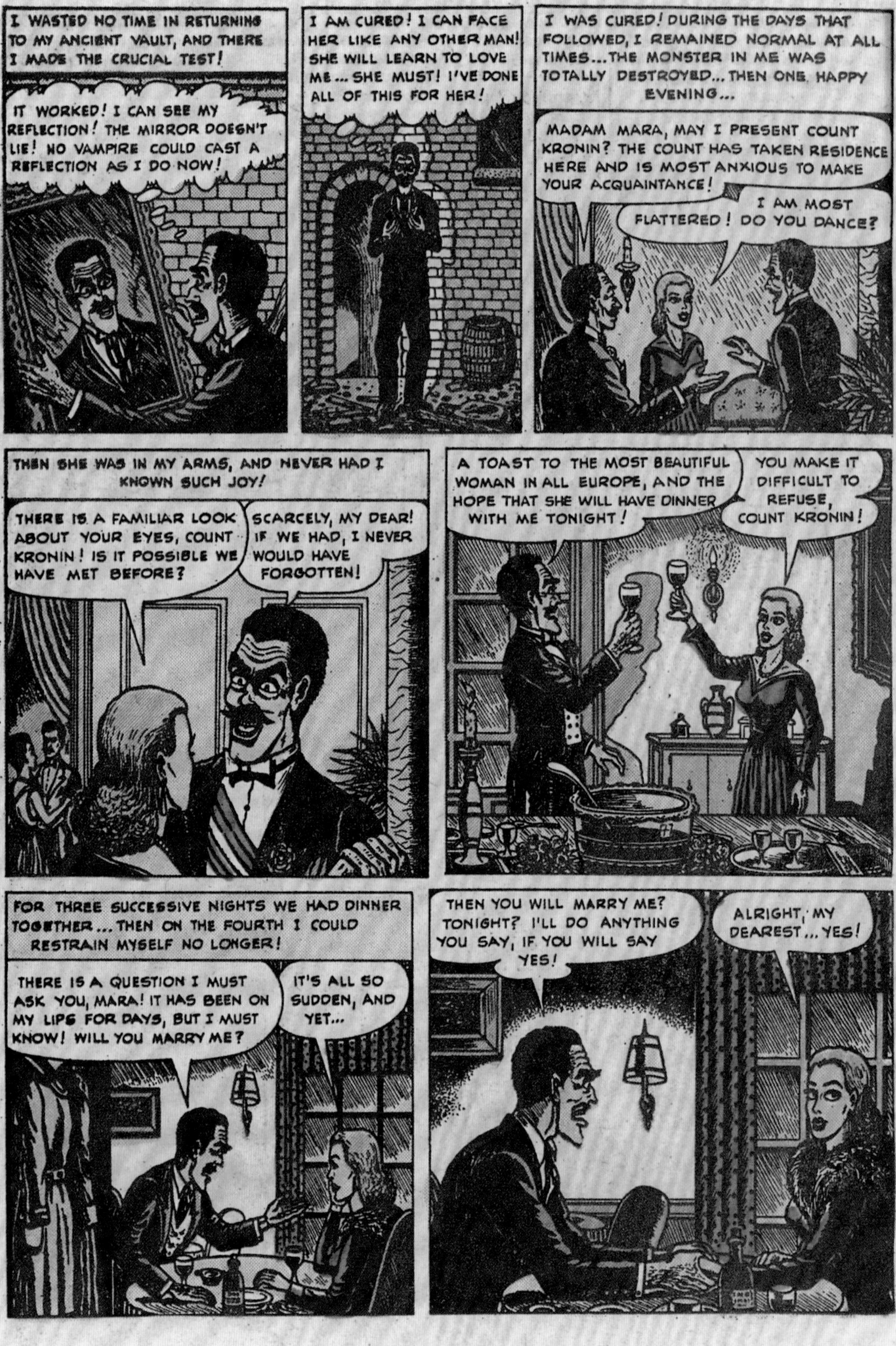
I WASTED NO TIME IN RETURNING TO MY ANCIENT VAULT, AND THERE I MADE THE CRUCIAL TEST!
IT WORKED! I CAN SEE MY REFLECTION! THE MIRROR DOESN'T LIE! NO VAMPIRE COULD CAST A REFLECTION AS I DO NOW!
I AM CURED! I CAN FACE HER LIKE ANY OTHER MAN! SHE WILL LEARN TO LOVE ME... SHE MUST! I'VE DONE ALL OF THIS FOR HER!
I WAS CURED! DURING THE DAYS THAT FOLLOWED, I REMAINED NORMAL AT ALL TIMES... THE MONSTER IN ME WAS TOTALLY DESTROYED... THEN ONE HAPPY EVENING...
MADAM MARA, MAY I PRESENT COUNT KRONIN? THE COUNT HAS TAKEN RESIDENCE HERE AND IS MOST ANXIOUS TO MAKE YOUR ACQUAINTANCE!
I AM MOST FLATTERED! DO YOU DANCE?
THEN SHE WAS IN MY ARMS, AND NEVER HAD I KNOWN SUCH JOY!
THERE IS A FAMILIAR LOOK ABOUT YOUR EYES, COUNT KRONIN! IS IT POSSIBLE WE HAVE MET BEFORE?
SCARCELY, MY DEAR! IF WE HAD, I NEVER WOULD HAVE FORGOTTEN!
A TOAST TO THE MOST BEAUTIFUL WOMAN IN ALL EUROPE, AND THE HOPE THAT SHE WILL HAVE DINNER WITH ME TONIGHT!
YOU MAKE IT DIFFICULT TO REFUSE, COUNT KRONIN!
FOR THREE SUCCESSIVE NIGHTS WE HAD DINNER TOGETHER... THEN ON THE FOURTH I COULD RESTRAIN MYSELF NO LONGER!
THERE IS A QUESTION I MUST ASK YOU, MARA! IT HAS BEEN ON MY LIPS FOR DAYS, BUT I MUST KNOW! WILL YOU MARRY ME?
IT'S ALL SO SUDDEN, AND YET...
THEN YOU WILL MARRY ME? TONIGHT? I'LL DO ANYTHING YOU SAY, IF YOU WILL SAY YES!
ALRIGHT, MY DEAREST... YES!

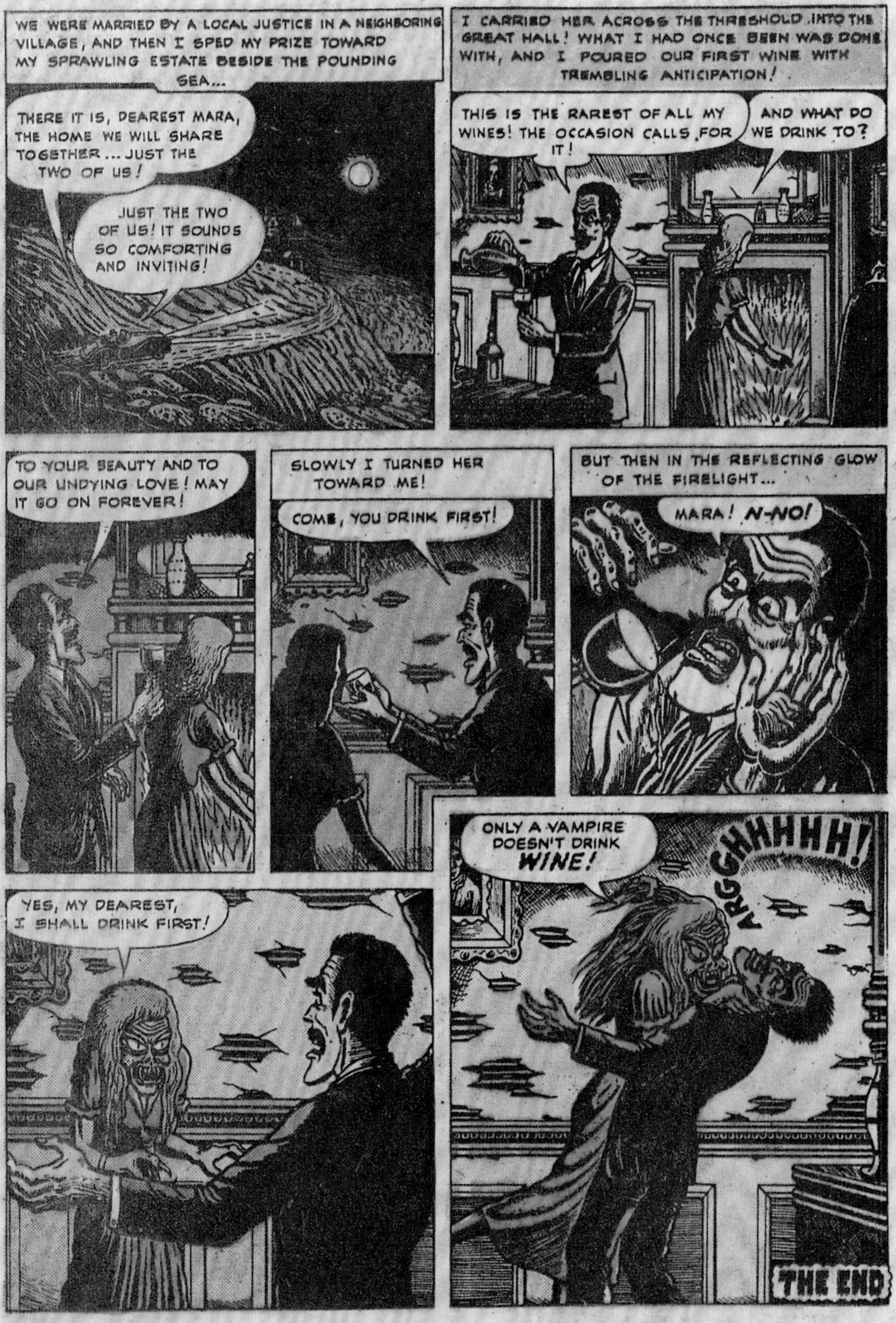
WE WERE MARRIED BY A LOCAL JUSTICE IN A NEIGHBORING VILLAGE, AND THEN I SPED MY PRIZE TOWARD MY SPRAWLING ESTATE BESIDE THE POUNDING SEA...
THERE IT IS, DEAREST MARA, THE HOME WE WILL SHARE TOGETHER ... JUST THE TWO OF US!
JUST THE TWO OF US! IT SOUNDS SO COMFORTING AND INVITING!
I CARRIED HER ACROSS THE THRESHOLD INTO THE GREAT HALL! WHAT I HAD ONCE BEEN WAS DONE WITH, AND I POURED OUR FIRST WINE WITH TREMBLING ANTICIPATION!
THIS IS THE RAREST OF ALL MY WINES! THE OCCASION CALLS FOR IT!
AND WHAT DO WE DRINK TO?
TO YOUR BEAUTY AND TO OUR UNDYING LOVE! MAY IT GO ON FOREVER!
SLOWLY I TURNED HER TOWARD ME!
COME, YOU DRINK FIRST!
BUT THEN IN THE REFLECTING GLOW OF THE FIRELIGHT...
MARA! N-NO!
YES, MY DEAREST, I SHALL DRINK FIRST!
ONLY A VAMPIRE DOESN'T DRINK WINE!
ARRGGHHHHHH!
THE END

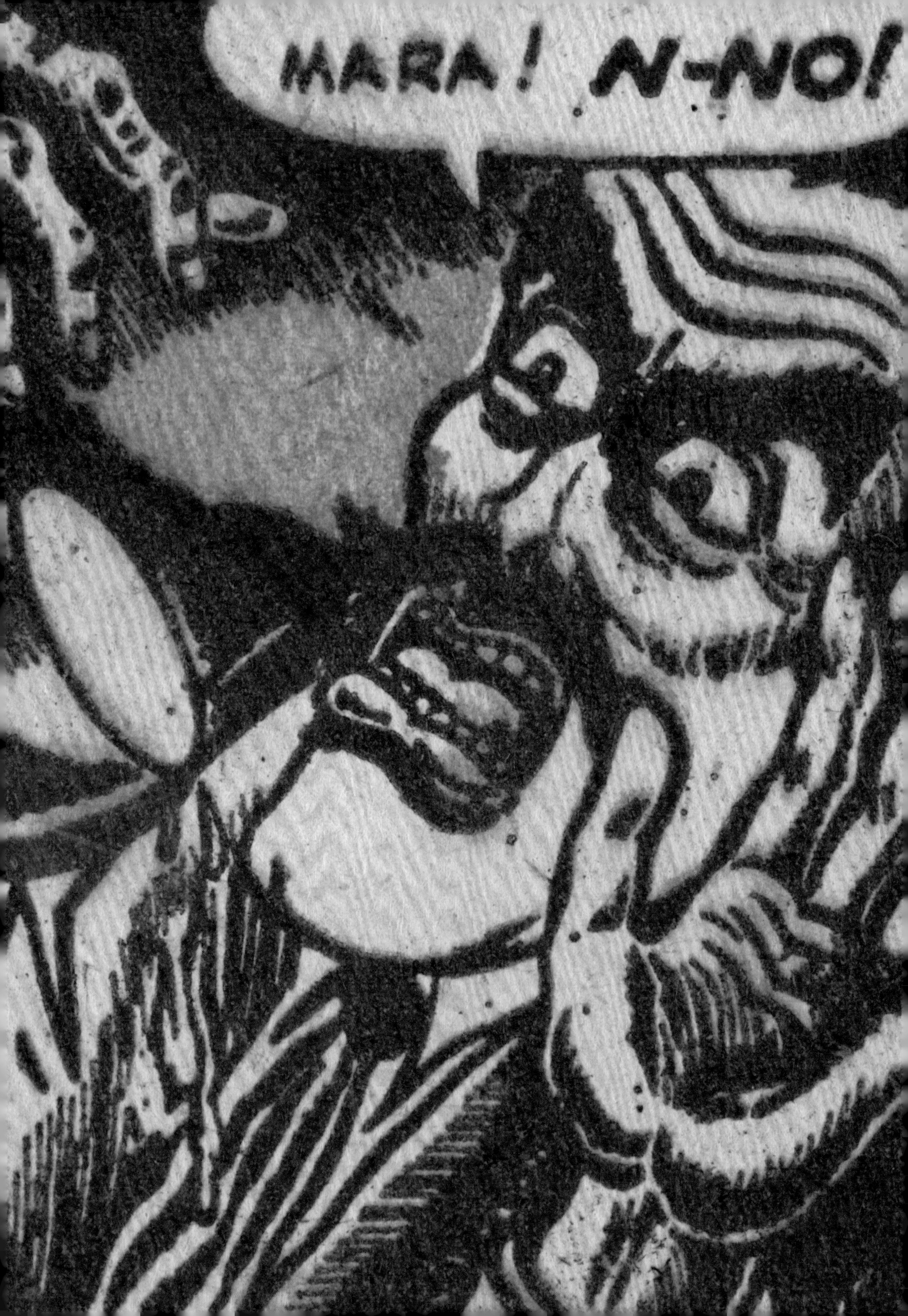
MARA! N-NO!

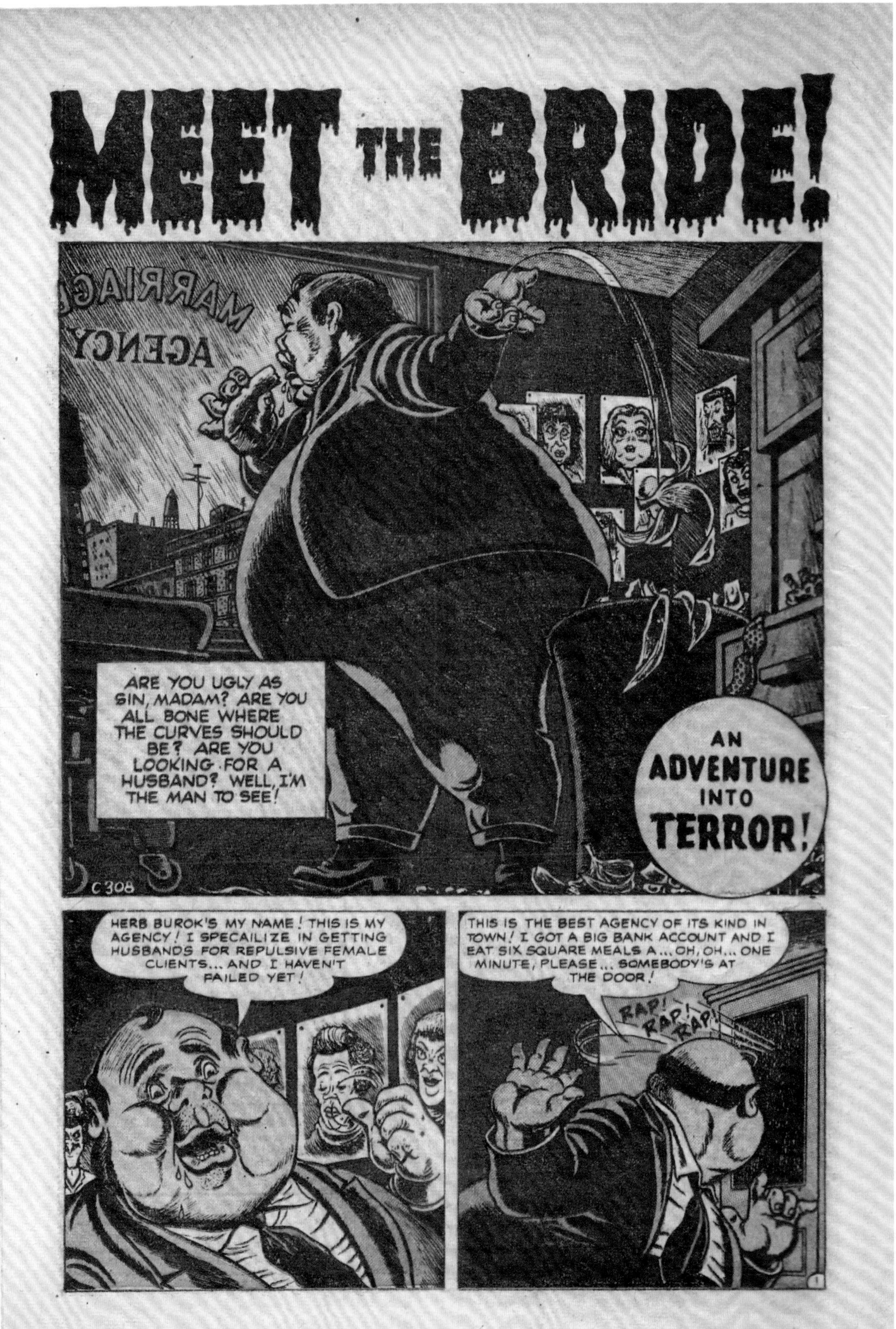
MEET THE BRIDE!
MARRIAGE AGENCY
ARE YOU UGLY AS SIN, MADAM? ARE YOU ALL BONE WHERE THE CURVES SHOULD BE? ARE YOU LOOKING FOR A HUSBAND? WELL, I'M THE MAN TO SEE!
AN ADVENTURE INTO TERROR!
C 308
HERB BUROK'S MY NAME! THIS IS MY AGENCY! I SPECAILIZE IN GETTING HUSBANDS FOR REPULSIVE FEMALE CLIENTS... AND I HAVEN'T FAILED YET!
THIS IS THE BEST AGENCY OF ITS KIND IN TOWN! I GOT A BIG BANK ACCOUNT AND I EAT SIX SQUARE MEALS A... OH, OH... ONE MINUTE, PLEASE... SOMEBODY'S AT THE DOOR!
RAP! RAP! RAP!

Uncanny Tales no. 6 (1953)

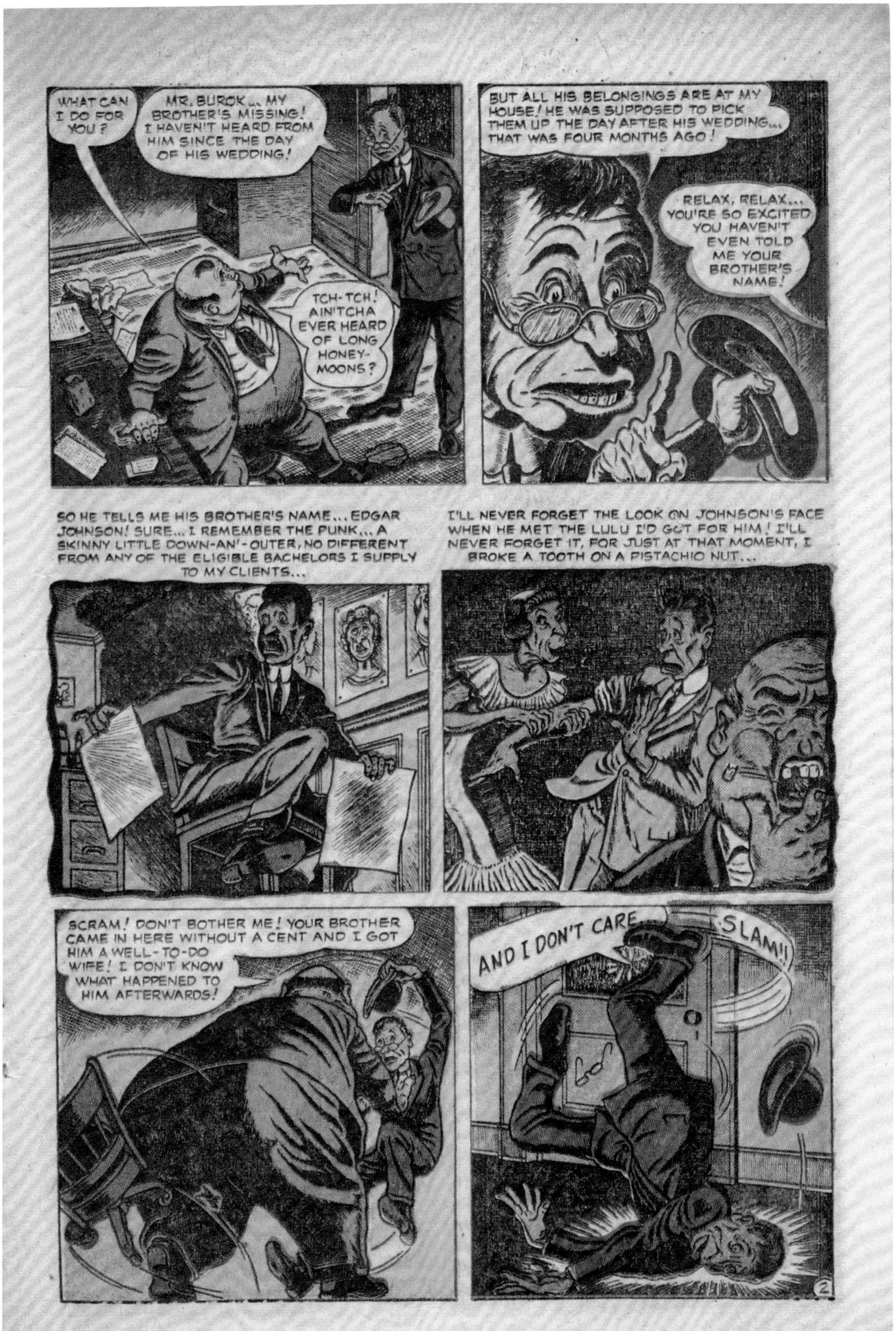
WHAT CAN I DO FOR YOU?
MR. BUROK... MY BROTHER'S MISSING! I HAVEN'T HEARD FROM HIM SINCE THE DAY OF HIS WEDDING!
TCH-TCH! AIN'TCHA EVER HEARD OF LONG HONEY-MOONS?
BUT ALL HIS BELONGINGS ARE AT MY HOUSE! HE WAS SUPPOSED TO PICK THEM UP THE DAY AFTER HIS WEDDING... THAT WAS FOUR MONTHS AGO!
RELAX, RELAX... YOU'RE SO EXCITED YOU HAVEN'T EVEN TOLD ME YOUR BROTHER'S NAME!
SO HE TELLS ME HIS BROTHER'S NAME... EDGAR JOHNSON! SURE... I REMEMBER THE PUNK... A SKINNY LITTLE DOWN-AN'-OUTER, NO DIFFERENT FROM ANY OF THE ELIGIBLE BACHELORS I SUPPLY TO MY CLIENTS...
I'LL NEVER FORGET THE LOOK ON JOHNSON'S FACE WHEN HE MET THE LULU I'D GOT FOR HIM! I'LL NEVER FORGET IT, FOR JUST AT THAT MOMENT, I BROKE A TOOTH ON A PISTACHIO NUT...
SCRAM! DON'T BOTHER ME! YOUR BROTHER CAME IN HERE WITHOUT A CENT AND I GOT HIM A WELL-TO-DO WIFE! I DON'T KNOW WHAT HAPPENED TO HIM AFTERWARDS!
AND I DON'T CARE...
SLAM!!
2

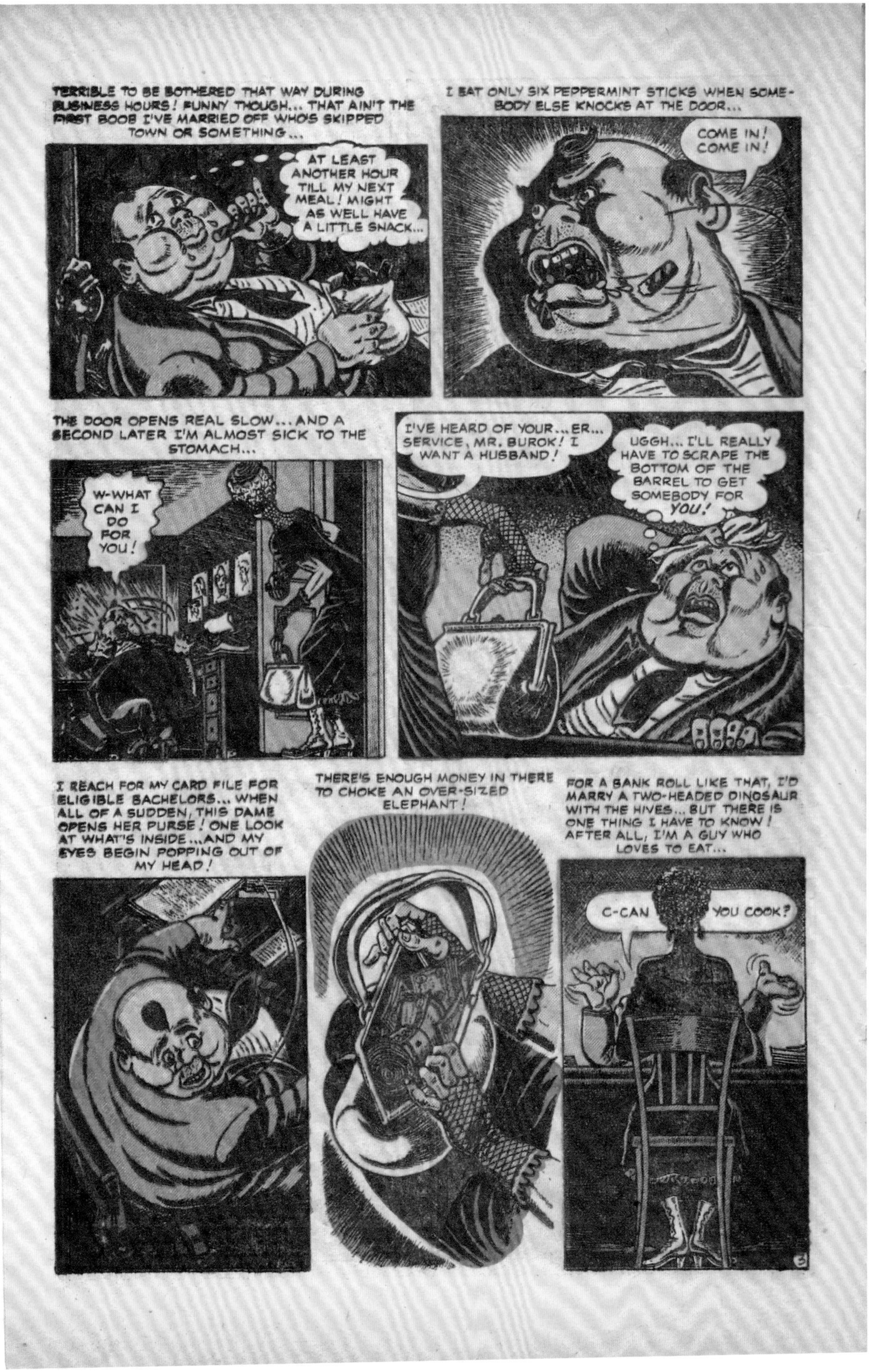
TERRIBLE TO BE BOTHERED THAT WAY DURING BUSINESS HOURS! FUNNY THOUGH... THAT AIN'T THE FIRST BOOB I'VE MARRIED OFF WHO'S SKIPPED TOWN OR SOMETHING...
AT LEAST ANOTHER HOUR TILL MY NEXT MEAL! MIGHT AS WELL HAVE A LITTLE SNACK...
I EAT ONLY SIX PEPPERMINT STICKS WHEN SOMEBODY ELSE KNOCKS AT THE DOOR...
COME IN! COME IN!
THE DOOR OPENS REAL SLOW... AND A SECOND LATER I'M ALMOST SICK TO THE STOMACH...
W-WHAT CAN I DO FOR YOU!
I'VE HEARD OF YOUR... ER... SERVICE, MR. BUROK! I WANT A HUSBAND!
UGGH... I'LL REALLY HAVE TO SCRAPE THE BOTTOM OF THE BARREL TO GET SOMEBODY FOR YOU!
I REACH FOR MY CARD FILE FOR ELIGIBLE BACHELORS... WHEN ALL OF A SUDDEN, THIS DAME OPENS HER PURSE! ONE LOOK AT WHAT'S INSIDE... AND MY EYES BEGIN POPPING OUT OF MY HEAD!
THERE'S ENOUGH MONEY IN THERE TO CHOKE AN OVER-SIZED ELEPHANT!
FOR A BANK ROLL LIKE THAT, I'D MARRY A TWO-HEADED DINOSAUR WITH THE HIVES... BUT THERE IS ONE THING I HAVE TO KNOW! AFTER ALL, I'M A GUY WHO LOVES TO EAT...
C-CAN
YOU COOK?
5

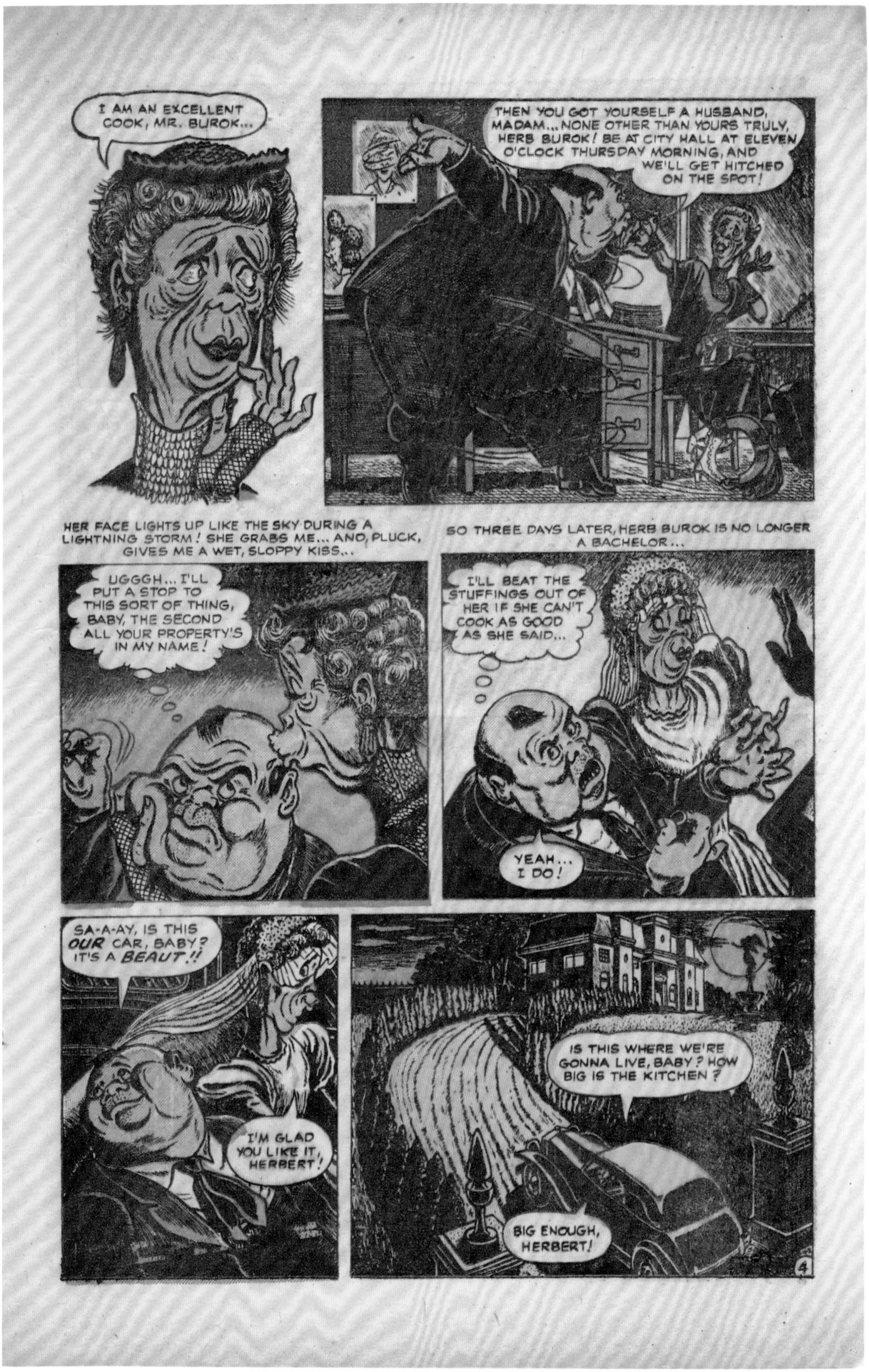
I AM AN EXCELLENT COOK, MR. BUROK...
THEN YOU GOT YOURSELF A HUSBAND, MADAM... NONE OTHER THAN YOURS TRULY, HERB BUROK! BE AT CITY HALL AT ELEVEN O'CLOCK THURSDAY MORNING, AND WE'LL GET HITCHED ON THE SPOT!
HER FACE LIGHTS UP LIKE THE SKY DURING A LIGHTNING STORM! SHE GRABS ME... AND, PLUCK, GIVES ME A WET, SLOPPY KISS...
UGGGH... I'LL PUT A STOP TO THIS SORT OF THING, BABY, THE SECOND ALL YOUR PROPERTY'S IN MY NAME!
SO THREE DAYS LATER, HERB BUROK IS NO LONGER A BACHELOR...
I'LL BEAT THE STUFFINGS OUT OF HER IF SHE CAN'T COOK AS GOOD AS SHE SAID...
YEAH... I DO!
SA-A-AY, IS THIS OUR CAR, BABY? IT'S A BEAUT!!
I'M GLAD YOU LIKE IT, HERBERT!
IS THIS WHERE WE'RE GONNA LIVE, BABY? HOW BIG IS THE KITCHEN?
BIG ENOUGH, HERBERT!
4

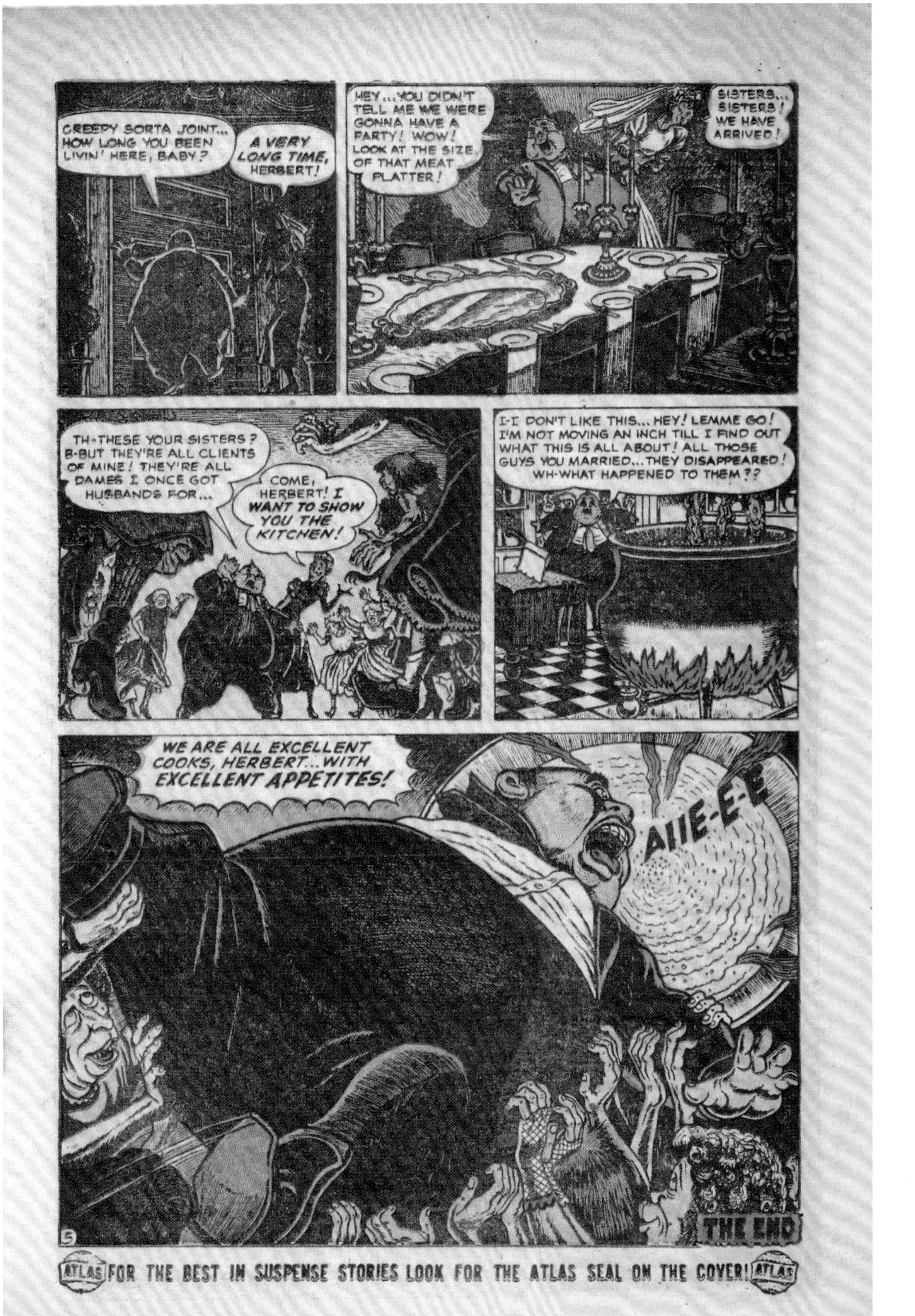
CREEPY SORTA JOINT... HOW LONG YOU BEEN LIVIN' HERE, BABY?
A VERY LONG TIME, HERBERT!
HEY... YOU DIDN'T TELL ME WE WERE GONNA HAVE A PARTY! WOW! LOOK AT THE SIZE OF THAT MEAT PLATTER!
SISTERS... SISTERS! WE HAVE ARRIVED!
TH-THESE YOUR SISTERS? B-BUT THEY'RE ALL CLIENTS OF MINE! THEY'RE ALL DAMES I ONCE GOT HUSBANDS FOR...
COME, HERBERT! I WANT TO SHOW YOU THE KITCHEN!
I-I DON'T LIKE THIS... HEY! LEMME GO! I'M NOT MOVING AN INCH TILL I FIND OUT WHAT THIS IS ALL ABOUT! ALL THOSE GUYS YOU MARRIED... THEY DISAPPEARED! WH-WHAT HAPPENED TO THEM??
WE ARE ALL EXCELLENT COOKS, HERBERT... WITH EXCELLENT APPETITES!
AIIE-E-E
THE END
5
ATLAS FOR THE BEST IN SUSPENSE STORIES LOOK FOR THE ATLAS SEAL ON THE COVER! ATLAS

JOHN THOMPSON

(b. 1945)

John Thompson was born in Carmel, California, and raised in San Francisco. Dyslexic from birth, he was an art history major at the University of California (Berkeley and Davis) and later earned a master's degree in art technology in 1970. As a result of his dyslexia, Thompson developed his own ways to negotiate reading texts and digesting lectures: he has cited that it was his "meticulously written and illustrated surreal lecture notes" that got him through school and anticipated his own visual narratives. As a child who had difficulty reading linearly for any length of time, Thompson found he was naturally attracted to the allover quality of art that would later be termed "psychedelic," as a way to soothe his mind. Thompson was not a comics reader, and never strove to be a comic book artist, but was drawn into the medium as part of the Bay Area culture of the time. He co-founded the underground comics anthology *The Yellow Dog* in 1968, and created numerous posters for local rock shows. *Cyclops Comics* was published in 1969.

Thompson's peers at the time were the likes of R. Crumb and psychedelic artist Rick Griffin. Like Griffin, Thompson says, "I also drove a large motorcycle, had very long hair, and could be friendly and outgoing, lived on very little money, collected ephemera, and lived with a strong grasp of what the Gospel of John points out." Thompson's work, which also includes a three-issue comic book called *Tales from the Sphinx*, is replete with private meanings and interior languages. It has neither the graphic precision of fellow underground comics artist Victor Moscoso nor the cartooned roughness of Crumb; instead it seems more related to the ecstatically detailed work of his beloved William Blake and even the pulp illustrator Virgil Finlay. No one else on the underground scene achieved his kind of aesthetic delicacy. Thompson's work represents an adventurous interior exploration of the symbology that he sought to understand and communicate with. The story printed in this book is best described by the artist himself:

I never read this comic all the way through, nor did I draw it sequentially from page 1 to 18. I penciled the boxes on eighteen sheets of illustration board and then jumped from page to page jotting down spontaneous ideas in a non-linear fashion. So it was more like a mural that I bounced around within, scribbling here and there. These pages do not reflect my "beliefs," nor were they intended to do so. At that time some non-academic teens thought "Whoah, this dude musta taken a lotta acid, and this is heavy shit that he like learned." Instead, it reflects that fact that a lot of art history students at top universities were being taught complex symbol systems. It was intriguing to learn that late Hellenist Greeks developed astrological symbolism: including myths imbued in "decanades" (three sets to each zodiacal set; each set consisting of ten degrees). Later, Pythagorean Revival ideas mixed with Celtic lore and Jewish mysticism to come up with some of the ideas hinted at on page [201], as in the Hebrew Greek and one Tibetan form imply as correlating. Later, Swedenborg (pictured in the lower right corner with his birthday) incorporated Pythagorean-Kabalistic ideas in his writings, which impressed William Blake, who is shown in the lower right corner of page [214].

Other artists I drew were Michelangelo—page [203] profile; Judas in profile—page [203]; at the bottom of page [204] is Mona Lisa with Julie Christie on her right; Durer on page [206]; Walt Whitman on page [208]; Cabalist character Adom Kadmon atop page [209] with the Bible's Amos and artist Rembrandt below. In the lower right corner of page [209] is the Friant Dam in the Sierra foothills where I lived briefly in 1968 while drawing this story. The top left of page [211] is a reference to a cryptic passage from Blake and a nursery rhyme mantra I learned as a child that is similar to Blake's musical celebration of The River of Life as a dream. Personally my favorite page is [216]. The Tibetan meanings are significant to me as a Nyingma Buddhist, and have more significance than the other pages.

John Thompson continued to make comics into the early 1970s. When the underground comics market faltered, Thompson maintained his work in schools and his sociopolitical activism, and pursued an active, if private, drawing practice. He lives with his family on the Monterey Peninsula.

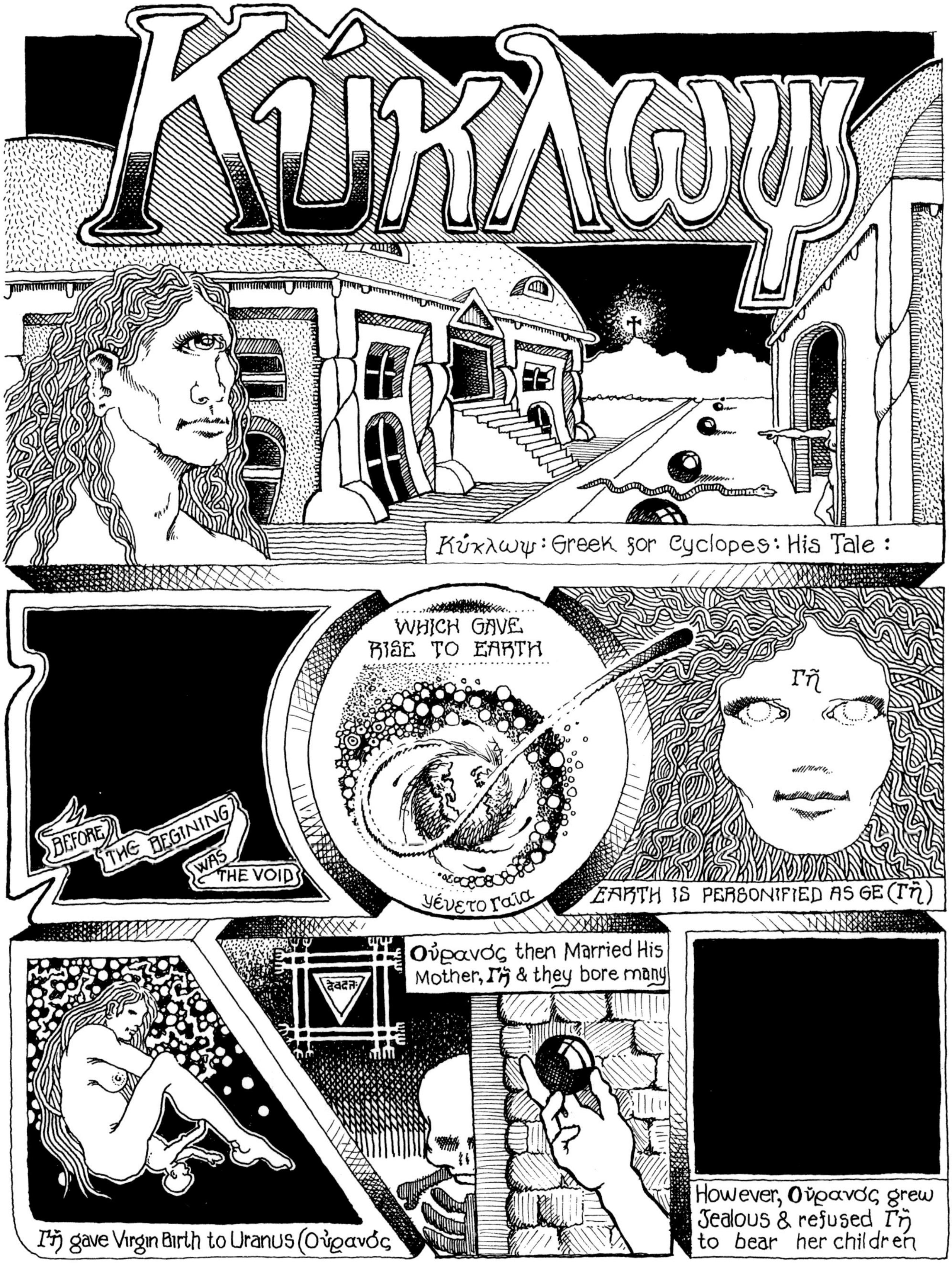
Κύκλωψ
Κύκλωψ: Greek for Cyclopes: His Tale:
BEFORE THE BEGINING WAS THE VOID
WHICH GAVE RISE TO EARTH
γένετο Γαῖα
Γῆ
EARTH IS PERSONIFIED AS GE (Γῆ)
Γῆ gave Virgin Birth to Uranus (Οὐρανός
Οὐρανός then Married His Mother, Γῆ & they bore many
However, Οὐρανός grew Jealous & refused Γῆ to bear her children

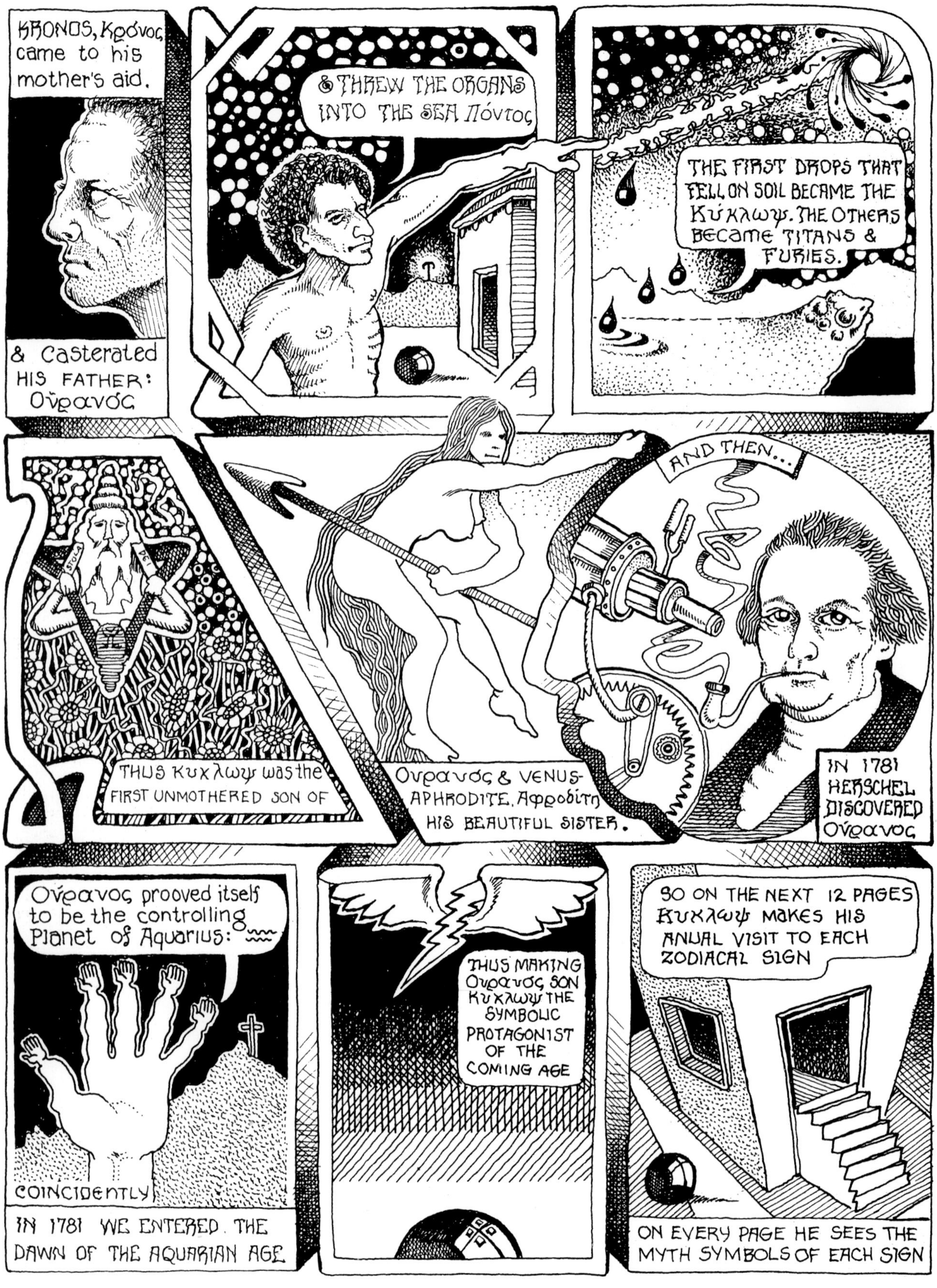
KRONOS, Κρόνος, came to his mother's aid.
& Casterated HIS FATHER: Οὐρανός
& THREW THE ORGANS INTO THE SEA Πόντος
THE FIRST DROPS THAT FELL ON SOIL BECAME THE Κύκλωψ. THE OTHERS BECAME TITANS & FURIES.
THUS Κυκλωψ was the FIRST UNMOTHERED SON OF
Ουρανός & VENUS-APHRODITE, Αφροδίτη HIS BEAUTIFUL SISTER.
AND THEN...
IN 1781 HERSCHEL DISCOVERED Οὐρανος
Οὐρανος prooved itself to be the controlling Planet of Aquarius: ♒
COINCIDENTLY
IN 1781 WE ENTERED THE DAWN OF THE AQUARIAN AGE
THUS MAKING Ουρανος SON Κυκλωψ THE SYMBOLIC PROTAGONIST OF THE COMING AGE
SO ON THE NEXT 12 PAGES Κυκλωψ MAKES HIS ANUAL VISIT TO EACH ZODIACAL SIGN
ON EVERY PAGE HE SEES THE MYTH SYMBOLS OF EACH SIGN

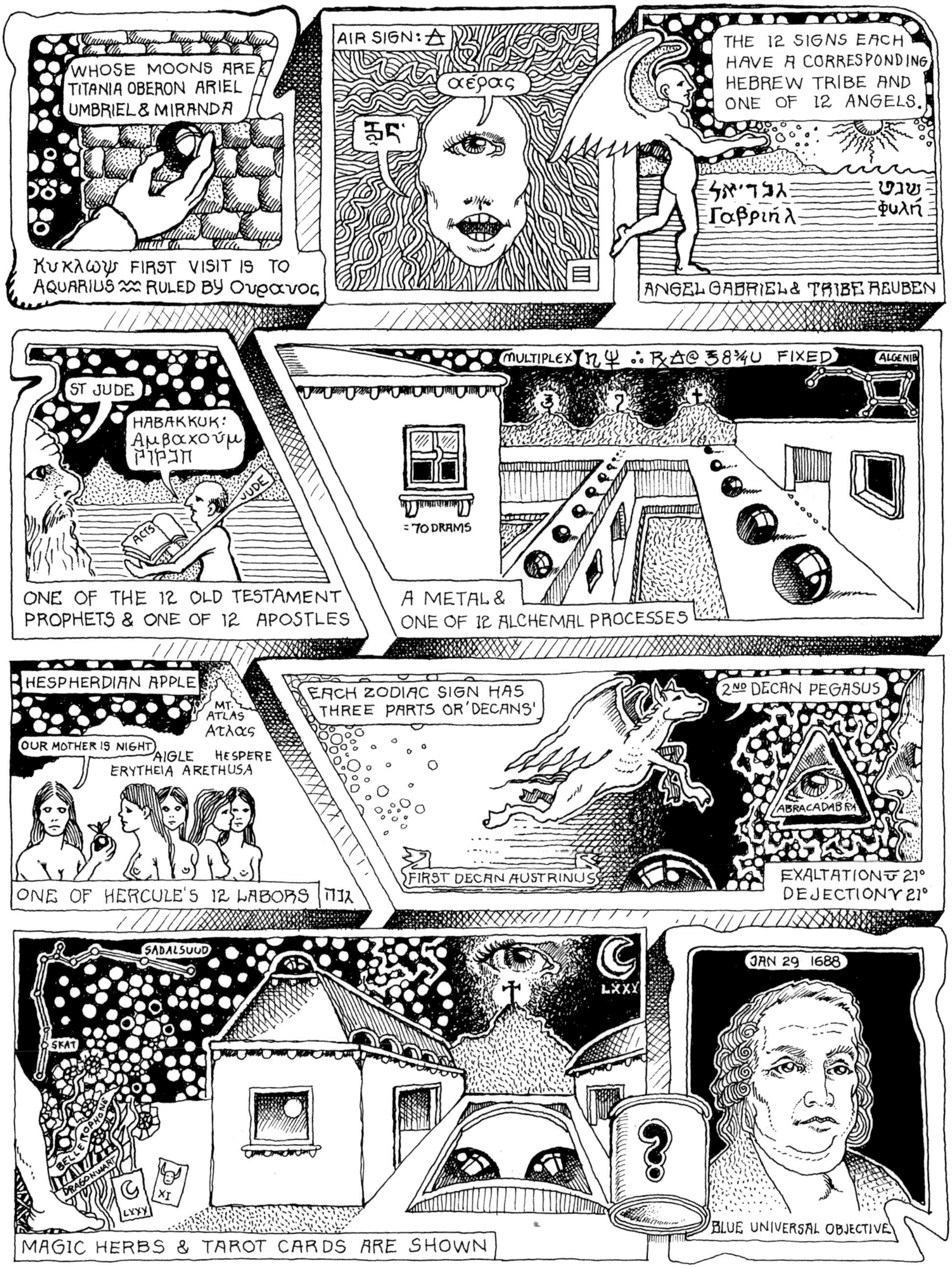
WHOSE MOONS ARE TITANIA OBERON ARIEL UMBRIEL & MIRANDA
Κυκλωψ FIRST VISIT IS TO AQUARIUS ♒ RULED BY Ουρανος
AIR SIGN: △
αέρας
THE 12 SIGNS EACH HAVE A CORRESPONDING HEBREW TRIBE AND ONE OF 12 ANGELS.
גבריאל
Γαβριήλ
שבט
φυλή
ANGEL GABRIEL & TRIBE REUBEN
ST JUDE
HABAKKUK: Αμβαχούμ חבקוק
JUDE
ACTS
ONE OF THE 12 OLD TESTAMENT PROPHETS & ONE OF 12 APOSTLES
MULTIPLEX
38¾U FIXED
ALGENIB
= 70 DRAMS
A METAL & ONE OF 12 ALCHEMAL PROCESSES
HESPHERDIAN APPLE
MT. ATLAS Ατλας
OUR MOTHER IS NIGHT
AIGLE HESPERE ERYTHEIA ARETHUSA
ONE OF HERCULE'S 12 LABORS
EACH ZODIAC SIGN HAS THREE PARTS OR 'DECANS'
2ND DECAN PEGASUS
ABRACADABRA
FIRST DECAN AUSTRINUS
EXALTATION 21°
DEJECTION ♈ 21°
SADALSUUD
LXXX
SKAT
BELLEROPHONE
DRAGONWART
XI
MAGIC HERBS & TAROT CARDS ARE SHOWN
JAN 29 1688
BLUE UNIVERSAL OBJECTIVE

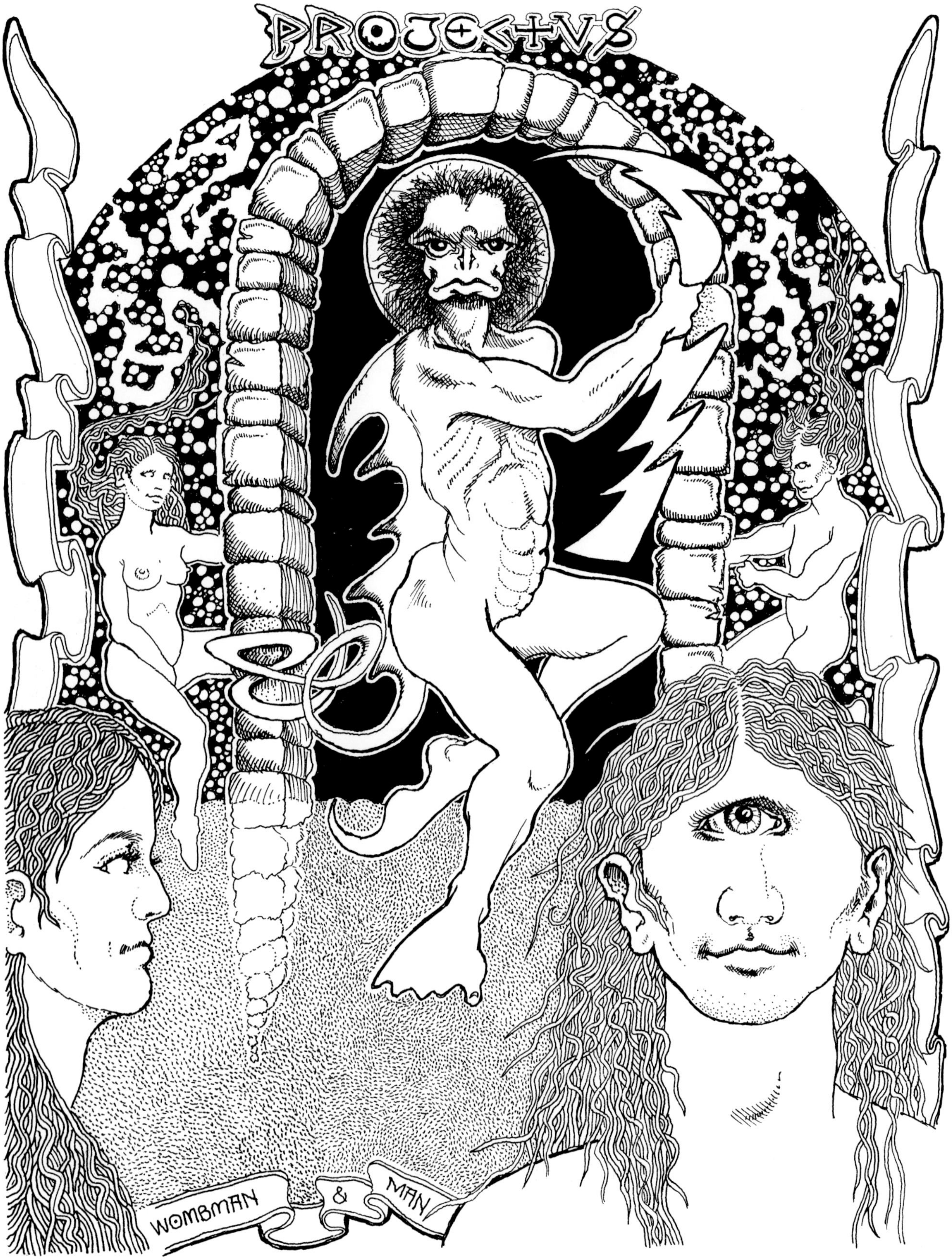
PROJECTVS
WOMBMAN
&
MAN

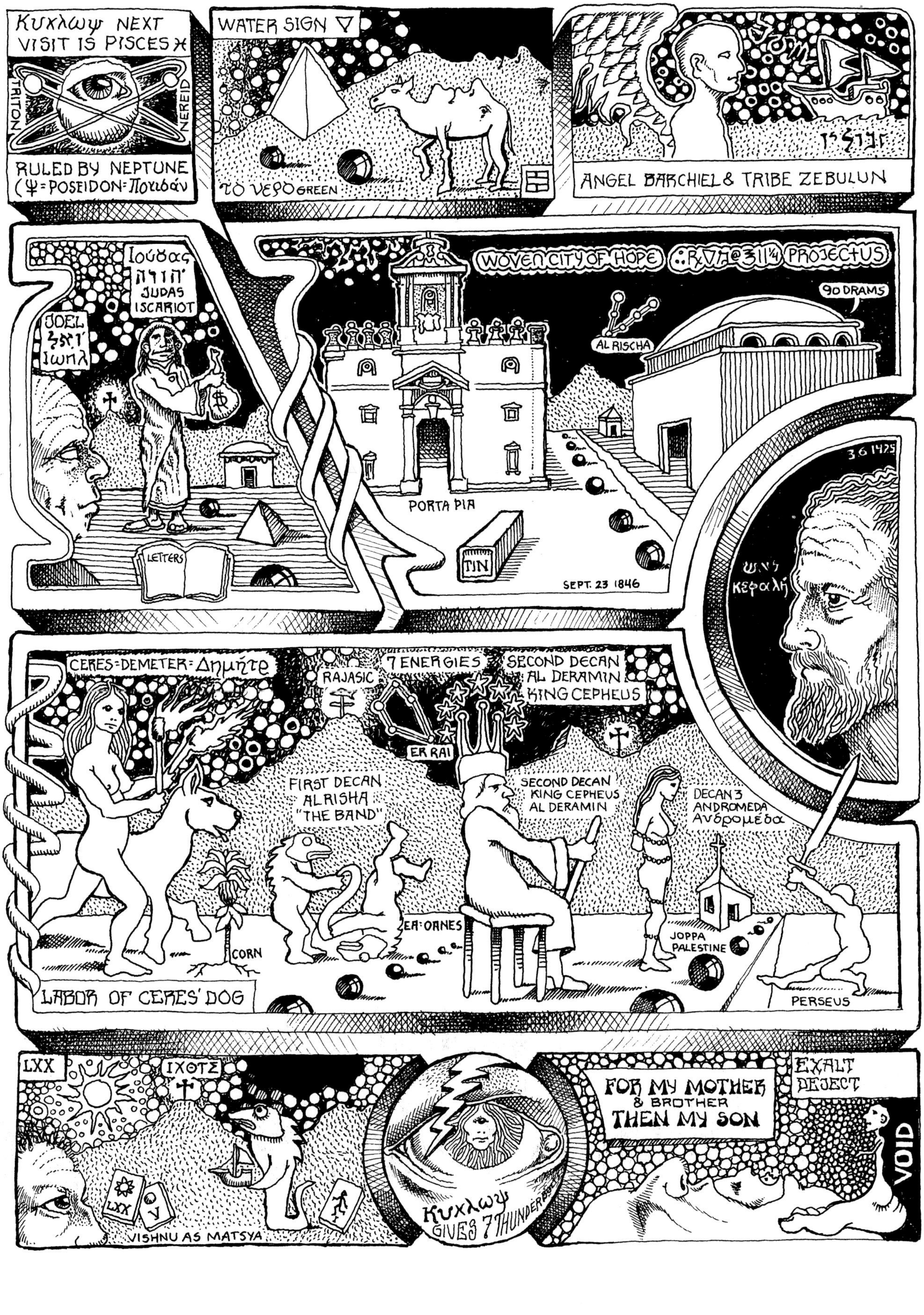
Κυχλωψ NEXT VISIT IS PISCES ♓
TRITON
NEREID
RULED BY NEPTUNE (Ψ=POSEIDON=Ποτιδάν
WATER SIGN ▽
τὸ νερὸ GREEN
ANGEL BARCHIEL & TRIBE ZEBULUN
Ιούδας יהודה JUDAS ISCARIOT
JOEL יואל Ιωηλ
LETTERS
WOVEN CITY OF HOPE
PROJECTUS
90 DRAMS
AL RISCHA
PORTA PIA
TIN
SEPT. 23 1846
3 6 1475
κεφαλή
CERES=DEMETER=Δημήτε
RAJASIC
7 ENERGIES
SECOND DECAN AL DERAMIN KING CEPHEUS
ER RAI
FIRST DECAN AL RISHA "THE BAND"
SECOND DECAN KING CEPHEUS AL DERAMIN
DECAN 3 ANDROMEDA Ανδρομέδα
EA: OANES
CORN
JOPPA PALESTINE
PERSEUS
LABOR OF CERES' DOG
LXX
ΙΧΘΥΣ
FOR MY MOTHER & BROTHER THEN MY SON
EXALT DEJECT
VOID
LXX
VISHNU AS MATSYA
Κυχλωψ GIVES 7 THUNDERS

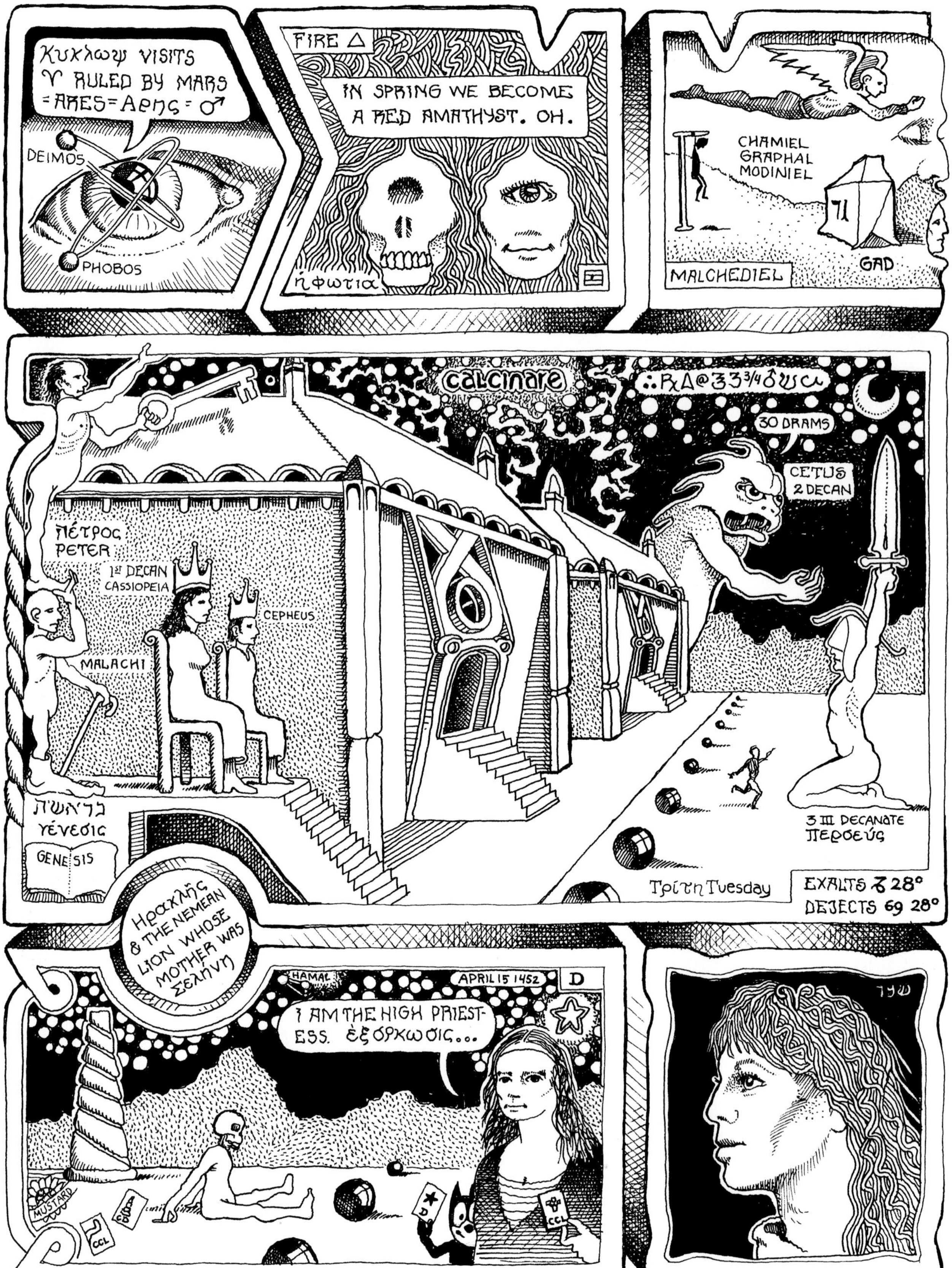
Κυκλωψ VISITS ♈ RULED BY MARS =ARES=Αρης=♂
DEIMOS
PHOBOS
FIRE △
IN SPRING WE BECOME A RED AMATHYST. OH.
ἡ φωτια
CHAMIEL
GRAPHAL
MODINIEL
MALCHEDIEL
GAD
calcinare
30 DRAMS
CETUS 2 DECAN
Πέτρος
PETER
1st DECAN CASSIOPEIA
CEPHEUS
MALACHI
בראשית
γένεσις
GENESIS
3 III DECANATE
Περσεύς
Τρίτη Tuesday
EXALTS 28°
DEJECTS 69 28°
Ηρακλῆς & THE NEMEAN LION WHOSE MOTHER WAS Σελήνη
HAMAL
APRIL 15 1452
D
I AM THE HIGH PRIESTESS. ἐξορκωσις...
MUSTARD
CCL
D
CCL

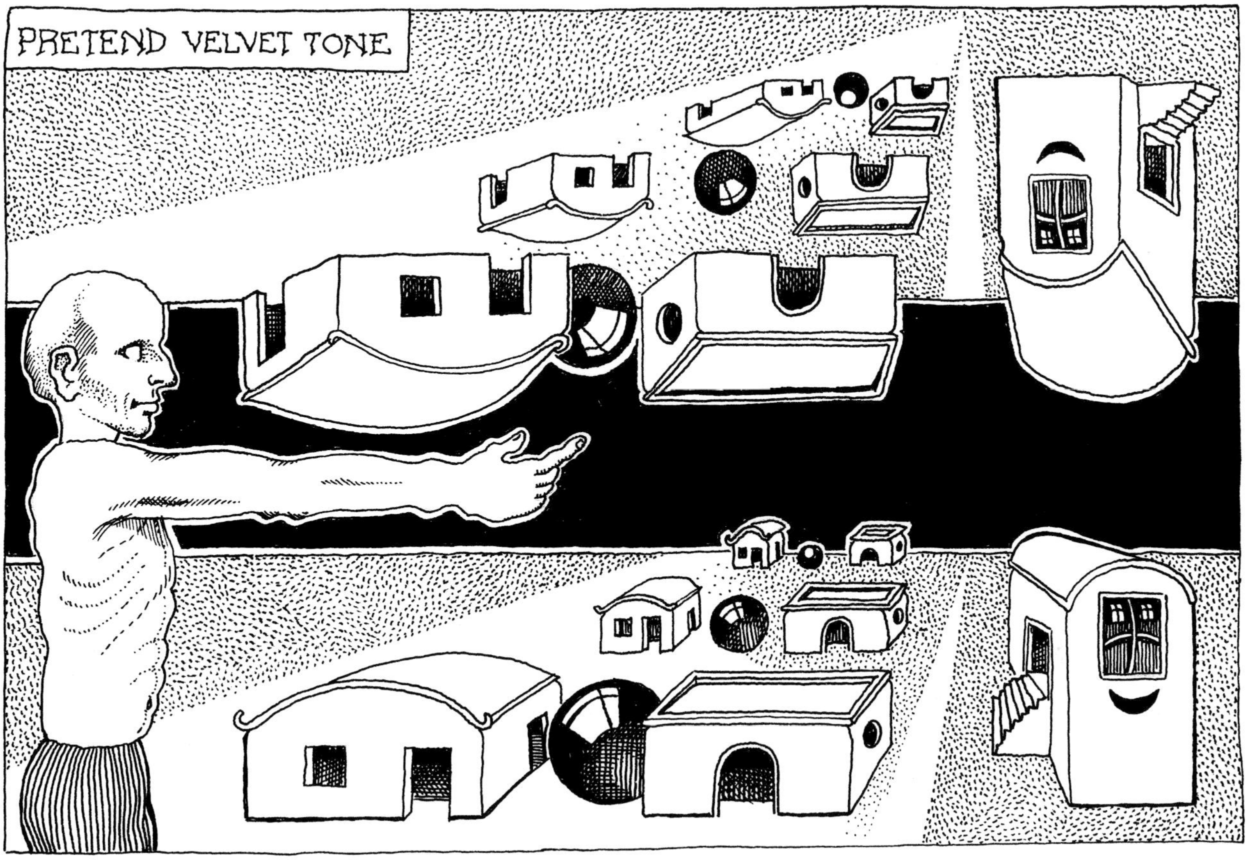
PRETEND VELVET TONE

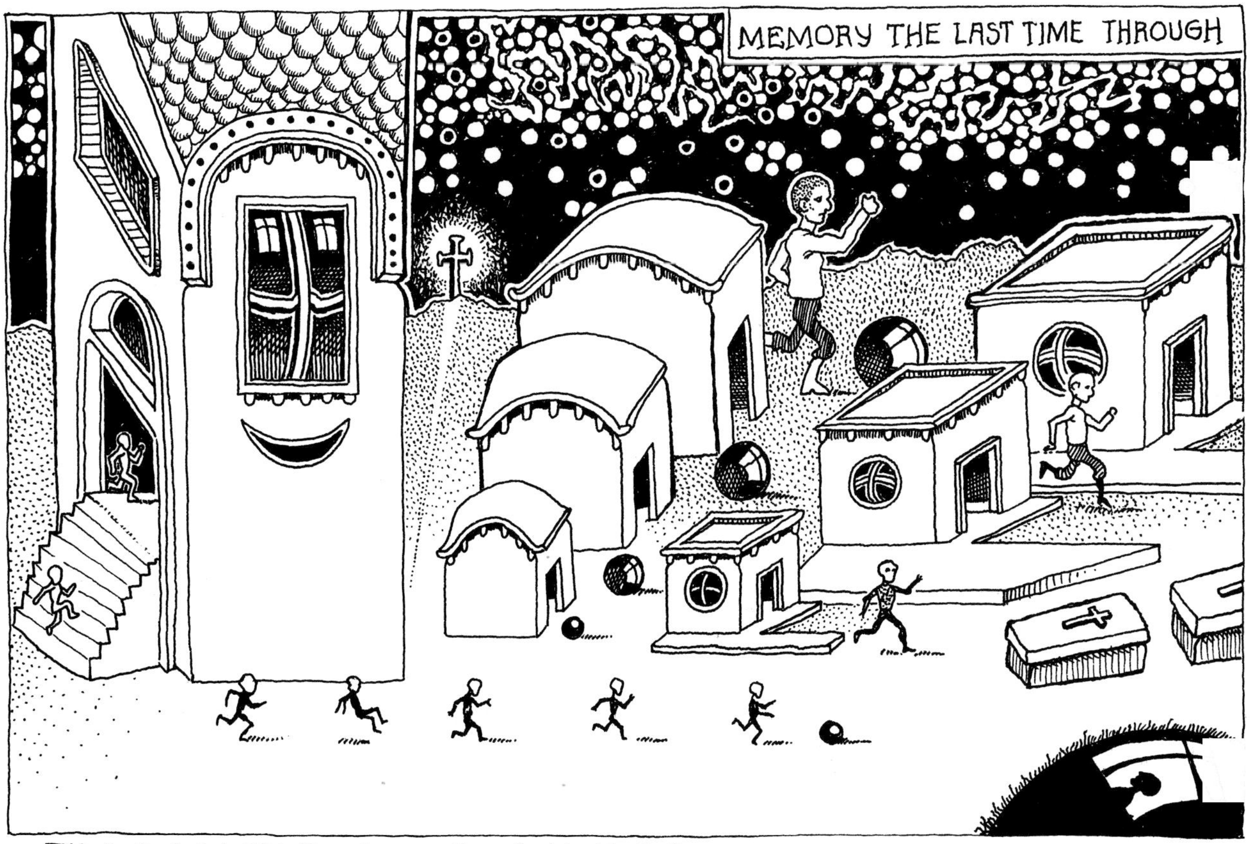
MEMORY THE LAST TIME THROUGH

B4. I. 8. I M BN BZ CN A GM & N IC C 2.

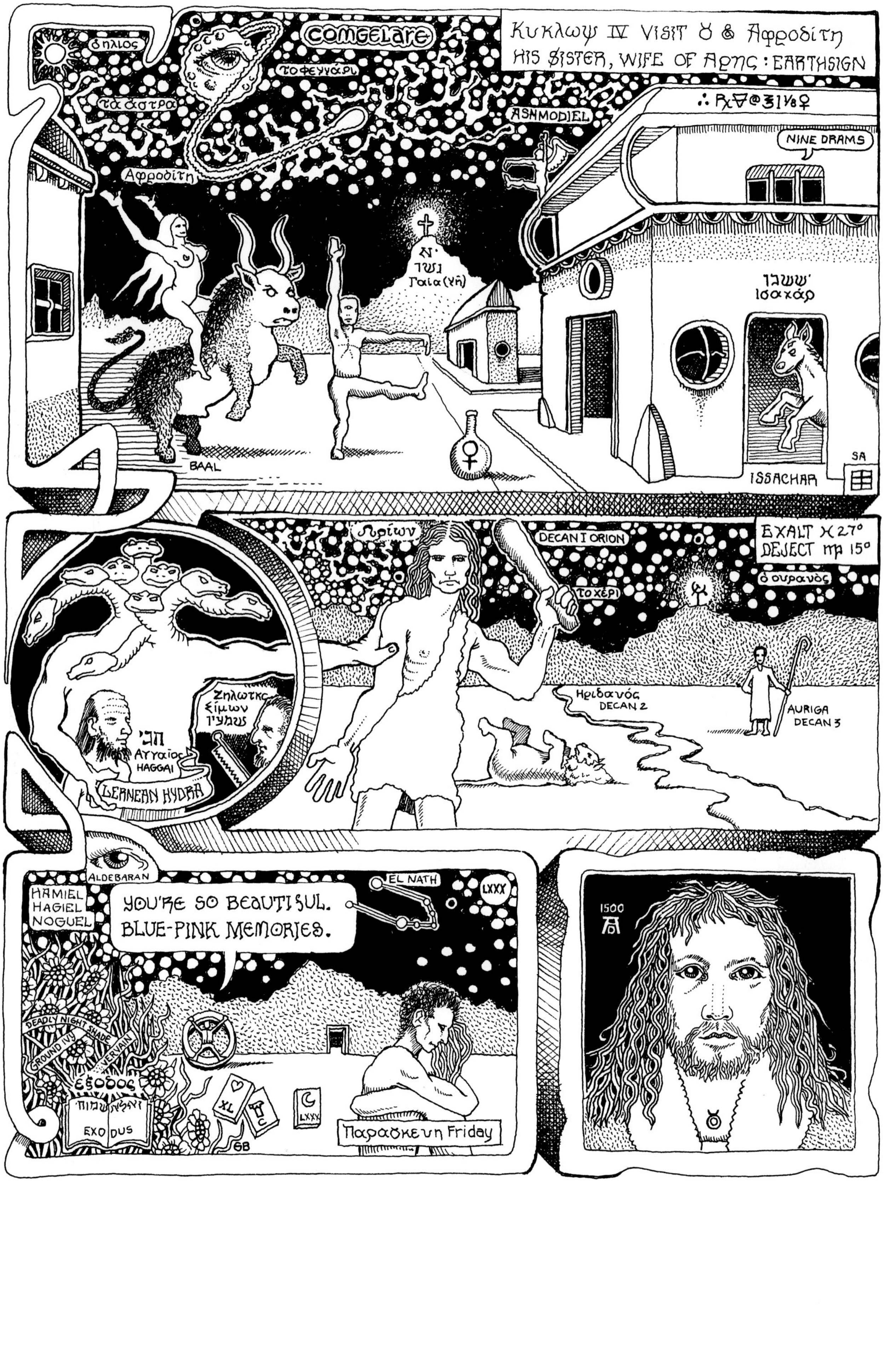
Κυκλωψ IV VISIT ♉ & Αφροδιτη
HIS SISTER, WIFE OF Αρης : EARTHSIGN
COMGELARE
ο ηλιος
το φεγγαρι
τα αστρα
Αφροδιτη
ASHMODIEL
NINE DRAMS
Ισαχάρ
BAAL
ISSACHAR
SA
Ωρίων
DECAN I ORION
EXALT ♓ 27°
DEJECT ♍ 15°
ο ουρανός
το χέρι
Ηριδανός
DECAN 2
AURIGA
DECAN 3
Αγγαίος
HAGGAI
LERNEAN HYDRA
ALDEBARAN
HAMIEL
HAGIEL
NOGUEL
YOU'RE SO BEAUTIFUL.
BLUE-PINK MEMORIES.
EL NATH
LXXX
DEADLY NIGHT SHADE
GROUND IVY
VERVAIN
έξοδος
EXODUS
XL
LXXX
Παρασκευη Friday
GB
1500

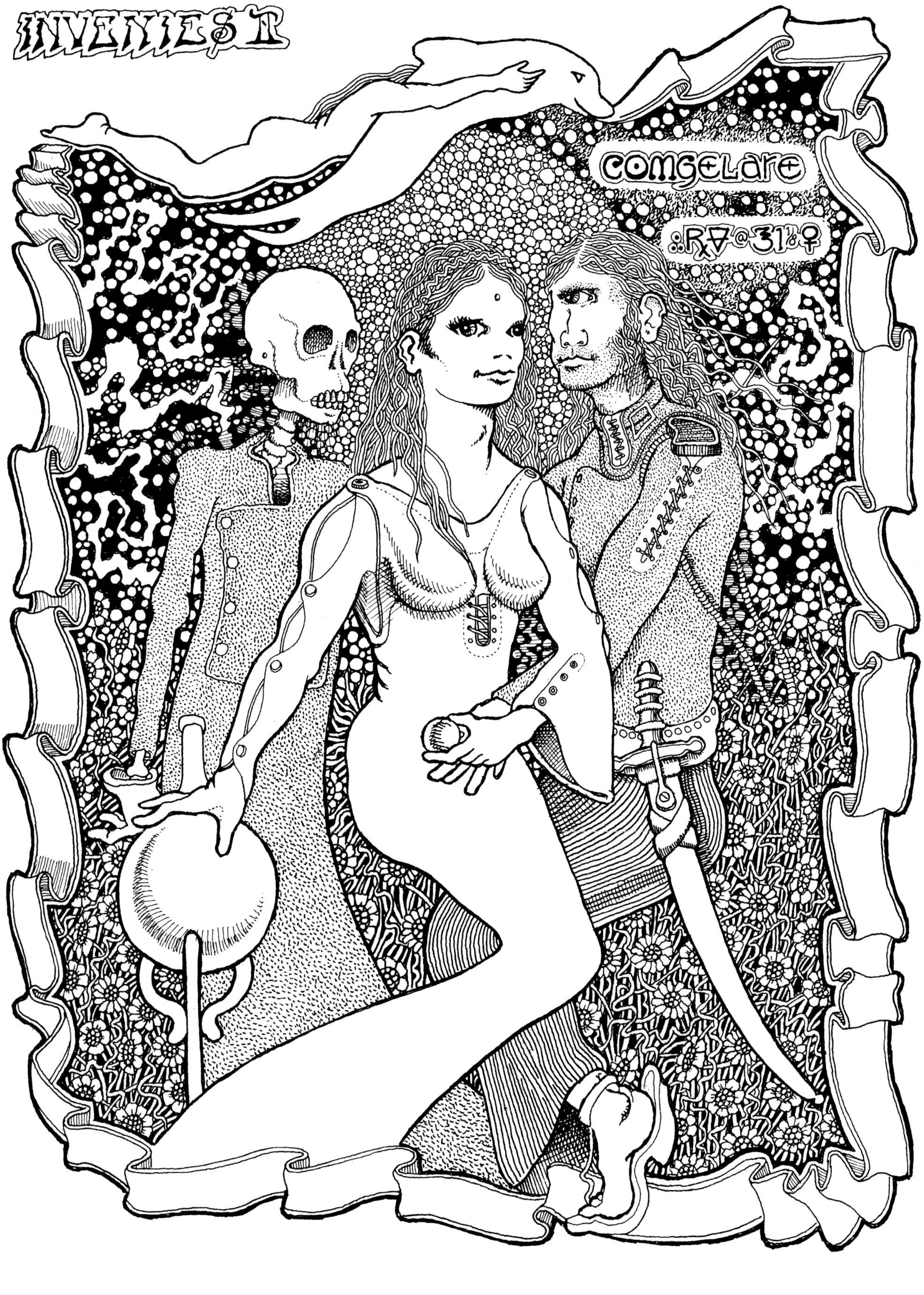
INVENIES R
COMGELARE

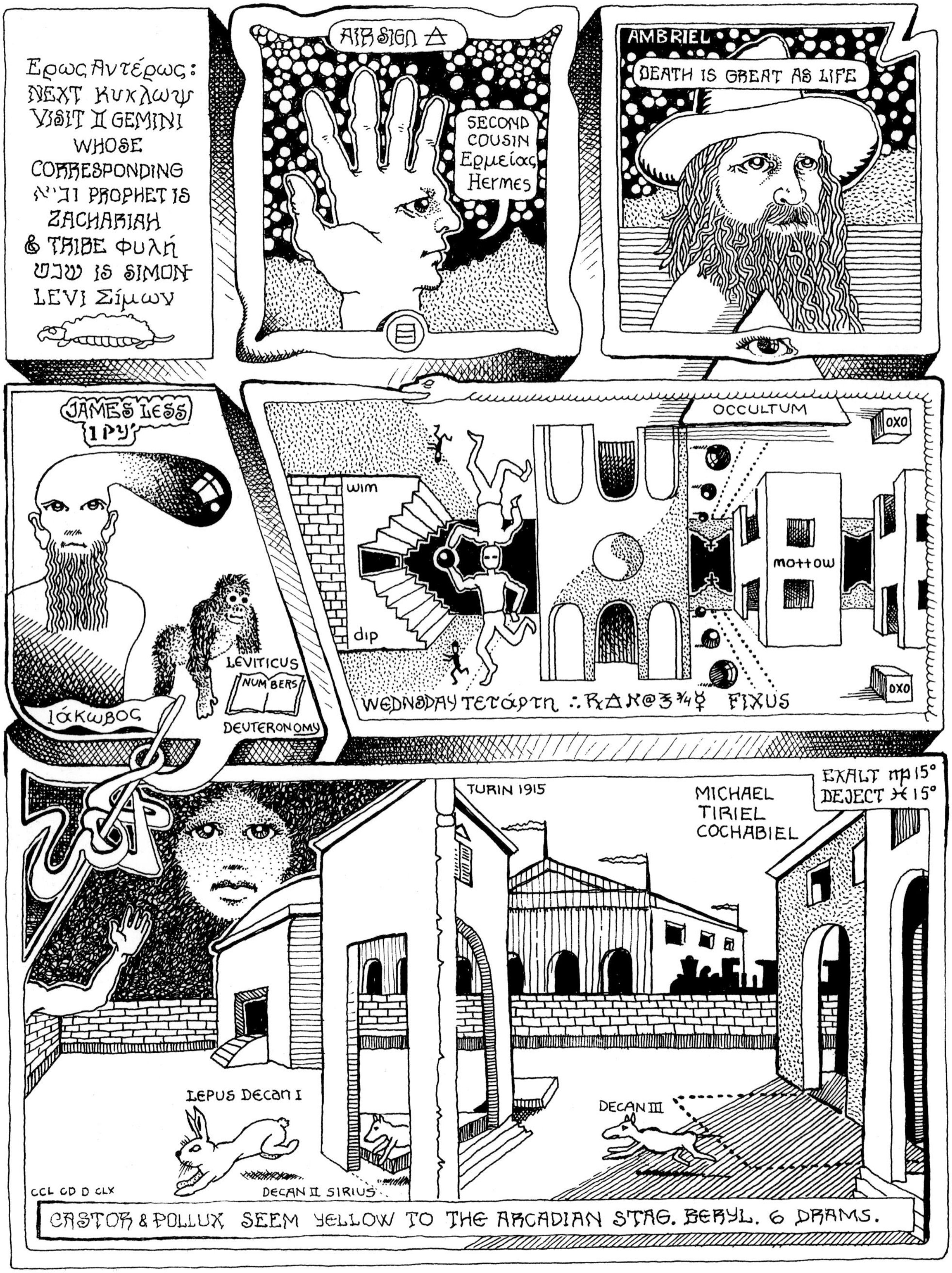
Ερως Αντέρως: NEXT Κυκλωψ VISIT II GEMINI WHOSE CORRESPONDING PROPHET IS ZACHARIAH & TRIBE φυλή IS SIMON-LEVI Σίμων
AIR SIGN △
SECOND COUSIN Ερμείας Hermes
AMBRIEL
DEATH IS GREAT AS LIFE
JAMES LESS 1 PY
Ιάκωβος
LEVITICUS
NUMBERS
DEUTERONOMY
OCCULTUM
OXO
wim
dip
mottow
OXO
WEDNSDAY Τετάρτη
FIXUS
TURIN 1915
MICHAEL TIRIEL COCHABIEL
EXALT 15°
DEJECT 15°
LEPUS DECAN I
DECAN III
CCL CD D CLX
DECAN II SIRIUS
CASTOR & POLLUX SEEM YELLOW TO THE ARCADIAN STAG. BERYL. 6 DRAMS.

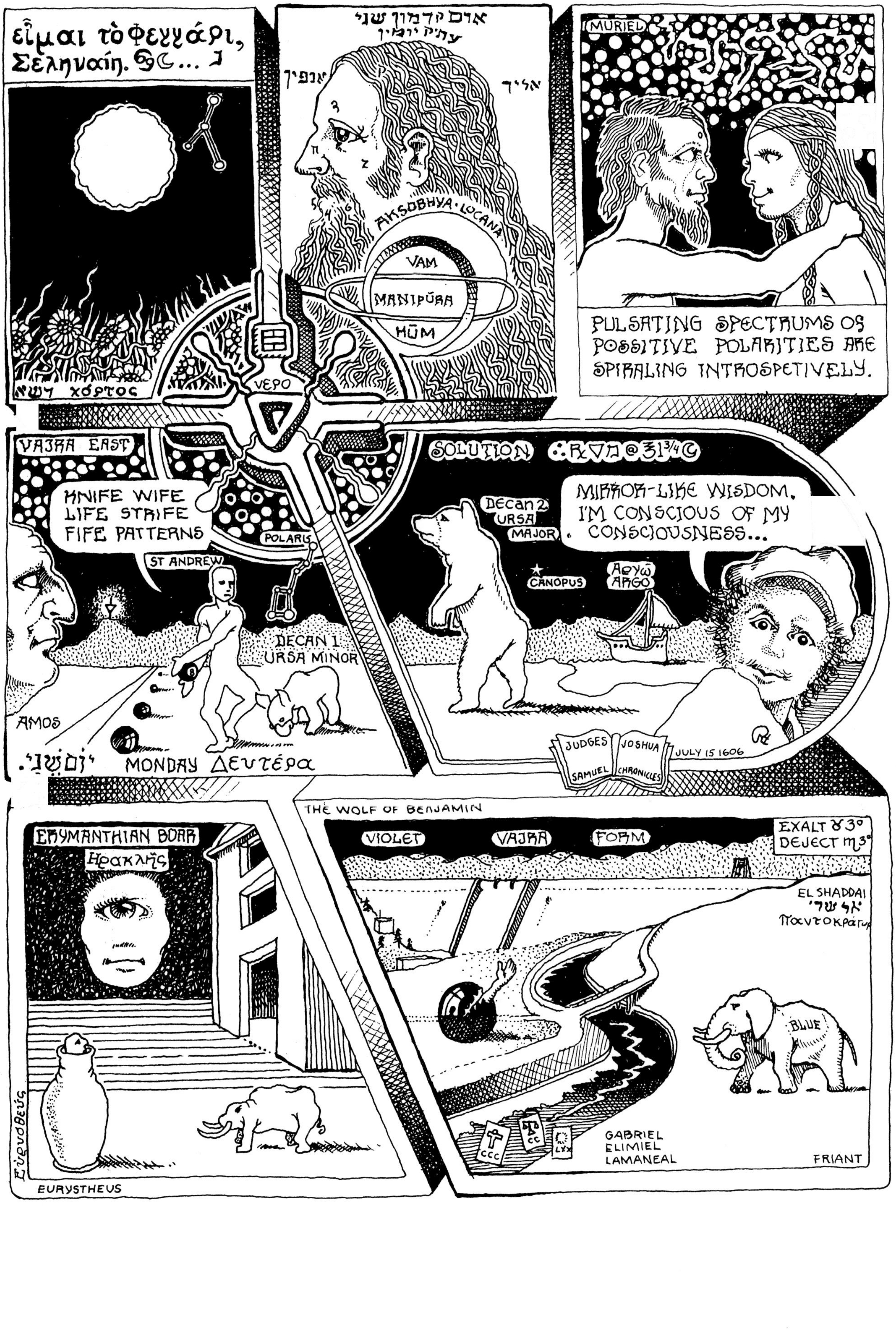
εἶμαι τὸ Φεγγάρι, Σεληναίη.
νωγ χόρτος
AKSOBHYA · LOCANA
VAM
MANIPŪRA
HŪM
VEPO
MURIEL
PULSATING SPECTRUMS OS POSSITIVE POLARITIES ARE SPIRALING INTROSPETIVELY.
VAJRA EAST
KNIFE WIFE LIFE STRIFE FIFE PATTERNS
POLARIS
ST ANDREW
DECAN 1 URSA MINOR
AMOS
MONDAY Δευτέρα
SOLUTION
DECAN 2 URSA MAJOR
MIRROR-LIKE WISDOM. I'M CONSCIOUS OF MY CONSCIOUSNESS...
CANOPUS
Αργώ ARGO
JUDGES JOSHUA SAMUEL CHRONICLES
JULY 15 1606
ERYMANTHIAN BOAR
Ηρακλῆς
Εὐρυσθεύς
EURYSTHEUS
THE WOLF OF BENJAMIN
VIOLET VAJRA FORM
EXALT ♉ 3° DEJECT ♍ 3°
EL SHADDAI
Παντοκράτωρ
BLUE
GABRIEL ELIMIEL LAMANEAL
FRIANT

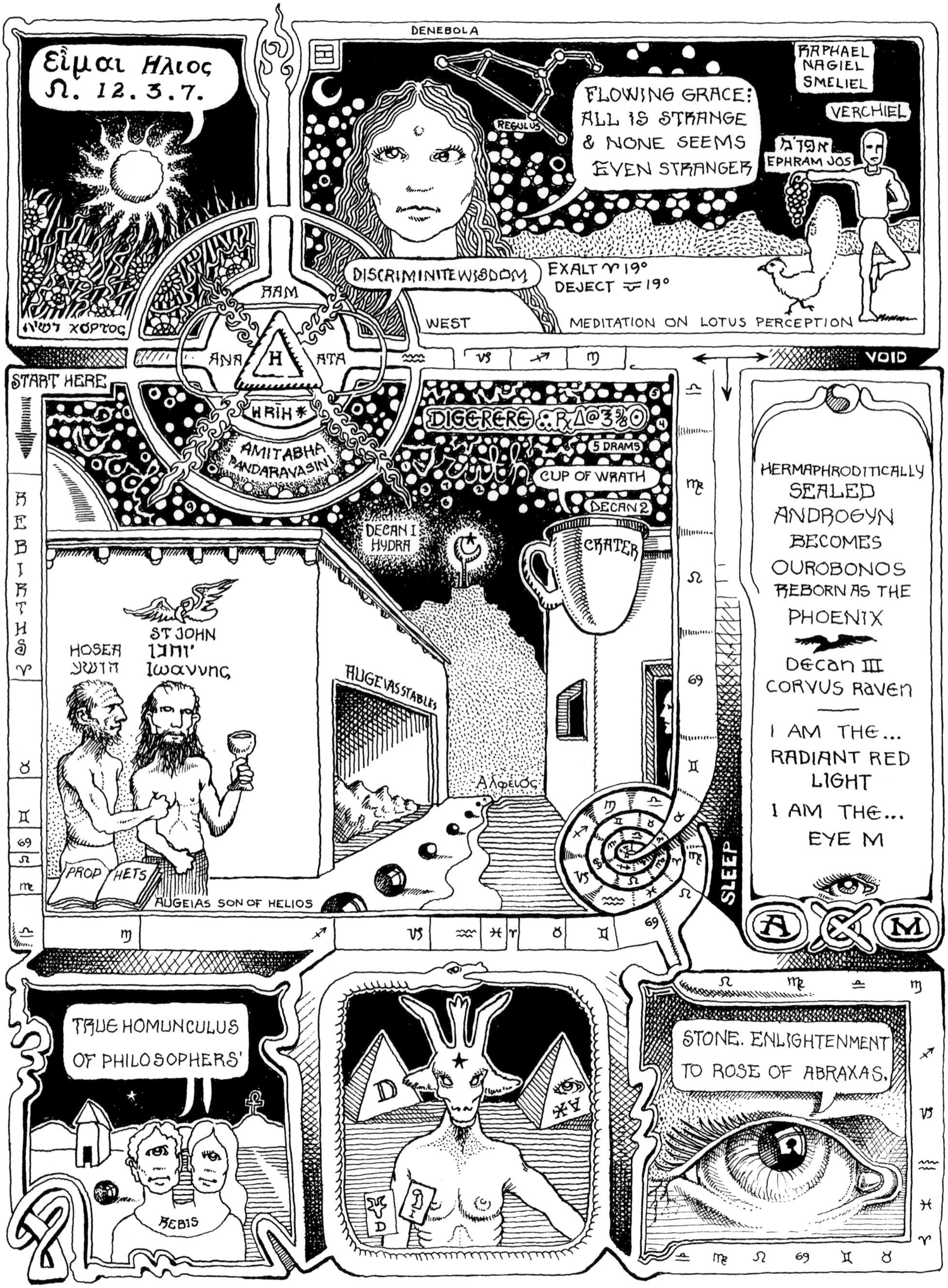
Εἰμαι Ηλιος
Ω. 12.3.7.
DENEBOLA
REGULUS
FLOWING GRACE: ALL IS STRANGE & NONE SEEMS EVEN STRANGER
RAPHAEL NAGIEL SMELIEL
VERCHIEL
EPHRAM JOS
DISCRIMINITEWISDOM
EXALT ♈ 19°
DEJECT ♎ 19°
WEST
MEDITATION ON LOTUS PERCEPTION
χορτος
RAM
ANA
H
ATA
HRIH *
AMITABHA PANDARAVASINI
VOID
START HERE
REBIRTHS ♈
DIGERERE
5 DRAMS
CUP OF WRATH
DECAN 2
DECAN I HYDRA
CRATER
ST JOHN
Ιωαννης
HOSEA
AUGEIAS STABLES
Αλφειός
PROP HETS
AUGEIAS SON OF HELIOS
SLEEP
HERMAPHRODITICALLY SEALED ANDROGYN BECOMES OUROBONOS REBORN AS THE PHOENIX
DECAN III CORVUS RAVEN
I AM THE... RADIANT RED LIGHT
I AM THE... EYE M
A
M
TRUE HOMUNCULUS OF PHILOSOPHERS'
REBIS
D
STONE. ENLIGHTENMENT TO ROSE OF ABRAXAS.

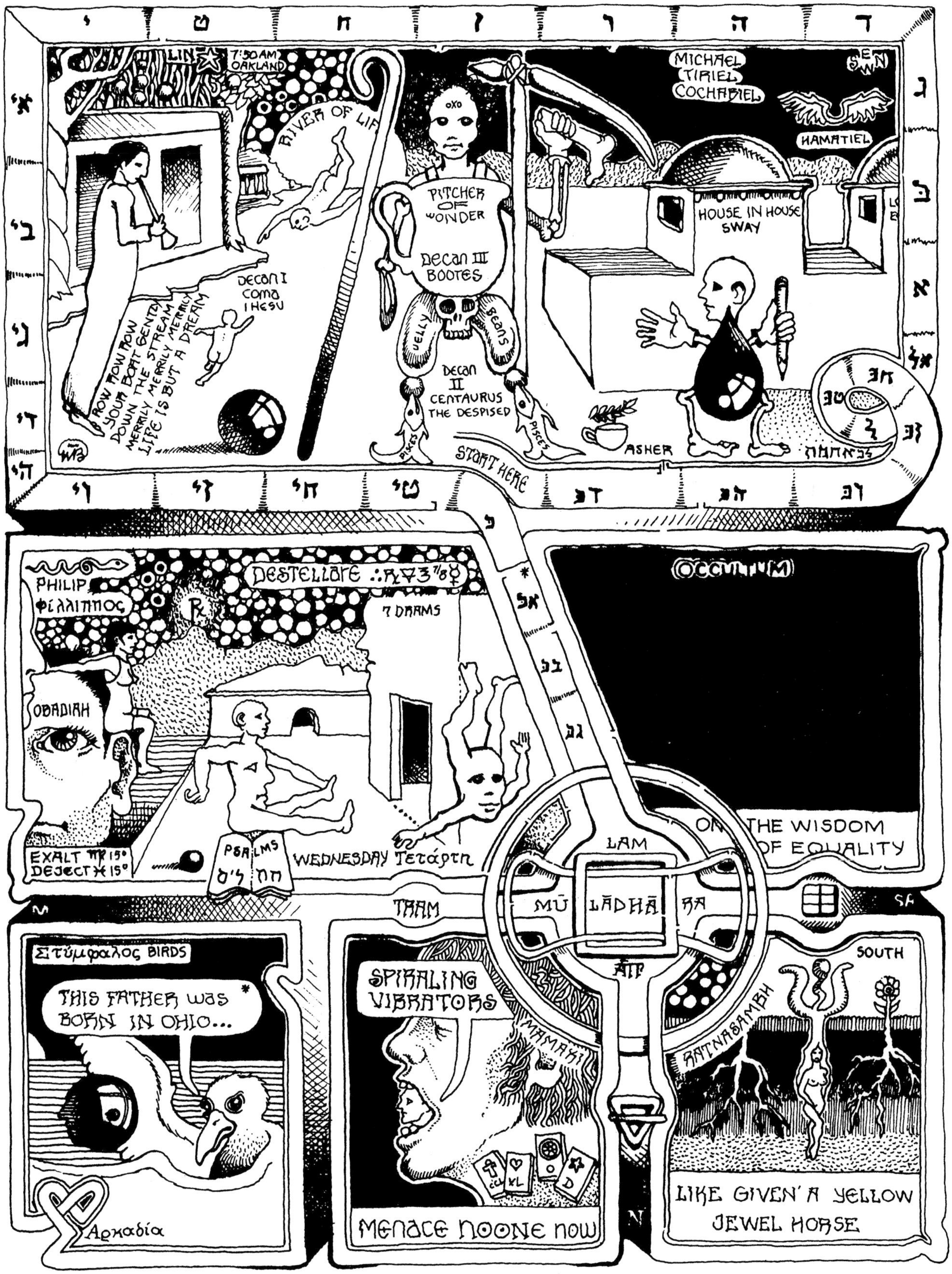
LIN
7:50 AM OAKLAND
RIVER OF LIFE
ROW ROW ROW YOUR BOAT GENTLY DOWN THE STREAM MERRILY MERRILY MERRILY MERRILY LIFE IS BUT A DREAM
Decan I Coma Ihesu
OXO
PITCHER OF WONDER
Decan III BOOTES
JELLY BEANS
Decan II CENTAURUS THE DESPISED
PISCES
PISCES
START HERE
MICHAEL TIRIEL COCHABIEL
HAMATIEL
HOUSE IN HOUSE SWAY
ASHER
PHILIP
φιλλιπποσ
DESTELLARE
7 DRAMS
OBADIAH
EXALT ♍ 15°
DEJECT ♓ 15°
PSALMS
WEDNESDAY Τετάρτη
OCCULTUM
ON THE WISDOM OF EQUALITY
LAM
MŪ LĀDHĀ RA
TRAM
Στύμφαλος BIRDS
THIS FATHER was BORN IN OHIO...
Αρκαδία
SPIRALING VIBRATORS
MAMAKI
MENACE NOONE NOW
SOUTH
RATNASAMBH
LIKE GIVEN A YELLOW JEWEL HORSE

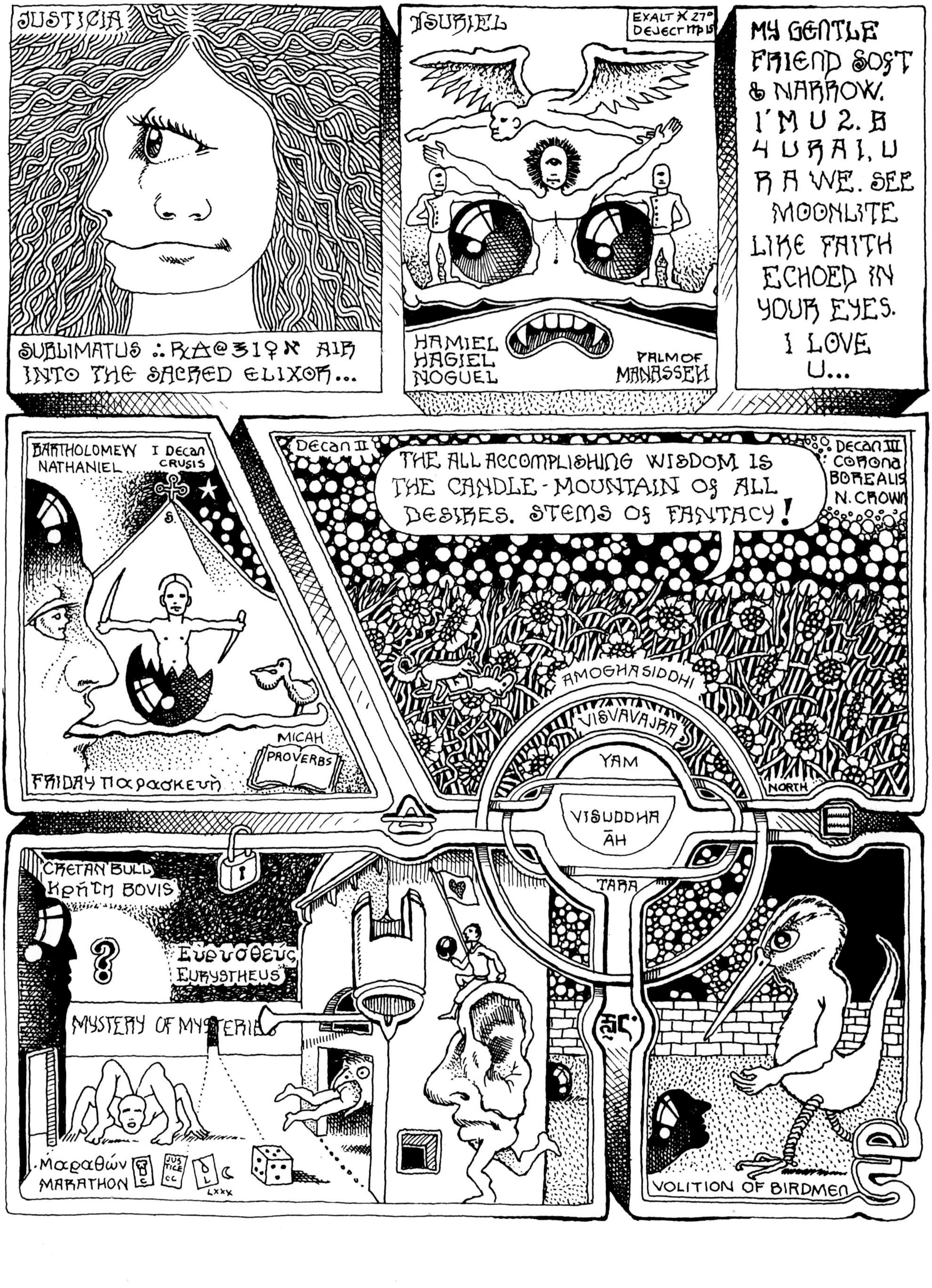
JUSTICIA
SUBLIMATUS AIR INTO THE SACRED ELIXOR...
ISURIEL
EXALT 27°
DEJECT
HAMIEL
HAGIEL
NOGUEL
PALM OF MANASSEH
MY GENTLE FRIEND SOFT & NARROW. I'M U 2. B 4 U R A I, U R A WE. SEE MOONLITE LIKE FAITH ECHOED IN YOUR EYES. I LOVE U...
BARTHOLOMEW NATHANIEL
I DECAN CRUSIS
MICAH
PROVERBS
FRIDAY παρασκευή
DECAN II
THE ALL ACCOMPLISHING WISDOM IS THE CANDLE-MOUNTAIN OF ALL DESIRES. STEMS OF FANTACY!
DECAN III CORONA BOREALIS N. CROWN
AMOGHASIDDHI
VISVAVAJRA
YAM
VISUDDHA
ĀH
NORTH
TARA
CRETAN BULL
Κρήτη BOVIS
Ευρυσθευς
EURYSTHEUS
MYSTERY OF MYSTERIES
Μαραθών
MARATHON
JUSTICE
LXXX
VOLITION OF BIRDMEN

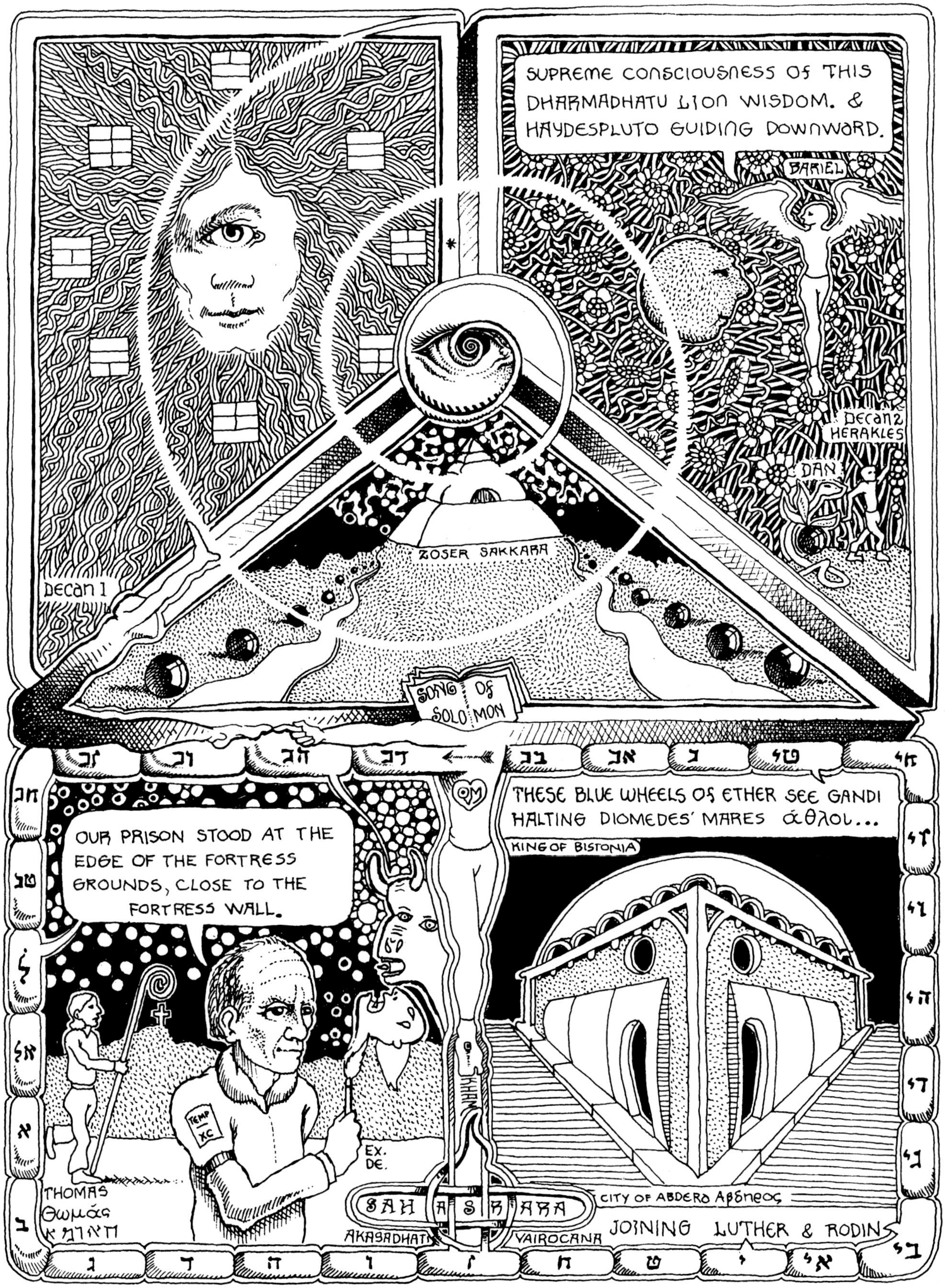
SUPREME CONSCIOUSNESS OF THIS DHARMADHATU LION WISDOM. & HAYDESPLUTO GUIDING DOWNWARD.
BARIEL
DECAN 2 HERAKLES
DAN
DECAN 1
ZOSER SAKKARA
SONG OF SOLOMON
OUR PRISON STOOD AT THE EDGE OF THE FORTRESS GROUNDS, CLOSE TO THE FORTRESS WALL.
THESE BLUE WHEELS OF ETHER SEE GANDI HALTING DIOMEDES' MARES άθλοι...
KING OF BISTONIA
OM
TEMP XC
EX. DE.
THOMAS
Θωμάς
SAH A S R ARA
AKASADHATU
VAIROCANA
CITY OF ABDERA
JOINING LUTHER & RODIN

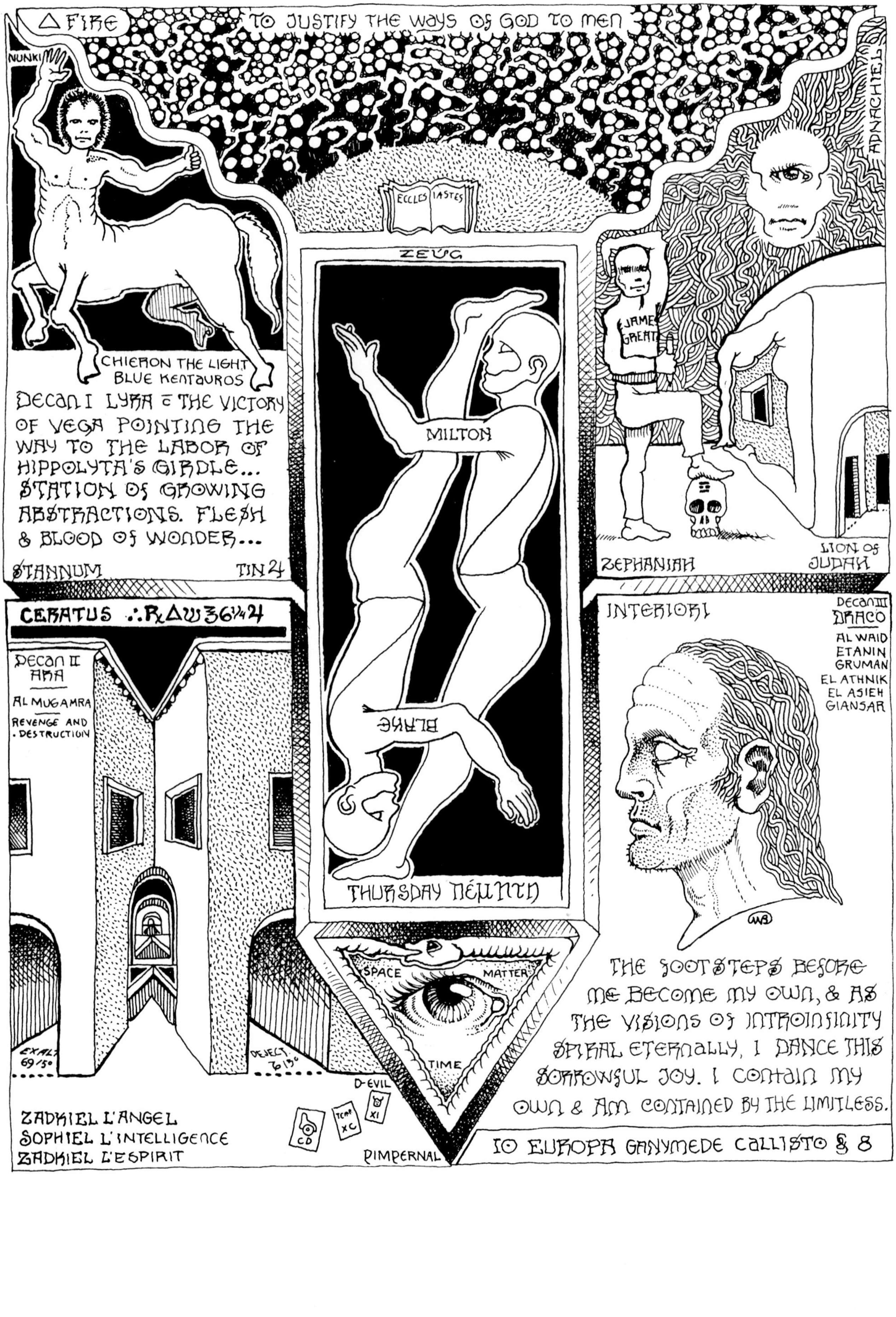
FIRE
TO JUSTIFY THE WAYS OF GOD TO MEN
NUNKI
ADNACHIEL
ECCLESIASTES
CHIERON THE LIGHT BLUE KENTAUROS
DECAN I LYRA = THE VICTORY OF VEGA POINTING THE WAY TO THE LABOR OF HIPPOLYTA'S GIRDLE... STATION OF GROWING ABSTRACTIONS. FLESH & BLOOD OF WONDER...
STANNUM
TIN
MILTON
ZEPHANIAH
LION OF JUDAH
CERATUS
DECAN II ARA
AL MUGAMRA
REVENGE AND DESTRUCTION
BLAKE
INTERIORI
DECAN III DRACO
AL WAID
ETANIN
GRUMAN
EL ATHNIK
EL ASIEH
GIANSAR
THURSDAY
SPACE
MATTER
TIME
THE FOOTSTEPS BEFORE ME BECOME MY OWN, & AS THE VISIONS OF INTROINFINITY SPIRAL ETERNALLY, I DANCE THIS SORROWFUL JOY. I CONTAIN MY OWN & AM CONTAINED BY THE LIMITLESS.
D-EVIL
PIMPERNAL
ZADKIEL L'ANGEL
SOPHIEL L'INTELLIGENCE
ZADKIEL L'ESPIRIT
IO EUROPA GANYMEDE CALLISTO & 8

Βάχχος DISGUISED FROM Τυφῶν

GERYON'S OXEN

WHITE GANESA

MAKARA — ISHWARA

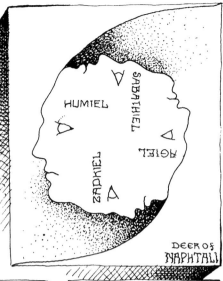

DEER OF NAPHTALI

VISTA FERMENTUM ∴ ℞ ℥ 7½ ℞ **PLUMBUM**

DECAN II ALTAIR AQUILA

DECAN I SAGITTA

DECAN III DELPHIN

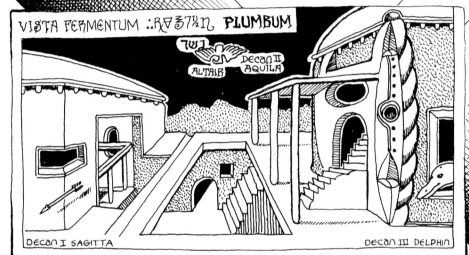

FOR EVERY SUNSET, A SUNRISE. INSIDE DESIRE IS THE ROOT OF MOTION, ALL DANCING IN THE MEDIA OF SPACE= TIME= MATTER. OH YOU ARE ALIVE IS BEING IS ALL IS GOD IS INFINITE IS ME... HI PAL!

NAHUM · SATURDAY Σαccατον

MATHEW

GOSPELS

DOCK

TITAN RHEA IAPETUS DIONE TETHYS ENCELADUS MIMAS HYPERION PHOEBE

THE END

IS TIME TO RETURN TO THE BEGINING!

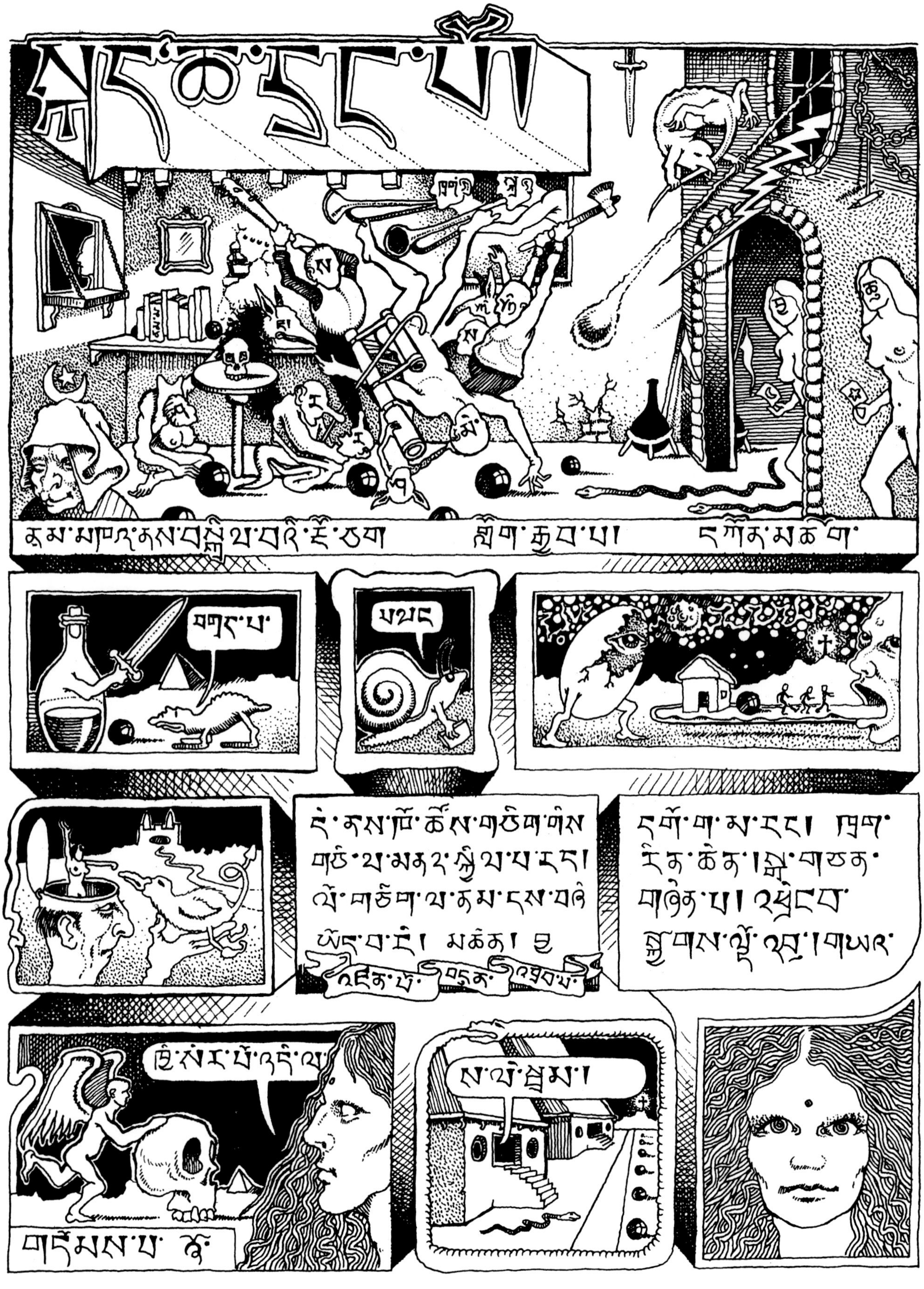

Expansive Palettes

Color and texture have often been under-used as visual signifiers in comics. Some artists, such as Willy Mendes, render stories with such strong blacks and patterns they don't need color. Other artists seem to have thought in color and so elements are left out of the drawings for color to fill in. When color is an active element on the page it can add new meaning or, as in the case of the cyan tones suffusing Bill Everett's "Tidal Wave of Terror," enhance the mood of a line drawing. Jesse Marsh's open swathes of color allow for a profound feeling of space in his comics. Marsh's sparse compositions and use of simple forms allow the colors of the West to come to the fore. With vistas of red and yellow, the actual landscape is pointedly evoked. Where Marsh succeeded by subtraction, Pat Boyette, on the other hand, succeeded by throwing a lot *in*. Boyette used Craft-Tint—a type of pre-colored board that enjoyed a popular resurgence in comic books after having been pioneered by Roy Crane in the comic strips—as well as the limited palette utilized by Charlton Comics' notoriously shoddy printing, to create an ominous mood in his illustrations. Boyette's muddy forms and discolored spaces are perfect signifiers for his post-apocalyptic future in "Children of Doom." In another mood, the technicolor palette of Mort Meskin's "Golden Lad: The Menace of the Minstrel!" makes its lyrical plot and solid forms sing along with the minstrel. There, color is used to create a bright world of fun and somewhat harmless heroics. In both cases, it's a world of color used to convey meaning—a world unto itself.

PAT BOYETTE

(1923–2000)

Pat Boyette took his time getting into comics, but when he finally entered the medium, he produced a remarkable body of work. Born and raised in San Antonio, Texas, Boyette spent the first part of his adult life as a radio and then television broadcaster in the San Antonio area. He began his career in cartooning fitfully, with a brief stint assisting Charlie Plumb on his comic strip "Ella Cinders," and with a strip of his own called "Captain Flame" in 1954 and 1955. In the early 1960s Boyette began yet another career as a low budget film auteur. He wrote, directed, and art directed at least one film himself, *Dungeon of Harrow* (1962), and scripted another two: *The Weird Ones* (1962) and *The Girls from Thunder Strip* (1966). These super-low-budget movies were made for television broadcast, and are firmly in the sub–Roger Corman school of genre exploitation. Yet despite his dedication and evident enjoyment, the business of film wasn't working for Boyette and in the mid-1960s he decided to return to comics. Boyette matter-of-factly submitted some samples to Charlton Comics and a year later received his first comic book assignment, which was published in 1966 when he was forty-three years old.

Boyette's approach to making comics was as close to being in complete control as possible: "I'd take a script, block out the pencils, doing all the lettering, then I would pencil it and I would ink it." As a result, all of his stories bear his complete visual sensibility, making it easy to pick them out from the stacks of other stories from that period. Boyette's artwork was influenced by the great science fiction illustrators of his youth: Virgil Finlay and Hannes Bok among them, as well as by his colleagues Alex Toth and Wally Wood. Focused on solid, realistic figuration, Boyette illustrated his work with an emphasis on clear, uncluttered panels and he excelled at the difficult task of bringing texture and mood onto the comics pages. Always adventurous in whatever medium he employed, Boyette's comics were some of the very first to actively experiment with color. One of the stories for which he is best known, "Children of Doom" (1967), was completed in just a handful of days under a very tight deadline from Charlton Comics. Written by Denny O'Neil under the name "Sergius O'Shaughnessy," it's a classic late 1960s apocalyptic science fiction story of survival and rebirth. Boyette, emboldened by the experimentation of Alex Toth and Jim Steranko (Nick Fury), told the story in a series of fractured panels taking whatever shape best served both the image and the overall page design. Making liberal use of Zip-a-Tone, he colored the book in gray tones and added the little splashes of color only at Charlton's insistence. In twenty-five pages Boyette takes readers across multiple visual landscapes and pictorial ideas. It's a genuinely beguiling story—purposefully disorienting in some parts, stunning in its visual daring, and, at the same time, true to his homegrown films. Boyette did quite a lot of work for Charlton Comics, enjoying the creative free-dom the company gave him; he even stepped in to draw Pete Morisi's *Thunderbolt* for a few issues. Boyette drew for Warren, DC Comics, and numerous other publishing companies throughout the 1970s and 1980s before his retirement in the late 1990s.

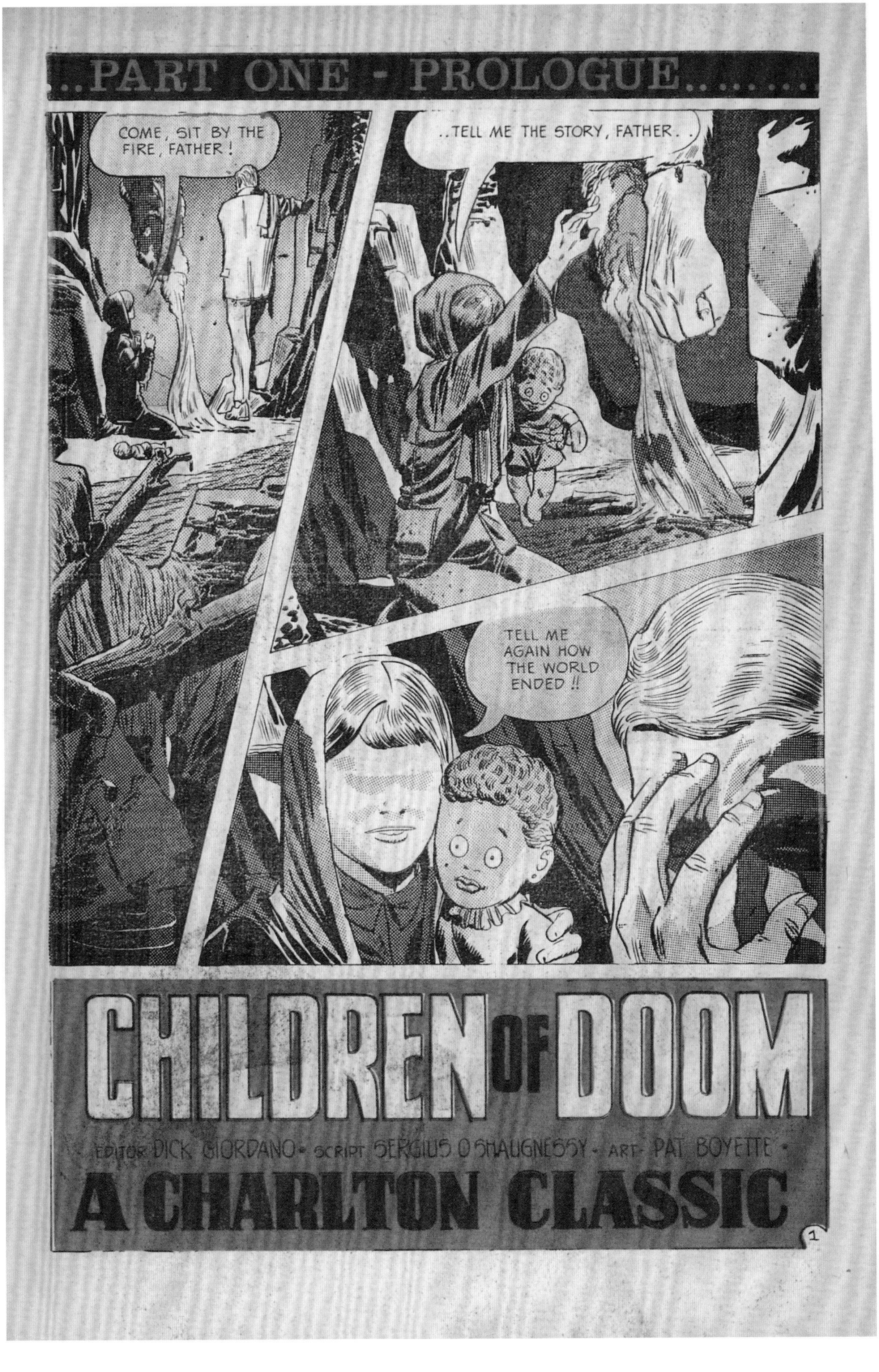
..PART ONE - PROLOGUE........
COME, SIT BY THE FIRE, FATHER!
..TELL ME THE STORY, FATHER..
TELL ME AGAIN HOW THE WORLD ENDED!!
CHILDREN OF DOOM
EDITOR DICK GIORDANO • SCRIPT SERGIUS O'SHAUGNESSY • ART PAT BOYETTE •
A CHARLTON CLASSIC
1

Charlton Premiere no. 2 (1967)

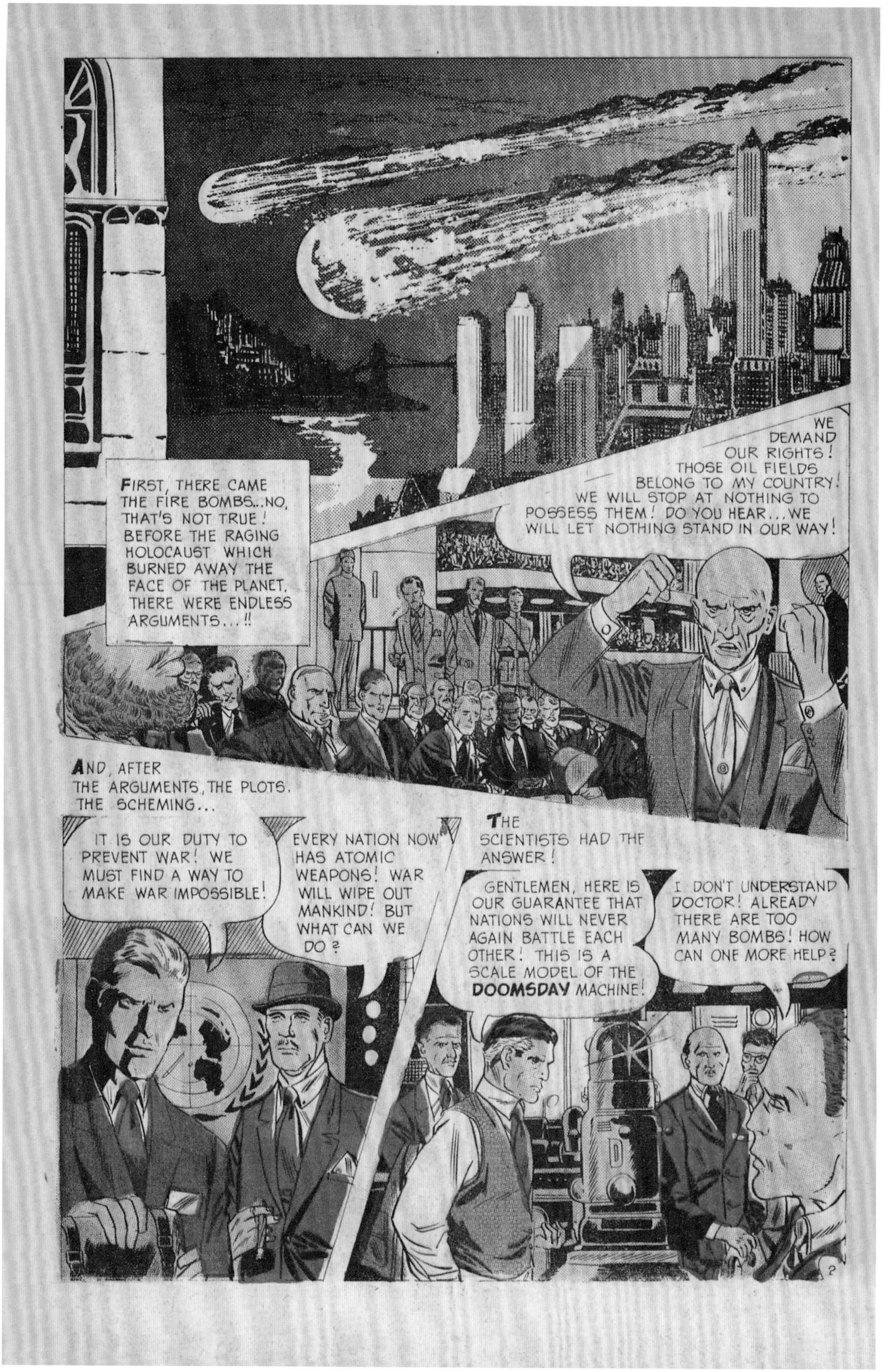
FIRST, THERE CAME THE FIRE BOMBS...NO, THAT'S NOT TRUE! BEFORE THE RAGING HOLOCAUST WHICH BURNED AWAY THE FACE OF THE PLANET, THERE WERE ENDLESS ARGUMENTS...!!
WE DEMAND OUR RIGHTS! THOSE OIL FIELDS BELONG TO MY COUNTRY! WE WILL STOP AT NOTHING TO POSSESS THEM! DO YOU HEAR...WE WILL LET NOTHING STAND IN OUR WAY!
AND, AFTER THE ARGUMENTS, THE PLOTS, THE SCHEMING...
IT IS OUR DUTY TO PREVENT WAR! WE MUST FIND A WAY TO MAKE WAR IMPOSSIBLE!
EVERY NATION NOW HAS ATOMIC WEAPONS! WAR WILL WIPE OUT MANKIND! BUT WHAT CAN WE DO?
THE SCIENTISTS HAD THE ANSWER!
GENTLEMEN, HERE IS OUR GUARANTEE THAT NATIONS WILL NEVER AGAIN BATTLE EACH OTHER! THIS IS A SCALE MODEL OF THE DOOMSDAY MACHINE!
I DON'T UNDERSTAND DOCTOR! ALREADY THERE ARE TOO MANY BOMBS! HOW CAN ONE MORE HELP?
2

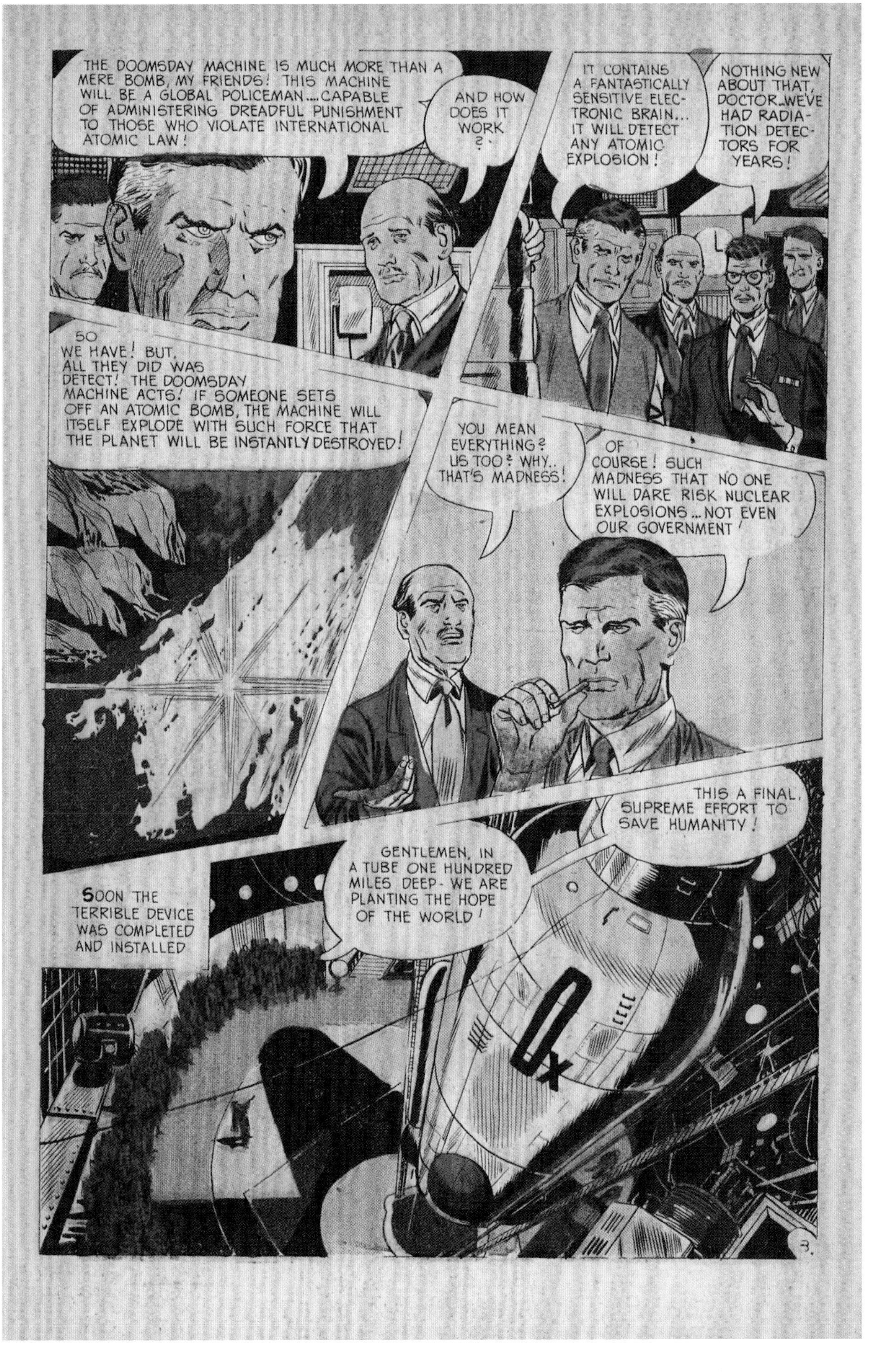
THE DOOMSDAY MACHINE IS MUCH MORE THAN A MERE BOMB, MY FRIENDS! THIS MACHINE WILL BE A GLOBAL POLICEMAN....CAPABLE OF ADMINISTERING DREADFUL PUNISHMENT TO THOSE WHO VIOLATE INTERNATIONAL ATOMIC LAW!
AND HOW DOES IT WORK ?
IT CONTAINS A FANTASTICALLY SENSITIVE ELECTRONIC BRAIN... IT WILL DETECT ANY ATOMIC EXPLOSION!
NOTHING NEW ABOUT THAT, DOCTOR..WE'VE HAD RADIATION DETECTORS FOR YEARS!
SO WE HAVE! BUT, ALL THEY DID WAS DETECT! THE DOOMSDAY MACHINE ACTS! IF SOMEONE SETS OFF AN ATOMIC BOMB, THE MACHINE WILL ITSELF EXPLODE WITH SUCH FORCE THAT THE PLANET WILL BE INSTANTLY DESTROYED!
YOU MEAN EVERYTHING? US TOO? WHY.. THAT'S MADNESS!
OF COURSE! SUCH MADNESS THAT NO ONE WILL DARE RISK NUCLEAR EXPLOSIONS...NOT EVEN OUR GOVERNMENT!
SOON THE TERRIBLE DEVICE WAS COMPLETED AND INSTALLED
GENTLEMEN, IN A TUBE ONE HUNDRED MILES DEEP- WE ARE PLANTING THE HOPE OF THE WORLD!
THIS A FINAL, SUPREME EFFORT TO SAVE HUMANITY!
3.

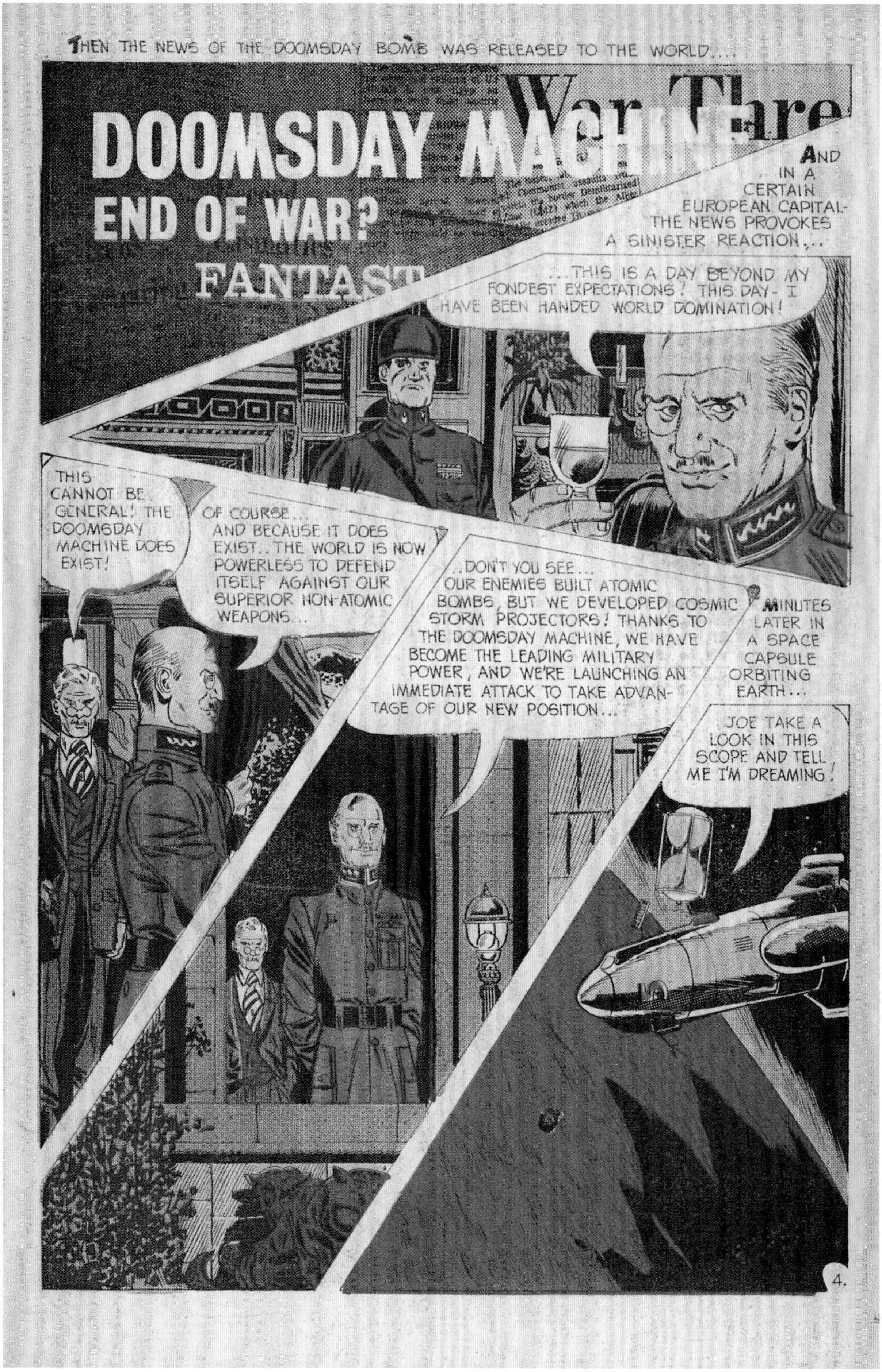
THEN THE NEWS OF THE DOOMSDAY BOMB WAS RELEASED TO THE WORLD....
DOOMSDAY MACHINE
END OF WAR?
FANTAST
AND IN A CERTAIN EUROPEAN CAPITAL- THE NEWS PROVOKES A SINISTER REACTION,..
...THIS IS A DAY BEYOND MY FONDEST EXPECTATIONS! THIS DAY- I HAVE BEEN HANDED WORLD DOMINATION!
THIS CANNOT BE GENERAL! THE DOOMSDAY MACHINE DOES EXIST!
OF COURSE... AND BECAUSE IT DOES EXIST.. THE WORLD IS NOW POWERLESS TO DEFEND ITSELF AGAINST OUR SUPERIOR NON-ATOMIC WEAPONS...
...DON'T YOU SEE... OUR ENEMIES BUILT ATOMIC BOMBS, BUT WE DEVELOPED COSMIC STORM PROJECTORS! THANKS TO THE DOOMSDAY MACHINE, WE HAVE BECOME THE LEADING MILITARY POWER, AND WE'RE LAUNCHING AN IMMEDIATE ATTACK TO TAKE ADVANTAGE OF OUR NEW POSITION...
MINUTES LATER IN A SPACE CAPSULE ORBITING EARTH...
JOE TAKE A LOOK IN THIS SCOPE AND TELL ME I'M DREAMING!
4.

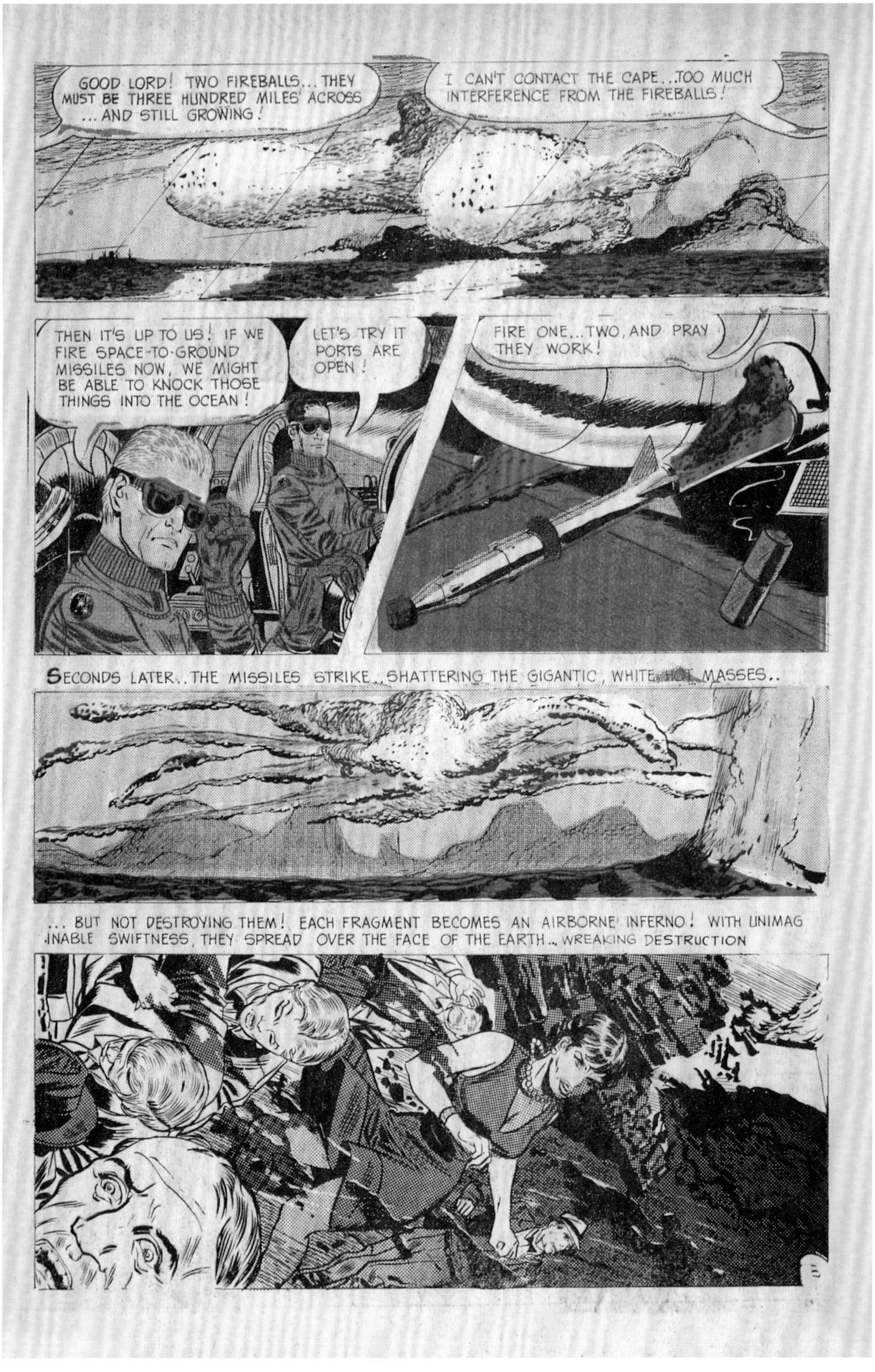
GOOD LORD! TWO FIREBALLS... THEY MUST BE THREE HUNDRED MILES ACROSS ... AND STILL GROWING!
I CAN'T CONTACT THE CAPE...TOO MUCH INTERFERENCE FROM THE FIREBALLS!
THEN IT'S UP TO US! IF WE FIRE SPACE-TO-GROUND MISSILES NOW, WE MIGHT BE ABLE TO KNOCK THOSE THINGS INTO THE OCEAN!
LET'S TRY IT PORTS ARE OPEN!
FIRE ONE...TWO, AND PRAY THEY WORK!
SECONDS LATER..THE MISSILES STRIKE..SHATTERING THE GIGANTIC, WHITE-HOT MASSES..
... BUT NOT DESTROYING THEM! EACH FRAGMENT BECOMES AN AIRBORNE INFERNO! WITH UNIMAGINABLE SWIFTNESS, THEY SPREAD OVER THE FACE OF THE EARTH... WREAKING DESTRUCTION
3

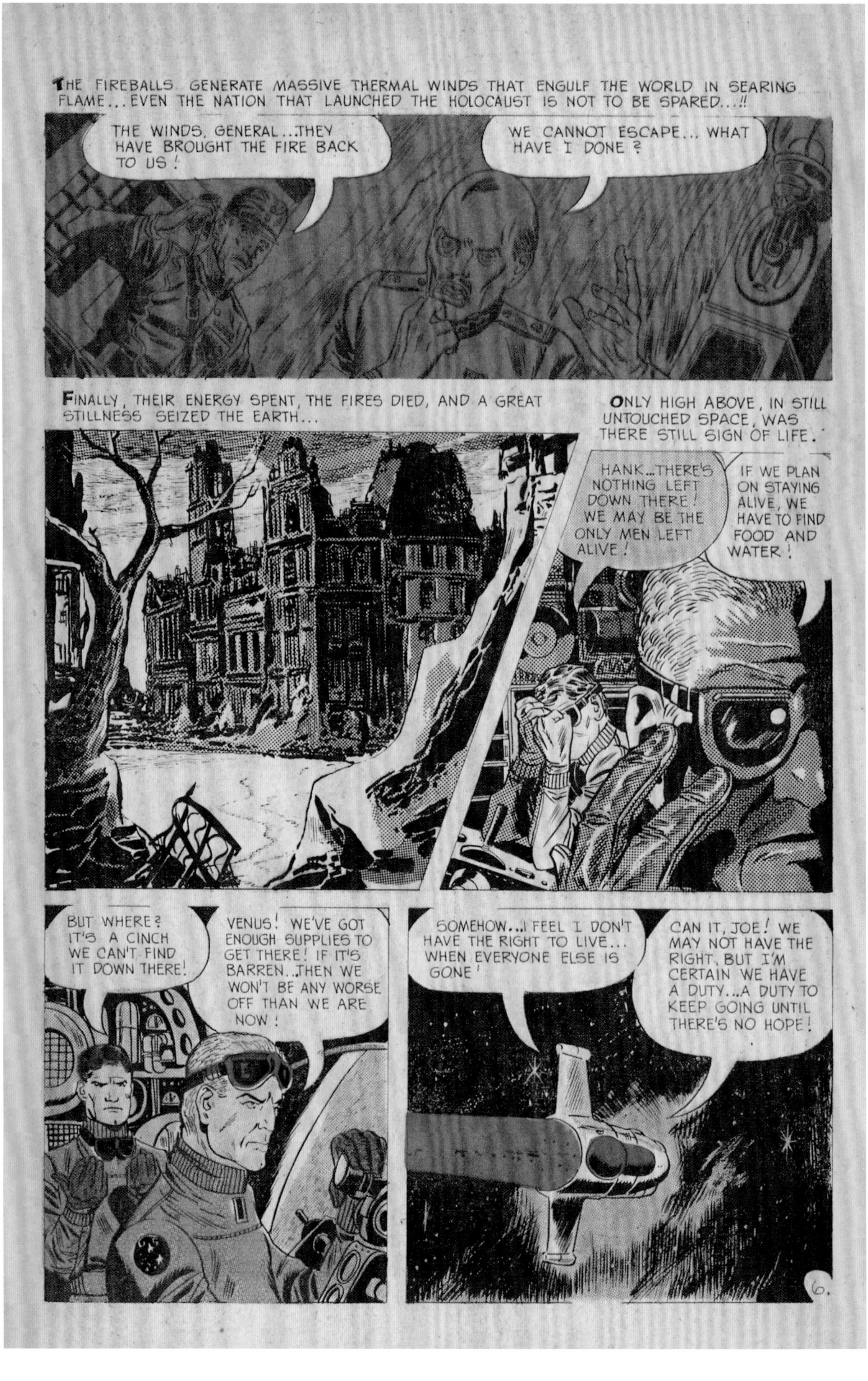
THE FIREBALLS GENERATE MASSIVE THERMAL WINDS THAT ENGULF THE WORLD IN SEARING FLAME... EVEN THE NATION THAT LAUNCHED THE HOLOCAUST IS NOT TO BE SPARED...!!
THE WINDS, GENERAL... THEY HAVE BROUGHT THE FIRE BACK TO US!
WE CANNOT ESCAPE... WHAT HAVE I DONE?
FINALLY, THEIR ENERGY SPENT, THE FIRES DIED, AND A GREAT STILLNESS SEIZED THE EARTH...
ONLY HIGH ABOVE, IN STILL UNTOUCHED SPACE, WAS THERE STILL SIGN OF LIFE.
HANK... THERE'S NOTHING LEFT DOWN THERE! WE MAY BE THE ONLY MEN LEFT ALIVE!
IF WE PLAN ON STAYING ALIVE, WE HAVE TO FIND FOOD AND WATER!
BUT WHERE? IT'S A CINCH WE CAN'T FIND IT DOWN THERE!
VENUS! WE'VE GOT ENOUGH SUPPLIES TO GET THERE! IF IT'S BARREN... THEN WE WON'T BE ANY WORSE OFF THAN WE ARE NOW!
SOMEHOW... I FEEL I DON'T HAVE THE RIGHT TO LIVE... WHEN EVERYONE ELSE IS GONE!
CAN IT, JOE! WE MAY NOT HAVE THE RIGHT, BUT I'M CERTAIN WE HAVE A DUTY... A DUTY TO KEEP GOING UNTIL THERE'S NO HOPE!
6.

IS THERE ANY HOPE? YES. MORE THAN THE SPACEMEN THINK... FOR NOT ALL HAVE PERISHED. FROM MINES... FROM SHELTERS... FROM THE FEW ISOLATED PLACES UNTOUCHED BY THE STORMS THE SURVIVORS COME. BUT THEY ARE NOT THE SAME... MANKIND HAS UNDERGONE DRAMATIC CHANGES...

FIRST THE PYROS WITH THE UNCANNY POWER TO WISH FIRE INTO EXISTENCE!

SAM LOOK... MY FINGERS! I CAN MAKE FIRE JUST BY THINKING ABOUT IT!

OTHERS LOST PHYSICAL SIGHT BUT GAINED THE ABILITY TO SEE WITH THEIR MINDS! THESE ARE THE "CLAIRVOYANTS"!

DON'T TOUCH THAT STONE...

WHY NOT?

THERE'S A SNAKE UNDERNEATH!

FINALLY... "THE MYSTERIOUS ONES"!

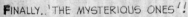

THAT ODD FELLA AGAIN! WHY WON'T HE JOIN US?

LET'S ASK HIM! LOOK... HE'S GOING IN THE CAVE! WE'VE GOT HIM CORNERED.. THERE'S ONLY ONE ENTRANCE!

WHERE'D HE GO? HE COULDN'T HAVE GONE THROUGH SOLID ROCK!

HE COULDN'T BUT HE DID!

7.

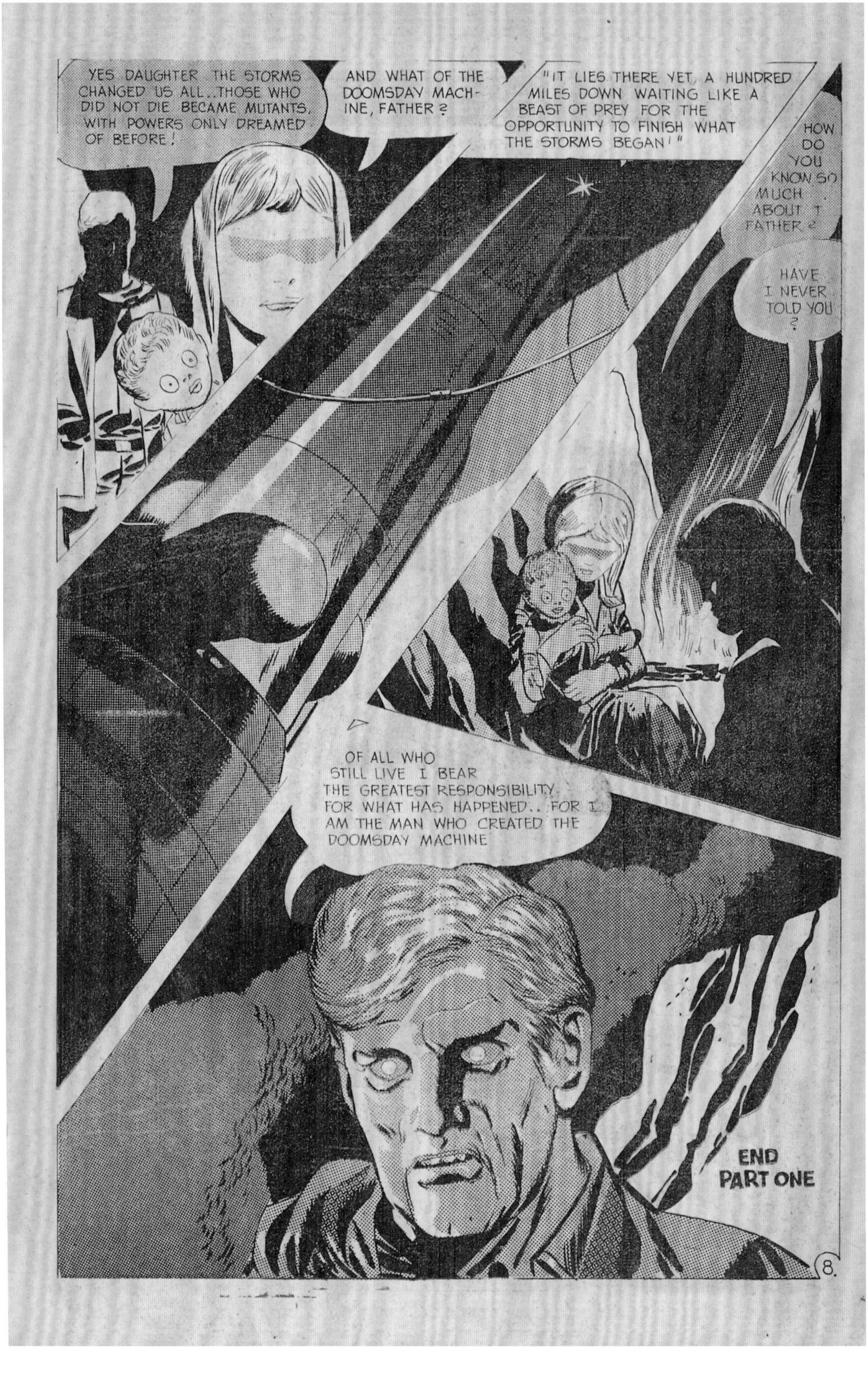
YES DAUGHTER THE STORMS CHANGED US ALL..THOSE WHO DID NOT DIE BECAME MUTANTS, WITH POWERS ONLY DREAMED OF BEFORE!
AND WHAT OF THE DOOMSDAY MACHINE, FATHER?
"IT LIES THERE YET, A HUNDRED MILES DOWN WAITING LIKE A BEAST OF PREY FOR THE OPPORTUNITY TO FINISH WHAT THE STORMS BEGAN!"
HOW DO YOU KNOW SO MUCH ABOUT IT FATHER?
HAVE I NEVER TOLD YOU?
OF ALL WHO STILL LIVE I BEAR THE GREATEST RESPONSIBILITY FOR WHAT HAS HAPPENED.. FOR I AM THE MAN WHO CREATED THE DOOMSDAY MACHINE
END PART ONE
8.

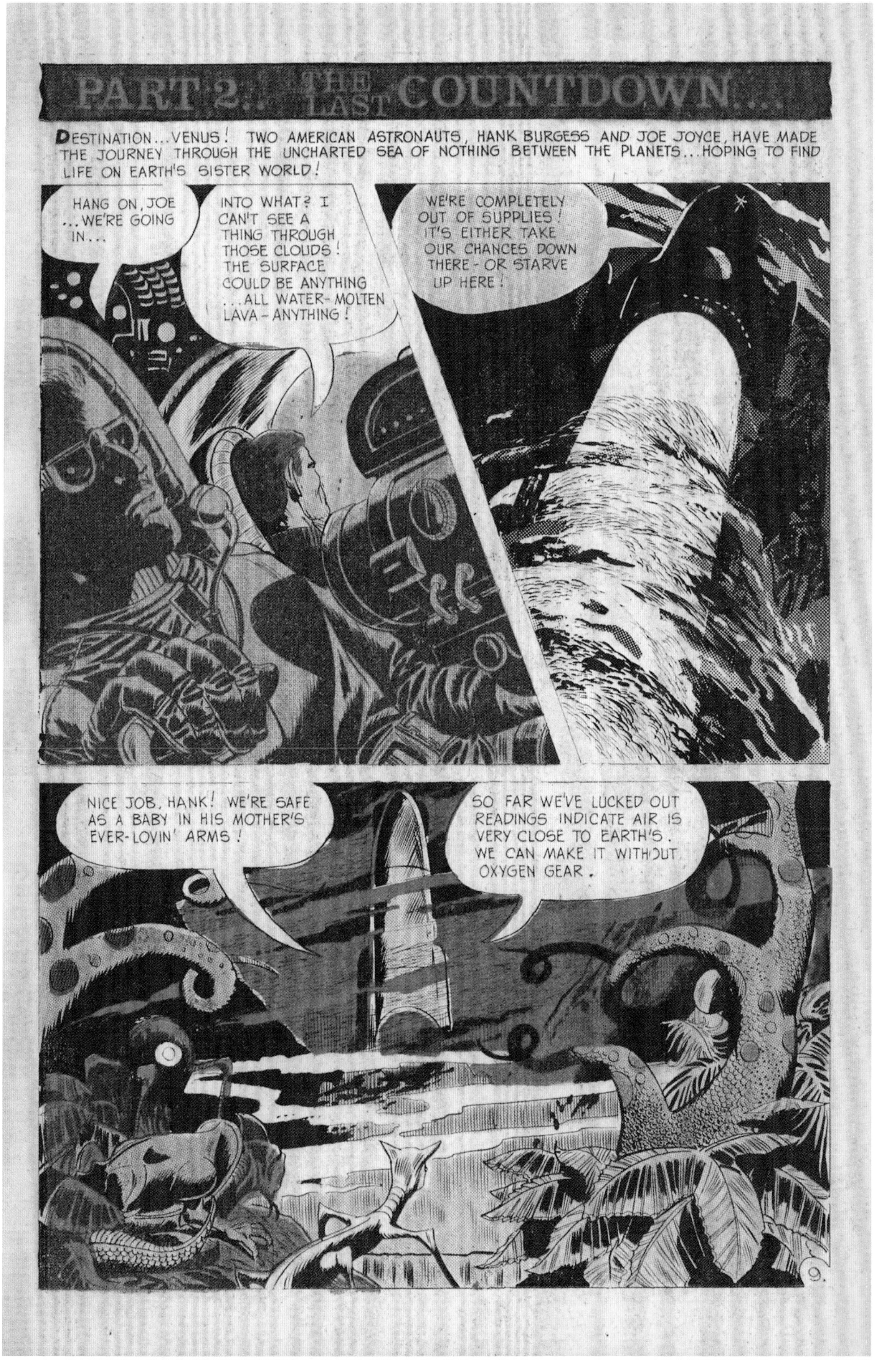
PART 2.. THE LAST COUNTDOWN...
DESTINATION... VENUS! TWO AMERICAN ASTRONAUTS, HANK BURGESS AND JOE JOYCE, HAVE MADE THE JOURNEY THROUGH THE UNCHARTED SEA OF NOTHING BETWEEN THE PLANETS... HOPING TO FIND LIFE ON EARTH'S SISTER WORLD!
HANG ON, JOE ...WE'RE GOING IN...
INTO WHAT? I CAN'T SEE A THING THROUGH THOSE CLOUDS! THE SURFACE COULD BE ANYTHING ...ALL WATER-MOLTEN LAVA-ANYTHING!
WE'RE COMPLETELY OUT OF SUPPLIES! IT'S EITHER TAKE OUR CHANCES DOWN THERE-OR STARVE UP HERE!
NICE JOB, HANK! WE'RE SAFE AS A BABY IN HIS MOTHER'S EVER-LOVIN' ARMS!
SO FAR WE'VE LUCKED OUT READINGS INDICATE AIR IS VERY CLOSE TO EARTH'S. WE CAN MAKE IT WITHOUT OXYGEN GEAR.
9.

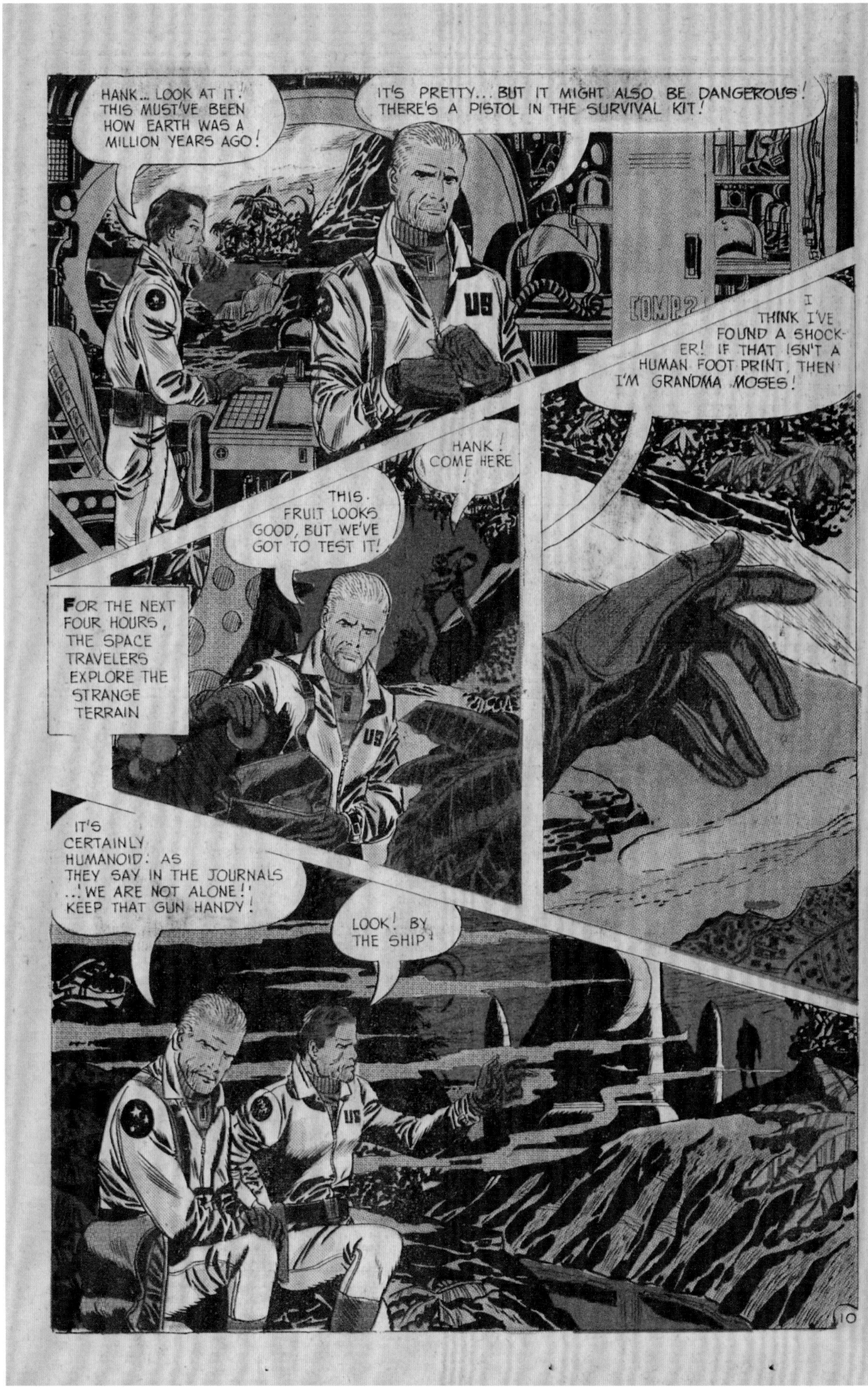
HANK... LOOK AT IT! THIS MUST'VE BEEN HOW EARTH WAS A MILLION YEARS AGO!
IT'S PRETTY... BUT IT MIGHT ALSO BE DANGEROUS! THERE'S A PISTOL IN THE SURVIVAL KIT!
COMP 2
THIS FRUIT LOOKS GOOD, BUT WE'VE GOT TO TEST IT!
HANK! COME HERE!
FOR THE NEXT FOUR HOURS, THE SPACE TRAVELERS EXPLORE THE STRANGE TERRAIN
I THINK I'VE FOUND A SHOCKER! IF THAT ISN'T A HUMAN FOOT PRINT, THEN I'M GRANDMA MOSES!
IT'S CERTAINLY HUMANOID! AS THEY SAY IN THE JOURNALS ..! WE ARE NOT ALONE! KEEP THAT GUN HANDY!
LOOK! BY THE SHIP!
10

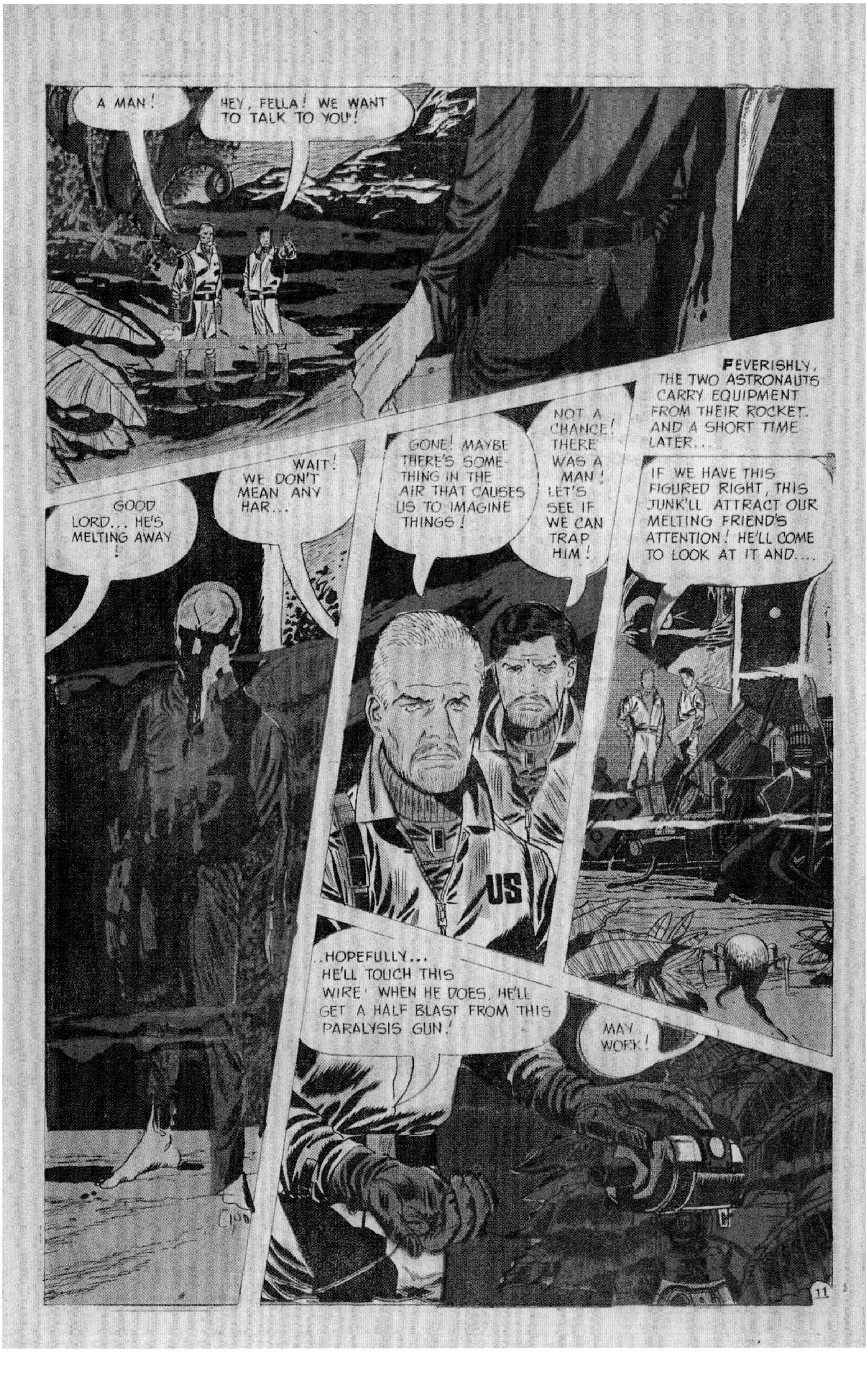
A MAN!
HEY, FELLA! WE WANT TO TALK TO YOU!
FEVERISHLY, THE TWO ASTRONAUTS CARRY EQUIPMENT FROM THEIR ROCKET. AND A SHORT TIME LATER...
GOOD LORD... HE'S MELTING AWAY!
WAIT! WE DON'T MEAN ANY HAR...
GONE! MAYBE THERE'S SOMETHING IN THE AIR THAT CAUSES US TO IMAGINE THINGS!
NOT A CHANCE! THERE WAS A MAN! LET'S SEE IF WE CAN TRAP HIM!
IF WE HAVE THIS FIGURED RIGHT, THIS JUNK'LL ATTRACT OUR MELTING FRIEND'S ATTENTION! HE'LL COME TO LOOK AT IT AND....
..HOPEFULLY... HE'LL TOUCH THIS WIRE! WHEN HE DOES, HE'LL GET A HALF BLAST FROM THIS PARALYSIS GUN!
MAY WORK!
US
11

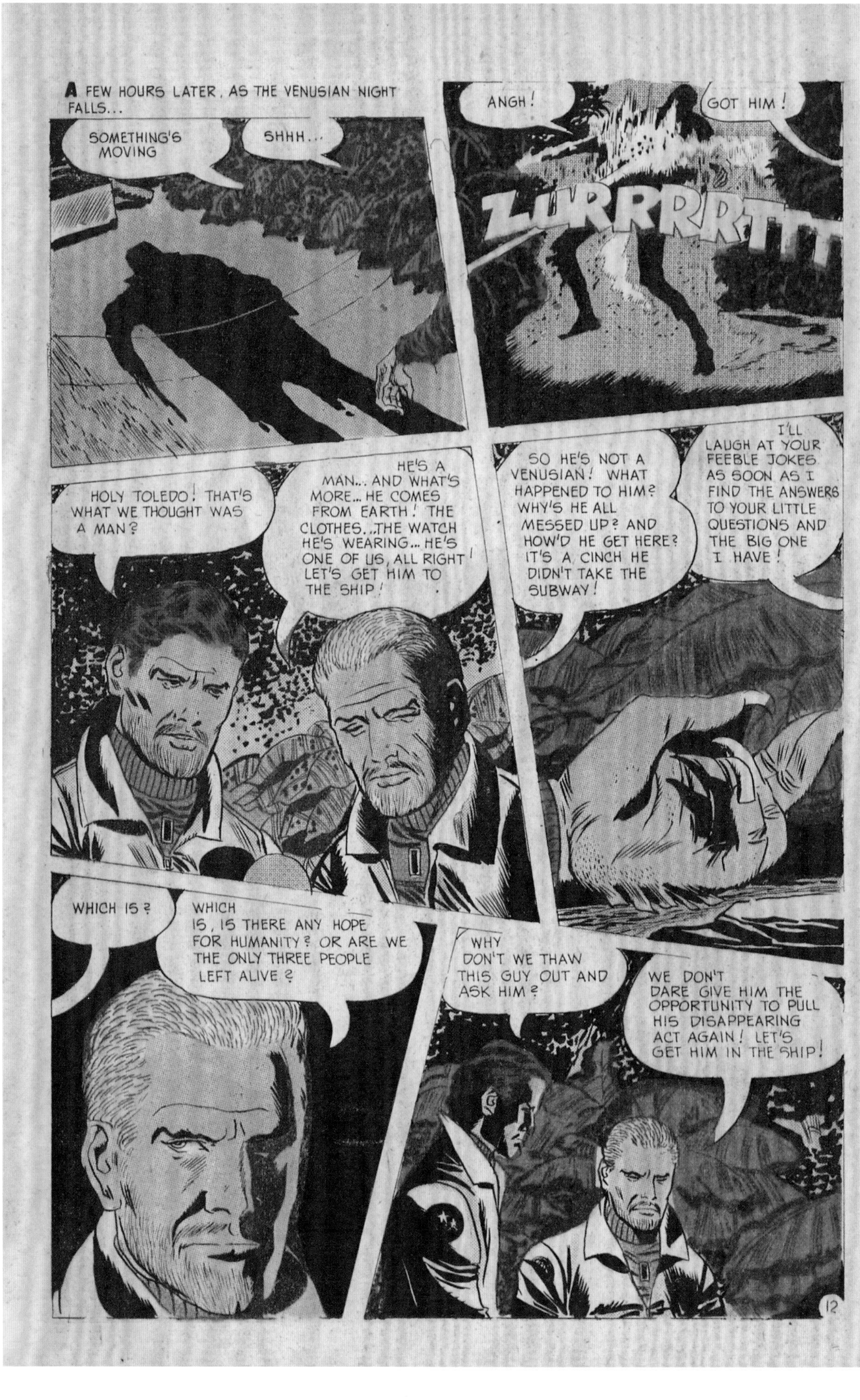
A FEW HOURS LATER, AS THE VENUSIAN NIGHT FALLS...
SOMETHING'S MOVING
SHHH...
ANGH!
GOT HIM!
ZURRRRTTT
HOLY TOLEDO! THAT'S WHAT WE THOUGHT WAS A MAN?
HE'S A MAN... AND WHAT'S MORE... HE COMES FROM EARTH! THE CLOTHES...THE WATCH HE'S WEARING... HE'S ONE OF US, ALL RIGHT! LET'S GET HIM TO THE SHIP!
SO HE'S NOT A VENUSIAN! WHAT HAPPENED TO HIM? WHY'S HE ALL MESSED UP? AND HOW'D HE GET HERE? IT'S A CINCH HE DIDN'T TAKE THE SUBWAY!
I'LL LAUGH AT YOUR FEEBLE JOKES AS SOON AS I FIND THE ANSWERS TO YOUR LITTLE QUESTIONS AND THE BIG ONE I HAVE!
WHICH IS?
WHICH IS, IS THERE ANY HOPE FOR HUMANITY? OR ARE WE THE ONLY THREE PEOPLE LEFT ALIVE?
WHY DON'T WE THAW THIS GUY OUT AND ASK HIM?
WE DON'T DARE GIVE HIM THE OPPORTUNITY TO PULL HIS DISAPPEARING ACT AGAIN! LET'S GET HIM IN THE SHIP!
12

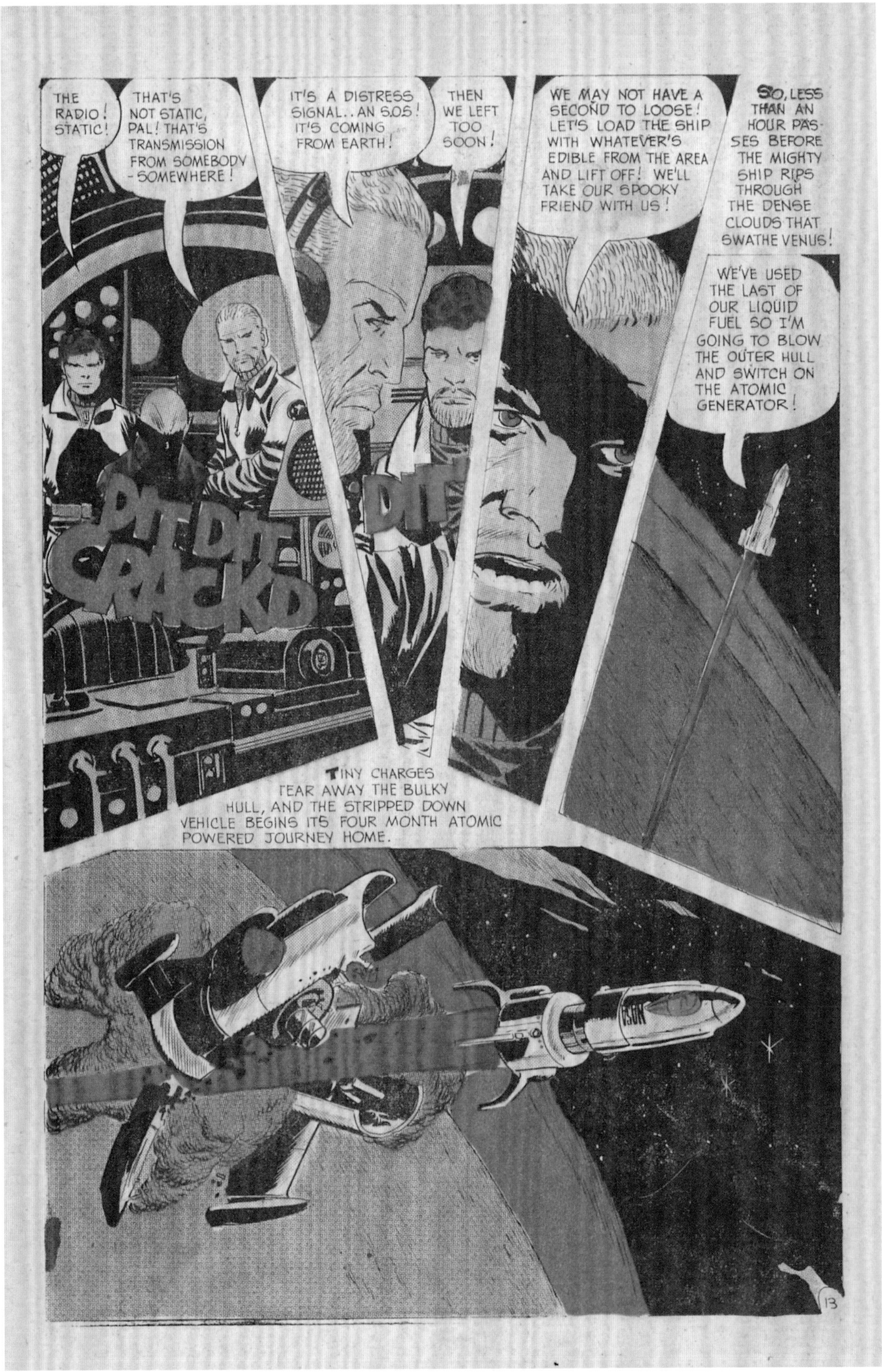
THE RADIO! STATIC!
THAT'S NOT STATIC, PAL! THAT'S TRANSMISSION FROM SOMEBODY - SOMEWHERE!
DIT DIT CRACKD
IT'S A DISTRESS SIGNAL.. AN S.O.S! IT'S COMING FROM EARTH!
THEN WE LEFT TOO SOON!
DIT
WE MAY NOT HAVE A SECOND TO LOOSE! LET'S LOAD THE SHIP WITH WHATEVER'S EDIBLE FROM THE AREA AND LIFT OFF! WE'LL TAKE OUR SPOOKY FRIEND WITH US!
SO, LESS THAN AN HOUR PASSES BEFORE THE MIGHTY SHIP RIPS THROUGH THE DENSE CLOUDS THAT SWATHE VENUS!
WE'VE USED THE LAST OF OUR LIQUID FUEL SO I'M GOING TO BLOW THE OUTER HULL AND SWITCH ON THE ATOMIC GENERATOR!
TINY CHARGES TEAR AWAY THE BULKY HULL, AND THE STRIPPED DOWN VEHICLE BEGINS ITS FOUR MONTH ATOMIC POWERED JOURNEY HOME.
13

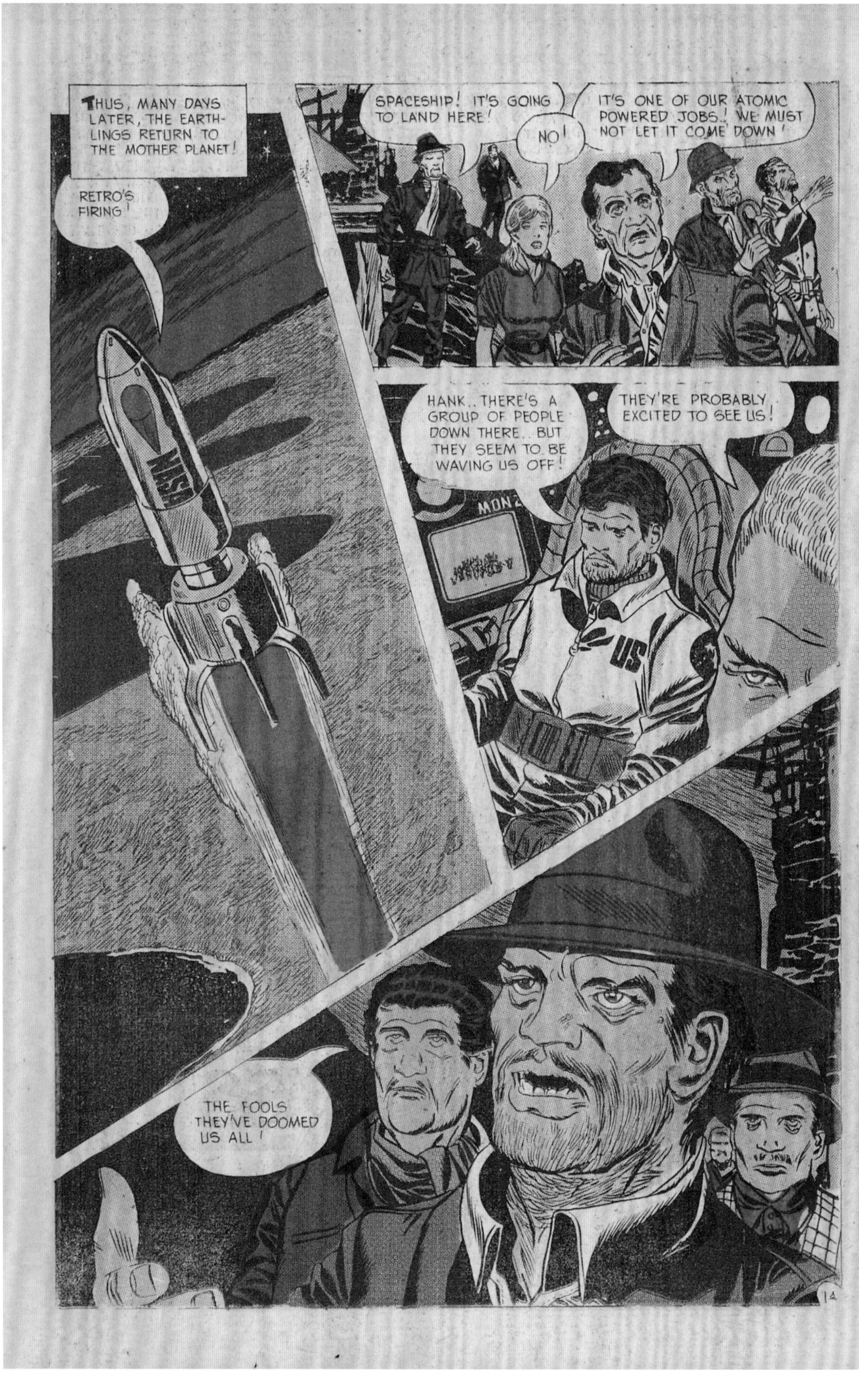
THUS, MANY DAYS LATER, THE EARTHLINGS RETURN TO THE MOTHER PLANET!
RETRO'S FIRING!
SPACESHIP! IT'S GOING TO LAND HERE!
NO!
IT'S ONE OF OUR ATOMIC POWERED JOBS! WE MUST NOT LET IT COME DOWN!
HANK.. THERE'S A GROUP OF PEOPLE DOWN THERE.. BUT THEY SEEM TO BE WAVING US OFF!
THEY'RE PROBABLY EXCITED TO SEE US!
THE FOOLS THEY'VE DOOMED US ALL!
14

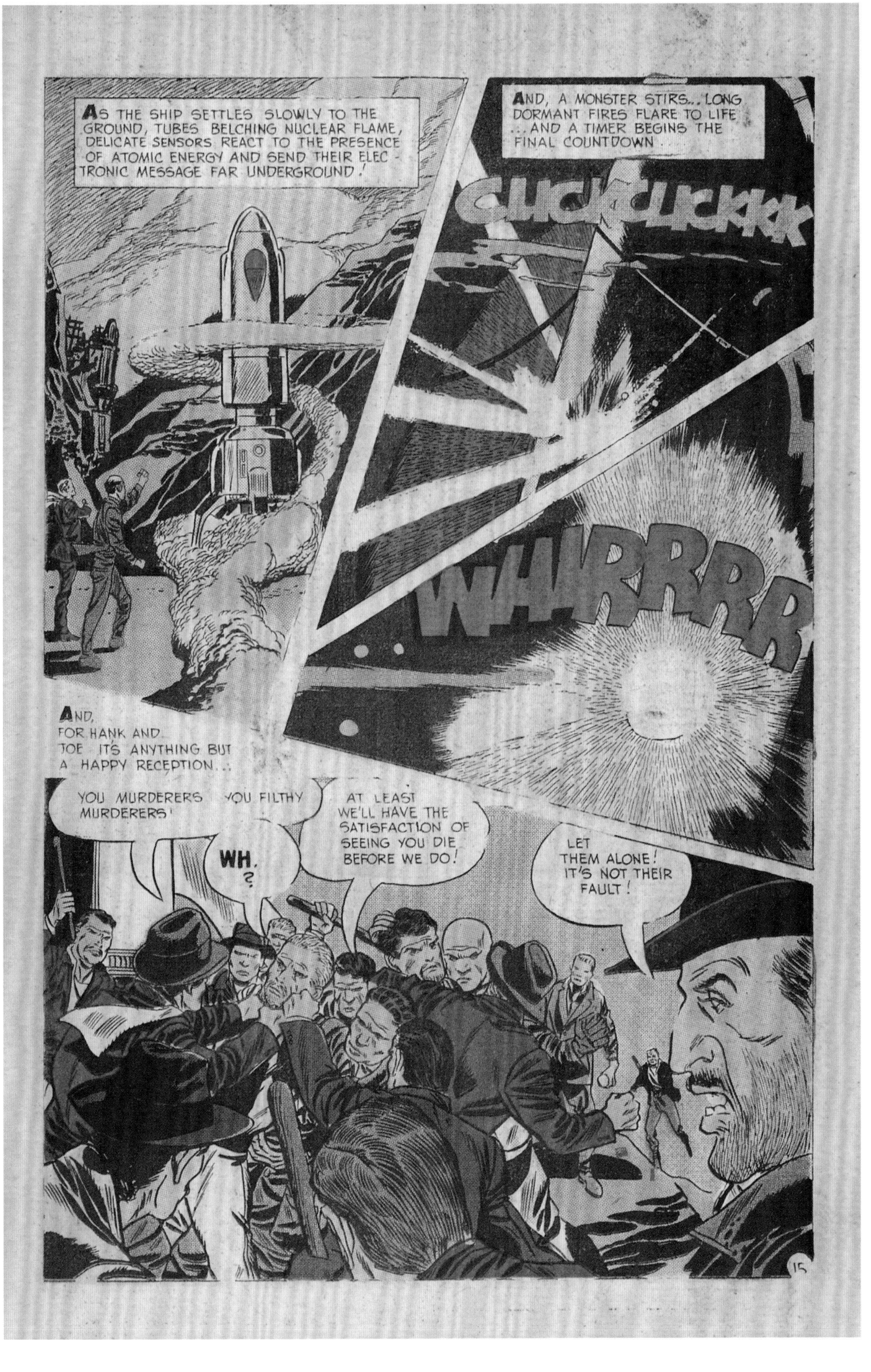
AS THE SHIP SETTLES SLOWLY TO THE GROUND, TUBES BELCHING NUCLEAR FLAME, DELICATE SENSORS REACT TO THE PRESENCE OF ATOMIC ENERGY AND SEND THEIR ELECTRONIC MESSAGE FAR UNDERGROUND!
AND, A MONSTER STIRS... LONG DORMANT FIRES FLARE TO LIFE ... AND A TIMER BEGINS THE FINAL COUNTDOWN.
CLICKCLICKKK
WHIRRRR
AND, FOR HANK AND JOE, IT'S ANYTHING BUT A HAPPY RECEPTION...
YOU MURDERERS... YOU FILTHY MURDERERS!
WH...?
AT LEAST WE'LL HAVE THE SATISFACTION OF SEEING YOU DIE BEFORE WE DO!
LET THEM ALONE! IT'S NOT THEIR FAULT!
15

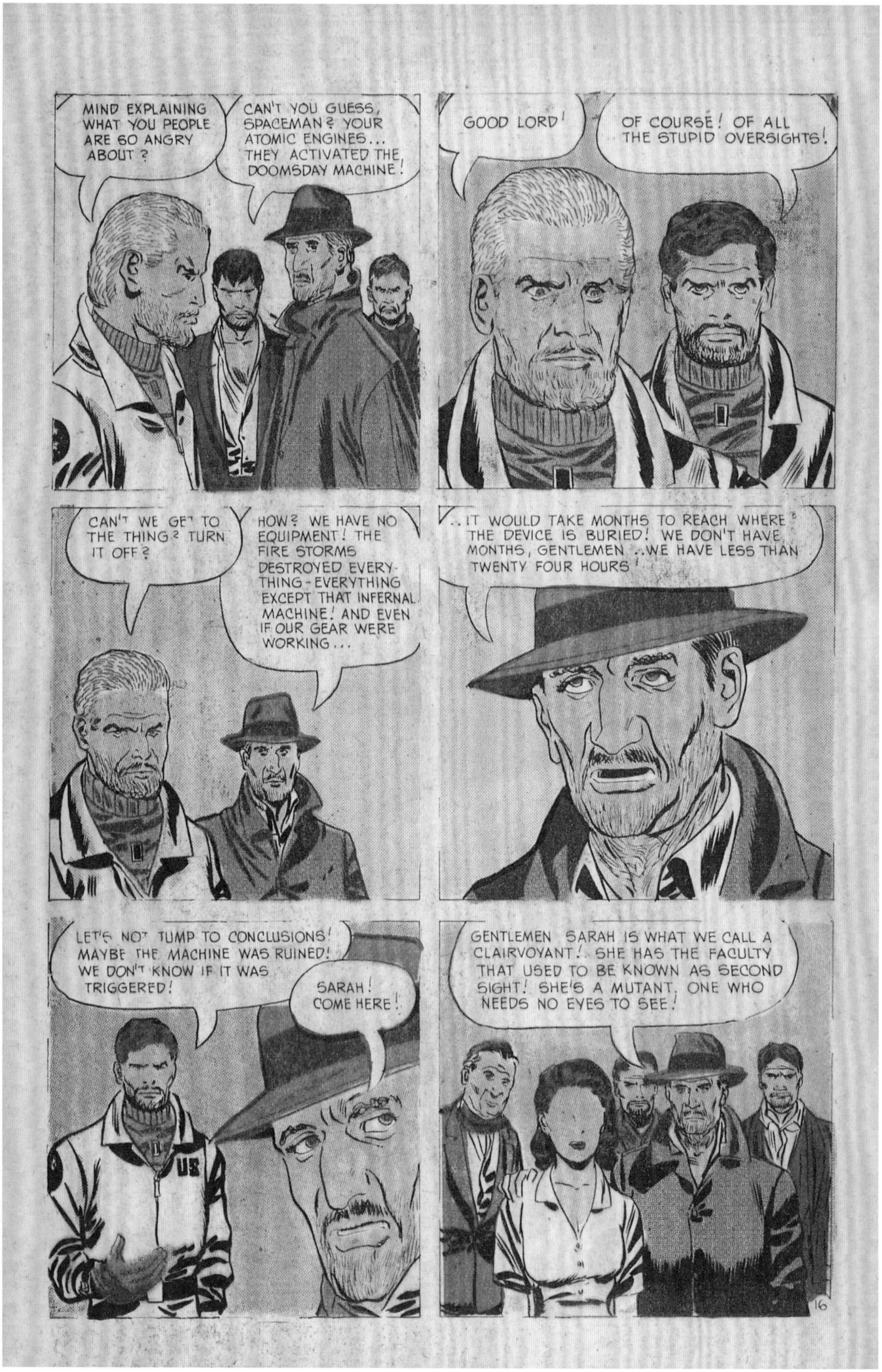
MIND EXPLAINING WHAT YOU PEOPLE ARE SO ANGRY ABOUT?
CAN'T YOU GUESS, SPACEMAN? YOUR ATOMIC ENGINES... THEY ACTIVATED THE DOOMSDAY MACHINE!
GOOD LORD!
OF COURSE! OF ALL THE STUPID OVERSIGHTS!
CAN'T WE GET TO THE THING? TURN IT OFF?
HOW? WE HAVE NO EQUIPMENT! THE FIRE STORMS DESTROYED EVERYTHING - EVERYTHING EXCEPT THAT INFERNAL MACHINE! AND EVEN IF OUR GEAR WERE WORKING...
...IT WOULD TAKE MONTHS TO REACH WHERE THE DEVICE IS BURIED! WE DON'T HAVE MONTHS, GENTLEMEN ...WE HAVE LESS THAN TWENTY FOUR HOURS!
LET'S NOT JUMP TO CONCLUSIONS! MAYBE THE MACHINE WAS RUINED! WE DON'T KNOW IF IT WAS TRIGGERED!
SARAH! COME HERE!
GENTLEMEN SARAH IS WHAT WE CALL A CLAIRVOYANT! SHE HAS THE FACULTY THAT USED TO BE KNOWN AS SECOND SIGHT! SHE'S A MUTANT, ONE WHO NEEDS NO EYES TO SEE!
16

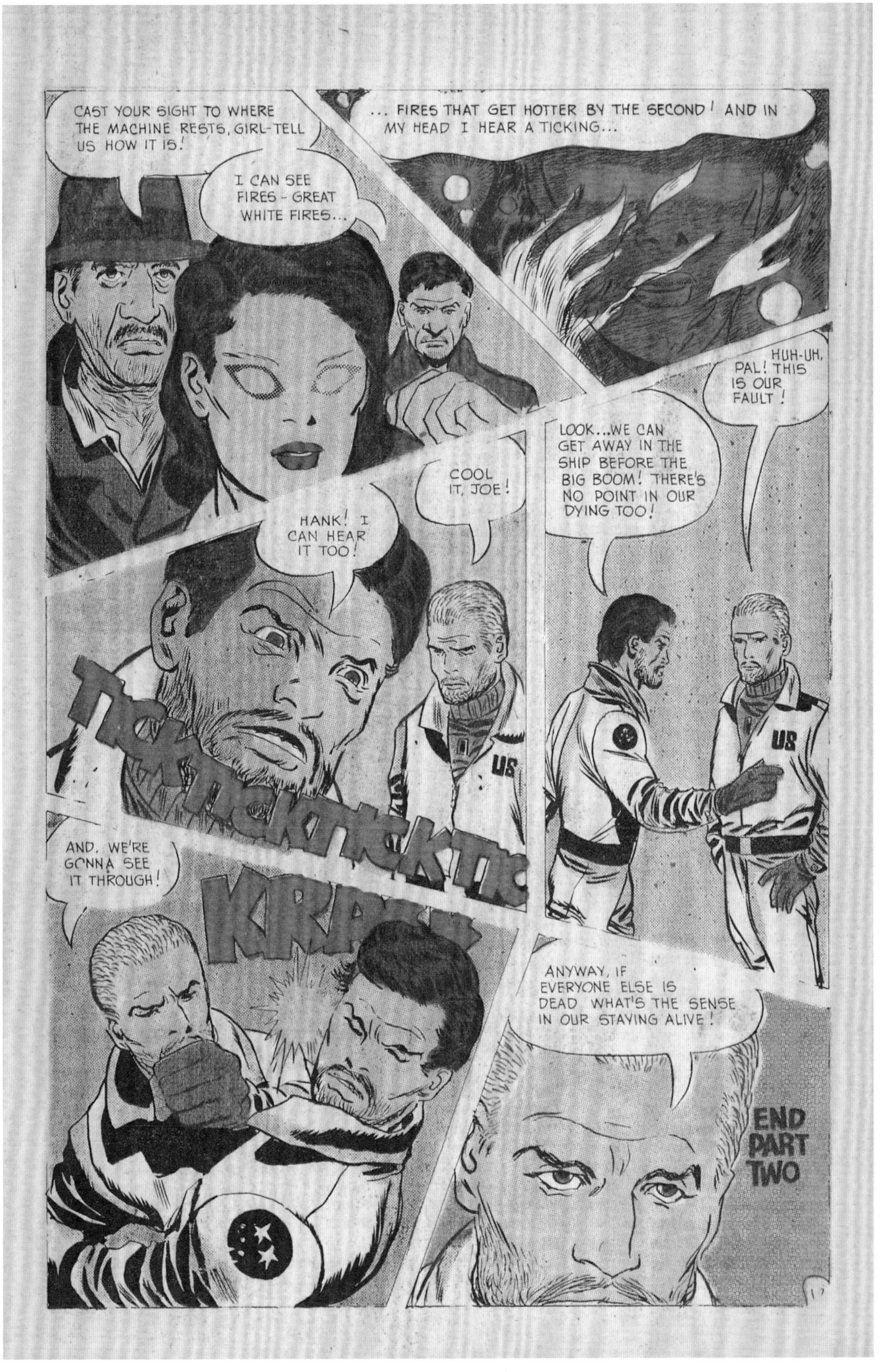
CAST YOUR SIGHT TO WHERE THE MACHINE RESTS, GIRL-TELL US HOW IT IS!
I CAN SEE FIRES - GREAT WHITE FIRES...
... FIRES THAT GET HOTTER BY THE SECOND! AND IN MY HEAD I HEAR A TICKING...
HANK! I CAN HEAR IT TOO!
COOL IT, JOE!
TICK TICK TICK TICK TIC
LOOK...WE CAN GET AWAY IN THE SHIP BEFORE THE BIG BOOM! THERE'S NO POINT IN OUR DYING TOO!
HUH-UH, PAL! THIS IS OUR FAULT!
AND, WE'RE GONNA SEE IT THROUGH!
ANYWAY, IF EVERYONE ELSE IS DEAD WHAT'S THE SENSE IN OUR STAYING ALIVE!
END PART TWO

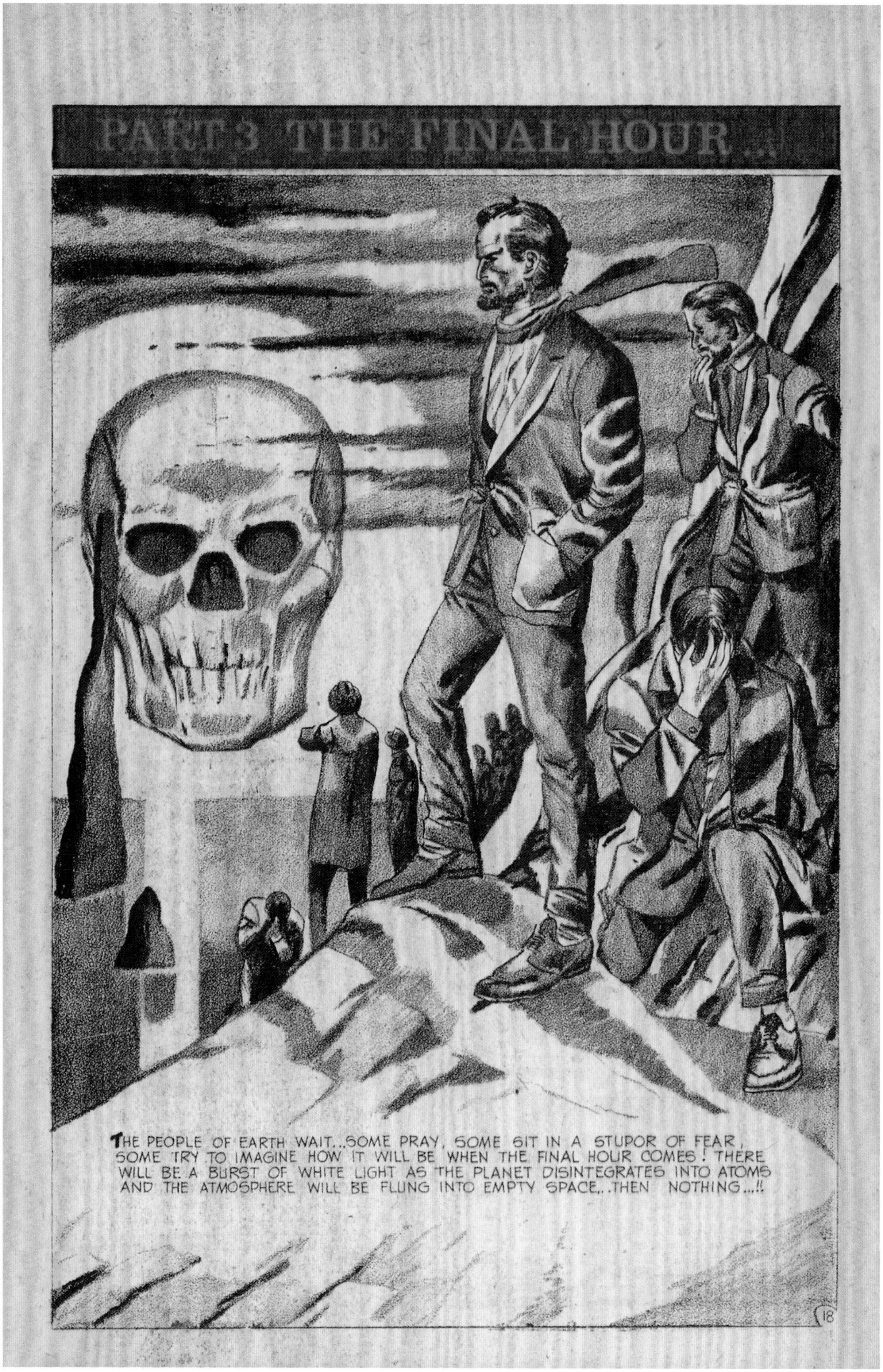
PART 3 THE FINAL HOUR...
THE PEOPLE OF EARTH WAIT...SOME PRAY, SOME SIT IN A STUPOR OF FEAR, SOME TRY TO IMAGINE HOW IT WILL BE WHEN THE FINAL HOUR COMES! THERE WILL BE A BURST OF WHITE LIGHT AS THE PLANET DISINTEGRATES INTO ATOMS AND THE ATMOSPHERE WILL BE FLUNG INTO EMPTY SPACE...THEN NOTHING...!!
18

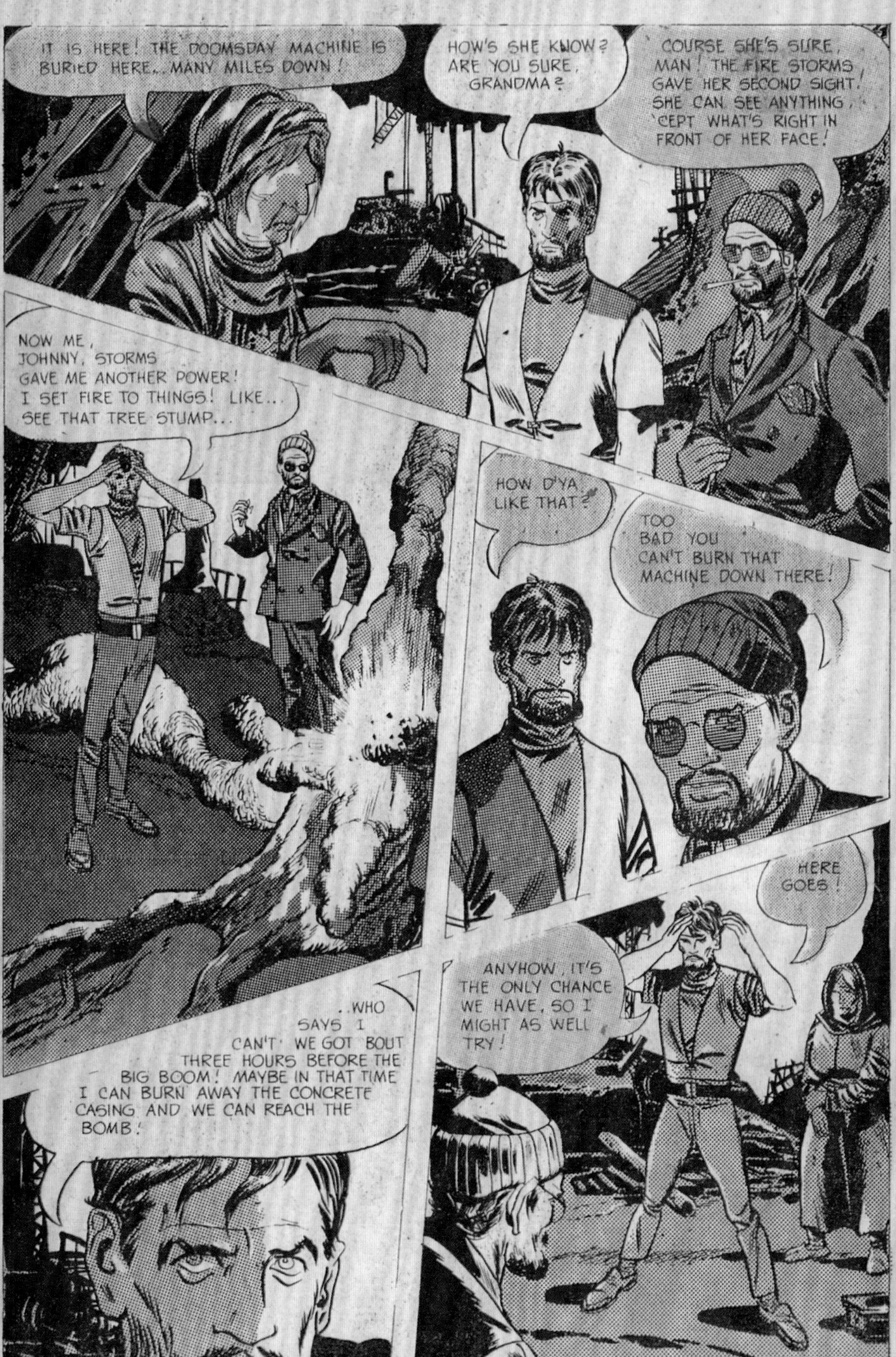
IT IS HERE! THE DOOMSDAY MACHINE IS BURIED HERE...MANY MILES DOWN!
HOW'S SHE KNOW? ARE YOU SURE, GRANDMA?
COURSE SHE'S SURE, MAN! THE FIRE STORMS GAVE HER SECOND SIGHT! SHE CAN SEE ANYTHING, 'CEPT WHAT'S RIGHT IN FRONT OF HER FACE!
NOW ME, JOHNNY, STORMS GAVE ME ANOTHER POWER! I SET FIRE TO THINGS! LIKE... SEE THAT TREE STUMP...
HOW D'YA LIKE THAT?
TOO BAD YOU CAN'T BURN THAT MACHINE DOWN THERE!
..WHO SAYS I CAN'T! WE GOT BOUT THREE HOURS BEFORE THE BIG BOOM! MAYBE IN THAT TIME I CAN BURN AWAY THE CONCRETE CASING AND WE CAN REACH THE BOMB!
HERE GOES!
ANYHOW, IT'S THE ONLY CHANCE WE HAVE, SO I MIGHT AS WELL TRY!
19

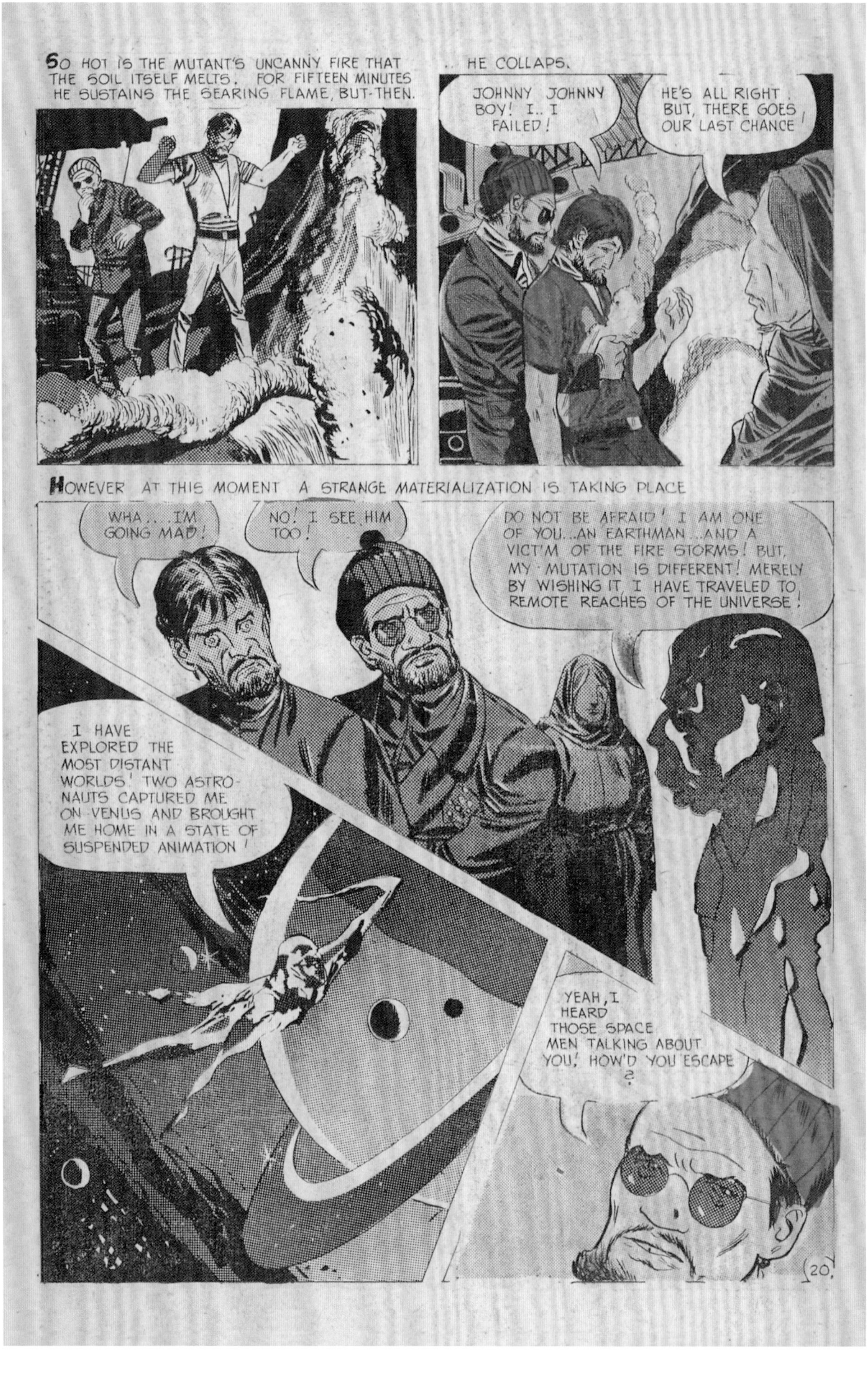
SO HOT IS THE MUTANT'S UNCANNY FIRE THAT THE SOIL ITSELF MELTS. FOR FIFTEEN MINUTES HE SUSTAINS THE SEARING FLAME, BUT-THEN.
.. HE COLLAPS.
JOHNNY JOHNNY BOY! I.. I FAILED!
HE'S ALL RIGHT. BUT, THERE GOES OUR LAST CHANCE!
HOWEVER AT THIS MOMENT A STRANGE MATERIALIZATION IS TAKING PLACE
WHA....I'M GOING MAD!
NO! I SEE HIM TOO!
DO NOT BE AFRAID! I AM ONE OF YOU...AN EARTHMAN..AND A VICTIM OF THE FIRE STORMS! BUT, MY MUTATION IS DIFFERENT! MERELY BY WISHING IT, I HAVE TRAVELED TO REMOTE REACHES OF THE UNIVERSE!
I HAVE EXPLORED THE MOST DISTANT WORLDS! TWO ASTRONAUTS CAPTURED ME ON VENUS AND BROUGHT ME HOME IN A STATE OF SUSPENDED ANIMATION!
YEAH, I HEARD THOSE SPACE MEN TALKING ABOUT YOU! HOW'D YOU ESCAPE ?
20

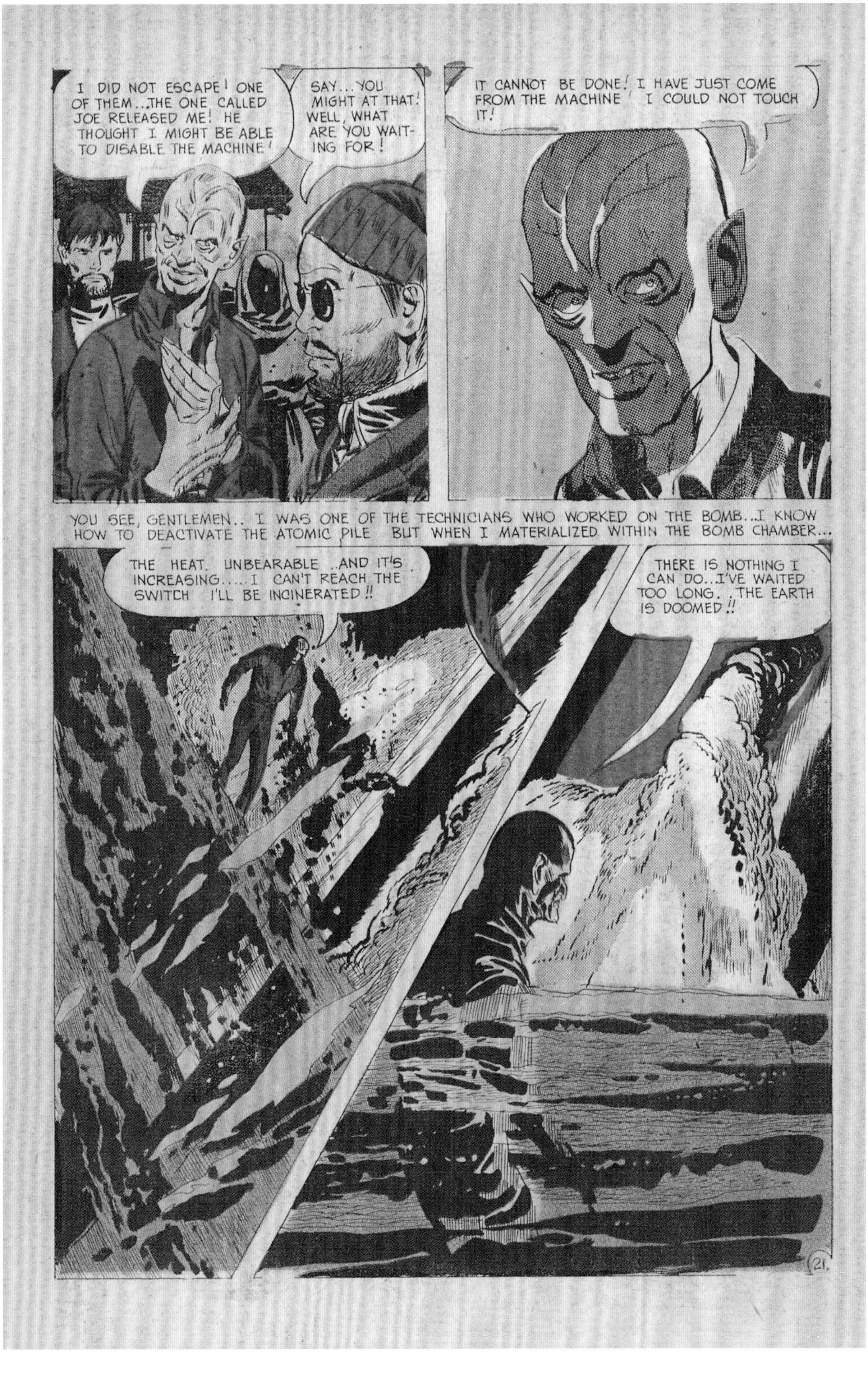
I DID NOT ESCAPE! ONE OF THEM...THE ONE CALLED JOE RELEASED ME! HE THOUGHT I MIGHT BE ABLE TO DISABLE THE MACHINE!
SAY...YOU MIGHT AT THAT! WELL, WHAT ARE YOU WAITING FOR!
IT CANNOT BE DONE! I HAVE JUST COME FROM THE MACHINE I COULD NOT TOUCH IT!
YOU SEE, GENTLEMEN.. I WAS ONE OF THE TECHNICIANS WHO WORKED ON THE BOMB...I KNOW HOW TO DEACTIVATE THE ATOMIC PILE BUT WHEN I MATERIALIZED WITHIN THE BOMB CHAMBER...
THE HEAT. UNBEARABLE ..AND IT'S INCREASING.....I CAN'T REACH THE SWITCH I'LL BE INCINERATED!!
THERE IS NOTHING I CAN DO..I'VE WAITED TOO LONG. .THE EARTH IS DOOMED!!
21

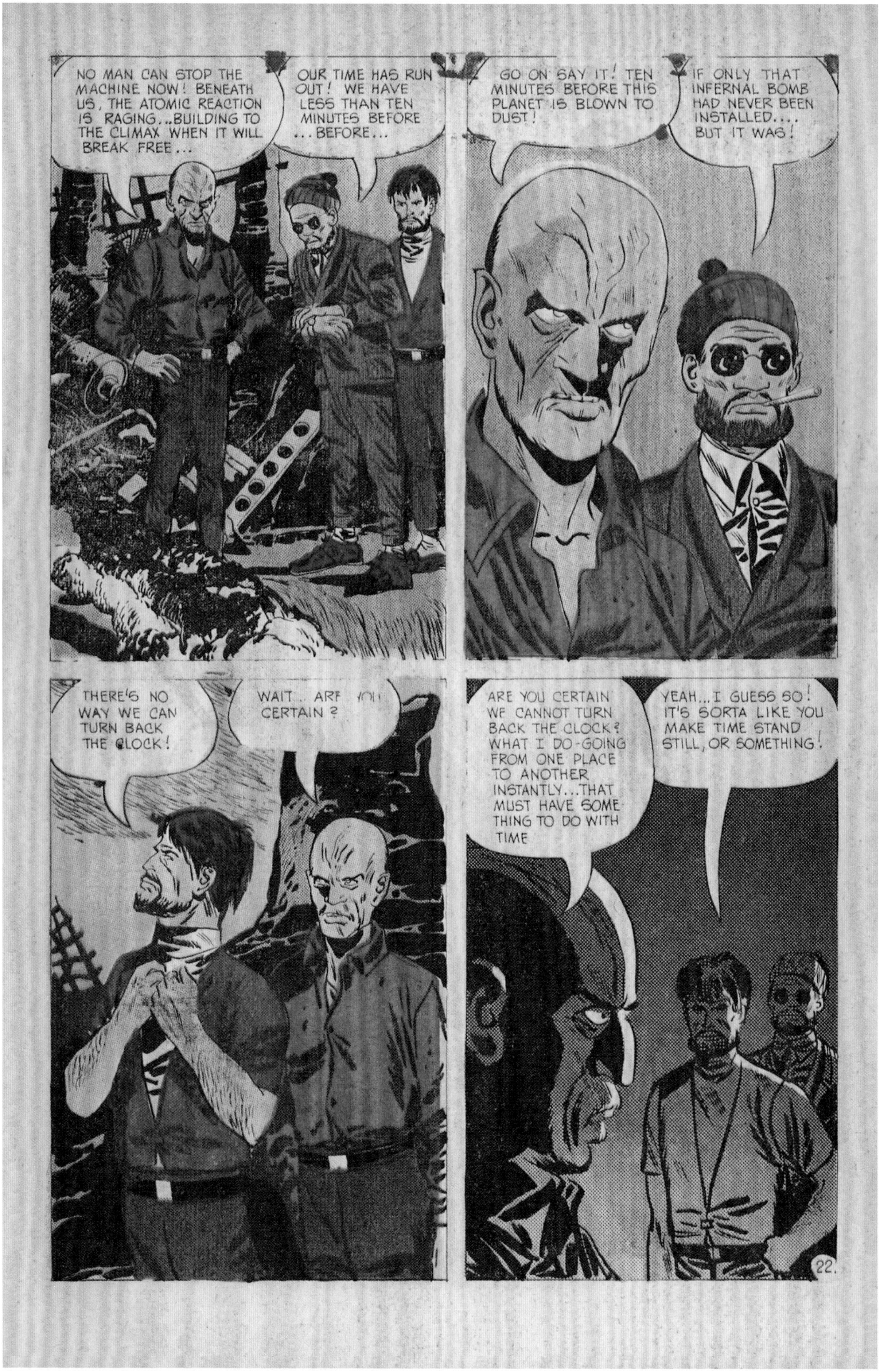
NO MAN CAN STOP THE MACHINE NOW! BENEATH US, THE ATOMIC REACTION IS RAGING...BUILDING TO THE CLIMAX WHEN IT WILL BREAK FREE...
OUR TIME HAS RUN OUT! WE HAVE LESS THAN TEN MINUTES BEFORE ...BEFORE...
GO ON SAY IT! TEN MINUTES BEFORE THIS PLANET IS BLOWN TO DUST!
IF ONLY THAT INFERNAL BOMB HAD NEVER BEEN INSTALLED.... BUT IT WAS!
THERE'S NO WAY WE CAN TURN BACK THE CLOCK!
WAIT.. ARE YOU CERTAIN?
ARE YOU CERTAIN WE CANNOT TURN BACK THE CLOCK? WHAT I DO-GOING FROM ONE PLACE TO ANOTHER INSTANTLY...THAT MUST HAVE SOME THING TO DO WITH TIME
YEAH...I GUESS SO! IT'S SORTA LIKE YOU MAKE TIME STAND STILL, OR SOMETHING!
22.

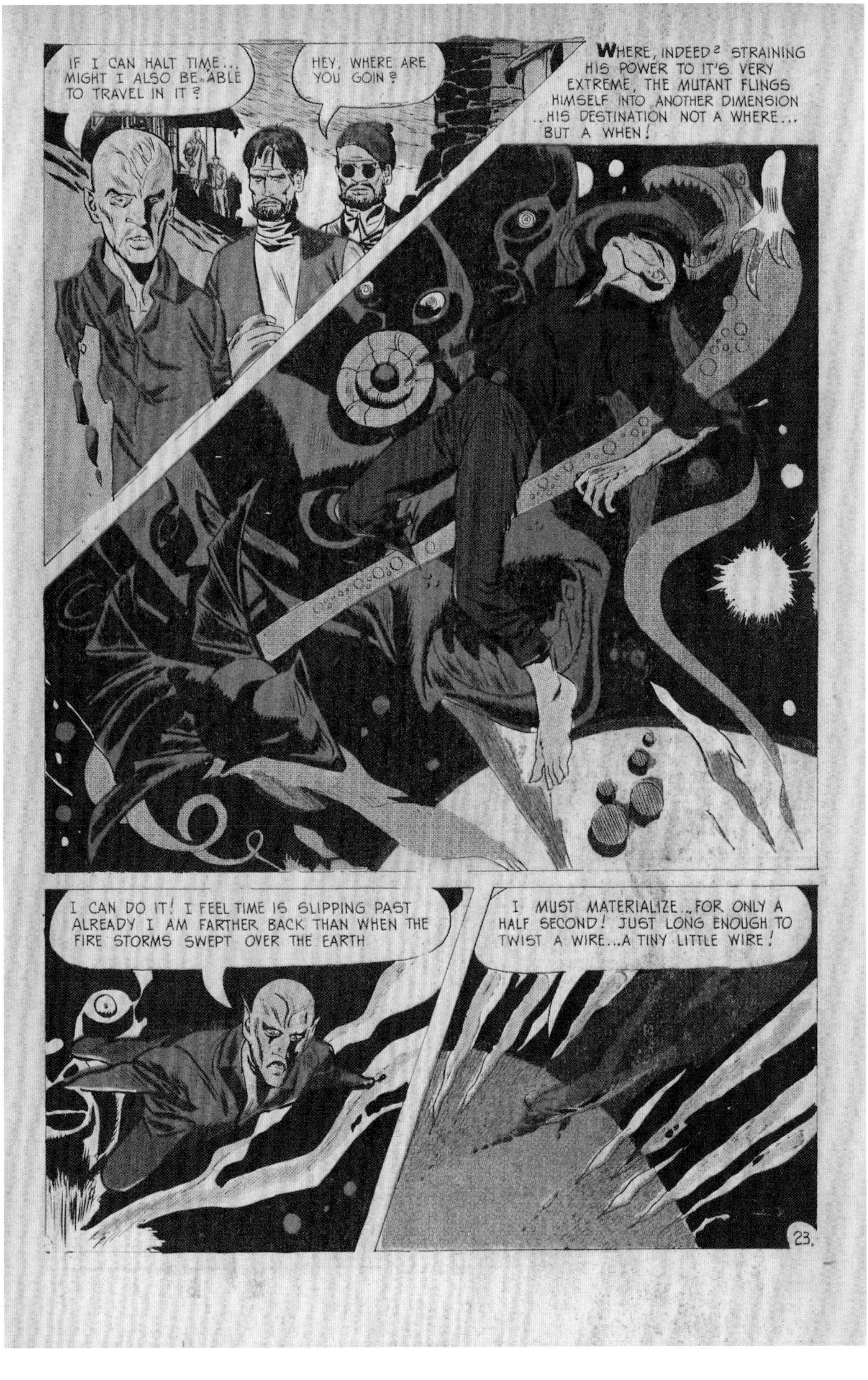
IF I CAN HALT TIME... MIGHT I ALSO BE ABLE TO TRAVEL IN IT?
HEY, WHERE ARE YOU GOIN?
WHERE, INDEED? STRAINING HIS POWER TO IT'S VERY EXTREME, THE MUTANT FLINGS HIMSELF INTO ANOTHER DIMENSION ..HIS DESTINATION NOT A WHERE... BUT A WHEN!
I CAN DO IT! I FEEL TIME IS SLIPPING PAST ALREADY I AM FARTHER BACK THAN WHEN THE FIRE STORMS SWEPT OVER THE EARTH
I MUST MATERIALIZE..FOR ONLY A HALF SECOND! JUST LONG ENOUGH TO TWIST A WIRE...A TINY LITTLE WIRE!
23.

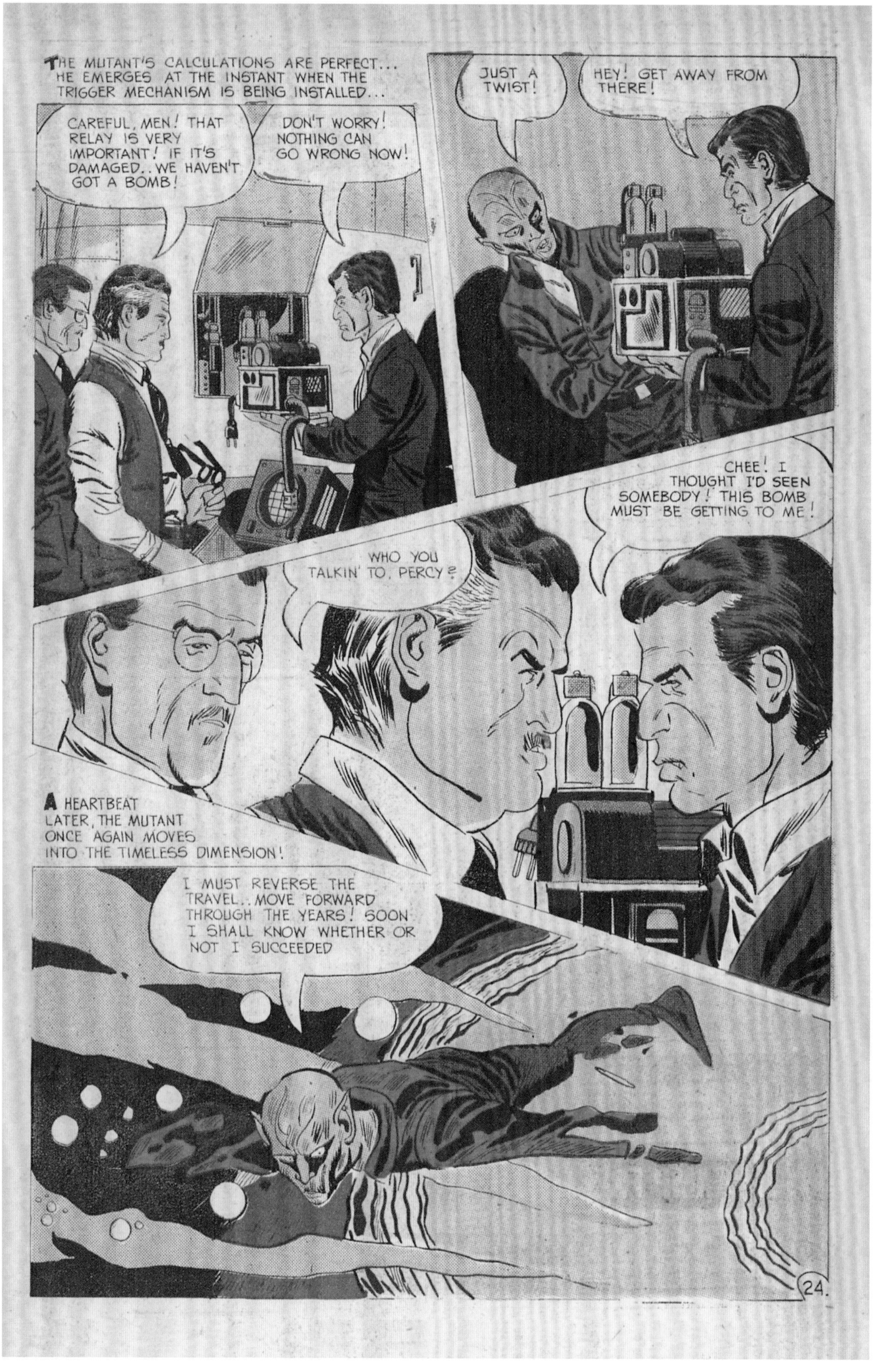
THE MUTANT'S CALCULATIONS ARE PERFECT... HE EMERGES AT THE INSTANT WHEN THE TRIGGER MECHANISM IS BEING INSTALLED...
CAREFUL, MEN! THAT RELAY IS VERY IMPORTANT! IF IT'S DAMAGED.. WE HAVEN'T GOT A BOMB!
DON'T WORRY! NOTHING CAN GO WRONG NOW!
JUST A TWIST!
HEY! GET AWAY FROM THERE!
CHEE! I THOUGHT I'D SEEN SOMEBODY! THIS BOMB MUST BE GETTING TO ME!
WHO YOU TALKIN' TO, PERCY?
A HEARTBEAT LATER, THE MUTANT ONCE AGAIN MOVES INTO THE TIMELESS DIMENSION!
I MUST REVERSE THE TRAVEL.. MOVE FORWARD THROUGH THE YEARS! SOON I SHALL KNOW WHETHER OR NOT I SUCCEEDED
24.

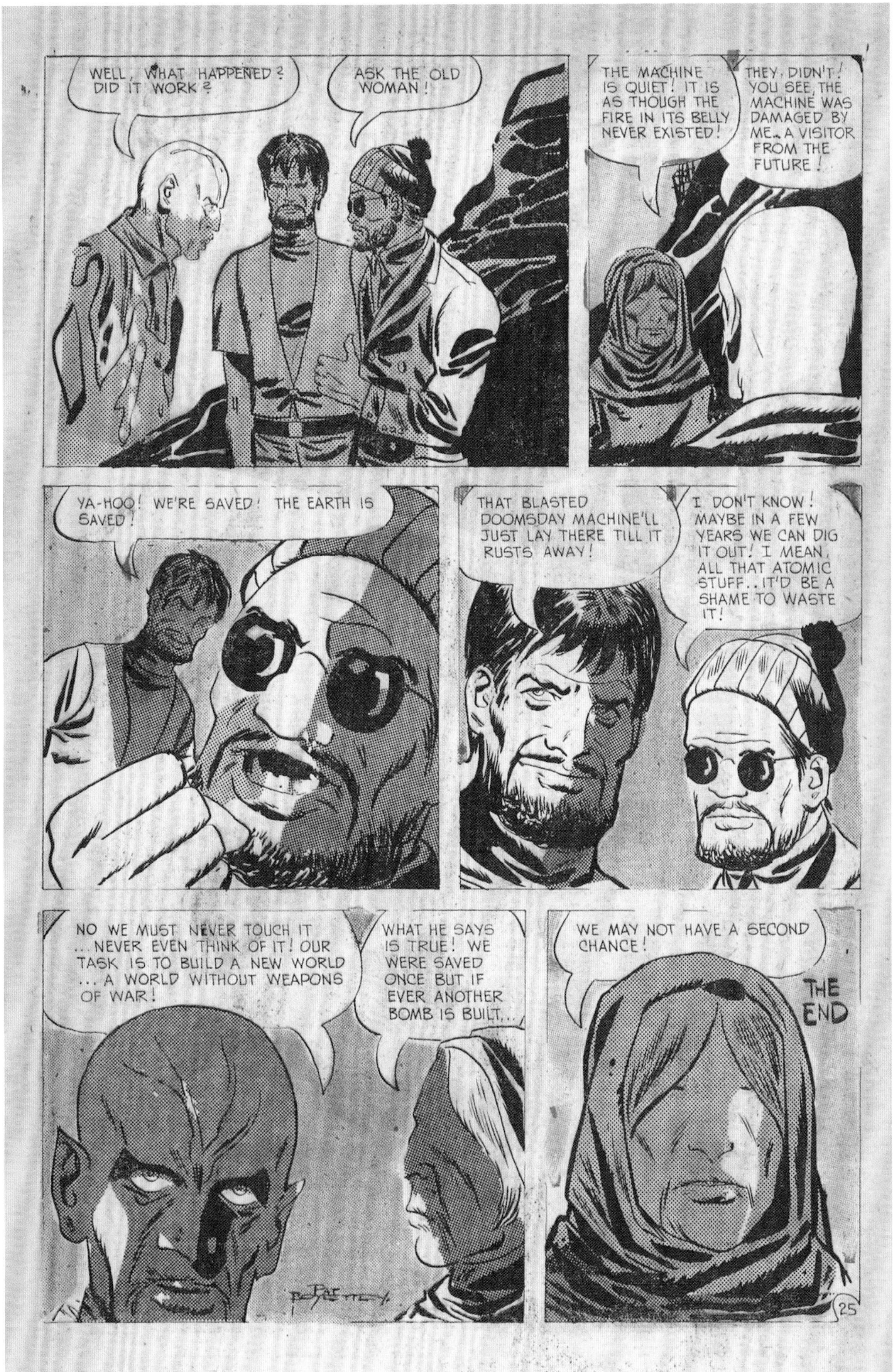
WELL, WHAT HAPPENED? DID IT WORK?
ASK THE OLD WOMAN!
THE MACHINE IS QUIET! IT IS AS THOUGH THE FIRE IN ITS BELLY NEVER EXISTED!
THEY DIDN'T! YOU SEE, THE MACHINE WAS DAMAGED BY ME.. A VISITOR FROM THE FUTURE!
YA-HOO! WE'RE SAVED! THE EARTH IS SAVED!
THAT BLASTED DOOMSDAY MACHINE'LL JUST LAY THERE TILL IT RUSTS AWAY!
I DON'T KNOW! MAYBE IN A FEW YEARS WE CAN DIG IT OUT! I MEAN, ALL THAT ATOMIC STUFF.. IT'D BE A SHAME TO WASTE IT!
NO WE MUST NEVER TOUCH IT ...NEVER EVEN THINK OF IT! OUR TASK IS TO BUILD A NEW WORLD ... A WORLD WITHOUT WEAPONS OF WAR!
WHAT HE SAYS IS TRUE! WE WERE SAVED ONCE BUT IF EVER ANOTHER BOMB IS BUILT...
WE MAY NOT HAVE A SECOND CHANCE!
THE END
PAT BOYETTE
25

JESSE MARSH

(1907–66)

Jesse Marsh's colleague and admirer, Alex Toth, put it best when he wrote, "Jesse epitomized West Coast comic book art with his simple, straightforward storytelling in evenly measured panels and pages. . . ." Nothing in comics evokes the legendary West as well as Marsh's pages: His enormous skies, rough plains scenery, and spacious panels speak volumes about the landscape he depicted and inhabited for much of his life.

Marsh was born in Alabama but moved to California with his family as a young adult. He was a self-taught artist, and was something of an autodidact, eventually accumulating some 750 volumes of art and reference books. In 1939 he went to work for Walt Disney doing lower-level story and breakdown tasks for *Pinocchio* and *Fantasia*. Marsh enlisted in the U.S. Army Air Forces in 1942 and was wounded in Italy. Upon his return to California at the end of World War II, he began working for Disney again as well as taking on his first comic book assignments for Western Publishing (known as Dell), then the only comic book company with offices in the West and publishers of primarily licensed properties, including *Little Lulu* and the entire Disney line of comics, among others. Western Publishing provided an outlet for numerous animators and cartoonists who were far from the hustle of New York and its teeming comic book production lines. Marsh first drew the *Gene Autry* comic book and then, in 1947, took on the assignment that would define his career: *Tarzan*. Working from original scripts first by Robert P. Thompson and then by Gaylord DuBois, Marsh drew 153 issues of *Tarzan* until he retired from comics in 1965. Along the way Marsh also worked on numerous other titles, all for Western Publishing, including *John Carter of Mars*, *Annie Oakley*, and *Robin Hood*.

Marsh lived with his parents in Monrovia, California. He was apparently a visual connoisseur of sorts—enjoying beautifully designed cars and fine clothes, and building a substantial library. He had hoped to spend his retirement making his own paintings, but his decade-long battle with diabetes unfortunately got the better of him just a year after he retired.

Johnny Mack Brown, a movie cowboy hero, was, like much of Marsh's material, an unlikely vehicle for good work; the spacious Western landscape is perfect for Marsh's often abstract notions of figures in space. Throughout *Johnny Mack Brown* we're reminded of the enormous Western sky above the flat plains. The scrappy underbrush and foliage is lit, like the characters, by either the glaring sun or flickering firelight. Marsh gets all of this in his comics with subtle compositions and quick, casual brushwork. The story in these pages, the best of the *Johnny Mack Brown* issues, shows Marsh's very finest early work. During this and later years, according to Alex Toth, Marsh would design his comics pages as entire abstract compositions before beginning to rough in figures or backgrounds. Marsh would then move swiftly to pen and brush rather than "redrawing" over his own pencils. This helps explain the liveliness of his marks—he was truly inventing the space as he drew.

Marsh also avidly consulted reference materials, which structured his architecture and scenarios, allowing him to draw freely over the "idea" of the thing. Ironically, for someone who spent much of his career drawing someone else's characters, likenesses and precise body language were not Marsh's strength as a storyteller: place and space and design were. While his style is certainly related to Milton Caniff's, Marsh's work occupies its own category: Only years later, in the work of Gilbert Hernandez (*Love and Rockets*), does one find such an assured sense of place and space in comics. Marsh, like many of the artists in this book, remained invisible for much of his career, hidden behind the famous character he rendered for so many years. But behind the property was a rare talent for the subtler aspects of the medium.

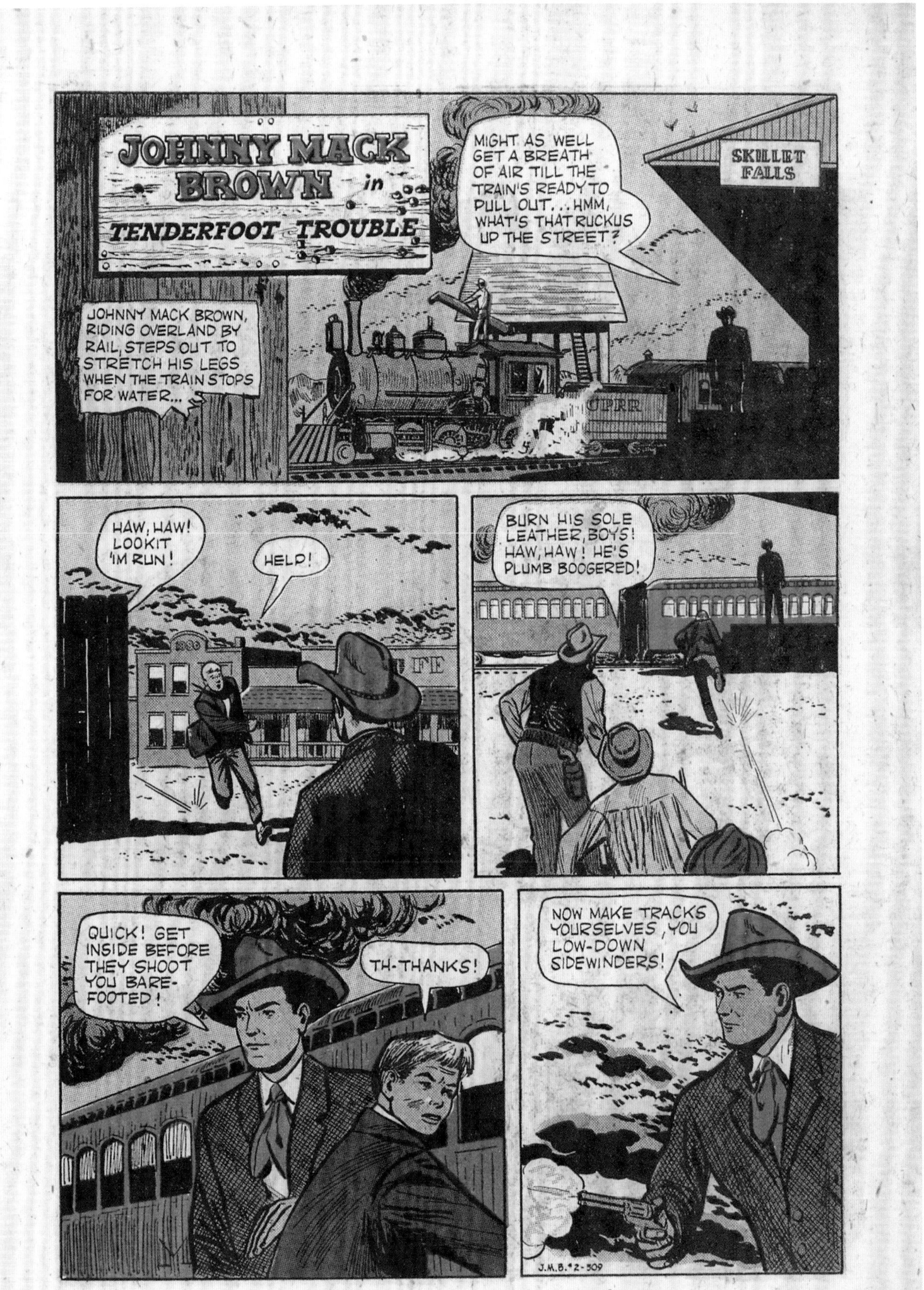
JOHNNY MACK BROWN in
TENDERFOOT TROUBLE
MIGHT AS WELL GET A BREATH OF AIR TILL THE TRAIN'S READY TO PULL OUT... HMM, WHAT'S THAT RUCKUS UP THE STREET?
SKILLET FALLS
JOHNNY MACK BROWN, RIDING OVERLAND BY RAIL, STEPS OUT TO STRETCH HIS LEGS WHEN THE TRAIN STOPS FOR WATER...
HAW, HAW! LOOKIT 'IM RUN!
HELP!
BURN HIS SOLE LEATHER, BOYS! HAW, HAW! HE'S PLUMB BOOGERED!
QUICK! GET INSIDE BEFORE THEY SHOOT YOU BARE-FOOTED!
TH-THANKS!
NOW MAKE TRACKS YOURSELVES, YOU LOW-DOWN SIDEWINDERS!
J.M.B.#2-509

Johnny Mack Brown no. 2 (1950)

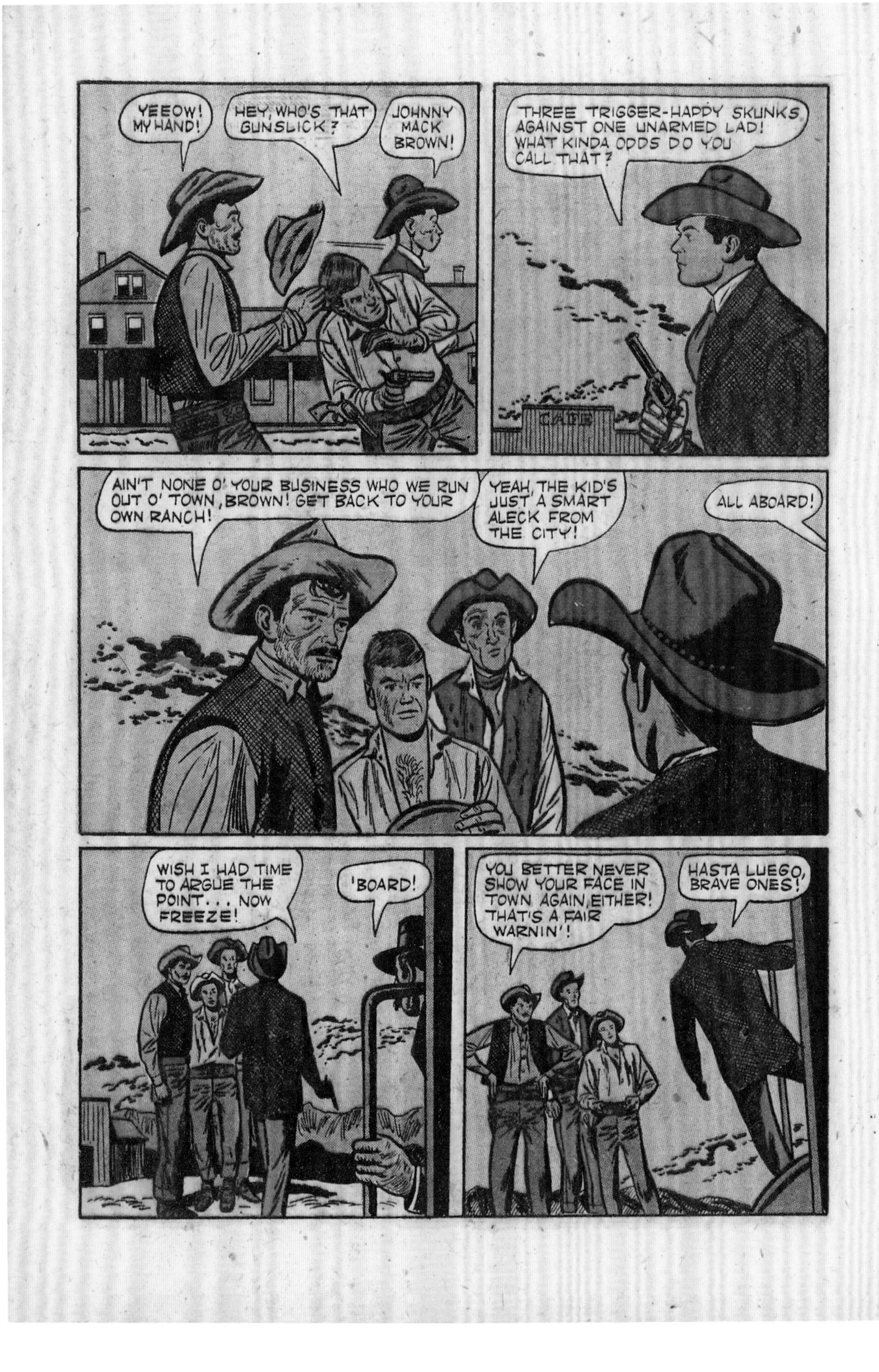
YEEOW! MY HAND!
HEY, WHO'S THAT GUNSLICK?
JOHNNY MACK BROWN!
THREE TRIGGER-HAPPY SKUNKS AGAINST ONE UNARMED LAD! WHAT KINDA ODDS DO YOU CALL THAT?
CAFE
AIN'T NONE O' YOUR BUSINESS WHO WE RUN OUT O' TOWN, BROWN! GET BACK TO YOUR OWN RANCH!
YEAH, THE KID'S JUST A SMART ALECK FROM THE CITY!
ALL ABOARD!
WISH I HAD TIME TO ARGUE THE POINT... NOW FREEZE!
'BOARD!
YOU BETTER NEVER SHOW YOUR FACE IN TOWN AGAIN, EITHER! THAT'S A FAIR WARNIN'!
HASTA LUEGO, BRAVE ONES!

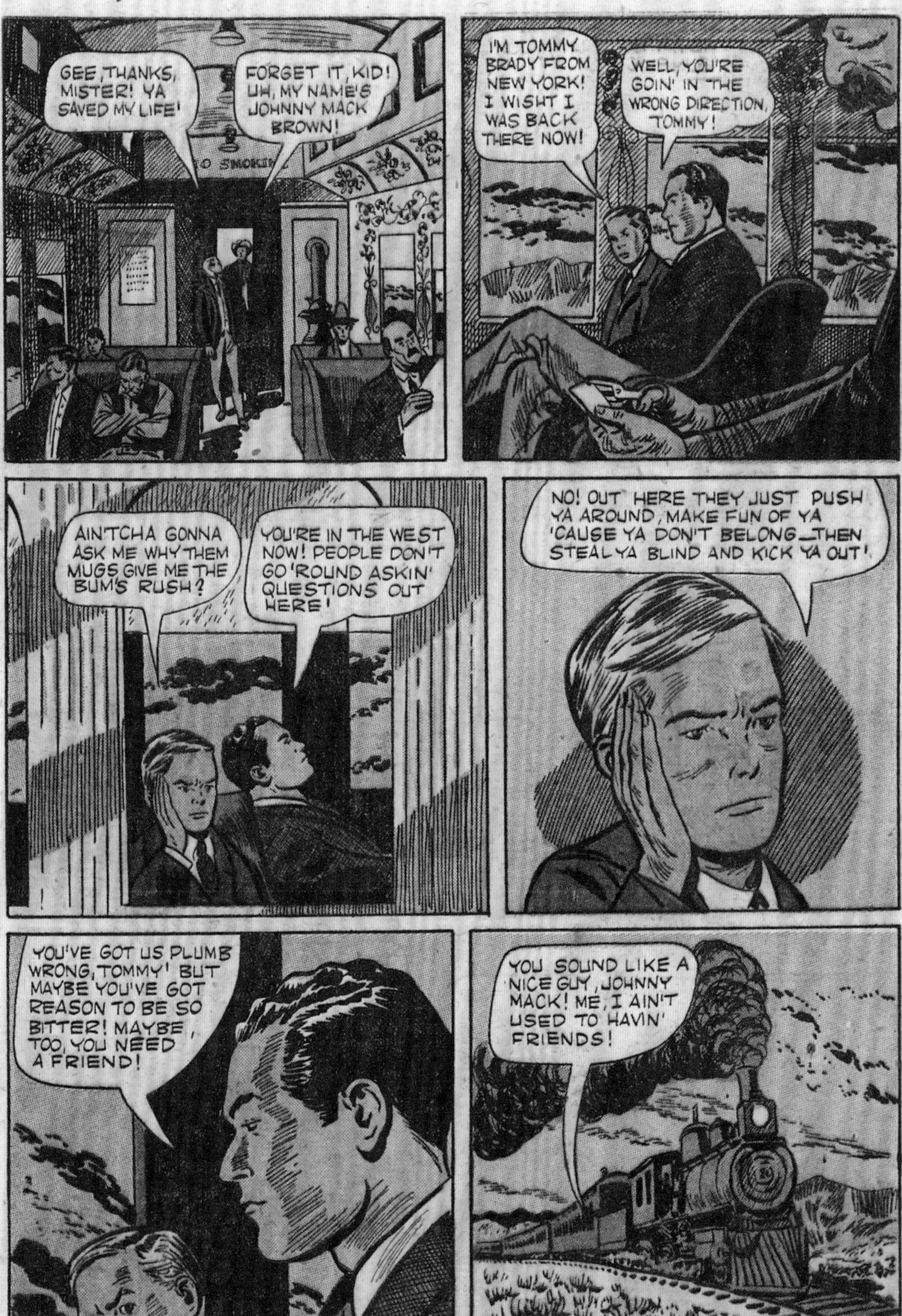
GEE, THANKS, MISTER! YA SAVED MY LIFE!
FORGET IT, KID! UH, MY NAME'S JOHNNY MACK BROWN!
I'M TOMMY BRADY FROM NEW YORK! I WISHT I WAS BACK THERE NOW!
WELL, YOU'RE GOIN' IN THE WRONG DIRECTION, TOMMY!
AIN'TCHA GONNA ASK ME WHY THEM MUGS GIVE ME THE BUM'S RUSH?
YOU'RE IN THE WEST NOW! PEOPLE DON'T GO 'ROUND ASKIN' QUESTIONS OUT HERE!
NO! OUT HERE THEY JUST PUSH YA AROUND, MAKE FUN OF YA 'CAUSE YA DON'T BELONG—THEN STEAL YA BLIND AND KICK YA OUT!
YOU'VE GOT US PLUMB WRONG, TOMMY! BUT MAYBE YOU'VE GOT REASON TO BE SO BITTER! MAYBE, TOO, YOU NEED A FRIEND!
YOU SOUND LIKE A NICE GUY, JOHNNY MACK! ME, I AIN'T USED TO HAVIN' FRIENDS!

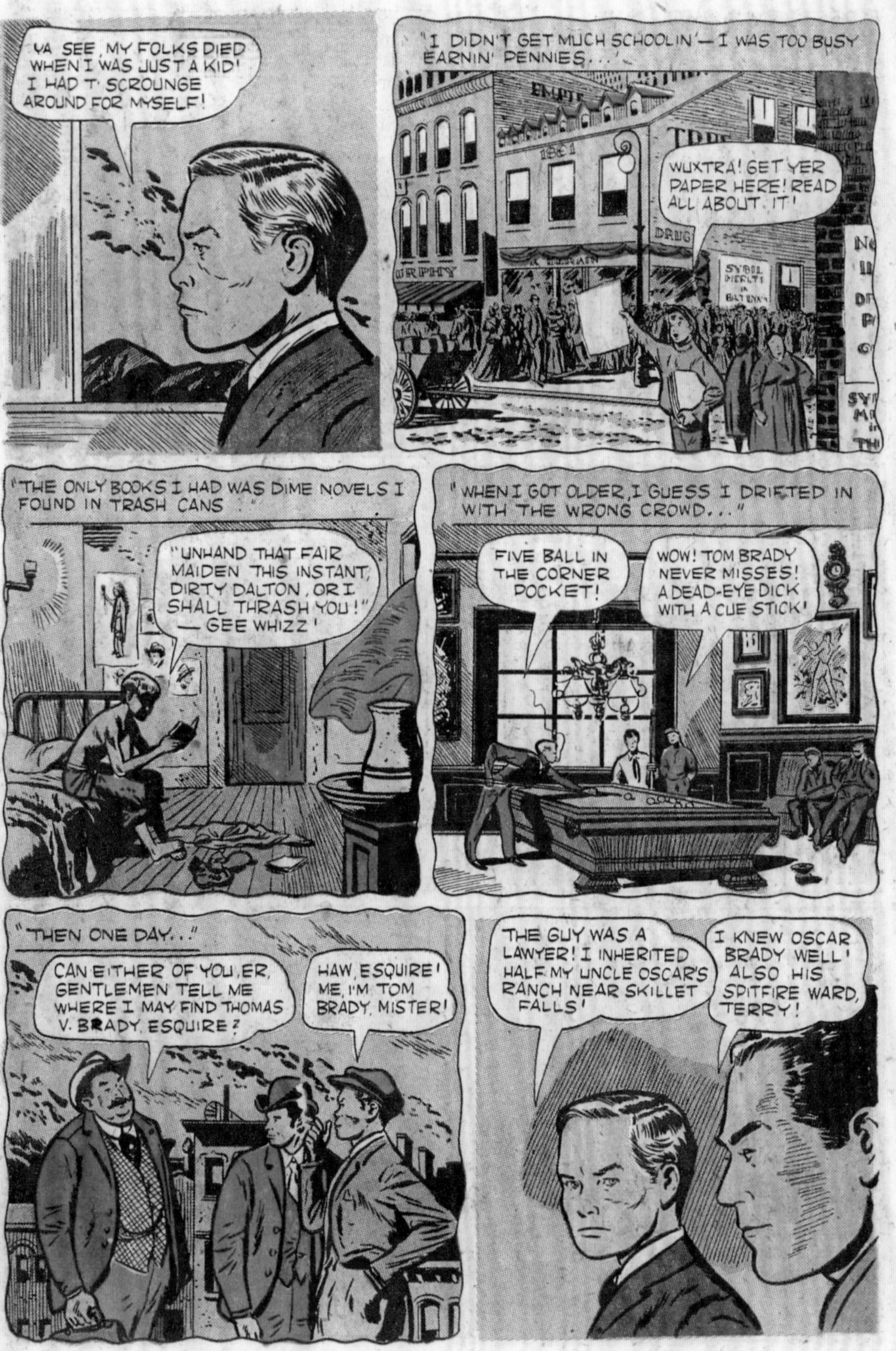
YA SEE, MY FOLKS DIED WHEN I WAS JUST A KID! I HAD T' SCROUNGE AROUND FOR MYSELF!
"I DIDN'T GET MUCH SCHOOLIN'— I WAS TOO BUSY EARNIN' PENNIES..."
WUXTRA! GET YER PAPER HERE! READ ALL ABOUT IT!
DRUG
"THE ONLY BOOKS I HAD WAS DIME NOVELS I FOUND IN TRASH CANS..."
"UNHAND THAT FAIR MAIDEN THIS INSTANT, DIRTY DALTON, OR I SHALL THRASH YOU!" — GEE WHIZZ!
"WHEN I GOT OLDER, I GUESS I DRIFTED IN WITH THE WRONG CROWD..."
FIVE BALL IN THE CORNER POCKET!
WOW! TOM BRADY NEVER MISSES! A DEAD-EYE DICK WITH A CUE STICK!
"THEN ONE DAY..."
CAN EITHER OF YOU, ER, GENTLEMEN TELL ME WHERE I MAY FIND THOMAS V. BRADY, ESQUIRE?
HAW, ESQUIRE! ME, I'M TOM BRADY, MISTER!
THE GUY WAS A LAWYER! I INHERITED HALF MY UNCLE OSCAR'S RANCH NEAR SKILLET FALLS!
I KNEW OSCAR BRADY WELL! ALSO HIS SPITFIRE WARD, TERRY!

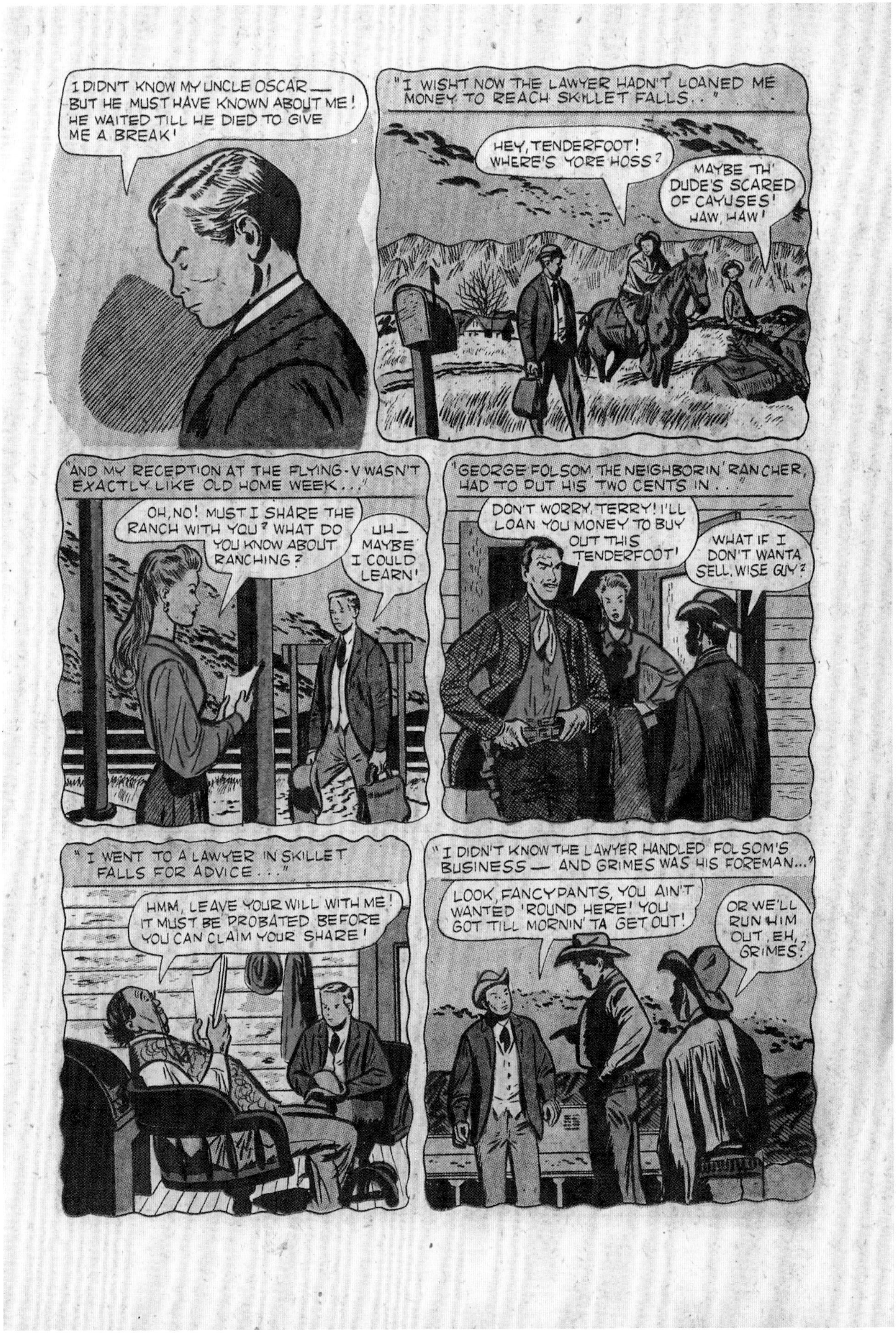
I DIDN'T KNOW MY UNCLE OSCAR— BUT HE MUST HAVE KNOWN ABOUT ME! HE WAITED TILL HE DIED TO GIVE ME A BREAK!
"I WISHT NOW THE LAWYER HADN'T LOANED ME MONEY TO REACH SKILLET FALLS.."
HEY, TENDERFOOT! WHERE'S YORE HOSS?
MAYBE TH' DUDE'S SCARED OF CAYUSES! HAW, HAW!
"AND MY RECEPTION AT THE FLYING-V WASN'T EXACTLY LIKE OLD HOME WEEK..."
OH, NO! MUST I SHARE THE RANCH WITH YOU? WHAT DO YOU KNOW ABOUT RANCHING?
UH— MAYBE I COULD LEARN!
"GEORGE FOLSOM, THE NEIGHBORIN' RANCHER, HAD TO PUT HIS TWO CENTS IN..."
DON'T WORRY, TERRY! I'LL LOAN YOU MONEY TO BUY OUT THIS TENDERFOOT!
WHAT IF I DON'T WANTA SELL, WISE GUY?
"I WENT TO A LAWYER IN SKILLET FALLS FOR ADVICE..."
HMM, LEAVE YOUR WILL WITH ME! IT MUST BE PROBATED BEFORE YOU CAN CLAIM YOUR SHARE!
"I DIDN'T KNOW THE LAWYER HANDLED FOLSOM'S BUSINESS— AND GRIMES WAS HIS FOREMAN..."
LOOK, FANCYPANTS, YOU AIN'T WANTED 'ROUND HERE! YOU GOT TILL MORNIN' TA GET OUT!
OR WE'LL RUN HIM OUT, EH, GRIMES?

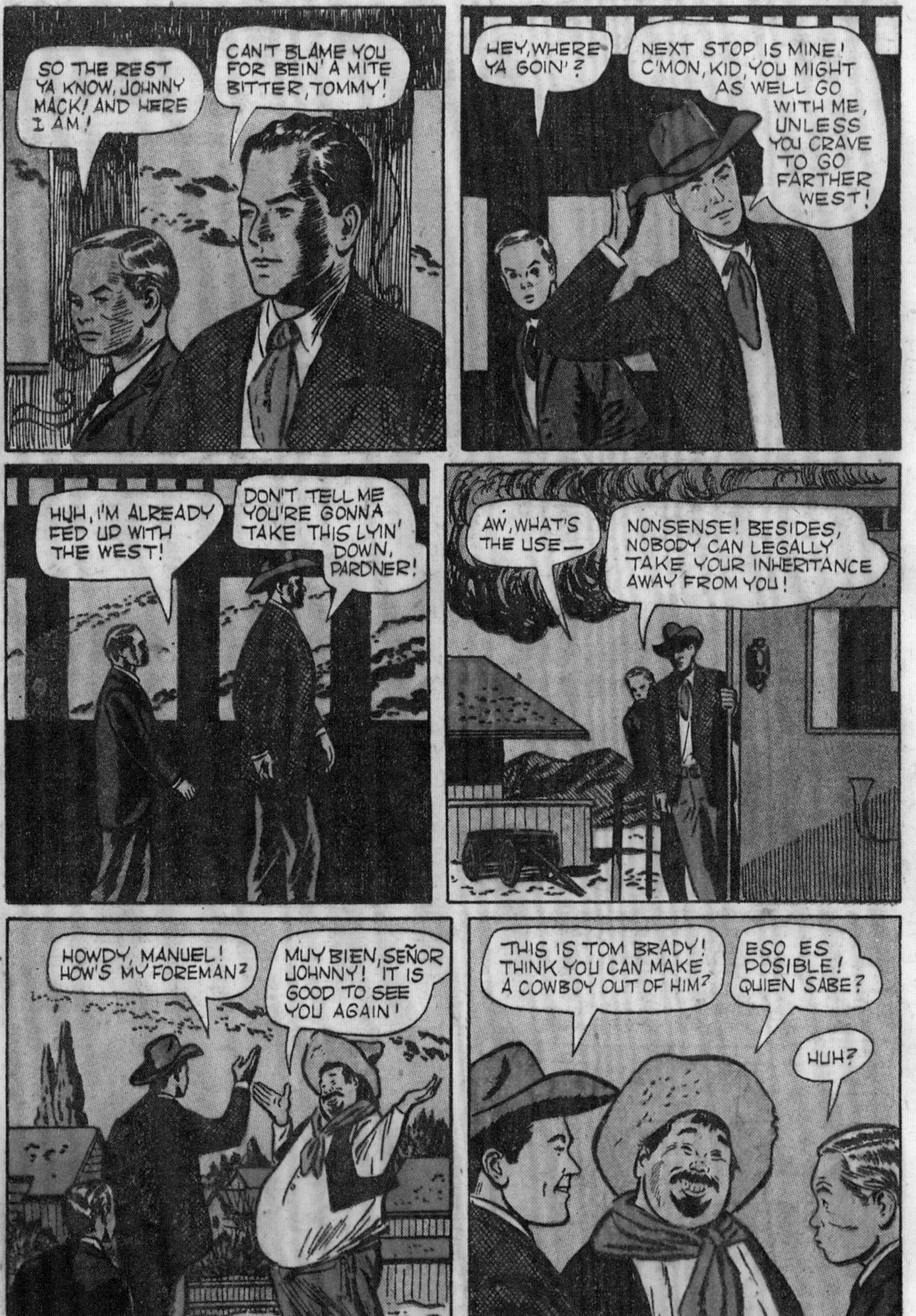
SO THE REST YA KNOW, JOHNNY MACK! AND HERE I AM!
CAN'T BLAME YOU FOR BEIN' A MITE BITTER, TOMMY!
HEY, WHERE YA GOIN'?
NEXT STOP IS MINE! C'MON, KID, YOU MIGHT AS WELL GO WITH ME, UNLESS YOU CRAVE TO GO FARTHER WEST!
HUH, I'M ALREADY FED UP WITH THE WEST!
DON'T TELL ME YOU'RE GONNA TAKE THIS LYIN' DOWN, PARDNER!
AW, WHAT'S THE USE—
NONSENSE! BESIDES, NOBODY CAN LEGALLY TAKE YOUR INHERITANCE AWAY FROM YOU!
HOWDY, MANUEL! HOW'S MY FOREMAN?
MUY BIEN, SEÑOR JOHNNY! IT IS GOOD TO SEE YOU AGAIN!
THIS IS TOM BRADY! THINK YOU CAN MAKE A COWBOY OUT OF HIM?
ESO ES POSIBLE! QUIEN SABE?
HUH?

WEEKS OF INTENSIVE TRAINING BEGIN FOR TOMMY AS JOHNNY MACK BROWN SLOWLY MOLDS THE RAW MATERIAL INTO A TRUE BUT RELUCTANT SON OF THE WEST— THE CURRICULUM INCLUDES RIDING...

REMEMBER WHAT I SAID NOW... HOLD THE REINS IN YOUR LEFT HAND!

AND SHOULD THE CABALLO BOLT, THEN YOU ARE READY FOR HIM!

THAT'S WHAT YOU SAY!

RODING...

FIRST OFF, TOMMY, THE PART IN MY LEFT HAND IS THE SPOKE, WHICH PASSES THROUGH THE EYELET, OR HONDA, TO FORM THE LOOP!

I SEE!

HOG-TYING...

THIS THREE-FOOT ROPE IS CALLED THE PIGGIN STRING! SLIP THE ROPE OVER ONE FORELEG AND MAKE A COUPLA TURNS AND HALF-HITCHES AROUND HIS HIND LEGS!

BRANDING...

BEFORE BRANDING THE CRITTER, ALWAYS SMACK THE IRON ON SOMETHING TO KNOCK OFF THE HOT COALS!

HERDING...

I'LL RIDE POINT WHILE YOU SHOO THESE FOOTSORE DRAGS ALONG!

WISHT I WAS ONLY FOOTSORE!

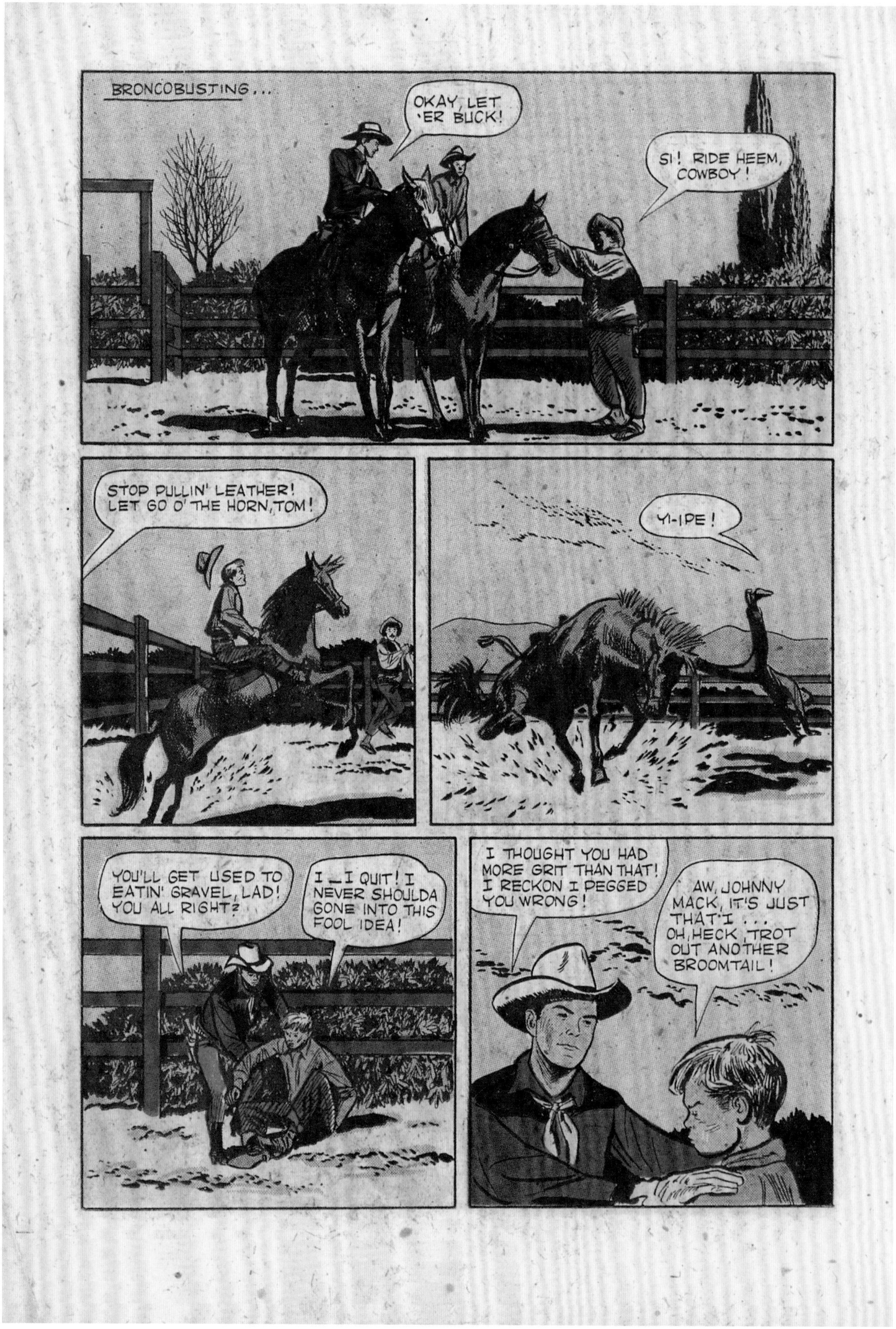
BRONCOBUSTING...
OKAY, LET 'ER BUCK!
SI! RIDE HEEM, COWBOY!
STOP PULLIN' LEATHER! LET GO O' THE HORN, TOM!
YI-IPE!
YOU'LL GET USED TO EATIN' GRAVEL, LAD! YOU ALL RIGHT?
I—I QUIT! I NEVER SHOULDA GONE INTO THIS FOOL IDEA!
I THOUGHT YOU HAD MORE GRIT THAN THAT! I RECKON I PEGGED YOU WRONG!
AW, JOHNNY MACK, IT'S JUST THAT I... OH, HECK, TROT OUT ANOTHER BROOMTAIL!

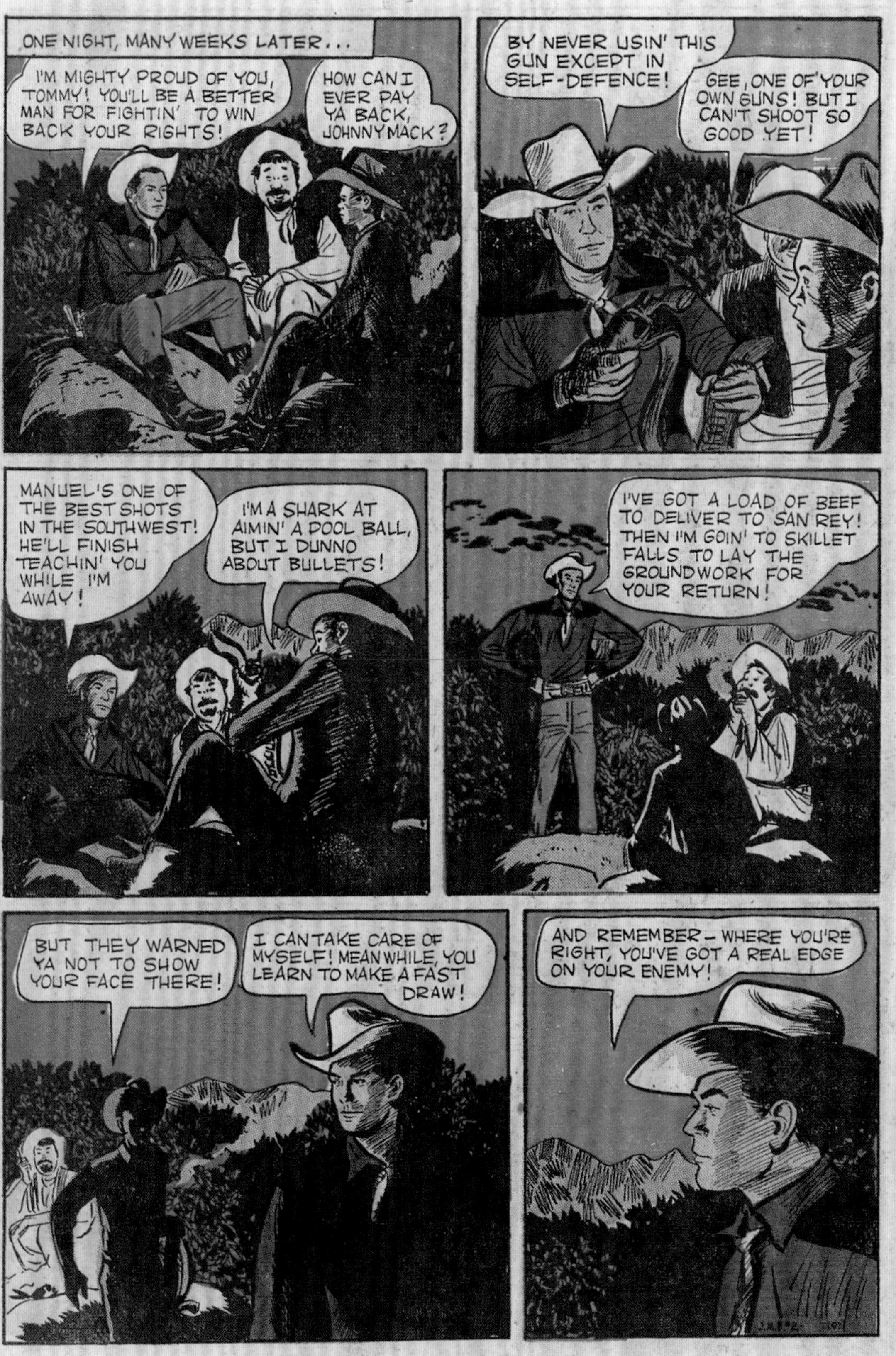
ONE NIGHT, MANY WEEKS LATER...
I'M MIGHTY PROUD OF YOU, TOMMY! YOU'LL BE A BETTER MAN FOR FIGHTIN' TO WIN BACK YOUR RIGHTS!
HOW CAN I EVER PAY YA BACK, JOHNNY MACK?
BY NEVER USIN' THIS GUN EXCEPT IN SELF-DEFENCE!
GEE, ONE OF YOUR OWN GUNS! BUT I CAN'T SHOOT SO GOOD YET!
MANUEL'S ONE OF THE BEST SHOTS IN THE SOUTHWEST! HE'LL FINISH TEACHIN' YOU WHILE I'M AWAY!
I'M A SHARK AT AIMIN' A POOL BALL, BUT I DUNNO ABOUT BULLETS!
I'VE GOT A LOAD OF BEEF TO DELIVER TO SAN REY! THEN I'M GOIN' TO SKILLET FALLS TO LAY THE GROUNDWORK FOR YOUR RETURN!
BUT THEY WARNED YA NOT TO SHOW YOUR FACE THERE!
I CAN TAKE CARE OF MYSELF! MEANWHILE, YOU LEARN TO MAKE A FAST DRAW!
AND REMEMBER - WHERE YOU'RE RIGHT, YOU'VE GOT A REAL EDGE ON YOUR ENEMY!

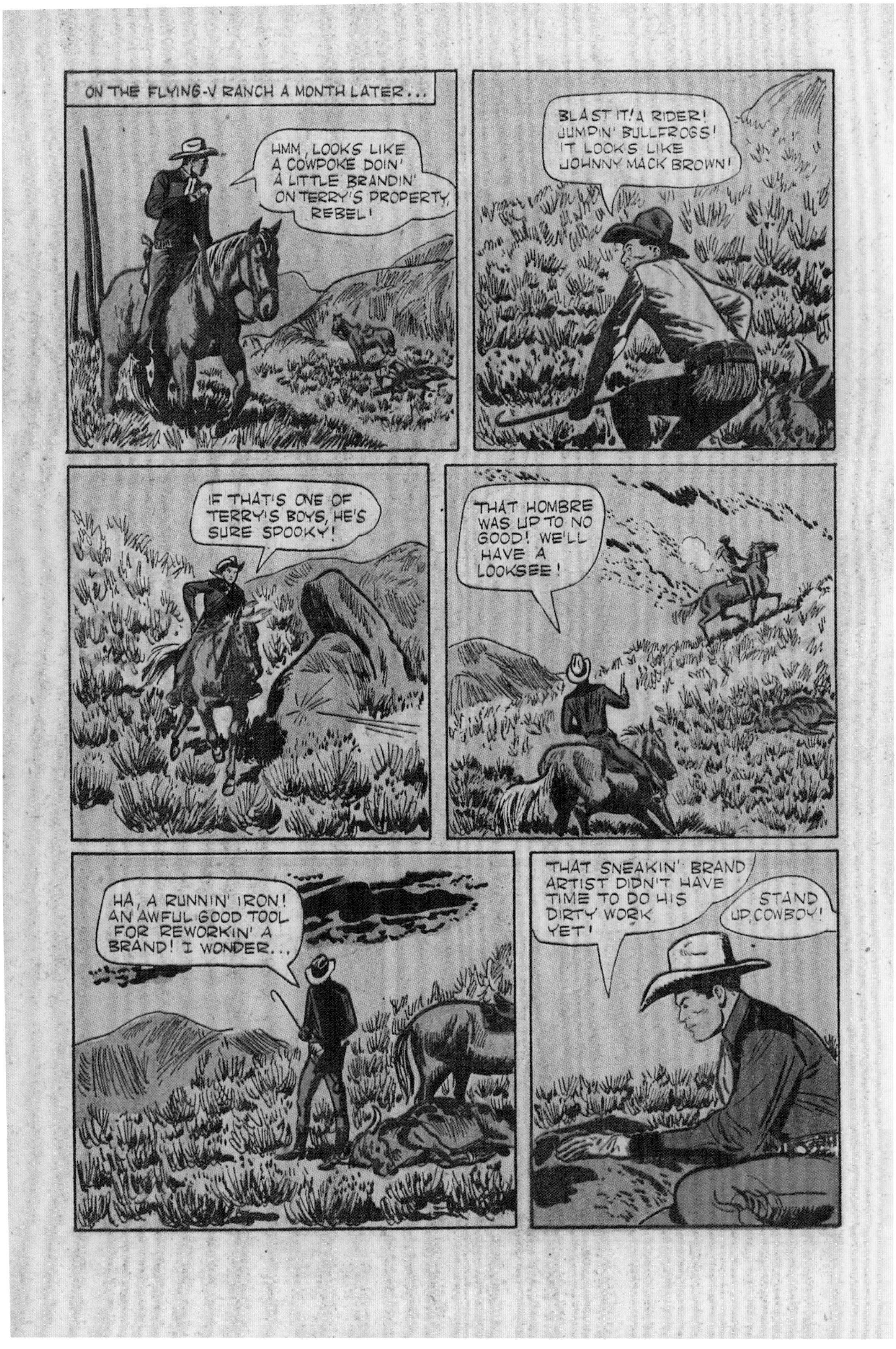
ON THE FLYING-V RANCH A MONTH LATER...
HMM, LOOKS LIKE A COWPOKE DOIN' A LITTLE BRANDIN' ON TERRY'S PROPERTY, REBEL!
BLAST IT! A RIDER! JUMPIN' BULLFROGS! IT LOOKS LIKE JOHNNY MACK BROWN!
IF THAT'S ONE OF TERRY'S BOYS, HE'S SURE SPOOKY!
THAT HOMBRE WAS UP TO NO GOOD! WE'LL HAVE A LOOKSEE!
HA, A RUNNIN' IRON! AN AWFUL GOOD TOOL FOR REWORKIN' A BRAND! I WONDER...
THAT SNEAKIN' BRAND ARTIST DIDN'T HAVE TIME TO DO HIS DIRTY WORK YET!
STAND UP, COWBOY!

CAUGHT YOU WITH THE GOODS, EH, RUSTLER?
HUH?
WHY, JOHNNY MACK BROWN! WHAT ARE YOU DOING HERE?
H'LO, TERRY! IF YOUR PAL HERE CAN READ SIGNS, HE'LL FIND THE TRACKS OF THE RUSTLER WHO FOGGED IT EAST!
IF BROWN'LL SEE YOU TO TOWN, I'LL PICK UP THE RUSTLER'S TRAIL!
I DON'T UNDERSTAND IT, JOHNNY! SINCE OSCAR BRADY DIED, I'VE BEEN LOSING CATTLE RIGHT AND LEFT!
YOU NEED SOMEBODY TO HELP YOU RUN THE SPREAD, TERRY!
THAT'S WHAT GEORGE FOLSOM SAYS, BUT I'M NOT READY TO MERGE OUR, UH, INTERESTS YET!
DID YOUR GUARDIAN LEAVE THE RANCH TO YOU?
NO, HE LEFT HALF TO A CITY NEPHEW— A NO-ACCOUNT, YOUNG SCALAWAG WHO KNOWS NOTHING ABOUT RANCHING!
A TENDERFOOT, EH? WHERE IS HE?

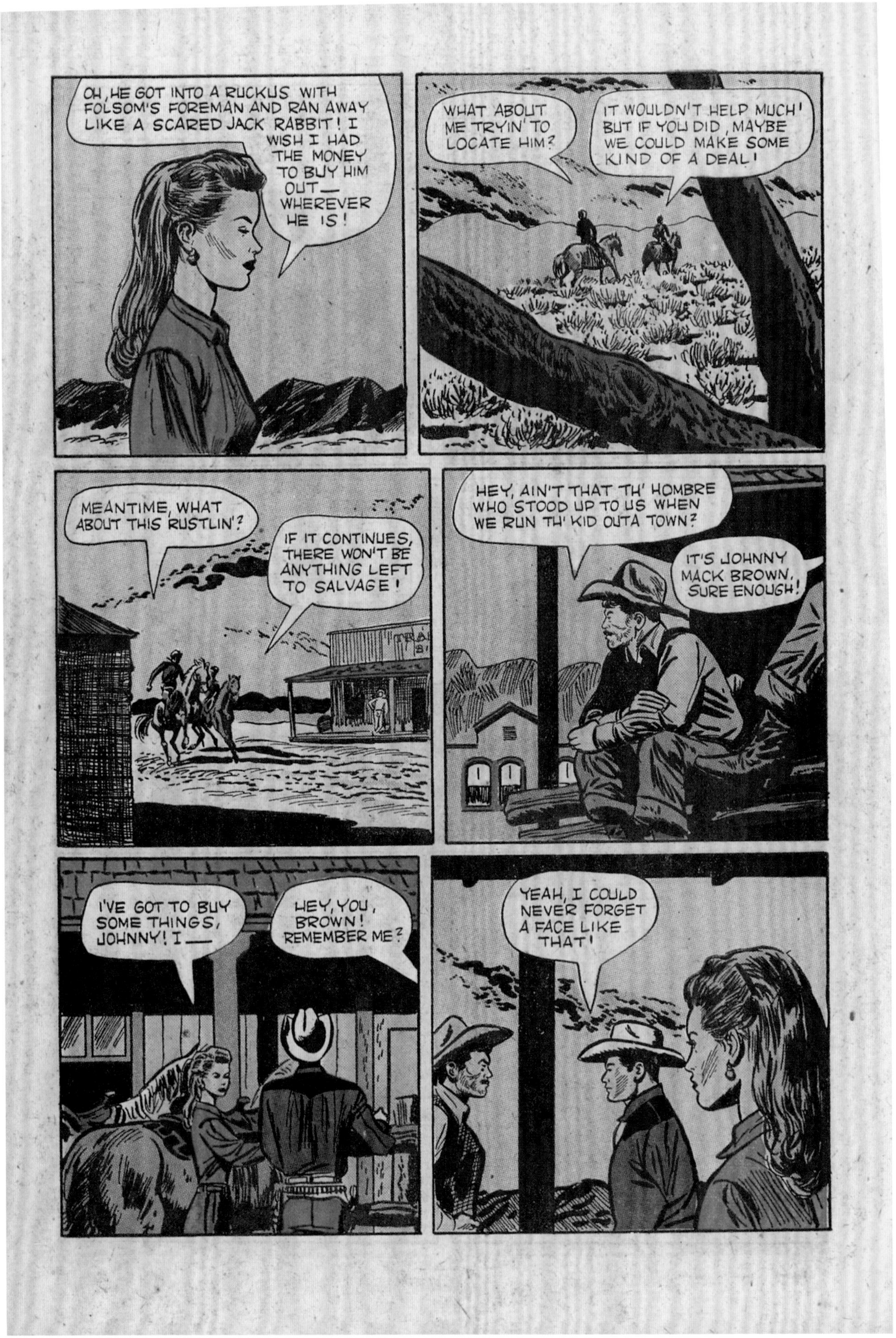
OH, HE GOT INTO A RUCKUS WITH FOLSOM'S FOREMAN AND RAN AWAY LIKE A SCARED JACK RABBIT! I WISH I HAD THE MONEY TO BUY HIM OUT— WHEREVER HE IS!
WHAT ABOUT ME TRYIN' TO LOCATE HIM?
IT WOULDN'T HELP MUCH! BUT IF YOU DID, MAYBE WE COULD MAKE SOME KIND OF A DEAL!
MEANTIME, WHAT ABOUT THIS RUSTLIN'?
IF IT CONTINUES, THERE WON'T BE ANYTHING LEFT TO SALVAGE!
HEY, AIN'T THAT TH' HOMBRE WHO STOOD UP TO US WHEN WE RUN TH' KID OUTA TOWN?
IT'S JOHNNY MACK BROWN, SURE ENOUGH!
I'VE GOT TO BUY SOME THINGS, JOHNNY! I—
HEY, YOU, BROWN! REMEMBER ME?
YEAH, I COULD NEVER FORGET A FACE LIKE THAT!

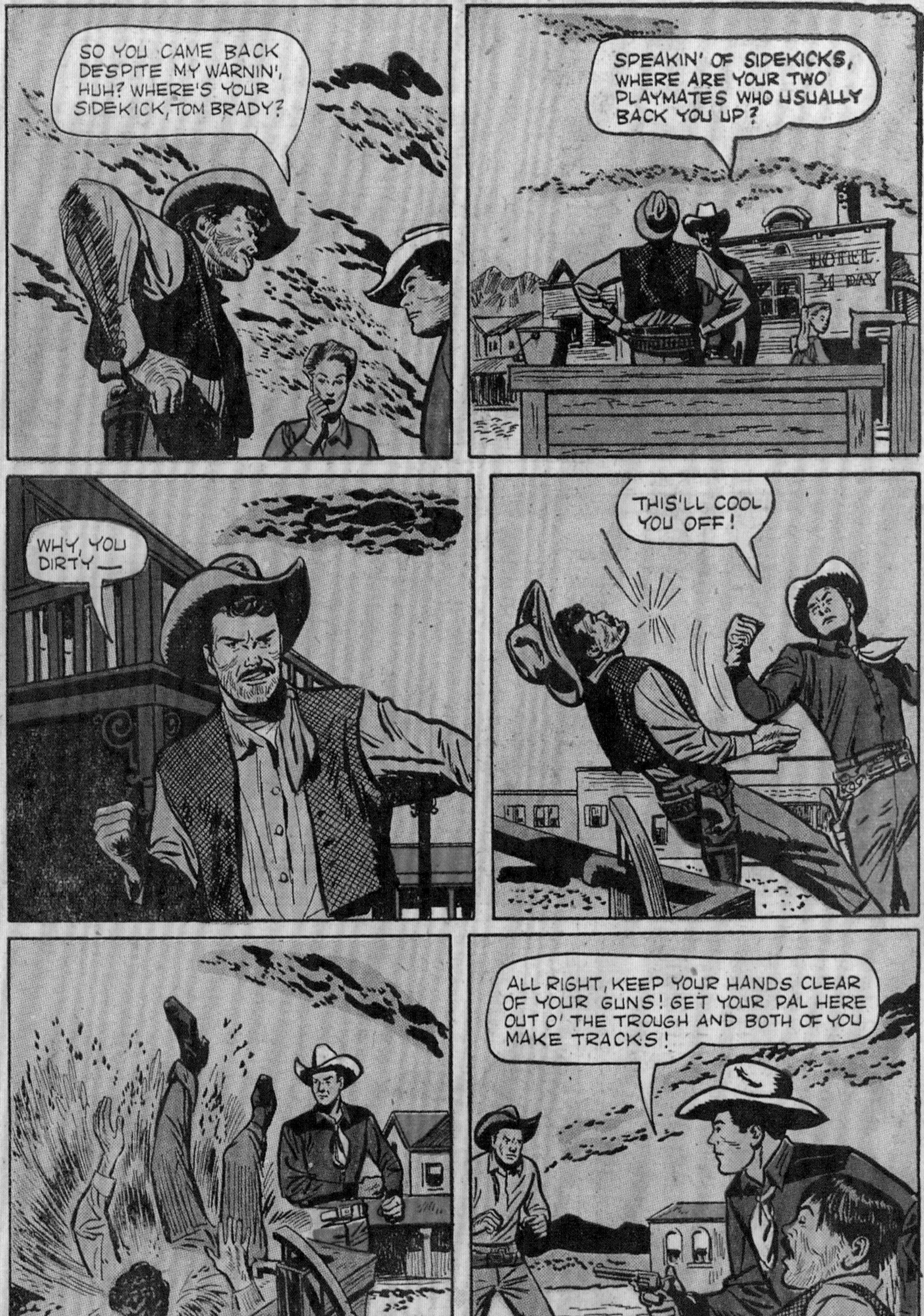
SO YOU CAME BACK DESPITE MY WARNIN', HUH? WHERE'S YOUR SIDEKICK, TOM BRADY?
SPEAKIN' OF SIDEKICKS, WHERE ARE YOUR TWO PLAYMATES WHO USUALLY BACK YOU UP?
HOTEL
WHY, YOU DIRTY—
THIS'LL COOL YOU OFF!
ALL RIGHT, KEEP YOUR HANDS CLEAR OF YOUR GUNS! GET YOUR PAL HERE OUT O' THE TROUGH AND BOTH OF YOU MAKE TRACKS!

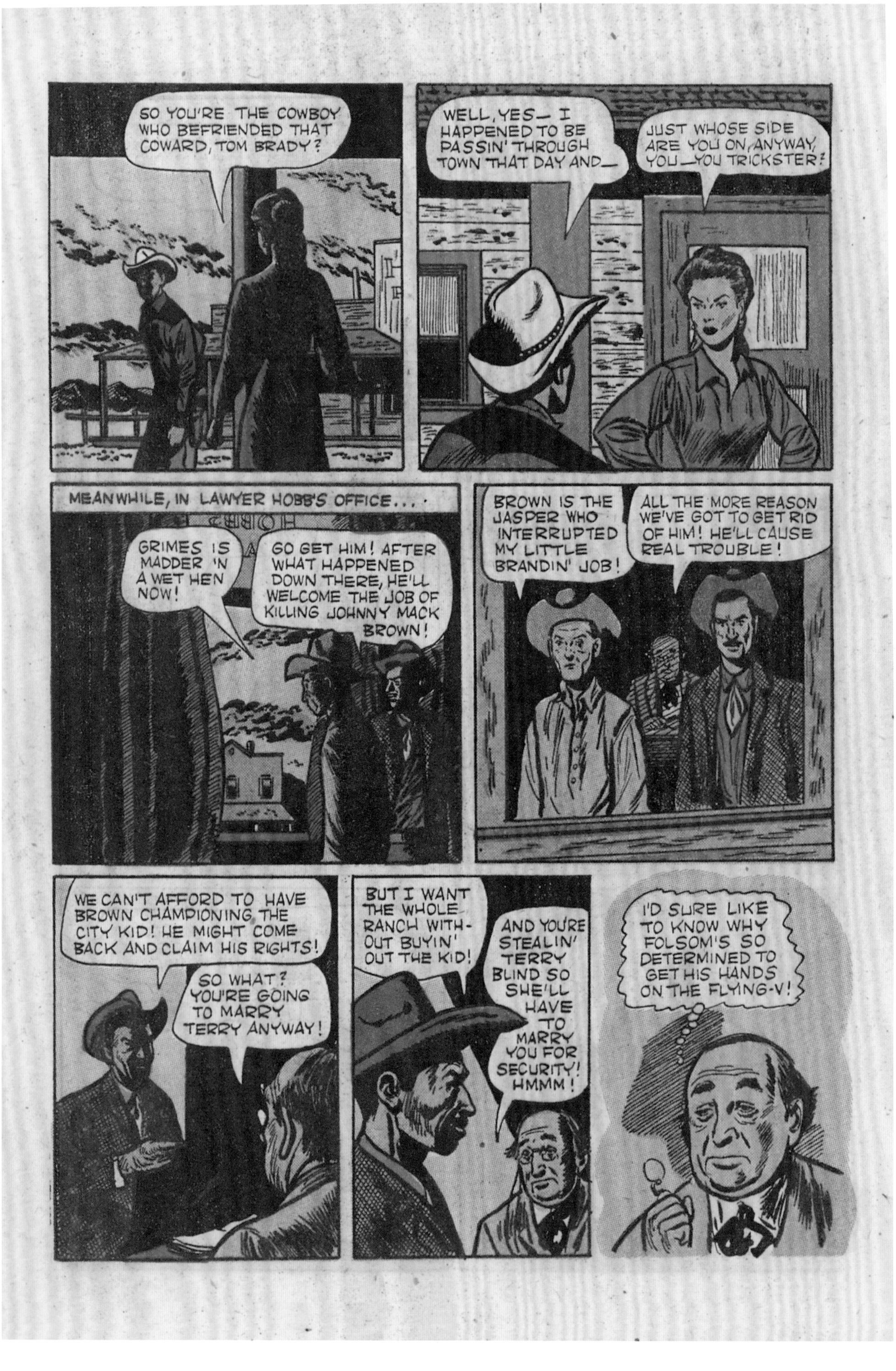
SO YOU'RE THE COWBOY WHO BEFRIENDED THAT COWARD, TOM BRADY?
WELL, YES— I HAPPENED TO BE PASSIN' THROUGH TOWN THAT DAY AND—
JUST WHOSE SIDE ARE YOU ON, ANYWAY, YOU—YOU TRICKSTER?
MEANWHILE, IN LAWYER HOBB'S OFFICE...
GRIMES IS MADDER 'N A WET HEN NOW!
GO GET HIM! AFTER WHAT HAPPENED DOWN THERE, HE'LL WELCOME THE JOB OF KILLING JOHNNY MACK BROWN!
BROWN IS THE JASPER WHO INTERRUPTED MY LITTLE BRANDIN' JOB!
ALL THE MORE REASON WE'VE GOT TO GET RID OF HIM! HE'LL CAUSE REAL TROUBLE!
WE CAN'T AFFORD TO HAVE BROWN CHAMPIONING THE CITY KID! HE MIGHT COME BACK AND CLAIM HIS RIGHTS!
SO WHAT? YOU'RE GOING TO MARRY TERRY ANYWAY!
BUT I WANT THE WHOLE RANCH WITH-OUT BUYIN' OUT THE KID!
AND YOU'RE STEALIN' TERRY BLIND SO SHE'LL HAVE TO MARRY YOU FOR SECURITY! HMMM!
I'D SURE LIKE TO KNOW WHY FOLSOM'S SO DETERMINED TO GET HIS HANDS ON THE FLYING-V!

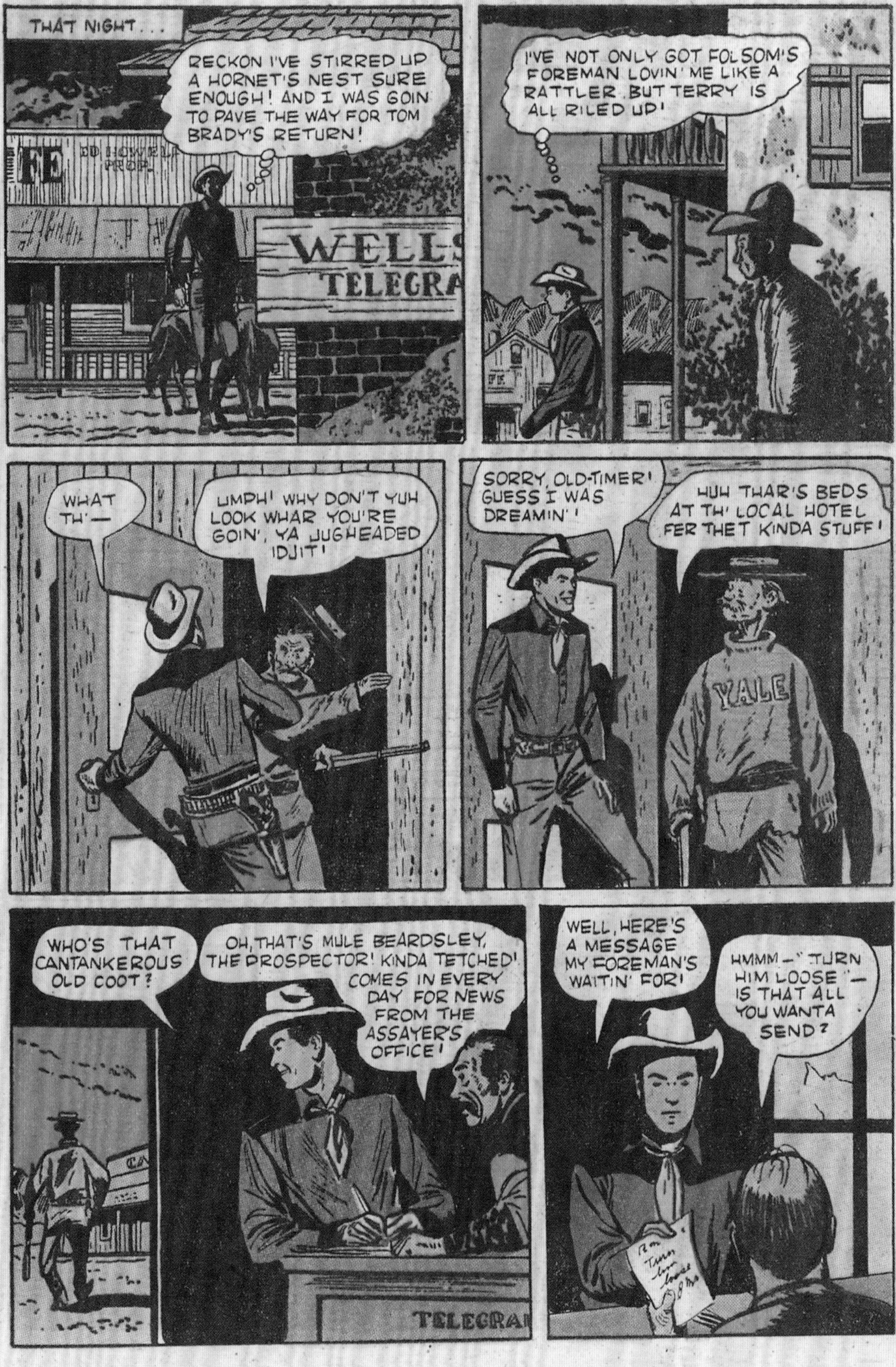
THAT NIGHT...
RECKON I'VE STIRRED UP A HORNET'S NEST SURE ENOUGH! AND I WAS GOIN TO PAVE THE WAY FOR TOM BRADY'S RETURN!
WELLS
TELEGRA
I'VE NOT ONLY GOT FOLSOM'S FOREMAN LOVIN' ME LIKE A RATTLER, BUT TERRY IS ALL RILED UP!
WHAT TH'—
UMPH! WHY DON'T YUH LOOK WHAR YOU'RE GOIN', YA JUGHEADED IDJIT!
SORRY, OLD-TIMER! GUESS I WAS DREAMIN'!
HUH THAR'S BEDS AT TH' LOCAL HOTEL FER THET KINDA STUFF!
YALE
WHO'S THAT CANTANKEROUS OLD COOT?
OH, THAT'S MULE BEARDSLEY, THE PROSPECTOR! KINDA TETCHED! COMES IN EVERY DAY FOR NEWS FROM THE ASSAYER'S OFFICE!
TELEGRA
WELL, HERE'S A MESSAGE MY FOREMAN'S WAITIN' FOR!
HMMM—"TURN HIM LOOSE"—IS THAT ALL YOU WANTA SEND?

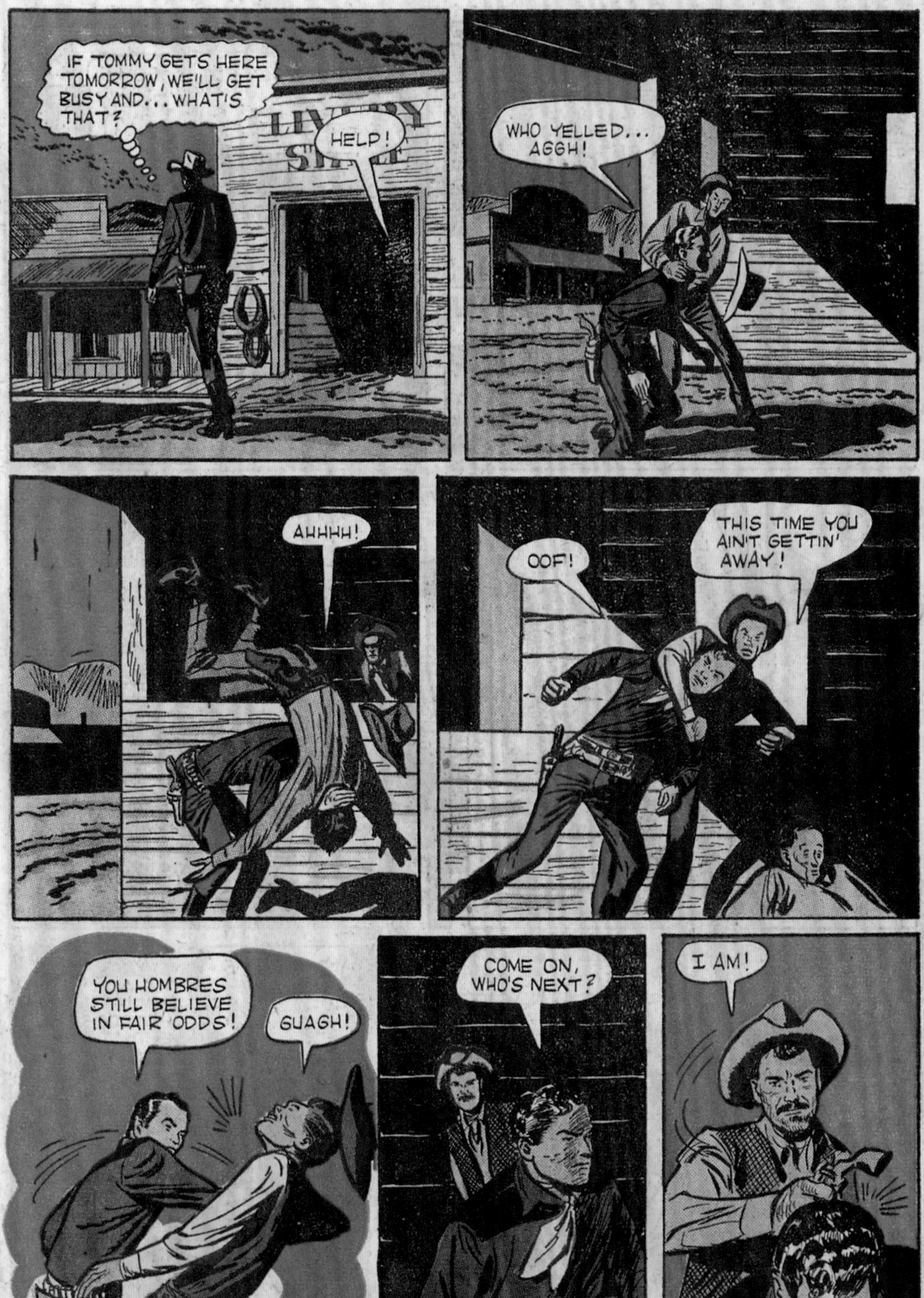
IF TOMMY GETS HERE TOMORROW, WE'LL GET BUSY AND... WHAT'S THAT?
HELP!
WHO YELLED... AGGH!
AHHHH!
OOF!
THIS TIME YOU AIN'T GETTIN' AWAY!
YOU HOMBRES STILL BELIEVE IN FAIR ODDS!
GUAGH!
COME ON, WHO'S NEXT?
I AM!

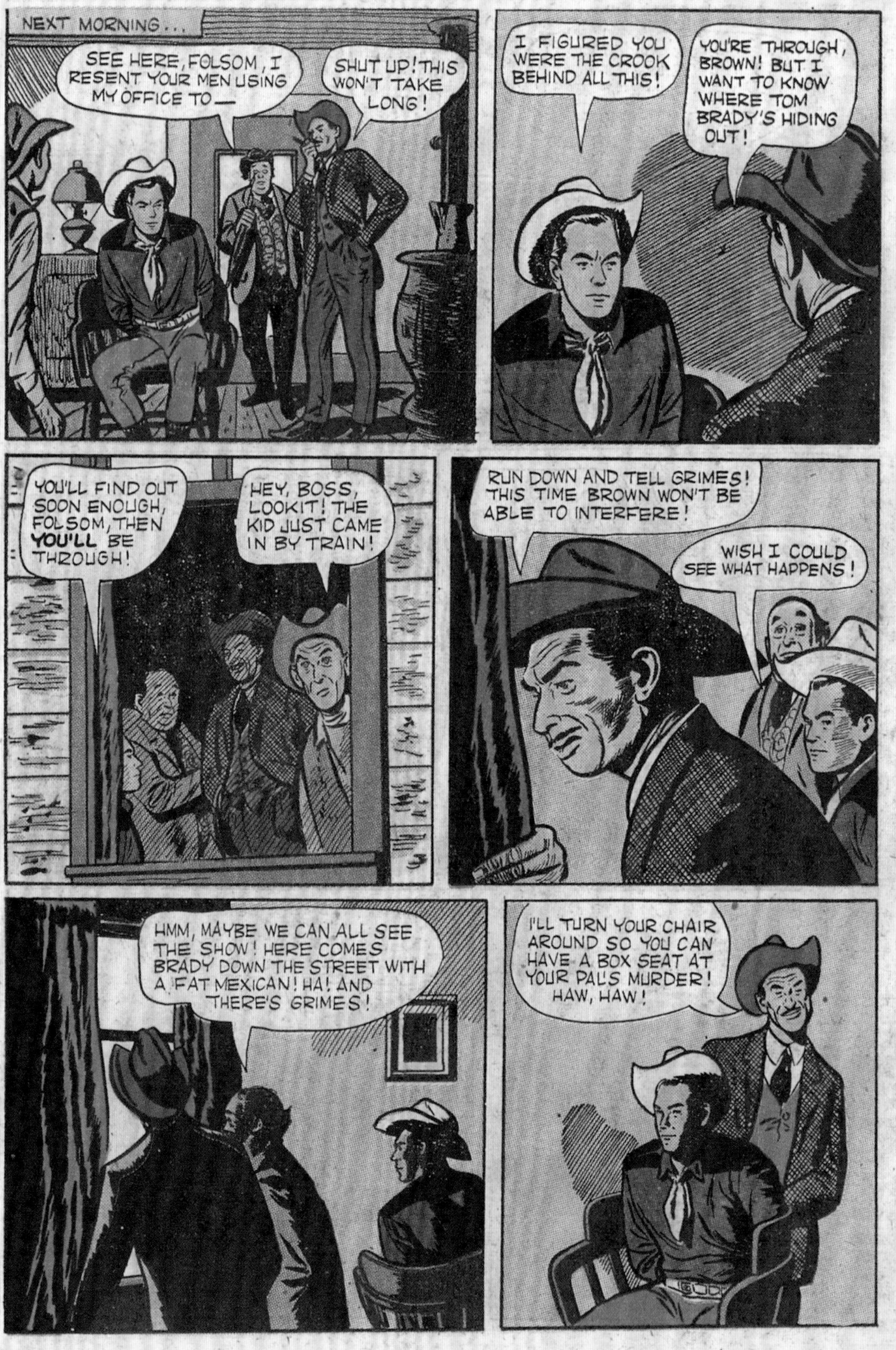
NEXT MORNING...
SEE HERE, FOLSOM, I RESENT YOUR MEN USING MY OFFICE TO—
SHUT UP! THIS WON'T TAKE LONG!
I FIGURED YOU WERE THE CROOK BEHIND ALL THIS!
YOU'RE THROUGH, BROWN! BUT I WANT TO KNOW WHERE TOM BRADY'S HIDING OUT!
YOU'LL FIND OUT SOON ENOUGH, FOLSOM, THEN **YOU'LL** BE THROUGH!
HEY, BOSS, LOOKIT! THE KID JUST CAME IN BY TRAIN!
RUN DOWN AND TELL GRIMES! THIS TIME BROWN WON'T BE ABLE TO INTERFERE!
WISH I COULD SEE WHAT HAPPENS!
HMM, MAYBE WE CAN ALL SEE THE SHOW! HERE COMES BRADY DOWN THE STREET WITH A FAT MEXICAN! HA! AND THERE'S GRIMES!
I'LL TURN YOUR CHAIR AROUND SO YOU CAN HAVE A BOX SEAT AT YOUR PAL'S MURDER! HAW, HAW!

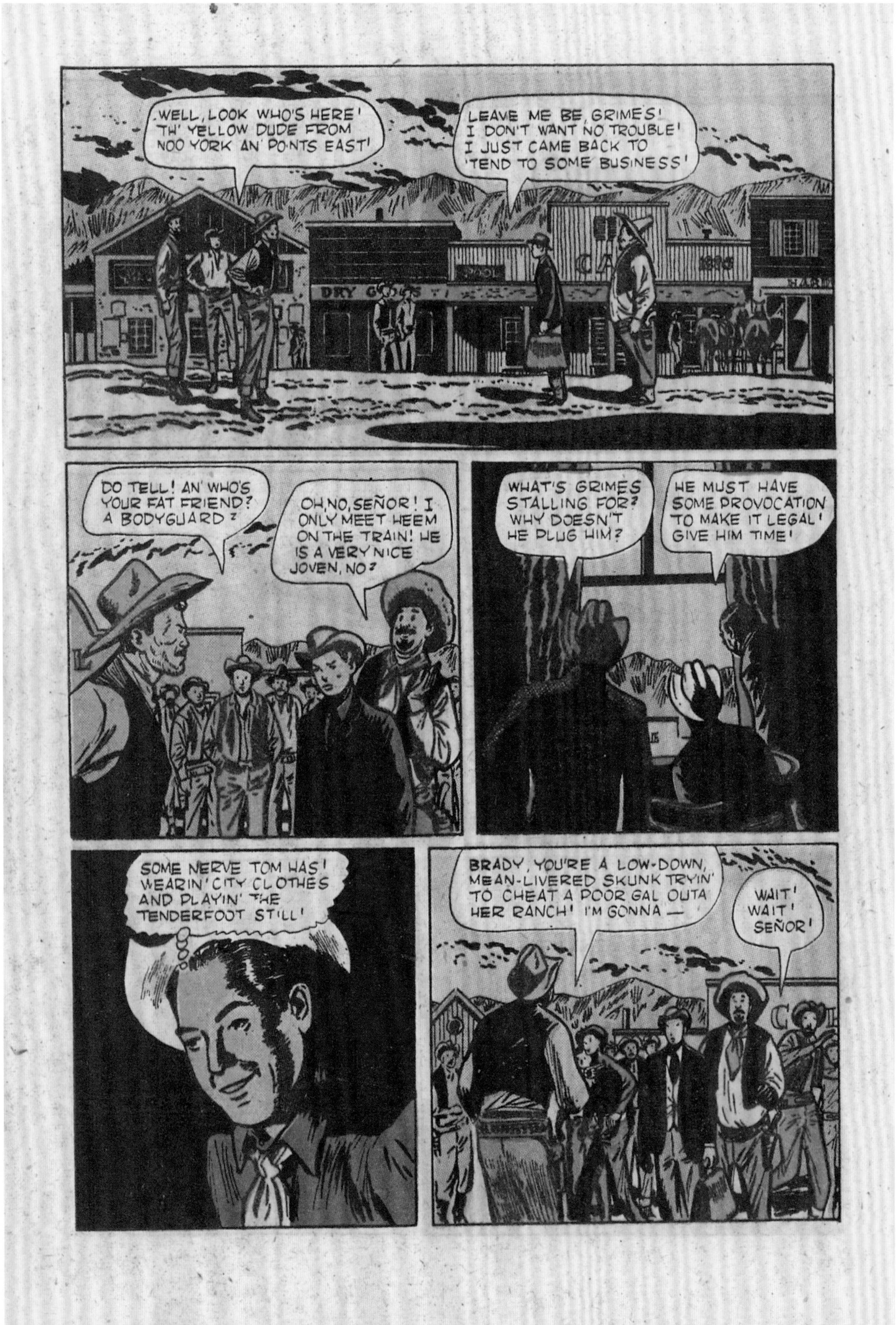
WELL, LOOK WHO'S HERE! TH' YELLOW DUDE FROM NOO YORK AN' POINTS EAST!
LEAVE ME BE, GRIMES! I DON'T WANT NO TROUBLE! I JUST CAME BACK TO 'TEND TO SOME BUSINESS!
DRY GOODS
POOL
DO TELL! AN' WHO'S YOUR FAT FRIEND? A BODYGUARD?
OH, NO, SEÑOR! I ONLY MEET HEEM ON THE TRAIN! HE IS A VERY NICE JOVEN, NO?
WHAT'S GRIMES STALLING FOR? WHY DOESN'T HE PLUG HIM?
HE MUST HAVE SOME PROVOCATION TO MAKE IT LEGAL! GIVE HIM TIME!
SOME NERVE TOM HAS! WEARIN' CITY CLOTHES AND PLAYIN' THE TENDERFOOT STILL!
BRADY, YOU'RE A LOW-DOWN, MEAN-LIVERED SKUNK TRYIN' TO CHEAT A POOR GAL OUTA HER RANCH! I'M GONNA —
WAIT! WAIT! SEÑOR!

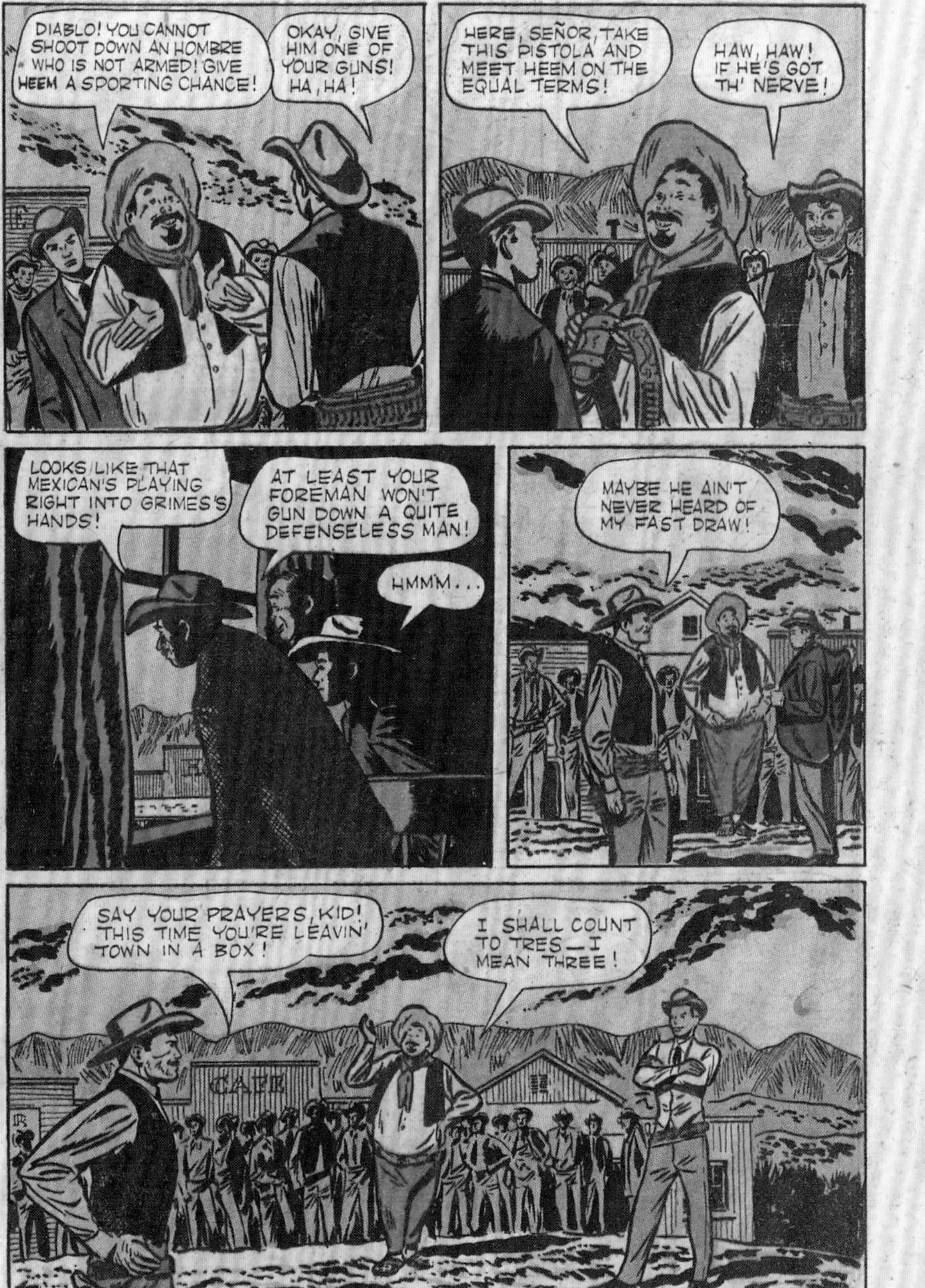
DIABLO! YOU CANNOT SHOOT DOWN AN HOMBRE WHO IS NOT ARMED! GIVE HEEM A SPORTING CHANCE!
OKAY, GIVE HIM ONE OF YOUR GUNS! HA, HA!
HERE, SEÑOR, TAKE THIS PISTOLA AND MEET HEEM ON THE EQUAL TERMS!
HAW, HAW! IF HE'S GOT TH' NERVE!
LOOKS LIKE THAT MEXICAN'S PLAYING RIGHT INTO GRIMES'S HANDS!
AT LEAST YOUR FOREMAN WON'T GUN DOWN A QUITE DEFENSELESS MAN!
HMMM...
MAYBE HE AIN'T NEVER HEARD OF MY FAST DRAW!
SAY YOUR PRAYERS, KID! THIS TIME YOU'RE LEAVIN' TOWN IN A BOX!
I SHALL COUNT TO TRES—I MEAN THREE!
CAFE

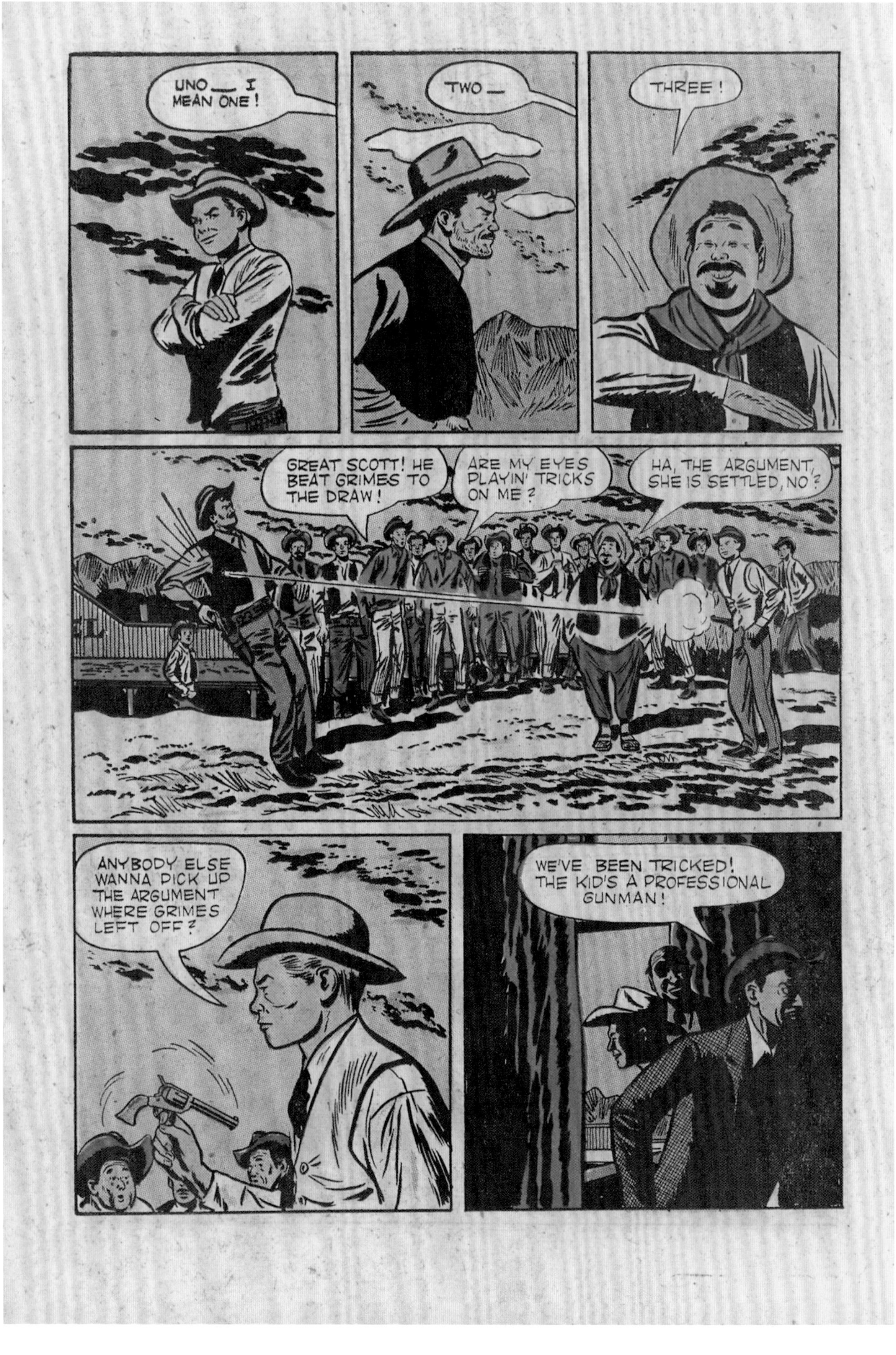
UNO — I MEAN ONE!
TWO —
THREE!
GREAT SCOTT! HE BEAT GRIMES TO THE DRAW!
ARE MY EYES PLAYIN' TRICKS ON ME?
HA, THE ARGUMENT, SHE IS SETTLED, NO?
ANYBODY ELSE WANNA PICK UP THE ARGUMENT WHERE GRIMES LEFT OFF?
WE'VE BEEN TRICKED! THE KID'S A PROFESSIONAL GUNMAN!

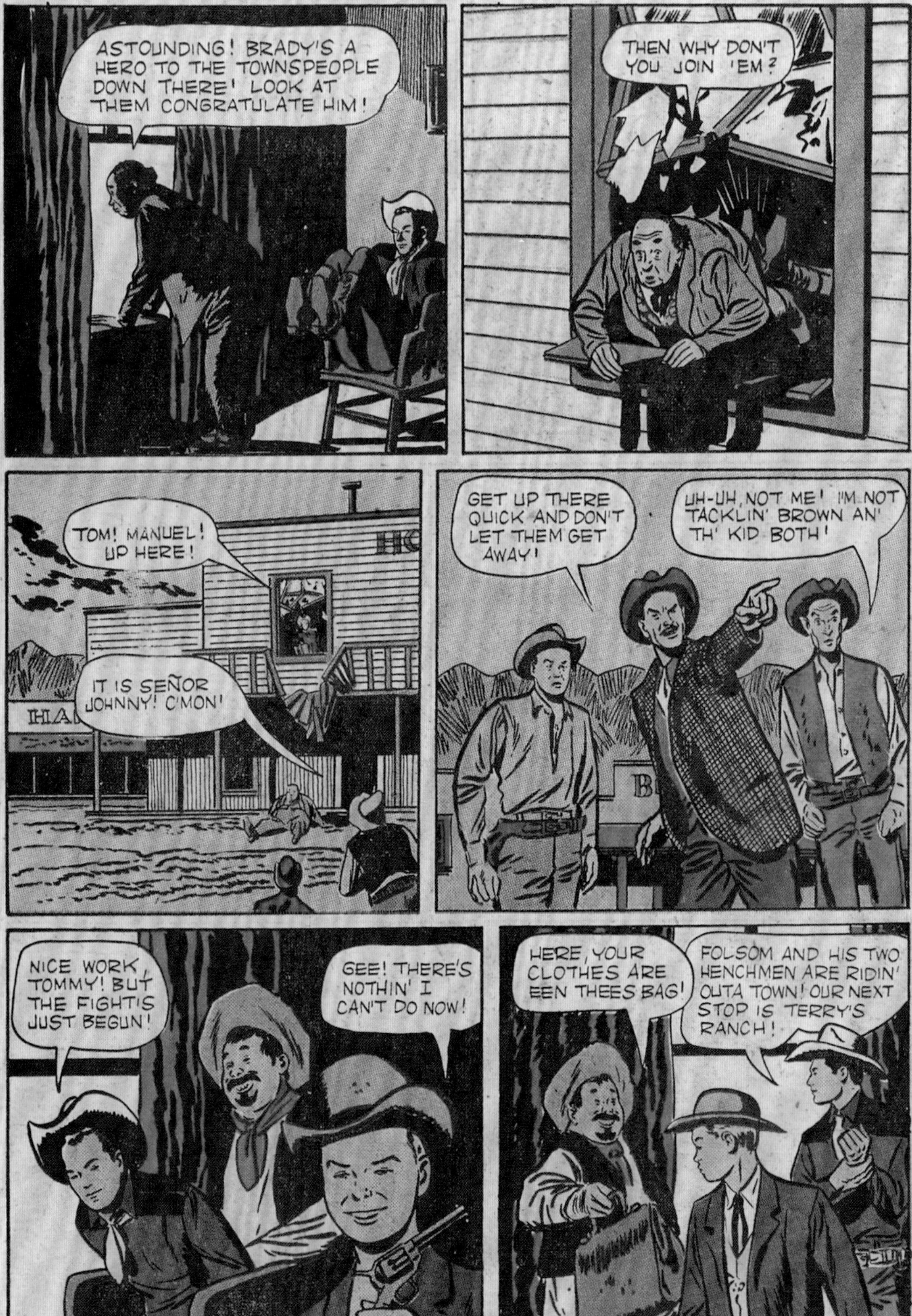
ASTOUNDING! BRADY'S A HERO TO THE TOWNSPEOPLE DOWN THERE! LOOK AT THEM CONGRATULATE HIM!
THEN WHY DON'T YOU JOIN 'EM?
TOM! MANUEL! UP HERE!
IT IS SEÑOR JOHNNY! C'MON!
GET UP THERE QUICK AND DON'T LET THEM GET AWAY!
UH-UH, NOT ME! I'M NOT TACKLIN' BROWN AN' TH' KID BOTH!
NICE WORK, TOMMY! BUT THE FIGHT IS JUST BEGUN!
GEE! THERE'S NOTHIN' I CAN'T DO NOW!
HERE, YOUR CLOTHES ARE EEN THEES BAG!
FOLSOM AND HIS TWO HENCHMEN ARE RIDIN' OUTA TOWN! OUR NEXT STOP IS TERRY'S RANCH!

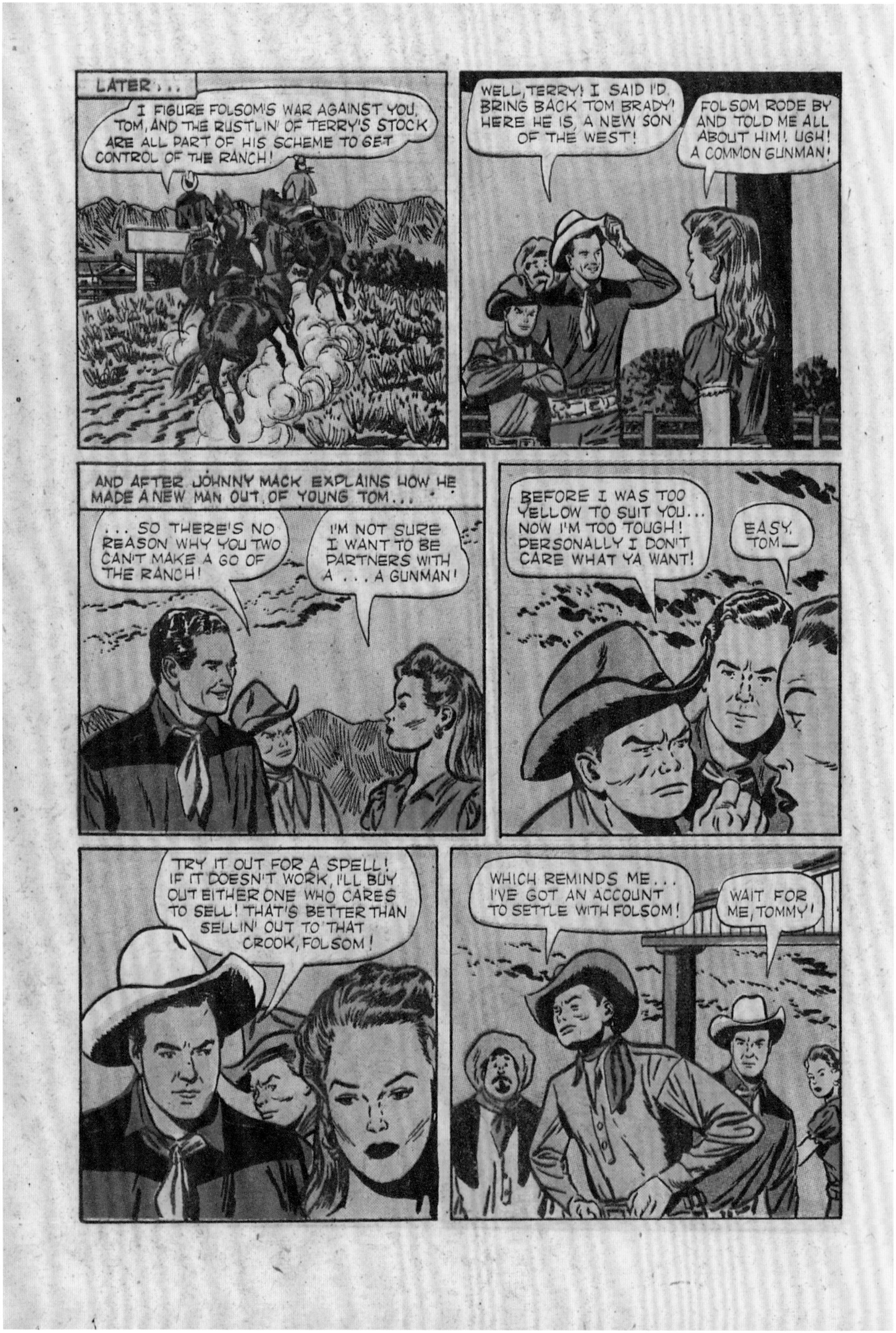
LATER...
I FIGURE FOLSOM'S WAR AGAINST YOU, TOM, AND THE RUSTLIN' OF TERRY'S STOCK ARE ALL PART OF HIS SCHEME TO GET CONTROL OF THE RANCH!
WELL, TERRY! I SAID I'D BRING BACK TOM BRADY! HERE HE IS, A NEW SON OF THE WEST!
FOLSOM RODE BY AND TOLD ME ALL ABOUT HIM! UGH! A COMMON GUNMAN!
AND AFTER JOHNNY MACK EXPLAINS HOW HE MADE A NEW MAN OUT OF YOUNG TOM...
... SO THERE'S NO REASON WHY YOU TWO CAN'T MAKE A GO OF THE RANCH!
I'M NOT SURE I WANT TO BE PARTNERS WITH A . . . A GUNMAN!
BEFORE I WAS TOO YELLOW TO SUIT YOU... NOW I'M TOO TOUGH! PERSONALLY I DON'T CARE WHAT YA WANT!
EASY, TOM—
TRY IT OUT FOR A SPELL! IF IT DOESN'T WORK, I'LL BUY OUT EITHER ONE WHO CARES TO SELL! THAT'S BETTER THAN SELLIN' OUT TO THAT CROOK, FOLSOM!
WHICH REMINDS ME... I'VE GOT AN ACCOUNT TO SETTLE WITH FOLSOM!
WAIT FOR ME, TOMMY!

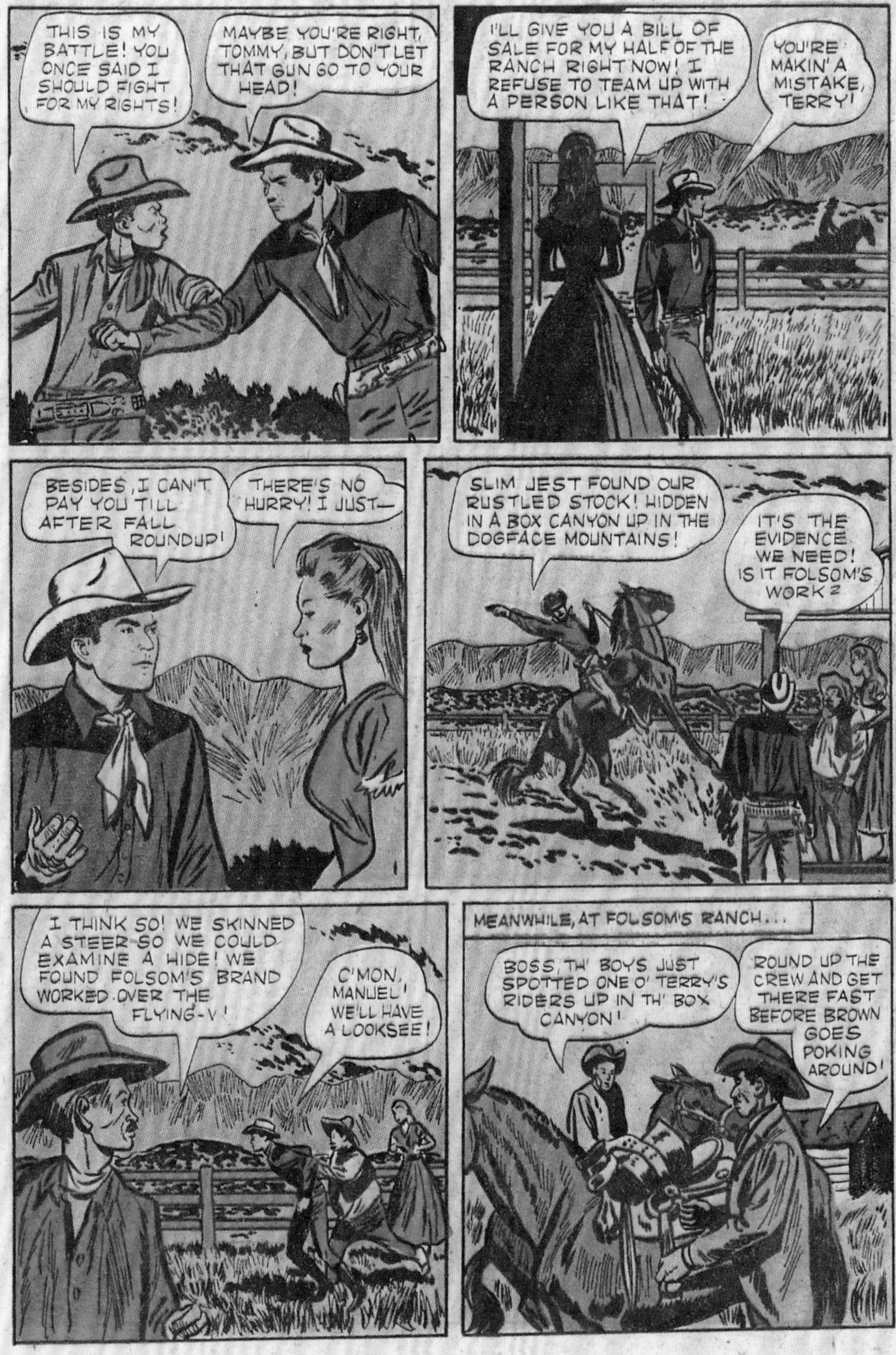
THIS IS MY BATTLE! YOU ONCE SAID I SHOULD FIGHT FOR MY RIGHTS!
MAYBE YOU'RE RIGHT, TOMMY, BUT DON'T LET THAT GUN GO TO YOUR HEAD!
I'LL GIVE YOU A BILL OF SALE FOR MY HALF OF THE RANCH RIGHT NOW! I REFUSE TO TEAM UP WITH A PERSON LIKE THAT!
YOU'RE MAKIN' A MISTAKE, TERRY!
BESIDES, I CAN'T PAY YOU TILL AFTER FALL ROUNDUP!
THERE'S NO HURRY! I JUST—
SLIM JEST FOUND OUR RUSTLED STOCK! HIDDEN IN A BOX CANYON UP IN THE DOGFACE MOUNTAINS!
IT'S THE EVIDENCE WE NEED! IS IT FOLSOM'S WORK?
I THINK SO! WE SKINNED A STEER SO WE COULD EXAMINE A HIDE! WE FOUND FOLSOM'S BRAND WORKED OVER THE FLYING-V!
C'MON, MANUEL! WE'LL HAVE A LOOKSEE!
MEANWHILE, AT FOLSOM'S RANCH...
BOSS, TH' BOYS JUST SPOTTED ONE O' TERRY'S RIDERS UP IN TH' BOX CANYON!
ROUND UP THE CREW AND GET THERE FAST BEFORE BROWN GOES POKING AROUND!

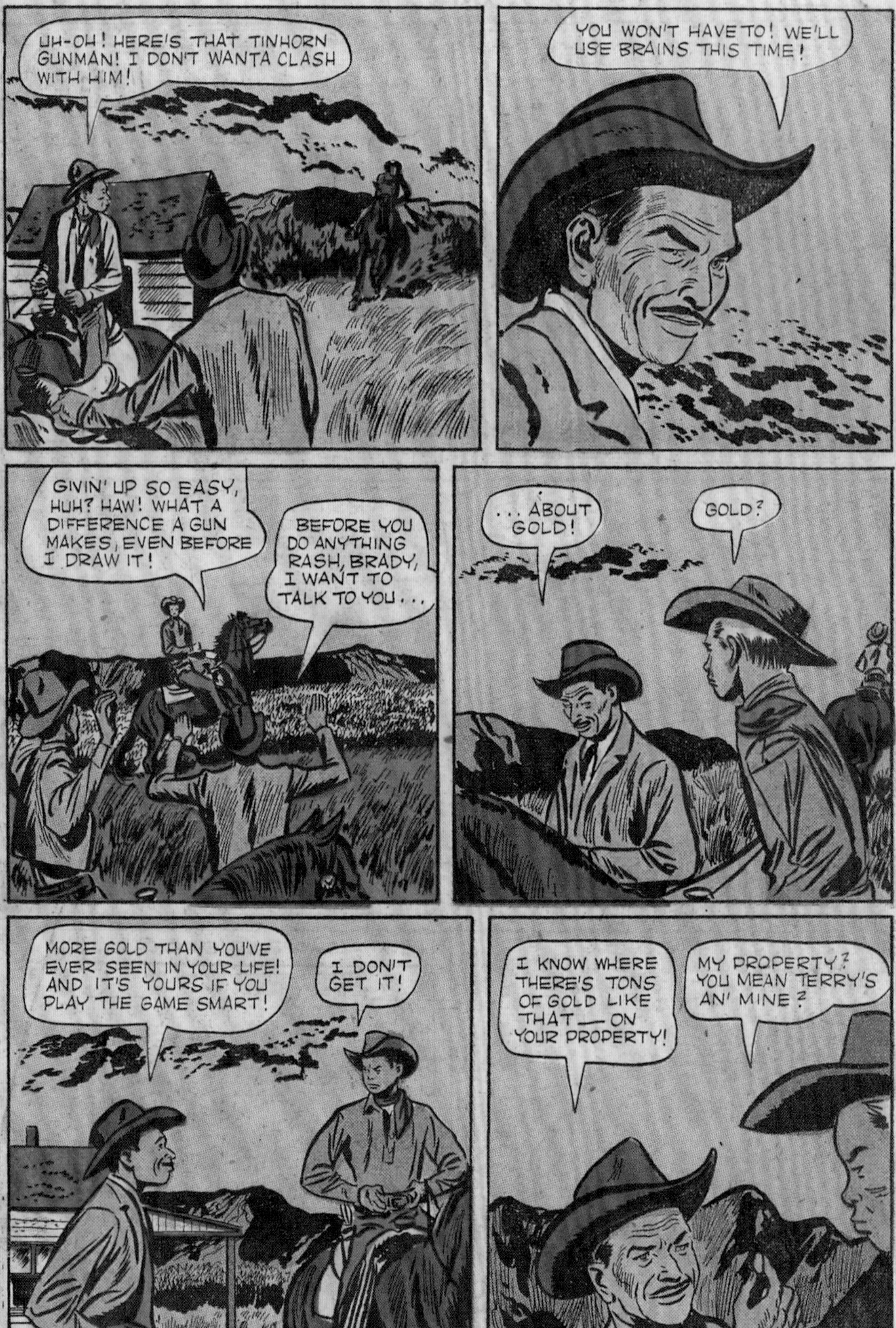
UH-OH! HERE'S THAT TINHORN GUNMAN! I DON'T WANTA CLASH WITH HIM!
YOU WON'T HAVE TO! WE'LL USE BRAINS THIS TIME!
GIVIN' UP SO EASY, HUH? HAW! WHAT A DIFFERENCE A GUN MAKES, EVEN BEFORE I DRAW IT!
BEFORE YOU DO ANYTHING RASH, BRADY, I WANT TO TALK TO YOU...
... ABOUT GOLD!
GOLD?
MORE GOLD THAN YOU'VE EVER SEEN IN YOUR LIFE! AND IT'S YOURS IF YOU PLAY THE GAME SMART!
I DON'T GET IT!
I KNOW WHERE THERE'S TONS OF GOLD LIKE THAT — ON YOUR PROPERTY!
MY PROPERTY? YOU MEAN TERRY'S AN' MINE?

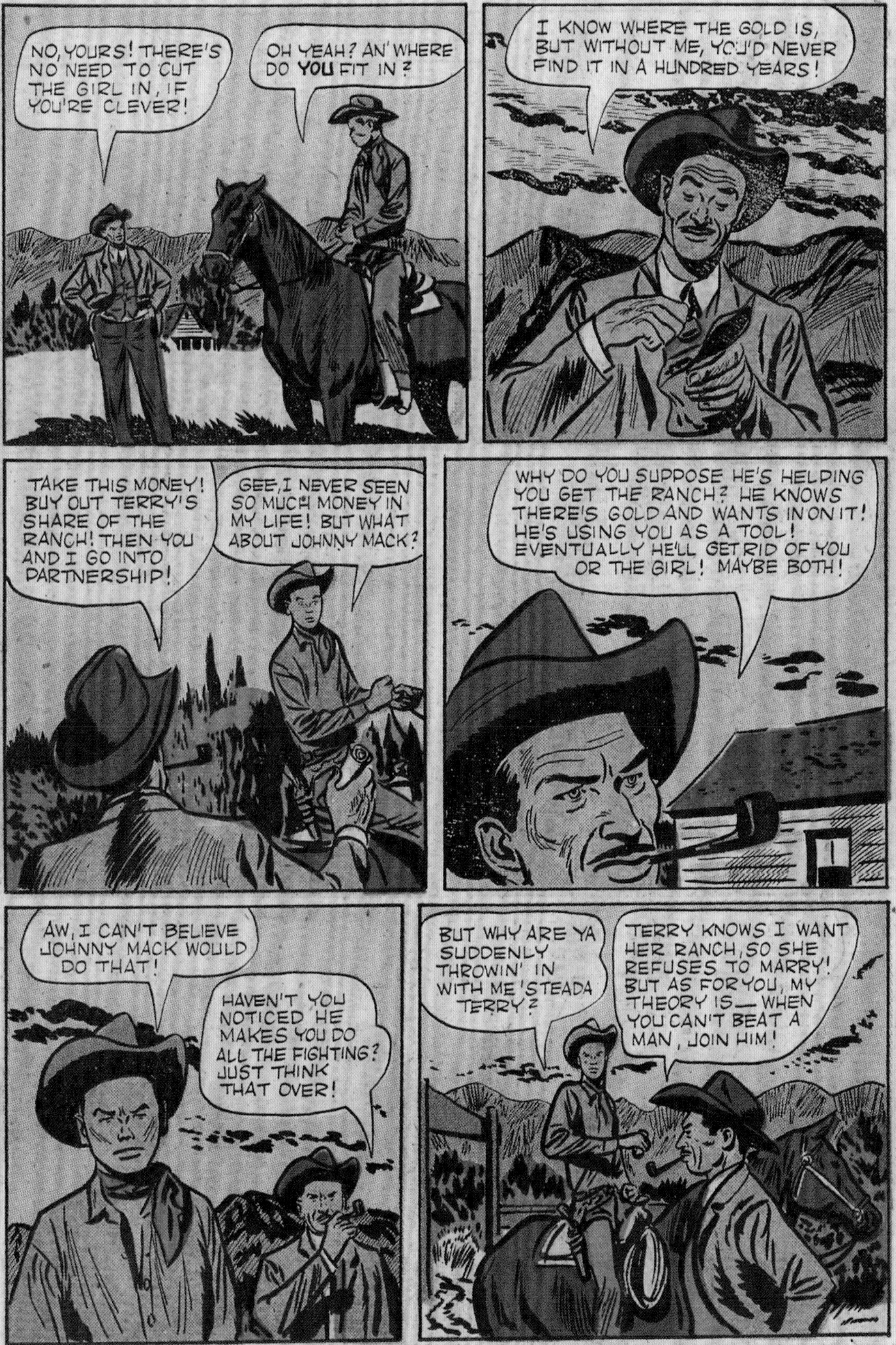
NO, YOURS! THERE'S NO NEED TO CUT THE GIRL IN, IF YOU'RE CLEVER!
OH YEAH? AN' WHERE DO YOU FIT IN?
I KNOW WHERE THE GOLD IS, BUT WITHOUT ME, YOU'D NEVER FIND IT IN A HUNDRED YEARS!
TAKE THIS MONEY! BUY OUT TERRY'S SHARE OF THE RANCH! THEN YOU AND I GO INTO PARTNERSHIP!
GEE, I NEVER SEEN SO MUCH MONEY IN MY LIFE! BUT WHAT ABOUT JOHNNY MACK?
WHY DO YOU SUPPOSE HE'S HELPING YOU GET THE RANCH? HE KNOWS THERE'S GOLD AND WANTS IN ON IT! HE'S USING YOU AS A TOOL! EVENTUALLY HE'LL GET RID OF YOU OR THE GIRL! MAYBE BOTH!
AW, I CAN'T BELIEVE JOHNNY MACK WOULD DO THAT!
HAVEN'T YOU NOTICED HE MAKES YOU DO ALL THE FIGHTING? JUST THINK THAT OVER!
BUT WHY ARE YA SUDDENLY THROWIN' IN WITH ME 'STEADA TERRY?
TERRY KNOWS I WANT HER RANCH, SO SHE REFUSES TO MARRY! BUT AS FOR YOU, MY THEORY IS— WHEN YOU CAN'T BEAT A MAN, JOIN HIM!

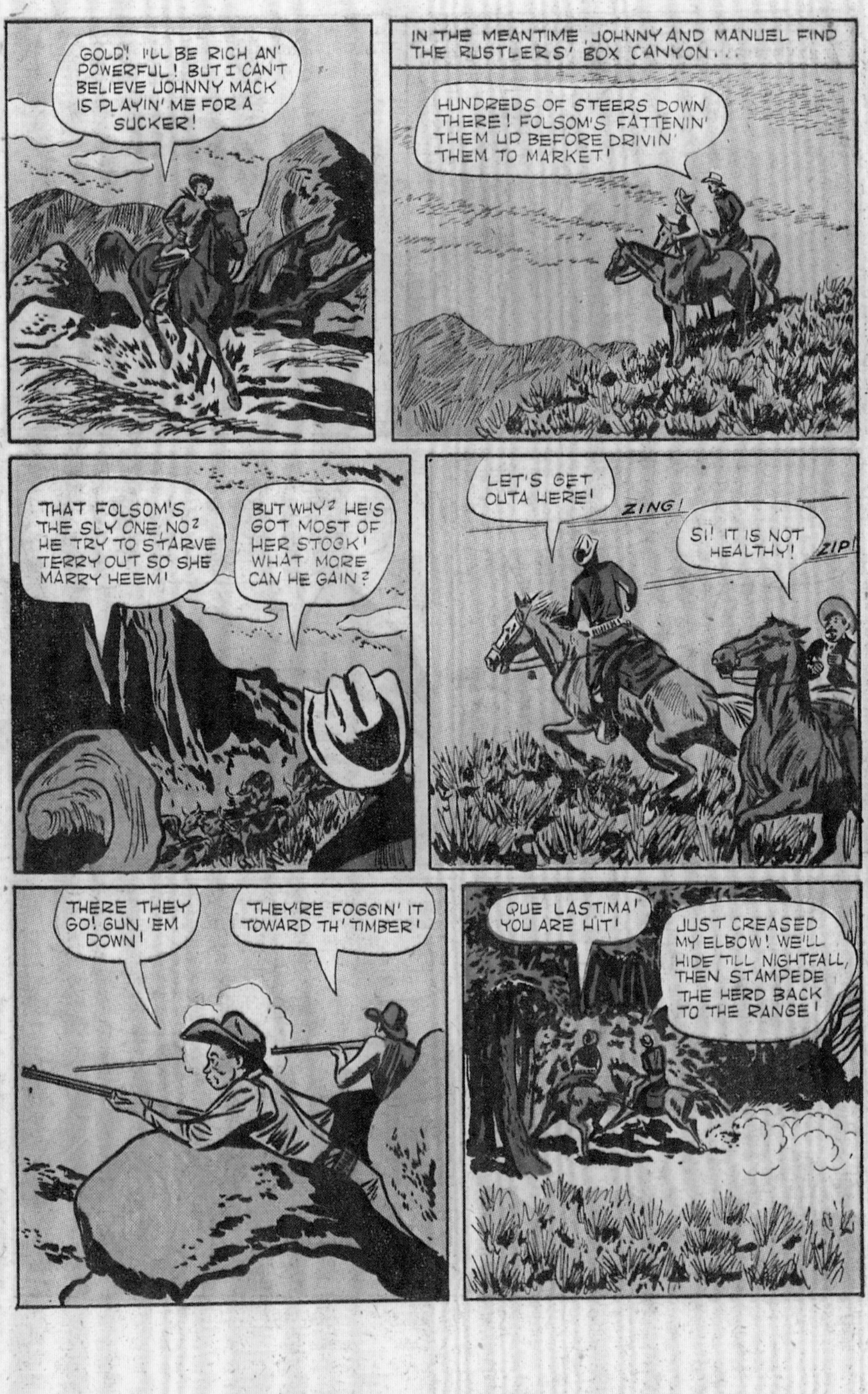
GOLD! I'LL BE RICH AN' POWERFUL! BUT I CAN'T BELIEVE JOHNNY MACK IS PLAYIN' ME FOR A SUCKER!
IN THE MEANTIME, JOHNNY AND MANUEL FIND THE RUSTLERS' BOX CANYON...
HUNDREDS OF STEERS DOWN THERE! FOLSOM'S FATTENIN' THEM UP BEFORE DRIVIN' THEM TO MARKET!
THAT FOLSOM'S THE SLY ONE, NO? HE TRY TO STARVE TERRY OUT SO SHE MARRY HEEM!
BUT WHY? HE'S GOT MOST OF HER STOCK! WHAT MORE CAN HE GAIN?
LET'S GET OUTA HERE!
ZING!
SI! IT IS NOT HEALTHY!
ZIP!
THERE THEY GO! GUN 'EM DOWN!
THEY'RE FOGGIN' IT TOWARD TH' TIMBER!
QUE LASTIMA! YOU ARE HIT!
JUST CREASED MY ELBOW! WE'LL HIDE TILL NIGHTFALL, THEN STAMPEDE THE HERD BACK TO THE RANGE!

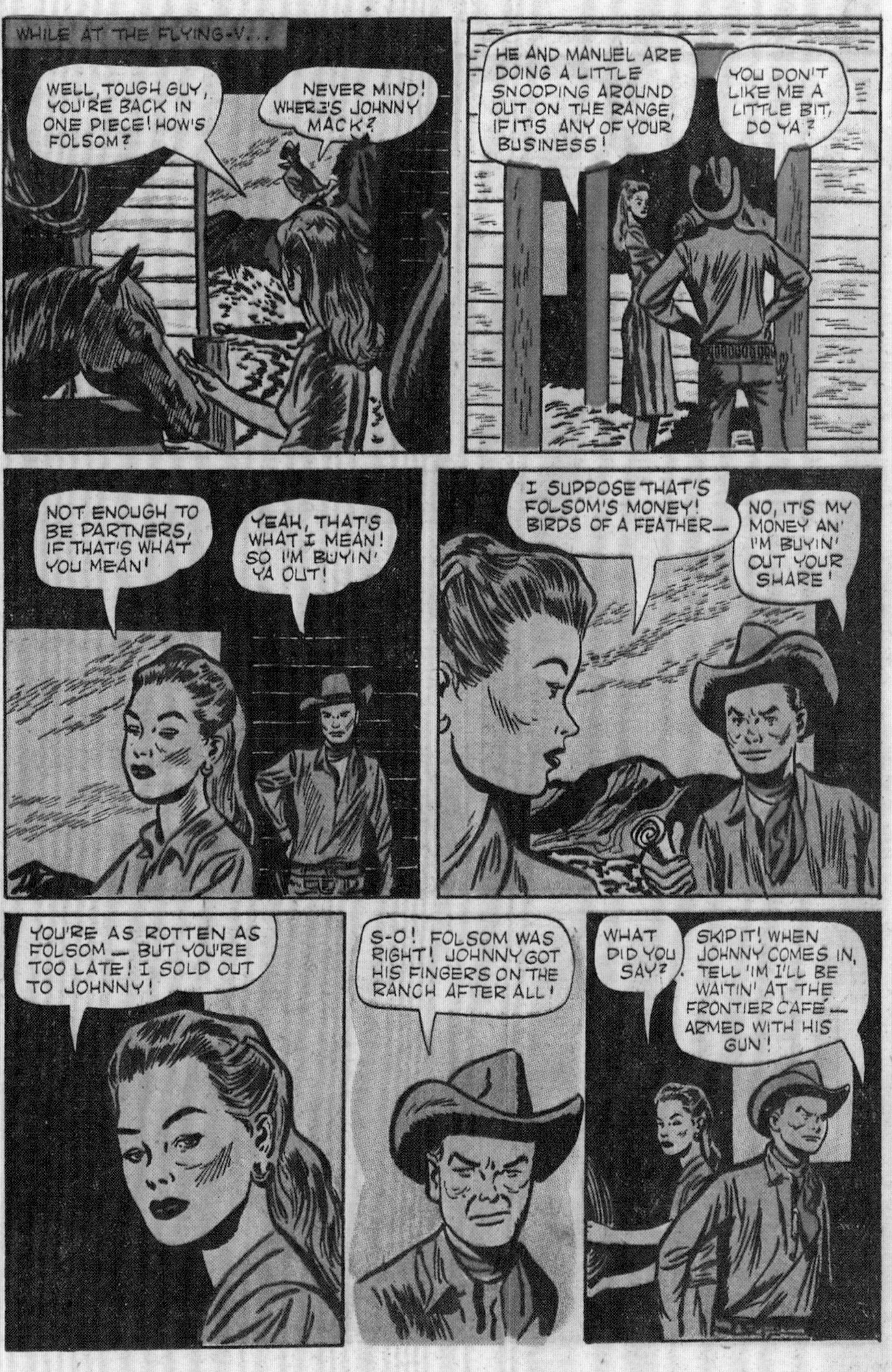
WHILE AT THE FLYING-V...
WELL, TOUGH GUY, YOU'RE BACK IN ONE PIECE! HOW'S FOLSOM?
NEVER MIND! WHERE'S JOHNNY MACK?
HE AND MANUEL ARE DOING A LITTLE SNOOPING AROUND OUT ON THE RANGE, IF IT'S ANY OF YOUR BUSINESS!
YOU DON'T LIKE ME A LITTLE BIT, DO YA?
NOT ENOUGH TO BE PARTNERS, IF THAT'S WHAT YOU MEAN!
YEAH, THAT'S WHAT I MEAN! SO I'M BUYIN' YA OUT!
I SUPPOSE THAT'S FOLSOM'S MONEY! BIRDS OF A FEATHER—
NO, IT'S MY MONEY AN' I'M BUYIN' OUT YOUR SHARE!
YOU'RE AS ROTTEN AS FOLSOM — BUT YOU'RE TOO LATE! I SOLD OUT TO JOHNNY!
S-O! FOLSOM WAS RIGHT! JOHNNY GOT HIS FINGERS ON THE RANCH AFTER ALL!
WHAT DID YOU SAY?
SKIP IT! WHEN JOHNNY COMES IN, TELL 'IM I'LL BE WAITIN' AT THE FRONTIER CAFÉ — ARMED WITH HIS GUN!

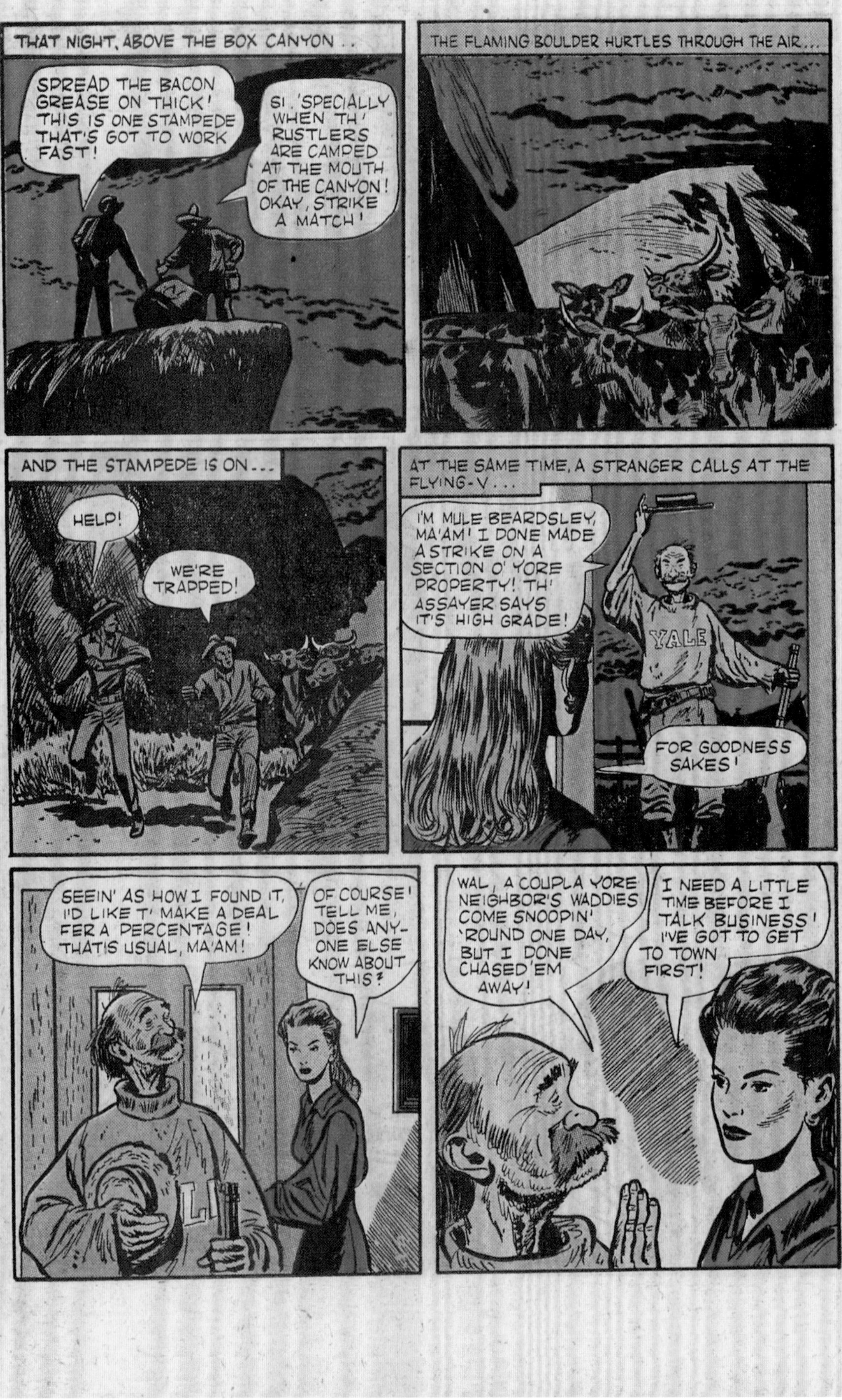
THAT NIGHT, ABOVE THE BOX CANYON . .
SPREAD THE BACON GREASE ON THICK! THIS IS ONE STAMPEDE THAT'S GOT TO WORK FAST!
SI. 'SPECIALLY WHEN TH' RUSTLERS ARE CAMPED AT THE MOUTH OF THE CANYON! OKAY, STRIKE A MATCH!
THE FLAMING BOULDER HURTLES THROUGH THE AIR...
AND THE STAMPEDE IS ON...
HELP!
WE'RE TRAPPED!
AT THE SAME TIME, A STRANGER CALLS AT THE FLYING-V...
I'M MULE BEARDSLEY, MA'AM! I DONE MADE A STRIKE ON A SECTION O' YORE PROPERTY! TH' ASSAYER SAYS IT'S HIGH GRADE!
YALE
FOR GOODNESS SAKES!
SEEIN' AS HOW I FOUND IT, I'D LIKE T' MAKE A DEAL FER A PERCENTAGE! THAT'S USUAL, MA'AM!
OF COURSE! TELL ME, DOES ANYONE ELSE KNOW ABOUT THIS?
WAL, A COUPLA YORE NEIGHBOR'S WADDIES COME SNOOPIN' 'ROUND ONE DAY, BUT I DONE CHASED 'EM AWAY!
I NEED A LITTLE TIME BEFORE I TALK BUSINESS! I'VE GOT TO GET TO TOWN FIRST!

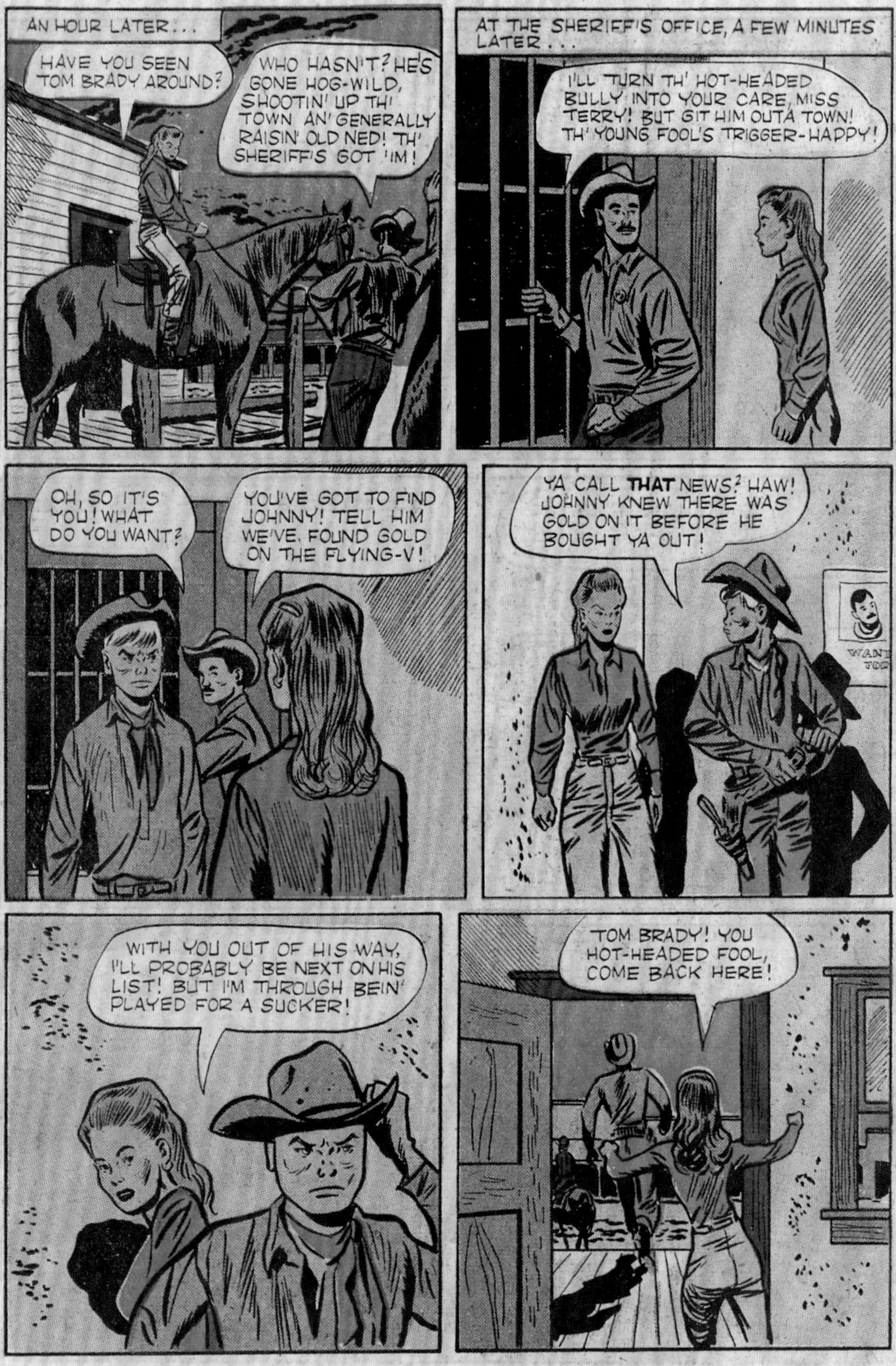
AN HOUR LATER...
HAVE YOU SEEN TOM BRADY AROUND?
WHO HASN'T? HE'S GONE HOG-WILD, SHOOTIN' UP TH' TOWN AN' GENERALLY RAISIN' OLD NED! TH' SHERIFF'S GOT 'IM!
AT THE SHERIFF'S OFFICE, A FEW MINUTES LATER...
I'LL TURN TH' HOT-HEADED BULLY INTO YOUR CARE, MISS TERRY! BUT GIT HIM OUTA TOWN! TH' YOUNG FOOL'S TRIGGER-HAPPY!
OH, SO IT'S YOU! WHAT DO YOU WANT?
YOU'VE GOT TO FIND JOHNNY! TELL HIM WE'VE FOUND GOLD ON THE FLYING-V!
YA CALL **THAT** NEWS? HAW! JOHNNY KNEW THERE WAS GOLD ON IT BEFORE HE BOUGHT YA OUT!
WITH YOU OUT OF HIS WAY, I'LL PROBABLY BE NEXT ON HIS LIST! BUT I'M THROUGH BEIN' PLAYED FOR A SUCKER!
TOM BRADY! YOU HOT-HEADED FOOL, COME BACK HERE!

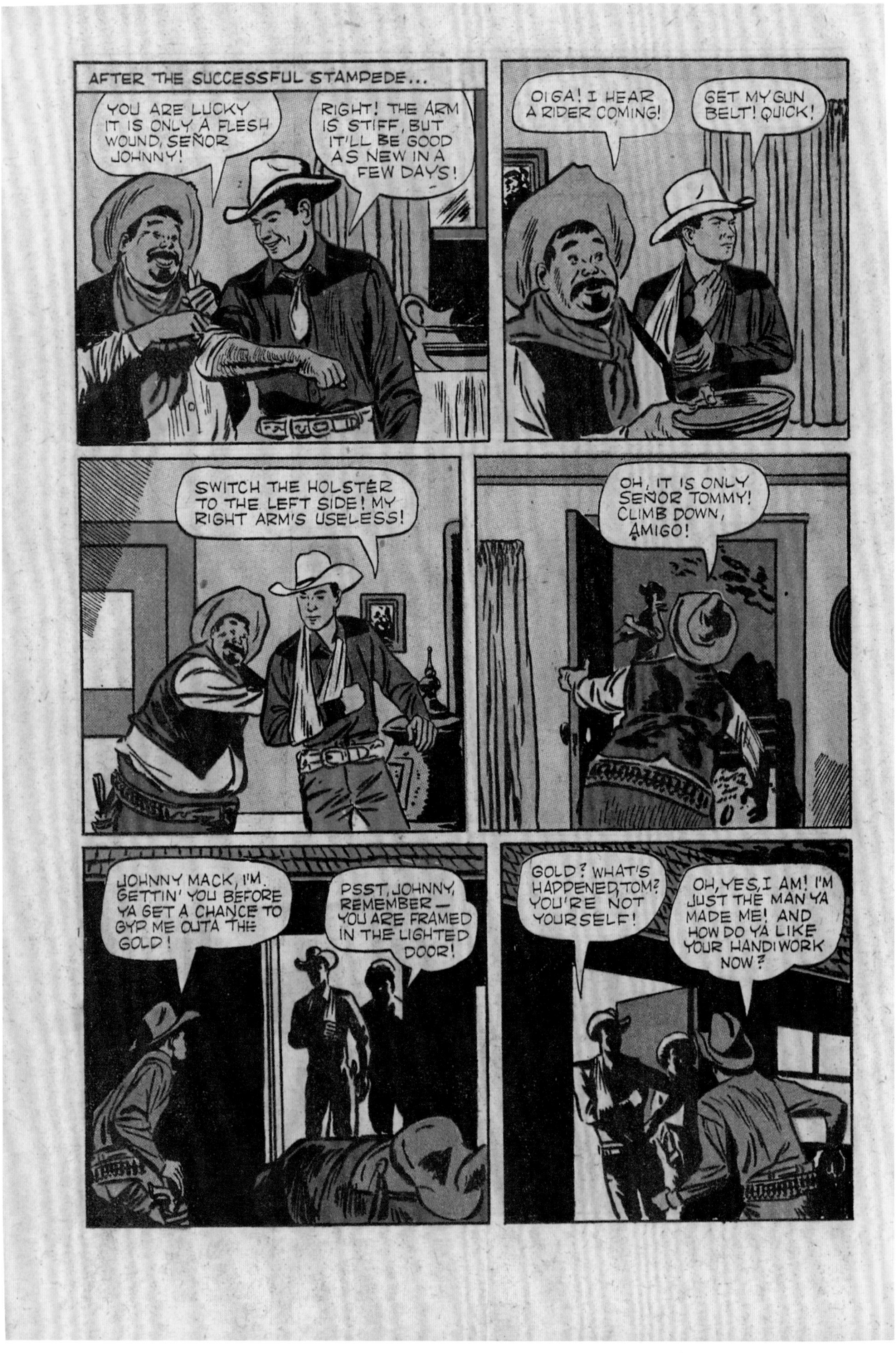
AFTER THE SUCCESSFUL STAMPEDE...
YOU ARE LUCKY IT IS ONLY A FLESH WOUND, SEÑOR JOHNNY!
RIGHT! THE ARM IS STIFF, BUT IT'LL BE GOOD AS NEW IN A FEW DAYS!
OIGA! I HEAR A RIDER COMING!
GET MY GUN BELT! QUICK!
SWITCH THE HOLSTER TO THE LEFT SIDE! MY RIGHT ARM'S USELESS!
OH, IT IS ONLY SEÑOR TOMMY! CLIMB DOWN, AMIGO!
JOHNNY MACK, I'M GETTIN' YOU BEFORE YA GET A CHANCE TO GYP ME OUTA THE GOLD!
PSST, JOHNNY, REMEMBER— YOU ARE FRAMED IN THE LIGHTED DOOR!
GOLD? WHAT'S HAPPENED, TOM? YOU'RE NOT YOURSELF!
OH, YES, I AM! I'M JUST THE MAN YA MADE ME! AND HOW DO YA LIKE YOUR HANDIWORK NOW?

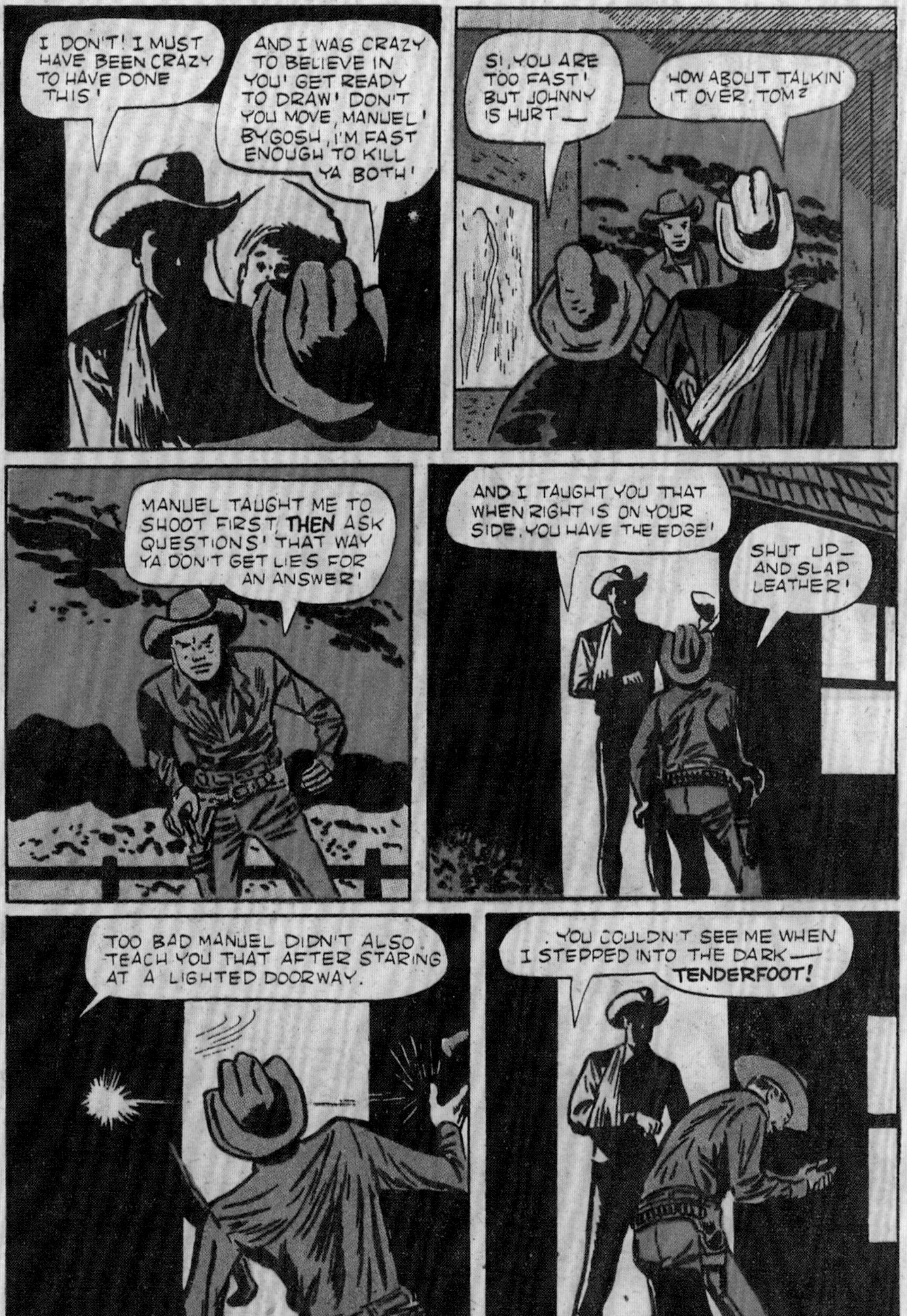
I DON'T! I MUST HAVE BEEN CRAZY TO HAVE DONE THIS!
AND I WAS CRAZY TO BELIEVE IN YOU! GET READY TO DRAW! DON'T YOU MOVE, MANUEL! BYGOSH, I'M FAST ENOUGH TO KILL YA BOTH!
SI, YOU ARE TOO FAST! BUT JOHNNY IS HURT —
HOW ABOUT TALKIN' IT OVER, TOM?
MANUEL TAUGHT ME TO SHOOT FIRST, THEN ASK QUESTIONS! THAT WAY YA DON'T GET LIES FOR AN ANSWER!
AND I TAUGHT YOU THAT WHEN RIGHT IS ON YOUR SIDE, YOU HAVE THE EDGE!
SHUT UP — AND SLAP LEATHER!
TOO BAD MANUEL DIDN'T ALSO TEACH YOU THAT AFTER STARING AT A LIGHTED DOORWAY.
. YOU COULDN'T SEE ME WHEN I STEPPED INTO THE DARK — TENDERFOOT!

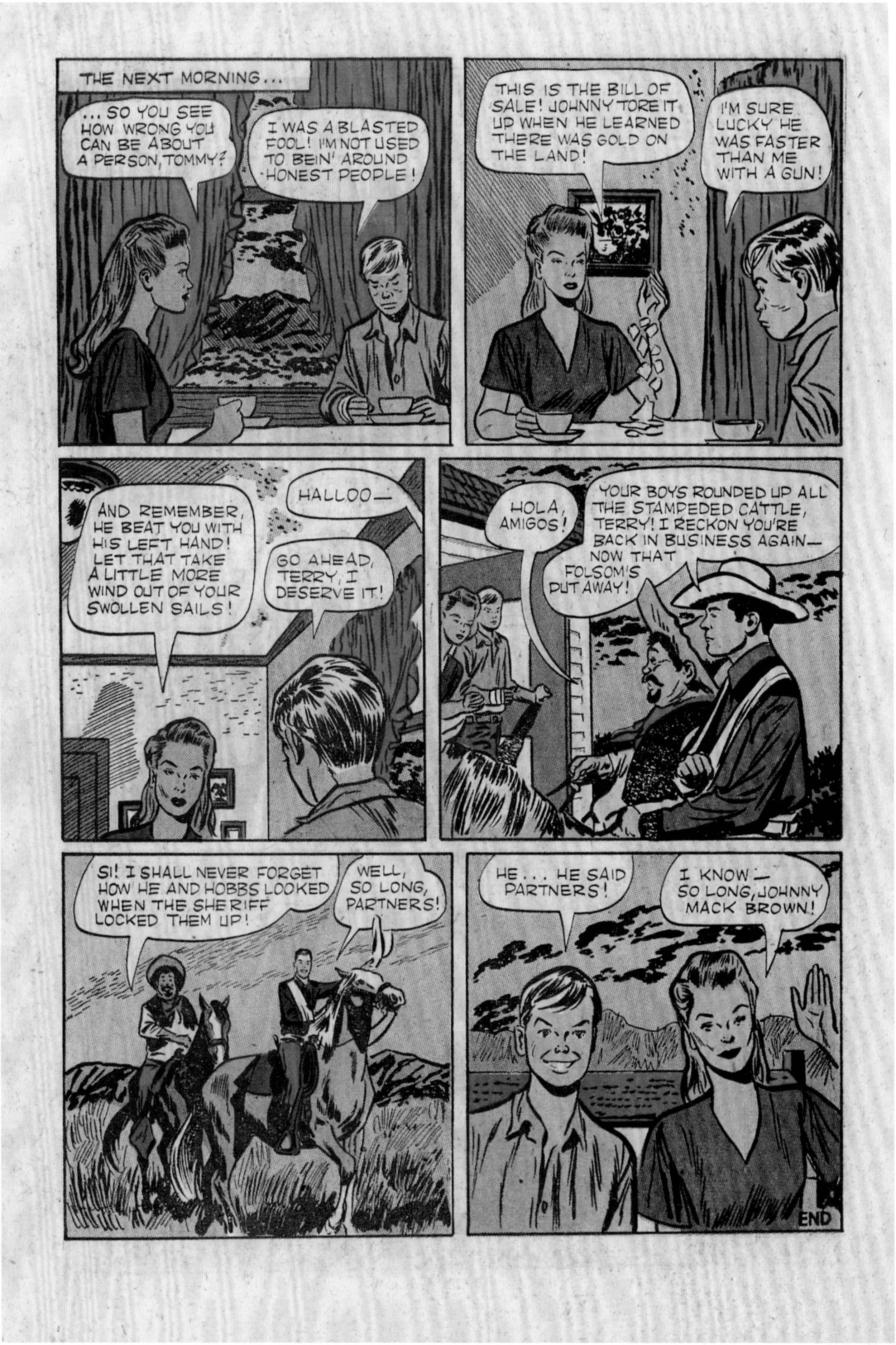
THE NEXT MORNING...
...SO YOU SEE HOW WRONG YOU CAN BE ABOUT A PERSON, TOMMY?
I WAS A BLASTED FOOL! I'M NOT USED TO BEIN' AROUND HONEST PEOPLE!
THIS IS THE BILL OF SALE! JOHNNY TORE IT UP WHEN HE LEARNED THERE WAS GOLD ON THE LAND!
I'M SURE LUCKY HE WAS FASTER THAN ME WITH A GUN!
AND REMEMBER, HE BEAT YOU WITH HIS LEFT HAND! LET THAT TAKE A LITTLE MORE WIND OUT OF YOUR SWOLLEN SAILS!
HALLOO—
GO AHEAD, TERRY, I DESERVE IT!
HOLA, AMIGOS!
YOUR BOYS ROUNDED UP ALL THE STAMPEDED CATTLE, TERRY! I RECKON YOU'RE BACK IN BUSINESS AGAIN— NOW THAT FOLSOM'S PUT AWAY!
SI! I SHALL NEVER FORGET HOW HE AND HOBBS LOOKED WHEN THE SHERIFF LOCKED THEM UP!
WELL, SO LONG, PARTNERS!
HE... HE SAID PARTNERS!
I KNOW— SO LONG, JOHNNY MACK BROWN!
END

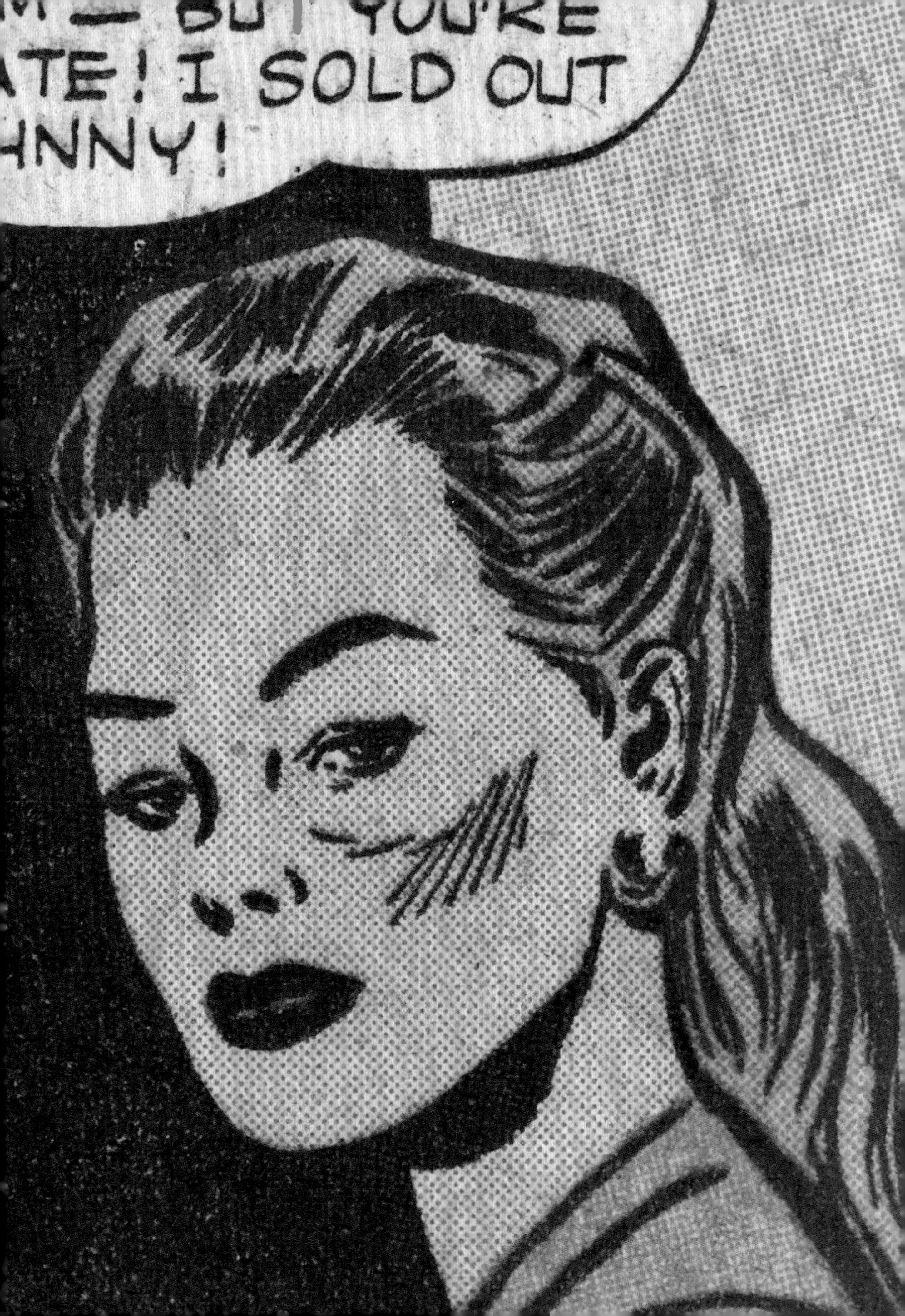
I SOLD OUT

BILL EVERETT

(1917–73)

Water seemed to follow Bill Everett wherever he went. In 1939 his most famous character, the Sub-Mariner, was the star of his own flagship feature for Timely Comics (which became Marvel Comics), and Everett revisited the character toward the end of his life in the *Sub-Mariner* comic book series in the early 1970s. In the late 1930s and early 1940s, another water-based character of his, the Fin, was also published by Timely Comics, and his Hydroman shared space with Man O'Metal in *Heroic Comics*. Speaking at a comic book convention in 1970, Everett remembered, "I suppose I've always liked water. If anything started it, I suppose it was when I got interested in Admiral Byrd's expedition to the South Pole. I read a lot about that, and the more I read, the more intrigued I became, so when the opportunity came to create a character I naturally thought of water. Jack London's adventures at sea were influential, too. I used to read a lot of sea stories."

William Blake Everett was born in Cambridge, Massachusetts, and raised in Arizona. He was a distant relative to the artist William Blake, a fact he enjoyed playing with—even sometimes signing his work "William Blake" or "Everett Blake." After a stint in the merchant marines, Everett studied art at the Vesper George School of Art from 1934 to 1935; afterward, he swiftly embarked on a checkered career as a commercial artist before happening into the just-burgeoning field of comic books in 1938. As a child, Everett was encouraged by his father to become a cartoonist, but Bill himself claimed to have no particular interest in comics as a medium, though he admired illustrators like Dean Cornwell and Mead Schaeffer, as well as cartoonists including Milton Caniff and Bill Holman. By 1939 Everett had formed Funnies, Inc. with art director Lloyd Jacquet and two other artists. Together they sold packages of comics to existing publishers, Timely Comics among them. Everett drew numerous comics in these early years before entering the U.S. Army in 1942. He returned home in 1946, settling in Nebraska, and after a brief break returned to both the Sub-Mariner and comics in general. When super-hero comic sales declined in the late 1940s, Everett moved on to horror and fantasy comics, working for the renamed Timely Comics. Under the new company name of Atlas Comics, Everett worked on *Mystic, Adventures into Weird Worlds*, and *Marvel Tales*. Among the many titles Everett contributed to was *Venus*, which featured the titular supernatural character acting as a guide through various fantastic adventures, including the water-logged "Tidal Wave of Terror." This story echoes both the wind-swept plains and innocence of the Midwest as well as Everett's own Sub-Mariner past, high-lighting many of Everett's finest qualities.

Visualizing the depths of the sea or the power of flowing water seemed to bring out Everett's maximalist, visionary tendencies. Everett usually wrote, drew, and even lettered his own stories, exerting a rare control over his work. He possessed the unusual ability to make complete, compelling pictures in each panel while still keeping the story moving. A reader can examine a panel for a long time, or can swiftly move through the story. Both approaches are rewarding. Into his lush land-scapes, Everett injected angular figures composed of a handful of confident marks. The same long strokes that delineate a wave are used to sculpt a figure. Everett always found the form with his lines: Though his pictures over-flow with ink, nothing is drawn unnecessarily.

When the comics industry began to falter in the mid-1950s, Everett went on to work for a greeting card company as well as a paper company as an art director. He returned to comics in 1964, cocreating and then drawing the first issue of *Daredevil* while still holding down a full-time job. Everett spent the rest of the decade working on and off for Marvel on characters including Dr. Strange and the Incredible Hulk, penciling, inking, and some-times also writing. He died too young, at age fifty-six, still creating lavish, beautifully rendered comics until the end.

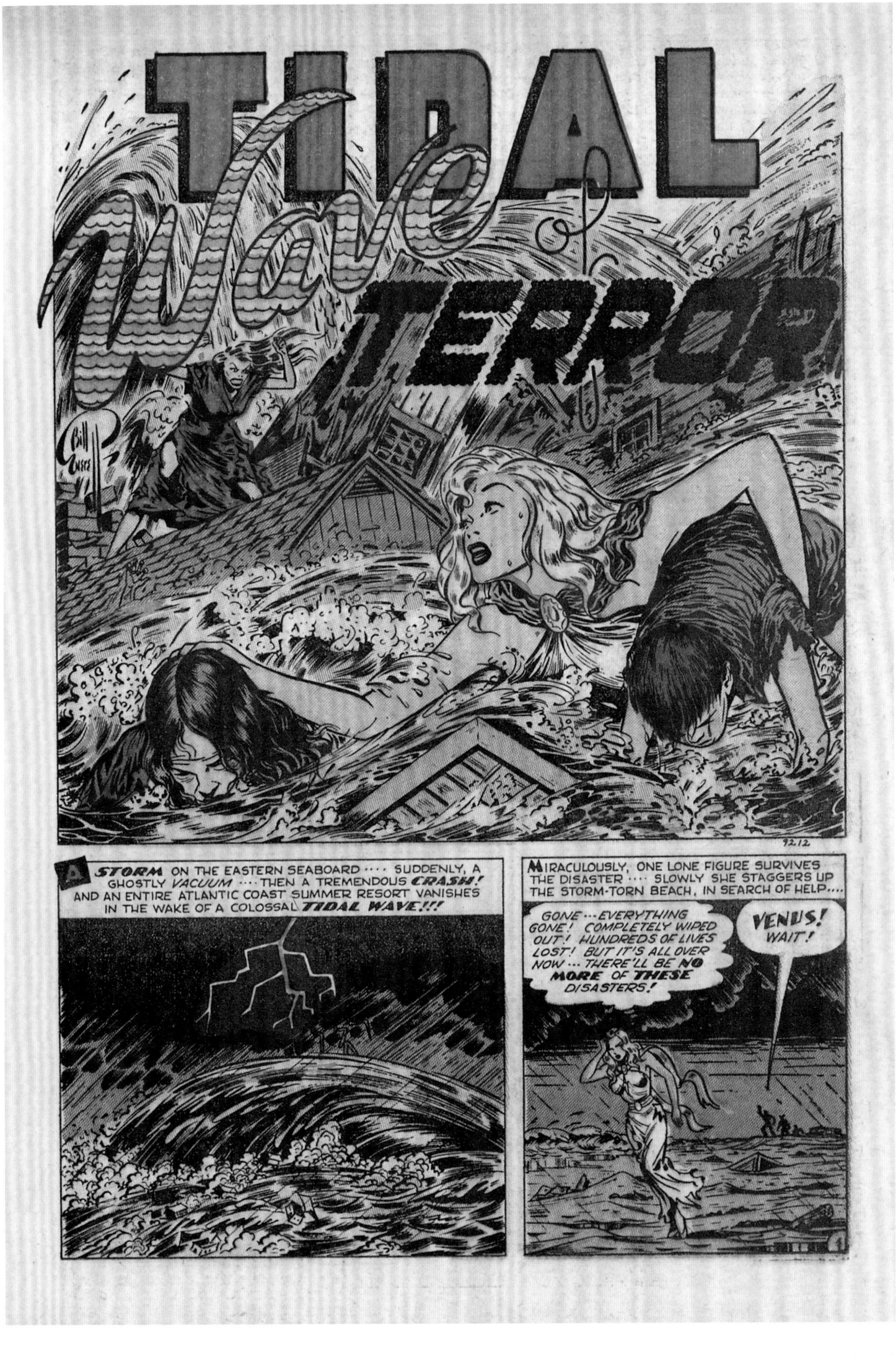
TIDAL
Wave of TERROR
A STORM ON THE EASTERN SEABOARD .... SUDDENLY, A GHOSTLY VACUUM .... THEN A TREMENDOUS CRASH! AND AN ENTIRE ATLANTIC COAST SUMMER RESORT VANISHES IN THE WAKE OF A COLOSSAL TIDAL WAVE!!!
MIRACULOUSLY, ONE LONE FIGURE SURVIVES THE DISASTER .... SLOWLY SHE STAGGERS UP THE STORM-TORN BEACH, IN SEARCH OF HELP....
GONE ... EVERYTHING GONE! COMPLETELY WIPED OUT! HUNDREDS OF LIVES LOST! BUT IT'S ALL OVER NOW ... THERE'LL BE NO MORE OF THESE DISASTERS!
VENUS! WAIT!

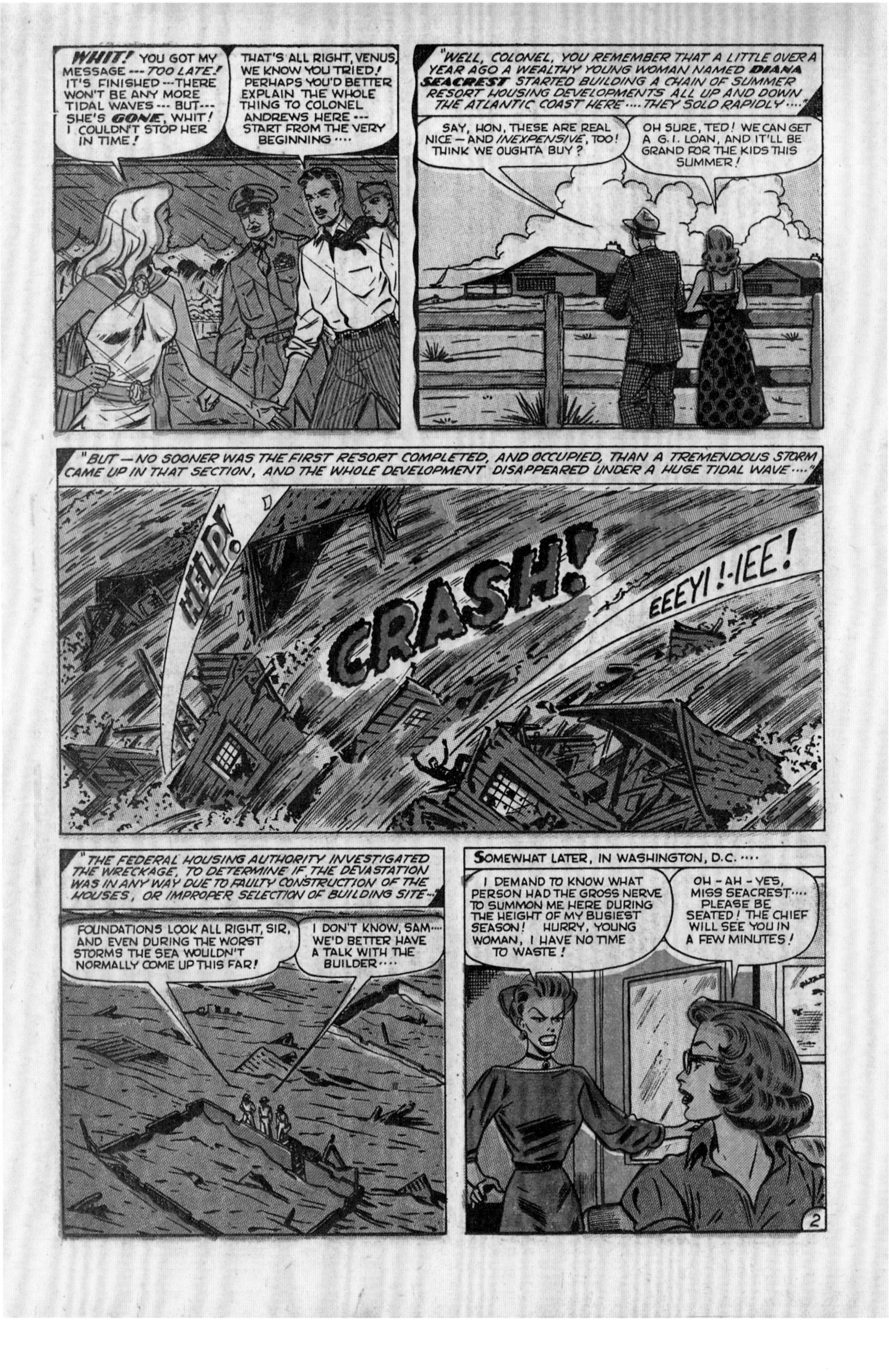
WHIT! YOU GOT MY MESSAGE --- TOO LATE! IT'S FINISHED --- THERE WON'T BE ANY MORE TIDAL WAVES --- BUT--- SHE'S GONE, WHIT! I COULDN'T STOP HER IN TIME!
THAT'S ALL RIGHT, VENUS, WE KNOW YOU TRIED! PERHAPS YOU'D BETTER EXPLAIN THE WHOLE THING TO COLONEL ANDREWS HERE --- START FROM THE VERY BEGINNING....
"WELL, COLONEL, YOU REMEMBER THAT A LITTLE OVER A YEAR AGO A WEALTHY YOUNG WOMAN NAMED DIANA SEACREST STARTED BUILDING A CHAIN OF SUMMER RESORT HOUSING DEVELOPMENTS ALL UP AND DOWN THE ATLANTIC COAST HERE.... THEY SOLD RAPIDLY...."
SAY, HON, THESE ARE REAL NICE — AND INEXPENSIVE, TOO! THINK WE OUGHTA BUY?
OH SURE, TED! WE CAN GET A G.I. LOAN, AND IT'LL BE GRAND FOR THE KIDS THIS SUMMER!
"BUT — NO SOONER WAS THE FIRST RESORT COMPLETED, AND OCCUPIED, THAN A TREMENDOUS STORM CAME UP IN THAT SECTION, AND THE WHOLE DEVELOPMENT DISAPPEARED UNDER A HUGE TIDAL WAVE...."
HELP!
CRASH!
EEEYI!-IEE!
"THE FEDERAL HOUSING AUTHORITY INVESTIGATED THE WRECKAGE, TO DETERMINE IF THE DEVASTATION WAS IN ANY WAY DUE TO FAULTY CONSTRUCTION OF THE HOUSES, OR IMPROPER SELECTION OF BUILDING SITE...
FOUNDATIONS LOOK ALL RIGHT, SIR, AND EVEN DURING THE WORST STORMS THE SEA WOULDN'T NORMALLY COME UP THIS FAR!
I DON'T KNOW, SAM.... WE'D BETTER HAVE A TALK WITH THE BUILDER....
SOMEWHAT LATER, IN WASHINGTON, D.C....
I DEMAND TO KNOW WHAT PERSON HAD THE GROSS NERVE TO SUMMON ME HERE DURING THE HEIGHT OF MY BUSIEST SEASON! HURRY, YOUNG WOMAN, I HAVE NO TIME TO WASTE!
OH - AH - YES, MISS SEACREST.... PLEASE BE SEATED! THE CHIEF WILL SEE YOU IN A FEW MINUTES!
2

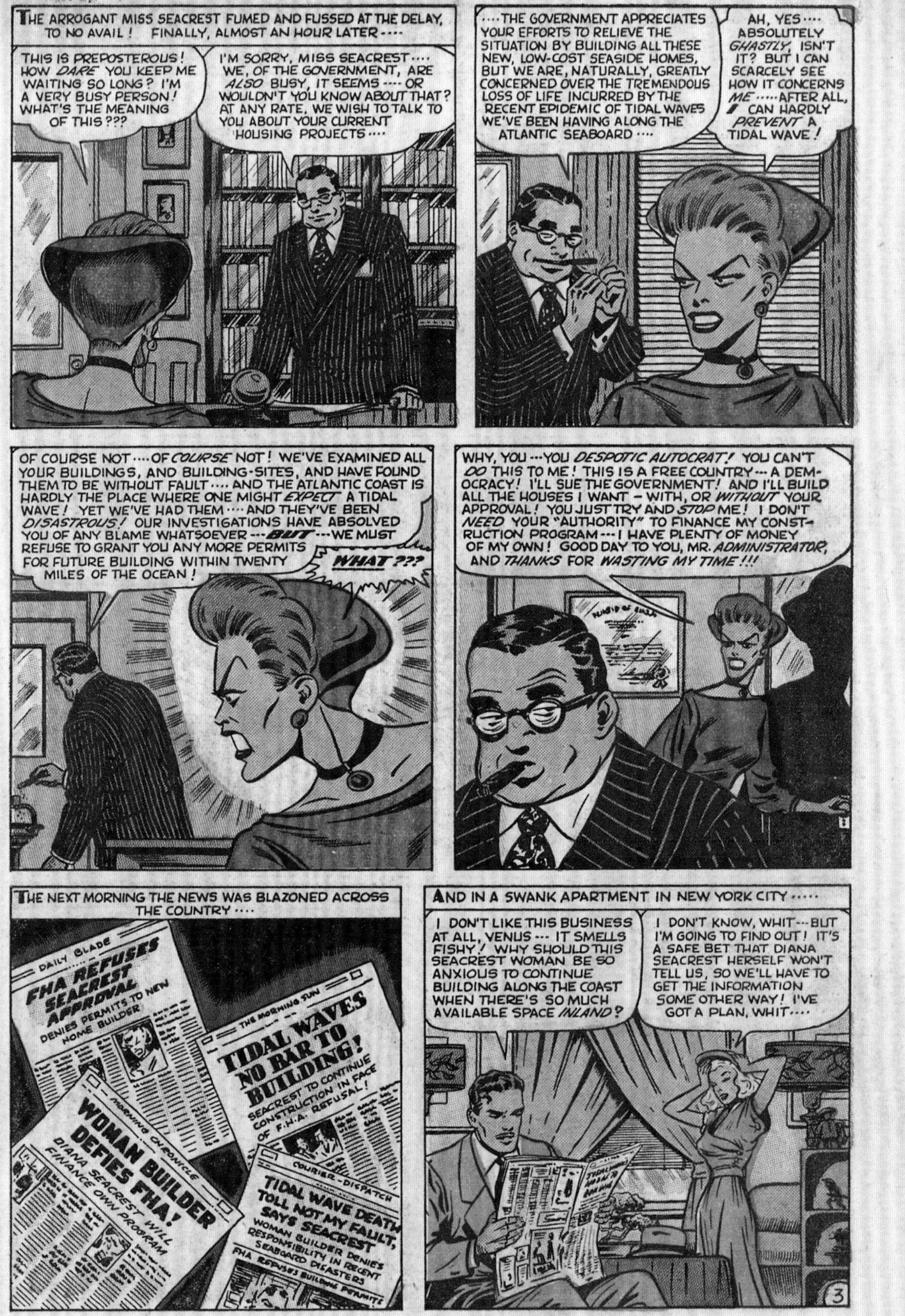
THE ARROGANT MISS SEACREST FUMED AND FUSSED AT THE DELAY, TO NO AVAIL! FINALLY, ALMOST AN HOUR LATER....
THIS IS PREPOSTEROUS! HOW DARE YOU KEEP ME WAITING SO LONG? I'M A VERY BUSY PERSON! WHAT'S THE MEANING OF THIS???
I'M SORRY, MISS SEACREST.... WE, OF THE GOVERNMENT, ARE ALSO BUSY, IT SEEMS.... OR WOULDN'T YOU KNOW ABOUT THAT? AT ANY RATE, WE WISH TO TALK TO YOU ABOUT YOUR CURRENT HOUSING PROJECTS....
....THE GOVERNMENT APPRECIATES YOUR EFFORTS TO RELIEVE THE SITUATION BY BUILDING ALL THESE NEW, LOW-COST SEASIDE HOMES, BUT WE ARE, NATURALLY, GREATLY CONCERNED OVER THE TREMENDOUS LOSS OF LIFE INCURRED BY THE RECENT EPIDEMIC OF TIDAL WAVES WE'VE BEEN HAVING ALONG THE ATLANTIC SEABOARD....
AH, YES.... ABSOLUTELY GHASTLY, ISN'T IT? BUT I CAN SCARCELY SEE HOW IT CONCERNS ME.....AFTER ALL, I CAN HARDLY PREVENT A TIDAL WAVE!
OF COURSE NOT....OF COURSE NOT! WE'VE EXAMINED ALL YOUR BUILDINGS, AND BUILDING-SITES, AND HAVE FOUND THEM TO BE WITHOUT FAULT.... AND THE ATLANTIC COAST IS HARDLY THE PLACE WHERE ONE MIGHT EXPECT A TIDAL WAVE! YET WE'VE HAD THEM.... AND THEY'VE BEEN DISASTROUS! OUR INVESTIGATIONS HAVE ABSOLVED YOU OF ANY BLAME WHATSOEVER ---BUT--- WE MUST REFUSE TO GRANT YOU ANY MORE PERMITS FOR FUTURE BUILDING WITHIN TWENTY MILES OF THE OCEAN!
WHAT???
WHY, YOU ---YOU DESPOTIC AUTOCRAT! YOU CAN'T DO THIS TO ME! THIS IS A FREE COUNTRY--- A DEMOCRACY! I'LL SUE THE GOVERNMENT! AND I'LL BUILD ALL THE HOUSES I WANT - WITH, OR WITHOUT YOUR APPROVAL! YOU JUST TRY AND STOP ME! I DON'T NEED YOUR "AUTHORITY" TO FINANCE MY CONSTRUCTION PROGRAM--- I HAVE PLENTY OF MONEY OF MY OWN! GOOD DAY TO YOU, MR. ADMINISTRATOR, AND THANKS FOR WASTING MY TIME!!!
THE NEXT MORNING THE NEWS WAS BLAZONED ACROSS THE COUNTRY....
DAILY BLADE
FHA REFUSES SEACREST APPROVAL
DENIES PERMITS TO NEW HOME BUILDER
THE MORNING SUN
TIDAL WAVES NO BAR TO BUILDING!
SEACREST TO CONTINUE CONSTRUCTION IN FACE OF F.H.A. REFUSAL!
MORNING CHRONICLE
WOMAN BUILDER DEFIES FHA!
DIANA SEACREST WILL FINANCE OWN PROGRAM
COURIER-DISPATCH
TIDAL WAVE DEATH TOLL NOT MY FAULT, SAYS SEACREST
WOMAN BUILDER DENIES RESPONSIBILITY IN RECENT SEABOARD DISASTERS
FHA REFUSES BUILDING PERMITS
AND IN A SWANK APARTMENT IN NEW YORK CITY.....
I DON'T LIKE THIS BUSINESS AT ALL, VENUS--- IT SMELLS FISHY! WHY SHOULD THIS SEACREST WOMAN BE SO ANXIOUS TO CONTINUE BUILDING ALONG THE COAST WHEN THERE'S SO MUCH AVAILABLE SPACE INLAND?
I DON'T KNOW, WHIT--- BUT I'M GOING TO FIND OUT! IT'S A SAFE BET THAT DIANA SEACREST HERSELF WON'T TELL US, SO WE'LL HAVE TO GET THE INFORMATION SOME OTHER WAY! I'VE GOT A PLAN, WHIT....
3

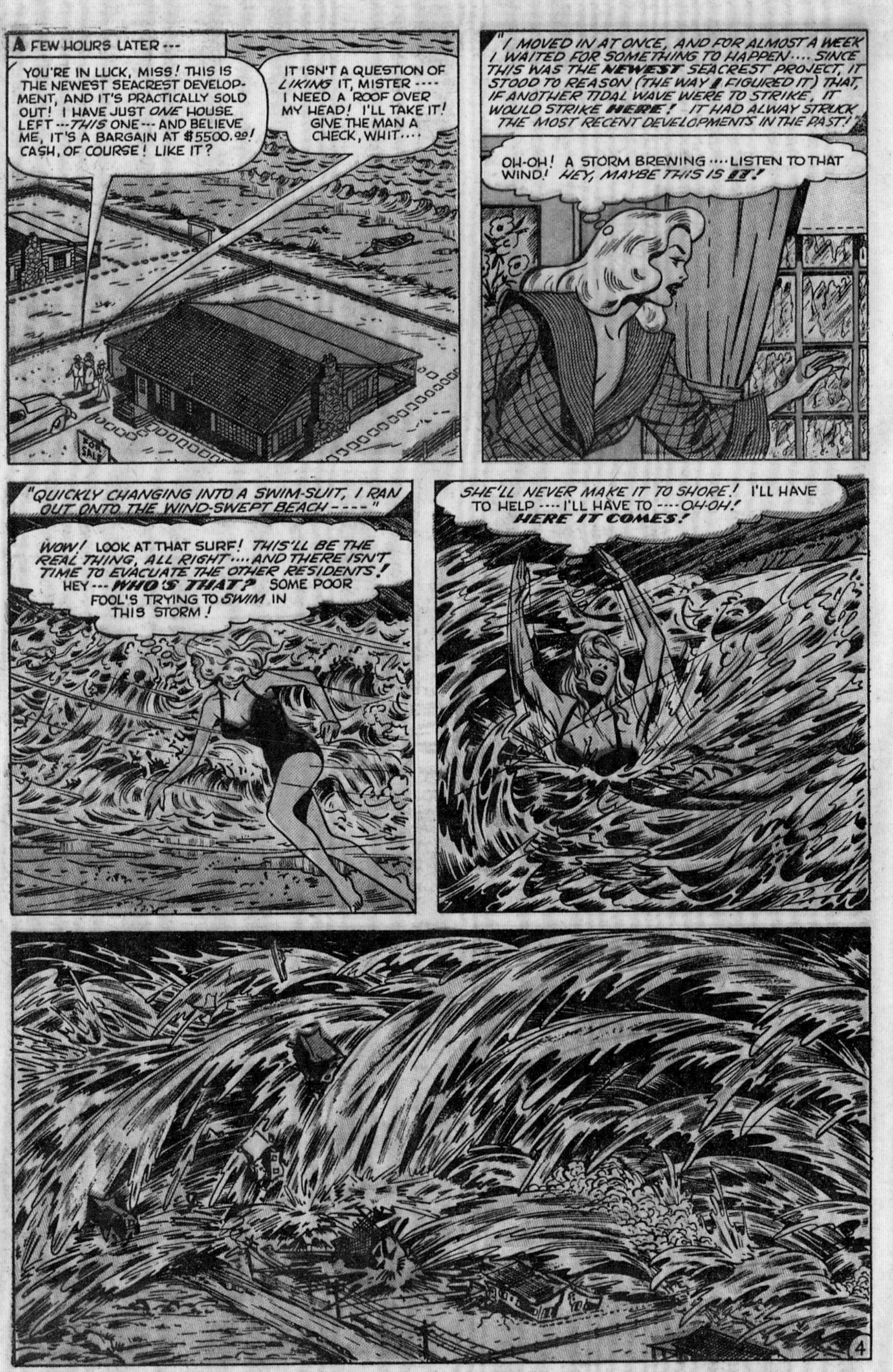
A FEW HOURS LATER ---
YOU'RE IN LUCK, MISS! THIS IS THE NEWEST SEACREST DEVELOPMENT, AND IT'S PRACTICALLY SOLD OUT! I HAVE JUST ONE HOUSE LEFT --- THIS ONE --- AND BELIEVE ME, IT'S A BARGAIN AT $5500.00! CASH, OF COURSE! LIKE IT?
IT ISN'T A QUESTION OF LIKING IT, MISTER ---- I NEED A ROOF OVER MY HEAD! I'LL TAKE IT! GIVE THE MAN A CHECK, WHIT ····
FOR SALE
"I MOVED IN AT ONCE, AND FOR ALMOST A WEEK I WAITED FOR SOMETHING TO HAPPEN .... SINCE THIS WAS THE NEWEST SEACREST PROJECT, IT STOOD TO REASON (THE WAY I FIGURED IT) THAT, IF ANOTHER TIDAL WAVE WERE TO STRIKE, IT WOULD STRIKE HERE! IT HAD ALWAY STRUCK THE MOST RECENT DEVELOPMENTS IN THE PAST!"
OH-OH! A STORM BREWING .... LISTEN TO THAT WIND! HEY, MAYBE THIS IS IT!
"QUICKLY CHANGING INTO A SWIM-SUIT, I RAN OUT ONTO THE WIND-SWEPT BEACH ----"
WOW! LOOK AT THAT SURF! THIS'LL BE THE REAL THING, ALL RIGHT .... AND THERE ISN'T TIME TO EVACUATE THE OTHER RESIDENTS! HEY --- WHO'S THAT? SOME POOR FOOL'S TRYING TO SWIM IN THIS STORM!
SHE'LL NEVER MAKE IT TO SHORE! I'LL HAVE TO HELP ---- I'LL HAVE TO ---- OH-OH! HERE IT COMES!
4

"WITH A DEVASTATING CRASH, THE GIGANTIC WAVE ENGULFED THE ENTIRE SEASIDE RESORT! HOUSES VANISHED .... AUTOMOBILES AND BOATS WERE TOSSED ABOUT LIKE MINIATURE TOYS.... TREES WERE SPLINTERED INTO TOOTHPICKS.... AND YET - MIRACULOUSLY - I MANAGED TO LIVE THROUGH IT, CLINGING DESPERATELY TO A STEEL BARREL TORN LOOSE FROM SOME DEMOLISHED PIER! MY EYES REMAINED GLUED ON THAT ONE LONE FIGURE IN THE WILD SEA!"
STILL THERE! I CAN'T BELIEVE IT!
"SUDDENLY THE FIGURE ROSE HIGH ON A BREAKER...."
GOOD GRIEF! IT'S --- IT'S DIANA SEACREST!!! WHAT'S SHE DOING OUT HERE?
HA HA! HO HO!
"FEARING THE WORST --- AND SCARCELY BELIEVING MY EYES --- I DOVE, AND SWAM AFTER HER...."
THIS IS IMPOSSIBLE! THE WOMAN MUST BE MAD! WITH DEATH AND DESTRUCTION ALL AROUND HER, SHE WAS LAUGHING!
HO HO! COME ON AND CATCH ME --- IF YOU CAN, YOU LITTLE FOOL!
"THE WAVE SUBSIDED .... I LASHED OUT DESPERATELY, GROPING FOR THAT ELUSIVE FIGURE! THEN, JUST AS IT CAME WITHIN MY GRASP — SHE VANISHED!"
GONE! SHE WENT DOWN --- STRAIGHT AS A ROCK! THE POOR, DEMENTED IDIOT! SHE COULDN'T HAVE BEEN A VERY STRONG SWIMMER --- YET, I DON'T SEE HOW ANYONE COULD LIVE THROUGH THIS MAELSTROM!
"I STRUGGLED BACK TO THE WRECKED BEACH..."
HOW LUCKY CAN I GET? IF IT HADN'T BEEN FOR THAT BARREL --- BRR-R-RR! --- I'D BE PLAYING TAG WITH DAVY JONES TOO! WOW! THIS IS A GHASTLY MESS! I'LL HAVE TO FIND DRY CLOTHES, AND GET THE NEWS BACK TO SEACREST'S OFFICE!
"THE GOVERNMENT AND THE AMERICAN RED CROSS TOOK OVER THE DISASTER AREA, AND I FOUND REFUGE IN A NEARBY TOWN .... THE NEXT MORNING I WENT DIRECTLY TO THE LATE DIANA SEACREST'S OFFICE..."
MY NAME IS VENUS, MISS .... I WAS THE SOLE SURVIVOR OF LAST NIGHT'S TIDAL WAVE UP THE COAST! I WANT TO REPORT THAT I WAS THE LAST PERSON TO SEE MISS DIANA SEACREST ALIVE!
YOU WERE WHAT???
5

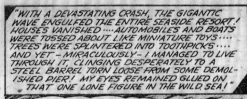

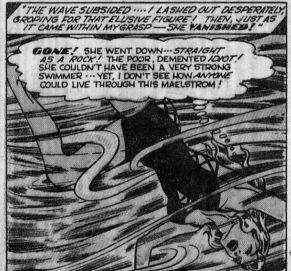

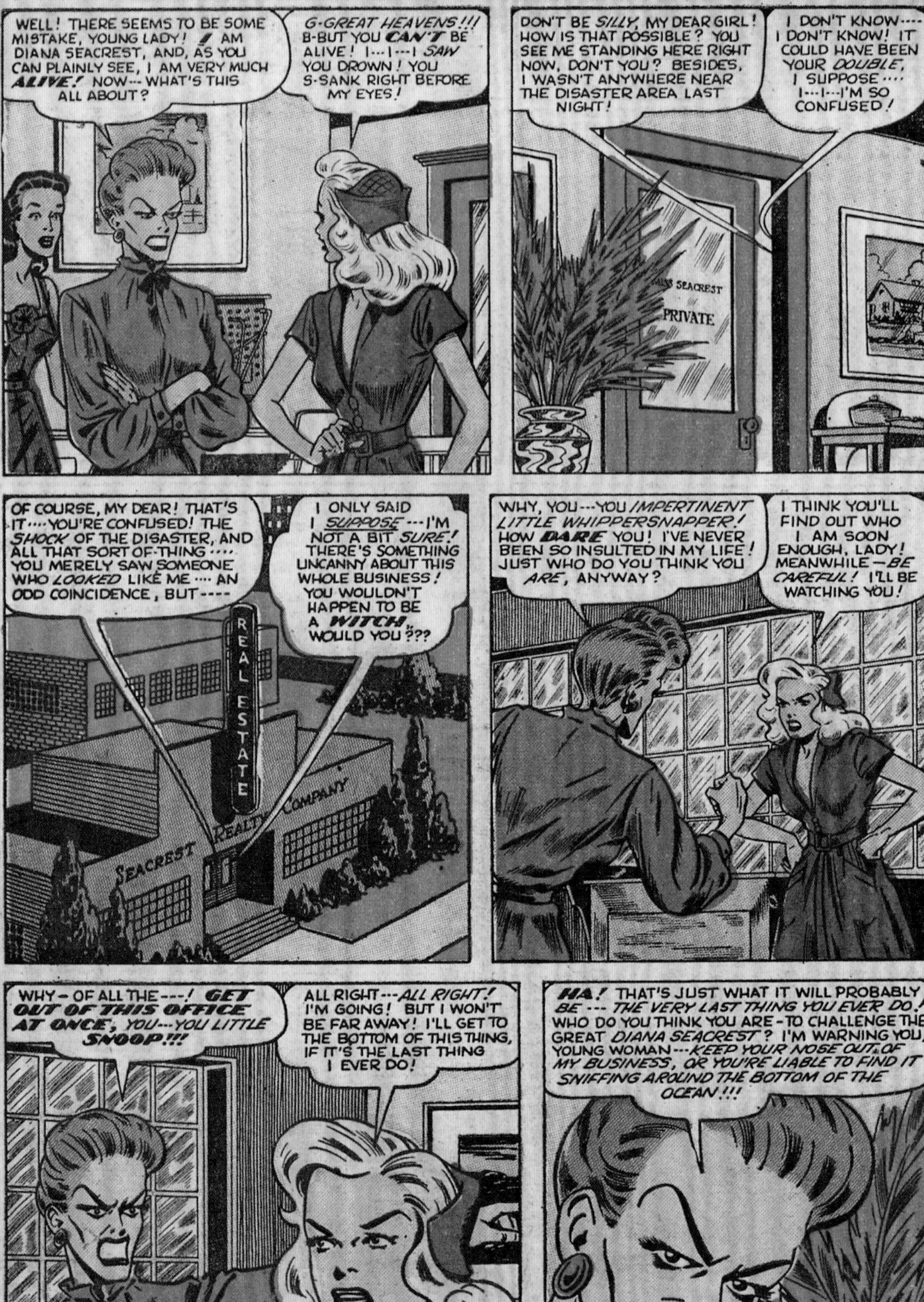
WELL! THERE SEEMS TO BE SOME MISTAKE, YOUNG LADY! I AM DIANA SEACREST, AND, AS YOU CAN PLAINLY SEE, I AM VERY MUCH ALIVE! NOW--- WHAT'S THIS ALL ABOUT?
G-GREAT HEAVENS!!! B-BUT YOU CAN'T BE ALIVE! I---I---I SAW YOU DROWN! YOU S-SANK RIGHT BEFORE MY EYES!
DON'T BE SILLY, MY DEAR GIRL! HOW IS THAT POSSIBLE? YOU SEE ME STANDING HERE RIGHT NOW, DON'T YOU? BESIDES, I WASN'T ANYWHERE NEAR THE DISASTER AREA LAST NIGHT!
I DON'T KNOW---- I DON'T KNOW! IT COULD HAVE BEEN YOUR DOUBLE, I SUPPOSE.... I---I---I'M SO CONFUSED!
MISS SEACREST
PRIVATE
OF COURSE, MY DEAR! THAT'S IT---- YOU'RE CONFUSED! THE SHOCK OF THE DISASTER, AND ALL THAT SORT OF THING.... YOU MERELY SAW SOMEONE WHO LOOKED LIKE ME.... AN ODD COINCIDENCE, BUT----
I ONLY SAID I SUPPOSE---I'M NOT A BIT SURE! THERE'S SOMETHING UNCANNY ABOUT THIS WHOLE BUSINESS! YOU WOULDN'T HAPPEN TO BE A WITCH, WOULD YOU???
REAL ESTATE
SEACREST REALTY COMPANY
WHY, YOU---YOU IMPERTINENT LITTLE WHIPPERSNAPPER! HOW DARE YOU! I'VE NEVER BEEN SO INSULTED IN MY LIFE! JUST WHO DO YOU THINK YOU ARE, ANYWAY?
I THINK YOU'LL FIND OUT WHO I AM SOON ENOUGH, LADY! MEANWHILE--BE CAREFUL! I'LL BE WATCHING YOU!
WHY - OF ALL THE---! GET OUT OF THIS OFFICE AT ONCE, YOU---YOU LITTLE SNOOP!!!
ALL RIGHT---ALL RIGHT! I'M GOING! BUT I WON'T BE FAR AWAY! I'LL GET TO THE BOTTOM OF THIS THING, IF IT'S THE LAST THING I EVER DO!
HA! THAT'S JUST WHAT IT WILL PROBABLY BE --- THE VERY LAST THING YOU EVER DO! WHO DO YOU THINK YOU ARE - TO CHALLENGE THE GREAT DIANA SEACREST? I'M WARNING YOU, YOUNG WOMAN --- KEEP YOUR NOSE OUT OF MY BUSINESS, OR YOU'RE LIABLE TO FIND IT SNIFFING AROUND THE BOTTOM OF THE OCEAN!!!
6

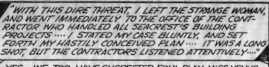

"WITH THIS DIRE THREAT, I LEFT THE STRANGE WOMAN, AND WENT IMMEDIATELY TO THE OFFICE OF THE CONTRACTOR WHO HANDLED ALL SEACREST'S BUILDING PROJECTS .... I STATED MY CASE BLUNTLY, AND SET FORTH MY HASTILY CONCEIVED PLAN .... IT WAS A LONG SHOT, BUT THE CONTRACTORS LISTENED ATTENTIVELY ...."

YES---WE, TOO, HAVE SUSPECTED FOUL PLAY, MISS VENUS---BUT IT SOUNDS UTTERLY *FANTASTIC!* HOWEVER --- WE'LL GO ALONG WITH YOU! WE'LL ---*OH-OH!* HERE COMES MISS SEACREST NOW! GET IN THE OTHER ROOM, QUICKLY!

AH, GOOD MORNING, MISS SEACREST, GOOD MORNING! WHAT A SHOCKING DISASTER LAST NIGHT! WE SEEM TO BE PLAGUED ----

YES, YES! I KNOW! BUT THERE'S NO ROOM FOR SENTIMENT IN THIS BUSINESS, MR. O'CONNOR! WE MUST NOT THINK ABOUT THE TRAGEDY.....WE MUST START TO REBUILD --- *IMMEDIATELY !!!*

REBUILD? *NOW?* SO *SOON*? BUT, MISS SEACREST! I---I'M AFRAID --- I MEAN --- WELL, THE INSURANCE PEOPLE ---THEY-*ER-*THEY DON'T THINK WE'RE SUCH A GOOD RISK NOW! YOUR CREDIT---WELL ---UH---I MEAN --- WELL, I'M AFRAID WE JUST CAN'T AFFORD TO DO ANY MORE BUILDING FOR YOU, MISS SEACREST !!!

WHAT ??? DO YOU *MEAN* THAT? YES---YES, YOU *DO* MEAN IT! I SEE IT ALL NOW - TOO, *TOO* CLEARLY! YOU---YOU'VE FORMED A *CONSPIRACY* AGAINST ME! YOU AND THE STUPID GOVERNMENT! *BUT YOU WON'T GET AWAY WITH IT! I'LL FIX YOU ALL !!!*

"AS I HEARD THE DOOR SLAM, I KNEW INSTINCTIVELY THAT THE WORST WAS YET TO COME! THERE WAS ONLY ONE THING TO DO .... I QUICKLY PICKED UP THE PHONE AND PUT A CALL THROUGH TO WASHINGTON"

---YES, I THINK THAT'S WHAT SHE'S GOING TO DO, SIR! I KNOW---IT SOUNDS IMPOSSIBLE---INCREDIBLE---BUT WHAT OTHER EXPLANATION IS THERE? YES---I THINK IT WILL *HAVE* TO BE TONIGHT ! --- OKAY--- DO WHAT YOU CAN, WILL YOU? YES---YES---I'LL STAY ON HER TRAIL! OKAY----

"INSTANTLY THE WHEELS OF GOVERNMENT BEGAN TO TURN! ALL UP AND DOWN THE ATLANTIC COAST, ASSISTED BY NATIONAL GUARD TROOPS AND MOBILIZED RED CROSS PERSONNEL, THE ENTIRE POPULATION COMMENCED A MASS EVACUATION EASTWARD --- INLAND---TOWARD HIGHER GROUND AND SAFETY---"

"WHILE I FOLLOWED THE MYSTERIOUS DIANA SEACREST ALL AFTERNOON ----THEN, AS EVENING FELL, SHE ARRIVED ON THE COAST, AND TOOK ONE LOOK AT THE VAST EMIGRATION --- "

WHAT ARE THEY *DOING?* OH---*NO!* THEY CAN'T *DO* THIS TO ME! THEY CAN'T LEAVE *NOW*--- I WON'T *LET* THEM! I'LL STOP THEM! I'LL STOP THEM! NOW--- *ARISE, NEPTUNUS! ARISE---NOW!!!*

7

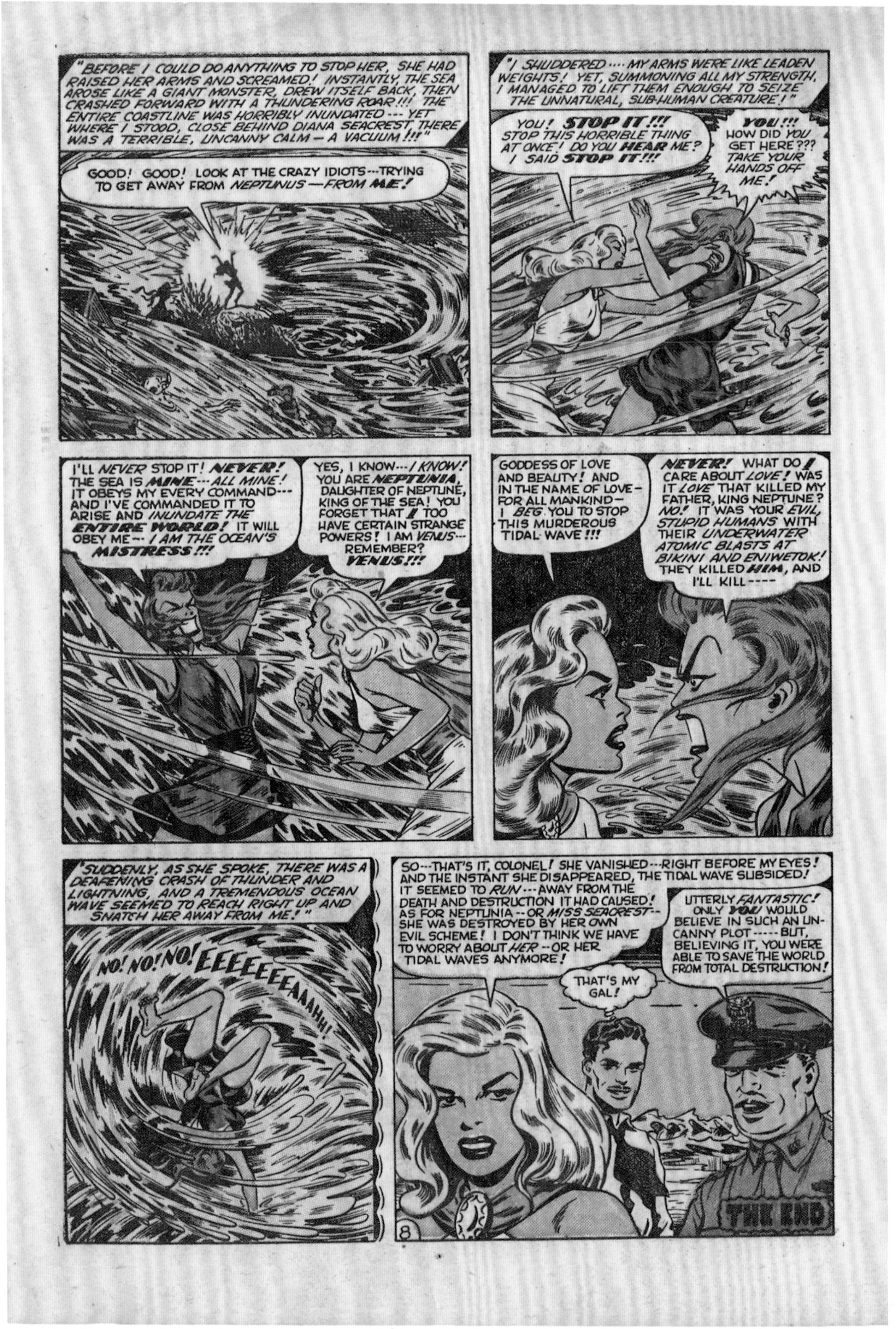
"BEFORE I COULD DO ANYTHING TO STOP HER, SHE HAD RAISED HER ARMS AND SCREAMED! INSTANTLY, THE SEA AROSE LIKE A GIANT MONSTER, DREW ITSELF BACK, THEN CRASHED FORWARD WITH A THUNDERING ROAR!!! THE ENTIRE COASTLINE WAS HORRIBLY INUNDATED --- YET WHERE I STOOD, CLOSE BEHIND DIANA SEACREST, THERE WAS A TERRIBLE, UNCANNY CALM — A VACUUM!!!"
GOOD! GOOD! LOOK AT THE CRAZY IDIOTS---TRYING TO GET AWAY FROM NEPTUNUS — FROM ME!
"I SHUDDERED.... MY ARMS WERE LIKE LEADEN WEIGHTS! YET, SUMMONING ALL MY STRENGTH, I MANAGED TO LIFT THEM ENOUGH TO SEIZE THE UNNATURAL, SUB-HUMAN CREATURE!"
YOU! STOP IT!!! STOP THIS HORRIBLE THING AT ONCE! DO YOU HEAR ME? I SAID STOP IT!!!
YOU!!! HOW DID YOU GET HERE??? TAKE YOUR HANDS OFF ME!
I'LL NEVER STOP IT! NEVER! THE SEA IS MINE---ALL MINE! IT OBEYS MY EVERY COMMAND--- AND I'VE COMMANDED IT TO ARISE AND INUNDATE THE ENTIRE WORLD! IT WILL OBEY ME -- I AM THE OCEAN'S MISTRESS!!!
YES, I KNOW---I KNOW! YOU ARE NEPTUNIA, DAUGHTER OF NEPTUNE, KING OF THE SEA! YOU FORGET THAT I TOO HAVE CERTAIN STRANGE POWERS! I AM VENUS--- REMEMBER? VENUS!!!
GODDESS OF LOVE AND BEAUTY! AND IN THE NAME OF LOVE - FOR ALL MANKIND - I BEG YOU TO STOP THIS MURDEROUS TIDAL WAVE!!!
NEVER! WHAT DO I CARE ABOUT LOVE! WAS IT LOVE THAT KILLED MY FATHER, KING NEPTUNE? NO! IT WAS YOUR EVIL, STUPID HUMANS WITH THEIR UNDERWATER ATOMIC BLASTS AT BIKINI AND ENIWETOK! THEY KILLED HIM, AND I'LL KILL----
"SUDDENLY, AS SHE SPOKE, THERE WAS A DEAFENING CRASH OF THUNDER AND LIGHTNING, AND A TREMENDOUS OCEAN WAVE SEEMED TO REACH RIGHT UP AND SNATCH HER AWAY FROM ME!"
NO! NO! NO! EEEEEEEAAAHH!
SO---THAT'S IT, COLONEL! SHE VANISHED---RIGHT BEFORE MY EYES! AND THE INSTANT SHE DISAPPEARED, THE TIDAL WAVE SUBSIDED! IT SEEMED TO RUN---AWAY FROM THE DEATH AND DESTRUCTION IT HAD CAUSED! AS FOR NEPTUNIA--OR MISS SEACREST-- SHE WAS DESTROYED BY HER OWN EVIL SCHEME! I DON'T THINK WE HAVE TO WORRY ABOUT HER--OR HER TIDAL WAVES ANYMORE!
UTTERLY FANTASTIC! ONLY YOU WOULD BELIEVE IN SUCH AN UNCANNY PLOT----- BUT, BELIEVING IT, YOU WERE ABLE TO SAVE THE WORLD FROM TOTAL DESTRUCTION!
THAT'S MY GAL!
8
THE END

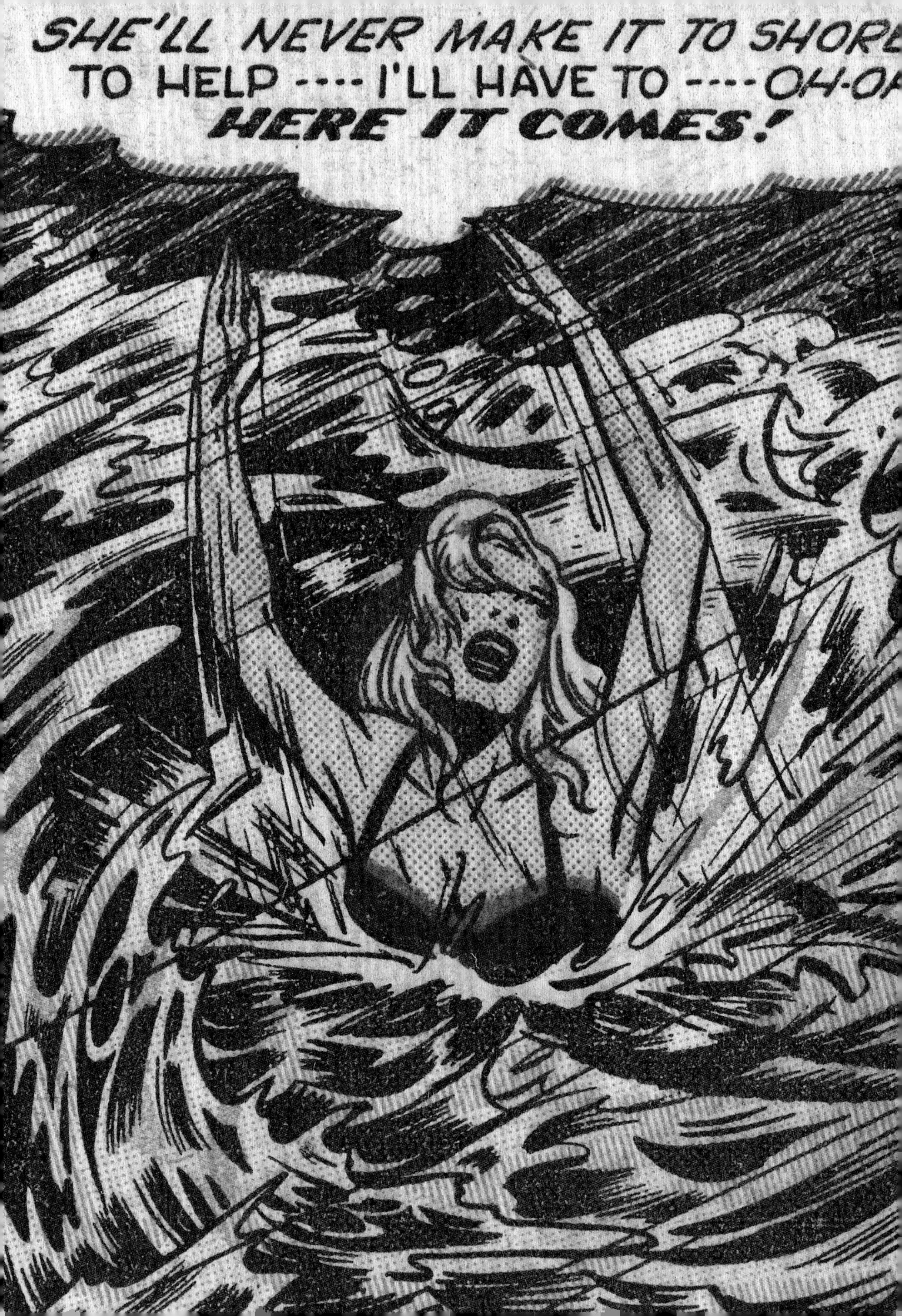
SHE'LL NEVER MAKE IT TO SHORE
TO HELP ---- I'LL HAVE TO ---- OH-OH
HERE IT COMES!

WILLY MENDES

(b. 1948)

Willy Mendes was the *nom de guerre* of Barbara Mendes, who was born in Montclair, New Jersey, and raised in Brooklyn Heights, New York. She grew up in a culturally rich environment and attended both the School of Visual Arts and Hunter College. Mendes fell into comics in New York City, first publishing her work in the *East Village Other*'s comics anthology, *Gothic Blimp Works*. She "tuned in, turned on and dropped out" to San Francisco in 1969 and made comics for anthologies including *All Girl Thrills; It Ain't Me, Babe*; and *Insect Fear*. By 1971 Mendes was confident in her abilities and created her own comic book, *Illuminations*. It contained her own lengthy story occasionally interrupted by full-page drawings by some of the best artists of the comics underground, including Rory Hayes, Kim Deitch, and Bill Griffith. The story "Jonny, Julie, and Harpo" was actually inspired by her life in Wonder, Oregon, where she moved in 1971 with her companion, Rick, and their baby, Oma. In correspondence Barbara describes Wonder as a kind of hippy eden:

> Rick wrote awesome songs, baby Oma glowed with growth and beauty, we immersed in icy creeks, and we made our second baby out in the ferns of the woods. When we arrived in Wonder we found a purple dome, a hand-worked sign saying "Miracles of Wonder," and a psychedelic school bus outside a blue house. Inside, we were greeted, got high, and then followed new friends to the weekly feast on Leonard's land in Wilderville. We put up in a chicken coop behind the blue house in Wonder, which was equipped with a tiny wood stove and a bed shelf, for a rainy week. Then we left and headed for the Mackenzie River outside Eugene. In the rainy dusk we picked up Cathye hitchhiking. She put us up in her cabin on the river, with jars of nuts and coconut, and *The Biography of Milarepa*. Amazing, as we loved the "100,000 Songs of Milarepa," and longed to read the biography. We talked so much about Wonder that we decided to go back and stay. I wrote and drew *Illuminations* there. I always believed that the comics medium could be a vehicle for fine drawings with inspiring subjects to be published.

"Jonny, Julie, and Harpo" is a pure narrative of utopian idealism, and in its spiritual yearning and literal journeying, it is a perfectly realized adventure story. Mendes, enthralled by her surroundings, her comics, and Eastern traditions of art, created a kind of tapestry in ink. She was uninterested, she has said, in notions of traditional realism, focused instead on her own interior vision, and slowed down in order to take in all the holy details. Each of Mendes's panels is filled with detail and drawn to its very edge—not cartooned, but built out of tiny, exacting marks. The ecstasy of the work is the heady hopefulness for a child to instruct its parents and bring the enlightenment, and for bio-spiritual claims made for humankind. If John Thompson's comics were attempts to explore and understand language and symbology, Mendes's were attempts to explore the new mental and physical landscape that (briefly) became available in the 1960s.

There was no sequel to *Illuminations*. When Mendes returned to San Francisco in 1973 with a new thirty-six-page comic, *Tales from the Modern Mystic*, the underground comics market had already begun to collapse and she couldn't find a publisher. Instead, she self-published *Tales* as a 200-copy edition. Eventually, Barbara Mendes left comics and embarked on a career as a painter. She lives in Los Angeles, California, where she continues to paint. Mendes illustrated a children's picture book, *Max Said Yes! The Woodstock Story*, which was published in 2009.

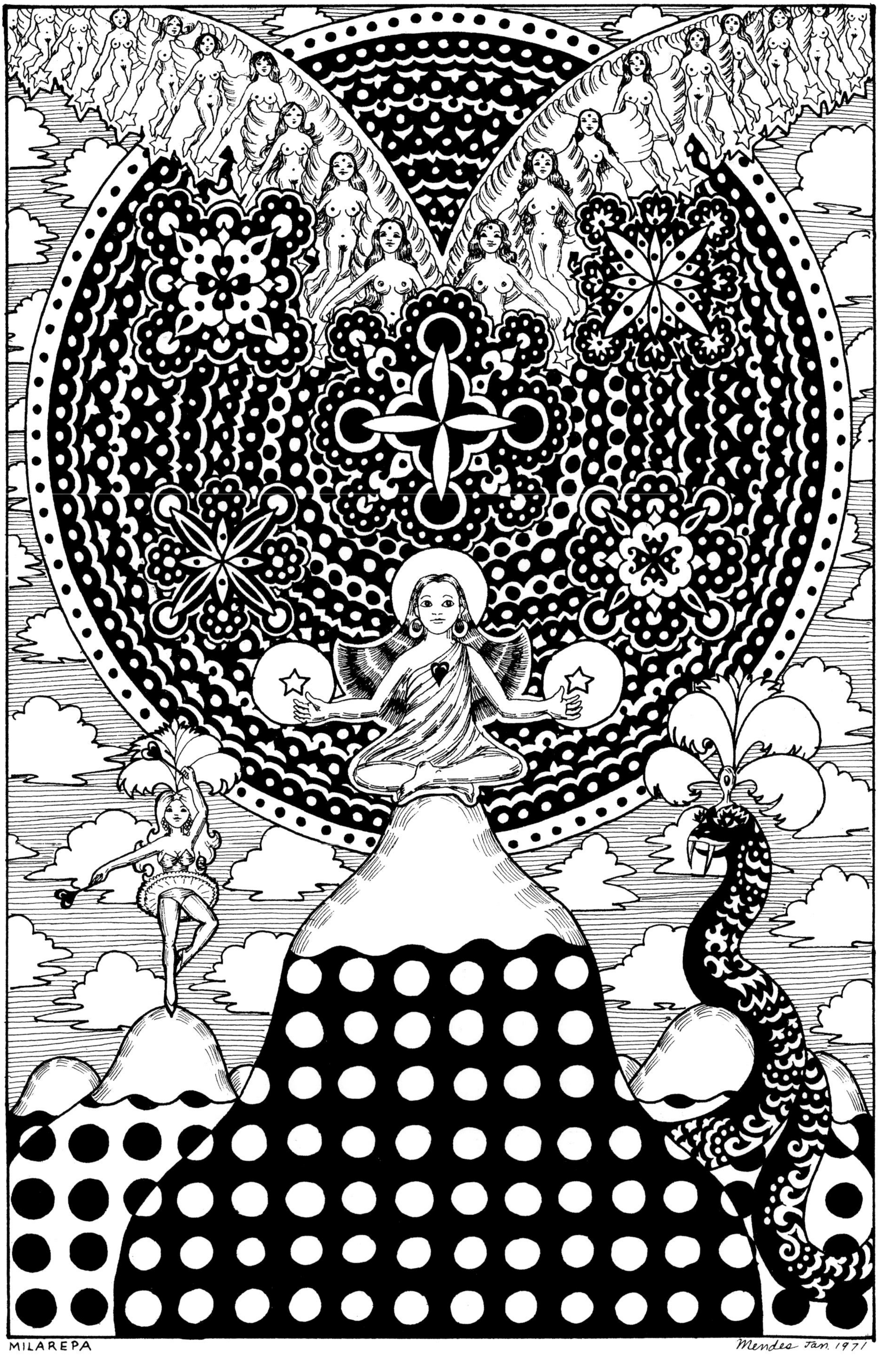
MILAREPA
Mendes Jan. 1971

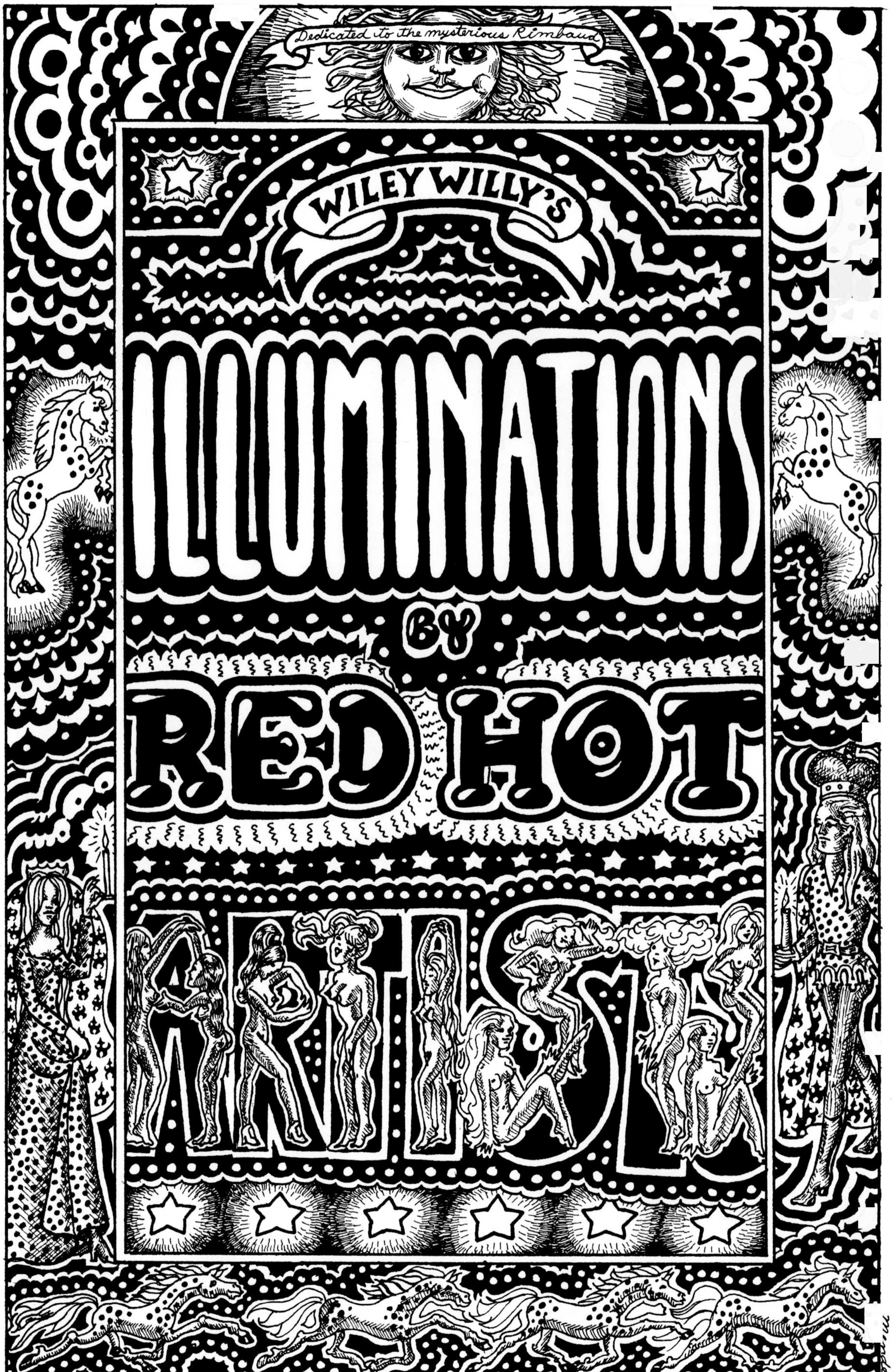
Dedicated to the mysterious Rimbaud
WILEY WILLY'S
ILLUMINATIONS
BY
RED HOT
ARTISTS
PUBLISHED BY THE PRINT MINT — 830 FOLGER AVE. BERKELEY, CAL. 94710

Illuminations (1971)

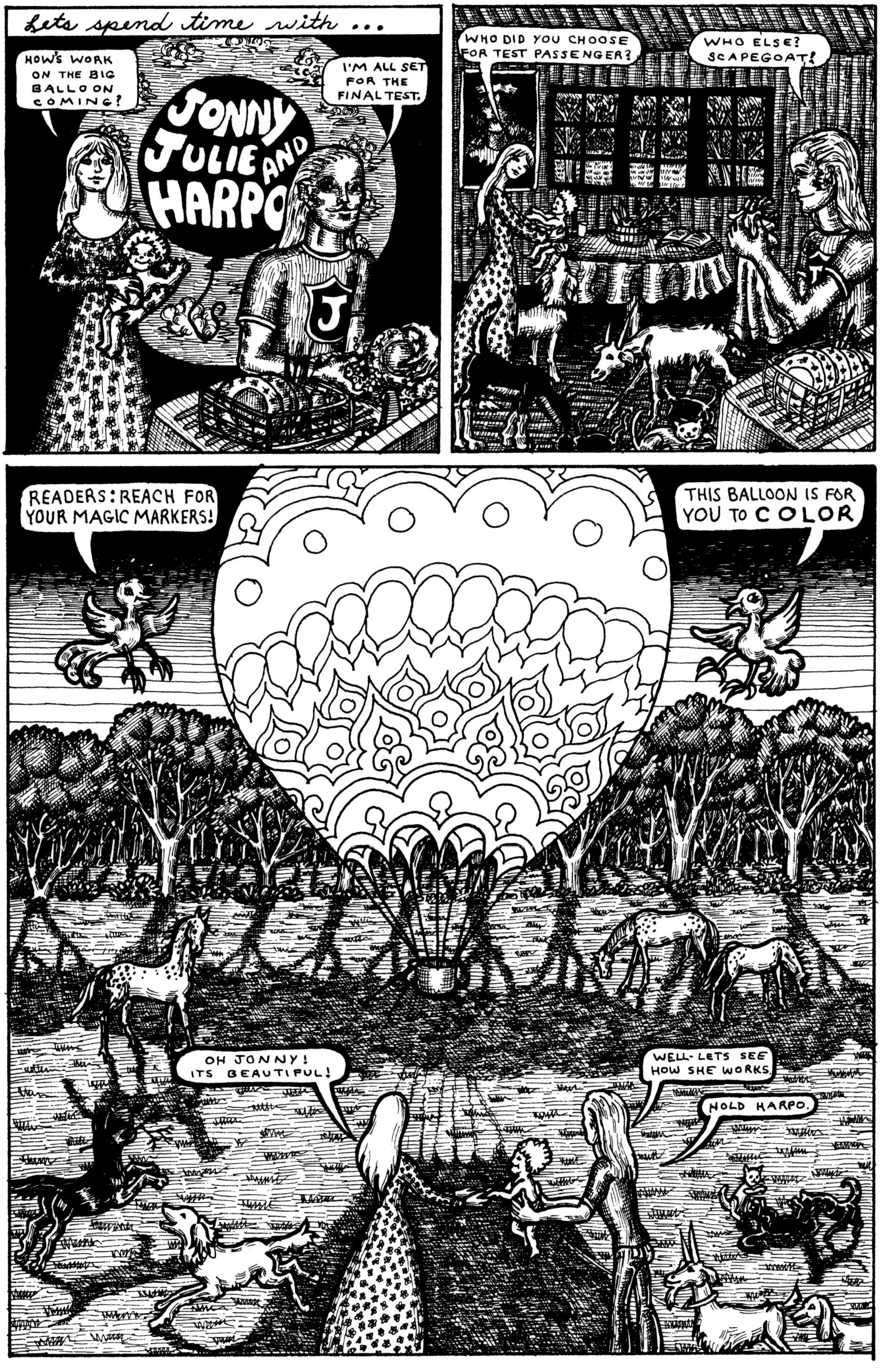
Lets spend time with ...
HOW'S WORK ON THE BIG BALLOON COMING?
JONNY JULIE AND HARPO
I'M ALL SET FOR THE FINAL TEST.
WHO DID YOU CHOOSE FOR TEST PASSENGER?
WHO ELSE? SCAPEGOAT!
READERS: REACH FOR YOUR MAGIC MARKERS!
THIS BALLOON IS FOR YOU TO COLOR
OH JONNY! ITS BEAUTIFUL!
WELL-LETS SEE HOW SHE WORKS.
HOLD HARPO.

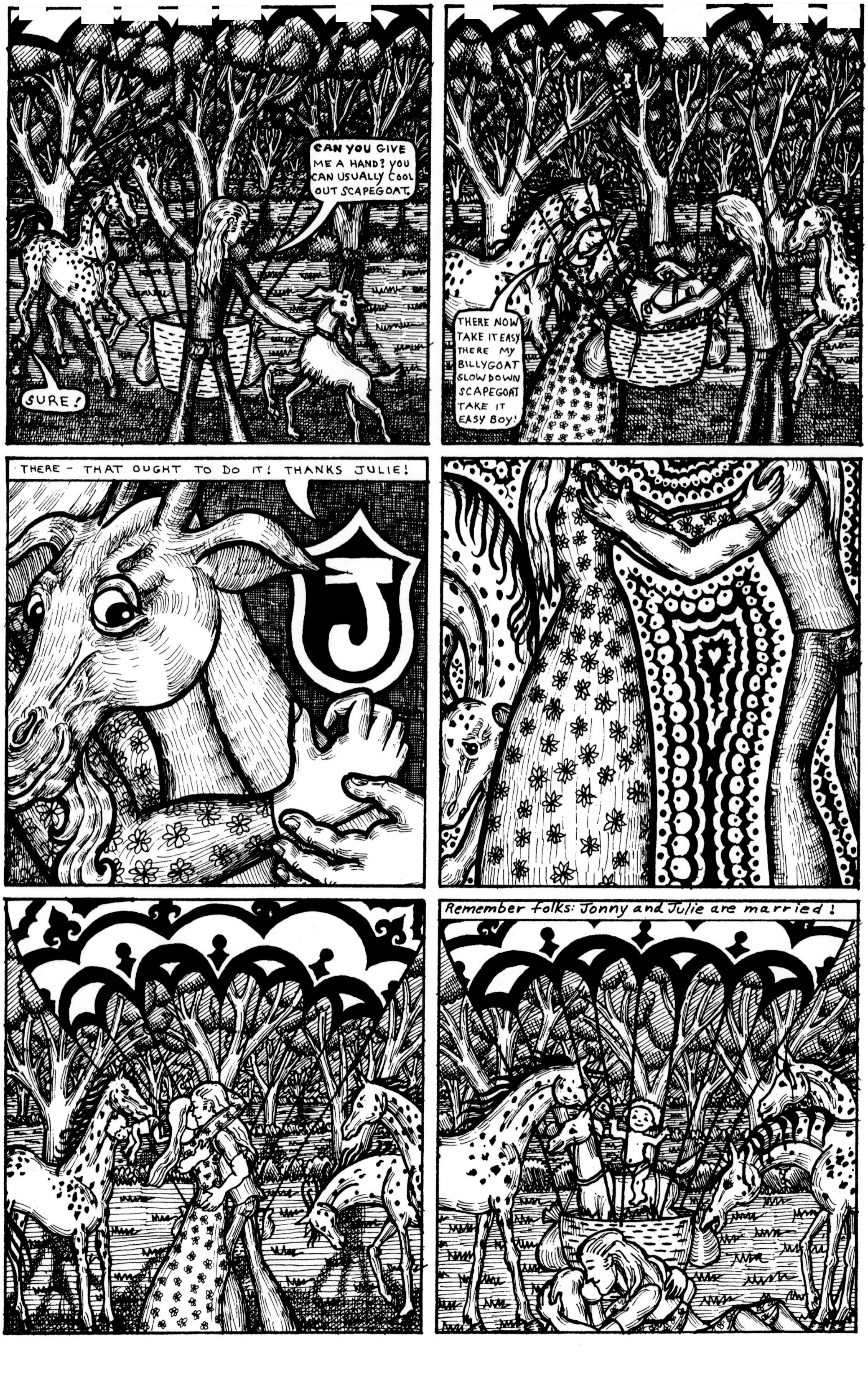

CAN YOU GIVE ME A HAND? YOU CAN USUALLY COOL OUT SCAPEGOAT.
SURE!
THERE NOW TAKE IT EASY THERE MY BILLYGOAT SLOW DOWN SCAPEGOAT TAKE IT EASY BOY!
THERE - THAT OUGHT TO DO IT! THANKS JULIE!
J
Remember folks: Jonny and Julie are married!

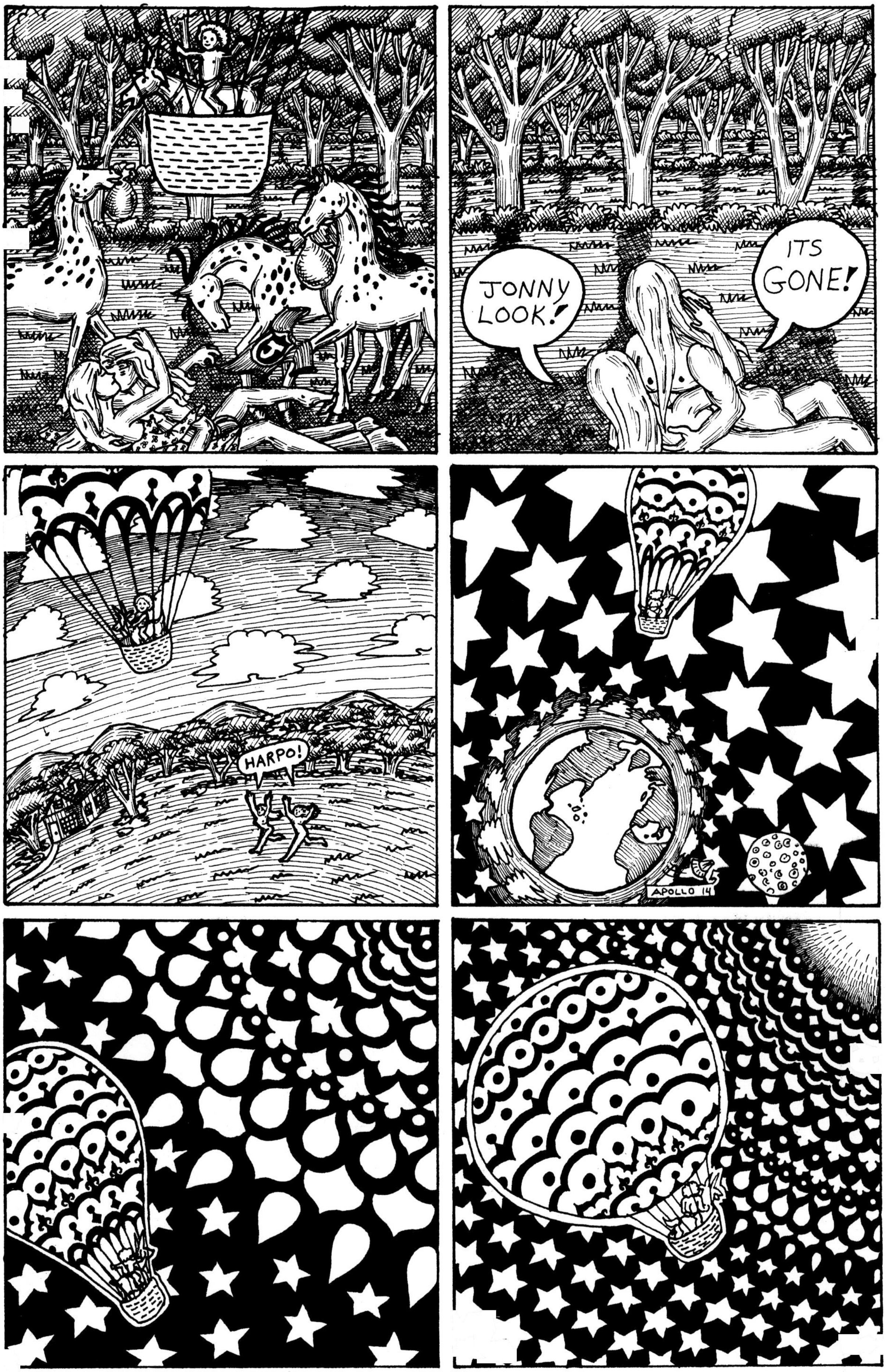
JONNY LOOK!
ITS GONE!
HARPO!
APOLLO 14

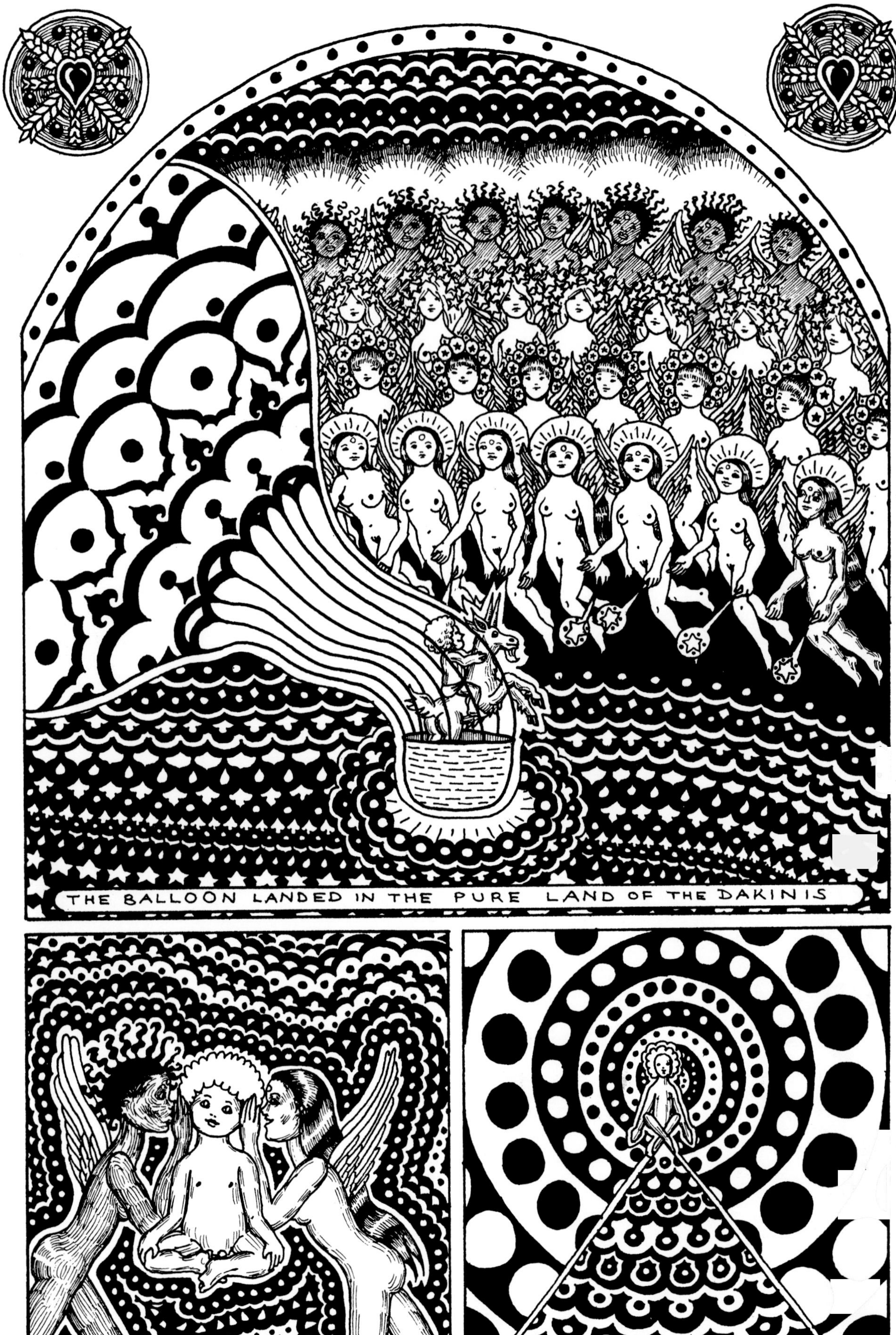
THE BALLOON LANDED IN THE PURE LAND OF THE DAKINIS
WHERE HARPO HEARD THE WHISPERED SOUND AND WAS ILLUMINATED

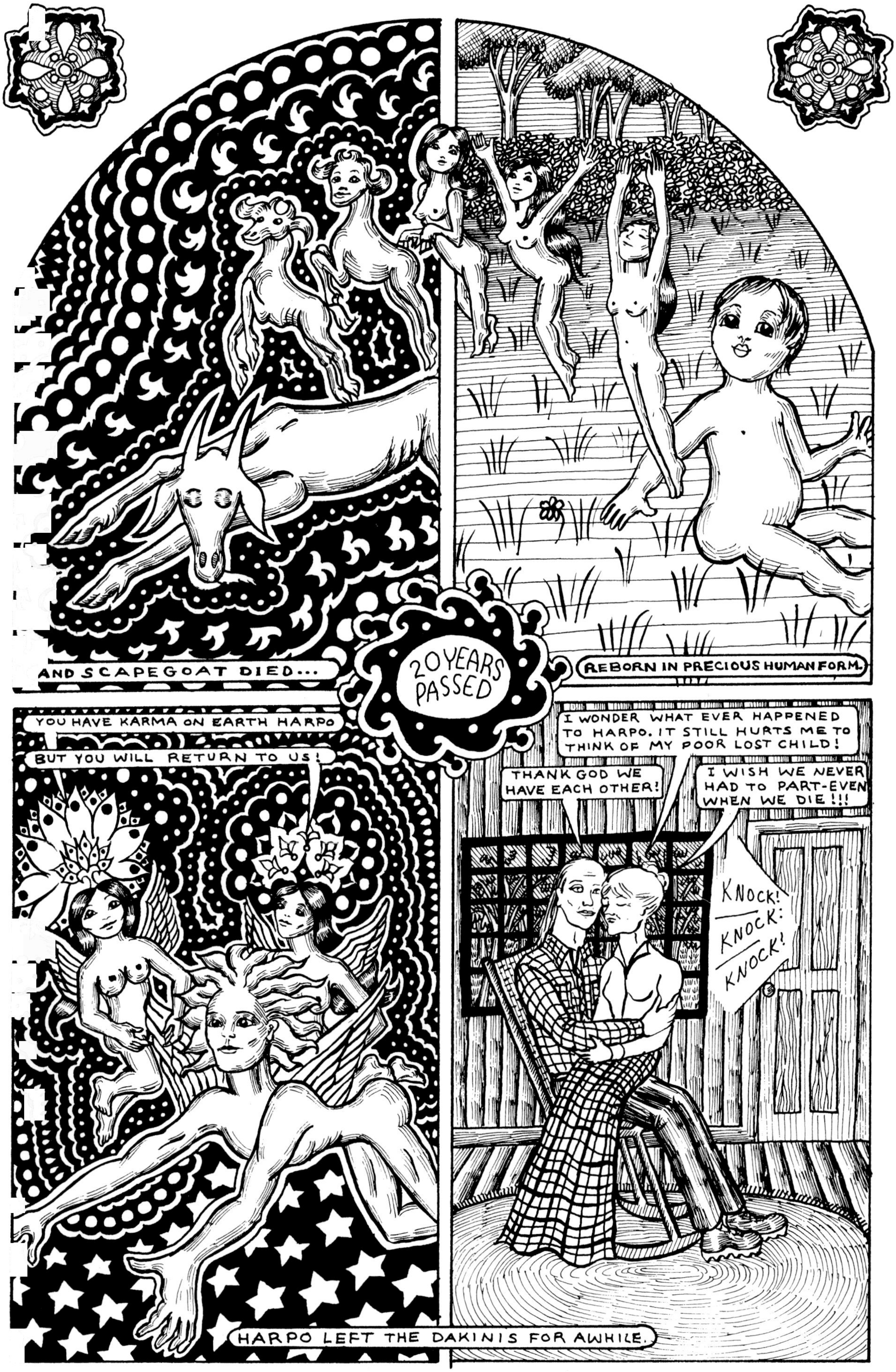
AND SCAPEGOAT DIED...
20 YEARS PASSED
REBORN IN PRECIOUS HUMAN FORM.
YOU HAVE KARMA ON EARTH HARPO
BUT YOU WILL RETURN TO US!
HARPO LEFT THE DAKINIS FOR AWHILE.
I WONDER WHAT EVER HAPPENED TO HARPO. IT STILL HURTS ME TO THINK OF MY POOR LOST CHILD!
THANK GOD WE HAVE EACH OTHER!
I WISH WE NEVER HAD TO PART-EVEN WHEN WE DIE!!!
KNOCK! KNOCK! KNOCK!

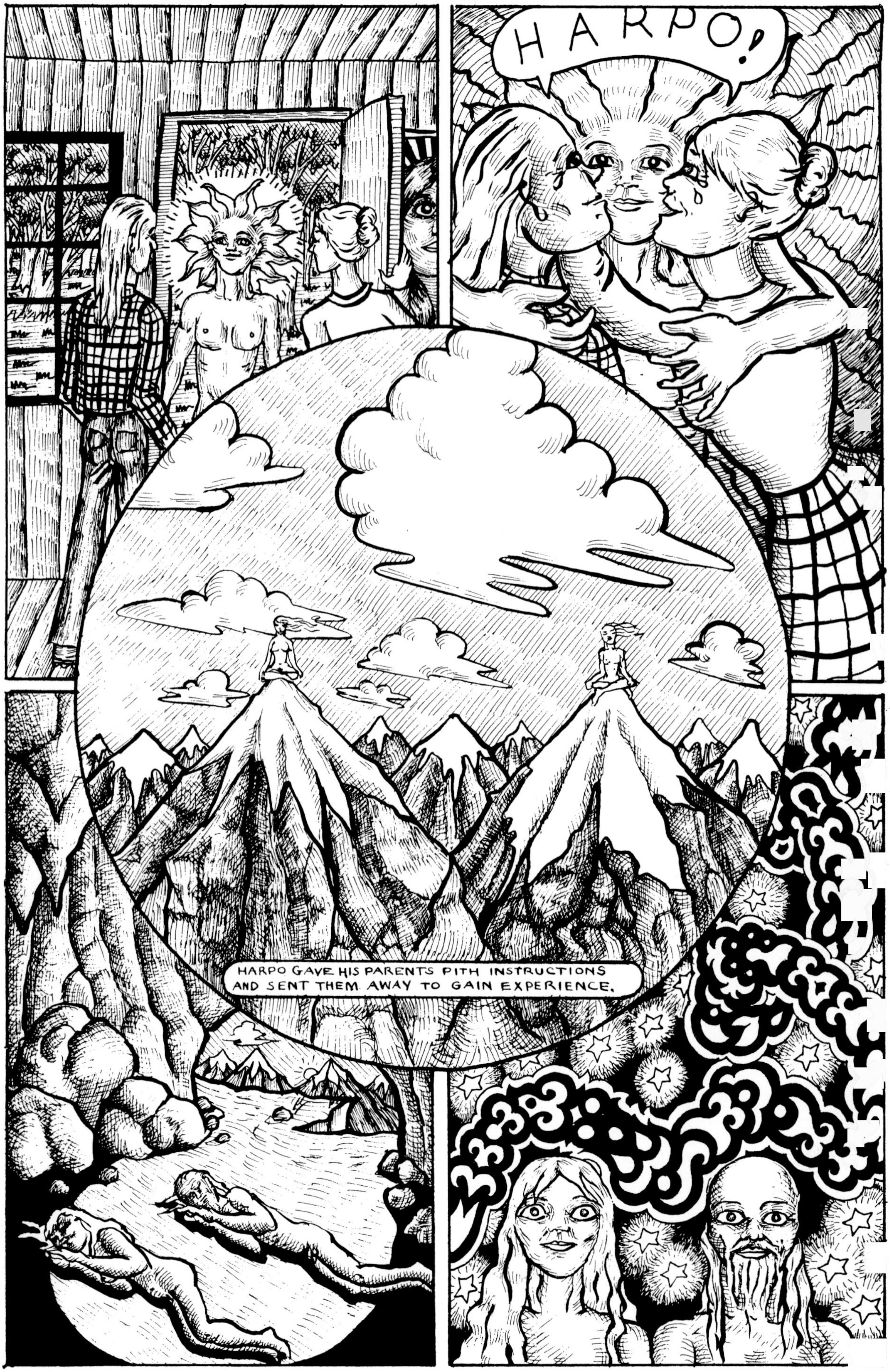
HARPO!
HARPO GAVE HIS PARENTS PITH INSTRUCTIONS AND SENT THEM AWAY TO GAIN EXPERIENCE.

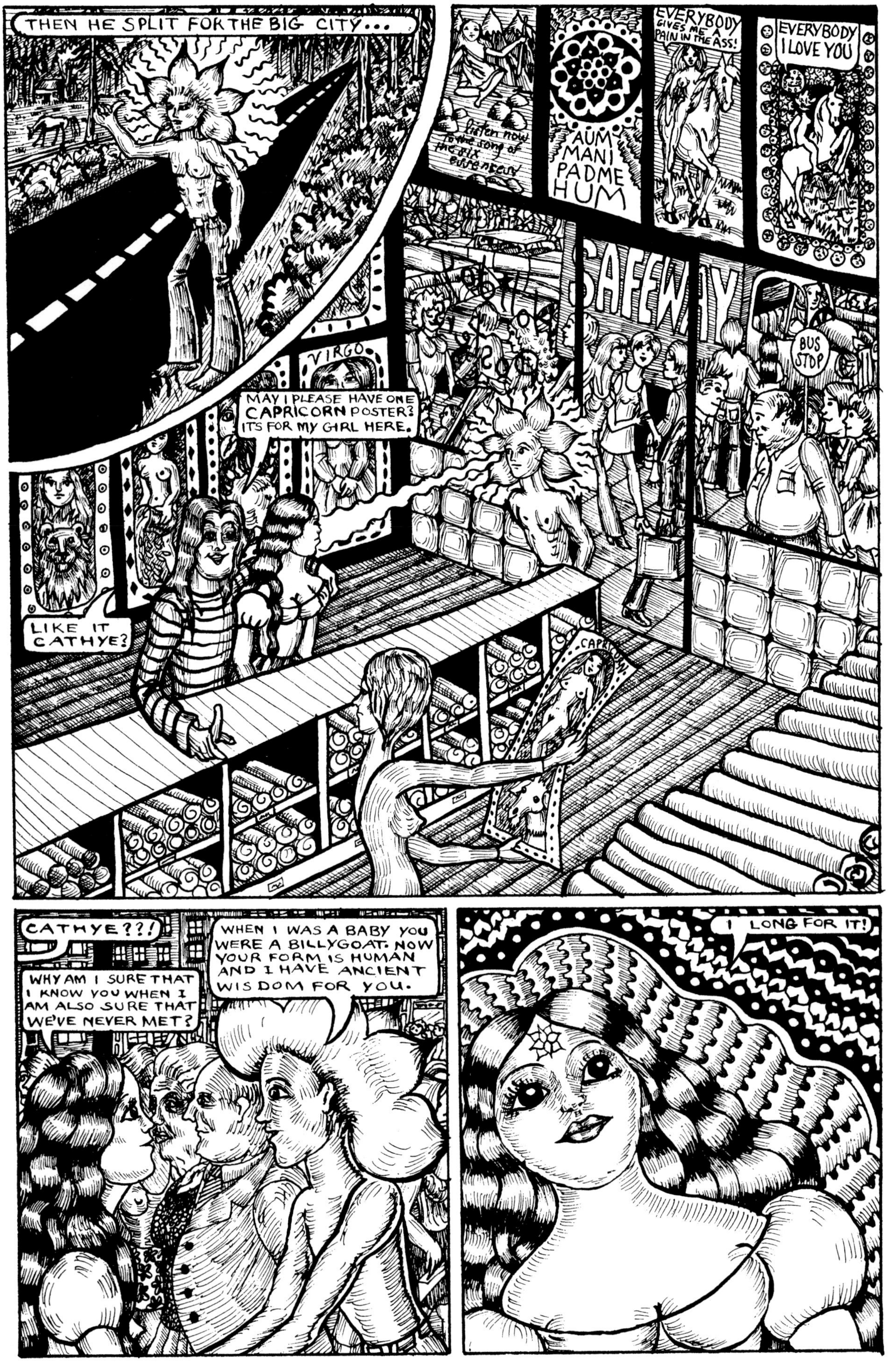
THEN HE SPLIT FOR THE BIG CITY...
AUM MANI PADME HUM
EVERYBODY GIVES ME A PAIN IN THE ASS!
EVERYBODY I LOVE YOU
SAFEWAY
BUS STOP
VIRGO
MAY I PLEASE HAVE ONE CAPRICORN POSTER? ITS FOR MY GIRL HERE.
LIKE IT CATHYE?
CATHYE???!
WHY AM I SURE THAT I KNOW YOU WHEN I AM ALSO SURE THAT WE'VE NEVER MET?
WHEN I WAS A BABY YOU WERE A BILLYGOAT. NOW YOUR FORM IS HUMAN AND I HAVE ANCIENT WISDOM FOR YOU.
I LONG FOR IT!

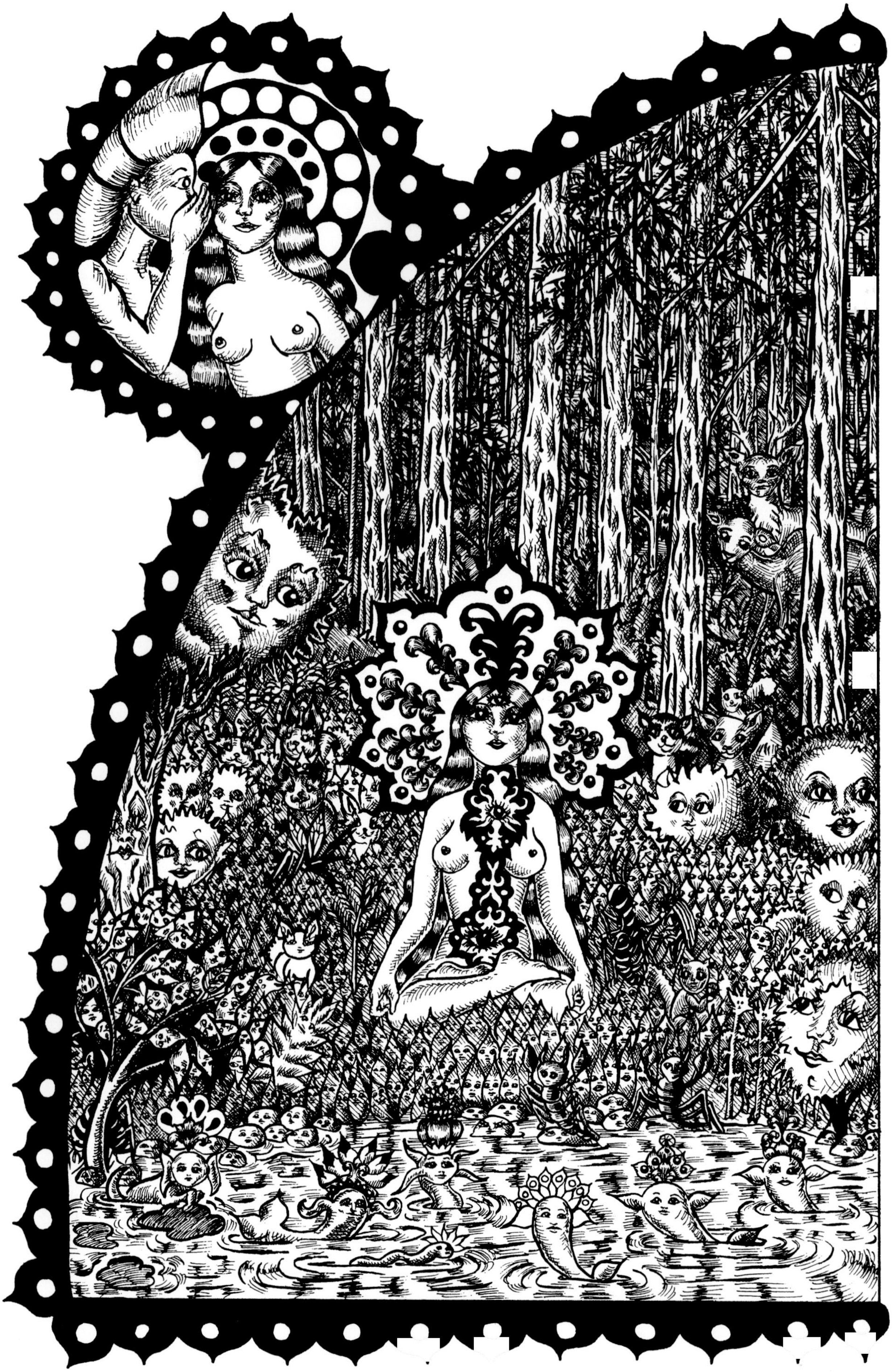

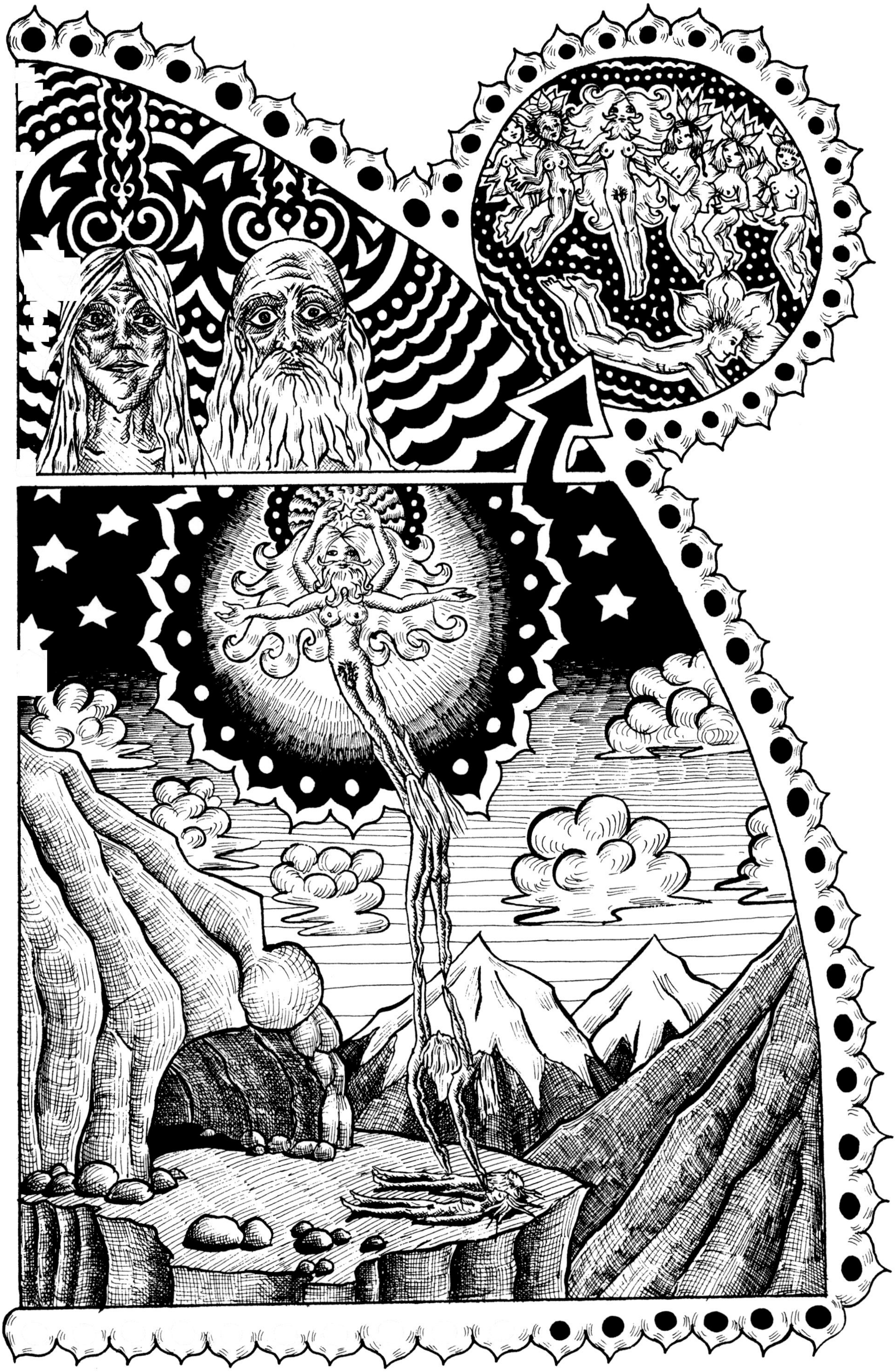

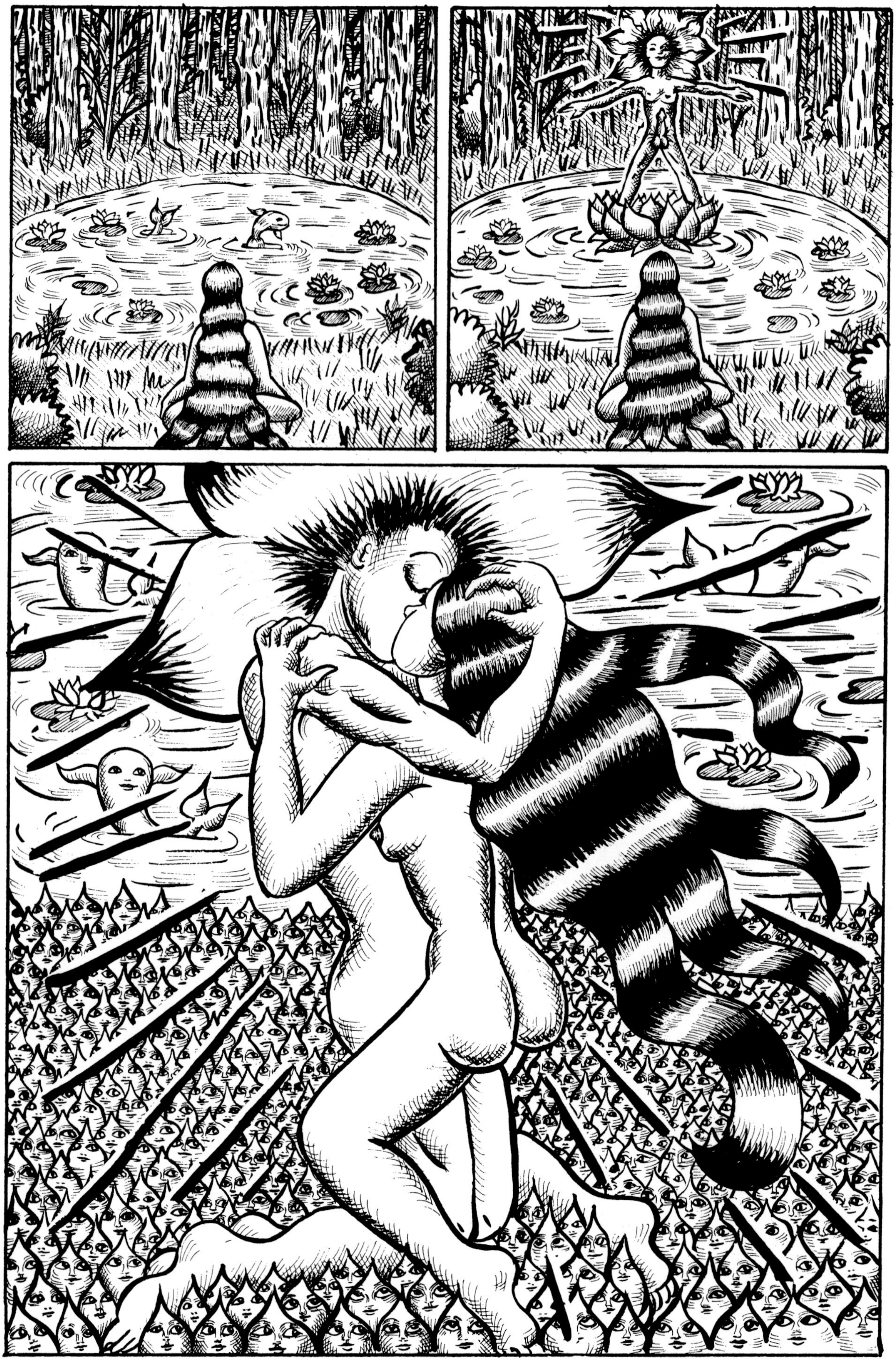

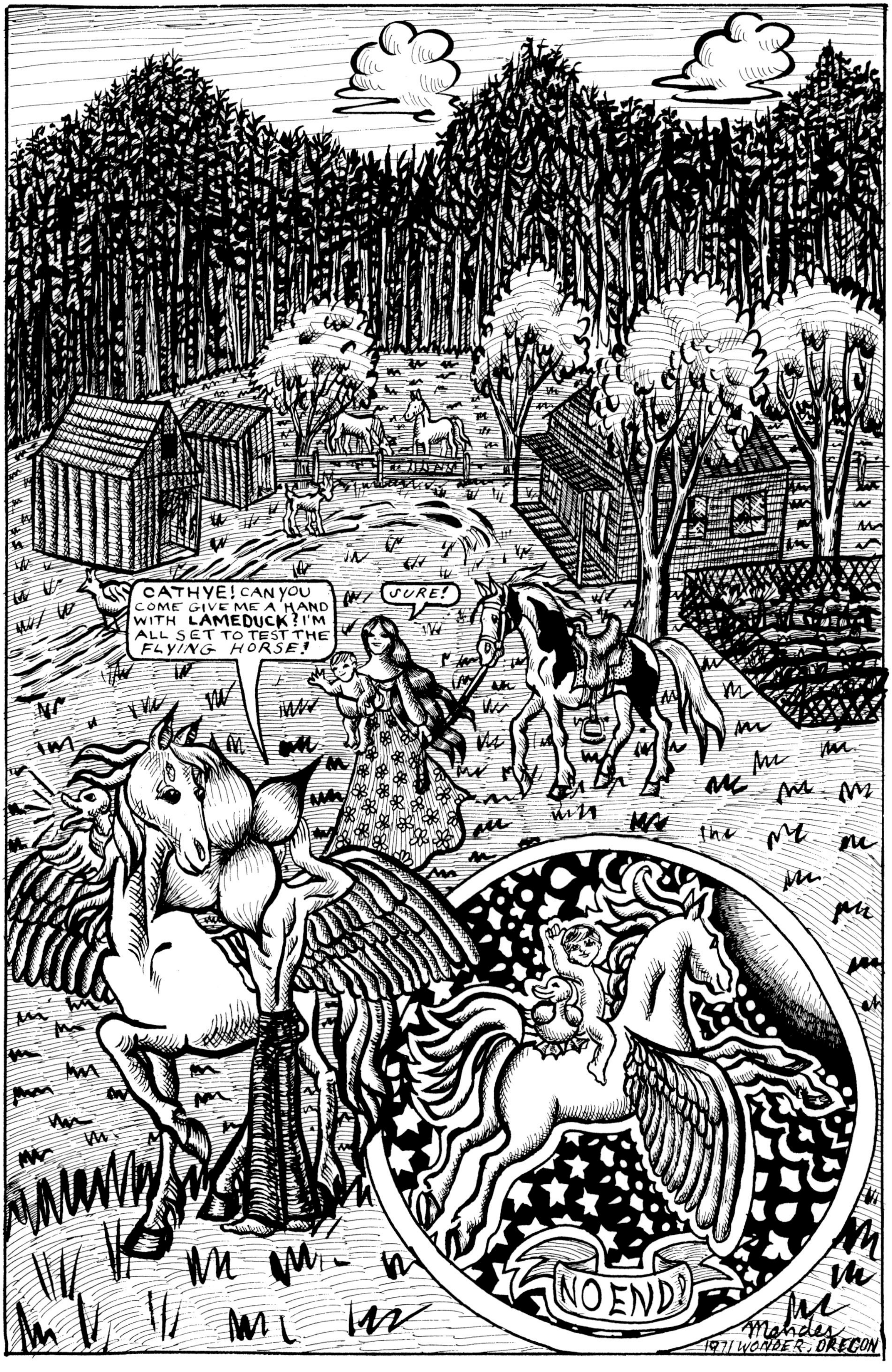
CATHYE! CAN YOU COME GIVE ME A HAND WITH LAMEDUCK? I'M ALL SET TO TEST THE FLYING HORSE!
SURE!
NO END!
Mendes
1971 WONDER, OREGON

Sources

Amash, Jim. "He Raised the Artistic Bar." *Alter Ego*, vol. 3, no. 24, May 2003.

——. "He Thought He Was a Great Comic Book Artist!" *Alter Ego*, vol. 3, no. 24, May 2003.

Ambrose, Michael. "PAM: Walking the Comics Beat." *Charlton Spotlight* no. 4, Summer/Fall 2005.

——. "Son of PAM." *Charlton Spotlight* no. 4, Summer/Fall 2005.

Antoni, Ralf. "A Biography of Sorts." The Jesse Marsh Site. www.angelfire.com/apes2/jessemarsh102, 2006.

Burbey, Mark. "The Explosive World of Johnny Dynamite." *Charlton Spotlight* no. 4, Summer/Fall 2005.

Daniels, Les. *Wonder Woman: The Complete History*. San Francisco: Chronicle Books, 2004.

Frantz, Ron. "Pete Morisi: Before and After Charlton." *Charlton Spotlight* no. 4, Summer/Fall 2005.

Glanzman, Sam J. Author interview, 2009.

Goulart, Ron. *The Great Comic Book Artists*. New York: St. Martin's Press, 1986.

——. *The Great Comic Book Artists Volume 2*. New York: St. Martin's Press, 1988.

——, ed. *The Encyclopedia of American Comics*. New York: Facts on File, 1991.

——. "Jesse Marsh: History of His Work in Comics." *Comic Art*, no. 9. Oakland, CA: Buenaventura Press, 1997.

Johnson, Glen. "Pete Morisi . . . Comic Book Artist." *Charlton Spotlight* no. 4, Summer/Fall 2005.

Kane, Gil. "Four of a Kind." *Alter Ego*, vol. 3, no. 22, March 2003.

Kyle, Richard. Letter. *Graphic Story Magazine*, no. 9, Summer 1968.

Mangus, Don. "Sam Glanzman's Autobiography: My Life as a Cartoonist." *Swag Report*, January–May, 1998.

——. "A Tribute to Pat Boyette." http://comicartville.com, 2003.

Manning, Russ. Letter. *Graphic Story Magazine* no. 8, Fall 1967.

McMillan, Michael. Author interview, 2009.

Mendes, Barbara. Author interview, 2009.

Pearson, Bill. "Mighty Tight: Stylized in Black and White." *Charlton Spotlight*, no. 4, Summer/Fall 2005.

Rudahl, Sharon. "Author's Note." *Dangerous Woman: The Graphic Biography of Emma Goldman*. New York: New Press, 2007.

——. Author interview, 2009.

Smith, Ken. "Pat Boyette." *The Comics Journal* no. 22, March 2000.

Spurgeon, Tom. "Pat Boyette Dies at 77." *The Comics Journal* no. 22, March 2000.

Stewart, Bhob. "Weird Tales of Matt Fox." *Potrzebie*, December 29, 2007.

Thomas, Roy. "Everett on Everett." *Alter Ego*, vol. 1, no. 11, 1978.

Thompson, John. Author interview, 2009.

Tomine, Adrian. "A Q&A with Gilbert Hernandez," *Comic Art* no. 9. Oakland, CA: Buenaventura Press, 1997.

Toth, Alex. "Jesse Marsh." *Panels* no. 2, Spring 1981.

——. "Homage to Mort Meskin: Maestro." *Alter Ego*, vol. 3, no. 24, May 2003.

Williams, Dylan, ed. The Art and Life of Mort Meskin, www.mortmeskin.com, 2004.

Acknowledgments

This book is the product of a series of friendships with an extraordinary group of artists and writers. They are the inspiration behind this project, as well as its future: Tim Hodler, Frank Santoro, Ben Jones, Christopher Forgues, Gary Panter, Brian Chippendale, Lauren Weinstein, Sammy Harkham, Matthew Thurber, and Bill Boichel.

For loans, suggestions, and help with research and production, I wish to thank Jason T. Miles, Kim Deitch, Tom Stein, Paul Karasik, Jack Peters, Dylan Williams, Glenn Bray, Jon Vermilyea, Will Luckman, Patrick Rosenkranz, Steve Banes, Blake Bell, Carlos Gonzales, and Mark Newgarden. I would also like to honor the example set by writer/historian/publishers who include Richard Kyle, Gary Groth, Bill Spicer, and John Benson. All of their respective magazines and texts have been invaluable to me—they led the way.

Thanks to Charlie Kochman, Sheila Keenan, Sofia Gutiérrez, and Abrams ComicArts for giving this one another go around, and for providing such expert guidance and support. Much appreciation is also due to Norman Hathaway for his gorgeous cover lettering and to Helene Silverman, dear friend and brilliant designer, whose work really makes these books sing. Finally, my gratitude to Marge Camras, Mark and Beverly Nadel and Matt and Amy Nadel for their love.

Editors: Sofia Gutiérrez, Sheila Keenan
Project Manager: Charles Kochman
Designer: Helene Silverman
Production Manager: Alison Gervais

Library of Congress Cataloging-in-Publication Data
Nadel, Dan.
    Art in time : unknown comic book adventures 1940–1980 / Dan
Nadel.
      p. cm.
    "PictureBox, Inc."
    Includes bibliographical references and index.
    ISBN 978-0-8109-8824-8 (hardcover with jacket : alk. paper)
    1. Comic books, strips, etc.—United States—History—20th century.
    2. Cartoonists—United States—Biography. I. Title. II. Title: unknown
    comic book adventures, 1940–1980.
    NC1426.N33 2010
    741.5'973—dc22

                          2009031672

Text and compilation © 2010 Dan Nadel
Unless otherwise indicated below, all comics are copyright their
respective owners or creators.
"Tidal Wave of Terror," "I Was a Vampire," "Meet the Bride,"
copyright © Marvel Entertainment Group. Reprinted with permission.

The following sources also provided images used in this anthology:
McMillan, Michael: 143–149, Michael McMillan comics
Rudahl, Sharon: 61–95, *The Adventures of Crystal Night*
Thompson, John: 199–216, *Cyclops Comics*

Case art: Pete Morisi
Title page art: Pat Boyette
Table of contents art: Pete Morisi

Published in 2010 by Abrams ComicArts, an imprint of ABRAMS.
All rights reserved. No portion of this book may be reproduced,
stored in a retrieval system, or transmitted in any form or by
any means, mechanical, electronic, photocopying, recording, or
otherwise, without written permission from the publisher.

Printed and bound in China
10 9 8 7 6 5 4 3 2 1

Abrams ComicArts books are available at special discounts when
purchased in quantity for premiums and promotions as well as
fundraising or educational use. Special editions can also be created to
specification. For details, contact specialmarkets@abramsbooks.com,
or the address below.

ABRAMS
THE ART OF BOOKS SINCE 1949

115 West 18th Street
New York, NY 10011
www.abramsbooks.com

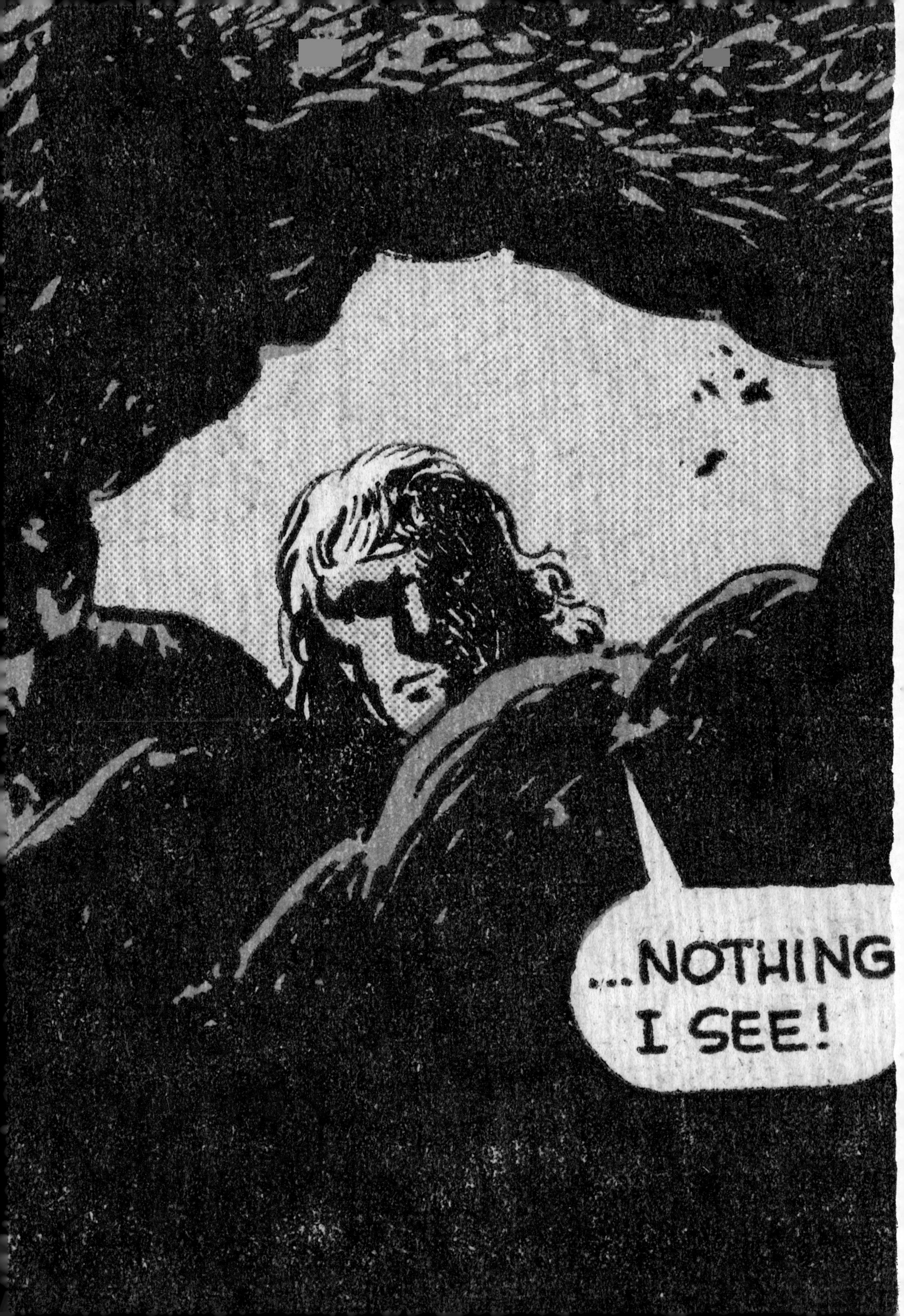
...NOTHING I SEE!

GRAPHIC
741.5973
NADEL

GRAPHIC
741.5973
NADEL

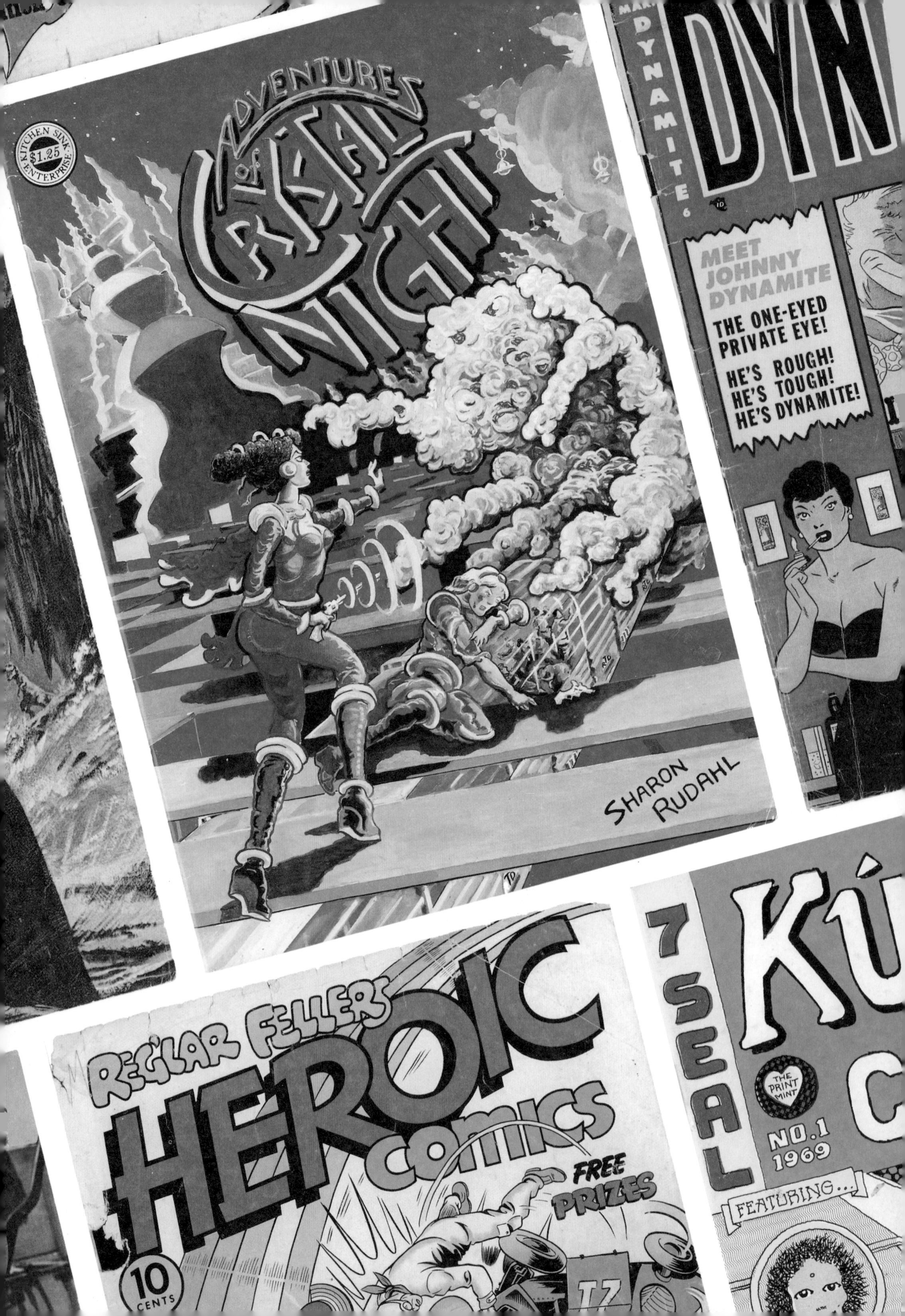
KITCHEN SINK ENTERPRISE
$1.25
ADVENTURES of CRYSTAL NIGHT
SHARON RUDAHL
DYNAMITE
6
MEET JOHNNY DYNAMITE
THE ONE-EYED PRIVATE EYE!
HE'S ROUGH! HE'S TOUGH! HE'S DYNAMITE!
REG'LAR FELLERS
HEROIC COMICS
FREE PRIZES
10 CENTS
7 SEAL
THE PRINT MINT
NO.1 1969
FEATURING...